RIGHT, WRONG, AND RISKY

RIGHT, WRONG, AND RISKY

A Dictionary of
Today's American English Usage

MARK DAVIDSON

W. W. NORTON & COMPANY

NEW YORK • LONDON

Definitions and usage examples within quotation marks are the
author's own. Citations are provided for material quoted from
dictionaries, usage and style manuals, and other sources.

Copyright © 2006 by the Estate of Mark Davidson

For information about permission to reproduce selections from this book,
write to Permissions, W. W. Norton & Company, Inc.,
500 Fifth Avenue, New York, NY 10110

Manufacturing by Maple-Vail Book Manufacturing Group
Book design by Anthea Lingeman
Production manager: Julia Druskin

Library of Congress Cataloging-in-Publication Data

Davidson, Mark, d. 2005.
Right, wrong, and risky : a dictionary of today's American English usage /
Mark Davidson.—1st ed.
p. cm.
Includes bibliographical references.
ISBN 978-0-393-06119-2
1. English language—United States—Usage—Dictionaries.
2. English language—Usage—Dictionaries. I. Title.
PE2835.D38 2005
423'.1—dc22
2005017628

W. W. Norton & Company, Inc., 500 Fifth Avenue, New York, N.Y. 10110
www.wwnorton.com

W. W. Norton & Company Ltd., Castle House, 75/76 Wells Street, London W1T 3QT

2 3 4 5 6 7 8 9 0

The greatest possible merit of style is, of course, to make the words absolutely disappear into the thought.

—Nathaniel Hawthorne

The greatest problem about communication is the illusion that it has been accomplished.

—George Bernard Shaw

[Language] is the most vivid and crucial key to identity. It reveals the private identity, and connects one with, or divorces one from, the larger public, or communal identity.

—James Baldwin

To Kubeshini

Contents

Acknowledgments

11

Four Questions about This Book

13

Some Words about Words

17

How This Book Is Organized

21

RIGHT, WRONG, AND RISKY: DICTIONARY ENTRIES

23

Sources

559

Acknowledgments

Thanks to my dedicated and wise literary agent, Susan Lee Cohen, for sending the manuscript of this book to the dedicated and wise W. W. Norton Vice President and Senior Editor Maria Guarnaschelli.

Thanks to Ms. Guarnaschelli for placing the manuscript in the capable and caring hands of Katya Rice, the best copy editor I've ever encountered.

And thanks for many years of encouragement and suggestions from my colleagues, students, friends, and loved ones.

Four Questions about This Book

WHY WATCH YOUR WORDS?

If you fail words, they will fail you. Throughout your personal and professional life, from your first date to a job-of-a-lifetime interview, you are judged by your ability to express yourself in language. It's trite but true: Nobody gets a second chance to make a first impression.

Your ability to express what you know is at least as important as what you know. Fairly or not, your use of language may cause people to decide if you are bright or bumbling, interesting or boring, sincere or pretentious, or just plain annoying like the sound of a fingernail scraping a blackboard. If you are judged deficient in communication skills, you may lose out in competition for a job or a promotion, often without your ever knowing why.

On the positive side, your communication skills can help you achieve your goals. To use a fashionable word, communication skills can *empower* you. They can enhance your ability to define your goals in your own mind and then gain support for those goals from others.

Language skill is especially useful today in Standard American English. The language of English, whose uniquely large vocabulary of more than half a million words came mostly from other languages, is not culturally superior to any of the six thousand or so other languages that our species speaks. Likewise, Standard American English is not culturally superior to the other varieties of American English that thrive in our nation. But Standard American English is a master key to success and interethnic communication in today's multilingual, multicultural America. Globally, English plays a uniquely influential role in world commerce, information technology, media, entertainment, science, diplomacy, air-traffic control, and communications for ships at sea. English, the official corporate language of many European banks and corporations, the dominant language of the European Union, and the dominant second language of the world, is the closest thing the world has ever had to an international language.

English, to quote *The Story of English*, the companion volume to the PBS television series of that name, "is more widely scattered, more widely spoken and written, than any other language has ever been." And, says *The Oxford Guide to World English,* "American English has a global role at the beginning of the 21st century comparable to that of British English at the start of the 20th—but on a larger scale than any previous language or variety of a language in recorded history."

ISN'T A DICTIONARY ENOUGH?

The principal role of dictionaries is to show how language is used, not how it *should* be used. Hence, along with such universally acceptable plurals as *criteria* and *phenomena*, you will find dictionary listings for *criterions* and *phenomenons*—two variant forms that could stigmatize you as someone seriously deficient in education. Likewise, dictionaries list not only the acceptable plural *communications media* but also the reputation-jeopardizing *communications mediums.*

Nowhere in the English-speaking world, from Toronto to Tasmania, will you find *the* authority on English usage comparable to France's "supreme court" of language: the Académie Française, established in 1634 by Cardinal Richelieu to adjudicate on grammar, vocabulary, and usage. England has repeatedly rejected the idea of an academy that would regulate the natural development of the English language. And American dictionary pioneer Noah Webster failed to win support for such a proposal in the newly formed United States of America. The closest thing to a bible of English is Britain's *Oxford English Dictionary*, whose 12-volume first edition was published in 1928 after 70 years of research. But the goal of the *OED* has been to describe, not prescribe. To quote a *User's Guide* to the 20-volume second edition, published in 1989: "Contrary to the popular view of the *OED* as an authority on the 'correct' usage of the language, the *Dictionary* is intended to be descriptive, not prescriptive; it records, non-judgmentally, the history of the language as mirrored in the written words of a democratic mix of novelists, playwrights, journalists, scholars, scientists, legislators, politicians, diarists, saints, and philosophers."

Some dictionaries offer helpful usage notes about certain words. But such advice is buried amid thousands of entries. That's why there are reference books that focus solely on questions of usage.

WHY USE THIS USAGE BOOK?

As opposed to the generally *descriptive* dictionary, the typical usage book tends to be dogmatically *prescriptive*. It cites "right" and "wrong" usage, too often without explanation and without acknowledging that many usage questions are the subject of widespread debate. For example, some usage books ignore the disagreement among language commentators about the "correct" meaning of such words as *aggravate, allude, anxious, collision, comprise, connive, continual, disinterested,* and *enormity.* (See my entries for those words.) Other usage books acknowledge such controversies but dismiss them as irrelevant and therefore expose their readers to the needless risk of criticism.

Usage guides that do acknowledge diverse viewpoints tend to leave the reader stranded in a swamp of indecision. Should one adopt the usage recommended by the sources that are the most prestigious, or should one look for the most persuasive argument? What if the "vote" on a usage question is virtually a tie? What if usage commentators support a usage—such as those cited in my book for *nauseous, transpire,* and *lion's share*—that many people are likely to misinterpret? In the words of poet-critic John Ciardi, what if you are "so right that you will be misunderstood"? For such pitfalls, I offer recommendations that are free of risk.

But let me emphasize that *Right, Wrong, and Risky* does not promote the myth that "correct usage" exists. Nor does it ignore the fact that the prominent usage commentators who have prescribed "correct usage" have a significant influence over *actual* usage. Instead, this book reports on what usage is generally *considered* correct, and by whom. This book views the real world of today's American English, identifying usage questions that are debatable, citing conflicting answers, and offering risk-free solutions for each conflict.

Though rejecting dogmatic "right" and "wrong" usage, this book does not surrender to "anything goes" permissiveness. Yes, some schoolteachers still impose nonsensical rules—for example, about never splitting infinitives and never beginning a sentence with a conjunction or ending a sentence with a preposition. But that does not mean *all* schoolroom instruction in English is worthless. And yes, change in language is common and inevitable, in grammar, in pronunciation, and most notably in the meaning of words. *Villain* once meant "village peasant." *Libertine* meant "liberated slave." *Nice* meant "foolish." *Silly* meant "happy." *Cute* was short for *acute.* And *pompous* meant "important" before it came to mean "self-important." But this book's approach also acknowledges that language evolution can and should be guided by socially beneficial criteria. The criteria applied here are grace, logic, clarity, precision, and the desirability of preserving useful word distinctions such as those between *imply* and *infer, lie* and *lay, simple* and *simplistic, unusual* and *unique.*

In summary, I believe the tree of language should be allowed to experience natural growth and change, but we should do what we can to protect it from vandals.

HOW DID THIS BOOK COME TO BE?

As a full-time professional writer and professor of communications, I tried in vain to find an American English usage book that would help students in my writing classes. Usually, the students obediently bought the book I assigned, but they didn't consult it. If they consulted it, they often couldn't find answers to their questions, or they found answers that were confusing, obscure, or outdated. So, back in 1991, I began researching and writing the kind of usage book that I thought my students would find helpful—the kind I wished I'd had when I was a student myself. I tried out several preliminary versions in my classes, making changes in response to reactions and questions from students and colleagues. In 1999, having quit teaching in order to devote all my time to writing, I continued to revise and update this book.

Now, after informally test-marketing innumerable versions, I believe I have finally come up with a usage dictionary worthy of your time. My goal has been to produce a usage dictionary that is grounded in scholarship and professional experience—and accessible, even entertaining, for the general reader.

Some Words about Words

The ability to use language is like the ability to drive a car. You can be an excellent driver without knowing the difference between a carburetor and a distributor, but you'd better be able to distinguish the brake from the gas pedal. Similarly, you can be an excellent writer without mastering all the terminology of grammar, but you need to be able to distinguish, for example, a noun from a verb.

Many people forget what they were taught about the parts of speech. Many others were never taught that subject adequately. So make sure you're aware that a person, place, thing, act, or idea is named by a *noun* or a substituting *pronoun,* introduced by an *article* (either *a/an* or *the*), modified ("described, qualified, limited") by an *adjective,* and involved in action by a *verb* that can be modified by an *adverb.*

An *adverb* (whose name literally means "near the verb") can modify not only a verb but also an adjective or another adverb: "She spoke *eloquently.*" "Her ideas were *uniquely* brilliant." "Her presentation was *very* well done."

Prepositions—such as *at, by, in, on, up, from,* and *with*—show the relationship of a noun or pronoun to a verb, an adjective, or another noun or pronoun. *Conjunctions*—such as *and* and *but*—link words, phrases, and sentences. *Interjections*—like *Oh!* and *Hey!*—are grammatically isolated words that express surprise or emotion.

Many words can play more than one role. For example, the word *love* can perform as a verb, a noun, and an adjective for people who *love* reading about *love* in *love* stories.

In a group of words, a *subject* (say, *kittens*) is the noun you're talking about, and a *predicate* is what you're saying about the subject with the help of a verb (*love to play*). A *phrase* consists of two or more related words (say, *tiny kittens*) that lack the combination of a subject and a predicate; a phrase that begins with a preposition (*with yarn balls*) is a *prepositional phrase*. A group of words with a subject and a predicate is a *clause*, and a clause is called *independent* when it can stand on its own as a sentence (*Tiny kittens love to play with yarn balls*). A clause that cannot form a sentence is a *dependent* clause, also known as a *subordinate* clause (*that are soft and brightly colored*). A single independent clause with one or more dependent (subordinate) clauses is a *complex sentence*. (Put the last two examples together.) Add a second independent clause to a complex sentence and you have a *compound-complex sentence*. (*Tiny kittens love to play with yarn balls that are soft and brightly colored, and then they like to take a nap.*) If you add any more clauses, you'll be subject to arrest for cruel and unusual composition.

RIGHT, WRONG, AND RISKY

How This Book Is Organized

I have arranged all entries in this book in a single alphabetical order, to help you find immediate answers to questions about words such as *comprise* and *paradox* as well as subjects such as the comma and the hyphen. Likewise, I have alphabetized the order of words and subjects within the titles of comparative entries—entries such as "*affect* or *effect*?" or "colon or semicolon?"— except in instances in which the out-of-order term is the one you're much more likely to be looking up. At any rate, I hope you do not hesitate to read this book randomly, at your leisure, or even methodically from A to Z, if you enjoy discovering answers to questions you never thought of asking.

A

***a* or *an*?**   Most of my hundreds of university writing students told me that they had been taught to change *a* to *an* before words that begin with a vowel. They should have been taught to change *a* to *an* before words that begin with a vowel *sound*. And they should have been taught to stay with *a* before words that begin with a consonant sound. Whether the first letter of the word being introduced is a vowel or a consonant is not decisive; what matters is the sound.

True, "*an* apple *a* day" is always okay. But remember that your choice is based solely on sound. Therefore, you would be wrong to say "a NBC newscast." *NBC* should be introduced by *an* because the consonant N at the beginning of *NBC* is pronounced with the vowel sound of *en* as in *entrance*. Likewise, *SUV* should be introduced by *an*, because the consonant *s* in that abbreviation is pronounced with the vowel sound of *es* as in *escape*. Conversely, *a* should introduce words like the noun *ukulele* and the adjective *ubiquitous* because the initial vowel *u* in such words is pronounced with the sound of the consonant *y* as in *yellow*. So don't imitate a 2004 U.S. State Department Web page in which travelers were advised that "the loss or theft abroad of an [should be *a*] U.S. passport should be reported immediately."

In a further application of the "sound rule," words that begin with the consonant *h* should be introduced by *a* when the *h* is pronounced, as in *honeydew*, and by *an* when the *h* is silent, as in *honor*. Note that you use *an* for the silent-h *herb* but *a* for the sounded-h *herbarium*.

Some American usage commentators accept the British *an* before a pronounced but unstressed *h*, as in the title of a 1956 book by British historian Arnold Toynbee, *An Historical Approach to Religion*. But in American English you run no risk if you use *a* before all words with an initial *h* that is pronounced with or without stress, as in a *New York Times* opinion-page essay (11/1/2000) referring to "a historic era." (See also "*historic* or *historical*?")

a pronunciation   Pronounce the article *a* softly, as in *applause*, unless you want to use a long *a*, as in *play*, to emphasize that what follows is singular. Example: "I did not ask for *a* [pronounced with emphasis] paper clip. I asked for a whole box." (See also entry for "*the*: when does it sound like *thee*?")

a/an or her/his?   In an example of a common error, a student of mine began a news article with this sentence: "State Senator Barbara Lane yesterday announced her plan to protect suburban wildlife." Unless the announcement of the plan had been widely expected by the public, the sentence should have read that Senator Lane announced *a* plan, not *her* plan. But "*her* plan" was appropriate in subsequent sentences, after the reader had learned of the plan's existence.

A similar mistake appeared in this opening sentence from a news story written by another of my student writers: "Millions of Americans fail to use seat belts, according to yesterday's report from the National Transportation Safety Board." That sentence should have referred to *a* report, not *yesterday's* report, because the phrase "yesterday's report" wrongly suggested that the public knew about the report before the news story was published. (For a variation of that usage problem, see the next entry.)

a/an or the?   When you *introduce a subject*, as I just did in italics, use the indefinite article *a/an* rather than the definite article *the*.

Usage examples: You would deserve *an* A for your use of *a* if you wrote: "A 1995 book, *When Elephants Weep*, presents evidence that animals have feelings at least as profound as those of humans." Once you have made the subject definite by introducing it to the reader, you should use the definite article *the* in your subsequent references: "*The* book acknowledges that people with animal companions have known about the feelings of animals all along."

Someone who writes for a living but is not widely known is referred to as "*a* writer." But internationally renowned author Mario Vargas Llosa was appropriately referred to in *The New York Times* (7/31/2001) as "*the* Peruvian novelist." (See also entries for *the*.)

a/an or *the* in a series   For clarity and consistency, use an article (*a/an* or *the*) before each noun in a series: "Please put *a* plate, *a* knife, and *a* napkin at each place at the table." But don't repeat the article in the case of nouns that commonly go together: "And don't forget *the* bread and butter."

abbreviated advice   Easily understood abbreviations, such as *St.* and *Ave.* in addresses, are often helpful to writers and readers. But don't show off your knowledge of technical abbreviations unless you're communicating with a technical audience. (See also "*acronym* or *initialism?*").

abdomen, belly, stomach, or *tummy?*   A few generations ago, the word *limb* was customarily substituted for *leg* because the word *leg* was considered vulgar. In an echo of such prudery, many people today continue an old practice of substituting the technical word *abdomen* (preferably stressed on the first syllable) for the supposedly indelicate word *belly*.

Belly (Old English for "bag, purse") is actually the appropriate nontechnical word for the portion of the human body between the chest and the thighs, according to *The Oxford English Dictionary*, Henry W. Fowler's *Dictionary of Modern English Usage*, and Theodore M. Bernstein's *Careful Writer*. Fowler, Bernstein, and other usage commentators acknowledged that their defense of belly was probably a lost cause. But such word guardians have refused to surrender to the baby-talk euphemism *tummy* and the inaccurate substitution of *stomach* or *gut* (two organs *inside* the belly).

Nobody will blame you if you lack the courage to rescue *belly*. But you need not censor *belly* so completely that you end up saying *abdomen* button, pot *tummy*, or *stomach* dancer.

ability or *capacity?*   Some birds have the *ability* ("skill, power") to migrate thousands of miles between their winter and summer habitats.

Capacity, which means "*potential* ability," can be used with the prepositions *to*, *for*, and *of*. For example: "Martha clearly has the capacity *to* acquire many professional skills, and she has the capacity *for* teaching such skills." The preposition *of* is appropriate when *capacity* refers to an inanimate object's potential to *contain* a certain amount of something: "Our neighborhood theater has a seating capacity *of* only 99."

abjure or **adjure**?   *Abjure* and *adjure* are listed as a puzzling pair in many usage books. Indeed, these two verbs sound so much alike that you are probably wise to avoid them in speech.

In writing, remember that each contains a clue to its meaning in its first syllable. *Abjure* means "solemnly renounce" (as in "*ab*dicate"), and *adjure* means "solemnly command" (as in "*ad*monish") or "earnestly appeal to."

Usage example of *adjure*, in the "earnestly appeal to" sense, in *The New York Times Book Review* (2/4/2001): "Donald Kagan and Frederick W. Kagan [father-and-son authors of *While America Sleeps*] adjure us to wake up lest America after the cold war repeat the grave errors of Britain after World War I."

able to or **able to be**?   You face no problem with the active-voice *able to*, as in "I'll be able to see you Friday at 6 p.m."

But don't let anyone catch you using the nonsensical, passive-voice *able to be*, as in "The Huntington Gardens *are able to be seen* by members of the public every day but Monday." This statement is nonsense because it is members of the public that are able, not the gardens. A simple solution: "Members of the public are able to see . . ."

ablution or **absolution**?   *Ablution*, usually used in its plural form, *ablutions*, means "washing the body as a religious ritual." As a reference to *ordinary* body-cleansing rituals, the word *ablutions* is usually intended to be jocular.

Absolution, the noun related to the verb *absolve* ("pardon"), means "formal declaration that one is forgiven one's sins."

abode is more than an address   In addition to being a pretentious or facetious synonym for *home*, the word *abode* serves as a past-tense form and the past participle of the verb *abide* ("to put up with, tolerate").

Also, note that a *law-abiding* person is one who abides *by* ("complies *with*") the law.

abolishment or **abolition**?   British linguist R. W. Burchfield assured readers of his *New Fowler's Modern English Usage* that both these forms "coexisted as synonyms" from the time they entered English in the sixteenth century until *abolition* began achieving "supremacy" over *abolishment* two centuries later.

Abolishment is still acceptable, but your risk-free choice is the more common form, *abolition*.

aboriginal and **aborigine** **can both be proper**   The nouns *aboriginal* and *aborigine*—both meaning "one of the original inhabitants of a region"—should be capitalized for the earliest known inhabitants of Australia. That rule from Down Under also applies to *aboriginal* as an adjective, as in "Aboriginal Australian art."

about **mistakes**   The phrase "about 79 books" is contradictory, because *about* promises an approximation, not an exact number. The phrase should be "about 80 books."
    The *about* in "estimated at *about* 800" is redundant.

about or **almost**?   Avoid *about* if you mean *almost*, as in "about ready." Use *about* when you want a short, unpretentious synonym for *approximately*, as in "about three o'clock."

about or **as to**?   In a sentence such as "The mother questioned the boy as to his poor grades," replace the stuffy *as to* with *about*.

about or **on**?   When you mean *concerning*, your risk-free choice is *about*. Someone who lectures *about* cruise ships is clearly someone who shares knowledge concerning that topic. But the topic could be anything under the sun when someone lectures *on* cruise ships.

above **is not above criticism**   Nobody objects to *above* as an adverb, as in "the sky above." But some word guardians object to *above* as an adjective (as in "the above paragraph"), a noun ("see the above"), or a substitute for the phrase *more than* ("she had to wait above an hour").
    If you decide to risk using *above* as an adjective, you can cite the support of lawyer-lexicographer Bryan A. Garner in *Garner's Modern American Usage* and a majority of the usage panel of *The American Heritage Dictionary*. Garner views *above* as a desirable abbreviation for *above-mentioned*. He notes that *above* has long been used "even by the best writers," despite a long-standing notion that it "could not properly act as an adjective."

abridgement or **abridgment?**   Americans generally *abridge* ("shorten, condense, diminish, reduce in scope") the British *abridgement* by spelling it *abridgment*. Memory hint: In England an *e* is used. (See similar entries for *acknowledgment, aging, ax,* and *judgment.*)

abrogate or **arrogate?**   *Abrogate,* which begins like *abolish,* means "abolish, annul, cancel, void, repeal by authority." Usage example: "The new treaty will abrogate the previous agreement."

Arrogate, which begins like *arrogant,* means "lay claim to without justification." Usage example: "Some U.S. presidents have arrogated the power of Congress to declare war."

absent **is present as a preposition**   In addition to serving as an adjective (as in "the absent student") and a verb ("the student said he would absent himself"), *absent* emerged in early 20th-century American English as a preposition, meaning "without."

The prepositional *absent* was denounced as "pompous" in the 1998 edition of Wilson Follett's *Modern American Usage* and dismissed as "unnecessary" legal jargon in the 1998 and 2003 edition of Bryan A. Garner's usage dictionary. But the prepositional *absent* remains present in leading publications. For example, *The New York Times* noted in an editorial (1/2/2001) that a president's Congressional-recess appointee to the U.S. Court of Appeals "can serve for only a year absent [without] Congressional confirmation."

absolute advice   Absolute words—including *absolute, complete, dead, equal, essential, excellent, eternal, final, full, impossible, infinite, integral, necessary, perfect, round, supreme, total, unique,* and *utter*—refer to ultimate conditions that cannot be intensified by *more, most,* or *especially.*

But you can qualify absolutes with *nearly, almost,* and *hardly,* because such words show that the ultimate condition does not exist. For example, although a task cannot be "*most* impossible," it can be "*nearly* impossible."

You can also use qualifiers to dismiss doubts about an absolute condition, as in "*absolutely* impossible," "*definitely* full," and "*really* excellent." (See also entries for *complete, equal, necessary, perfect, state of the art,* and *unique.*)

abstemious* or *abstinent?   As a host, you should offer only one or two glasses of wine to a guest who is *abstemious* (practicing moderation) and no drinks at all to a guest who is *abstinent* (practicing complete self-denial).

Abstemious is from a Latin combination of "away" and "intoxicating drink." In Shakespeare's *Tempest*, the adjective *abstemious* was extended to moderation in sex. And *abstemious* has been widely used for moderation in general. But today's writers tend to restrict the word to its original Latin association with intoxicating beverages.

abuse* or *abusage?   *Abusage*, an archaic synonym for *abuse*, was revived in the 1940's as a word meaning "improper use of language" in the title of a book by British literary critic and lexicographer Eric Partridge, *Usage and Abusage*. You'll find that modern sense of *abusage* in England's *Oxford English Dictionary* and America's unabridged Merriam-Webster and Random House dictionaries. (See also "*usage* or *use?*")

***abyss:* the bottom lines**   The *abyss* (from a Greek word for "bottomless") was once thought to be a bottomless pit, the site of hell, beneath the earth. Russian-born American novelist Vladimir Nabokov (1899–1977) wrote in *Speak, Memory*, a book about his childhood and youth, "The cradle rocks above an abyss, and common sense tells us that our existence is but a brief crack of light between two eternities of darkness." Today, *abyss* means "anything literally or figuratively of profound depth" or "the deepest levels of the ocean."

The related adjectives are *abyssal* ("relating to the ocean depths, unfathomable, immeasurable") and the more commonly used *abysmal* ("bottomlessly low, hopelessly bad").

Usage example of *abysmal* in the sense of "hopelessly bad": According to *Newsweek* (3/6/2000), "It's no secret that [America's customer] service is abysmal."

academe,* Academy, or *academy?   The uppercase *Academy* refers to the school of philosophy founded by Plato in the fourth century B.C. and continuing for about nine hundred years until it was suppressed, along with other "pagan" influences, by the Roman emperor Justinian. The school acquired the name *Academy* because Plato used to meet his students at Akademia, an olive-grove estate (near Athens) named in honor of Akademos, a Greek hero in the Trojan War.

Today, the word *academy* may be applied to any place, society, or institution dedicated to the pursuit of knowledge, from the Académie Française to the Academy of Motion Picture Arts and Sciences. Though *academy* is often used in the title of a private secondary or college preparatory school, the phrase "the academy" is synonymous in higher education with "the academic community, academe, academia." The word *academe*, introduced by Shakespeare to refer to a school of higher education in his *Love's Labor's Lost*, and the newer and less common word *academia* both sometimes refer today to "the world of higher education, the academic community."

academese: an infectious disease   Scholars are supposed to simplify complexity, but too often they complicate simplicity. The result is *academese*, which is characterized by what the *Harper Dictionary of Contemporary Usage* calls "polysyllabic monstrosities" and what *Webster's New World Guide to Concise Writing* refers to as new terminology to "categorize what the rest of us have always known." Here are some meaningless monstrosities concocted for an exposé of academese in *The Wilson Quarterly* (Spring 1984): *integrated reciprocal contingencies*, *systematized operational flexibility*, and *synchronized modular mobility*.

University of Southern California Journalism Professor Roy H. Copperud spent much of his life (1915–1991) defending academe from academese. In his *American Usage and Style: The Consensus*, Copperud wrote that "some academicians avoid plain English on principle; others are incapable of expressing themselves plainly. Both varieties tend, by example, to infect students with the noxious idea that what is difficult to understand is necessarily deep."

Academics who write in the pedantic style of academese are committing a victimless crime to the extent that their writing is unpublished or is published in journals that are obscure, irrelevant, and destined for the dustpile. But, sadly, such writing is frequently imitated by eager-to-please students. And unless such students themselves pursue a career in academic language corruption, they are likely to graduate with a severe communication handicap.

In a term paper submitted to me in one of my classes on media law, a student imitating her pedantic role models wrote that the purpose of the U.S. Constitution is "to codify the premises, assumptions, behaviors and actions, necessary and sufficient for a free society." One of those assumptions, she wrote, is that our society is based on "a moral construct predicated on the ethics and moralities of the Judeo-Christian religions." Other assumptions, she added, involve "a freedom/responsibility construct" and "an applicational boundary" of free expression. Notice that the author of that term paper, as a typical perpetrator of academese, flaunted redundancies such as "behaviors and actions" and "ethics and moralities." In producing such prolixity, she was engaging in the time-honored pedantic practice of using repetition in a futile attempt to conceal insufficient content. (See also "*jargon* is not really for the birds.")

academic counseling   Be sure you clearly indicate whether you are using the adjective *academic* to mean "scholarly" (as in "an academic career") or "hypothetical, unrealistic, not directly useful" (as in "That question is purely academic").

academic degrees, titles, and departments   For degree abbreviations, write *B.A., M.A., Ph.D.* Example: "Elsa Manning, Ph.D., will be the colloquium speaker." Otherwise, write *bachelor's degree, master's degree, doctorate.* Example: "Elsa Manning has a doctorate in physics."

Lowercase such titles as *professor, chair, dean,* and *president,* except before a person's name. Lowercase the name of departments except for proper nouns or adjectives. Examples: "Make an appointment with Professor Rudy Walker *of the philosophy department.*" "Rudy Walker, *a professor of philosophy,* has many friends in the department of English." (See also "capital punishment.")

accede or **exceed?**   *Accede* ("to agree") should be pronounced carefully to distinguish it from *exceed* ("to surpass").

accept no substitutes   People often write the preposition/conjunction/verb *except* when they intend to write the verb *accept.*

access or **accession?**   After a politician's *accession* ("elevation in rank") to the presidency, his aides are sometimes suspected of raising re-election campaign funds by selling *access* ("the right to approach") to the White House to representatives of special interests.

Access is also a computer-jargon verb, meaning *acquire,* as in "access the company's personnel files." But the nontechnical use of this verb, as in "access your cash at automatic tellers," has been rejected by 82 percent of the *American Heritage Dictionary* usage panel.

accident or mishap?   The word *mishap* (like *mischance*) is appropriate only for accidents that are minor, according to *The American Heritage Dictionary*, the *Harper Dictionary of Contemporary Usage*, Bernstein's *Careful Writer*, and the stylebooks of the Associated Press, *The Washington Post*, *The Boston Globe*, *The New York Times*, and *The Wall Street Journal*.

Careless headline writers tend to misuse the conveniently short *mishap* for accidents of just about any type. Example of such abusage in the winter 1998 magazine of the University of Southwestern Louisiana chapter of the Society of Professional Journalists: "Veteran Reporter Drowns in Mishap."

accidentally or accidently?   *Accidently* has been a variant of *accidentally* for nearly four centuries. But *Merriam-Webster's Dictionary of English Usage* and *The Columbia Guide to Standard American English* warn that you may be accused of a spelling error if you don't use the currently prevailing *accidentally*. Indeed, *accidently* is listed as nonstandard by *The New Fowler's Modern English Usage* and is dismissed as incorrect by *Garner's Modern American Usage*, *The Scott, Foresman Handbook for Writers*, and *The Beacon Handbook*.

To avoid the debatable spelling of this adverb, build it on *accidental*, not *accident*. (See also "spelling traps.")

accomodate or accommodate?   The many people who misspell this word might benefit from remembering that one of its meanings is "make room for." You need to make room here not only for two *c*'s but also for two *m*'s.

Other senses of *accommodate*: "do a favor for, provide for, lend money to, provide with a room, make suitable, bring into harmony, become adjusted."

accompanied by or with?   *The American Heritage Book of English Usage* cites what it calls "a traditional rule" under which *people* are *accompanied by* and *things* are *accompanied with*. But as that source and *Merriam-Webster's Dictionary of English Usage* acknowledge, that rule no longer prevails. *The Columbia Guide to Standard American English* says things can be *accompanied with* or *by*, as in "The potato salad was accompanied with (or *by*) a limp dill pickle." *Garner's Modern American Usage* says *accompanied by* is now the only correct usage for both people and things.

Risk-free suggestion: Always use *accompanied by*, inasmuch as that usage is prescribed for people and is now permitted, even when not prescribed, for things.

accord or ***accordance?***   You may choose to be in *accord* ("agreement") with a proposal that a local safety regulation be in *accordance* ("conformity") with prevailing national standards.

***accost*: guilty or innocent?**   Paul W. Lovinger, in his *Penguin Dictionary of American English Usage and Style*, corrected the impression that someone who *accosts* somebody is guilty of engaging in an "assault or attack." But Lovinger was wrong in stating that the verb *accost* has only the innocent meaning of "approach and speak to someone first."

   "Approach and speak to" is only *one* of the dictionary definitions of *accost*. Other definitions, more reflective of common usage, are "approach and speak to boldly," "confront boldly," and "solicit for sexual purposes." And the most realistic definition, quoted here from Microsoft's *Encarta World English Dictionary*, is "to approach and stop somebody in order to speak, especially in an aggressive, insistent or suggestive way."

accouterments or ***accoutrements?***   The first spelling is preferred in American English, the second in British English. Likewise, our verb *accouter* is spelled *accoutre* by the British. (See also "*theater* or *theatre?*")

   The verb *accouter* ("ah-KOO-ter"), from a French word for *equip*, means "to equip, as for military duty." Hence, *accouterments* are "military equipment in addition to weapons and uniforms" or "auxiliary items of equipment or dress." By extension, the word *accouterments* refers to "trappings" (that is, "the things usually associated with something as an outward sign of its existence"), as in "the accouterments of wealth." Usage example from *The New York Times* (8/4/2000): "Egypt boasts of having a Constitution and democratic accouterments like courts, elections, a lively private business sector and a Parliament."

"accuracy, accuracy, and accuracy"   Journalism professors, echoing newspaper publisher Joseph Pulitzer (1847–1911), tell their students that the three most important criteria for nonfiction writing are "accuracy, accuracy, and accuracy." (See also "Pulitzer and his prizes.")

   No writer should ever assume that something is true, as *New York Times* columnist Anna Quindlen apparently did (5/16/1991) when she referred to California's 1960 gas-chamber execution of "convicted murderer" Caryl Chessman. Actually, the Chessman case had nothing to do with murder. Convictauthor Chessman, who died insisting on his innocence after nearly 12 years on death row, had been convicted of lovers'-lane holdups defined as capital kidnapping under a then-existing California law.

Triple-check your information, especially when misinformation could cause serious harm. You don't want to be in the position of Ruth Whitney, editor in chief of *Glamour* magazine, who had to mail a warning to all her subscribers when she discovered that the health column in her June 1992 issue suggested that yeast infections could be prevented by taking "500 mg. of boric acid tablets three times a day with meals." When taken orally, boric acid is poisonous.

Achilles: **a casualty of carelessness**   The phrase *Achilles' heel* ("vulnerable spot") recalls the legend of the hero of the *Iliad*, the epic poem ascribed to the ancient Greek poet Homer and the source of the 2004 movie *Troy*.

When Achilles was a baby, his mother, the sea nymph Thetis, dipped him into the sacred River Styx to make him immortal, but she failed to immerse the heel by which she held him. Consequently, after slaying the Trojan hero Hector, Achilles was mortally wounded in his heel by a poisoned arrow shot by Hector's younger brother, the Trojan prince Paris.

Usage example from a story about computer vandals in *The New York Times* (2/10/2000): "The attributes that make the Internet an engine for innovation—its openness and lack of central control—are also its Achilles' heel." (Don't forget to add the possessive apostrophe in *Achilles' heel*.)

acknowledgement **or** *acknowledgment*?   The preferred American spelling drops the British *e* after the *g*, as is also true with *abridgment* and *judgment*.

acme **or** *epitome*?   *Epitome* ("summary, abridgment, embodiment, a part that's representative of an entire class or type") is sometimes wrongly used as if it were a synonym for *acme* ("highest point, peak of perfection").

Acme is appropriate for praise. But *epitome* can embody the good, the bad, or the ugly. A scene from a movie can epitomize the movie's greatness or its mediocrity.

acoustics is **or** *acoustics are*?   See "*-ics* words: some are singular and plural."

acquiesce in, to, or *with*?   Always *acquiesce* ("passively submit, comply, cooperate") *in* something, such as a plan. The phrase *acquiesce to* poses a needless risk, because it is not always appropriate. *Acquiesce with* is obsolete.

acronym or *initialism*?   An *acronym* is an abbreviation, pronounced as if it were a word, from the initial letters or other parts of a name or expression, as with NASA (National Aeronautics and Space Administration) and WYSIWYG (pronounced "WIS-ee-wig" and meaning "What you see is what you get"). Some acronyms are uncapitalized words, from the initial letters or other parts of a group of words, as with *laser* (*l*ight *a*mplification by *s*timulated *e*mission of *r*adiation) and *modem* (*mo*dulator *dem*odulator). (See also "*Amtrak, AMTRAK,* or *Amtrack?*")

An *initialism* is an abbreviation formed like an acronym but pronounced letter by letter, such as *SUV* (sport utility vehicle).

acronym-initialism impostors   You have the word of David Wilton's copiously researched *Word Myths* (Oxford, 2004) that *news* is not an acronym for "north, east, west, and south," and that *SOS* does not mean "Save our ship" or "Save our souls." Wilton says *news* arose as an obvious reference to "new things or events." *SOS*, says Wilton, "was chosen as a universal distress signal by the International Radio Telegraph Convention of July 1908 simply because the [*SOS* Morse Code] combination of three dots followed by three dashes followed by three dots was easy to send and easy to recognize."

acronym-initialism punctuation   Everybody knows that it would make no sense to insert periods in words. But many people make the mistake of inserting periods in initialisms that are abbreviations for a single word, such as *TV* and *ID*.

You should also omit periods for the initialisms of the many organizations that do so in their name, as with *AAA* (American Automobile Association), *ABC* (American Broadcasting Co.), *BBC* (British Broadcasting Corp.), *FBI* (Federal Bureau of Investigation), *IBM* (International Business Machines Corp.), and *IRS* (Internal Revenue Service).

For non-organizational initialisms formed from more than one word, follow any style that you choose or that's chosen for you by your employer. Note that the stylebook of *U.S. News & World Report* omits periods for *HMO* (health maintenance organization), and the stylebook of *The Washington Post* omits periods for *GNP* (gross national product). But the stylebook of *The New York Times* prescribes *H.M.O.* and *G.N.P.*

Never omit periods from an initialism if the result can be misleading, as in removing the periods from *a.m.* to form what looks like the verb *am*.

acronym-initialism redundancy   See "redundant acronyms and initialisms."

acronym-initialism warning   Though acronyms and initialisms are time-savers for the writer, they can be time-wasters for the reader when they are not used sparingly. As cultural historian Jacques Barzun warned in *From Dawn to Decadence*, published in 2000, too many writers are addicted to "using initials instead of names and to giving institutions long titles that yield a pseudo-word acronym." Barzun added that this addiction wastes the reader's time because it "taxes the memory and creates ambiguity as identical letter groups multiply."

act or **action?**   These words are sometimes interchangeable, as in "His act [action] was inexcusable." But *act* usually means a single deed, as in "a heroic act," and *action* means a process involving more than one act, as in "a demand for action."

In an acceptable, idiomatic exception, we use *act* for a process involving more than one act when we say "She cleaned up her act" or "He got his act together."

act or **bill?**   A *bill* is a proposed law, submitted for the consideration of a legislature. If the bill becomes law, which is to say it is *enacted*, it can be called an *act*. (See also "*enact* or *enact into law?*")

activate or **actuate?**   *Actuate* used to be a common synonym for *activate* ("making something function"), as in triggering a chemical process or an emergency plan. Today, *actuate* is a rarely used synonym for *motivate*, as in "actuated by greed." To avoid confusion, activate things, motivate people, and actuate nothing.

active or passive voice?   See "passive voice should not be silenced."

acuity or *acuteness*?   Both words are synonyms for "sharpness, keenness." But precise writers tend to save *acuity* to express an acuteness ("keenness") of hearing, vision, or understanding.

A.D.: before or after the numeral?   Because A.D. stands for *Anno Domini* ("[in] the year of our Lord"), the logical, time-honored practice is to place A.D. before the numeral and to avoid the redundancy of adding "in" or "in the year."

In an illustration of the comparative use of A.D. and B.C., Jared Diamond wrote in his 2005 bestseller, *Collapse: How Societies Choose to Fail or Succeed*, about "the destruction of Carthage by Rome in 146 B.C." and the Western Roman Empire's fall "being taken somewhat arbitrarily as A.D. 476."

Usage commentator William Safire has repeatedly confessed in his *New York Times* "On Language" column that he positioned A.D. incorrectly in his "most far-reaching" usage error. As a speechwriter in the Nixon White House, Safire instructed a plaque maker to use "July 1969 A.D." for the sign the astronauts would leave on the moon. Too late, Safire realized that he should have said "July A.D. 1969."

adage: an *old* problem   You risk being accused of a redundancy if you join the many professional writers who use the phrase *old adage* ("old saying"). That's because some usage guides—for example, *The New York Times Manual of Style and Usage*—maintain that *adage* means "old saying" all by itself. Indeed, *adage* is defined as an "old saying" by *Webster's New World College Dictionary*. And the other dictionary definitions of *adage*—"traditional saying" and "proverb"—unquestionably refer to a saying that is old.

The American Heritage Dictionary, though acknowledging that all adages are old, suggests that the phrase *old adage* should be accepted as an established idiom because *old* has accompanied *adage* since *adage* first entered English in the 16th century. But if you want to avoid 21st-century criticism for using *old adage*, just say "old saying."

adapter or *adaptor*?   Dictionaries list *adapter* as the preferred spelling and *adaptor* as an alternate spelling for "a person or device that adapts." But some professional writers prefer *adaptor* for the device.

addressing your pronunciation   Stress the first syllable of *address* when you mean "location," the second syllable when you mean "formal speech," "to give a speech," or "to deal with."

adduce or deduce?   *Adduce* means "cite evidence to support an opinion," as in "adducing statistics to prove one's point." *Deduce* means "infer, draw a conclusion."

adequate is enough already   *Adequate* means "sufficient for the purpose," so *enough* is redundant in the phrase *adequate enough*.

If you are using *adequate* to mean "*barely* sufficient," make sure your sentence conveys your intended message. Example: "His performance on that job was only adequate." (See also "*ample enough* for you?")

adherence or adhesion?   Careful communicators use *adhesion* in the literal sense of "the act of sticking to" and *adherence* in the figurative sense of "the act of sticking to faithfully," as in "adherence to an agreement."

adieu or au revoir?   The internationally adopted French expression *adieu* ("ah-DYOO")—like its equivalents in Spanish and Italian, *adios* and *addio*—is a straight *good-bye*, couched in the polite phrase "[I commend you] to God."

The internationally adopted French expression *au revoir* ("oh re-VWAH")—like its equivalents in Spanish and Italian, *hasta la vista* and *arrivederci*—means "until we meet again." Usage example: In a *Mary Worth* comic strip by Karen Moy and Joe Giella (4/23/2002), a scheming woman dumps her lovestruck admirer with the words "Just think of this as 'au revoir,' Wilbur, not 'good-bye'!"

adjacent or adjoining?   *Adjacent* can mean "joined, touching," but it also can mean "near." Precise writers therefore use *adjacent* for "near" and *adjoining* for "joined, touching." In line with that distinction, only rooms that are next door or connected can be described as *adjoining*. Memory hint: *Adjoining* contains *join*.

adjectives: comparative and superlative   See "comparatives and superlatives: what Alice didn't know."

adjectives: how many deserve to die? Voltaire said, "The adjective is the enemy of the noun." Echoing that sentiment in a letter about writing style to a 12-year-old boy, Mark Twain advised: "When you catch an adjective, kill it. No, I don't mean utterly, but kill most of them—then the rest will be valuable. They weaken when they are close together. They give strength when they are wide apart."

How do you decide which adjectives to keep? Sir Ernest Gowers, in his *Complete Plain Words*, urged writers to favor adjectives that denote kind rather than degree. For example, note that *economic* in "economic crisis" adds important information but *acute* in "acute crisis" is redundant.

You can justify the killing of many adjectives by making your nouns more precise. For example, *skyscraper* is better than *tall building*. Likewise, you can justify the killing of many adverbs by making your verbs more precise, as in saying that freeway traffic was *crawling* rather than *moving slowly*.

Novelist and writing instructor Anne Bernays, in a *New York Times* essay (2/28/2000), recalled that her students "hated" writing assignments of hers in which they were not allowed to use adjectives or adverbs. But, she said, such assignments "made them realize how strong verbs and nouns are, especially when they stand alone."

administer or **administrate?** *Merriam-Webster's Dictionary of English Usage* says *administrate* is "unstigmatized" and can be traced all the way back to the British English of the 17th century. But you risk some criticism today if you use *administrate* instead of the less awkward synonym *administer*.

Depending on your occupation, you can *administer* ("manage") an agency, *administer* ("apply in a formal way") last rites, *administer* ("apply as a remedy") a medication, or *administer* ("mete out") justice.

admissable is not **admissible** The correct spelling is *admissible*. (See also "spelling traps.")

admission or **admittance?** Which sign is correct, "No admission" or "No admittance"? Both, depending on the intended meaning. "No admission" may mean "No one can go in" but also can mean "No money will be charged." "No admittance" clearly means "No one can go in."

You will be in the mainstream of usage if you save *admittance* for "physical access to a place" and *admission* for being admitted to membership in something or for the sense of "confession," as in "admission of guilt."

admit or **admit to?**   Use *admit* when you mean "acknowledge, confess," as in "I freely admit my inadequacy." Use *admit to* when you mean "permit entrance, give access," as in "I was admitted to the palace" and "That door admits to the garden."

admit or **say?**   Journalism students who try too hard to find a substitute for the word *say* will sometimes wrongly pick the word *admit*. Notice that error in a sentence from a story submitted by one of my journalism students, about a woman who teaches dance: "She admits [should be *says*] she has considered a career in dance therapy." In a variation of that error, another student journalist wrote that a professor "admittedly is intrigued by Russian culture."

Save *admit* and *admittedly* for disclosures that are made reluctantly: "He admitted that the accident was his fault."

ad nauseam: look again   Take a second look at the correct spelling—*ad nauseam*—of this Latin-derived phrase meaning "to the point of causing nausea; to a sickening, disgusting, or ridiculous degree." The mistake of ending the phrase with *-um* is so common that you will find it in leading newspapers such as the *Los Angeles Times* (6/5/1993) and even in a highly regarded reference book, *The New York Public Library Desk Reference*.

In an example of correct spelling and usage, with a bonus pun, a *Time* magazine article (11/13/2000) about ridiculously repetitive television commercials was titled "Campaign Ad Nauseam."

adonis or **Adonis?**   In Greek mythology, Adonis was a strikingly attractive youth whom the goddess of love, Aphrodite, hid in a chest, trying unsuccessfully to keep him for herself. Today, an *Adonis* or *adonis* is any "very handsome young man."

adopted or **adoptive?**   In adoption, adults become the *adoptive* parents of *adopted* children.

The New Fowler's Modern English Usage announced in 1996 that "the traditional distinction between *adopted* and *adoptive* appears to be crumbling." But the distinction was still being upheld in the 2003 *Garner's Modern American Usage.*

Both *adoptive* and *adopted* may be used, without risk, for a resettled person's "new" country, city, or state.

adrenaline or *Adrenalin?*
The energizing hormone secreted by the adrenal gland is adrenaline. The capitalized, no-final-*e Adrenalin* is the trademark for the adrenaline extracted from animals or prepared synthetically.

adult: an adulterated word
As dictionaries now acknowledge, *adult* no longer necessarily means "mature." *Adult* now also means "not suitable for children," as in "adult entertainment." (See also *"explicit."*)

Adult is preferably pronounced "a-DULT" in American English, "AD-ult" in British English.

advance or *advancement?*
Advance is a verb meaning "to move or cause to move forward" and a noun meaning "a forward movement," either physical (as in "the army's advance") or figurative (as in "advances in public transportation").

As a noun, *advance* differs from *advancement* in two ways. *Advancement* generally is used only in the figurative sense of *advance* ("progress, development, improvement"). And *advancement* usually implies that the progress is a result or intended result of a deliberate effort, as illustrated by the name of the American Association for the Advancement of Science.

advance planning may be too much
The *advance* in *advance planning* is redundant unless you are emphasizing the idea of planning that is long-range rather than planning for the immediate future.

The same applies to the *advance* in *advance notice* and *advance reservations,* to the *ahead* in *planning ahead,* and to the *future* in *future plans.*

advantage, vantage, or *vantage point?*
An *advantage* is, of course, "a state or circumstance favorable to a desired end."

A *vantage* is "an advantage in a competition" or "a position likely to provide an advantage." A *vantage point* is "a place affording a good view."

advent, Advent, or **Adventist?**　　The word *advent*—from the Latin *adventus* ("the coming to, the arrival")—means the coming or arrival of something, usually something very important. For example, an article in *The New York Times* (11/16/2000) referred to the "advent of sophisticated new computer technology."

The capitalized *Advent* refers to the period beginning with the fourth Sunday before Christmas, which is observed by many Christians as a time to pray, fast, and otherwise commemorate the birth of Christ.

Adventist identifies a member of any Christian denomination that believes the Second Coming of Christ is near.

adventitious is not always advantageous　　Derived from the Latin *adventicius* ("extraneous"), *adventitious* means "associated with in an accidental, extraneous manner, not essentially inherent." For example, consider "the adventitious beauty of a nuclear-bomb mushroom-cloud." In that sense, the beauty is obviously unrelated ("extraneous") to the cloud's macabre origin.

adverbs: comparative and superlative　　See "comparatives and superlatives: what Alice didn't know."

adverbs that look like adjectives　　Many people think it is wrong to tell somebody to "drive slow." They think only "drive slowly" will do, on the grounds that the adverb *slowly* is needed to modify the verb *drive*. But "drive slow" is as acceptable as "drive slowly," because *slow* is not just an adjective but also the "flat" form of the adverb *slowly*. The adverbial *slow* tends to sound better in short messages, *slowly* in long ones.

The Columbia Guide to Standard American English explains: "Flat adverbs are old, mostly high-frequency adverbs that in Old English usually had an *-e* ending. When they lost it, they looked and sounded like adjectives, and some of them then added the *-ly* suffix of modern adverbs, often being used adverbially then in both forms."

In addition to *slow*, the flat forms of *-ly* adverbs include *bad, bitter, bright, close, fair, hard, high, loud, near, right, sharp, sure, tight,* and *wrong.* Some adjectives, including *straight* and *fast*, assume the role of adverb only without the *-ly* ("Go straight," "Drive fast"). (*Fastly* exists but is archaic.)

Your choice of adverbial form—with or without the *-ly*—may be determined by your intended meaning. For example, *high* means "up," and *highly* can mean "extremely." *Late* means "tardy," but *lately* means "recently." The adverbial *short* can mean "lacking" ("He came up short"), but *shortly* means "soon." The adverbial *right* means "directly," and *rightly* can mean "justifiably." As Follett's *Modern American Usage* points out, "To think hardly of a person or idea is not the same thing as to think hard." Likewise, "to hit *hard*" obviously does not mean the same as "to *hardly* hit."

When the same adverb can be used with or without an -*ly*, your choice usually depends on which version works better for your style and context. But remember that English idiom requires a clock to run *slow* (not *slowly*) and a night watchman to stay *wide* (not *widely*) awake. And all of us should learn to take it *easy* (not *easily*). (See also entries for *bitter, clean, deep, easy, quick, slow,* and *tight*.)

adverbs that modify sentences   See "commas for sentence adverbs."

adverse **or** *averse*?   "Never be adverse to checking facts," says a journalism instructor's handout at a Southern California community college. If the instructor had checked a dictionary, he would have discovered that he should have used *averse*.

Adverse and *averse* are both adjectives that speak of opposition. But you should apply *averse* to *people* (who are "unwilling, reluctant") and *adverse* to *events* or *effects* (that are "unfavorable, harmful"). The *Financial Times* (5/12/2000) used *adverse* correctly when quoting a scientific panel on mobile-phone microwave radiation: "If there are any adverse effects, children would be most vulnerable."

To help you remember the distinction between these words, note that *adverse* has the related noun *adversity* ("misfortune"), and *averse* has the related noun *aversion* ("strong feeling of dislike").

advice **or** *advise*?   Typo gremlins often cause people to confuse the verb *advise* ("to recommend") with the noun *advice* ("recommendation").

advise **or** *inform*?   To avoid criticism from some word guardians, use the verb *advise* when you mean "to offer advice" or "to recommend" but not when you mean "to inform." Advisable usage: "When the new employee was informed about the meeting, she was advised that she should make every effort to attend."

adviser or *advisor?*   Dictionaries list both as correct. Most dictionaries assign the preferred listing to *adviser*. But others, perhaps influenced by the sole spelling of *advisory*, assign the preferred listing to *advisor*.

So choose either, as long as you avoid the inconsistency shown by following a *Chronicle of Higher Education* (7/17/1998) article about the problems confronting the student-newspaper *adviser*. In the article, a college president was quoted about the proper role of the student-newspaper *advisor*.

aegis, **Aegis,** or *escutcheon?*   In Greek mythology, the impregnable shield of the god Zeus was named the Aegis ("EE-jis"), from a Greek word for "goat," because the shield was said to be covered with the skin of a she-goat named Amalthea who had suckled Zeus as an infant.

The word *aegis*—as used in the phrase "under the aegis of"—has acquired the meanings "protection, patronage, sponsorship, auspices, authority, guidance, controlling influence, leadership."

An *escutcheon* ("eh-SKUTCH-en"), from a Latin word for "shield," is a shield that displays a coat of arms. A "blot on one's escutcheon" is a stain on a person's reputation. *Escutcheon* is also a word for a protective plate around a keyhole, light switch, or the like.

aeolian or *Aeolian?*   The adjective *Aeolian* ("ee-OH-lee-an") means "pertaining to Aeolus" ("EE-oh-les"), the ancient Greek god of the winds. Hence, *Aeolian* and *aeolian*—the lowercase form is more common—mean "caused by the wind, wind-driven."

An *aeolian harp* (also known as a *wind harp*) is in the form of an open box over which are stretched strings that sound when the wind blows over them.

aerate and *aerie*: keep the *air* out   Though the verb *aerate* sounds like "AIR-ate" and means "expose to the circulation of air," you won't find any *air* in the word. Note too the lack of *air* in the noun *aerie*, which refers to "a nest, such as that of a bird of prey, high up in the air" or "a house or other structure in a high place." *Aerie* is preferably pronounced to rhyme with *dairy*.

aesthetics or *esthetics?*   A tendency is developing to change the *ae* in our Greek-originated words to *e*. For example, *anesthesia* is now preferred over *anaesthesia*.

But dictionaries still reflect a preference for *aesthetics* over *esthetics* (used with a singular verb and meaning "the branch of philosophy dealing with theories of beauty in art and in general"). The preference for preserving the *ae* also applies to *aesthetic* ("of or relating to aesthetics"), *aesthetically* ("according to aesthetics" or "in an aesthetic manner"), *aestheticize* ("to depict in an artistic or idealized manner"), and three related words discussed in the next entry: *aesthete*, *aestheticism*, and *aesthetician*. (See also "*archaeology* or *archeology*?")

aesthetics-related confusion   With the following three words, you will need to make sure that your context clarifies your intended meaning.

Aesthete means "one who cultivates an unusually high sensitivity for beauty" or "one who pretends to have an unusually high sensitivity for beauty" or "one whose sensitivity for beauty is decadently excessive or superficial."

Aestheticism means "the doctrine that beauty is the basic principle from which all other principles, especially moral ones, are derived." But *aestheticism* can also mean "an exaggerated devotion to art, music, or poetry, with indifference to practical matters."

Aesthetician means "one versed in the theory of beauty." But it can also mean "beautician," especially with the alternate spelling *esthetician*.

affect or effect?   These words are so easily confused that you can find an example of the confusion even in the files of *The Journal of the Writers Guild of America, West*. The table of contents for the July 1992 issue summarized an article about "how the entertainment industry . . . is effected [should have been *affected*] by censorship."

To deal with this eternally troublesome pair of words, the first thing to remember is that *affect* is the *verb* for influence and *effect* is the *noun* for influence. When you *affect* something, the result is an *effect*. And just as a cause comes before a result, the initial letter of *affect* alphabetically precedes the initial letter of *effect*.

The verb *affect* can also mean "pretend, feign," as in "to affect an accent." From that meaning you get the adjective *affected* ("pretentious") and the noun *affectation* ("pretension").

Effect can also play the role of a verb, meaning "cause, accomplish, execute," as in a *New York Times* observation (8/6/2000) that presidential candidates' ideas about school reform "rarely effect change."

Let us hope this usage dictionary will *affect* its readers by producing a beneficial *effect* and perhaps *effect* a greater appreciation of communication that is not what critics would call *affected*. (See also "*cause* or *effect*.")

affinity: must the feeling go both ways?   You would be taking a risk at a job interview if you said you had an *affinity* ("aptitude") for a particular skill or an *affinity* ("natural liking") for hard work.

Such usage, though listed as standard by the Merriam-Webster and Random House dictionaries, has been rejected by Fowler's *Dictionary of Modern English Usage*, *The Oxford Guide to English Usage*, *The Economist Style Guide*, Follett's *Modern American Usage*, and a majority of the *American Heritage Dictionary* usage panel. Fowler and Follett argued that *affinity*—originally "a relationship by marriage," then "a feeling of kinship inspired by common interest" and "a mutual attraction binding atoms together in compounds"—must refer only to attractions that are mutual. From that perspective, you can have an affinity *with* somebody, or an affinity can exist *between* you. But, so this argument goes, you cannot have an affinity *for* someone or *to* something, because *affinity* does not apply to someone or something not also attracted to you.

Here is an illustration of the mutual nature of *affinity*, from *The Economist* (2/7/1998): "To celebrate their intellectual affinity, the [Prime Minister] Blair and President Clinton camps are due to hold a policy seminar this weekend."

afflict or inflict?   These words are often used interchangeably, and they are therefore listed by some dictionaries as synonyms. But precise communicators observe the following distinction: With *afflict*, they immediately say *who* is involved; with *inflict*, they immediately say *what* is involved. *Afflict* means "to cause suffering to some living thing." Therefore, the object of *afflict* is the victim: "Poverty too often afflicts children." *Inflict* means "to impose [something unpleasant]." The object of *inflict* is that unpleasant thing: "Poverty too often inflicts suffering upon children."

Note that *afflict* takes the preposition *with*, but *inflict* takes *upon*.

affluent and effluent go with the flow   Both these words have a preferred pronunciation that stresses the first syllable, and both refer to a flow.

As adjectives, *affluent* means "wealthy, abundant, flowing freely," and *effluent* means "flowing out."

As nouns, an *affluent* is "a stream or river that flows into a body of water," and an *effluent* is "a stream flowing out of a body of water" or "an outflow of a storage tank, irrigation canal, or sewer."

Afghan or afghani? The *Afghans*, the south-central Asian people of Afghanistan, call their basic monetary unit the *afghani*.

afraid, aghast, frightened, or scared? People who avoid air travel because of a phobia are not *scared* or *frightened* of flying. They are *afraid* of it. Being scared or frightened is temporary, as when one watches a horror movie. The word *afraid* connotes fear that is chronic.

Aghast, derived from an Old English word for *ghost*, means "suddenly struck by shock, terror, or amazement."

African-American See "ethnic and racial classifications."

after or following? Avoid the artificially formal *following* in such sentences as "They went to the movies following dinner." Use *after* instead.

after or when? Some students who ordinarily know the difference between *after* and *when* will sometimes write *after* when they mean *when*. The result is that a single incident is made to seem like two incidents. Here is an example from one of my university classes in newswriting: "A bulletproof vest saved the life of a policeman last night after [should have been *when*] a holdup man fired two shots at his chest."

aftermath: an unpleasant crop A few centuries ago, a *math* (from an Old English word for "mowing") was a mowing of grass or similar grazing vegetation, and the *aftermath* was the usually inferior grazing vegetation that sprang up after the first crop had been harvested. Today, *aftermath* means "the consequences of, or period following, an event, usually a misfortune or disaster."

Merriam-Webster's Dictionary of English Usage speculates that *aftermath* acquired its unpleasant connotation because farmers discovered that their livestock became sick from grazing on aftermath that was infested with parasites. Whether or not that is correct, today's precise writers use *aftermath* only for situations that are unpleasant. For example, the *Columbia Journalism Review*

(May/June 2002) noted that "all but five of the fourteen Pulitzers this year were related to September 11 and its aftermath." Similarly, *New York Times* columnist Paul Krugman (7/29/2003) wrote about "the aftermath of the Iraq war."

afterward or afterwards? American English favors *afterward* for this adverb; British English, *afterwards*. (See also "*backward* or *backwards?*" "*forward* or *forwards?*" and "*toward* or *towards?*")

again you must choose a pronunciation The customary American pronunciation of *again* rhymes with *hen*. But some people in the Atlantic states, echoing a British pronunciation, pronounce *again* so that it rhymes with *pain*. In parts of our South, *again* rhymes with *fin*.

agape can express amazement or love The adverb and adjective *agape* (rhyming with *escape*) means "open-mouthed with amazement."

A separate *agape*, preferably pronounced "ah-GAH-pay," is a noun used in the broad sense of "brotherly love." As President Jimmy Carter wrote in an op-ed essay for *The New York Times* on Christmas Eve 1996, "Most great religions espouse the golden rule, based on agape—love or self-sacrifice, for the benefit of others."

aged: one syllable or two? *Aged* as the past tense of the verb *age*—"he aged quickly under stress"—should be pronounced as one syllable. But in the role of a noun—as in "caring for the aged"—make it two syllables.

In the role of an adjective, *aged* is two syllables when applied to people and one syllable when applied to process. For example: "Some [two-syllable] aged people enjoy [one-syllable] aged wine."

ageing or aging? This is another of those words—including *abridgment*, *acknowledgment*, and *judgment*—in which Americans typically drop an *e* (as in *England*) from the British English spelling. (See also "spelling traps.")

ageism or agism? This term for "age prejudice," attributed to a 1969 coinage by geriatric physician Robert Butler of Washington, D.C., contains the full word *age*.

agenda is **or** *agenda are?*   Your best bet is to say, "agenda *is*," though that violates *agenda*'s original Latin meaning.

Agenda is the plural of the Latin *agendum*, which means "something that needs to be done." But in English, *agendum* is used so infrequently and is considered so pedantic, even archaic, that many usage commentators approve of *agenda* as singular, meaning "a *list* of things that need to be done."

Recommendation: Replace *agendum*—on the rare occasions when you need to use it—with *agenda item*. Use *agenda* for a single list of agenda items. For more than one such list, say *agendas*—as in a headline in *The New York Times* (8/8/1997), "Israelis and Palestinians Have Different Agendas." (See also "*data is* or *data are?*")

aggravate **can irritate**   If you want to avoid the risk of being accused of an aggravated assault on the English language, don't join the millions of people who use *aggravate* as a synonym for *annoy*. Use *aggravate* only in its uncontroversial meaning of "worsen," as in this example from *The New York Times* (3/24/2004): "Troops [in Syria fired] on the [Kurdish] demonstrators, aggravating long-standing tensions."

As word connoisseur Robert Claiborne observed in *Our Marvelous Native Tongue*, "The use of *aggravate* to mean 'annoy' [is] seen by many educated people as evidence of ignorance." If you need a synonym for *annoy*, consider *anger, arouse, bother, exasperate, irritate, nettle, outrage, provoke, rile, upset*, or *vex*.

Though both the "annoying" and "worsen" meanings of *aggravate* have been traced as far back as the early 17th century, grammarians in the late 19th century began denouncing the "annoying" *aggravate* for being too far removed in meaning from the word's Latin root, *aggravare* ("to make heavier").

Henry W. Fowler declared in the 1926 first edition of his *Dictionary of Modern English Usage* that the "annoying" *aggravate* "should be left to the uneducated." Fowler's verdict was sustained in Theodore M. Bernstein's 1972 book, *The Careful Writer*, and in the 1972, 1979, and 2000 editions of Strunk and White's *Elements of Style*. The 1975 and 1985 *Harper Dictionary of Contemporary Usage* reported that its usage panel had cast a 57 percent vote against the "annoying" *aggravate* in writing and a 47 percent vote against its use in speech. In 1988, the *Longman Guide to English Usage* advised that the "annoying" *aggravate* was avoided by "careful stylists." In 1993 *The Columbia*

Guide to Standard American English reported, "Edited English uses the 'make worse' sense [of *aggravate*] almost exclusively."

In 1997, lexicographer Eugene Ehrlich wrote in his *Highly Selective Dictionary for the Extraordinarily Literate*, "If you wish to speak and write well . . . reserve *aggravate* for *worsen*." The 1998 American edition of Kingsley Amis' *King's English* cited the "annoying" *aggravate* as "improper." Paul W. Lovinger's 2000 *Penguin Dictionary of American English Usage and Style* and Bryan A. Garner's 2003 *Garner's Modern American Usage* said the "annoying" *aggravate* should be avoided in all formal communication. The 2002 *Wall Street Journal Guide to Business Style and Usage* included this listing for *aggravate*: "It means *make worse*. Don't use it to mean *irritate*."

ago or **since**?   *Ago* counts backward from the present ("Four score and seven years ago . . ."). *Since* counts forward from the past ("Since time began . . .").

agreement: noun-pronoun   See "pronouns can be agreeably nonsexist."

agreement: subject-verb   See "verbs must agree in number with their subject."

ahold or **hold**?   Hold back on *ahold* except as a colloquialism ("an informal expression"). For example: An advertisement for Lucent Technologies in *U.S. News & World Report* (3/24/1997) noted that, thanks to communications innovations such as cordless phones, "it seems that anyone can get ahold of you no matter where you are." For risk-free, standard usage, say "[get, take, grab, etc.] *hold* of."

aides, aids, AIDS, Aids   *Aides* are people who provide help. *Aids* are objects that provide help. *AIDS* (note caps and lack of periods) is the acronym for "acquired immune deficiency syndrome."

In British English, the last-named acronym is often written *Aids*. In both British and American English, the human immunodeficiency virus is written *HIV* or *H.I.V.* Avoid the redundant *virus* in "HIV virus."

ain't it a shame?   *Ain't* is "a perfectly good and useful word" that earned its bad reputation by mistake, according to language scholar Stuart Berg Flexner. In his 1976 book *I Hear America Talking*, Flexner wrote that *ain't* had been traced back to *an't*, a contraction for *am not* in early 18th-century England. He explained: "By 1778–79 *an't* had become *ain't* on both sides of the Atlantic [and] was completely acceptable and used by 'gentlemen and scholars.' [But] *ain't* got into serious trouble in the 1830's [after] many people had come to use it to mean 'is not,' 'are not,' 'has not,' and 'have not.' . . . Now so many people began to criticize or disdain the other uses of *ain't* that it became socially unacceptable in all its uses, including its legitimate use as the contraction of *am not*."

Poet-critic John Ciardi, a president of the National College English Association, vigorously defended *ain't* when he served as a panelist for the 1975 and 1985 *Harper Dictionary of Contemporary Usage*: "*Ain't* is the right and inevitable contraction the language demands and will have. No amount of schoolmarming will suppress it. It is about time to end the conspiracy against it." Nevertheless, the "conspiracy" against *ain't* continued. As the year-2000 edition of *The American Heritage Dictionary* reported, "Criticism of *ain't* by usage commentators and teachers has not subsided, and the use of *ain't* is often regarded as a sign of ignorance." In a typical response to *ain't* by mainstream media, the year-2000 edition of *The Associated Press Stylebook* dismissed it as "substandard."

Risk-free recommendation: Save *ain't* for enduring expressions such as "If it ain't broke, don't fix it" and "You ain't heard nothin' yet" (which originated as an ad lib by Al Jolson, when he played the title role in the first talking motion picture, *The Jazz Singer* [1927]).

aka is also known as *a k a*, **a.k.a.**, and ***AKA*** You can find support for all those ways to abbreviate "also known as." For example, *The Associated Press Stylebook* prescribes *aka*. *The New York Times Stylebook* and *Webster's New World Dictionary* prescribe the same abbreviation with spaces, *a k a*. The *Random House Webster's Unabridged Dictionary* prefers *AKA* but accepts *aka*. *The American Heritage Dictionary* lists only *AKA*. The *Microsoft Encarta College Dictionary* prefers *a.k.a.* but accepts *aka*.

I prefer the form used by *Time* magazine, *a.k.a.*, because the periods clearly show that it's an abbreviation. Here's a usage example from a *Time* letter to the editor (6/10/2002): "The reason that the character Peter Parker (a.k.a. Spider-Man) and many of the other Marvel comic-book heroes strike a chord with my generation is that Parker is a conflicted young man."

***à la* is fashionably French**   The compound preposition *à la* is a short adaptation of the French phrase *à la mode de* ("in the fashion, manner, or style of"). In English, *à la* is usually written with the accent mark over the *a*, but the preposition has been in English so long (since the end of the 16th century) that using italics is purely optional. When the English *à la* is followed by a proper name, the French feminine article *la* is used even when the name is masculine, as in a *New York Review of Books* reference (9/24/1998) to a demand that Attorney General Janet Reno "appoint an independent counsel, à la Kenneth Starr, to investigate charges that [Vice President] Gore raised campaign funds on federal property."

The term *à la carte* means "with a separate price for each dish offered on the menu." Depending on context, the phrase *à la mode* can mean "served with ice cream" or "fashionable."

***alarm* or *alarum*?**   The three-syllable *alarum* ("a-LAR-um"), a centuries-old variant of the two-syllable *alarm* ("warning or fear of danger"), survives today despite the premature announcements of its death. But be aware that its use is rare and is usually limited to the meaning of "a call to arms."

Alarum has been dismissed as "obsolete" by *The New Shorter Oxford English Dictionary* and as "archaic" by the *Random House Webster's Unabridged Dictionary* and *Merriam-Webster's Collegiate Dictionary*. *The New Fowler's Modern English Usage* says the use of *alarum* as an alarm signal is "virtually obsolete," and the word *alarum* is used today mainly in a phrase echoing stage directions in Elizabethan drama: *alarums and excursions* ("off-stage sounds of battle"), extended today to mean "clamor, feverishly disordered activity."

But the year-2000 edition of *The American Heritage Dictionary* reports that *alarum* is in current use as "a warning or alarm, especially a call to arms." In an example of such usage, *The New York Times* reported (12/9/1996) that Robert Hass, the nation's poet laureate, had been "traveling to business and civic meetings across the nation with [an] alarum that literacy standards have been plummeting."

***albatross*: the bird and the symbol**   The word *albatross* literally means any of several large web-footed seabirds of the Diomedeidae family, found mostly in the South Pacific.

The symbolic meaning of *albatross*—"a seemingly inescapable burden of guilt," as in the phrase "an albatross around one's neck"—recalls the English poet Samuel Taylor Coleridge's allegorical classic, "The Rime of the Ancient Mariner" (1798). The poem is the tale of a sailor who thoughtlessly uses his crossbow to kill an albatross (a symbol of good luck) that had been adopted as a beloved companion by his fellow crewmen. The death of the albatross brings horribly bad luck to the ship, and the crewmen make the sailor wear the albatross around his neck as a sign of his guilt. One night, suddenly becoming aware of the beauty of water snakes around the ship, the sailor realizes that all God's creatures are beautiful and precious. The spell of bad luck is thus broken, and the albatross falls from the sailor's neck into the sea.

A related symbolic meaning of *albatross* is "obstacle to success," as in a *New York Times* article (9/12/2000) in which a political observer was quoted as saying that the generally pro-Republican National Rifle Association had decided not to endorse Republican presidential candidate George W. Bush because the organization had become "a real albatross for candidates."

albeit: an oldie but goodie   In the early 20th century, some usage commentators dismissed *albeit* as "archaic." Near the end of the century, in 1990, Professor of English J. N. Hook wrote in his *Appropriate Word* that *albeit* imparts "an old-time touch reminiscent of a Dickensian lawyer's office." But according to *Merriam-Webster's Dictionary of English Usage*, the word *albeit* has remained in style for centuries, with a "considerable increase" in use since the 1930's.

Pronounced "ahl-BEE-it" and derived from a Middle English compound for *although it be*, this synonym for "although, though, even though, even if, notwithstanding, conceding the fact that" has been employed by Shakespeare, Thackeray, Yeats, Kipling, and many writers of our own time.

Usage examples: *The Economist* (3/4/2000) commented that Andres Pastrana, the president of Colombia, "leads a democracy, albeit an imperfect one." An editorial in the national weekly edition of *The Washington Post* (4/3/2000) noted that Vladimir Putin, then the acting president of Russia, had won the presidency—"albeit with a smaller majority than expected."

Apparently, you need not be afraid that *albeit* will mark you as old-fashioned. But you will be marked as a perpetrator of redundancy if you use the needless *but* in "but albeit."

***alibi* is no excuse**   Nobody disputes the use of *alibi* (Latin for "elsewhere") in its centuries-old legal sense of "proof that a suspect was not at the scene of the crime." But you risk criticism if you contribute to the widespread use of *alibi* in the sense of "an excuse offered to evade responsibility."

Opponents of the "excuse" *alibi* include slightly more than half of the usage panel of *The American Heritage Dictionary*, along with the stylebook editors of *The Wall Street Journal* and *The Economist*. B. A. Phythian argued in his *Concise Dictionary of Confusables*: "This [use of *alibi* to mean excuse] is inexcusable, there being plenty of words that will serve (*defense, justification, pretext, reason, explanation*) without abusing *alibi* in this way. . . . Alibi has a specific, useful and unique [legal] meaning, which is worth preserving intact."

The *Longman Guide to English Usage* reports that an even more intense objection is raised by "some people" to the use of *alibi* as a verb, meaning "to offer an excuse."

Risk-free recommendation: Leave *alibi* to defense attorneys.

***aliterate* or *illiterate*?**   *Illiterate* has been used for centuries as a noun and adjective for people who are "unlettered, unlearned" or "completely unable to read and write."

The noun and adjective *aliterate* (coined as television began to seriously challenge print media in the 1960's) applies to the millions of people who know how to read and write but hardly ever use those skills. The early 1980's saw the emergence of the word *aliteracy* as the name for a condition reportedly at least as widespread as *illiteracy*.

***all-around* or *all-round*?**   See "*around* or *round*?"

***all but one is* or *all but one are*?**   The *all* in the phrase *all but one* clearly has a meaning that is plural. For example: "Of the 500 tickets, *all* but one [of those *tickets*] *were* sold." But grammarians say that *one* "attracts" a singular verb when it is followed by its matching singular noun. Example: "All but *one ticket is* sold." Notice that "one ticket *are*" would sound silly. (See also "*one of those plural problems*.")

all* can be incompatible with *not   You risk ambiguity when you say *all* of something is *not* something.

Consider this sentence: "All the students in the class were not present." That statement can convey the idea that there was less than 100 percent but more than zero attendance. But inasmuch as "not present" means "absent," the same statement can be taken to mean that all the students were gone. To clearly communicate your intended meaning, say either "*Some* students were absent" or "*All* students were absent."

all, none, always, never: how do you know?   Consider those words guilty until proven innocent when you are tempted to use them in a generalization about any category of person or thing. Be honest. Have you really observed *all* of whatever it is you are talking about? Do you know enough to exclude an entire category with the word *none*? How do you know something has *always* or *never* been a certain way? The only safe generalization you can make is that none of us knows everything about anything.

all or all of ?   That question has produced "a morass of conflicting opinion," according to Roy H. Copperud's *American Usage and Style: The Consensus.* But you can avoid sinking into that morass if you simply always drop the unnecessary word *of* whenever Standard English gives you the option of doing so.

You are given that option before the possessive pronouns *its, my, your, our, his, her,* and *their* and the relative pronoun *that,* so you should choose *all* rather than *all of* in such phrases as "all my children," "all your life," and "all that jazz." Likewise, you should exercise your option to choose *all* in place of *all of* before collective and plural nouns, as in "He cut all the [collective] grass, then trimmed all the [plural] trees."

But Standard English usage gives you no choice—you must use *all of*—before singular nouns ("Search all of the house"), before the impersonal pronoun *it* ("The dog ate all of it"), and before the objective-case pronouns (objects of verbs or prepositions) *me, you, us, them,* and *whom* ("All of us are leaving"). (See "*both* or *both of* ?")

all ready or already?   *All ready* is an adjectival phrase meaning "completely prepared." ("She is all ready to go.") *Already* is an adverb meaning "previously, by this time, so soon." ("She is back already?")

"all that glitters" is not Shakespeare   The actual saying, from Shakespeare's *Merchant of Venice*, is "All that *glisters* [a now-archaic word for "glistens" or "sparkles"] is not gold."

all time or all-time?   A hyphen is not needed for the noun phrase *all time*, as in "the most successful pitcher of *all time*." But use a hyphen to designate a compound adjective when you write about "the *all-time* greatest pitcher."

all together or altogether?   The adjectival phrase *all together* means "everyone together, in a group, all at once, all in one place, gathered," as in "They arrived *all together*." Use *all together* only if the two words could be separated. For example: "They arrived *all together*" means the same as "They *all* arrived *together*."

   Altogether, an adverb, means "completely, wholly, totally, entirely, utterly, thoroughly, quite, all told." Usage examples: "Their appearance was *altogether* [entirely] too informal." "He owes me $5,000 *altogether* [all told]."

all told isn't telling   The word *told* in the idiomatic phrase *all told* refers not to communicating but to counting. In the "counting" sense of *tell*, we say "The nun *tells* her beads" and we refer to a person who counts money at a bank as a *teller*. Therefore, *all told* is properly used in the sense of "in all."

   So you should use *all told* only when an explicit total is involved: "All told, *75 books* were written by that author." Replace the *all told* in "All told, she was a good mayor" with something like "all things considered."

all ways or always?   *All ways* is a noun phrase meaning "all the ways." *Always* is an adverb meaning "without exception, all the time, at any time, or forever. Usage examples: "The teacher *always* [without exception] says you should study *all ways* [all the ways] of solving a problem.

alleged is for accusations   For the sake of clarity, use *alleged* only for accusations. Say "alleged guilt" but "apparent innocence."

   If you want to avoid accusations from word guardians—such as the editors of *The New York Times Manual of Style and Usage*—apply *alleged* only to an offense or condition, not to a person. For example, say "alleged perjury," not "alleged perjurer."

allegory, fable, parable, or *roman à clef* ?   An *allegory* is a narrative, such as a novel or drama, in which the characters, places, and incidents are symbolic of various moral truths. In John Bunyan's 17th-century allegory, *The Pilgrim's Progress From This World to That Which Is to Come,* a character named Christian undertakes a journey that is meant to symbolize every Christian's journey through life toward the gate of heaven. Along the way, Christian encounters such characters as Hypocrisy, Mistrust, and Despair as well as Piety, Prudence, and Discretion. Christian is nearly led astray by Mr. Worldly-Wiseman and Mr. Legality, but he is helped by a character named Help and by Mr. Good-will. At one point in the journey, Christian and a traveling companion named Faithful visit the town of Vanity, where they are arrested for refusing to buy anything at the year-round Vanity Fair, which sells all the empty things of the world. Finally, Christian and another traveling companion, Hopeful, bravely cross the River of Death and are met on the other side by angels who lead them to heaven.

A *fable* is a brief allegory that usually involves talking animals, as in the fables attributed to the ancient Greek slave named Aesop ("EE-sahp"). The Aesop fable called "The Fox and the Grapes," about a fox who dismissed as sour the grapes he could not reach, inspired one of the most common expressions in our language: *sour grapes* ("pretended disdain for something one does not or cannot have").

A *parable* is a brief allegory, as in Jesus' parable of the prodigal son, who leaves home and squanders his inheritance but returns repentant and thus earns forgiveness. (See also "*prodigal son* was no conservative.")

A *roman à clef* ("romahn ah KLAY") is French for "novel with a key." It is a novel in which real people appear under fictitious names, as in *Primary Colors,* the best-selling, thinly veiled portrait of Bill and Hillary Clinton and the national press corps, written under the name Anonymous by *Newsweek* columnist Joe Klein and subsequently produced as a movie.

allergic or *allergenic*?   The material (an *allergen*) that causes an *allergic* reaction such as sneezing or itching is described as *allergenic*.

alliteration is not always apt   Alliteration—the repetition of sounds at the beginnings of words or in their accented syllables—attracts attention and may facilitate memory for a key phrase or message.

Sometimes alliteration combines memory enhancement with poetic grace, as when Shakespeare had Hamlet declare, "So foul and fair a day I have not seen," or when the Rev. Martin Luther King Jr. spoke of his dream of a world in which all people would be judged not "by the color of their skin but by the content of their character." But beware of the temptation to overdo it. As *Los Angeles Times* staff writer Bob Baker warned in an investigatory piece on alliteration (5/31/2004), today's "word merchants of politics, advertising and publishing seem to be stacking alliterative words on top of one another like cordwood."

allow, *let,* or *permit*?   These synonyms for "to grant or to consent to something" express three degrees of influence.

Allow implies that you won't be stopped from doing something. You are *allowed* to park in restricted areas on Sunday.

The strongest word, *permit,* suggests formal, authoritative *consent.* A government license *permits* you to practice a certain profession.

Let, the weakest word, may involve a *failure to stop* something. You *let* people take advantage of you.

allude: a risky way of saying *refer*   You invite criticism from word guardians if you imitate the many people who use *allude* as if it were a synonym of *refer* (in the sense of "make reference").

To avoid that risk, preserve the useful distinction between *allude* and *refer* by using *allude* to mean "make reference *indirectly*, without naming the subject of the reference." In President George W. Bush's first inaugural address, he alluded (referred indirectly) to Mother Teresa, Nobel Peace Prize–winning founder of the Missionaries of Charity, when he recalled without mentioning any name that "a saint of our times has said, every day we are called to do small things with great love."

Allude entered early 16th-century English, from the Latin *alludere* ("to play toward," as in pun), and in that sense Christ subsequently was said to have *alluded* to the apostle Peter's name by calling him "a rock." (Note the root in the modern word *petrology,* the study of rocks.)

Consistent with *allude's* history, today's careful writers apply *allude* and *allusion* to references that are indirect and thus not mentioned by name, according to *The New Oxford American Dictionary.*

In a dissenting opinion, the permissive *Merriam-Webster's Dictionary of English Usage* says *allude's* and *allusion's* widespread modern American sense of *direct* reference has become as "impeccably standard" as *allude*'s centuries-old sense of *indirect* reference (and a lesser-known sense of *casual* reference).

But support for adhering exclusively to the "indirect" *allude* and *allusion* can be found in Fowler's *Dictionary of Modern English Usage,* Strunk and White's *Elements of Style,* Bernstein's *Careful Writer,* Follett's *Modern American Usage,* Copperud's *American Usage and Style,* Lovinger's *Penguin Dictionary of American English Usage and Style,* Garner's *Dictionary of Modern American Usage,* the American Heritage and Random House dictionaries, and the style-books of the Associated Press, *The New York Times, The Washington Post, The Wall Street Journal,* and the *Los Angeles Times.*

allusion or illusion?   As if *allusion* (see preceding entry) were not the cause of enough confusion, careless writers confuse it with *illusion* ("deception"). (See also "*delusion* or *illusion?*")

almighty or Almighty?   Capitalize this word only as a noun synonymous with God, as in *the Almighty.* The adjective is lowercase, even in *almighty God.*

almond is a mouthful   Many people say "AL-mund" or "AHL-mund." But *The Columbia Guide to Standard American English* reports that "most Standard English speakers keep the *l* silent," as in "AH-mund."

almost means a lot   A student in one of my newswriting classes wrote, "Almost $40 was taken in the holdup." Though *almost* (meaning "very nearly") was technically correct, that use of the word misleadingly implied that $40 added up to a major robbery. The same misleading implication would have existed if the holdup had involved a few more dollars and the student had written "more than" or "over" $40. The student should have used a neutral word such as *about* or *approximately.* (See also "*most* as a synonym for *almost.*")

a lot they don't know   Many teachers would give a lot to know how to stop students from writing the nonexistent word *alot.* According to *The American Heritage Book of English Usage,* "The fusion of an article and a noun into a single word is a normal linguistic phenomenon, having occurred in *another* and *awhile,* so it is very possible that we all may write *alot* one day." But *alot*'s day of acceptance has not yet arrived.

The single word *allot* means "distribute by share or portion," as in a head-line from *The New York Times* (12/29/2000): "Argentina Plans to Allot Public Works $20 Billion."

alpha and omega   Separately, *alpha* and *omega* are the first and last letters of the Greek alphabet. The phrase *alpha and omega* ("the beginning and the ending" or "the most important part") recalls a statement attributed to Jesus in the Bible (Revelation 1:8): "I am Alpha and Omega, the beginning and the ending, saith the Lord."

already existing: enough already   Just say *existing*.

alright is not right   *Alright* is common in advertising, as in this advertising pitch in *The New York Times* (10/1/1997): "Alright, there is a catch to our free Chase Online Banking. You have to ask for it." That spelling can also be found in some newspaper stories, as in a *Salt Lake Tribune* reference (3/24/2000) to a mother "who calls often to make sure [her son] is alright."

In the view of many usage commentators, however, *alright* is as wrong as *alwrong*. *The New Oxford American Dictionary* lists *alright* as a "logical" spelling variant that is nevertheless nonstandard. *The Oxford Guide to English Usage* says that "*alright*, though widely seen in the popular press, remains non-standard." The *Longman Guide to English Usage* notes that *alright* "is considered to be uneducated, and should be avoided in formal writing." *The American Heritage Dictionary* warns that *alright* has never been accepted as a standard variant of *all right*.

Dennis ("Dr. Grammar") Baron of the University of Illinois at Urbana-Champaign, in his *Guide to Home Language Repair* (1994), wrote: "I predict that *alright* will continue to spread, and that it will continue to be attacked even after it begins to be considered Standard English. But I wouldn't be caught dead using it."

Example of correct usage: In 1954, a 19-year-old delivery boy named Elvis Presley recorded his first single, "That's All Right."

also is also misused   Many students wrongly use the conjunctive adverb *also* ("in addition to") when the appropriate word is the conjunction *and*. For example, the statement, "Sally enjoys walking, also bird watching" should be, "Sally enjoys walking *and* bird watching."

The use of *also* to begin a sentence, as in "Also, she enjoys walking," is forbidden by Follett's *Modern American Usage* but approved by 63 percent of the usage panel of *The American Heritage Dictionary*. However, nobody objects to the use of *also* to begin a sentence when *also* modifies another word in the sentence, as in "Also present at the city council meeting were opponents of the proposed ordinance."

also or too?   The words *also* and *too* both mean "besides, moreover, in addition." But these words differ in three ways:

1. *Also* cannot substitute for *too* when *too* means "overly, excessively." Obviously, "too much" can never be expressed as "also much."
2. As British novelist-critic Kingsley Amis reported in his posthumously published 1997 usage guide, *The King's English*, the word *too*, but not *also*, "is sometimes used by Americans, and increasingly here [in the United Kingdom], to mean *very*, as in [such informal use as] 'I don't feel too well.'"
3. *Too* should never substitute for *also* to begin a sentence. Amis playfully wrote in *The King's English*, "Not even Americans should be allowed to get away with that."

altar or alter?   A student of mine wrote in an autobiographical essay that he once was an "*alter* boy." He should have replaced *alter*, the verb meaning "to change," with *altar*, the noun meaning "platform for religious rituals."

alternate or alternative?   As adjectives, these words are frequently used interchangeably. But to quote the Modern Language Association manual of editing, *Line by Line*, "Why not maintain a distinction that enriches the language?"

Here's how to maintain that risk-free distinction: Use *alternate* as an adjective meaning "every second one," as in "a club that meets on *alternate* Mondays." Use *alternative* as an adjective meaning "providing a choice," as in "an *alternative* lifestyle."

alternatives: can there be too many?   An *alternative*, as compared with an ordinary choice, implies an opportunity to choose from among available options. But considering that the Latin *alter* means "the other of two," can you have more than two alternatives?

Certainly, say the 49 percent of *The American Heritage Dictionary* usage panel who accept that dictionary's broad definition of *alternative* (noun or adjective) as "one of a number of things from which one must be chosen." But 51 percent of the usage panel say they abide by the same dictionary's strict definition of *alternative* as the required choice between "two mutually exclusive possibilities." That 49–51 percent vote reflects disagreement about this question among usage critics in general. The *Harper Dictionary of Contemporary Usage,* which accepts the broad definition of *alternative,* nevertheless includes a warning: "To the purist, one should never speak of three alternatives, rather of three 'choices' or three 'possibilities.' "

Risk-free advice: If you are worried about close encounters with purists, limit your *alternatives* to two. (See also "choice words about *choice.*")

***although* and *though* are not identical twins**   *Although* is more commonly used for "in spite of the fact that," as in "*although* she was rich." *Though* is more commonly used in the sense of *but,* as in "richer *though* not happier."

You cannot use anything but *though* in the conjunctive phrases *as though* and *even though.* Likewise, only *though* can be used as a terminal adverb meaning "however," as in "He continued to bank there, though."

altogether   See "*all together* or *altogether?*"

aluminium* or *aluminum?   Though the spelling *aluminium* ("al-you-MIN-ium") is consistent with that of other chemical elements—like *sodium* and *potassium*—it is acceptable only in British English. In American English, the correct spelling is *aluminum* ("a-LOOM-in-um").

alumnus, alumni, alumna, alumnae   An *alumnus* is the "foster son" of an *alma mater* ("mother who fosters or nourishes"), a term that originally applied to such Roman goddesses as Ceres and Cybele and in the 17th century began to be applied to a person's former school or college. *Alumni* (final sound "eye") may be used as the plural of *alumnus* or as the term for a group of men and women intellectually "nourished" by an educational institution.

The "foster-daughter" words are *alumna* and its plural *alumnae* (final sound "ee"). The year-2000 edition of *The American Heritage Dictionary* notes that "the choice of many women's colleges that have begun to admit men" is the phrase *alumnae and alumni* or the term *alumnae/i.*

These designations apply to anyone who attended a particular campus, whether or not that person graduated. *Graduate* is the correct noun for someone who earned a degree.

a.m. and p.m.   These abbreviations stand for *ante meridiem* (Latin for "before noon") and *post meridiem* (Latin for "after noon").

In American English (as distinguished from British English), *a.m.* and *p.m.* are commonly capitalized, except by publications and organizations that follow a lowercase style, such as *The Wall Street Journal* and the Associated Press. If the abbreviations are capitalized, either full caps (*A.M.* and *P.M.*) or small caps (*A.M.* and *P.M.*) can be used.

Without periods, the capitalized *AM* stands for "amplitude modulation" broadcasting, as compared with *FM* for "frequency modulation" broadcasting.

amateur, neophyte, or novice?   The meaning of *amateur* depends on its context, because it can be used as a compliment or as criticism. Derived from the Latin *amare* ("to love"), *amateur* can refer to a person who engages in an activity for the sheer love of it (nonprofessionally), or it can mean "one who lacks competence."

Novice, from the Latin *novus* ("new"), and *neophyte,* from the Greek *neophutos* ("newly planted"), are synonyms for "beginner."

In a religious sense, both *novice* and *neophyte* can mean "new convert." Also, a neophyte can be a newly ordained priest, and a novice can be someone in a religious order who has not yet taken final vows.

amazon, Amazon, or the Amazon?   In classical mythology, an *Amazon*—from the Greek words *a* ("without") and *mazos* ("breast")—was a member of a tribe of warlike women who fought the Greeks and were so named because they burned or chopped off their right breast to facilitate bending the bow in military archery.

The Amazon, the South American river second in length only to the Nile, is said to have been given its name by the 16th-century Spanish explorer-soldier Francisco de Orellana after he reported that his expeditionary forces were attacked from the shores of the river by tribes of female warriors. (But some scholars say the formidable river derived its name from a Native American word, *amassona,* meaning "boat destroyer.")

The often-lowercase *amazon*—a disparaging term for a tall, powerful, aggressive woman—is clearly a relic of linguistic sexism in a society that has no disparaging term for a tall, powerful, aggressive man.

***ambiance* or *ambience*?** This noun, meaning "the special atmosphere or mood created by a particular environment," was imported from France in the late 19th century. A related adjective, *ambient* ("surrounding"), had entered our language three centuries earlier.

The anglicized form of the noun, *ambience* ("AM-bee-ents"), is prescribed by *The New Fowler's Modern English Usage* and *The New York Times Manual of Style and Usage*, and is preferred by *Merriam-Webster's Collegiate Dictionary* and *Webster's New World Dictionary*.

The alternate form, *ambiance* ("AHM-bee-YAHNS"), is dismissed by *Garner's Modern American Usage* as "a Frenchified affectation." And *The Columbia Guide to Standard American English* warns that some Americans regard the form *ambiance* to be "precious." But *ambiance* is listed as an "equally acceptable variant" in Copperud's *American Usage and Style*, and it is listed as the preferred form by *Random House Webster's College Dictionary* and *The American Heritage Dictionary*.

Suggestion: Pick the form you prefer—or the one preferred by the organization you work for—and don't waste time criticizing those who prefer the other.

ambiguity alert Ambiguities—messages capable of more than one interpretation—can be clever when intentional. For example, there is the old joke about a letter of recommendation that contains these deliberately ambiguous sentences: "I can't even begin to list his good qualities. All I can say is that you'll be lucky if you can get him to work for you. I therefore urge you to waste no time calling him for an interview."

But writers must be constantly on guard against committing ambiguities by accident. For example, if you write "They are cooking apples," your intention may be to refer to *people* cooking apples, but your reader may think you are referring to *apples* suitable for cooking. Watch for such ambiguous phrases as "the French teacher," which could mean a teacher who is French or one who teaches French. Clarify such statements such as "The child hit the man with the baseball bat," which leaves the reader wondering whether the baseball bat was held by the child or the man.

And if you say "I've read Ron's letter to Russell," it could mean either that you've taken the liberty of reading a letter Ron had actually addressed to Russell, or that you read aloud to Russell a letter Ron had written to you or somebody else.

Here are examples of ambiguities in newspaper headlines, reprinted in the *Columbia Journalism Review*: "Alternative to Jail Is Working in Albany" (*Daily Gazette*, Schenectady, N.Y., 2/26/1998); "Dog Chews on Recall List" (*Fresno Bee*, 12/31/1999); "Cubans March Over 6-year-old" (*Amarillo Globe-Times*, 1/28/2000). (See also "*as* ambiguity," "*more* ambiguity," "*since* ambiguity," and "*while* ambiguity.")

ambiguity can always be cured   Writers who have been asked by their editors to explain or replace an ambiguous word or phrase sometimes argue that their intended meaning is made clear by the end of the sentence or in a subsequent sentence. But responsible writers communicate clearly to the reader during every stage of every sentence. Readers should never be forced to waste time and effort wrestling with ambiguity, even momentarily. And under no condition should a writer make it necessary for a reader to stop, back up, and re-read.

Here's an anti-ambiguity prescription: When your context does not instantly convey your intended meaning of a word that has more than one meaning, replace that word with one that conveys only the meaning you want. For example, if you use *still* to mean *nevertheless*—as in "Still, he remained in bed"—your reader might momentarily think you are using *still* in one of its other senses, such as "silent" or "motionless." The reader would probably ascertain your message after reading and pondering the sentence. But you should never force your reader to engage in needless effort. Your clear choice in that sentence is *nevertheless*, because it instantly conveys only the meaning that you intended: "after taking everything into consideration."

ambiguous or **ambivalent?**   *Ambiguous* ("having more than one meaning") applies to *things*, including things that people may say or do.

Ambivalent ("having contradictory feelings")—a word coined in early 20th-century psychiatry—applies only to *people*. It means "the simultaneous existence of opposing feelings, such as love and hate, for the same thing or person." Usage commentators warn that *ambivalent* should not be used for indecision about choosing a thing or person, and that the word does not suggest deception and therefore should not be used to mean two-faced.

Historical note: *The New Fowler's Modern English Usage* calls *ambivalent* "a Jungian word," in reference to Swiss psychiatrist and early Freudian disciple Carl Gustav Jung (1875–1961). But psychiatrist Franz G. Alexander's *History of Psychiatry* credits that coinage to Swiss psychiatrist Eugene Bleuler (1857–1939), who defected from Freud's psychoanalytic movement in 1910, long before the defection of Jung.

ambiguous or **equivocal?**   A statement may be *ambiguous* ("having more than one meaning") by accident or by intent. Only if the ambiguity is intentional ("for the purpose of evasiveness") should you refer to it as *equivocal*. A deceitful person *equivocates*.

amend or **emend?**   Slightly change the verb *amend* ("modify, improve") and you get *emend*, a verb meaning "improve by critical editing." Use *emend* only in writing, and only when you are addressing scholars. Otherwise, people are likely to assume you meant *amend*.

Americans or **United Statesians?**   Our nation's exclusive use of the term *American* "has historically rankled Latin Americans and Canadians," linguist Richard Lederer observed in *The Miracle of Language*. Lederer noted that many alternative names for us have been proposed—including *United Statesians, Unisians,* and *Columbards*—"but none has earned a thumbs-up from the American people, or whatever it is we are."

The term *America* originated with German geographer Martin Waldseemuller. He suggested that name in 1507, in a book detailing the explorations of Italian navigator Amerigo Vespucci, who had sailed to the new land four times between 1497 and 1503. Vespucci himself had suggested that the continent be called *Mundus Novus* ("New World").

Though the name *United States of America* was introduced in our Declaration of Independence, our government called itself the *United States of North America* until *North* was deleted in 1778 by an act of the Continental Congress.

amiable or **amicable?**   The first form refers to people, the second, to relationships. An *amiable* ("friendly, cheerful, pleasing") person is likely to have relationships that are *amicable* ("characterized by goodwill and cooperation").

amid or **among**?   To preserve a useful distinction between these prepositions, use *amid* to mean "in the middle of [things or circumstances]," and use *among* to mean "in the company of [people]."

Usage example for *amid*: In a story about the 2004 race for the presidency, *The New York Times* (9/6/2004) reported that the Kerry team's "recruitment of old Clinton hands came amid rising concerns among Democrats about the state of Mr. Kerry's campaign. "

amidst and **amongst**   Our dictionaries list *amidst* and *amongst* as secondary, chiefly British alternatives to *amid* and *among*. Moreover, *amidst* and *amongst* are rejected by the stylebooks of *The New York Times* and *The Wall Street Journal*, and are dismissed as old-fashioned and pretentious in *Garner's Modern American Usage*.

amok or **amuck**?   *Amok* is the preferred form for this adverb meaning "in a murderous frenzy or otherwise wild manner."

Though *amuck* is listed as the primary spelling by the Random House and American Heritage dictionaries, *amok* is prescribed by the Merriam-Webster unabridged and collegiate dictionaries, *Webster's New World Dictionary*, the *Encarta World English Dictionary*, *The New Oxford American Dictionary*, *The Oxford English Dictionary*, the *Longman Dictionary of the English Language*, Evan Morris' *Word Detective*, and the stylebooks of the Associated Press, *The Washington Post*, *The Wall Street Journal*, and the *Los Angeles Times*.

Amok/amuck entered English in the 16th century, from the Malay *amoq*, and was defined in William Marsden's 18th-century *Malay Dictionary* as "engaging furiously in battle, attacking with desperate resolution, rushing in a state of frenzy to the commission of indiscriminate murder." Today, the word is more likely to be used in the milder sense of "[behaving] in a wild manner."

among or **amongst**?   See "*amidst* and *amongst*."

among or **between**?   You will *usually* be safe if you follow the advice laid down by Samuel Johnson in his dictionary of 1755: "*Between* is properly used of two, and *among* of more." That advice, by the way, is consistent with the fact that -*tween* is derived from an Old English word meaning "two." Usage example: "We must choose *between* good and evil, though there is disagreement about the meaning of those terms *among* philosophers."

But no matter what you may have been taught in school, *between* is the right word for *more* than two if you are focusing on pairs of relationships. For example, in "an agreement between the World Health Organization and 25 nations," each relationship consists of the organization and one nation. Likewise, you brush *between* your teeth, because the phrase refers to the area between each tooth and one next to it. (See "*between you and I* or *between you and me?*")

among other things: not for people   Remember that the phrase "among other things" refers *only* to things, as in "The house needs new plumbing and a new roof, among other things."

Don't fall into the trap of saying something like "Among other things, he was an actor and a director." Acting and directing are not things. That sentence should be changed to "In addition to his other careers, he pursued acting and directing."

amorous words   *Amorous* means "full of or showing love." The Latin phrase *amor patriae* means "love of one's country." The hyphenated French noun *amour-propre* ("ah-moor-PRO-pr") literally means "love of self" but is used in the sense of "self-esteem." An *amour* is a love affair, especially one that is illicit or secret.

amount or number?   Use *amount* for a quantity that cannot be counted—that is, for singular mass nouns, as in "a large amount of structural *damage*." Use *number* for a quantity that can be counted—that is, for plural nouns, as in "a large number of damaged *structures*." (See also "*fewer or less?*")

ample enough for you?   The *enough* in "ample enough" is redundant, because *ample* means "more than enough." (See also "redundancy: a vice and a virtue.")

Amtrak, AMTRAK, or Amtrack?   *Amtrak*, an acronym for "American travel by track," is the correct way to refer to the federally subsidized National Railroad Passenger Corporation.

amuse used to *bemuse*   *Bemuse* and *amuse*—linguistic offspring of the verb *muse* ("to become lost in thought")—both formerly meant "to throw thoughts into disorder" so as to "utterly confuse, bewilder, muddle, stupefy, distract." *Bemuse* retained that meaning while *amuse* evolved separately.

Amuse meant "distract for the purpose of deception" through the 18th century, then developed its present sense of "distract for the purpose of entertainment, entertain in a playful manner." (See also *"muse* or *Muse?"*)

anachronisms: time will tell   Beware of anachronisms—chronological misplacements—when you write about the past or place characters in a setting from the past. For example, you would be guilty of an anachronism if you wrote about an American of the 1930's using a ballpoint pen, an electric blanket, or penicillin. Hollywood has committed plenty of these mistakes: in *The Babe Ruth Story*, for example, a scene set in 1927 showed baseball-stadium ads for beer and whiskey, though 1927 was a Prohibition year. But Hollywood can take comfort in the fact that anachronisms can be found even in the plays of Shakespeare. In Shakespeare's *Julius Caesar*, for example, Cassius says, "The clock has stricken three," though striking clocks would not be invented for another 14 centuries.

anagrams and *antigrams*   An *anagram* is a word, phrase, or sentence made from another by rearranging its letters. Examples: *angel* produces *glean*, *the Morse code* produces *here come dots*, and the memorable moon-landing sentence, "That's one small step for a man, one giant leap for mankind," produces "A thin man ran; makes a large stride, left planet, pins flag on moon. On to Mars."

The word *antigram*, according to *The Oxford Companion to the English Language*, is an anagram that has the opposite meaning to the original word or phrase, as in the utopian vision that *violence* can be changed to *nice love*.

Anagramming, for Scrabble-like amusement and as a technique of hiding secret messages, has been traced back to the ancient Greeks, Romans, and Jews. The practice was so popular in medieval Europe that an official position was created in France called "anagrammatist to the king." In 17th-century Europe, Galileo and other leading scientists recorded their discoveries in anagrams so they could prevent rivals from stealing the credit during the final stage of verification. In recent decades, thousands of reader letters to *The New Yorker* have been answered by "Owen Ketherry," a nonexistent staffer whose name is an anagram for *The New Yorker*. (For more wordplay, see "*palindrome* is not a sports arena.")

anchors usually don't go *away*   Seamen *weigh* ("raise") anchor. The word *aweigh* in "Anchors aweigh!" is an adjective meaning "just clear of the bottom."

and to begin with?   Generations of schoolteachers have warned that it is a mortal sin to begin a sentence with *and*. Actually, as the 1970 and 1998 editions of Follett's *Modern American Usage* pointed out, "the supposed rule" against the initial *and* is "without foundation in grammar, logic or art."

The "rule" against the initial *and* is just a "superstition," according to *Webster's New World Guide to Current American Usage*, *Garner's Modern American Usage*, and Fowler's *Dictionary of Modern English Usage*. In *The New Fowler's Modern English Usage*, linguist R. W. Burchfield wrote: "An initial *and* is a useful aid to writers as the narrative continues. . . . It is also used for other rhetorical purposes, and sometimes just to introduce an improvised afterthought." In further acceptance of the initial *and*, the usage was unanimously approved by the authorities consulted for Copperud's *American Usage and Style* and was classified as "appropriate at any Standard level" by *The Columbia Guide to Standard American English*. And you'll find a vigorous defense of the initial *and* in William F. Buckley Jr.'s 1996 compendium of his writings on "the uses and abuses of language," *Buckley: The Right Word*.

The Oxford English Dictionary notes that the initial *and* was used in the Gospel of St. John, 21:21. You'll find the initial *and* in the writings of Shakespeare (*King John* act 4, scene 1), E. L. Doctorow (*Loon Lake*), and Russell Baker (*Growing Up*). And the initial *and* appears regularly in *The New York Times*, *The Wall Street Journal*, *The Washington Post*, the *Los Angeles Times*, *Time*, *Newsweek*, *U.S. News & World Report*, *The New Yorker*, *Harper's*, *Vogue*, *National Geographic*, *The Nation*, *The American Spectator*, *The Chronicle of Higher Education*, *Glamour*, *Modern Maturity*, *Town & Country*, *Vanity Fair*, *The Economist*, *Natural History*, *Technology Review*, *Reader's Digest*, and the *Columbia Journalism Review*.

A childhood addiction to the initial *and*, according to *Merriam-Webster's Dictionary of English Usage*, may be responsible for much of the anti-initial-*and* prejudice: "Most of us think the prohibition goes back to our early school days [when teachers corrected] the tendency of children to string together independent clauses or simple declarative sentences with *and*'s. [Consequently] many of us go through life thinking it wrong to begin a sentence with *and.*"

At any rate, be careful to use the initial *and* sparingly. If you become addicted to it, says *The Columbia Guide to Standard American English*, your style may seem unpleasantly garrulous and mechanical. (See also "*but* is a starter.")

and/or: a punishable offense?   This legalistic, bureaucratic usage has the virtue of expressing three possibilities—*and, or,* or both of those—with two little words and a slash mark called a *virgule.* But *and/or* is regarded by many usage critics as a grotesque eyesore that perhaps ought to be punishable in nontechnical writing by a fine and/or imprisonment.

The *and/or* combination has been denounced as "ugly" by Fowler's *Dictionary of Modern English Usage,* "ungraceful" by Follett's *Modern American Usage,* "graceless" by Wilson's *Columbia Guide to Standard American English,* "graceless, unsightly and unnecessary" by Freeman's *Wordwatcher's Guide to Good Writing and Grammar,* "stilted" by *The New York Times Manual of Style and Usage,* "a visual and mental monstrosity" by Bernstein's *Careful Writer,* and "[justifiably] vilified" by *Garner's Modern American Usage.*

Risk-free recommendation: If you find yourself using *and/or,* try getting by with *and.* Or try the word *or.* In the example cited in the second sentence of this entry, "a fine and/or imprisonment" the *and/or* can easily be replaced by "a fine or imprisonment or both."

anecdote: don't swallow it   Some people pronounce *anecdote* as if it were *antidote.* Pronounce *anecdote* carefully, the way it is spelled.

angry or mad?   Is it acceptable to use *mad* as a synonym for *angry?* The maddening answer to that question is "Yes, no, and watch out."

According to Copperud's *American Usage and Style:* "the idea that *mad* should not be used to mean 'angry' is now a nearly forgotten pedantry." But Freeman's *Words to the Wise* states with equal certainty that a person should be described as *mad* only if "deranged." American-language scholar Stuart Berg Flexner, in his *I Hear America Talking,* wrote: "Some Englishmen had used *mad* to mean angry since the 13th century, but after the 1750's this archaic use was condemned as a new and vulgar Americanism. . . . By the 1840's, however, *mad* meaning *angry* was accepted and becoming standard, formal English."

The Oxford English Dictionary states that "*mad* implies maniacal, violent excitement or extravagant delusions" and is appropriate as an adjective for "furious, beside oneself with anger" only in communication that is informal.

The *Random House Webster's Unabridged Dictionary* defines *mad* as "deranged" and also as "angry," but adds, "Because some teachers and usage critics insist that the only correct meaning of *mad* is 'mentally disturbed, insane,' *mad* is often replaced by 'angry' in formal contexts." Similarly, *The American Heritage Dictionary* first defines *mad* as "suffering from a disorder of the mind," then lists the "angry" definition as "informal."

Risk-free solution: Nobody will become angry with you if you use *mad* only for "deranged."

angst: anxiety-proof pronunciation   The German-derived noun *angst*—"a feeling of anxiety or dread, often associated with depression"—is preferably pronounced "AHNKst." Usage example from a *New York Times* article about television dramas (12/10/2000): "The budding romance between two teachers seems to burn with more angst than passion."

Don't expect thanks for saying "ANKst" unless you are using the *angst* that is an abbreviation for *angstrom* (named after 19th-century Swedish physicist Anders Jonas Ångström), a unit of length equal to one hundred-millionth of a centimeter.

animadversion or aversion?   *Animadversion* ("hostile criticism") is sometimes wrongly used as if it were an elegant or more emphatic form of *aversion* ("an intense dislike of something and a desire to avoid it"). People can have an *aversion to,* not an *animadversion to,* spiders.

Animadversion and its verb, *animadvert,* require the prepositions *on* or *upon*: "Jones animadverted *on* [or *upon*] the irresponsibility of columnists who engage in unjust animadversions *on* [or *upon*] the Los Angeles lifestyle."

animalist means confusion   An award should go to anyone who can use this word in such a way that the intended meaning is clear. Since the early 19th century, *animalist* has been used to designate "a person driven by carnal, sensual appetites" or a person who believes in *animalism* ("the theory that humans lack a spiritual nature"). *Animalist* also has been used to mean "an artist who treats animal subjects." During the mid-1980's, *animalist* became a contraction for "animal liberationist." To add still more confusion, the 1991 *Oxford Dictionary of New Words* reported that *animalist* was sometimes used in England as an adjective (comparable to *sexist*) meaning "discriminating against, or opposing the rights of, animals."

animals aren't groupies   Say a *bed* of oysters, a *bevy* of quail, a *brood* of chickens, a *clutch* of chicks, a *covey* of partridges, an *exaltation* of larks, a *flock* of sheep, a *gaggle* of geese, a *muster* of peacocks, a *pack* of wolves, a *pride* of lions, a *school* of fish, a *troop* of monkeys, and a *herd* of antelope, cattle, cranes, deer, goats, oxen, or seals. (See also "*schools of fish* are not accredited.")

animals as linguistic sitting ducks   People are justifiably criticized when they project their own faults on others, as when a self-centered person habitually accuses others of being self-centered. But in our everyday language we routinely project human faults on other species.

We call crazy people *loons*, we call crude people *baboons*, and we call sadistic criminals *beasts* or *animals*. A German word for an utterly contemptible villain, *Schweinhund*, means "pig dog." And our words *pig* and *dog* join *skunk*, *jackal*, *leech*, *vixen*, *vulture*, and *weasel* in an arsenal of insults.

Our animal-projection expressions include such adjectives as the ass-like *asinine* ("stupid"), the ox-like *bovine* ("dull, stolid, listless"), the elephant-like *elephantine* ("awkward"), the fox-like *vulpine* ("crafty"), and the serpent-like *serpentine* ("subtly sly").

A personal observation: Animal-projection expressions are deeply embedded in human history and psychology. Nevertheless, as inhabitants of an increasingly fragile biosphere, each of us might want to think twice about continuing to use such expressions. Perhaps our environmentally reckless human behavior would be easier to control if we kept reminding ourselves of the cautiously optimistic conclusion of author-scholar Jared Diamond's 2005 bestseller, *Collapse: How Societies Choose to Fail or Succeed*. He wrote that humanity can solve all the most serious problems threatening our global society today if only we act on the fact that "we are the cause." I would add that one small step in the direction of that enlightenment would be to linguistically face the truth that our worst, most destructive behavior is not really animal-like. It's strictly human. (See also "*birdbrain* should be a compliment.")

animal talk   *Brewer's Dictionary of Phrase and Fable* warns against the indiscriminate naming of the "cry, call or voice" of animals. That source advises that asses *bray*, bees *hum*, bulls *bellow*, calves *bleat*, cocks *crow*, doves *coo*, geese *cackle*, mice *squeak*, monkeys *chatter*, owls *hoot*, pigeons *coo*, ravens *croak*, and vultures, eagles, and peacocks *scream*.

animation, animosity, animus   *Animation* is "a condition of being spirited, lively." *Animosity* and *animus* have evolved the sense of "spirited hostility."

anniversary can't be rushed   No matter how much newlyweds love each other, they can't celebrate their wedding anniversary every month. The noun *anniversary*, derived from a Latin word meaning "returning yearly," is a date that comes only once a year.

annunciation or Annunciation?   An *annunciation* is an "announcement." The uppercase *Annunciation* refers to the announcement by the angel Gabriel to the Virgin Mary that she was to give birth to the Messiah, or the commemoration of that announcement in an annual church festival on March 25.

anoint or annoint?   The correct spelling, *anoint*, can be recalled by associating this word with "an ointment." The verb *anoint* means "apply ointment or oil to, especially as an act of consecration at a religious ceremony." It also means "to choose by divine intervention." The name *Christ* can be traced to Hebrew, Greek, and Latin words for *anointed. Anoint* can also be used to mean "install somebody ceremonially in an important position," as in a *New York Times* news story (6/11/2000) that began: "The party and nation that Hafez al-Assad ruled for 30 years until his death this weekend moved swiftly today to anoint his son Bashar as Syria's new president." (See also "spelling traps.")

another word trap   In a typical misuse of *another*, a caption for an Associated Press photo from Las Vegas (4/22/1991) read: "Los Angeles Police Chief Daryl Gates receives the baton from *another* [italics added] unidentified runner in the Seventh Annual Challenge Cup Relay Race." Obviously Police Chief Gates was not himself an "unidentified runner." The error could have been easily corrected by separating *unidentified* from *another* with a comma or parentheses, by removing the nonessential *unidentified*, or by changing *another* to *an*.

Another way *another* can trap you is if you use it to say *additional*. For example, you would be illogical if you said "Five guests came early and *another four* came later." *Another* in that context refers to "a duplication of a given quantity," as in "*Five guests* came early, and *another five* came later." When the two figures differ, eliminate *another* and reword your sentence.

antecedents   See "pronouns are preferably followers" and "pronouns are prone to getting lost."

antediluvian: **an old put-down**   The adjective *antediluvian* ("before the flood") literally means "belonging to the era before the Flood written about in the Bible." But *antediluvian* is used today mostly to describe someone or something as "hopelessly old-fashioned."

antennas **or** *antennae*?   *Antennas* send and receive radio waves. *Antennae* are the sensory organs on the heads of insects or a metaphor for human alertness.

anti- **is not always opposed**   Don't assume every word beginning with *anti-* is negative. Sometimes *anti-* is a spelling variant of *ante-* (meaning "before, first, or in front of"). *Antipasto*, for instance, is Italian for "before the meal." The cartoonist Scott Adams played with the ignorance of that meaning of *anti-* in a *Dilbert* comic strip in which Dogbert asks, "If a man eats a pound of pasta and a pound of antipasto, would they cancel each other out, leaving the man still hungry?"

anticipate: **what can you expect?**   According to *The New Fowler's Modern English Usage*, you risk being a target of "insults" if you join in the widespread use of *anticipate* as a synonym for *expect*. That's because many word guardians want to preserve *anticipate* as a way of saying "*prepare* for the expected." For example: "He anticipated rain by taking an umbrella."

The "prepare for the expected" sense of *anticipate* is the only approved definition in Strunk and White's *Elements of Style*, Bernstein's *Careful Writer*, *The Oxford English Dictionary*, and the stylebooks of the Associated Press, the *Los Angeles Times*, *The New York Times,* and *The Wall Street Journal.*

antique show   Exhibit your collection of antique (archaic) words only when such a display is called for to achieve a special literary or humorous effect.

Otherwise, avoid such words as *abed* (in bed), *anent* ("about") *betimes* ("early"), *betwixt* ("between"), *coolth* ("opposite of warmth"), *forsooth!* ("truly!"), *methinks* ("I think"), *nether* ("lower"), *nigh* ("near"), *perchance* ("perhaps"), *saith* ("says"), *verily* ("truly"), and *yclept* ("named"). (See also "*ye olde* controversy.")

anxious or **eager?**   If you use *anxious* sometimes to mean "eager" and sometimes to mean "worried," you could create confusion in a sentence such as "He was anxious to hear from her." To avoid such ambiguity, use *eager* ("marked by keen desire") about what is desirable, and use *anxious* ("uneasy, worried") about what is not.

Risk-free usage: Normally, people look forward to New Year's Eve *eagerly*. But, as *The New York Times* noted (1/2/2000), predictions of end-of-the-century terrorism and Y2K computer failures caused that New Year's Eve to be "anxiously anticipated."

Anxious, from the Latin *anxius* ("worried"), entered the English language in the early 17th century. Ever since, *anxious* has been used in the sense of "uneasy, troubled, causing or full of anxiety." In the mid-18th century, it acquired the additional meaning of "eager." Though the "eager" *anxious* is now so common that it is listed as correct (along with the "worried" *anxious*) by *The Columbia Guide to Standard American English* and *Reader's Digest Success With Words*, those guidebooks acknowledge that some language guardians have been less than eager to accept that meaning. And *The American Heritage Book of English Usage* reports that its usage panel "splits down the middle on this issue."

According to Theodore M. Bernstein's *Careful Writer*, "The careful writer will discriminate between [*anxious* and *eager*], reserving *anxious* for the situation in which some anxiety is involved." Echoing Bernstein, *The New Oxford American Dictionary* states that "careful writers" do not use *anxious* in the sense of *eager*. Similar sentiments have been expressed by Follett's *Modern American Usage*, the Modern Language Association's editing manual, *Line by Line*, Freeman's *Handbook of Problem Words and Phrases*, Ehrlich's *Highly Selective Dictionary for the Extraordinarily Literate*, and the stylebooks of *The New York Times* and *The Wall Street Journal*.

any and all: pick one   To avoid redundancy in the phrase *any and all*, use the word *any* or the word *all*. "Any [or all] of the students in my class are eligible to apply for the award."

any is or **any are?**   *Any* as a pronoun can be singular or plural, depending on context and intended meaning. Usage example: "Any seat in that auditorium *is* a good one. But *are* any seats still available?"

any or **any other?**   If you say "Sally is smarter than any student in her class," you are making the illogical statement that Sally is smarter than herself, because she is one of the students in her class. To be logical, you must say "Sally is smarter than any *other* student in her class."

anybody or **any body?**   The informal pronoun *anybody*—as in "Anybody here?"—is always written as one word. *Any body* is a noun phrase that means "any group" or "any physical body."

anymore or **any more?**   A compulsive gambler who promises his wife not to gamble *anymore* ("any longer") is of course promising that he will stop gambling. But he might have no intention of putting a stop to his gambling if he promises not to gamble any *more*, because that merely means he will not gamble any more than he *has* been gambling.

Use one word when you are being adverbial: "I don't live there *anymore* [any longer]." Make it two words when you are using *more* as an adjective or a pronoun: "At that intersection, there haven't been any *more* [additional] accidents." (In that sentence, *more* was an adjective modifying *accidents*.) "After three drinks, the bartender wouldn't serve him *any more*." (That *more* is a pronoun standing for *drinks*.)

anyone or **any one?**   *Anyone* is a slightly more formal version of the pronoun *anybody*, as in "Anyone can grow up to be president." The phrase *any one* means "any single member of a group of persons or things," as in "Any one of the leading candidates would make a good president" or "Any one of those computers can do the job."

anyplace or **any place?**   The risk-free answer is to use only the two-word form, *any place* (meaning "any location"). For example: "Any place in Big Sur is a photo opportunity."

Anyplace, an informal synonym for *anywhere* that apparently emerged in America about a century ago, has yet to win acceptance from usage commentators. In 2003, Bryan A. Garner, in his *Modern American Usage*, called *anyplace* "much inferior" to *anywhere*. Here's a usage reminder: "He said he hasn't gone anyplace [replace with *anywhere*] all day."

anytime or any time? Your risk-free choice is the phrase *any time*, as in "Any time is the right time for exercise," or "She rarely has any time to go out for lunch," or "It's liable to rain at any time." If you choose to use the American adverb *anytime*, make sure you use it only in the dictionary sense of "*at* any time."

You can write, "My veterinarian is available for emergency housecalls *at any time.*" Or you can write, "My veterinarian is available for emergency housecalls *anytime.*" But if you write that your vet is available *at anytime*, you're redundantly stating that the vet is available at *at* any time.

Sometimes the sense of "*at* any time" is your only choice: "My supervisor says I'm now performing better than *at any time* in the past." It's important to use *at* in that sentence because an employee cannot perform better than a previous *time* but can perform better than that employee performed *at* a previous time.

anyway or any way? *Anyway* means "in any case, at any rate, nevertheless." ("He had no invitation, but he went to the party *anyway.*")

Any way means "by any course, direction, or means." ("She couldn't think of *any way* to get there on time.")

You are safe using either form if your intended meaning is "in any way or manner." ("Dress *anyway* [or *any way*] you wish.") You are never safe using the nonstandard adverb *anyways*.

apiary or aviary? The first is a place for keeping bees; the second, birds.

Apocalypse or Armageddon? The uppercase *Apocalypse* (from a Greek word for "uncovering" or "revealing") is another name for the New Testament Book of Revelation, which echoes ancient Jewish prophecies that God will end the world in a catastrophe in which evil is destroyed and the righteous are rewarded. But the word *Apocalypse* usually refers to the world-ending catastrophe itself.

The uppercase *Armageddon*, the site of the Book of Revelation's final battle between good and evil, usually means that horrendous battle itself.

The lowercase *apocalypse* and its adjective, *apocalyptic*, can refer to any vision of catastrophe. For example, *New York Times* television critic Caryn James (12/17/2000) wrote that, during the post-election drama of 2000, "anchors and commentators maintained a relentlessly hysterical tone, an apocalyptic attitude far removed from the general public's."

The lowercase *armageddon* can refer to any catastrophic situation. For example, the *Boston Herald* (11/23/2004) quoted investment-banking economist Stephen Roach as warning groups of fund managers that America's record trade deficit was inviting an "eventual armageddon" in which the falling value of the dollar forces interest-rate increases that deal a crushing blow to U.S. households already mired in record debt.

apogee* or *perigee? In the orbit of the moon or of an artificial satellite, the farthest (highest) point from the earth is the *apogee*, and the closest (lowest) point is the *perigee*. That pair can also be used figuratively to denote the highest and lowest point.

Figurative example of *apogee*: Political columnist Paul A. Gigot complained in *The Wall Street Journal* (9/11/1998) that "the Clinton years have seen the apogee [highest point] of spin and political artifice." (See also "*zenith* or *nadir?*")

Apollonian* or *Dionysian? This pair of capitalized adjectives provides a contrast in discipline. *Apollonian* ("apa-LOW-nee-an")—from *Apollo*, the Greek god of poetry and music who personified manly beauty—means "disciplined, calm, well-balanced." *Dionysian* ("dye-ah-NISH-an")—from *Dionysus*, the Greek god who personified the joy-giving, intoxicating power of nature and consequently became known as the god of wine and ecstasy—means "undisciplined, frenzied, sensuous."

Both words can also be used as nouns, to refer to people who are disciplined (*Apollonians*) or undisciplined (*Dionysians*). In an example of the noun use of *Dionysian*, a character in E. L. Doctorow's novel *World's Fair* recalls discovering in himself "the double personality engendered by school: the good attentive boy in class, the raucous, unstrung Dionysian in the schoolyard at recess."

Dionysus was known to the Romans as *Bacchus*. Roman festivals honoring Bacchus—*bacchanalia*—were outlawed by the Roman senate in 186 B.C. because of the drunkenness and licentiousness for which they had become known. The word *bacchanalia* has survived in modern English as a term for "a drunken feast or orgy."

***a posteriori* or *a priori*?**   *A posteriori* (Latin for "from what comes later") and *a priori* (Latin for "from what precedes") are adjectives that describe methods of reasoning.

A posteriori reasoning—also called "inductive, empirical, experimental"—examines particulars to develop a generalized rule or theory.

A priori reasoning—also called "deductive"—begins with a generalized rule or theory and applies it to particulars. (For other Latin terms in our language, see "Latinisms.")

apostrophes for contractions   The apostrophe, named after the Greek word *apostrephein* ("to turn away"), is a punctuation mark often used when you "turn away" from using one or more letters or numbers to form contractions. For example: *can't, don't, o'clock* ("of the clock"), *ne'er-do-well* ("never-do-well"), *rock 'n' roll* (with apostrophes for both of the missing letters of *and*), and the class of *'03*.

Apostrophes are also used in abbreviations with an *-er* ending, as in *4-H'er*, and in the past tense of verbs composed of numerals or individually pronounced letters: "Congress *86'ed* [threw out] the amendment." "In his first bid for public office, he was defeated but not *KO'd* [knocked out]."

apostrophes for possessives   To show possession, add an apostrophe and an *-s* to nouns not ending in *-s*, as in "a child's toy" and "children's toys." For singular and plural nouns ending in *-s* or the sound of *-s*, add only an apostrophe, as in "squirrels' tails," "that witness' testimony," "General Motors' profits" and "for appearance' sake."

If your boss challenges you about your use of the advice in this entry, you can cite the authority of Merriam-Webster's *Standard American Style Manual* and *The Associated Press Stylebook*. If your boss insists that you follow another style on this issue, submit gracefully. The choice of style in which you express possessiveness is not as important as your paycheck.

With names of organizations that *sound* possessive, check before you add an apostrophe. Note that *Writer's* Digest Books are read by members of the *Writers* Guild of America.

apostrophes that accent plurals   Use apostrophes with plurals that would otherwise be confusing, as in "Watch your *p*'s and *q*'s," "Dot your *i*'s and cross your *t's*," and "an academic record of straight A's." Note, too, how the apostrophe helps you recognize the plural *do's* in the phrase *do's and don'ts*.

Some publications, including *The New York Times* and this usage dictionary, exercise the option to use apostrophes to aid readability in reference to decades, as in "the 1990's." Other publications, including the *Los Angeles Times*, prefer "the 1990s."

apostrophes that show signs of abuse A retired Lincolnshire County, England, newspaper copy editor, John Richards, achieved international renown when the Associated Press reported (5/12/2001) that he and his son, Stephen, had founded the Apostrophe Protection Society. The Society encourages local merchants to end apostrophe abuse, as with a restaurant that forgot to include the apostrophe in its own name, *Bennys Café*, but served *chip's*, *roll's*, and everything else on the menu with an inappropriate apostrophe on the side.

Note the five apostrophe errors in a flier recently distributed by a storefront psychic in Los Angeles (italics added): "The Psychic World of Palmistry and Tarot cards *draw's* many people to *it's* door. Once you are there, Psychic Sophia tears away the veil of mystery to reveal what she *view's* as a natural phenomenon. Sophia can help and advise you with all your *problem's*. Remember you have not had a reading unless *its* been done by Psychic Sophia. . . . " (See also next entry and "*its* or *it's?*")

apostrophizing **is not about punctuation** The Greek word *apostrephein* ("to turn away"), which inspired the noun *apostrophe* for a punctuation mark that abbreviates by "turning away" letters and numbers, also inspired the separate word *apostrophe* that means an exclamatory digression ("a turning away") in a speech or composition to address an absent or imaginary person or personified abstraction. Based on that definition of *apostrophe*, here are examples of *apostrophizing*: The English poet William Wordsworth (1770–1850) began his sonnet about the 17th-century English poet and prose writer John Milton by writing, "Milton, thou shouldst be living at this hour." The 19th-century British historian-essayist Thomas Carlyle wrote, "O Liberty, what things are done in thy name!"

apotheosis **can be sacred or secular** *Apotheosis* (preferably pronounced "apoth-ee-OH-sis")—based on the Greek word for god, *theos*—literally means *deification*, as in "elevation to divine status." But usually it is used in the sense of "perfect example," as in a *New Yorker* reference (6/9/1997) to the Washington law firm of Patton, Boggs & Blow as "the apotheosis of [political] connectedness."

apparatus is or **apparatus are?** *Apparatus* ("equipment, organization") can be used as a singular or a plural. An acceptable but rarely used plural is *apparatuses*.

apparent: an ambiguity trap When used before a noun, the adjective *apparent* means "seeming; what only *appears* to be true." Example: "His apparent wealth helped him make influential contacts."

But beware: When *apparent* follows a noun, it can mean either "seeming; what only *appears* to be true" or "obvious; what is *clearly* true." Example of such ambiguity: "His wealth was apparent." In such cases, you'll need to make your meaning unmistakably clear. Say either "His wealth was apparent [seeming] until his real financial condition became known" or "His wealth was apparent [obvious] from his major donations to charity."

appraise or **apprise?** In a typical example of the confusion caused by this pair of verbs, a CNN newscaster (5/5/2004) reported accusations that Defense Secretary Donald H. Rumsfeld had not been kept sufficiently "appraised" by U.S. military leaders. About a minute later, the newscaster noted that he should have used the word *apprised*, meaning "informed." The newscaster should actually have avoided the problem by using *informed* instead of trying to remember the pretentious synonym *apprised*.

The other verb, *appraise,* means "to estimate the value of," as when the county assessor appraises somebody's home to set that person's property taxes.

apprehend: a word that grabs A police officer's job is to *apprehend* ("arrest") criminals. A criminologist's job is to *apprehend* (same word, but meaning "understand") crime.

Apprehend, which comes from the Latin *prehendere* ("seize") and *apprehendere* ("lay hold of"), entered English more than six centuries ago with the meaning "seize with the mind, learn, comprehend." In the 16th century, *apprehend* acquired today's senses of "catch the meaning or idea of, understand" and "arrest, take into custody."

Another meaning of *apprehend*—"anticipate, especially with fear or dread"—is related to the adjective *apprehensive* and the noun *apprehension.*

approximate or proximate?   Some dictionaries show both these adjectives as meaning "nearly exact," but *proximate* is usually reserved for "nearest, next, imminent."

The "nearest" use of *proximate* keeps it consistent with the meaning of *proximity* ("nearness") and *proxemics* ("the study of how near individuals stand when they are in conversation, depending on their culture and degree of intimacy").

apropos or *a propos*?   In English the single word *apropos* is used, though it retains the pronunciation of the French *a propos* ("ah pruh-PO").

Apropos as an adjective means "fitting, appropriate." As an adverb, it means "fittingly, appropriately." As a preposition meaning "with reference to," *apropos* is used alone or with the preposition *of,* as in "apropos [of] your proposal." Avoid "apropos *to*."

apt, liable, or *likely*?   A person who drinks before driving is *apt* ("has a tendency") to cause an accident. That person is *liable* to be ("exposed to the unpleasant possibility of being") arrested and will *likely* ("probably") be punished.

arbitrator or *mediator*?   An *arbitrator* issues binding decisions. A *mediator* makes suggestions.

arch can throw you a curve   The noun *arch* means, of course, "a curved structure that supports material over an open space such as a bridge or doorway." But be careful how you use *arch* as an adjective: It can mean "mischievous, cunning," as in an "arch smile," but it can also mean "chief, principal," as in "arch rival."

The combining form *arch-* can signify "principal," as in *archangel* (pronounced "ARK-angel"); "having authority over others," as in *archbishop*; or "extreme," as in "the archconservative radio commentator."

Arche- is a combining form that means "original," as in *archetype* ("original pattern or model").

archaeology or *archeology*?   For this word meaning "the study of past cultures by examination of their physical remains," leading U.S. dictionaries accept both spellings but assign preferred status to the traditional spelling, *archaeology*.

arctic: **remembering both *c*'s is cool**   As noted in a popular pronunciation manual—Charles Harrington Elster's *There Is No Zoo in Zoology*—*arctic* should be pronounced "ARK-tik" but is "almost universally mispronounced" as "AR-tik."

Dictionaries list both pronunciations but do assign the preferential first listing to "ARK-tik." The same preference applies, of course, to *antarctic* and the continent surrounding the South Pole, *Antarctica*.

The adjective *arctic*—often capitalized, as in "Arctic marine life"—means "of or pertaining to the North Pole or the region near it." Uncapitalized, *arctic* can mean "frigid, either literally or in temper or mood."

arguably **must go**   Now is the time for all good persons to come to the aid of our language by stamping out *arguably*, an adverb that serves no purpose other than to infect communication with irresponsibility.

Burling Lowrey, a contributor to the *Quarterly Review of Doublespeak* (April 1993) of the National Council of Teachers of English, observed that writers in many fields use *arguably* to "create the illusion of being fearlessly unequivocal while at the same time pulling back with the wimpish qualifier *arguably*." Case in point: An online advertisement for UltimateBet.com (1/24/2005) declared Phil Hellmuth of Team UB "arguably the best player . . . in all of poker."

As Associate Professor of English Ben Yagoda of the University of Delaware wrote in *The Chronicle of Higher Education* (7/10/1998), *arguably* has become "a sort of wildcard adverb designed to cover the posterior of writers who would like to make a statement but are unable to verify it." For example, Citibank became "arguably the most technologically advanced" bank (*Fortune*, 7/26/2004), Paul Celan became "arguably the greatest European poet in the postwar period" (*New York Times Book Review*, 12/31/2000), and Emanuel "Squeak" Manson III of Oxnard, California, became "arguably the greatest bowler in Ventura County today" (*Ventura County Star*, 4/1/1998).

The wimpish qualifier *arguably* has even been dragged into statements that are already qualified. An article in Britain's *Tatler* magazine (April 1994) said Tessa

Kennedy was "arguably *one of* England's finest interior decorators." The Duluth *News-Tribune* (10/16/1997) stated that "Duluth's Woodland Avenue arguably ranks *among* the most traveled arteries in the city." And the Greensboro *News & Record* (8/2/1998) deserved a Wimp Award for reporting that the Eastern Philharmonic Orchestra had presented "what arguably *might have been* its finest presentation all season."

The adjective *arguable* seems to have entered English in the mid-19th century, followed by the adverb *arguably* near the end of that century. Researchers for *Merriam-Webster's Dictionary of English Usage* found "occasional use of the adjective during the first half of the 20th century, and very little of the adverb." Those researchers determined that "usage of both begins to pick up noticeably" in the 1960's. And "noticeably" has been an understatement regarding *arguably* ever since. In a particularly flagrant pair of examples, an article in *The Economist* (3/16/2002) about academic celebrities accused of plagiarism called Stephen Ambrose "arguably America's favorite historian" and in the next paragraph stated that Doris Kearns Goodwin's "handling of the plagiarism charges against her has arguably been worse than the charges themselves."

Here's how you can help fight the *arguably* epidemic: If you feel the urge to imitate the many people now using *arguably*, reach immediately for such responsible substitutes as "I believe," "I think," or "judging from my experience." If you feel driven to endorse an opinion that's arguable, take the time and space to spell out the argument yourself, or quote someone who has done so. If you simply want to express a personal reaction or feeling, just do it. For instance, instead of saying that a movie is "arguably the funniest ever made," say that no other movie ever made you laugh that much.

arguments need not be nasty   When you use the noun *argument*, make sure your intended meaning is clear. *Argument* can mean "a quarrel" or "a presentation of facts and reasoning in support of a conclusion." For example, two scientists may argue with each other over a parking space before attending a conference during which they jointly present an argument in favor of their theory about the origin of the universe.

Argus: the eyes have it   The phrase *Argus-eyed*, meaning "keenly observant, vigilantly watchful," was inspired by a creature in Greek mythology with a hundred eyes.

The story of the hundred-eyed Argus was one of many episodes involving the supreme god Zeus' failed attempts to hide his amorous adventures from his wife, Hera. When Zeus realized that he was about to be caught by Hera in a compromising position with a princess named Io, Zeus transformed Io into a cow. Hera, pretending to be fooled, talked Zeus into letting her have the cow as a gift. And Hera assigned Argus, who never had what we would call complete "shuteye," to guard the cow night and day to prevent Zeus from changing it back into the princess. Zeus had his musically talented son Hermes charm Argus to sleep with his lyre and slay him. Hera then managed to delay (but not prevent) Zeus' reunion with (and retransformation of) Io by driving off Io's cow-form with a stinging gadfly. Meanwhile Hera kept alive the memory of Argus by setting his eyes in the tail of her favorite bird, the peacock.

**around* or *round?*   *Around* is preferred in American English, *round* in British English, for most prepositional and adverbial senses of these words. In contrast to the British, we Americans sit *around* (not *round*) the breakfast table while there's plenty of food to go *around* (not *round*) before we decide to look *around* (not *round*) for a mailbox that we discover is *around* (not *round*) the corner.

American English accepts the British *all-round* but prefers the American *all-around* as an adjective for "having many abilities," as in "all-around athlete."

If you're one of the increasing number of Americans who use the British form when you complain year-*round* about *round*-the-clock traffic congestion, don't write *'round,* as if the word were a contraction. It's not.

**arouse* or *rouse?*   *The American Heritage Dictionary* says both these adjectives "suggest awakening, as from inactivity or apathy." But that source adds that *rouse* "more strongly implies vigorous or emotional excitement." Usage example: "Once we *arouse* [awaken] the people of America, we can *rouse* [prod] them to seek fundamental reform."

**arrant* or *errant?*   The adjective *errant*, from a Latin word meaning "to wander," entered our language in the early 14th century, with the meaning "wandering, roving, especially in search of adventure"—hence "knights errant." Gradually, *errant* acquired today's more common meaning of the word, "wandering away [straying] from the proper course." Usage example from a headline in *The New York Times* (7/29/1998): "Government Easy on Errant Nursing Homes, Investigators Say."

Arrant, an early spelling variant of *errant*, also shifted from "wandering" to "straying." But it shifted again to become an intensifier—"complete, utter, thorough, downright, unmitigated"—usually for that which is objectionable. For example, Shakespeare wrote in *Hamlet* about "arrant knaves." And common usage today involves such phrases as "arrant fool" and "arrant nonsense."

arrive, arrivé, or arriviste?   One often-used meaning of the verb *arrive*—other than the obvious one of reaching one's destination—is "to attain a position of success." In line with the latter meaning, the imported French word *arrivé* ("ah-ree-VAY") means "one who has swiftly gained success," and the imported French word *arriviste* ("ah-ree-VEEST") means "one who has swiftly gained success, especially by questionable means."

artful and artless are risky adjectives   If you use either of these adjectives, you must make sure your context clearly shows whether your intention is to convey a compliment or a criticism.

Artful is defined by dictionaries in its original sense of "exhibiting art or skill." But *artful* is *likely* to be interpreted according to its subsequently developed dictionary definition of "deceitful." The "deceitful" sense of this word has been used for quite some time, as illustrated by Charles Dickens' use of the nickname *Artful Dodger* for a skillful child pickpocket in *Oliver Twist* (1839). In a recent usage example, a *New York Times* feature article from London (12/9/2000) described Prince Philip's evasive responses to questions at a press luncheon as a "demonstration of the skill—royal class—of the artful dodge."

Artless can be used as the uncomplimentary opposite of the *artful* that means "exhibiting art or skill." For example, a critic in *The Boston Globe* (5/22/1994) wrote, "In an age of artless novels, here was an artful book." But *artless* can also be used as the complimentary opposite of the *artful* that means "deceitful." In that sense, *artless* can mean "not deceitful." That complimentary *artless* can also mean "not artificial," as in "her artless charm."

artisan or artist?   *Artisan*, once synonymous with *artist* ("one who creates paintings or other works of fine art"), now means *craftsman* ("a manual worker who is skilled in making a particular product").

artiste: **a risky noun**   *Artiste* ("ahr-TEEST," from a French word for "artist") is misleadingly listed by most English dictionaries as just a synonym for "performing artist, such as singer or dancer." But as *The American Heritage Dictionary* points out, *artiste* can now also mean "a person with artistic pretensions." And *The Columbia Guide to Standard American English* contains the following warning: "To describe someone as an *artiste* may once have been a compliment, but today it is facetious, deliberately overblown, and uncomplimentary."

Risk-free suggestions: If you mean "performing artist," say so. If you are tempted to use *artiste* as a put-down, be as clear as *The New York Times* was when it referred (2/6/2000) to the Sundance Film Festival as not only "a career-advancing opportunity for young filmmakers [but also] a stage for artiste poseurs [pretenders]."

as **ambiguity**   *As* is not a usage problem when it's an adverb, meaning "to the same extent" (as in "high as the sky"), or when it's a preposition, meaning "in the role of" (as in "act as moderator"). But *as* can cause confusion when it's a conjunction, if the reader must guess whether *as* refers to *cause* or to *time*.

Suppose somebody writes, "As Andy was driving to work, he suffered an anxiety attack." Does that mean Andy suffered an anxiety attack *because* he was driving to his job or *while* (during the time) he was driving to his job? In that sentence, the reader cannot know what the conjunction *as* means.

Risk-free solution: If your conjunctive *as* is unclear, replace it with an unmistakably clear word or phrase such as *because, inasmuch as,* or *during the time that*. (See also "ambiguity alert" and "ambiguity can always be cured.")

as **and** *than* **comparisons need to be complete**   Incomplete and therefore illogical comparisons involving *as* or *than* are easy to correct. Just make sure you're comparing, so to speak, apples with apples and oranges with oranges rather than apples with oranges.

For example, you have an incomplete comparison involving *as* in this type of sentence: "We had four times the audience as last year's performance." In that sentence, the size of this year's audience should be compared with the size of last year's audience. Instead, the sentence compares the size of this year's audience with something quite different: last year's *performance*. But you can complete the comparison if you say, "We had four times the audience as *at* last year's performance."

Here are two incomplete *than* examples, with my italicized corrections in brackets, from staff-written stories in the *Los Angeles Times*: That newspaper noted (6/25/2001) that "Japanese live longer than anyone [*else*] in the world." Without the added word *else*, the statement would have made sense only if the Japanese lived on another planet. About three years earlier (8/13/1998), the newspaper reported that U.S. automakers "are making cars more affordable today than [*at*] any time since 1980." In that statement, the writer illogically compared today's car prices with a period of time. With the addition of *at*, the sentence correctly compares the car prices of today with the car prices of the earlier period. (See also next entry.)

as and *than* comparisons that only *seem* incomplete   Which is a better sentence, "His cat is as playful as a kitten" or "His cat is as playful as a kitten *is*"?

How about "No 20th-century figure spoke or wrote more eloquently than British statesman and Nobel Prize–winning author Winston Churchill"? Should that sentence end with an added *did*?

If you chose the first version of each of those examples, pat yourself on the back. Such *as* and *than* comparisons are complete because the final verb is understood. You would be technically correct to include the understood verb, but you would be needlessly ending the sentence with a dull thud.

as far as: a phrase of concern   *As far as* is widely used conversationally as a preposition meaning "as for, regarding." For example: "As far as generosity, you can count on Lawrence." But that use is rejected by leading language guardians. If you want to avoid criticism when you use *as far as*, make sure you follow it with a clause (a unit containing not only a subject but also a verb). For example: "As far as *Lawrence is concerned*, there is no rush about returning the money."

as good or better than is not good   Nothing is "as good or better than" anything else. The phrase needs a double helping of *as*: "*as* good *as* or better than." (See also "*than* comparisons need to be complete.")

as if or as though?   The risk-free answer is *as if*.

You can cite a whole library of dictionaries and usage manuals that say *as if* and *as though* are interchangeable. One such source, *Garner's Dictionary of Modern American Usage*, says that "attempts to distinguish between these idioms have proved futile" and advises you to choose whichever sounds better to you. But the influential *Associated Press Stylebook*, though it calls *as though* "acceptable," says (without explanation) that *as if* is "the preferred form." And an uncompromising choice of *as if*, with a brief explanation, appears in *The New York Times Manual of Style and Usage*: "*As if* is shorter and more logical." The manual explains that the *if* is consistent with the implied, bracketed words in this example: "It looks as [*it would look*] if the Yankees won." Though the manual doesn't say so, you presumably would be committing an offense against logic if you said "It looks as [*it would look*] though the Yankees won."

A fuller, more helpful explanation of why you should choose *as if* instead of *as though* appears in *Words on Words: The Columbia Dictionary for Writers*. The adverbial conjunction *if* speaks of condition ("If she agrees . . . "), but the adverbial conjunction *though* speaks of concession ("Though she has agreed . . . "). To cite the *Columbia Dictionary* example: "He looks as if he is disgusted" means "He looks as *he would look* if he were disgusted." So you're clearly stating that he has an expression of disgust. But if you said "He looks as he would look *though* he were disgusted," you wouldn't really be telling us anything about the man's expression. In the blunt words of *The Columbia Dictionary*, the *as though* version "doesn't make sense."

If the above explanation gives you a headache, you can cure it quickly and permanently by resolving to always choose *as if* over *as though*.

as or *like*?   Careful communicators frown on the common practice of using *like* in place of *as* to introduce a phrase or clause containing a subject with a verb.

Many TV personalities say, "Like I said." But Standard English grammar won't permit *like* to assume the role of a conjunction, as it does when it introduces a phrase or clause containing a subject (such as *I*) with a verb (such as *said*). In that conjunctive usage, grammar requires that *like* be replaced by an authentic conjunction, *as*.

Feel free to use *like* as a verb ("She *likes* [enjoys] jazz"), an adjective ("He's of like [similar] mind"), or a preposition ("There's nothing *like* [similar to] freshly baked bread"). But if you want to stay on the right side of grammatical law, avoid the conjunctive *like* by saying "as [not *like*] I said," "as [not *like*] she thought," "as [not *like*] they admitted," and so forth.

Take your cue from Shakespeare, who called one of his comedies *As You Like It*, not *Like You Like It*. And take a hint from the title of a *Reader's Digest* article (September 2000) called "Why Men Act As They Do," not "Why Men

Act *Like* They Do." Likewise, use *as* rather than *like* even when a verb is only implied, as (*is* true) in the example that you are now reading.

The generally permissive Merriam-Webster and Random House dictionaries defend the use of *like* before subject-verb constructions on the grounds that such usage is logical and extremely common in today's spoken English, and that some examples of it can be found in English literature for the past five centuries. But the most highly regarded source of information about the English language, England's *Oxford English Dictionary*, reports that *like* before subject-verb constructions has been "generally condemned as vulgar or slovenly." Strunk and White's *Elements of Style* declared in its editions of 1959, 1979, and 2000: "*Like* has long been widely misused by the illiterate. Lately it has been taken up by the knowing . . . who use it as though they were slumming. . . . For the student, perhaps the most useful thing to know about *like* is that most carefully edited publications regard its use before [subject-verb] phrases and clauses as simple error."

The conjunctive *like* has also been rejected by the usage-panel consensus of the *Harper Dictionary of Contemporary Usage* and *The American Heritage Dictionary*; by Bernstein's *Careful Writer,* Follett's *Modern American Usage, Garner's Modern American Usage,* and Lovinger's *Penguin Dictionary of American English Usage and Style*; and by the stylebooks of the Associated Press, *The New York Times, The Washington Post, The Wall Street Journal,* and the *Los Angeles Times.*

So if you don't want to sound *like* a fool, do *as* I say.

Exception: Use the conjunctive *like* to "tell it like it is," because that expression is an established idiom. (See also "*idioms* do their own thing.")

as well as   See "*together* but alone."

ascension or **Ascension?**   An *ascension* is an act of ascending, including (in astronomy) the rising of a star above the horizon. The *Ascension* refers to the bodily ascending of Christ from earth to heaven on the 40th day of the Resurrection, now celebrated on the 40th day after Easter. The British island of Ascension in the South Atlantic is so named because its discovery by the Portuguese in 1501 occurred on Ascension Day.

ask, examine, inquire, interrogate, query, question, or **quiz?**   *Ask* is the simplest of all these verbs that mean "to seek information by posing a question."

Examine involves detailed questioning, as when a teacher examines the knowledge of a student. *Inquire* means either "ask about" or "make an investigation." *Interrogate* is best used for official questioning, as when police interrogate a suspect. *Query* indicates the need to settle a doubt, as when a copy editor queries writers about their intended meaning. *Question* implies the asking of a series of questions, as when a prosecutor questions a witness. *Quiz* means "test the knowledge of," usually informally, as when a teacher gives a "pop quiz" about current events. (See also *"enquire* or *inquire?"*)

askance or **askew?**   Dictionaries say you can look at someone *askance* or *askew* (both meaning "sidewise, to express disapproval"). But some people might look askance at you if you don't reserve *askew* to mean "to one side, in a crooked position."

assault changes meaning in court   The word *assault* ordinarily means "violent attack." In the terminology of law, *assault* means "threatened or attempted violent attack," and the actual attack is called *battery.*

assay or **essay?**   The verb *assay* entered Middle English from Old French as an alternative spelling of *essay,* meaning "to try, attempt."

But though *assay* is still used occasionally as an alternative spelling of *essay*—and dictionaries list that usage—you'll avoid confusion if you use *assay* only in its currently prevailing sense of "to assess, evaluate, test."

assemblage or **assembly?**   Refer to an *assemblage* of things but an *assembly* of people.

assent or **consent?**   To *assent* is to "concur, concede." To *consent* is to "permit, approve."

In the words of semanticist S. I. Hayakawa's guide to synonyms, *Use the Right Word,* "[Assent] is most often limited to the affirmative response to a statement or opinion. [Consent] is restricted to the giving of permission or the accepting of a proposal or request." People who *assent* to the opinion that they need to exercise do not always *consent* to a proposed exercise program.

Caution: *Assent* is sometimes written by mistake when the writer means *ascent* ("upward motion, upward path").

***assume* or *presume*?** *New York Herald* correspondent Henry Morton Stanley demonstrated precise diction (word choice) on the historic day in 1871 in central Africa when he located the missionary-explorer he had been searching for: "Dr. Livingstone, I presume?" *Presume* and *assume* both mean "suppose, take for granted, inferring something as true without proof." But *presume* tends to be more positive—approaching the outskirts of certainty—because it implies a factual or logical reason for the inference.

Warning: In some contexts, *presume* means "take *too* much for granted, dare to act without permission, take liberties." For example: "He presumed to speak for me." The two faces of *presume*—a word derived from the Latin *praesumere* ("to take in advance")—have produced the distinct meanings of the two adjectives *presumptive* and *presumptuous*.

***assure, ensure,* or *insure*?** Here's how you can avoid criticism about your use of these three confusibles: Assure some*body*. Ensure some*thing*. And insure somebody or something by buying or issuing *insurance*.

Assure means "to state emphatically in an attempt to remove doubt and thereby set someone's mind at ease." Inasmuch as *assure* requires a person to receive the assurance, *assure* can be used only as a transitive verb (one with a direct object). Thus, a student of mine needed to be corrected when he wrote, "'I'll be home on time,' her husband *assured*." Correct version: " 'I'll be home on time,' her husband assured *her* [the receiver of the act of assuring]."

Ensure means "make sure," as in the following examples: "The enormous divide in agricultural productivity ensures that standards of living in tropical areas are likely to remain stagnant" (*Foreign Policy* magazine, January/February 2001).

Insure, as dictionaries point out, is often used to mean both "make sure" and "provide insurance for." But the exclusive use of *ensure* in the sense of "make sure" and the limitation of *insure* to the business of insurance is endorsed by *The American Heritage Book of English Usage, Garner's Dictionary of Modern American Usage*, Follett's *Modern American Usage*, 62 percent of the usage panel of the *Harper Dictionary of Contemporary Usage*, and the stylebooks of *The New York Times, The Washington Post, The Wall Street Journal*, the *Los Angeles Times, U.S. News & World Report*, and the Associated Press.

asterisk* requires *risk   As the *Random House Webster's Unabridged Dictionary* points out, the pronunciation "AS-teh-rik" for the star-shaped symbol (*) is "occasionally heard among educated speakers [but] is usually considered nonstandard." The only risk-free pronunciation includes the sound of *risk*: "AS-teh-risk."

An *asterisk,* from the Greek *asteriskos* ("little star"), is commonly used in printing to follow a word, phrase, or sentence that is footnoted and to precede the footnote itself. In such cases, a second footnote is designated by a downward-pointing *dagger* (†).

_at_ is not always where it's at		*The American Dialect Dictionary* describes as "painfully common" the practice of attaching a redundant *at* to the end of a question: "Where were you at?" "Where's my jacket at?" "Where's the movie playing at?" That *at* may be forgiven in conversation when it seems needed for emphasis. But you are unlikely to be forgiven for it in your writing.

"*ation*-itis"		This is what you are afflicted with if you employ too many *ation*-ending words in a sentence, as in "The installation of that abomination has caused nothing but consternation." A readily available cure is a rewrite.

A similar affliction, "*ention*-itis," can be cured by rewording such sentences as "His abstention caused contention at the convention."

atlas or *Atlas*?		After Greece's Olympian gods waged a successful war to overthrow the Titans who had been ruling the universe, a Titan named Atlas was punished in a manner that would mock his great strength. Atlas was sentenced by the new supreme god, Zeus, to spend eternity bearing the weight of the sky on his shoulders—just as the Atlas mountain range in northwest Africa seems to be doing. (See also "*titan* or *Titan*?")

The word *atlas* came to mean "a book of maps" after 16th-century Flemish geographer Gerardus Mercator's collection of maps was published with a title page decorated with a picture of the mighty Atlas bearing the weight of the world. The word *atlas* is also used for any "book of tables, charts, illustrations, etc., on a specific topic."

attenuate or *extenuate*?		*Extenuate* means "to reduce the seriousness of, especially by providing partial excuses." ("The defense attorney asked the judge to reduce the sentence because of extenuating circumstances.")

Attenuate means "to "reduce in force, intensity, value, amount, or degree; to weaken." *Attenuate* also means "to make thin, slender, or fine." Hence, an *attenuant* is a medicine that thins the blood.

attest is not something you take   *Attest* is a verb, meaning "to bear witness to, to affirm the truth or validity of, to supply or be evidence of." Note that, in those senses, a preposition (*to* or *of*) is included in the meaning and therefore need not be used in the sentence: "His record attests his loyalty."

But you need to include a preposition after *attest* if you are thinking of the word as meaning "to declare to be true or genuine, to testify or certify." Example: "My former employer can attest to my long experience in that field."

attorney or lawyer?   Contrary to what popular usage suggests, an attorney is not necessarily a lawyer. Under our laws, the word *attorney* retains the meaning it had when it entered English in the late 13th century as a noun—adapted from the Old French verb *atorner* ("turn to")—meaning anybody you "turn to" for help in handling your affairs. That's why non-lawyers as well as lawyers can be given *power of attorney* ("the authority, spelled out in a contract, to act on your behalf in the management of a business or single transaction"). So it's not redundant for lawyers to list themselves as *attorneys at law* ("those who are licensed to act on your behalf in a court of law").

By the way: Don't be confused by attorneys at law who introduce themselves, in person or on a shingle, as attorneys. They do so because the less prestigious *attorney* ironically sounds classier than the licensed professional *lawyer*, as witness the prevalence of jokes about lawyers but not attorneys.

attribute, ascribe, or impute?   In the words of Hayakawa's *Use the Right Word*, the word *attribute* means "to consider one thing as belonging to or stemming from another," *ascribe* means "to attribute a cause, quality, source, etc., to something as a property or as being characteristic of it," and *impute* means "to attribute a fault, crime, etc., to a person."

Impute may also be used to mean simply "to consider as the source or cause of," as in "He imputed his happiness to having mastered stress."

attribution   See entries for "'fortune telling' and 'mind reading,'" "quoting sources," and "sources: when should they be trusted?"

Augean is a dirty word   In Greek mythology, one of the seemingly impossible Twelve Labors assigned as challenges to the mighty Heracles (called Hercules by the Romans) was to quickly clean King Augeas' neglected stables of the mess left by 3,000 oxen for 30 years. Heracles, the strongest man in the world, accomplished the job by diverting the water of two rivers into the stable.

In accord with that story, the adjective *Augean* ("aw-GEE-uhn") means "filthy or corrupt from long neglect" or "requiring heroic efforts to clean up or correct." The phrase "cleanse the Augean stables" means "remove a massive amount of physical filth or moral corruption."

Usage example: *The Economist* (3/4/2000) used *Augean stables* to describe Japan's scandal-ridden banking system.

auger or *augur*?   *Auger* is a noun for a tool that bores holes and a verb for boring holes.

An *augur*, a religious official in ancient Rome, predicted future events by interpreting omens derived from the flying, singing, and feeding of birds and from an examination of bird entrails. Today, *augur* is a noun for someone who predicts the future from omens in general and a verb for such soothsaying.

The verb *augur* also means "foreshadow, give promise of," as in "Increased holiday sales augur an economic revival." The verb *augur* is frequently used intransitively (without a direct object), as in "The early negotiations augur well for an early settlement."

Augury means "omen."

augment or *supplement*?   These verbs are often used interchangeably. But careful communicators use *augment* to mean "increase something that exists" and *supplement* to mean "add something new." For example, your existing salary is augmented (increased) by a raise but supplemented (joined by something new) with a paycheck from a second job. (See also "*eke out* a living if you want to.")

aunt: a perilous pronunciation   If you use the pronunciation for *aunt* that's listed as standard in American dictionaries—"ant"—you'll annoy the many Americans, especially from New England, who favor the British "ahnt." But if you say "ahnt," many other Americans will think you are pretentious.

Recommendation: Pick the pronunciation that sounds right to you. If you're criticized, don't waste time defending yourself. Just cry uncle.

aural or *oral?*   *Aural* means, "relating to the sense of hearing." *Oral* means "relating to spoken communication" and "of or relating to the mouth." (See also "*oral* or *verbal?*")

authentic or *genuine?*   Both mean "a lack of falsehood or misrepresentation." But whereas *genuine* applies to a "real" person or thing, *authentic* suggests fidelity to the truth ("an authentic biography") or a lack of falsehood demonstrated by a certification process ("an authentic Rembrandt").

author as a verb   Nobody doubts that editors edit. But not everybody agrees that authors *author*, as in a Clarence Page column (9/18/1998) in which he referred to a book about affirmative action "authored by two former Ivy League presidents."

Some dictionaries list *author* as a verb without comment. But as Bryan A. Garner writes in *Garner's Modern American Usage,* "careful writers" avoid *author* as a verb. Using the word as a verb has been described as "needless" by Follett's *Modern American Usage,* and it has been dismissed as unacceptable by the *World Almanac Guide to Good Word Usage,* 74 percent of the *American Heritage Dictionary* usage panel, and by the stylebooks of the Associated Press, *The New York Times, The Washington Post, The Wall Street Journal,* and the *Los Angeles Times.*

Saying that someone authored a book, according to Freeman's *Words to the Wise,* "is as silly as saying that he poeted a poem." (See also "nouns as verbs.")

authoress: **the meaning is demeaning**   The English novelist Jane Austen referred to herself as an *authoress* in a letter she penned on December 1, 1815. But *authoress* is among the gender-specific occupational names now considered demeaning. (See also "*-ess*: an insufferable suffix?")

autocrat, autocracy, autarchy, or *autarky?*   *Autocrat* (from a Greek word meaning "ruling by oneself") means "a ruler or other person with unlimited power, a despot." A government ruled by such a person is an *autocracy* or *autarchy.*

Autarky (from a Greek word meaning "self-sufficient") means "a country that is economically self-sufficient."

avatar is descended from Hinduism   Once you know the origin of this word, you are likely to have no difficulty remembering its meaning.

Avatar, from a Sanskrit word for "descent," literally means the bodily form taken when a Hindu god descends to Earth. By extension, *avatar* means "the embodiment of a quality, concept, or view of life."

Usage example: A *New York Times* review (6/6/2000) of a biography of Groucho Marx referred to him as "the very avatar of iconoclasm and irreverence and plain old-fashioned mayhem."

avenge or revenge?   Both verbs mean "inflict punishment for injury." But precise writers tend to use *avenge* in the sense of "just" retribution for wrongs done to others and *revenge* in the sense of "spiteful" retaliation for wrongs done to oneself. *Vengeance* covers both *avenging* and *revenging*.

average, mean, median, or mode?   In statistics, the *average* is the sum of the quantities in a group divided by the number of quantities. Thus the average of the quantities 2, 8, 3, 7, and 10 is their sum of 30 divided by the number of quantities, 5. The answer, of course, is 6.

The *average* is also called the *arithmetic mean*, so dictionaries list *average* and *mean* as synonyms. If you want to show off to friends in math, tell them you're aware of the *geometric mean* ("the middle term in a geometric progression") and the *harmonic mean* ("the middle term in a harmonic progression"). Then quickly switch to another topic before they ask you to define those concepts.

The *median* is the middle number in a group, above and below which lie an equal number of other numbers. The median of 1, 3, 5, 10, 20, 30, 40 is 10, since there are three numbers above it and three numbers below it.

The *mode* is the number that occurs most frequently in a series. The number 2 is the mode in 2, 2, 2, 3, 3, 4.

avert, avoid, or evade?   You must take action to *avert* ("prevent") or *evade* ("avoid by dexterity or stratagem") something undesirable. You often can *avoid* ("keep away from, stay clear of") that which is undesirable by doing nothing.

If you are unable to *avert, avoid,* or *evade* the undesirable, you can always *avert* (in the sense of "turn away") your eyes.

aware or *conscious?*   You are *aware* of the outside world (for example, the faults of others) and *conscious* of your inner world (your own faults).

awesome has lost some awe The adjective *awesome*—from the noun *awe* ("an emotional response of reverence, respect, and wonder")—became a widely used synonym for *awe-inspiring* in the 19th century. But *awesome* has lost much of its power to inspire awe, now that it has been reduced to a generalized slang term of approval by trendy teens and adults who imitate them. ("Those jeans are awesome!")

Hint: The awe is still present and powerful in *awe-inspiring* and *awestruck*. (See also next entry and "devalued words.")

awful **usage**   Caution: *Awful* may be harmful to your communication.

You risk offense if you use *awful* in its common meaning as *extremely objectionable* ("awful food") or just plain *extremely* ("awful cute"). Though such meanings of *awful* have been well established for well over a century, some word connoisseurs insist that *awful* be used only in its original, Middle English sense of "inspiring awe." But if you take the word of those word connoisseurs, your communication could be awfully confusing. For example, imagine a TV critic telling viewers that an awe-inspiring performance was "truly awful."

Suggestion: To quote the *Longman Guide to English Usage*, "It is safer today to avoid *awful* and *awfully* altogether in serious writing." If you mean *awe-inspiring*, say so.

awhile or *a while?*   *A while* is a noun phrase meaning "a period of time." *Awhile* is an adverb meaning "*for* a period of time."

Usage rule: Use only the two-word form when it's preceded by a preposition, as with "*in* a while" or "*for* a while."

Note that you can stay *for a while* (a period of time) or you can stay *awhile* (*for* a period of time). But you cannot stay *for awhile*, because that would mean you are redundantly staying *for* "*for* a period of time."

ax or *axe?*   The preferred spelling in the United States is *ax*; in England, *axe*.

B

babble, **Babel,** or *babel?*   The word *babble* (also rhyming with *rabble*) is a verb ("to talk foolishly") and a noun ("meaningless talk").

Babel (preferably pronounced to rhyme with *table*) was the Hebrew name for the city of Babylon and the place cited in the Book of Genesis where Noah's descendants tried to build a tower to heaven but were prevented by God from doing so by a confusion of tongues. As *Benét's Reader's Encyclopedia* notes, "The story provides a biblical explanation for the diversity of languages in the world."

The lowercase *babel* (preferably pronounced to rhyme with *rabble*) entered English in the 16th century as a word meaning "a confusion of voices or sounds" or "a scene of noise and confusion."

As a suffix-like ending, *-babble* means jargon characteristic of the subject named in the first part of the word. *Psychobabble,* popularized in a 1977 book, inspired the coining of *technobabble.* (See also "*jargon* is not really for the birds.")

Babylon: **city and symbol**   The capitalized *Babylon* stands for the capital of the ancient empire of Babylonia or "any place of luxury, pleasure-seeking and, often, vice and corruption." Such a place can be described by the adjective *Babylonian.*

Usage example: *Time* celebrity-watcher Belinda Luscombe (4/6/1998) called the Academy Awards ceremony a "Babylonian backslapping fest."

back-forming new words   *Back-formation* is the term coined by Sir James Murray, chief editor of the first edition of *The Oxford English Dictionary,* for verbs and nouns formed "backwards" from established words. For example, *esthesia* ("the ability to feel") is a back-formation of *anesthesia* ("the loss of feeling").

Some back-formations, such as *donate* from *donation* and *diagnose* from *diagnosis,* have won complete acceptance.

Surveil, which has been traced by word sleuths to Pentagon jargon of the 1960's, established itself in *The Oxford English Dictionary* (1989) as a verb meaning "to subject [a person or place] to surveillance." Bryan A Garner, in his American usage dictionary editions of 1998 and 2003, described *surveil* as "relatively new, and decidedly useful."

But many back-formations remain in the Risk Zone. For example, the adjectives *drowsy* and *lazy* produced the questionable verbs *drowse* and *laze*. *Burglar* inspired W. S. Gilbert of Gilbert and Sullivan to back-form the jocular verb *burgle*. Other back-formations that have yet to achieve widespread acceptance include *butle* from *butler*, *liaise* from *liaison*, *commentate* from *commentator*, and *enthuse* from *enthusiasm*.

Here are some candidates for a Back-Formation Hall of Infamy: *to frivol, to gregare, to hilare, to incent, to obnox,* and *to sarcaz.* (See also "lost positives.")

backward or backwards?   Never "sneak a backwards glance," because only *backward* is acceptable as an adjective.

For adverbial use, you may step or otherwise move *backward* or *backwards*, except for the idioms "bend over *backward*" and "move *backwards* and *forwards*." And *backwards* is favored for adverbial uses in British English. (See also "*afterward* or *afterwards?*" "*forward* or *forwards?*" and "*toward* or *towards?*")

bad or badly?   See "*feel bad* or *feel badly?*" and "verbs that link subjects with adjectives."

bade sounds bad   *Bade*, the past tense of *bid*, is pronounced as if it were *bad*.

baedeker or Baedeker?   The word *baedeker* ("BAY-dicker") became a synonym for "guidebook, especially for tourists" because of the success of the series of tourist guidebooks introduced early in the 19th century by German printer Karl Baedeker.

baited or bated breath?   If you feel as if you are holding your breath in suspenseful anticipation of some important disclosure or occurrence, you are said to be waiting with *bated* ("suspended or shortened") breath.

The adjective *bated* is an abbreviation of *abated*, which means "restrained, moderated" and is related to the noun *abatement* ("moderation, reduction"), as in "noise abatement." The phrase *bated breath* has been traced back more than four centuries, to Shakespeare's *Merchant of Venice*.

Save *baiting* for "setting a trap" or "taunting somebody for the malicious purpose of provoking a reaction."

balance: the *remainder* of the story   Everybody agrees to the use of *balance* to mean "a state of equilibrium." Likewise, *balance* is acceptable in the accounting sense of "the equality in an account between total credits and debits," "the difference between those totals," or simply "the remainder of funds" you owe or have in an account.

But the use of *balance* as an all-purpose synonym for "remainder, something left over" has been opposed by a number of conservative critics ever since that extended sense was introduced in the United States two centuries ago. As *Merriam-Webster's Dictionary of English Usage* notes, "No solid reason for avoiding the [extended] sense has been brought forward in all that time." But *The Columbia Guide to Standard American English* says that because of the continuing opposition you should avoid that usage "in most formal contexts."

Risk-free advice: Replace *balance* with *remainder* or *rest* in a sentence such as "A third of the audience left the mayor's boring speech during the first 15 minutes, but the balance [replace with *rest*] stayed until the bitter end."

baleful or baneful?   Both these adjectives spell "harmful," but word connoisseurs try to preserve some distinction.

The American Heritage Dictionary, Merriam-Webster's Dictionary of English Usage, and *The Columbia Guide to Standard American English* note that *baleful* generally refers to that which *threatens* harm, as in a *New York Times* reference (6/8/2001) to "baleful forecasts about California's worsening energy situation."

Baneful usually refers to that which *causes* harm, as in a reference in *The New Yorker* (3/6/2000) to "the baneful influence of money" on political campaigns.

The noun *bane* means "a person or thing that ruins or spoils," as in an observation by pamphleteer Thomas Paine in *Common Sense* (1776) that "suspicion is the companion of mean souls, and the bane of all good society." *Bane* originally meant "that which causes death" and still has that meaning in the compound names of such poisonous plants as *wolfsbane* and *baneberry*.

Balkan or Baltic?   "Balkan Economies Stagnate," reported a *New York Times* headline (8/20/1996) about continuing crises in Bosnia, Croatia, and

Serbia. The adjective *Balkan*—"of or related to the Balkan Peninsula"—also embraces Albania, Bulgaria, continental Greece, southeastern Romania, and European Turkey.

Because the Balkan Peninsula is divided into all those nations, the sometimes capitalized verb *balkanize* means "to divide [a region or effort] into smaller, often competitive, units." For example: "Many Americans . . . believe that immigration from Mexico and Latin America is of a scale that could linguistically Balkanize the United States." (That observation is from Robert MacNeil and William Cran's companion volume to their 2005 PBS television series, *Do You Speak American?*)

Baltic is an adjective meaning "of or related to the Baltic states—Estonia, Latvia, and Lithuania—on the eastern coast of the Baltic Sea." These former Russian provinces became independent countries after World War I, were incorporated into the Soviet Union in 1940, and regained their independence in 1991.

baloney, boloney, or bologna?   All three spellings are pronounced "buh-LOW-nee" and are appropriate for a seasoned smoked sausage or a slang noun, adjective, or interjection denoting "nonsense."

If you capitalize the third spelling, you have the Italian city ("buh-LOAN-yuh"), the birthplace of the famous sausage. (See also "*bunk* is an American tradition.")

banal: a choice of syllables   This French-derived term for "trite, uninspired, boringly commonplace" is often heard in the United States today with an anglicized emphasis on the first syllable. But the risk-free pronunciation retains the French accent, rhyming with *canal*.

bandana or bandanna?   Dictionaries assign the preferred listing to *bandanna*. The other form is listed as a spelling variant for this "large, colored handkerchief, often worn as a scarf."

barbarism is crude, not cruel   *Barbarism* means "uncivilized behavior characterized by crudity or ignorance," including sloppy use of language. A linguistic *barbarism*, related to our word *babble*, can be traced back to the ancient Greek viewpoint that non-Greeks spoke gibberish that the Greeks called *barbarismós*.

The word for uncivilized behavior that's cruel is *barbarity*. The adjective *barbarous* can mean "crude" or "cruel."

bare or **bear** secrets?   *Bears* ("shaggy-coated mammals of the family Ursine") will not *bear* ("carry in the mind") a grudge against you if you *bare* ("reveal") secrets regarding the *bare* ("naked") truth about them.

The verb *bear* has many other meanings, including "carry on one's person, conduct oneself in a specified way, give birth to, support, relate, exhibit, produce, offer, endure."

basal or **basic**?   *Basal*, which is acceptable as a technical adjective ("pertaining to a base, as in basal metabolism"), is otherwise a pretentious, ambiguous, and needless synonym for "basic, fundamental."

based on confusion   The phrase *based on* causes no problem when it's used in the figurative sense of "rests on," as in a scientific theory "*based on* [supported by] extensive research," or a movie "*based on* [derived from] a true story."

But *based on* causes confusion when it's used in the sense of "because of." For example, consider this sentence: "Based on poor earnings, Randy decided not to invest in those companies." No matter how many times you read that sentence, you will not be able to determine if Randy's decision was based on *his* poor earnings, or the poor earnings of the *companies*. For a simple solution, say "Because of [his or the companies'] poor earnings, Randy decided against those investments." (See also "participles that dangle.")

bastille or **Bastille**?   The noun *bastille* ("a prison, especially one operated in a tyrannical way") comes from the fortress-prison called the *Bastille* (from a French word for "fortress"). A hated symbol of pre-revolutionary France, the Bastille was used to incarcerate political prisoners, and its guns commanded one of the gates of Paris. The storming of the Bastille by a Parisian crowd hoping to capture ammunition, on July 14, 1789, marked the beginning of the French Revolution and inspired France's July 14 observance of Bastille Day.

bathos or **pathos**?   *Pathos* is the quality (say, in a novel or movie) of "eliciting pity." *Bathos* is pathos that is counterfeit: "an insincere or excessive attempt to elicit pity."

beating around the bush   Call it circumlocution, periphrasis, a roundabout way of saying something, or just plain beating around the bush. Whatever you call this problem, you can solve it by getting to the point.

Do not "come to a realization" when you can *realize*. Do not "reach an agreement" when you can *agree*. Do not "have an opinion that" when you can *believe*.

Use *except* when you're tempted to say "except for the fact that," "with the exception of," or "apart from the fact that." Likewise, use *because* when you're tempted to say "because of the fact that," "by virtue of the fact that," or "on account of the fact that."

***beatitude* or *Beatitude*?**   The noun *beatitude* ("bee-AT-itude") is derived from a Latin word *beatitudo*, meaning "perfect happiness," and indeed means "supreme happiness or blessedness."

The *Beatitudes* are the sayings of Jesus in the opening verses of the Sermon on the Mount (Matthew 5:3–12), including "Blessed are the meek: for they shall inherit the earth" and "Blessed are the merciful: for they shall obtain mercy." The term *Beatitude* is a title and form of address (*Your Beatitude*) for a patriarch in the Armenian Church or a metropolitan (bishop) in the Russian Orthodox Church.

In Roman Catholicism, *beatification* is a declaration by the pope that a deceased person is one of the blessed, is worthy of public veneration, and is in the first stage of canonization.

***beauteous* or *beautiful*?**   Use *beautiful* unless you're trying for a poetic effect. (See "*plenteous* or *plentiful*?")

***because* can be a starter**   Because poorly prepared schoolteachers sometimes mislead their students about usage, some people grow up with a fear of using *because* as the first word in a sentence. In fact, *because* is fully accepted by usage authorities in sentences such as the one you just read. But don't make the mistake of using *because* to begin an unjustifiable sentence fragment, as in the following example from a student writer: "I hate math. Because it's really boring."

***because* can cause confusion**   Beware of the confusion that may occur when *because* follows a negative statement.

Consider this ambiguous sentence: "Rod did not fail the exam because of

Fred's advice." That could mean Rod *passed*, thanks to Fred's advice. Or it could mean that, though Rod *failed*, the failure wasn't caused by Fred's advice.

If the first of those two meanings is intended, the sentence should read "Rod *passed* the exam because of Fred's advice." The second meaning could be conveyed unambiguously with either "Rod *failed* the exam, but not because of Fred's advice" or "It was not *because of* Fred's advice *that* Rod failed the exam."

In some negative-plus-*because* sentences, the meaning may depend on the presence or absence of a comma: "Arnold didn't buy the house, because it was near a golf course" means that Arnold rejected the house because he didn't want to live near a golf course. "Arnold didn't buy the house because it was near the golf course" means that he *did* buy the house, but not because it was near a golf course. (See also "commas can change your meaning," "*since* ambiguity," and "*to* can cause confusion.")

begging the question is risky business   If you use the phrase *begging the question*, you have three risky choices.

First choice: You may be accused of ignorance if you imitate the popular but inaccurate use of the phrase to mean—quoting from a cautionary entry of *Garner's Modern American Usage*—"evade the issue." For example, many politicians are said to *beg the question* of how their proposed reforms would be funded.

Second choice: Another popular but inaccurate definition of the phrase is listed without any cautionary comment by the generally permissive *Merriam-Webster's Collegiate Dictionary*: "to elicit a question logically as a reaction or response." For example, the writer of an essay in the *Los Angeles Times Magazine* (12/19/2004) recalled his purchase of a home whose only evidence of a previous owner was a framed, half-century-old request for a building variance to erect an addition. The writer continued: "For me, that brown, brittle paper hanging on the wall begged the question: What lives had been lived in this now empty home?"

Third choice: You risk being misunderstood if you use *begging the question* in the accurate and only sense listed in the ultimate compilation of the English language, *The Oxford English Dictionary*: "a taking for granted of the thing to be proved." For example, a king *begs the question* of his competence by arguing that he can do no wrong because he's the king.

Usage advice: If you take the risk of using the correct, circular-logic meaning of *begging the question*, you'll need to explain what you mean. But, in return for that extra effort, you'll be able to take pride in helping to preserve a concept introduced more than 23 centuries ago by the philosopher Aristotle. He called *begging the question* "assumption at the outset," which in Aristotle's Greek was *en archei aiteisthai* and was translated by the Romans as *petitio principii* (literally, "seeking the start").

behalf (*in* or *on*)?   Someone who acts *on* behalf of others (represents them) does not necessarily act *in* their behalf (help them).

behaviorist is not synonymous with *behavioral scientist*   A *behaviorist* is a scientist who subscribes to *behaviorism*, a century-old school of psychology that assumes all organisms are essentially nothing but biological robots. To quote *The Columbia Encyclopedia*, behaviorists reject the study of mental processes as unscientific and instead focus on animal and human behavior "entirely in terms of observable and measurable responses to environmental stimuli."

behest or *request*?   A disc jockey may have to deny a *request* ("something asked for") from a listener at the *behest* ("command, emphatic request") of a station executive.

Example of *behest* usage from *The New York Times* (8/29/1999): "Last year the school board in Post Falls, Idaho, at the behest of creationists in the community, wrote a policy statement that would have allowed creation scientists considerable latitude in making their views known in public schools."

bellweather or *bellwether*?   This word for a trendsetter is correctly spelled *bellwether*, because the word refers not to weather but to sheep. *Bellwether* originated in a traditional method of herding sheep, in which a bell-wearing *wether* (male sheep) leads the flock. *Bellwether* figuratively means "a person or thing that leads or shows the way." Usage example: A *New York Times* news story (1/15/2001) noted that Switzerland was "considered an important bellwether of smoking trends in Europe."

beloved pronunciation   *Beloved* ("dearly loved") is preferably pronounced with three syllables ("bee-LOVE-id") rather than two.

benefactor or **beneficiary?** A *benefactor* is someone who gives money or other help to someone. The receiver of such help is a *beneficiary*.

beside or **besides?** If you add an *s* to the preposition *beside*, you get another preposition with an entirely different meaning. For example: "Nobody was parked *beside* [next to] me in that lot" is not at all the same statement as "Nobody was parked *besides* [except for] me in that lot."

    Beside may also be used in comparisons: "My son looks short *beside* yours." And *beside* can mean "apart or disjoined from," as in "Her wealth is *beside* the point" or "The customer was *beside* himself with anger."

    Besides means not only "except for" but also "in addition to." For example: "*Besides* her two cats, she has three dogs." *Besides* can also serve as an adverbial conjunction meaning "moreover, furthermore," as in "*Besides*, she won't be arriving until next month."

best or **better?** The word *better* compares two. *Best* is the superlative of more than two. Idiomatic exception: "Put your best foot forward." (See also "idioms do their own thing.")

"best-kept secrets" are best kept to yourself The new manager of a neighborhood swimming facility in Pasadena, California, tells the press that the facility is the area's "best-kept secret." In the same community, the new manager of a theater group tells the press that *his* worthy project is the area's "best-kept secret." Also in that community, a local newspaper publishes an advertising supplement—with small display ads for chiropractors, lawyers, hair stylists, and so on—under the heading "Best Kept Secrets."

    The worst-kept secret about the "best-kept secret" pitch is that it is used by advertisers and publicists who can't think of anything better to say about something or someone you may never have heard of.

best of all or **best of any?** When you use the superlative degree—*best, worst, most, least, tallest, shortest*—you are comparing something with *all*, not *any*. Usage example: "Octavio Paz was considered the best of any [replace with *all*] Mexican poets of the 20th century."

better than or ***more than?*** Word guardians recommend that you not say "*better* than" when you mean "*more* than."

better or ***bettor?*** Both can mean "one who bets." But, for that meaning, your best bet is the preferred spelling, *bettor*, to avoid confusion in sentences such as "Always listen to your betters [people who are superior in merit or rank]."

between or ***among?*** See "*among* or *between*."

between **must really come between** The phrases *between each* and *between every*, as in "between each act of the play" and "between every row in the garden," are not logical. That is because *between* means "*between* two things," not "*within* one thing." Correct usage: "between *the acts*," "between *rows*."

between Scylla and Charybdis **is not a good location** This expression, meaning "between two equally perilous alternatives," refers to the dangerous waters at the Strait of Messina between Italy and Sicily, where ships must navigate between the menacing rock named *Scylla* ("SIL-a") and a deadly whirlpool named *Charybdis* ("ka-RIB-dis").

In Greek mythology, the sorceress Circe—a rival of the nymph Scylla for the affections of a hero named Glaucus—turned Scylla into a ferociously barking monster with twelve feet and six heads, each with three rows of menacing teeth, who sat on Scylla rock and swallowed all sailors within her reach.

Across from Scylla, the god Zeus punished a woman named Charybdis for stealing oxen from him by hurling her into the sea, where she had to keep sucking in and spewing out huge amounts of water, creating the Charybdis whirlpool.

between you and I or ***between you and me?*** People who say "between you and *I*" are engaging in what usage commentators call hypercorrection, which means they are overcorrecting their language. The correct usage is "between you and me." The objective-case *me*, not the nominative-case *I*, is required in "between you and me," because the personal pronoun *me* is needed as the object of the preposition *between*. "Between you and *I*" is as objectionable as "between *we*."

In another example of this *me*-avoiding hypercorrection, *Just Shoot Me* sitcom star Laura San Giacomo told a *Los Angeles Times* writer (8/9/1998) that doing the series meant that she could stay in one place to care for her young child, and thus the series had been "really good for my son and I." She should have said "for my son and *me*," because *me* was needed as the object of the preposition *for*. The phrase "for my son and *I*" is as objectionable as "for *we*." (See also "*me* is nothing to be afraid of.")

bi- warning   If an employer promises to pay you *bimonthly*, that can mean either "twice a month" or "every two months." That's because *bi* can mean "twice" or "two."

The same "twice or two" ambiguity applies to *biweekly* and *biannually*.

Some usage sources—including *The American Heritage Book of English Usage, Webster's New World Dictionary of Media and Communications*, and *The Associated Press Stylebook*—say that *bi-* means "every two" and *semi-* means "twice." But for clarity in your own communication, use expressions such as "every two months" and "twice a month."

billet and billet doux are both notable   *Billet* (which rhymes with "skillet") once meant "a short document or note." Then it meant "an official document directing that military personnel be provided with board and lodging, typically in a private home." Next, it became synonymous with "the military lodging assigned by billet and then with military lodging in general."

Billet doux (which has a French pronunciation that sounds like "billy DO" and the literal French meaning of "sweet note") is used in English as a playful way of saying "love letter."

billion can mean trillion   The American definition of a billion—1,000,000,000—is gaining wide acceptance around the world. But be careful: a billion in Canada, England, and Germany is commonly defined by three additional zeros—1,000,000,000,000—which Americans call a *trillion*.

birdbrain should be a compliment   The insulting slang term *birdbrain*, defined in dictionaries as "a stupid, silly person," illustrates human ignorance about real birds. As science writer Michael Specter wrote in a *New Yorker* article (7/23/2001) about canaries and other songbirds that learn entirely new melodies each year, "The bird brain has an undeservedly bad reputation."

Bird brains are as complex and inventive as the brain of any mammal, with crows, parrots, and some other birds exhibiting intelligence at least comparable to that of chimpanzees. Such levels of intelligence were established by a team of 29 scientists from six countries in a seven-year study whose results were published February 1, 2005, in the journal *Nature Neuroscience Reviews.*

In one example cited in that monumental study, a group of carrion crows were seen carefully placing walnuts in a crosswalk at a university campus in Japan while vehicular traffic was halted by a red light. The crows then patiently waited on the sidewalk for oncoming cars to smash open the walnuts. When the traffic light showed that the crows could safely re-enter the crosswalk, they rushed back to retrieve their now-accessible food.

In a 1989 tribute to the role of the bird brain in transcontinental bird migrations, nature writer Jake Page and bird zoologist Eugene S. Morton wrote in *Lords of the Air:* "Just how so diminutive an organ as the much-maligned bird brain is capable of programming into itself such changing environmental information as is garnered on its maiden voyages is beyond our present understanding. But it surely deserves the respect of a species that requires a printed map to find its way around a shopping mall." (See also "animals as linguistic sitting ducks.")

bit about computers   The computer's numeric computer symbol, usually represented by 0 or 1, is a *bit* (short for *BI*nary digi*T*). A sequence of 8 bits forms a *byte,* the amount of memory needed to store one character of data such as a letter or number. Bytes are measured by the thousand (*kilobyte, K,* or *KB*), by the million (*megabyte, meg,* or *MB*), and by the billion (*gigabyte* or *GB*).

bitter truth   Should you say "*bitter* cold" or "*bitterly* cold"? Say either. *Bitter* serves not only as an adjective but also as a "flat adverb," one without an *-ly.* (See also "adverbs that look like adjectives.")

bizarre or bazaar?   Many people probably would not want to shop at a *bazaar* ("marketplace") that's *bizarre* ("odd, strange, outlandish, grotesque"). *Bazaar* is from a Persian word for "market." The French acquired *bizarre* from an Italian word, *bizzarro* ("marked by hot temper").

black or Black?   When the U.S. Supreme Court ruled that the Constitution does not permit "racial gerrymandering" for the purpose of electing minority candidates, the *Los Angeles Times* (6/29/1993) described the ruling as "a potentially far-reaching political setback for blacks and Latinos."

By lowercasing *blacks* while capitalizing *Latinos* and other group designations, the *Times* was following a mainstream-media practice, as prescribed by *The Associated Press Stylebook*. The AP lists *black* as the "preferred usage for those of the Negro race."

But as *The American Heritage Dictionary* points out in a usage note, the use of the capitalized ethnic *Black* "has the advantage of acknowledging the parallel with other ethnic groups and nationalities such as *Italian* and *Sioux*." In support of that view, Berkeley linguist John McWhorter wrote in an op-ed essay in the *Los Angeles Times* (9/8/2004): "It's time we descendants of slaves brought to the United States let go of the term 'African American' and go back to calling ourselves Black—with a capital B."

Though journalists would not think of depriving the term *African-American* or *Negro* of the respect shown by capitalization, they lowercase *black* on the grounds that the media also lowercase *white*. An obvious answer to this question of orthographic consistency would be to use an uppercase *White* as well as an uppercase *Black*. Inasmuch as nobody's skin is actually colored white or black, the uppercasing of those words for group identification would be a clear indication that such usage reflects social rather than scientific reality.

Note also that the uppercase *Black* helps avoid confusion with the term *black* in other contexts. To cite just one example: A *Black comedy* would clearly refer to a comedy involving race, as distinguished from a *black comedy*, which, as defined by the *Random House Webster's Unabridged Dictionary*) "employs morbid, gloomy, grotesque, or calamitous situations in its plot." (See "ethnic and racial classifications" and "*Caucasian*: the fact and the fable.")

blame only the guilty   As the old song goes, you can "put the blame on Mame, boys." But careful communicators don't *blame* an accident *on* carelessness. They say "carelessness was blamed *for* the accident."

blandish or **brandish**?   You can be more persuasive if you *blandish* ("coax by gentle flattery") than *brandish* ("to wave, as in waving a weapon, menacingly"). The noun *blandishment* refers to "action or speech that tends to flatter, coax, entice," as in "Our blandishments no longer seemed to work on the boss."

***blatant* or *flagrant*?**   These adjectives, both meaning "conspicuous," are often used interchangeably. But careful communicators employ them for separate purposes.

The American Heritage Book of English Usage suggests you think of *blatant* as "offensively *conspicuous*" and *flagrant* as "conspicuously *offensive*." Applying the same distinction, Professor J. N. Hook's *Appropriate Word* prescribes *blatant* for that which is conspicuous in a *shameless* way ("blatant display of nudity") and *flagrant* that which is conspicuous in an *evil* way ("flagrant violation of professional ethics").

blends and compounds   Linguistic *blends* are formed from word mixtures, as in the blending of *motor hotel* in *motel* and the blending of *breakfast* and *lunch* in *brunch*. (See also "*chortle* and other Carroll coinages.")

Compound words are formed by attaching one word to another, as in *birdcage*. (See also "spelling compound words.")

***blind* or *purblind*?**   *Blind*, in addition to its literal meaning of "sightless," can figuratively mean "unable or unwilling to perceive or understand." For example: "Love is blind."

Purblind ("PURR-blind"), a blend of *pure* and *blind* that used to mean "completely blind," now means "deficient in understanding." Author Simon Winchester wrote in his 2001 book, *The Map That Changed the World*, that the 18th-century father of geology, William Smith, "was brought up in a society still in the firm grip of purblind churchly certainty."

***bloc* this mistake**   This word for a group united for a common cause, such as the former Soviet *bloc* of nations, is often misspelled *block*.

"blood, sweat, and tears"   This echo of Winston Churchill's wartime rhetoric is slightly distorted. Churchill's actual phrase was "blood, toil, tears, and sweat."

***boast*: a question of pride**   The risk-free meaning of the verb *boast* is "brag, especially with excessive pride."

You face a small risk of criticism if you use the verb *boast* to mean "be proud in having," as in a city that "boasts excellent restaurants." That meaning of *boast* has been around for more than three centuries, and it's well established in our language today. But some word guardians just don't like it, judging from a 38 percent vote against it on the usage panel of *The American Heritage Dictionary* and a 44 percent vote against it on the usage panel of the *Harper Dictionary of Contemporary Usage.*

boat or *ship*?   A *boat*, most nautical authorities seem to agree, is any vessel that is small enough to be put on a *ship*. An exception is a ferry boat.

body, as in victim   In the context of criminal violence and other tragedies, the word *dead* in the phrase *dead body* is redundant. (See also "redundancy: a vice and a virtue.")

bogey, bogie, or bogy?   *Bogey*, a noun and a verb, designates the golf score of one stroke over par. ("He bogeyed the fourth hole.") *Bogie* and *bogy* are two ways to spell "evil spirit, goblin, hobgoblin, bugbear, object of obsessive dread." And *Bogie* is also the nickname Spencer Tracy created for the iconic actor Humphrey Bogart.

bohemian or *Bohemian*?   A *Bohemian* is someone from Bohemia, an area in what is today the Czech Republic. The lifestyle of Bohemia's Gypsies is said to have inspired the lowercase noun *bohemian* ("someone, usually an artist or writer, with an unconventional lifestyle"). (See also "*Gypsy, Gipsy*, or neither?")

bombs: desirable and otherwise   A play that *bombed* in America was a flop. A play that *went like a bomb* in England was a smash hit.

bona fide or *bona fides*?   The adjective and adverb *bona fide* (preferably pronounced in English to rhyme with *hide* rather than *Heidi*) is Latin and English for "in good faith." *Bona fide* has acquired the extended English meaning of "made in good faith, without intent to deceive, authentic, genuine, real," as in "a *bona fide* offer."

    Bona fides ("FI-deez")—a Latin and English noun phrase for "good faith"—has acquired the additional English meaning of "*evidence* of good faith or authenticity." Hence, *bona fides* is as singular as *faith* and *evidence*. But because *bona fides* looks and sounds plural in English, it is now used by many professional writers to mean *"credentials* of good faith."

bon appétit spells money   You know you're in a restaurant where you're expected to pay at least a 20 percent tip if the server correctly pronounces the French expression *bon appétit* ("boh-na-pay-TEE"), which literally means "good appetite" but actually means "Enjoy your meal."

boor or bore?   A *bore* ("someone who is boring") and a *boor* are annoying in different ways. A *boor*, originally a peasant and therefore someone whose manners were rustic, is now someone who is "unmannered, crude, insensitive." Usage example: According to *The New York Times* (12/30/2000), hostesses at Italy's conventions and public ceremonies are "trained to smile pleasantly at even the most boorish clients."

born or borne?   To choose between these two forms of the past participle of the verb *bear*, use *born* only when referring to a person's birth, actual or figurative. ("She was born in Russia." "The candidate called himself a born-again Christian.") Use *borne* when referring to a person's *giving* birth ("She had borne nine children") and for all other meanings originating in the verb *bear,* as well as *bear up, down, with, on, upon,* and *out.*

Usage example of *borne out* ("confirmed") from *The New York Times* (1/1/2001): "But the notion that women want to quit their jobs after only a few years of work in order to get married . . . was not borne out by interviews with many young women who are college job applicants."

In an example of *borne* in the sense of "endured," Danish short-story writer Isak Dinesen (1885–1962) wrote, "All sorrows can be borne if you put them into a story or tell a story about them." And a *Los Angeles Times* writer reported (4/3/2002), "Recent university research shows that those younger than 25 have borne the brunt of the employment decline."

both or both of?   The answer to this question parallels the answer to the question (asked in the title of an earlier entry) *"all* or *all of*?" When English usage gives you a choice between *both* and *both of*, choose the simple *both* in order to avoid the redundant *of.*

English usage requires *both of* before the pronouns *you*, *us*, *them*, and *whom*. But you should take advantage of your option to choose *both* in place of *both of* before the possessive pronouns *its*, *my*, *your*, *our*, *his*, *her*, and *their*, and also before plural nouns. Notice the unnecessary *of* in "Both [of] her sisters have lived in both [of] those countries."

***both* tips continued**   Delete *both* when the idea is expressed by other words: "They are [both] alike," "They [both] arrived at the same time" and "They are [both] equally tall." But feel free to add a redundant *both* when needed for emphasis: "The governor's educational proposals are supported by *both* Democrats and Republicans."

In "both . . . and" phrases, make sure the linked items are presented in the same way. For example, say "both *the* city and *the* county parks," not "both *the* city and county parks," and say "both *in the* morning and *in the* afternoon," not "both *in the* morning and *the* afternoon."

In possessive constructions, say "of both." For example, say "the mothers of both men," not "both men's mothers."

Avoid the ambiguous *both* that could mean either "each one" or "two together." For example, instead of making the ambiguous statement "Both suits cost $300," say "Each suit cost $300" or "The two suits together cost a total of $300," depending on your intended meaning.

***bouillon* or *bullion*?**   *Bouillon* means "broth," and its first syllable contains the letters and sound of "ou" as in *soup*.

Bullion means gold or silver considered in mass (bars or ingots) rather than value, and the word begins with the letters and sound of "bull" as in *Wall Street bull*.

***bounce* or *jounce*?**   *Jounce* is a noun meaning "a bounce with a rough, jolting movement." Both *jounce* and *bounce* can also be used as transitive and intransitive verbs.

***boundary* or *boundry*?**   This word for "something that indicates bounds or limits" is usually pronounced as if it were spelled *boundry*. But you won't get an A in spelling if you omit the *a*.

boycott or *embargo*?   A *boycott* is an organized refusal to patronize some-one or something. (For the origin of *boycott*, see "*eponymous* means never hav-ing to say you're anonymous.")

An *embargo* is a punitive restriction against trade, typically prohibiting goods from entering or leaving a country. A news embargo, to quote *Webster's New World Dictionary of Media and Communications*, "forbids the use of news material by a publication or broadcast medium; generally a time is specified, after which the embargo is released."

brackets and parentheses   Use parentheses (sparingly, please) when you must interrupt the flow of your sentence, or the flow of thought between sen-tences, with a separate thought. (If you must resort to a parenthetical sentence or sentences, make sure you place your closing punctuation before the closing parenthesis.)

You should use parentheses sparingly (only when you really *must*) because some people's reaction to them is similar to Mark Twain's: "A parenthesis is evi-dence that the man who uses it does not know how to write English or is too indolent to take the trouble to do it; a man who will wantonly use a parenthesis will steal. For these reasons I am unfriendly to the parenthesis. When a man puts one into my mouth, his life is no longer safe."

In a quoted sentence, *parentheses* mean an interruption or aside by the per-son being quoted, and *brackets* mean an insertion by a writer or editor for the purpose of clarification, commentary, or a smooth transition. An example of bracket use: "He often had lunch with [Mayor] Rodriguez."

Brahman or *Brahmin*?   Both spellings are acceptable for a member of the highest, priestly caste in Hinduism. In the United States, a *Brahmin* is a member of a social elite, especially of one of the elite old families of New England. Usage example: *The Wall Street Journal* (7/29/1997) referred to Republican William F. Weld as Massachusetts' "Boston Brahmin Governor."

breach or *breech*?   The noun *breach*, as in "breach in the dam" or "breach of contract," shares an *a* with its synonym *break*. As a verb, *breach* means "to make a hole in, rupture, disrupt, violate."

A *breech* is the back or lower part, as in a *breech birth* (feet or buttocks first). That's why trousers (clothing that covers a person's lower part) have been called *breeches* and, in slang, *britches.*

breadth, breath, or breathe? *Breadth* is a noun for "expanse," *breath* is a noun for "air inhaled and exhaled," and *breathe* is the verb "to inhale and exhale."

"break a leg" Why do we say "Break a leg" as a way of wishing good luck to someone facing a challenge such as a stage performance? Why, in the same spirit, do Germans say "Break your neck and leg"?

The *American Heritage Dictionary of Idioms* says nobody knows. But you can find a plausible explanation in *Webster's New World Dictionary of Media and Communications*: During the time of the classical Greek theater, "it was believed that the gods would send the opposite of a wish, so a wish for a mishap would trick the gods into bringing 'good luck.'"

break or brake? Never *brake* down and cry. In other words, make sure you don't confuse *brake* ("to slow and stop") with *break* ("take a break" or "fracture, damage").

breakup or break up? The noun *breakup* ("disruption") becomes a verb ("to disrupt") when it's broken up into two words: *break up.* Likewise, the nouns *breakdown* and *breakthrough* become verbs when you break them up.

brevity is the best policy See "cut it out," "cut out statements that go without saying," and "readability and reality."

bridal or bridle? *Bridal,* an adjective, means "of or pertaining to brides or weddings."

Bridle is a noun meaning "harness that fits on a horse's head" or "anything that restrains." *Bridle* also is a verb meaning "restrain" or "take offense." Here's an example of the "take offense" *bridle* in the *Los Angeles Times* (12/17/1997): "[President] Clinton bridled at the suggestion that his own efforts to spur racial unity . . . have amounted to a lot of talk with few apparent results."

bright or brightly? See "adverbs that look like adjectives."

bring or **take**?   *Bring* involves movement of an object *toward* the speaker. *Take* involves *any* movement *not* toward the speaker. If you have a problem distinguishing *bring* and *take*, remember that you naturally ask a restaurant server to *bring* you a plate of food and to *take* the empty plate away afterward.

In a situation in which your location is irrelevant to the movement, choose *bring* or *take* depending on the point of view you wish to adopt. For example, you can say your friend *brought* a defective computer back to the dealer if you want to visualize the action from the position of the dealer. But you say your friend *took* the computer back to the dealer if you want to visualize the action from the position of your friend.

When no movement is involved, *bring* can mean *produce*, as in "April showers bring May flowers."

Some *bring/take* decisions depend solely on idiomatic practice: *bring to bear, bring to mind, take to task.*

Brit or **Briton**?   The people of Great Britain call themselves *Britons*, as in a London *Economist* editorial (6/17/2000) stating, "Britons abhor cruelty to animals." But you enter the Risk Zone if you use *Brit*, the clipped synonym that emerged in the early 20th century. Although *Brit* has been adopted in the informal speech of some Britons, and even *The Economist* has used the term (12/22/2001), others find the word offensive.

According to *The New Fowler's Modern English Usage*, outside Great Britain *Brit* is "usually employed with more than a suggestion of teasing or, quite commonly, of hostility." *Merriam-Webster's Dictionary of English Usage* reports that *Brit* "has been used with a certain edge of derogation in some English-speaking nations, including Australia, New Zealand and Ireland." In an American echo of that derogation, Charlton Heston, president of the National Rifle Association, told ABC's *This Week* (3/19/2000): "I am not comfortable about the Brits telling us how to deal with our [right to bear arms]. I think we settled that in 1776, didn't we?"

Here in the United States, *Brit* is usually used in non-hostile contexts, as when *Time* magazine (4/15/2002) reviewed "the delightful new Brit film, *Crush*." But if you offend a Briton by using *Brit*, don't say you weren't warned.

British or **English**?   All *English* people are *British*, but not all *British* people are *English*. The *British* are the people of Great *Britain*, which consists not only of England but also of Scotland and Wales.

Great Britain and Northern Ireland (what the British call *Ulster*) constitute the *United Kingdom*.

broadcast or **broadcasted**?   The past tense and past participle of *broadcast* is the same word, *broadcast*. *The Columbia Guide to Standard American English* says that *broadcasted* is also standard, but some word guardians strongly object to it.

Long before radio and television, beginning in the 18th century, *broadcast* was a word that meant "the scattering of seed in all directions."

***Bronx* must have its article**   The Bronx is famous for its Yankee Stadium and Bronx Zoo. But it has another distinction that most people, even residents of the Bronx, would rather not discuss. That's because they can't explain it. Unlike the other boroughs of New York City, the Bronx has the definite article *the* as part of its name.

Born and bred in the Bronx, I used to ask my teachers why the other boroughs—Manhattan, Brooklyn, Staten Island, and Queens—needed no article to introduce them. Maybe Bronx was somehow a plural name, and this, like "Netherlands," needed *the*, I speculated. But then why didn't anyone ever refer to "the Queens"? In every case, my teachers deftly avoided further discussion by assuring me, and the rest of the class, that my question would never be on the test.

Such reassuring responses from teachers are often effective in silencing youthful curiosity. But I swore that someday I would learn the answer, and that I would reveal to the world that my birthplace was distinguished by something more than a stadium and a zoo.

So here goes: In the mid-17th century, a prosperous, Scandinavian-born immigrant from Holland, Jonas Bronck, settled and farmed a large parcel of land—to be called Bronck's Land—in the New York area between the Harlem River and what became known first as Bronck's River and later as the Bronx River. The borough took its name directly from the Bronx River, retaining the definite article *the* that you'll find introducing rivers in general. So the name for the *area* of the Bronx River was eventually referred to in the abbreviated form of "the Bronx."

That information may not change your life. But now you're able to make a memorable impression on anyone who loves, or is at least interested in, or has even heard about, New York.

brown belt, Brown belt, or Browne belt?   A *brown belt* is a brown cloth waistband signifying that a student of martial arts has reached intermediate rank, between those of the beginning rank (*white belt*) and the highest one (*black belt*).

A military and police belt that has a shoulder strap running diagonally across the chest is called a *Sam Browne belt*, named after Sir Samuel James Browne (1824–1901), a British general. There is no such thing as a Sam *Brown* belt, despite the reference to one in the *Los Angeles Times Magazine* (8/18/1996).

bug or insect?   Scientists use the term *bug* only for members of one insect order, Hemiptera, which includes bedbugs, mealy bugs, lice, aphids, and other insects with oval flattened bodies and a pointed beak for piercing and sucking. (See also "insects and non-insects.")

bugs: where they come from   Word historians suspect that *bug* in the sense of "insect" emerged more than four centuries ago from the Middle English word *bugge*, meaning *scarecrow* or *hobgoblin*. The insect *bug*, in turn, is credited by word historians with inspiring three *bugs* of American slang: the 1889 coinage of *bug* as an insect-like interference in a machine or plan, the 1919 coinage of *bug* as an insect-tiny eavesdropping microphone, and the 1949 coinage of the verb *bug* that *Cassell's Dictionary of Slang* defines as "annoy like a bug [insect]."

bully pulpits are not for bullies   *Bully* as a verb means, of course, to behave like a *bully* ("someone who picks on the weak"). But, informally, *bully* can also mean "excellent, splendid," either as an interjection (for example, "Bully for you!") or as an adjective, as in a *bully pulpit* ("an excellent position from which to make one's views known").

The term *bully pulpit* was coined by Theodore Roosevelt, to describe the presidency. As the *San Francisco Chronicle* has editorialized (5/21/2000), "A president can clearly use the White House as a bully pulpit to influence public opinion and prod local school boards to do the right thing."

bunch or crowd?   Usage commentators prescribe *bunch* for things, *crowd* for people.

***bunk* is an American tradition**   Ever since Ali MacGraw said the *bull*-word in the 1969 movie *Love Story*, many people on all social levels have been acting as if that word were the only available exclamatory synonym for "nonsense." But American English gave the world an equivalent with a much more interesting history: *bunk!*

Bunk is the shortened form of *bunkum*, a variant of *buncombe*, from Buncombe County, North Carolina (named for Colonel Edward Buncombe, who was killed while fighting for U.S. independence at the Battle of Germantown in 1777). The word *buncombe* began its life as a synonym for "political nonsense" in the 1820's, after Congressman Felix Walker of North Carolina confessed that he had delivered a long, irrelevant speech in Congress just to please the folks back home—"to make a speech for Buncombe."

The word *bunk* evolved from *buncombe* about 1900 and was popularized in 1916 in Henry Ford's famous comment that "history is more or less bunk." *Bunk* is now a relevant response to any insincere talk or action. The verb *debunk* ("to expose sham") emerged in the early 1920's.

buoy oh buoy   The order of preference in the pronunciation of *buoy*, the floating marker or warning device, is "BOO-ee" then "boy" in the Merriam-Webster, Random House, and American Heritage dictionaries. The reverse order is cited in *Webster's New World Dictionary*. And *Bryson's Dictionary of Troublesome Words* dismisses the pronunciation "BOO-ee" as "mistaken and misguided."

For *buoy* as a verb, meaning "to lift up in spirits, encourage," you can't go wrong by choosing the pronunciation "boy," as in "buoyed by the applause." In support of that advice, all the dictionaries mentioned above prefer "boy" to "boo" for the first syllable of the adjective *buoyant* ("able to float, lighthearted, cheerful") and its noun, *buoyancy* ("ability to float, lightheartedness, cheerfulness").

Reminder: Say "BOO-ee" when you're floating on water. Say "boy" when you feel as if you're floating on air, or at least being uplifted. You should use the "boy" pronunciation if you were to read aloud this headline from *The Wall Street Journal* (6/10/2002): "Alternative Lenders Buoy the Economy But Also Pose Risk."

burgeon: a blooming controversy   *Burgeon* has one dictionary meaning that is safe and one that is risky.

You are safe if you use *burgeon* in its original sense of "bud, sprout, emerge," as in "the young artist's burgeoning talent."

The word's other common meaning, "spread, rapidly grow"—as in "the world's burgeoning population"—has won the acceptance of leading dictionaries and *The Columbia Guide to Standard American English.* But that sense of *burgeon* has been branded as a "loose use" by Lovinger's *Penguin Dictionary of American English Usage and Style* and as a misusage by Follett's *Modern American Usage* and Bernstein's *Careful Writer.* And *The New York Times Manual of Style and Usage* agrees: "Careful writers and knowing readers still use [*burgeon*] only to mean budding."

Whatever your decision about *burgeon,* you'll need to make sure your intended meaning is clear from your context.

burned or **burnt?**   For the past tense and past participle of the verb *burn,* American English favors *burned.* British English favors *burnt.* In other usage, American or British, prolonged stress can cause a person to be *burned out* or *burnt out.* And an offering *burned* upon an altar as a sacrifice to a deity must be a *burnt* offering.

bus or **buss?**   Before being *bused* to school, a child may be *bussed* (kissed) by a parent.

but, however, nevertheless, nonetheless, still, still and all, or **yet?**   All these expressions can mean "in spite of that." But there are shades of difference.

The conjunctive *but* communicates a contrast that is simple and direct, as in the previous sentence.

However says "Notice this also," as this sentence: "I hate the smog in Southern California; however, I'm moving there for the job opportunities."

Nevertheless and *nonetheless* say "Do not forget that . . . " as in this sentence: "I've decided not to sue; nevertheless, I cannot forgive what they did."

Still says "In spite of what happened, be assured that . . . " as in this sentence: "I know that both presidential candidates have broken their promises; still, I'm going to do my duty and vote."

Still and all, which means the same as *still,* offends some usage commentators on the grounds that the added words *and all* add no meaning. But as

Merriam-Webster's Dictionary of English Usage reports, a number of professional writers have adopted the phrase in recent years because of its "casual, conversational quality."

Yet says "There is a chance to change things," as in this sentence: "I know that every truce has been violated; yet we must keep trying for a peace that will last."

but and commas   Use a comma after *but* only when the comma is one of a pair setting off an expression that interrupts the flow of a sentence: "But, *if I'm not mistaken*, she's the same person who called you five minutes ago." Here is an example of a *needless* comma after *but*, from the 1995 *Saturn Owner's Handbook*: "But, airbags would not provide protection in many types of collisions."

but ins and outs   When you use *but* as a coordinating conjunction, make sure you mean it.

In a typically illogical use of *but*, a writer for a community newspaper referred to author Ray Bradbury's living room as "compact but unassuming"—illogically implying that *compact* somehow contrasted with *unassuming*.

The conjunctive *but* means "on the other hand." It says that the adjective, phrase, clause, or sentence that follows is something that contrasts with what came before. In an example of correct usage, a *New York Times* article (8/4/1998) about the construction in Chile of an astronomical facility called the Very Large Telescope noted, "It is not one instrument but actually a planned complex of four equally large telescopes and three smaller ones."

When *but* is a preposition (meaning "except"), the noun or pronoun following it must be in the objective case: "She invited everyone *but him*."

but is a starter   Contrary to what you may have been told by misguided schoolteachers or carelessly programmed computer grammar-checkers, the conjunctive *but*, like the conjunction *and*, is an acceptable way to start a sentence in all levels of Standard English.

But don't overdo it. Limit such usage, as did the writer of a *New York Times* feature article (1/20/2005) about the impact on New Yorkers of increasing commuter-train fares, in which *but* introduced only 3 of 50 sentences. (See also next entry and "*and* to begin with?")

buzzwords and catchphrases: don't go there   Did you ever find yourself saying "Don't go there," "Been there, done that," "Same old, same old," "In your dreams," "Get over it," "Give me a break," or "Get a life"? If so, according to *Time* magazine essayist Leslie Savan (12/16/1996), you were infected by movie- and TV-generated catchphrases that numb the mind.

A similar warning was issued by columnist Erma Bombeck five years earlier (9/26/1991), in connection with buzzwords such as *bonding* ("cementing a relationship") and *closure* ("ending a relationship"). Bombeck argued that buzzwords ("impressive expressions that come into vogue in a particular culture") gain popularity because they make the user feel sophisticated but that they are often used not to convey thoughts but to conceal a lack of thought.

byzantine or **Byzantine**?   The capitalized *Byzantine* refers to the Byzantine Empire or that empire's art and architecture. The Byzantine Empire began early in the fourth century, when Emperor Constantine, a convert to Christianity, established the capital of his Eastern Roman Empire in ancient Byzantium (now Turkey's port of Istanbul).

The lowercase adjective *byzantine* ("BIZ-in-teen") means "characterized by complicated political intrigue."

Usage example: *Time* magazine (4/7/1997) noted that "Bruce van Voorst, who spent a decade covering defense and national security issues for *Time*, is no stranger to byzantine bureaucracies."

C

cache or **cachet**?   *Cache* (pronounced "cash"), a 19th-century coinage from the French *cacher* ("hide"), is "a hidden store of treasure" or "a safe place for hiding valuables."

Cachet ("cash-AY"), another 19th-century coinage from the French, was adapted from a word meaning "seal affixed to a letter of document." In English, *cachet* became "a personal stamp, distinguishing characteristic, sign or mark of distinction or prestige." Usage example from an article about the history of the

Rolls-Royce (in the Sunbury, Pennsylvania, *Daily Item*, 1/29/2005): "Today, the cachet of the name is nearly magical in car circles." (See also "French toast.")

caduceus: a medical staff The medical symbol called the *caduceus* ("ka-DUE-see-us")—the winged staff with two serpents coiled about it—derived its name from a Greek word for "herald." It was so named because it was carried by the herald—that is, the messenger—of the gods, Hermes (known to Romans as Mercury), and by many heralds of ancient Greece and Rome.

caesar salad: a long way from Rome Reflecting the widespread belief that *caesar salad* was named for Roman emperor Julius Caesar, the syndicated Jim Unger cartoon *Herman* (7/17/2002) showed a restaurant customer being given a plate of the salad by a server wearing an ancient Roman helmet. Actually, the salad was named for Caesar Gardini, a restaurateur in Tijuana, Mexico, who is credited with originating the dish.

caldron or cauldron? Both spellings for this "large kettle or vat for boiling" are classified as standard. But most American and British dictionaries list *cauldron* as the preferred spelling, with *caldron* as its variant. The most famous usage example can be found in Shakespeare's *Macbeth*, act 4, scene 1: "Double, double, toil and trouble; / Fire burn and cauldron bubble."

By extension, *cauldron* means a violently agitated situation, as in "Kosovo's cauldron bubbles on," a headline for a London *Economist* article about violence against ethnic Albanians in Serbia's province of Kosovo during the fall of 1998.

calendar, calender, or colander? The spelling of the *calendar* that reminds us of the date is sometimes confused with *calender* ("machine for processing paper, fabric, etc.") and *colander* ("a bowl for draining food"). Memory tip: *Calendar* ends with the same two letters as *year*.

calliope or Calliope? The word *calliope* ("a musical instrument consisting of a set of steam whistles activated by a keyboard") comes from the *Calliope* of Greek mythology who was the Muse of epic poetry and mother of the poet-musician Orpheus. (See also "*muse or Muse?*")

callous or callus?   *Callous* is an adjective meaning "unfeeling, insensitive" and a verb meaning "to make or become unfeeling, insensitive." Usage example: A *New York Times* editorial (5/24/2000) referred to New York's "often callous foster care system."

Callus is a noun meaning "thickened, hardened skin" and a verb meaning "to form or develop thickened, hardened skin." Memory tip: Dermatologists say, "*Call us* if you are worried about a *callus*."

calvary, Calvary, or cavalry?   The word *calvary* refers to a representation of the Crucifixion or an experience of intense mental suffering, *Calvary* to the hill near Jerusalem on which Jesus was crucified, and *cavalry* to mounted military.

can or may?   Traditionally, *can* has been used for ability and *may* for permission: "Now that Irwin *can* [is able to] drive, *may* he [have permission to] borrow your car?"

The Oxford Companion to the English Language refers to the tradition of distinguishing *can* from *may* as if it were dead on both sides of the Atlantic, and *The Columbia Guide to Standard American English* says, "In actual practice [*can* and *may*] are nearly interchangeable in most uses." But the consensus of usage commentators is that careful communicators still observe the *can/may* distinction.

In any event, avoid *can/may* usage that may be misinterpreted by the many people who are not sensitive to the *can/may* distinction. For example, note the potential misunderstanding in "We have no right to tell disabled people what they *can* do." Does that mean "what they *are able to* do" or "what they *are permitted to* do?"

Even if you are generally careful about the distinction, you can use the "permission" *can* in negative questions such as "*Can't* I go?" In fact, that seems preferable to the "correct" usage: "*Mayn't* I go?"

can hardly or can't hardly?   Are you thinking that you *can* hardly wait for the answer to this question or that you *can't* hardly wait?

The safe answer is *can*. That is because the adverb *hardly* has a negative quality, and therefore its combination with a negative word like *can't* produces what usage researchers such as Roy H. Copperud and the editors of *The American Heritage Book of English Usage* have dismissed as a substandard double negative.

cannon or canon?   A *cannon* ("a large, mounted piece of artillery") is not to be confused with a *canon* ("a rule or body of rules accepted as sacred or standard").

A *canon* also denotes "a set of books accepted as sacred or standard." Author Garry Wills in *The New York Times Magazine* (2/16/1997) describes the canon as "that body of Western thought and art that is supposed to be at the core of all our education."

cannot or can not?   Your clear choice is *cannot*. Depending on which dictionary or usage book you consult, *cannot* is the *only* acceptable form, the *preferred* form, or the form that is by far the more *common*.

cannot but: too negative?   *Cannot but,* as in "I cannot but admire her candor," is part of a cluster of expressions that many usage commentators accept as idiomatic but some denounce as double negatives. The *cannot but* risk also applies to its variants, *cannot help but, cannot choose but,* and the same phrases using the informal *can't.*

Safe alternative: "I cannot *help* admiring her candor." (See also "double negatives.")

can't cannot be cant   Your computer spellchecker won't notice, but your readers will, if you carelessly replace *can't*, the contraction for *cannot*, with the word examined in the next entry.

cant can say too much   If you use *cant*, make sure your context clearly highlights your meaning. *Cant*, which may share with *chant* an origin in the Latin *cantare* ("sing"), can mean "talk that's singsong or whining"—or more commonly "talk that's affected, hypocritically pious, or filled with boring platitudes or fashionable but mindless catchwords."

Cant also can mean "the private language of the underworld" or "the jargon of a particular group, class, sect, or profession."

Another *cant*—apparently related to Teutonic, Slavonic, Romanic, and Celtic words meaning "corner, edge, angle"—can mean "conspicuous angle, outer corner, sudden movement that may tilt or overturn something, slanting position, or slanted edge or surface."

***canvas* or *canvass*?**   *Canvas* is the noun for "firm, closely woven cloth" long associated with tents and sails.

Canvass is a noun and a verb referring to the solicitation of opinions or votes, or an examination or discussion of a subject in painstaking detail. According to John Ciardi's *Good Words to You*, the "detailed examination" sense of *canvass* derives from the fact that coarse canvas was once used for sifting. Another historical connection: As can be verified in dictionaries and in Shakespeare's *Henry VI*, the verb *canvass* once meant "to toss in a canvas sheet in sport or punishment."

***capital, capitol,* or *Capitol*?**   The lowercase noun *capitol* means a building that houses a legislative body, and you might want to associate the *o* with the capitol *dome*. Use the *-al* ending for all other meanings. The uppercase *Capitol*, which begins with a *capital* letter, denotes the building that houses the U.S. Congress in our nation's *capital* city of Washington, D.C.

The word *capital* also means "money, assets, accumulated goods devoted to the production of other goods." As an adjective, *capital* means "excellent," "chief in importance," or "punishable by death."

capital punishment   Many of us recall our childhood lessons on capitalization as a form of punishment. Capitalize this, we were told, but not that. Never capitalize some words, always capitalize others, and capitalize still other words on certain occasions. As a general rule, we were ordered to capitalize nouns that are "proper," but all nouns looked proper enough to some of us.

Today, you may still be somewhat puzzled—unless you now do all your writing in German, in which nouns are capitalized routinely, or you restrict your writing to a language without capitals, such as Chinese, Japanese, Hebrew, or Arabic. So let's review what is "proper" in English.

As *The Associated Press Stylebook* points out, proper nouns are those that "constitute the unique identification for a specific person, place, or thing." Some nouns—such as *Carl, California, Canada,* and *Coca-Cola*—are always proper. But many proper nouns are common nouns that are dressed up for a special reference. For example, a *first amendment* becomes our nation's *First Amendment*. A *prohibition* becomes *Prohibition*, the period (1920–1933) during which the 18th Amendment prohibited the manufacture and sale of alcoholic beverages.

And you may work in a *white house* with an *oval office*, but only the *White House* has an *Oval Office.*

The words *day* and *month* are common nouns, but specific days and months (*Monday, January,* and so on) are proper nouns. The particular seasons—*fall, winter, spring,* and *summer*—used to be considered proper nouns but are no longer capitalized. The common nouns *street* and *avenue* become proper in *Main Street* and *Fifth Avenue.* The common noun *island* becomes proper in *Rhode Island.* The noun *language* does not qualify as a proper noun because it applies to a variety of examples. *English* is a proper noun because there's only one English language. Students study *English history* in a class called *English History 101.*

Major print media, reflecting the style of *The Associated Press Stylebook,* use lowercase for academic departments, such as the department of history and the department of English. Do not be confused by the indiscriminate capitalization in the publications of many educational, corporate, and governmental institutions, which use an uppercase style as if to add prestige to every department in their organization. On the other hand, do capitalize federal departments such as the U.S. State Department.

capitalizing adjectives   Capitalized nouns almost always produce capitalized adjectives, as in *Danish* pastry, *English* muffins, *German* shepherd, and *Swiss* cheese.

You'll discover the exceptions only by routinely checking your dictionary. There, you'll find (for example) that you must capitalize *Venetian* glass but you must not capitalize *venetian* blind. You must capitalize *French* bread, but you have the option of lowercasing *french* fries. And you have the option of lowercasing *dutch* treat, *manila* envelope, and *india* ink.

capitalizing flora and fauna   The scientific name of an organism consists of a lowercase *species* introduced by an uppercase *genus* ("a group of related organisms ranking above a species and below a family"). For example, humans are classified as *Homo sapiens.* (See also "*specie* or *species?*")

capitalizing sentences with two beginnings   Have you ever wondered, What is the meaning of life? In a sentence like that, capitalize not only the first word of the sentence but also the first word of the sentence-like thought that completes the sentence.

capitalizing titles   Some editors will tell you they never "cap the CAP's"—*c* as in conjunctions, *a* as in articles, and *p* as in prepositions—for titles of books, articles, music, movies, and so on. But many editors capitalize all prepositions of four or more letters, including *from, with, after, before,* and *against,* and capitalize shorter prepositions when they are part of the verb (*Follow Up, Give In*).

Of course, you should always "cap the CAP's" at the beginning of a title, as in Ernest Hemingway's *For Whom the Bell Tolls,* and at the end of a title, as in Russell Baker's *Growing Up.* And you should always capitalize any other types of words, no matter how small. For example, note the capitalization of the little verb *is* in Mark Twain's *What Is Man?* Likewise, note the capitalization of the little pronoun *its* in historian Isaiah Berlin's posthumously published *Freedom and Its Betrayal.*

capitalizing titles of people   When you use a title that has been formally assigned to somebody, capitalize it before that person's name, but not after. For example: "He met with *Time* Senior Editor Mary Jane Romero." "He met with Mary Jane Romero, *Time*'s senior editor."

When a word simply tells what somebody does, don't capitalize it even when you use the word as if it were a title: "The speaker will be editor [or, for example, author, novelist, poet] Mary Jane Romero."

Let's review: "Allow me to introduce Professor Barbara Adler of UCLA." "Allow me to introduce Barbara Adler, a professor at UCLA." "Allow me to introduce UCLA educator Barbara Adler."

capitalizing trade names   See "*yo-yo* and *zipper*: why they're in the same entry."

***cardinal*: from pivotal noun to major adjective to colorful noun**   As an adjective, *cardinal* means "basic, fundamental, chief, principal, major, of special importance, of the highest rank." For example, *Newsweek* columnist Robert J. Samuelson wrote during the Gore-Bush campaign (8/7/2000), "We are now testing a cardinal [fundamental] rule of American politics: that a presidential election is essentially a referendum on the economy."

The word *cardinal* has been traced to the Latin noun *cardo,* a pivot, axis, or hinge on which something turns. By extension, a *cardo* became either of the pivots or poles on which the universe supposedly rotated about the Earth, then any of the four points of the horizon (north, south, east, and west) that we now call *cardinal points* of the compass.

In Medieval Latin, the related adjective *cardinalis,* meaning "pivotal," acquired the extended meaning of "basic, fundamental, chief, principal, of special importance, of the highest rank." That inspired the Roman Catholic Church's four *cardinal virtues* (justice, prudence, fortitude, temperance) and the naming of *cardinals* to the Church's *highest rank* under the pope (the Sacred College of Cardinals, which elects the pope).

The Church's cardinals traditionally wore robes of *cardinal red* (scarlet), and the word *cardinal* subsequently became synonymous with *scarlet,* and with a scarlet hooded cloak for 18th-century women, a scarlet tropical fish, a North American scarlet flower, a scarlet North American songbird, and a North American baseball team.

cardinal or ordinal?   *Cardinal* numbers—1, 2, 3, and so on—designate quantity rather than order. For memory-jogging purposes, you might want to remember that *cardinal* numbers are the types you find on playing *cards.*

Ordinal numbers refer to order: *first, second, third,* and so on.

careen or career?   Both these verbs are risky.

If you correctly write, as did *Time* (5/6/2002), that an amusement-park ride "provides careering [wildly speeding] thrills," many people will think you chose the wrong word. But if you write "*careening* thrills," word guardians will *know* you chose the wrong word.

Careen is a nautical word, meaning "to turn a ship on its side for cleaning, caulking, or repairing." By extension, *careen* can mean "to lean or tip to one side [like a ship] while in motion." Popular American usage has extended *careen* to a third sense, "to run wild, to rush headlong, especially with an unsteady motion." And that sense has won the approval of *The Columbia Guide to Standard American English, The American Heritage Book of English Usage* and *The Wall Street Journal Guide to Style and Usage.*

But Follett's *Modern American Usage,* Garner's *Modern American Usage,* and *The New York Times Manual of Style and Usage* say *careen* should be used only for "leaning like a ship." They add that the correct verb for "moving quickly and erratically" is *career,* which can be traced to the Latin *carrus* ("wheeled vehicle") and the Vulgar Latin *cararia* ("track for wheeled vehicles") and which entered English as a word for "racecourse." Using the "quickly and erratically" sense of *career*, a *Reader's Digest* article (December 2000) told about a motorist who risked his life to save a pregnant woman in another vehicle "who was blacked out, accelerator jammed, careering down the highway."

Risk-free recommendation: The obvious escape from the *careen/career* dilemma is to say, for example, that a car "moved so fast that it swerved erratically." Save *career* for its clearly understood meaning as a synonym for the noun *profession*. Save *careen* for posing showoff questions to sailors: "Careened any good ships lately?"

carom is more than a *collision* Carom ("KAHR-um") is a noun and a verb in billiards for a shot in which the player's ball is intentionally bounced off one ball into another.

Carom is also a general-usage American verb for actions involving encounters followed by a rebound, as in an accident in which a car caroms off a wall into oncoming traffic. Usage example: A *New York Times* book reviewer (1/4/1998) referred to a character in an Isaac Bashevis Singer story who "caroms from one woman to another and back again, each time with ungovernable intensity and in full awareness that he is behaving like a barbarian." (See also "*collision*: a moving experience.")

carousal or carousel? A *carousal* ("riotous drinking party") can be dangerous on a *carousel* ("merry-go-round" or "a rotating baggage conveyor at an airport"). For the second word, a double *r* is permitted but not preferred.

The word *carouse* ("ka-ROWZ") is a variant form of the noun *carousal* ("ka-ROWZ-uhl") and also a verb meaning "to engage in drunken merrymaking." *Carouse* comes from a German phrase meaning "all out," which was used to tell bar patrons that it was time to drink up and leave. The British adopted the term in the middle of the 16th century as a noun and then a verb for sitting around a pub drinking until closing time.

carrot, carat, caret, or karat? Bugs Bunny's favorite food, the *carrot*, is not to be confused with a *carat* ("a unit of weight for gems"), a *caret* ("a wedge-shaped symbol used by copy editors and proofreaders to mark a place in text where something is to be inserted"), or a *karat* ("a unit of fineness in gold").

cartoons **aren't all funny**   The word *cartoon*, usually used in the sense of "humorous drawing," as in an animated movie cartoon or a political cartoon, is also a term in fine art for "a preliminary sketch for a fresco, tapestry, oil painting, or stained glass."

cases **of wordiness**   Many sentences can be improved if you replace the phrase *in case* with *if*, the phrase *in most cases* with *usually*, and *in all cases* with *always*.

cashier **can be verbal**   The noun *cashier,* "someone whose job it is to handle cash transactions," is from a French word for "money box." *Cashier* is also a verb, from a French word for "dismiss," meaning "dismiss for disciplinary reasons from a position of responsibility." Usage example: A *New York Times* headline (1/24/1998) announced, "Argentina Cashiers an Officer Who Defended 70's Brutality."

Cassandra's curse   A *Cassandra* is defined by Merriam-Webster and Random House dictionaries as "one who predicts doom." But if you wish to demonstrate your knowledge of the word's origin in Greek mythology, you can apply the definition of a *Cassandra* from the *American Heritage Dictionary* and *Webster's New World Dictionary* as "one whose predictions of doom are *unheeded.*"

The mythological Cassandra, daughter of King Priam of Troy, was a devoutly chaste priestess who served at the shrine of the god Apollo. According to one version of the story, Apollo himself appeared before his altar and offered to release Cassandra from her vow of chastity if she would share her womanly charms with him. When she refused to violate her vow even for him, he angrily gave her what he called the "gift" of prophecy, filling her mind with a vision of her father lying dead in a pool of his own blood.

Cassandra pleaded with Apollo to make the vision go away. Apollo asked again if she would yield to him. When she continued to refuse, he added to his "gift" by cursing her with the ability to foresee the horrible events leading to the destruction of Troy in the Trojan War but the inability to persuade others that her prophecies were accurate.

When Cassandra started screaming at her father (the king) and others in the Trojan palace to take her visions seriously, she was considered insane and carried away to a cell under the palace. After the war, she became a slave of

Agamemnon, the king who had led the victorious Greek forces, and was killed with him by his treacherous wife, Clytemnestra.

casuistry: **a Jekyll-Hyde word**   Like the split personality depicted in Robert Louis Stevenson's *Strange Case of Dr. Jekyll and Mr. Hyde*, the word *casuistry* ("KAZ-oo-is-tree") lives separate lives of good and evil. That makes *casuistry* one of those words requiring that you double-check your context to make sure your intended meaning is clear.

Casuistry began with its good role—in early Jewish, Christian, and Islamic societies—as a word signifying rejection of the common practice of enforcing moral laws with blind rigidity. Supporters of *casuistry* (literally meaning "concern with individual cases") favored carefully reasoned arguments for forgiveness or leniency in appropriate cases of individual moral offenses. And today *casuistry* refers to such arguments, based on the goal of flexible and humane enforcement.

But because casuistry has sometimes been employed to excuse offenses that are inexcusable, the word *casuistry* is now most commonly used in its evil sense—to mean "specious or excessively subtle reasoning intended to rationalize or mislead, especially about questions of ethics." (See "*specious*.")

cataclysm **or** *catastrophe*?   A *cataclysm*, which originally meant "a huge flood," now refers to a violent upheaval, such as a hurricane or a battle. A *catastrophe* (literally, "an overturning") is a disaster of any kind.

The words *cataclysm* and *catastrophe* were unavoidable in the Week in Review section of *The New York Times* (1/2/2005) following the tsunami of December 26, 2004. One writer, recalling three disasters during which "whole civilizations . . . met watery dooms," noted that "the least-studied of these cataclysms took place in 5500 B.C., when the Mediterranean, rising as the last Ice Age melted, burst through the hills surrounding a brackish lake to the northeast, and created the Black Sea." Another writer noted that, "unimaginable as it may seem, future catastrophes may be far grimmer."

catalyst: **a cause to consider**   In chemistry, a *catalyst* is "a substance that causes or accelerates a chemical reaction without itself being changed."

Catalyst is commonly used figuratively, to refer to any thing or person that causes change or that stimulates action. But you risk criticism from some word guardians if you don't make your figurative use reflect, to some extent, the word's technical meaning. A safe figurative use, therefore, would apply to "a person or thing that *causes* an event without being directly involved in the *consequences*." For example, a subhead in *The Salt Lake Tribune* (3/21/2000) stated that Pope John Paul II "hopes [his] spiritual tour of the Holy Land also will be a catalyst for peace."

catastrophes or *catastrophies*?　　The second is a common misspelling of the first.

catch-22: not just a dilemma　　The expression *catch-22*, from the title of Joseph Heller's classic 1961 novel about World War II, has been described by linguist Richard Lederer as "the most frequently employed allusion in all of American literature." Unfortunately, the allusion is often employed inaccurately.

The darkly comic novel *Catch-22*, based on Heller's World War II experiences as a U.S. Air Force bombardier in Europe, is about a bombardier named John Yossarian who wants to stop flying death-defying missions. Yossarian learns that a military regulation says he can be excused from further combat duty if he is declared insane. All he has to do is ask. But there is a catch—called catch-22—that says anyone who asks to be disqualified for combat must be sane and therefore must return to combat.

So many people have carelessly reduced *catch-22* to a mere synonym of "dilemma" that some dictionaries now list "dilemma" as one of the definitions. But if you want to preserve the uniqueness of this literary allusion, use *catch-22* only in its original sense of "a situation in which a goal is made impossible by a contradictory policy." For example, the Florida Supreme Court (12/8/2000) ordered a partial vote recount in the Gore-Bush presidential election after concluding that a lower court had presented Gore "with the ultimate catch-22, acceptance of the only evidence [thousands of unexamined ballots] that will resolve the issue but a refusal to examine such evidence."

catchphrases　　See "buzzwords and catchphrases: don't go there."

catchup, catsup, or *ketchup*?　　This tomato-based, spicy sauce is spelled *ketchup* by Heinz and Hunt's and *catsup* by Del Monte and some leading cookbooks. *Catchup* has yet to catch up with the other spellings, though it was used by Ernest Hemingway. American and British dictionaries suggest that *ketchup* may be the most widely used of the three spelling variants, which tomato-sauce sleuths have traced to a Malay fish sauce called *kechap*.

catholic or Catholic?   Lowercase *catholic*, from the Greek word *katholikos* ("universal"), is an adjective meaning "universal, all-embracing, broad-minded, tolerant and sympathetic with all," as in "catholic interests" or "catholic taste."

The Church of Rome, regarded by its adherents as the only church that is truly *catholic* in the sense of "universal," is therefore named the *Catholic* Church. The *Random House Wesbter's Unabridged Dictionary* observes that the name *Catholic Church* is "often qualified, especially by those not acknowledging [its claim to unique universality] by prefixing the word *Roman*."

Caucasian: the fact and the fable   People who use *Caucasian* to mean "white person" are contributing to ignorance about the subject of what society calls "race." Caucasians are natives of the region of the Caucasus mountain range—between the Black Sea and the Caspian, occupying Russian-occupied Chechnya and parts of Georgia, Armenia, and Azerbaijan. That explains a report in *The New York Times* (5/3/2002) that Russia's war in Chechnya had "engendered negative attitudes [in Moscow] toward minorities, in particular Caucasians."

It was Johann Friedrich Blumenbach (1752–1840), the German "father" of physical anthropology, who was responsible for the misleading practice of using *Caucasian* to include all "members of the White Race." Blumenbach, a comparative anatomist who studied human skulls, divided humanity into five "races," with all "Whites" supposedly originating in the Caucasus. Blumenbach's naive assumption was soundly rejected by the scientific community about a century ago. And the year 2000 edition of *The American Heritage Dictionary* reminds its readers that the "white race" sense of *Caucasian* is "no longer in scientific use."

But the term *Caucasian* is described as "somewhat more scientific" than *white* by Paul W. Lovinger's year-2000 *Penguin Dictionary of American Usage and Style*. And the year-2000 edition of *The Associated Press Stylebook*, whose publishers call it "the journalist's bible," lists *Caucasian* without any comment, as if the AP's only concern about the use of *Caucasian* is that it be capitalized. No wonder that pseudoscientific usage is still circulated in our media, as in a *Newsweek* story (7/20/1998) telling how nicotine affects African-American men compared with "their Caucasian counterparts."

Recommendation: Unless you are referring to people of the Caucasus mountain range, forget *Caucasian*. (See also "*race*: a question of reality.")

cause célèbre: another kind of celebration   *Cause célèbre* does not mean "a cause for celebration." The phrase, a French import that should be italicized and pronounced "cawz say-LEH-bre," *literally* means "a cause [case] that is celebrated." But the *célèbre* in *cause célèbre* is derived not from the *celebrate* that means "mark a happy occasion" but from the *celebrate* that means "to make publicly known." Hence, *cause célèbre* is a term in law for "highly publicized legal case," and it is more commonly used as a general term for "any highly publicized *controversy*."

Usage examples: The *Baltimore Sun* reported (5/30/2000), "Emmett E. Molloy, whose brushes with the law have become a *cause célèbre* or an outrage, depending on whom you talk to, has not given up the fight to feed the birds and other creatures in his backyard." *The Boston Globe* reported (6/17/2000), "The disappearance of two computer hard drives from a vault in the X Division, or nuclear weapons section, of the Los Alamos National Laboratory was a *cause célèbre* for grandstanding politicians and wisecracking comedians." (See also "French toast.")

cause and effect as verbs   The verbs *cause* and *effect* have the same meaning. But inasmuch as the verb *effect* is somewhat pretentious, *The HarperCollins Concise Dictionary of English Usage* wisely urges writers to substitute *cause* "whenever they are inclined to use *effect* as a verb."

cause was due to redundancy   To remove the redundancy from "the cause was due to," omit either *the cause* or *due to*. Instead of "The cause of the team's loss was due to low morale," say either "The cause of the team's loss was low morale" or "The team's loss was due to low morale." (See also "redundancy: a vice and a virtue.")

cavalier: use with caution   Be careful about using the adjective *cavalier* in accordance with its dictionary sense of "carefree, casual, indifferent." People are likely to interpret *cavalier* in its *other* dictionary sense of "*arrogantly* indifferent," as in "a cavalier attitude toward the poor."

celebrant or ***celebrator*?**   Use *celebrator* for "someone who celebrates." Save *celebrant* for the special meaning it had when it entered the English language in the 19th century: "a person who performs a rite, especially a priest at the Eucharist."

cellphone or ***cell phone*?**   The abbreviated form for *cellular phone* is *cellphone.*

Celsius, centigrade, or ***Fahrenheit*?**   On the *centigrade* (now preferably called *Celsius*) scale of temperature, sea-level water freezes at zero degrees and boils at 100. With the *Fahrenheit* scale, used mainly in the United States, the comparable degrees are 32 and 212.

The Celsius and Fahrenheit scales are capitalized because they were named after their inventors, Swedish astronomer Anders Celsius (1701–1744) and German physicist Gabriel Daniel Fahrenheit (1686–1736).

cement or ***concrete*?**   *Cement* is the limestone-clay powder that, when wet, forms a paste that holds together the sand or gravel that is the main ingredient of the building material called *concrete.*

censer, censor, or ***censure*?**   The spelling of the verb and noun *censor* ("to ban" or "one who bans") is sometimes confused with the noun *censer* ("container for incense") and with the verb *censure* ("to condemn").

center or ***centre*?**   *Center* is American. *Centre* is British. (See also "*theater* or *theatre?*")

centers around **is pointless**   The common phrase *centers around* makes no sense. The center of something is a point in the middle, and, obviously, a point cannot go around anything.

In typical examples of this illogical usage, a Cornell professor of English wrote in *The New York Review of Books* (12/16/1999), "The plot of each book [about the adventures of Harry Potter] essentially centers around the attempts of dark forces to destroy him"; a *Los Angeles Times* staff writer (4/13/2003) referred to an 18-year-old student who "centered her life around academics"; and a Washington correspondent for National Public Radio reported (12/21/2004) that the Securities and Exchange Commission's case against Fannie Mae, the government-sponsored mortgage company, "centers around" alleged bookkeeping violations.

Astonishingly, the error also appears in Simon Winchester's *The Meaning of Everything: The Story of the Oxford English Dictionary*. In that major publication of 2003, Winchester wrote that "George Orwell . . . publicly yearned for Englilsh to be purged of all its Latin, French, Greek, and Norse loans, and to be centered around and dominated by the short, simpler words that were of undeniable 'Anglicity.'"

In an example of *correct* usage, *Newsweek* recalled (1/3/2005): "When the Dems' House leader [Nancy Pelosi] introduced a party platform centered on 'six core values' back in September, the GOP leadership snickered."

Another way to avoid the illogical *centers around* is to substitute *revolves around*. For example: In an essay about American politics, *The Economist* noted (11/9/2002) that "Senate and gubernatorial races tend to revolve around local issues and personalities."

centuries of mistakes   When you're referring to a previous century, remember to avoid the mistake of matching the first part of the number of the year with the number of the century. Remind yourself, for example, that 1776 was in the 18th century, and 1865 was in the 19th century. And note that you're in the Error Zone if you capitalize the word *century*, except in titles or company names (such as *21st Century Insurance Company*).

But the question of spelling out century numbers is just a matter of style. People who abide by *The Chicago Manual of Style* will spell out all century numbers. But people who abide by the stylebooks of *The New York Times*, the Associated Press, and the New York Public Library will spell out only the numbers under 10, as in *ninth century* but *10th century*. Feel free to choose either of those two styles, as long as the choice is applied consistently.

ceremonial *or* ceremonious?   Both mean "characterized by ceremony" and "involved with ritual." But careful communicators save *ceremonial* for referring to occasions and apply *ceremonious* only to people, specifically to their fondness for ceremony or ritualistic formality. *Ceremonious* also can suggest the idea of a ritual meaninglessness, as in "the ceremonious exchange of pleasantries before the rival candidates began their debate." *Unceremonious* means "without politeness or dignity."

certain **uncertainty**   Here's an ambiguity alert: A *certain* approach to a challenging task or social dilemma can mean an approach that is certain to succeed or merely one of various approaches.

As with all such ambiguity, you can eliminate the problem by making sure your intended meaning is clear from the context, or by rephrasing.

certainty **or** *certitude?*   *Certainty* refers to "the fact, quality, or state of unquestionable existence or inevitability," as in "the certainty of death and taxes." *Certitude* refers to one's *belief* that something is a certainty. Memory hint: *certitude* shares most of its letters with *attitude*.

As *The New Yorker* reminded its readers (11/20/2000), "Certitude, [Justice] Oliver Wendell Holmes once said, is not the test of certainty." Justice Holmes added, "We have been cocksure of many things that were not so."

chad **or** *Chad?*   As much of the world learned from media coverage of America's hotly contested presidential election of the year 2000, *chad* means the paper covering on the holes in punch cards given to voters. The word, of unknown origin, also has been used to signify the tiny rectangles punched out from data cards, as well as the perforated edges of paper for tractor-feed printers.

The capitalized *Chad* refers to a country, with a population of about seven million, bordering Libya and Sudan in north-central Africa.

chafe **or** *chaff?*   *Chafe*, which rhymes with *safe*, can be a transitive verb meaning "to irritate" or an intransitive verb meaning "to feel irritated." The national weekly edition of *The Washington Post* (2/23/1998) recalled that President Clinton "once chafed at the confinements of his job by calling the White House 'the crown jewel in the American penal system.' "

Chaff, which rhymes with *laugh*, is a noun that figuratively means "trivial or worthless matter." Literally, *chaff* refers to the husks of grains and grasses that are removed by winnowing or threshing, or to coarsely chopped hay or straw used to feed livestock.

chaise longue **or** *chaise lounge?*   *Chaise lounge* is a common spelling in American advertising for *chaise longue* (pronounced like "shays long"), which is French for "long chair."

Chaise lounge is rejected by some arbiters of American usage. For example, Copperud's *American Usage and Style* says that spelling is "a corrupted form," and *The American Heritage Dictionary* calls it "mistaken."

champagne or *Champagne*? This sparkling white wine originated about 300 years ago in the Champagne region of northeastern France and was thus called *vin de* (wine from) *Champagne*. It is now known by the shortened name *Champagne*.

For a sparkling white wine produced elsewhere, says The *New York Times Manual of Style and Usage*, use lowercase for the beverage, as in *Australian champagne*. The manual adds that you should do likewise for any other wine or spirit named for the area that first produced it, as in *Burgundy* but *California burgundy*, *Cognac* but *Russian cognac*. Lowercase all wines named after types of grapes, such as *pinot noir, cabernet sauvignon*, and *zinfandel*.

charivari or *shivaree*? A Latin word for "headache" (*caribaria*) apparently inspired the French word *charivari* for "a head-throbbing mock serenade for newlyweds" involving kettles, pans, horns, and other noisemakers. Word historians speculate that, early in the 19th century, French traders and settlers in the Mississippi Valley taught *charivari* to Americans, who changed the spelling to *shivaree* and made it a popular regional term for noisy celebrations in general.

In its original form, *charivari*, the word became part of the literary history of England with the founding in 1841 of the influential weekly satirical magazine calling itself *Punch or The London Charivari*.

Either way the word is spelled, it is pronounced "shiv-ah-REE."

chastened or *chastised*? To be *chastised* means "to be punished, as by beating" or "to be severely criticized." Usage example for the second sense: University of Illinois media scholar Robert W. McChesney wrote in his 1999 book, *Rich Media, Poor Democracy*, "Richard Branson, founder of Virgin Records, chastised U.S. radio stations in 1998 for continually playing the same old material, hence making it nearly impossible to launch new musical genres or original acts."

To be *chastened* means "to be humbled by corrective punishment or suffering." Usage example: Syndicated columnist Robert Scheer (1/9/2001) wrote that George W. Bush was "not at all chastened by being the first president in more than a century to have lost the popular vote."

chauvinism, ethnocentrism, jingoism, or *xenophobia*?   All these nouns identify a social pride that is dangerously distorted by prejudice.

Chauvinism ("exaggerated, militant, belligerent, unreasoning patriotism") derives from the name of Nicolas Chauvin, a soldier in Napoleon's army who was notorious for his patriotic fanaticism. *Chauvinism* has acquired the extended meaning of "prejudiced belief in the superiority of one's own group, including race or gender."

The extended meaning of *chauvinism* produced the term *male chauvinist*, reportedly coined by *Time* magazine in 1950. The term *male chauvinist* has become so popular that the term *chauvinist* by itself is sometimes used to convey that meaning, as in the following *Los Angeles Times* headline (6/20/1997) about France's strikingly few female business and political leaders: "French Still Engender Chauvinist Tendencies."

Ethnocentrism is "the belief in the inherent superiority of one's own ethnic group or culture."

Jingoism ("excessive, belligerent nationalism") got its meaning from the use of a centuries-old exclamation—"By jingo!" (possibly a euphemism for "By Jesus!")—in a warmongering anti-Russian song that was popular in English music halls during the Russo-Turkish War (1877–78):

> We don't want to fight, but by jingo if we do
> We've got the ships, we've got the men, and got the money too.
> We've fought the Bear before, and while we're Britons true,
> The Russians shall not have Constantinople.

Xenophobia ("zen-o-FO-bia") combining *phobia* with a prefix based on a Greek word for "stranger," is "a fear or hatred of anything or anyone foreign."

cheap prices are impossible to find   You may occasionally hear about "cheap prices," as in an article in *The Salt Lake Tribune* (5/1/2000) about "thousands of old books on sale for cheap prices at the Salt Lake City Public Library." But it makes no sense to call prices cheap, inasmuch as *cheap* in this context describes a product, not a price. As Roy H. Copperud pointed out in his *American Usage and Style*, "*Goods* may be cheap but prices are *low*." (See also "*cost* or *price*?" and "*thrifty*: what money can't buy.")

check your calendar   If you're writing about something scheduled for *today, tomorrow, next week, next month*, or *next year*, use those words rather than the actual dates. You'll be saving your reader the mental effort of calculating, for example, that "the week of March 23" is really "next week."

chic or *chichi*?   In the mid-19th century, English adopted the French noun and adjective *chic* ("sheek"), meaning "sophistication, subdued elegance in dress or manner."

In the early 20th century, English adopted the French noun and adjective *chichi* ("SHE-she"), meaning "*ostentatiously* chic, trendy, showy."

childish or *childlike*?   *Childish* means "similar to or suitable for a child" when applied to children, and "as immature and foolish as a child" when applied to adults.

Childlike, which of course should always be used to describe adults, means "as innocent and trusting as a child."

Chile, chile, chili, or *chilli*?   The capitalized *Chile*, of course, is the country in southwestern South America with a long Pacific coastline. The uncapitalized *chile* and *chili* are American spelling variants of the Mexican Spanish *chilli*, the word for the seasoning made from the dried pod of a tropical American hot red pepper.

chimera or *Chimera*?   Greek mythology gave us the original *Chimera* ("kai-MEER-uh," from a Greek word for "she-goat"), a fire-breathing she-monster with the body of a goat, the head of a lion, and the tail of a serpent. Drawing on that image, 17th-century French philosopher Blaise Pascal wrote in his posthumously published *Pensées* ("Thoughts") about religion: "What a chimera then is man! What a novelty! What a monster, what a chaos, what a contradiction, what a prodigy! Judge of all things, feeble earthworm, depository of truth, a sink of uncertainty and error, the glory and the shame of the universe."

Today, the word *chimera* has a number of related meanings that emphasize unreality: "a wild dream, a mere illusion, the product of sheer imagination, an unfounded notion." Usage example: An item in *George* magazine (September 1997) about the sexual harassment suit brought by Paula Jones against President Clinton asked, "Is Jones's story true, or is it a chimera concocted by the president's enemies?"

The adjective *chimerical* means "visionary, absurd, impossible, indulging in unrealistic fancies."

choice words about *choice*   The adjective *choice* in "choice words" clearly means "carefully chosen." And we all know what it means to say we have made a *choice*—we have selected one of the possibilities offered to us. But beware of the confusion that can arise from offering someone *one choice*.

Suppose you run a restaurant with a dinner menu offering two choices of beverage, coffee and tea. Now suppose you run out of tea. That would seem to mean your customers have the one remaining choice of coffee. But if they are left with only one choice, doesn't that mean they have none?

The problem is that *choice* has several meanings. It can mean "an item offered or chosen," as it does in the question "What are my choices?" and in a menu's offering of "the choices of coffee and tea." But *choice* can also refer, of course, to "the *chance to select* from among multiple alternatives." A restaurant that has run out of one of its two *choices* (one of its offered items) cannot offer its customers a *choice* (an opportunity to select).

Solution: Avoid using *one choice* when there is only one item or possibility being offered. In the restaurant example, you should simply say to your customers, "Sorry, but all we have tonight is coffee."

choppy writing   See "sentences should not be choppy."

***chord* or *cord*?**   A string quartet produces a *chord*—derived from the word *accord*—that is "a combination of at least three harmonious tones sounded together."

A *cord* is a unit of wood stacked for fuel, or a thin rope or piece of string. Note that the spelling *cord* is also used for *vocal cord* and *spinal cord*, though *chord* may be used for those purposes in British English.

***chortle* and other Carroll coinages**   *Chortle*, one of the useful words introduced in 1872 by Lewis Carroll in his *Through the Looking-Glass*, means "to chuckle [laugh to oneself] joyfully, in celebration."

Chortle—like *chuckle*, a noun as well as a verb—identifies a chuckle that is a response to welcome news. For example: "[Republicans] lost no time chortling," wrote columnist Dan Schnur in the *Los Angeles Times* (8/30/1996), "when news broke that [President Clinton's] chief political adviser [Dick Morris] was resigning from the campaign over allegations that he had allowed a $200-an-hour professional escort to listen in on his phone conversations with the president."

Carroll, the pen name of British mathematician and writer Charles L. Dodgson (1832–1898), created *chortle* by blending *chuckle* and *snort*. Also in *Through the Looking-Glass*, he invented a term to describe such blends: *portmanteau* words ("two meanings packed into one word," from a French-derived word meaning "large suitcase that opens into two compartments").

Another Carroll coinage, *galumph*, which scholars believe is a blend of *gallop* and *triumph*, means "to move with a clumsy, heavy tread." Carroll's title for a *Looking-Glass* nonsense poem, "Jabberwocky," entered the English language as a lowercase term for "meaningless speech or writing."

chutzpah: dare to use it correctly   "Chutzpah!" (as in "daring") was the title of a *Time* magazine cover story (8/21/2000) on Democratic presidential candidate Al Gore's choice for his running mate, Senator Joe Lieberman, the first Jew ever placed on a major-party presidential ticket. The following week, *Newsweek* Wall Street editor Allan Sloan observed that *chutzpah* had gotten "positively trendy lately, thanks to Joe Lieberman's nomination." But, as Sloan added, the widespread use of this Yiddish expression in the sense of "daring" was a mistranslation.

Chutzpah ("CHOOTS-pah," with the *ch* pronounced as in the German *Ach!*) conveys much more meaning than "daring." Leo Rosten points out in *The Joys of Yiddish*, no other word in any language communicates so much "insolence, audacity, gall, nerve, effrontery and presumption-plus-arrogance." Rosten adds a "classic" definition: "*Chutzpah* is that quality enshrined in a man who, having killed his mother and father, throws himself on the mercy of the court because he is an orphan." (See also "*schmooze* is a valuable verb.")

Cinco de Mayo   Mexico's *Cinco de Mayo* (Fifth of May) is not the same as our Fourth of July. *Cinco de Mayo* is the anniversary of the Mexican Army's victory over French invaders in the battle of Puebla in 1862. Mexico's Independence Day, commemorating the beginning of its 1810–1821 struggle for freedom from Spain, is celebrated September 16.

Cinderella's glass slippers: still in style   At the ball where Cinderella won the heart of her handsome prince, she wore slippers made of glass. Right?

Well, we're led to assume so from the Disney movie adaptation of English translations of the "Little Cinder Girl" fairy tale published by French poet Charles Perrault in 1697. But *Benét's Reader's Encyclopedia* says that "Perrault is believed to have confounded *vair*, 'ermine,' with *verre*, 'glass,' thus first giving Cinderella this unlikely footwear."

Pop word historian Hugh Rawson writes in his *Devious Derivations* that "the standard explanation" for Cinderella's glass footwear is that it is the result of a mistake by some English translator. But Rawson adds that "this is definitely not a question of mistranslation," inasmuch as Perrault's "original text" did contain *verre*, the French word for "glass."

At any rate, according to the 2005 *Encyclopaedia Britannica* CD, no glass slippers are found in the earliest known version of the Cinderella story, appearing in China in the ninth century, or in the hundreds of other versions that have been published around the world. Most commonly, Cinderella wears slippers of gold or silver.

In the classic 19th-century German collection, *Grimm's Fairy Tales*—in which the brothers Jakob and Wilhelm Grimm, pioneering linguists, sought with painstaking accuracy to record more than two hundred folk stories—Cinderella wore sensibly comfortable slippers "embroidered with silk and silver."

Nevertheless, at Cinderella-theme weddings today, you're likely to find the bride wearing vinyl "slippers of glass." Which suggests that what Cinderella really wears to the ball in our popular versions of the story, as with the "real" meanings of the words and phrases in our language, is *ultimately* whatever we the people choose.

cipher or cypher?   This word, a noun for "zero, a nonentity, or a coded message" or a verb meaning "to calculate," is preferably spelled *cipher* in American English and *cypher* in British English.

cite for sore editors   You risk a citation for wrongful usage if you *cite* that something is true, as in "He *cites* [should be *says*] that many bridges need repair." Likewise, you also risk a citation if you write "The bridges need repair, he cited [should be *said*]."

Never use *cite* as a substitute for *says*. Unlike *says*, the word *cite* is invariably a transitive verb and therefore must always act directly on an object (a noun).

Appropriate usage of *cite*: "He cites *the fact* that many bridges need repair." "He cites the *many bridges* that need repair." (See also "verbs: transitive and intransitive.")

cite, sight, site for sore eyes   To *cite* ("refer to") an example of how *sight* ("vision") may be confused with *site* ("location"), usage commentators have warned against "*on-sight* inspections." The correct phrase, of course, is "on-site inspections."

claim: you don't say   You may disturb people who keep Strunk and White's *Elements of Style* or Fowler's *Modern English Usage* next to their computer if you use the verb *claim* as a synonym for "assert, contend declare, maintain, say." You'll avoid criticism from such people if you use *claim* only to mean "lay claim to," as in "She claimed the title and rights of empress."

clamber or clamor?   *Clamber* is a verb meaning "to climb with difficulty, or to climb awkwardly as if by scrambling." Usage example: Columnist Maureen Dowd (6/7/2000) wrote, "Hillary Rodham Clinton remains a go-getter, clambering up the ladder."

Risk-free pronunciation of *clamber*: So many people pronounce *clamber* as if it were *clamor* that the silent-*b* option for *clamber* is listed in many dictionaries. But if you pronounce the full second syllable, *-ber*, you'll be using the preferred pronunciation, you'll be maintaining an oral distinction between *clamor* and *clamber*, and you'll be faithful to *clamber*'s apparent origin in a Middle English verb for "climb," *clambren*.

Clamor is a noun for "loud noise, shouting, public outcry" or "the making of an insistent demand," and a verb for engaging in such activity. The "insistent demand" sense of the verb *clamor* appeared in a *New York Times* essay about the continuation of the longest economic expansion in America's history (2/20/2000): "Companies everywhere are thriving and sharing this prosperity with workers clamoring for raises."

claque or clique?   *Claque* (pronounced "klack") is "a group of people paid to applaud a performance" or "a group of fawning followers."

Clique (preferably pronounced "cleek" rather than "click") means "an exclusive, snobbish group of persons."

classic or classical?   Use *classic* when you mean "serving as a standard of excellence" and *classical* when you mean "related to a classical period," as in the music of Bach and Beethoven or the literature of ancient Greece and Rome. Thus, in a music review, "a *classic* performance" means that the performance was superb, but "a *classical* performance" simply means that classical music was performed.

Classic can also mean "serving as a model of its kind," as in a *New York Times* reference (9/5/1998) to "a classic clash of Hollywood egos and New York investors."

classy words   The informal adjective *classy* ("high class, highly stylish, elegant")—along with other words that have *class*—can be traced back to the fact that the ancient Romans were class-conscious. Roman citizens who belonged to the highest of their five levels of social status were called *classicus*. The rest were *infra classem* ("beneath the class"). Today, people who have fallen from a classy status are dismissed with a French adjective, *déclassé* (*déclassée* if the reduced-status person is a woman).

A *classified advertisement* is so called because it is published under a heading with others of the same class ("category"). *Classified documents* contain a class ("category") of information that some government official has decided not to publish on the grounds that it should be kept secret for security reasons. Before such information can be made public, it must be *declassified*.

clean or cleanly?   *Cleanly*, like *clearly*, is obviously an adverb, as in "She fought all her campaigns cleanly." *Clean*, like *clear*, is obviously an adjective, as in "a clean campaign." But *clean* can also be used as a "flat adverb," as in "No matter how dirty they fought, he always fought clean." (See also "adverbs that look like adjectives.)

clean or cleanse?   The verb *cleanse*, dating back at least to the 10th century, originally meant "to make clean" in both literal and figurative senses. The verb *clean*, which emerged in the 15th century, gradually was assigned the job of removing dirt literally. That left *cleanse* for figurative uses, such as "cleansing the world of evil." Idiomatically, however, you may be asked to "clean up your act."

clear or clearly? *Clear* can be an adjective meaning, "free from obscurity," as in "clear sky," or an adverb meaning "all the way," as in "soaked clear through." *Clearly*, always an adverb, means, "without doubt, in a clear manner, it is clear." (See also "adverbs that look like adjectives.")

cleave: a question of context The verb *cleave* is a contranym, which means a word with contradictory meanings. *Cleave* can mean "to split, to separate from," as suggested by *cleaver, cleavage, cloven hoof,* and *cleft palate. Cleave* can also mean "to stick, adhere, cling, remain faithful to," as in a *New York Times* headline (4/30/2000), "As Vietnamese Modernize, Villages Cleave to the Past."

If you are not sure that your context will make your usage clear, choose another word. (For warnings about other contranyms, see entries for *oversight, sanction,* and *scan.*)

cliché does not need these adjectives Never describe a cliché as trite or hackneyed. Those adjectives are redundant when used to modify *cliché,* inasmuch as *cliché* means "an expression that is trite or hackneyed."

The adjective *trite,* from a Latin verb for "rub, wear down," means "formerly striking but now lacking in effectiveness because of excessive use."

The adjective *hackneyed*—recalling 17th-century Hackney, England, where broken-down horses were rented for carriages—describes expressions that have been worn out through overuse.

By the way: The noun *hack,* as defined by the unabridged Random House dictionary, is "a person, as an artist or writer, who exploits, for money, his or her creative ability or training in the production of dull, unimaginative, and trite work."

cliché: give it a rest or a spin In *Saying What You Mean,* Robert Claiborne defines *cliché* as "a once-colorful phrase whose color has faded with time and use."

A colorful phrase can become a cliché when too many people in the media seize upon it at the same time. Example: During a three-week period early in 1994, the *American Journalism Review* observed that *firestorms of criticism* appeared in totally unrelated stories in *USA Today,* the *Atlanta Journal and*

Constitution, *The Boston Globe*, the *San Bernardino Sun*, *Newsday*, the *Washington Times*, and Agence France-Presse.

Many ideas are quickly and vividly conveyed by common expressions, such as *needle in a haystack* and *tip of the iceberg*. We are reminded of basic truths by old sayings, including *Actions speak louder than words, Experience is the best teacher, An ounce of prevention is worth a pound of cure, A penny saved is a penny earned,* and *Two wrongs don't make a right.*

But you should stay informed about contemporary speech and writing so that you don't make the embarrassing mistake of using a cliché as if it were a new expression. For example, a futile reform is vividly but too often described as "rearranging the deck chairs on the Titanic." If you appear to think that this comparison is *your* creation, you may earn ridicule rather than respect.

Clever variations of a cliché may be effective, as when a book reviewer described Nancy Reagan biographer Kitty Kelley as "a woman who leaves no stone unthrown." In one of the most famous examples of a cliché with a devilishly clever spin, critic Dorothy Parker once commented that Katherine Hepburn, in an early performance, "ran the gamut of emotions from A to B."

Cliché (spelled in English with or without the acute accent over the *e*) is French for "stereotype," an 18th-century term for a metal mold used for making type or for copying wood engravings. By the late 19th century, *cliché* and *stereotype* referred to literary and other creative work that was so lacking in originality that it appeared to be produced from a mold. Subsequently, *stereotype* was applied to a lack of originality in thinking, specifically the assumption that all members of a group are as alike as prints made from a stereotype plate.

cliché **synonyms**   *Platitude*, from a French word for "flatness," means a flat, dull remark, especially one presented as if it were original.

The word *bromide*—derived from *potassium bromide*, a compound once sold as a sedative—means an expression that is tiresome.

A *truism* is an obvious truth, such as a politician's declaration that "children are society's future."

client or **customer?**   When you purchase professional services, you're a client. When you purchase anything else, you're a customer.

***climactic* or *climatic*?**   Be wary of writing *climactic* ("of or relating to a cli-max") when you mean *climatic* ("of or relating to climate"). That error has appeared even in *The New York Times* (9/6/2004): In an article about the *cli-mate*-shifting disappearance of glaciers in a region of northern Canada, the paper reported that the local streams were "becoming shallower because of cli-mactic shifts."

clipped words   The slang shortening of *delicatessen* to *deli* and *neighborhood* to *hood* are part of a long linguistic tradition of word clipping. Other well-established examples are *bus* from *omnibus*, *flu* from *influenza*, *groom* from *bridegroom*, *gym* from *gymnasium*, *piano* from *pianoforte*—and *drawing room* from the old British term for a home's formal reception room: *withdrawing room*.

***close* or *closely*?**   See "adverbs that look like adjectives."

***closing, closure,* or *cloture*?**   To quote William Safire's "On Language" col-umn in *The New York Times* (6/29/1997): "When you shut the doors, you have a *closing*. When you cut off debate [as in Congress], you have *cloture*. When you wrap up and tie a ribbon around an emotion, you have *closure*."

In an article in the *Los Angeles Times* (8/18/1997), staff writer Ken Ellingwood pointed out that *closure* originated as a "psychotherapy buzzword." But, Ellingwood wrote, *closure* is now applied to so many different situations that the concept has spawned what might be called a whole new self-help move-ment. He added: "*Closure* can encompass widely varying concepts. It refers to the last step of therapy and is a common theme in literature and film, describing the way a work ends. Most often, it means acceptance or resolution—to go on living by putting a tragedy in its place."

***cloth* or *clothe*?**   To *clothe* is to drape or outfit someone or something with *cloth*.

clue or clew?   *Clew* and its more recent and more common form, *clue*, both mean "information that can help solve a mystery" or "a ball of thread." (To learn what a ball of thread has to do with solving a mystery, see the entry on *labyrinth*.)

Risk-free usage: Use *clew* only for "ball of thread" or in its nautical sense as either "the lower corner of a square sail" or "the lower corner of a fore-and-aft sail."

cognate words   See "*metal* or *mettle?*"

cognizable or *cognizant?*   The first adjective means "knowable, perceivable." The second means "informed, aware."

cognoscente or *cognoscenti?*   If you are tired of using the French-flavored word *connoisseur* ("a person of expert knowledge or training, or of discriminating taste"), switch for a while to the Italian-flavored *cognoscente* ("konya-SHEN-tay," from an Italian word meaning "to know"). The plural, which is much more widely used, is *cognoscenti* (ending in the sound "tee").

cohort: **a group or an individual?**   *Cohort* originally meant a group of soldiers, specifically "one of the ten divisions (with each division consisting of 300–600 men) of a Roman legion." In mid-20th-century American English, *cohort* became any group sharing a statistical, demographic, or other characteristic, as in a *New York Times* reference (3/21/2001) to the "huge post-World War II cohort of baby boomers."

Today, *cohort* is widely used in an additional American sense, as an individual who is considered a buddy or, often, an accomplice. For example, an article in *Wired* magazine (December 2001) stated that "Osama bin Laden and his cohorts are tribal, medieval, absolutist, and messianic."

Risk-free advice: Use *cohort* only for a group with some common characteristic. Though both the group and individual senses of *cohort* are listed as standard by *The Columbia Guide to Standard American English*, the individual sense is rejected by *The New York Times Manual of Style and Usage*, the *New York Public Library Writer's Guide to Style and Usage*, Follett's *Modern American Usage*, and Lovinger's *Penguin Dictionary of American English Usage and Style*.

coiffeur or *coiffure?*   *Coiffure* ("kwah-FYOOR") means "hairdo." *Coiffeur* (pronounced "kwah-FER") is our borrowed French word for "male hairdresser." The female version of *coiffeur* is *coiffeuse* ("kwah-FYOOZ").

coincidental or *ironic?*   See "*irony* is no *coincidence.*"

Cold War: the good old days?   During the Cold War, America's students had to remember that *Russia* was not synonymous with the entire *Union of Soviet Socialist Republics*. Now, instead of merely distinguishing Russia from the Soviet Union of which it was a part, our students must contend with the former Soviet republics that became the independent nations of *Armenia, Azerbaijan, Belarus, Georgia, Kazakhstan, Kyrgyzstan, Moldova, Tadzhikistan, Turkmenistan, Ukraine,* and *Uzbekistan*—not to mention the regained independence of the Baltic states of *Estonia, Latvia,* and *Lithuania.*

coleslaw or cold slaw?   The word is *coleslaw*, from the Dutch *koolsla* (*kool* meaning "cabbage" and *sla* meaning "salad"). But some people have been misspelling it *cold slaw* ever since the term entered the English language in the late 18th century.

collectable or *collectible?*   For "an object worth collecting," the preferred spelling is *collectible* in American English, *collectable* in British English.

collective nouns   See "nouns that can be singular or plural."

collision: **a moving experience**   If a car crashes into your parked car, is that a *collision*? The answer is yes and no.

Yes, says *Merriam-Webster's Dictionary of English Usage*, which traces the single-moving-object *collision* back to the mid-18th century. You can find support for that viewpoint in *The Columbia Guide to Standard American English*, in *The New Fowler's Modern English Usage*, and in a number of current dictionary definitions, such as the *New Lexicon Webster's Dictionary* reference to a collision as "the violent coming together of a moving body with another, either moving or stationary."

But the stylebooks of the Associated Press, *The New York Times*, and *The Wall Street Journal*, echoing warnings of journalistic handbooks going back to the end of the 19th century, say that two objects must be in motion before they can collide. Many newspaper editors and journalism educators consequently maintain that it takes two to tangle.

How do you avoid a collision with critics about this usage? In *The Appropriate Word*, Professor of English J. N. Hook says "a valuable but seldom-used word" for the crashing of an object into a stationary object is *allision*.

But that word is used so infrequently that it is of no value in most communication. If you want to be safe and easily understood about a single-moving-object crash, say that a stationary object was *struck* or that a moving object *hit* or *crashed into* the stationary one.

Note that the *together* in the phrase *collided together* is redundant.

colloquial or **informal**?   The dictionary designation *colloquial*, from the Latin *con-* ("together") and *loquor* ("to speak"), means "informal, conversational."

Colloquial applies to expressions, such as "cooked up" and "big deal," that lie somewhere between Standard English and slang. "But," says the *New York Public Library Writer's Guide to Style and Usage*, "*colloquial* has acquired a derogatory association with inferior 'everyday, ordinary speech' versus 'formal, correct speech' [and consequently] many dictionaries have stopped using the term and have adopted 'informal' in its place."

colon or semicolon?   The colon (:) is an abbreviated way of saying, "Here comes an example" or "Here's what I'm talking about." A colon can introduce anything from a single word to several sentences, as in "The boy enjoyed only one thing about school: lunch" and "Our political system does not encourage long-range planning: Elected officials tend to focus only on measures that will help their image during their term of office.

The colon also does mechanical chores, as in "9:30 a.m." and "a ratio of 2:3."

The semicolon—contrary to what many amateur writers believe—is not a fancy comma. The semicolon (;) is appropriately called a "weak period," because it joins closely related independent clauses that otherwise could be presented as separate sentences. A model of this usage was Mark Twain's introductory warning to readers of *The Adventures of Huckleberry Finn*: "Persons attempting to find a motive in this narrative will be prosecuted; persons attempting to find a moral in it will be banished; persons attempting to find a plot in it will be shot."

The semicolon can substitute for a comma only in a series, and only when it helps readers perceive units that themselves contain commas: "Mary Jackson, president; John Smith, vice president; and Phil Robinson, treasurer."

Here, from *Time* magazine (10/19/1998), is a sentence illustrating the proper use of both the colon and the semicolon: "The brick house on a tree-lined street in Newark, N.J., is impeccable: the iron fence gleams with fresh black paint; the emerald grass looks newly mowed."

comic or comical? Dictionaries define both adjectives as "pertaining to comedy" or "causing laughter." But usage commentators recommend that *comic* be used when the humor is intended, *comical* otherwise. To abide by that distinction, you would say that a *comical* situation developed during the intermission of a *comic* opera.

comma or semicolon? See "colon or semicolon?"

comma splices (alias comma faults) See "sentences that run on" and "sentences that run on into adverbs."

commas are advisable before the last item in a series The serial comma—the one before the concluding conjunction at the end of a series, as in "the good, the bad, and the ugly"—will never cause a problem for the reader, but its absence can. For example: The *Journal of Court Reporting* (July–August 2000) noted that a serial comma might be necessary to establish the intended meaning of a legal document. Suppose you intend to write a will designating that your estate be divided equally among "Manny, Fanny, and Danny." That clearly means that each of those three individuals receives a third. But if you omit the serial comma—assigning equal portions of your estate to "Manny, Fanny and Danny," Manny could argue that he gets not just a third of your estate but half, with the other half being split by Fanny and Danny.

commas before *who* Suppose you're writing a computer-equipment ad in which you want to assure customers that your technical-support consultants are highly skilled. Do you invite the customers to "call our technical-support consultants who are highly skilled?" No. Inasmuch as that invitation says customers should call those consultants of yours who are highly skilled, you're suggesting that you have consultants who are *not* highly skilled. But all you need is a comma to assure your customers that *all* your consultants are highly skilled: "Call our technical-support consultants, who are highly skilled."

commas can change your meaning   The comma, our most frequently used punctuation mark, can be as meaningful as words.

Consider the change in meaning if you remove the comma that signals a highly meaningful pause in "Help, a robber," "No, one must resist," and "Let's eat, Grandma."

Consider the reversal of meaning if you *add* commas to the statement "Pat says Mike is guilty." The finger of guilt moves from Mike to Pat: "Pat, says Mike, is guilty."

Finally, notice what happens to the meaning of the sentence "A woman without her man is nothing" when you add a colon and a comma: "A woman: without her, man is nothing." (See also entries on hyphens.)

commas for introductory phrases and clauses   You don't need a comma after a short introduction if there's no natural pause: "*Next time* he'll be more careful." But watch for the natural pause and therefore the need for a comma after a short introduction like this: "At the age of four, she was able to draw realistic pictures of many animals." Count on the need for a comma when your introduction is obviously long: "Next time will be an entirely different experience, he was assured."

Always use a comma to set off an introductory clause or phrase when the lack of a comma might cause even *temporary* confusion. For example, imagine reading the following sentence if it had no comma: "While Hannibal Lecter cooked, his girlfriend set the table." (See also "*such as* this comma issue.")

commas for missing words   A comma can be a stand-in for one or more missing words. In the sentence "For some people the motive is money; for others, glory," the comma before *glory* takes the place of a repetition of the three words "the motive is."

commas for sentence adverbs   For readability, use commas with adverbs that modify an entire statement: "*Clearly*, humanity needs to develop alternative sources of energy."

Such adverbs—called sentence adverbs because they modify sentences and clauses that could stand on their own as sentences—include *happily* and *sadly*, *justly* and *unjustly*, *logically* and *illogically*, *luckily* and *unluckily*, *predictably* and *unpredictably*, *surprisingly* and *unsurprisingly*, and *wisely* and *foolishly*.

Usage examples: "*Fortunately*, she and he finally met. *Unfortunately*, their relationship was derailed by a misunderstanding. *Happily*, they solved their problem by taking the time to listen to each other."

Remember that adverbs should not have a comma when they modify only a word or phrase: "*Happily working* together, they never had a boring day. And so they *lived happily* ever after." (See also "*hopefully* can sentence you to criticism.")

commas for transitions   Commas should follow introductory transitional expressions, words, and phrases that relate a preceding idea to one that follows. For example, note the need for a comma after the two-word transitional phrase that began the sentence you are now about to finish reading. Other introductory transitional expressions include *first, further, finally,* and *in conclusion.*

commas linking clauses   Use a comma before a conjunction (*and, but, for, or, nor,* or *while*) that introduces an independent clause (one that could stand alone as a sentence): "He likes opera, and she likes football." (Without the comma after *opera,* the reader would momentarily expect to be told something else that *he* likes.)

Exception to this rule: Short, crystal-clear sentences, such as "Jim left but Wayne stayed."

commas separating adjectives   Independent adjectives in a series—as in "a dark, cold, lonely night"—must be separated with a comma so that the reader can see that the adjectives are not combined in a single thought.

You can be certain that adjectives in a series are independent if you can separate them with the conjunction *and* without changing the meaning. For example, the phrase used above has the same meaning if you say "a dark and cold and lonely night." But note that "a great big painting" changes its meaning if you say "a great and big painting."

commas separating identical words   You need a comma to help your reader make sense of the following advice from an incurable optimist: "Whatever happens, happens for the best."

commas separating nonessential information   Consider the pair of commas in this sentence: "Frank's wife, Flora, loves to garden."

The commas separating *Flora* from the rest of the sentence show that the name *Flora* is not essential to the meaning of the sentence. In other words: If you were to delete *Flora*, the meaning would not change. We would still know the essential information that Frank's wife loves to garden.

Now, suppose you write the original sentence without the commas: "Frank's wife Flora loves to garden." As a result of that slight change, you are communicating the idea to many educated readers that *Flora* is an essential part of the sentence. And the name *Flora* is essential only if Frank has more than one wife—which might come as a surprise to Flora.

The same principle of punctuation applies if Frank has a sister named Fannie. You're saying Frank has only one sister if you use commas to separate the sister's name from the rest of the sentence: "Frank's sister, [whose name happens to be] Fannie, speaks French." But you're saying Frank has *more* than one sister if you remove the commas to show that the name *Fannie* is essential to the meaning of the sentence: "Frank's sister Fannie [not some other sister of his] speaks French."

You may also change your meaning if you insert commas that *wrongly* signify information as nonessential. In a recent edition of a college newspaper, the news editor wrote, "All students, who have advance-registered for their next semester's classes, might have noticed a message printed on their schedule confirmation." That sentence, with its needless set of commas, wrongly addressed itself to all students, because it wrongly communicated the idea that all students had registered in advance. Without the commas, the words "who have advance-registered" would have been correctly presented as an *essential* (grammatically "restrictive") part of the sentence, and the sentence would have correctly addressed itself only to those students who had registered in advance. (See also "*such as* this comma issue.")

commas separating nonessentials called appositives   An *appositive*, in the language of grammar, is a word or phrase that follows a subject with an alternate identification or further description of that subject, and which can be removed without seriously changing the meaning or structure of the sentence. Note that the appositive phrases in the following sentence are set off by commas from the rest of the sentence: "Henry David Thoreau, *the 19th-century naturalist-essayist*, was unable for five years to find a publisher for the book that would become his best-known work, *Walden*."

Leave out the comma when you use identifying information as if it were a title: "*Naturalist-essayist* Henry David Thoreau was one of America's most influential authors." But you need commas when you present the same information as an appositive: "Henry David Thoreau, *a naturalist and essayist*, was one of America's most influential authors."

Clearly, no comma should be used in a phrase such as Catherine the Great. But you need commas if the subject is followed by an appositive: "Catherine, one of the great figures of Russian history, was a leader who did not shy from controversy." No comma is needed if you write "Assistant Dean Rebecca Smith." That's the same grammatical construction as "President George W. Bush." But you need commas if you follow Ms. Smith with an appositive: "Rebecca Smith, the assistant dean, will soon be appointed dean." The same comma rule applies if you reverse the order: "The assistant dean, Rebecca Smith, will soon be appointed dean."

commas that make reading easier Commas set off adverbial clauses ("*When he was ready*, he gave the signal"), transitional expressions ("His personality, *on the other hand*, was not at all pleasant"), conjunctive adverbs ("*However*, we must reconsider"), and illustrative expressions ("*That is to say*, all went well").

commas to go Try to remember this jocular reminder from the late Ernest Tucker, penned when he was assistant city editor of the old *Chicago American*: "Don't use commas, that aren't necessary." A few years ago, I noticed an unnecessary comma on an official sign posted for English-speaking pedestrians on the main street of the shopping district of Tijuana: "A well behaved tourist, is a welcome tourist."

No comma is necessary to link a direct quote with its attribution when the direct quote ends with a question mark or an exclamation point: "'Have I been nominated?' he asked." "'If so, I will never accept!' he declared."

Sentences that contain commas can sometimes be improved if they are rewritten so that the commas are not needed. But, of course, you will damage a sentence if you remove commas that are necessary.

***commemorate*: to honor the memory**   If you want to honor the memory of how this word should be spelled, think of the prefix *com-* introducing most of the word *memory*. (See also "spelling tips.")

***commendable* or *commendatory*?**   If you use these words correctly, word guardians will respond to your *commendable* ("praiseworthy") usage in a manner that is *commendatory* ("characterized by the *bestowing* of praise").

***comment* or *commentate*?**   The verb *commentate*, according to Kenneth G. Wilson's *Columbia Guide to Standard American English*, has a specialized sense that reflects what commentators do that is not quite the same as what the verb *comment* means. But *commentate* is risky, because some word guardians view *commentate* as just a pretentious, longer version of comment.

Recommendation: When commenting about commentators, avoid both *comment* and *commentate*. Instead, talk about such people "doing" or "giving" a commentary. (See also "verbs pretentiously ending in *-ate*.")

***common* or *mutual*?**   These words have been used interchangeably for nearly four hundred years. But reference books ranging from Samuel Johnson's 1755 *Dictionary of the English Language* to the 2001 *Webster's New World College Dictionary* have prescribed the following distinction: If two people adore each other, their feeling is reciprocal and therefore *mutual*. If two people adore ice cream, that feeling is merely something they have *in common*.

Risk-free suggestion: If you restrict *mutual* to expressions of reciprocity, nobody will find fault with you and some may admire your precision.

***common* or *ordinary*?**   Save *common* to communicate the idea of sharing, as in "common interests." For "commonplace, plain," use *ordinary*.

***common sense* or *commonsense*?**   The two-word form, *common sense*, is the noun. *Commonsense*—as in "commonsense approach"—is the adjective.

***comparable* pronunciations**   The preferred pronunciation of *comparable* accents the first syllable. But some educated people accent the second in imitation of the only acceptable pronunciation of *comparative* ("com-PAR-a-tiv").

comparatives and superlatives: what Alice didn't know　Being only seven, Lewis Carroll's Alice could be excused for abuse of the English language when she observed that her adventures in Wonderland were becoming "curiouser and curiouser." But you are old enough to know better. You are expected to know when you can intensify adjectives and adverbs with the comparative ending, *-er,* or the superlative ending, *-est,* and when you must instead use the comparative word *more* or superlative word *most.*

When you're in doubt, consult your dictionary. Intensify adjectives and adverbs with *-er* or *-est* only when your dictionary lists forms of the word with those endings. If the dictionary does not list those endings, that means you can intensify a modifier only by preceding it with *more* or *most.*

Warning: Ignore all grammar-manual rules about this subject. They are so contorted by complexities and contradictions that they will drive you crazy. Just follow the simple instructions in the previous paragraph. And have a nice day.

compare or **contrast?**　*Compare* means to examine similarities and perhaps some differences. *Contrast* means to examine only the differences.

Inasmuch as *contrast* is a perfectly clear word for examining differences, you cannot go wrong if you use *compare* only for examining *similarities*. If you are focusing on both differences and similarities, say "compare and contrast." Better yet, say "identify the similarities and differences."

compare to or **compare with?**　The distinction is not always carefully observed, but dictionaries and usage commentators suggest using "compare *to*" in the sense of "to liken"—that is, to say one thing resembles another—and "compare *with*" when you are literally making a comparison. Examples: "His paintings were compared *to* Picasso's." "Compared *with* his previous home, his new one is no more costly but much more comfortable."

comparisons that aren't　"How's your wife?" asks the straight man in an old vaudeville routine. The comedian replies, "Compared to what?"

Consumers may well ask that same question—or its preferred cousin, "Compared *with* what?—in response to advertisements that proclaim a product "better!" "faster!" or "twice as effective!" without stating any basis for comparison. Review what you write to make sure you haven't committed this offense by accident. (See "double comparison" and "*so* what?")

comparisons without logic   Illogical comparisons typically occur when a writer carelessly omits words needed to clearly identify the objects of comparison. You'll find illustrations and solutions to this problem in the entry for "*as* and *than* comparisons need to be complete."

compass encompasses two instruments   *Compass* (preferably rhymed with *rumpus*) refers to devices used to determine geographic direction or a device (sometimes called "a pair of compasses") for measuring or drawing circles.

compendium: a comprehensively concise case of confusion   When something is identified as a *compendium* or described as *compendious*—borrowing from a Latin word for "small"—some people will picture something small, but others will picture something large.

   The Oxford English Dictionary will tell you that the noun *compendium* and its adjective, *compendious*, refer to that which is "comprehensive, though brief." In American English, however, "comprehensive, fully detailed" is the *popular* meaning; but "brief" (as in "a concise summary or abridgment") is our standard *dictionary* meaning.

   Risk-free suggestion: If you use *compendium*, make clear whether you mean something small or something large, as in a *Financial Times* reference (6/12/2000) to public-policy researcher Mark Baldassare's book *California in the New Millennium* as "a fat compendium of his findings."

complacent or complaisant?   *Complacent* describes people who are overly contented with themselves or their situation and therefore may be unconcerned about, or even unaware of, serious problems. The sound-alike adjective *complaisant* is an adjective that describes people who are eager to please.

   Both words are from the Latin *complacere* ("to please greatly"), and both entered English in the middle of the 17th century. But they came to English by separate routes. *Complaisant* entered English by way of the French *complaire* ("gratify"), with its still-current meaning of "eager to please." (Example: "The complaisant child gave away her favorite toy.") *Complacent* came to us directly from Latin, originally with the simple meaning of "pleasant, delightful." *Complacent* then acquired the same meaning as *complaisant*: "eager to please." In fact, that was the only sense of *complacent* listed in Samuel Johnson's *Dictionary of the English Language* (1755). Today's dictionaries list that old meaning as an option. But the word's subsequently acquired, derogatory meaning—"overly pleased with oneself, self-satisfied, smugly unconcerned"—has been identified by certain language critics for the last hundred years or so as the only correct meaning.

The noun *complacency* means "smug satisfaction with an existing situation," as in a *New York Times* quote (1/11/1998) of a warning from former Surgeon General C. Everett Koop about obesity: "It is difficult to justify complacency in the face of this growing epidemic now afflicting more than 58 million Americans."

compleat or **complete**? *Compleat*, a spelling variant of *complete* with the same pronunciation, is sometimes used in the sense of "being an outstanding example." But *compleat* is usually reserved for the sense of "very highly skilled," as in *The Compleat Angler*, English author Izaak Walton's 1653 classic discourse on fishing. Conductor-composer-musician Gunther Schuller used the word recently in the title of his 1997 book, *The Compleat Conductor*.

As an adjective, *complete* can mean not only "entire" (as in "complete collection") but also "very highly skilled" (as in "complete musician") or "being an outstanding example of a [category]" (as in "complete idealist" or "complete bore").

complected or **complexioned**? *Complected* ("having a particular facial complexion") as in "light or dark complected"—is a long-established and completely acceptable "Americanism," according to *Merriam-Webster's Dictionary of English Usage*. But *complected* is classified as "informal," "dialectical," "nonstandard," and "illiterate" by other usage books.

Risk-free solution: If a person's color really is relevant, use *complexioned*.

complement or **compliment**? No matter how hard you work at your job, don't expect anyone to pay you a complement. What you want is a compliment.

Compliment, which shares an *i* with *praise*, is the noun meaning "an expression of praise" and a verb meaning "to pay a compliment to."

Complement, which contains most of the word *complete*, is a noun meaning "something that completes or makes perfect" and a verb meaning "to complete by providing something that was lacking."

complementary or *complimentary?* If you remember that *compliments* ("expressions of praise") are free, you'll remember to distinguish *complimentary* ("no charge") from *complementary* ("serving to complete" or "mutually supplying each other's lack"). Colors can be *complementary*; supermarket food samples are *complimentary*.

complete confusion   Can something be more complete than something else? The answer is yes and no, depending on which sources you consult.

Let's begin with the side that says no. You will never see a book called *The Most Complete Works of Shakespeare*. Such a book is either *complete* (defined by dictionaries as "entire, total, whole") or not. As noted by *The Columbia Guide to Standard American English*, the adjective *complete* and the adverb *completely* are considered by careful users of Standard English to be absolutes—"not modifiable by qualifiers such as *more* or *most*." As a matter of fact, one of the synonyms of *complete* is *absolute*, as in "absolute silence."

Nevertheless, you will often see "more complete" and "most complete" in advertising and journalism. For example, an advertising brochure described *Britannica Almanac 2004* as "The Most Complete Almanac for Today's World." And *The New Yorker* ran an article (11/6/2000) about what that magazine called "the most complete map" of New York City. Moreover, the qualifying of *complete* is condoned by *Merriam-Webster's Dictionary of English Usage*, the *Random House Webster's Unabridged Dictionary*, and a majority of the usage panel of *The American Heritage Dictionary*.

Risk-free recommendation: If you want to completely avoid criticism for your use of *complete*, don't qualify it unless you use *nearly*, *almost*, or another word that conveys the idea that something is *not* complete. If you feel tempted to say "more complete" or "most complete," switch to "more comprehensive" or "most comprehensive."

compound adjectives   See "hyphens protect the meaning of these adjectives," and "hyphens never need to protect these adjectives."

compound nouns   See "spelling compound words."

compound subjects: singular or plural?   When two subjects form one entity, they take a singular verb: "Strawberries and cream *is* their favorite dish."

comprise should not be compromised   If words were automobiles, a special license would be required for the use of the much-abused verb *comprise*. That license would be granted only after the applicant memorized the following instructions: The whole *comprises*—consists of—all its parts. The United States *comprises* fifty states.

Licenses to use the word *comprise* would be revoked for anyone who uses *comprise* in the passive sense of "composed" (as in "the United States *is comprised of* fifty states") and "constitute" (as in "Fifty states *comprise* the United States"). Those widespread violations of the five-century-old "consists of" definition of *comprise* are currently listed as alternative definitions by some dictionaries. But nearly all usage and style books endorse the "consists of" *comprise* exclusively.

Risk-free usage: A *New Yorker* article (5/3/2004) referred to "an audience comprising New York's most sparkling intelligentsia."

comptroller needs control   *Comptroller* may seem more prestigious than *controller* for "financial officer," especially in government. But *comptroller* is merely an old misspelling of *controller*. Word historians think the perfectly clear word *controller* somehow got mixed up with the Middle French word *compte*, meaning "account." At any rate, *comptroller* today is preferably pronounced as if it were spelled "controller."

conceit is more than _vanity_   The noun *conceit*, like *concept*, is from a Latin verb meaning "to conceive." Hence, *conceit* originally meant "that which is conceived in the mind; a conception, notion, or idea." *Conceit* today may refer to "a literary device" or "a fanciful idea" as well as "a conception, usually of oneself, that is excessively favorable."

Here's a literary conceit cited in *The New York Review of Books* (3/9/2000): "A prevailing conceit of [the E. L. Doctorow novel] *City of God* is that it's a film on an enormous reel with frequent interruptions, flashbacks and flash-forwards, quick cuts, dissolves."

Using *conceit* in the sense of a fanciful idea, a writer in *American Prospect* magazine (January 1–14, 2002) argued that the scandalous behavior of Enron Corporation executives prior to the surprising bankruptcy of that energy-trading giant "impeaches the conceit that a market economy can be efficiently self-policing."

concern or *firm*?   Use *concern* for a business or manufacturing organization, *firm* for a group of professionals such as lawyers or architects. (See also "*client* or *customer*?")

concert or *recital*?   Music recitals are given by soloists and very small groups. Concerts are given by larger groups, like bands and orchestras.

conciseness or *concision*?   They both mean "the quality of being concise; using few words to say much." But if you want to be perfectly clear, make a decision against the rarely used *concision*. (See also "cut it out.")

conclave: a key word   This word, derived from the Latin *clavis* ("key"), literally refers to a locked room where the Vatican's College of Cardinals meets to elect a pope. By figurative extension, *conclave* means any "private assembly or meeting in which the proceedings are secret."

Many writers have further extended *conclave* to include nonsecret meetings, as illustrated by a *New York Times* report of "an annual conclave that has become perhaps the world's largest biker rally" (8/9/1990). Such elastic usage of *conclave* has been accepted by the Merriam-Webster and Random House dictionaries, by *Webster's New World College Dictionary*, and by *The Columbia Guide to Standard American English*, but not by *The Associated Press Stylebook* or by the Oxford, Longman, and American Heritage dictionaries.

Risk-free advice: Bernstein's *Careful Writer*, rejecting the "nonsecret" *conclave*, prescribed such alternatives as *meeting, convention, conference, get-together, reunion, parley, assemblage, colloquium, palaver*, and *Kaffeeklatsch*.

condemn or *contemn*?   *Condemn* ("to express strong disapproval of") should not be confused with *contemn*, a word that contains most of the word *contempt* and indeed means "to treat with scorn or contempt." (See also "*contemptible* or *contemptuous*?")

condominiums or *condominia*?   Do you know people who boast about investing in *condominia*? Explain to them that *condominia* is a Latin plural that never existed. Nobody in ancient Rome owned a condominium—not even Caesar. The correct plural for *condominium* has an English ending: *condominiums*.

Condominium, from the Latin *com-* ("with, together") and *dominium* ("domain"), seems to have been coined in the 18th century, when it meant "joint international sovereignty." According to Merriam-Webster's *Word Histories*, "It was not until 1962 that we began using the word in its more familiar sense: 'individual ownership of a unit (as an apartment) in a multiunit structure, or a unit so owned.'"

confidant, confidante, confident, confidence *Confidant* means "someone you trust enough to share your secrets with." Though dictionaries list *confidante* as "a woman confidant," that gender distinction should be shunned by anyone enlightened enough to avoid such patronizing terms as *woman lawyer* and *woman doctor.*

People sometimes write the noun *confidant* when their intended meaning requires the adjective *confident* ("self-assured, having strong beliefs"). Actually, the two words are related historically, in the sense that the adjective *confident* used to mean "trustful, confiding." And the noun *confidence* currently means not only "self-assurance" but also "full trust" and "confidential [secret] information, as in exchanging confidences." If you tell somebody something *in confidence*, that always means you're entrusting that person with a secret. (See also "*disclose, divulge,* and *reveal* only what's been hidden.")

confused by prepositions? *Confused with* means "mistaken for," as in "Infatuation can be confused *with* love." *Confused by* means "bewildered, perplexed," as in "Lovers can be confused *by* conflicting advice given by well-meaning friends."

congenial or genial? Say *genial* when you mean "having a pleasant disposition," as in "the TV quiz show's genial host." Say *congenial* for persons or things that are "compatible," as in "a congenial couple" or "congenial surroundings."

congeries is or congeries are? Though *congeries* ("kon-JEER-ease" or "KON-jer-ease") sounds plural, it is a Latin-derived singular for "a pile, heap, collection of things in one mass." Don't turn *congeries* into a counterfeit singular by reaching for the unacceptable *congerie* or *congery.*

The plural of *congeries* is identical with the singular. So you may say *congeries is* or *congeries are,* depending on whether you mean one or more than one.

conglomerate or corporation?   A *conglomerate*, usually a family of *corporations*, is involved in a number of diverse enterprises.

congratulate those who pronounce this correctly   The word *congratulate* is widely mispronounced as if the second syllable were *grad*. If you pronounce this word the way it's spelled, you deserve congrats.

Congressional Medal of Honor has never been awarded   This medal, much mentioned by the media, does not exist. It is the *Medal of Honor.*

conjunctions: coordinating or subordinating?   When you want to join words or groups of equal rank, use a *coordinating* conjunction such as *and, but, for, or, nor,* or *yet.*

When you want to join a main clause to a dependent clause, use a *subordinating* conjunction such as *if, since, because, as, while, so that, although,* or *unless.* (See also "sentences that run on" and "sentences that run on into adverbs.")

conjunctions used in pairs   Paired conjunctions—mutually *related* and therefore described as cor*relative*—include *although . . . nevertheless, both . . . and, either . . . or, neither . . . nor, not only . . . but also,* and *whether . . . or.*

If you don't want to be accused of using correlative conjunctions carelessly, make sure they link nouns with nouns, verbs with verbs. For example, don't say "She loves both *the mountains* [a noun] and *to sail* [a verb] the sea." Instead, say "She loves both *the mountains* [a noun] and *the sea* [another noun]." (See "*either . . . or/neither . . . nor?*" "*not only . . . but also,*" and "parallel construction.")

conjure, conjurer, conjure up   The verb *conjure,* from an Old French word for "use a spell," means, "to use magical power to summon a demon or some other spirit, or to exercise influence as if by magic." Hence, *conjurer* means, "a magician or other person who uses magical powers."

Conjure up means "to call to mind, evoke," as when a severely injured and isolated man tries to "conjure up some image from a Red Cross handbook he'd once memorized" (in *Assorted Fire Events,* an award-winning recent collection of short stories by David Means).

connecting your ideas   See "transitions."

***connive* or *conspire*?** The word *connive* is commonly used in the sense of "conspire." But many word guardians insist that *connive* should be used only in its original sense, to mean "pretend not to see something evil." For example, Follett's *Modern American Usage* declares that "the careful writer will protect this distinct meaning [because] no synonym exists for the subtle action and motive the word denotes."

Connive is derived from Latin and French words meaning "to wink or shut the eyes." In that sense, a cowardly district attorney *connives at* ("winks at" or "shuts his eyes to") organized crime, choosing not to see the Mafia-like activities in his or her jurisdiction. That meaning of *connive* is endorsed by *The Oxford English Dictionary*, Bernstein's *Careful Writer*, Copperud's *American Usage and Style*, Freeman's *Handbook of Problem Words and Phrases*, *Reader's Digest Success With Words*, and *The New York Public Library Guide to Style and Usage*.

The "conspire" *connive*, however, has been around since about 1800, and the many people today who think *connive* means "conspire" would assume that the district attorney mentioned in the previous paragraph is being accused of working *with* the Mafia.

Risk-free suggestion: Use *connive*, with its original, "see no evil" meaning, only when you are certain that you are communicating with people who know that meaning. Otherwise, say *wink at*. And instead of calling somebody a *conniver* or a *conniving so-and-so*, call that person a *schemer* or a *sneak*.

***connoisseur*: don't forget to double-dip** Connoisseurs ("people with expert knowledge") of words make sure to spell this word with a double *n* and a double *s*.

***connote* or *denote*?** What a word *connotes* ("implies, suggests") is as important as what it *denotes* ("means literally").

Synonyms have the same *denotation*, but they often differ in *connotation*. For example: The synonyms *collusion* and *cooperation* both denote "working together, agreeing," but *collusion* connotes that the purpose of the cooperative venture is wrongful." *Lucre* ("LU-ker") is a synonym for "money," but as *Webster's New World College Dictionary* notes, the word *lucre* is now used "chiefly in a humorously derogatory sense," as in the phrase *filthy lucre*. An expression that English speakers borrowed from France, *nouveau riche* ("noo-vo REESH"), denotes "someone newly wealthy" but connotes that the person flaunts his or her wealth because he or she lacks the refinement of those who are used to being wealthy. (See also "*scheme*: not the American plan.")

consensus: it makes sense "Possibly the most commonly misspelled word in the English language, excepting 'supercede' for *supersede*, is 'concensus' for *consensus*," says Morton S. Freeman in *Words to the Wise*. Memory hint: Associate *consensus* with *common sense*.

consensus is a matter of opinion   Some usage commentators condemn the word *opinion* in *consensus of opinion* as redundant, on the grounds that *consensus* means "generally shared opinion." Those commentators point to the fact that *consensus*—derived from the Latin words for "together" (*con*) and "thinking" (*sentire*)—literally means "a thinking together."

But *Merriam-Webster's Dictionary of English Usage*, citing the apparently original English meaning of *consensus* as "harmony" or "cooperation," argues that the *opinion* in *consensus of opinion* is needed to distinguish that idea from such other expressions of harmony and cooperation as *consensus of support, consensus of behavior*, and *consensus of values*.

Risk-free suggestion: When you mean *consensus of opinion*, avoid the appearance of redundancy by just saying *consensus*. But make sure your intended reference to opinion is made clear in your context. Usage example from *Business Week* (5/15/2000): "While there's no consensus on Capitol Hill on how to regulate [Internet] privacy, lawmakers and regulators could be forced into action if Net companies keep engaging in digital eavesdropping."

consist of or **include?** Use *consist of* to introduce a full list, *include* to introduce a partial list.

consistency is not debatable   Though much language usage is debatable and some usage is purely optional, there is no debate about consistency. For example, if you capitalize *Third World* (as does *The Washington Post*) in one place, don't lowercase the term (as does *The New York Times*) elsewhere.

consummate: the adjective and verb   As an *adjective*, preferably pronounced "kon-SUM-it," *consummate* means "complete or perfect in every way" or "of the highest degree." Usage example from *The New York Times*

(6/13/2000): "William Gilbert [16th-century English physician-physicist] was the consummate observer, seeing wonder in nature and pondering its secrets."

As a *verb*, pronounced "KON-suh-mate," *consummate* means "to bring to completion," as in consummating a business transaction or the intimate relationship of a marriage. The verb also means "to fulfill," as in consummating one's dream of becoming an Olympic champion.

contact: a touchy verb Everybody agrees that it is good to have contacts. But not everybody agrees that contacts should be contacted.

Contact, from the Latin *tangere* ("touch"), can safely be used as a noun, for "the state of touching" or for "physical or personal connection." But *contact* as a verb, meaning "get in touch with," was once widely rejected for formal usage, and it is still rejected for formal usage by some college handbooks of English.

Acceptance of the verb *contact* among the usage panelists of *The American Heritage Dictionary* nearly doubled from 1969 to 1992, from about one-third of the panel to nearly two-thirds. Opposition to the usage now comes mostly from "elderly readers and listeners," according to *The Columbia Guide to Standard American English*. Some usage commentators say that opposition to the verb *contact* is likely to disappear. For now, if you want to avoid the risk of criticism for this usage, substitute such words and phrases as *see, ask, consult, approach, confer with*, or *get in touch with*. (See also "*impact* could have a negative impact on you" and "noun verbification.")

contagious or infectious? Any disease you can catch—from food, water, air, or human or animal contact—is *infectious*. Bacteria, viruses, and parasitic worms are infectious agents.

The word *contagious*, derived from a Latin term for "in touch with," describes only those infectious diseases that are communicated by contact. As a memory tip, note that *contagious* contains most of the word *contact*.

contemporary: now or then? Think twice before suggesting that people judge the morality of Attila the Hun by *contemporary standards*. Many people will wonder whether you mean the standards of *his* contemporaries or *ours*.

Contemporary's predominant meaning today is "modern, present-day." The word's older sense of "existing or occurring at the same time" is gradually being taken over by *contemporaneous*. But *contemporary* remains in the Risk Zone of ambiguity, so you may need to accompany it with clarifying words or phrases such as *now, then, at that time, in the past,* or *at the same time.*

contemptible or contemptuous?   Shakespeare and other writers of his time used *contemptible* to mean "show contempt for." Today, *contemptible* is acceptable only to mean "*deserving* contempt, despicable." When we want to "talk about *showing* contempt," we say we are *contemptuous* of something.

Usage review: People are *contemptuous* of someone or something they regard as *contemptible.*

continual or continuous?   Use *continual* to mean "*frequently repeated,* like drops of water from a leaking faucet." Use *continuous* to mean "*uninterrupted,* like the flow of water from an open faucet."

Continual and *continuous* are used interchangeably so often that most people won't notice when you observe the distinction. But you'll be admired by people who are aware that such word distinctions help maintain language precision. (For similarly useful distinctions, see "*convince* or *persuade?*" "*imply* or *infer?*" "*farther* or *further?*" "*fewer* or *less?*" "*lend* or *loan?*" "*lie* or *lay?*" and "*that* or *which?*")

continuance or continuation?   Both words mean "the act or fact of continuing." But *continuation* should be applied to the prolongation or resumption of *action,* as in "the continuation of the debate." And *continuance* should be applied only to the duration of a *condition,* as in "the continuance of prosperity." In law, *continuance* means "the postponement of a proceeding such as a trial."

continuity is not just for movies   If you watch movies closely, you may notice mistakes in continuity, resulting from the fact that some scenes are shot many times or are shot over a period of days. For instance, an actor will be wearing a wedding ring, then suddenly appear without one in the same scene.

Here is an example of the kind of continuity problem you need to watch for in your writing: In an article about how to earn good grades, a student in my feature-writing class quoted a fellow student as saying he was "never really afraid of having to write term papers." Four pages later, the same student was quoted as saying that he had "conquered" that fear.

contract: read this carefully In addition to being a noun (pronounced "KON-tract") for a formal agreement, this word is also a verb (preferably pronounced "kon-TRACT") that enables you to contract ("formally arrange") a marriage, contract ("incur") obligations, contract ("acquire") a disease, or contract ("shrink, by abbreviation") a word.

contractions: when you do and when you don't *Let's* use contractions when we want to communicate informally. For formal communication, *let us* not.

contranyms speak with forked tongue Proceed with extreme caution when you use words with contradictory meanings. Such words—called contranyms, autoantonyms, antagonyms, and Janus ("two-faced") words—should be used only when the intended meaning is clear from the context.

Here are some notorious two-faced examples, cited in other entries: *Cleave* means "to separate" or "to cling," *sanction* means "permission" or "punishment," *sanguine* means "cheerful" or "bloody," *scan* means "examine thoroughly" or "examine superficially," and *suspicious* means "suspecting" or "being suspected." (See also entries on "*oversight* and "*showstopper*." For the link with Janus, see "*Janus-faced*.")

conversely: thinking in reverse Contrary to widespread misusage, *conversely* does not mean "on the other hand." *Conversely* refers to a relationship *in reverse*: "Anxiety may cause a low score on an exam. *Conversely*, a low score on an exam may cause anxiety." If someone admires you but you don't admire that person, you may say, "He admires me, but the *converse* isn't true."

convince or *persuade*? *Convince* means "satisfy by argument or evidence." *Persuade* means "influence to take action."

For example, *USA Today* reported (7/14/2000) that U.S. Defense Secretary William Cohen was visiting Beijing "to *convince* [italics added] the Chinese that the United States was not trying to isolate China or check its power." Secretary Cohen's purpose was to *persuade* China's leaders to be more cooperative with the United States.

The New Fowler's Modern English Usage reports that *convince* "began to be controversially used in the 1950's to mean *persuade*. . . . It is [now] a classic example of a new construction that is acceptable or at least unexceptionable to some and repugnant to others." The use of *convince* to mean *persuade* has won acceptance from Kenneth Wilson's *Columbia Guide to Standard American English*, the usage scholars of Merriam-Webster and Random House, and 74 percent of the usage panel of *The American Heritage Dictionary*. But you cannot go wrong if you help maintain the *convince/persuade* distinction, for which you can find support in Follett's *Modern American Usage*, Bernstein's *Careful Writer*, Newman's *Strictly Speaking*, Freeman's *Handbook of Problem Words and Phrases*, Garner's *Modern American Usage*, Lovinger's *Penguin Dictionary of American English Usage and Style*, and the stylebooks of *U.S. News & World Report*, the Associated Press, and *The Economist*.

The New York Times, whose stylebook also supports the *convince/persuade* distinction, demonstrated its consistency by choosing *convincingly* over *persuasively* in a report (1/12/2005) that astronomers "had convincingly seen, in the patterns of galaxies scattered across the night sky, the vestiges of sound waves that rumbled through the universe after the Big Bang."

cool **is still hot**   Slang is always risky. That's because the very thing that makes slang appealing, its novelty, can place you in the embarrassing position of using expressions that have fallen out of fashion.

A notable exception is the slang use of *cool* as an all-purpose adjective of approval—as in a *Parade* magazine cover story (11/23/2003) entitled "Today's Coolest Electronics" and a *Fortune* magazine cover story (5/17/2004) entitled "15 Cool Companies We Love." That use of *cool* has outlived generations of predecessors, including *hot*, *bully*, *capital*, *groovy*, *hep*, *hip*, *crazy*, *far-out*, *rad*, and *tubular*.

As far back as 1825, a British magazine called *English Spy* referred to a young man from Eton College as "a right cool fish." *Cool's* current popularity has been traced to its adoption as an emphatic synonym for "excellent" by American jazz musicians of the 1930's. By the late 1940's, *cool* was being used by a wide variety of people who wanted to *sound* cool. And so it went with the beatniks of the 1950's, with the hippies of the 1960's and early 1970's, and with people in many walks of life ever since.

In a *Wall Street Journal* cartoon (9/30/1999), a clergyman officiating at a wedding says to the young ponytailed groom, "I'd appreciate it, Larry, if you'd drop the 'cool' and just say 'I do.'" *Time* magazine (6/26/2000) titled an article about Morocco's "hip and charming" young monarch, Mohammed VI, "The King of Cool." The year-2000 edition of *The American Heritage Dictionary* noted that *cool* "has even been borrowed into other languages, such as French and German." And in a 2001 book, *Birth of the Cool*, poet and documentary filmmaker Lewis MacAdams solemnly declares that "to use the word *cool* well is to partake of a central ritual of global culture as profound and as universal as a handshake."

The New York Times (8/27/1995) identified *cool* as "the favorite expression of [Microsoft chairman Bill] Gates and just about everyone else in computerdom." In a book about the corporate culture of Microsoft, called *I Sing the Body Electronic*, author Fred Moody wrote about *cool* as used by Microsoft employees: "Depending upon the context in which it is used and the tone of voice with which it is uttered, *cool* can mean perfect, phenomenal, awesome, ingenious, eye-popping, bliss-inducing, pretty clever, enchanting, fine, adequate, acceptable, okay, or any of hundreds or so of other such words." According to *Newsweek* columnist Steven Levy (5/15/2000), Apple Computer CEO Steve Jobs "restored the company and its products to respectability and coolness." And *Time* (1/22/2001) reported that "Apple had a lot of cool new stuff to show off" at a Macworld convention.

Usage advice: Enjoy the all-approving *cool* while it lasts—and that may be forever. But resist the temptation to allow *cool* to become half of your vocabulary. (See also entries for *cute* and *neat*.)

cop-calling   Some police officers don't mind being called a *cop*. Others do. *The Associated Press Stylebook* warns that this slang term is often considered "derogatory" and therefore should be confined to "quoted matter."

There is controversy about the word's origin as well. Some word historians say that *cop*, an abbreviation of *copper*, was inspired by the fact that early police, in London and elsewhere, wore large copper buttons. Some say *cop* originated in "constable on patrol" or "constabulary of police" or "chief of police"—as in "John Smith, C.O.P."

Language scholar Stuart Berg Flexner, in *I Hear America Talking*, said *cop* "probably" came from the Latin *capere* ("to catch, to capture"). In unqualified support of that view, Merriam-Webster's *Word Histories* says "the truth" is that *cop* began as 18th-century English slang for "to catch, to capture"—a sense that *cop* the verb retains today in the slang term *cop a plea*. In the 19th century, according to Merriam-Webster's word sleuths, police were said to *cop* ("catch") criminals, then the police were called *coppers* ("those who cop criminals"), and then *coppers* was shortened to *cops*.

copyright or copywrite?   *Copyright* can be a verb, an adjective, or a noun. For example, you can *copyright* what you write by obtaining a *copyright* form to apply for a *copyright* from the United States Copyright Office of the Library of Congress in Washington, D.C.

To *copywrite* is "to write advertising or publicity copy [text]."

cornucopia or Cornucopia?   The word *cornucopia* ("symbol or source of abundance") literally means "horn of plenty." The *corn* in *cornucopia* means "horn," as it does in *unicorn*. The *copia* means "plentiful," as it does in *copious*.

The original *Cornucopia* of Greek mythology was the horn of the goat that suckled the god Zeus. The horn broke off and became filled with endless supplies of whatever food and drink the owner desired.

corps is or corps are?   A *corps* is "a body of people having a common activity or occupation," as in the press corps, or "a branch of the armed forces having a specialized function," as in the Marine Corps. You change *corps* from singular to plural—as in "Three nations sent corps of engineers"—simply by changing the pronunciation from "kor" to "korz."

corpus delicti may be no body   This term does not necessarily refer to the body of a murder victim. A *corpus delicti* (Latin for the figurative "body of a crime") is any evidence that a crime has been committed.

correlative conjunctions   See "conjunctions used in pairs," "*either . . . or/neither . . . nor?*" and "*not only . . . but also.*"

cost or price?   The *price* of an article is what the seller asks. The *cost* is what the buyer actually pays.

could care less or couldn't care less?   The many people who say they *could care less* when they mean they *couldn't care less* are risking the accusation that they are careless.

People who correctly say they "*couldn't* care less" are emphasizing that they don't care *at all* and therefore could not possibly care any less than they do. But people who mistakenly say "*could* care less" are unintentionally saying they really *do* care, because they are saying that they could care *less* than they do.

The Columbia Guide to Standard American English says the *could care less* usage invites "the scorn of logic lovers and cliché haters alike." *Line by Line*, the Modern Language Association's editing manual, observes, "It is true that idioms are not necessarily logical, but since both the logical and the illogical versions [of this expression] are idiomatic, why not make sense?" Even the generally permissive *Merriam-Webster's Dictionary of English Usage* emphasizes that "most writers, faced with putting the words on paper, choose the clearer *couldn't care less.*"

Merriam-Webster researchers say it is "plausible" that *couldn't care less* was brought to the United States by GI's returning from World War II, and that, at any rate, "it was clearly established by the late 1950's and early 1960's." The *could care less* version appears to have emerged, first in speech and then print, in the late 60's. By 1975, *could care less* had attracted so much attention that the *Harper Dictionary of Contemporary Usage* denounced it as "an ignorant debasement of the language."

Risky usage: *The New York Times* (2/15/2004) quoted the author of *A Dog's History of America,* Mark Derr, as observing that dog-show dogs "could care less about the ribbon and trophy."

Risk-free usage, from an opinion essay in the *Los Angeles Times* (5/5/2000): "the media giants could not care less about the public."

could have or **could of**? See "*of:* to have and have not."

councilor or **counselor**? As the spelling of these words suggests, a *councilor* is a member of a *council* ("a group with legislative or administrative functions"), and a *counselor* is a person who offers *counsel* ("advice"), typically as a lawyer or someone who supervises young people at a summer camp.

In both words, a double *l* is permitted but not preferred.

count noun or mass noun? See "nouns that don't count."

coup de grâce might be a blow to your reputation This French phrase—meaning "deathblow that ends the misery of a mortally wounded victim" or "any finishing or decisive stroke"—should be pronounced "koo duh GRAHSS." If you pronounce it "koo duh GRAH," warns *The Columbia Guide to Standard American English*, "the knowing may snicker at your ignorance."

Usage example from *The New York Times* (8/25/2001): "In a [Central American] region battered over the years by earthquakes, hurricanes and conflict, the drought is a potential coup de grâce."

couple is* or *couple are? For *couple* in the sense of a pair of socially related people, use a singular verb when you are focusing on them as one unit ("The couple in the rear of the restaurant is still waiting to be served"). Use a plural verb with *couple* when you are focusing on two individuals. ("The couple are planning to get married on Valentine's Day").

Avoid coupling the same *couple* with both a singular and a plural verb, as in the following caption in *The Daily Herald* of Provo, Utah (6/28/2000): "This couple has [should be *have*] been married for 31 years and have [correctly plural] had more time together since their two daughters, who are grown, left home eight years ago." The writer should have noticed that the *couple* in that sentence needed to be consistently plural because of the reference to *their* (a plural pronoun) daughters.

***coupon*: a risk-free pronunciation** Nobody objects if you pronounce this French-derived word "KOO-pon." Though "KYOO-pon" is a widely accepted American pronunciation variant, it annoys some usage critics.

***Court of St. James's*: a royal test of spelling** The British royal court, to which foreign diplomats are accredited, is called the *Court of St. James's*, because it is named after St. James's Palace, which was built by Henry VIII on the site of St. James's Leper Hospital.

Copperud's *American Usage and Style* recalled that knowledge of the correct spelling for the British royal court (along with the correct spelling for *restaurateur*) "was for many years what marked the difference between cubs and more experienced reporters on American newspapers." (See also "*restaurateur* or *restauranteur?*")

coverup, cover-up,* or *cover up? *New York Times* language columnist William Safire (10/6/1991) recommended that the attempt to hide political corruption be written unhyphenated (*coverup*), to distinguish that word from the *cover-up* that means *beach towel, caftan,* or other article that somebody might reach for in order to *cover up.*

craft or *crafts*?   *Crafts* is appropriate only in the sense of *arts and crafts*. For ships and planes, *craft* is the plural form as well as the singular. Usage example: "The air*craft* is flying over the many *craft* that *are* entering the harbor."

crass is bad enough   *Crass*, which entered English in the 16th century as an adjective for "thick, coarse," now means "coarse" in the sense of "gross, unrefined, insensitive, stupid."

Crass is often mistakenly used as if it meant "mercenary, greedy," perhaps because of the popularity of the term *crass* ("coarse") *commercialism*.

credence, credibility, or *credulity*?   *Credence* is the belief in something or someone's credibility. *Credibility* is the quality of being believable. *Credulity* is the tendency to give credence too easily.

credible or *creditable*?   *Credible* means "worthy of belief." *Creditable* means "worthy of praise."

crescendo: take it gradually?   Though many people use *crescendo* to mean "*peak* of intensity," the risk-free choice is to use *crescendo* to mean "*gradual* increase in intensity."

As a music term—from an Italian word for "increasing"—*crescendo* ("kruh-SHEN-doe") means "a gradual increase in loudness or force." Figuratively, the word refers to any gradual increase in intensity or effect, as in the following *New York Times* dispatch from Rome (3/31/2002): "Pope John Paul II offered an Easter prayer today that the crescendo of attacks and revenge between the Israelis and the Palestinians would be ended by discussions between them."

In the 1920's, some influential American writers (notably F. Scott Fitzgerald and William Faulkner) began using *crescendo* to mean "*peak* of intensity or effect." That meaning is now "fully established" in American English, in the view of *Merriam-Webster's Dictionary of English Usage*. But *The Oxford English Dictionary* classifies it as an American colloquialism, and OED editor R. W. Burchfield wrote in his *New Fowler's Modern English Usage* that "the new use still lies rawly in disputed territory, eschewed by anyone knowing the meaning of the Latin participial ending." Moreover, many American guardians of precise writing—including the style-guide editors of *The New York Times*, *The Washington Post*, and *The Wall Street Journal*—

still limit the meaning of *crescendo* to "a gradual increase in intensity or effect." That meaning is also preserved when *crescendo* is precisely used as a verb, as in a *New York Times Magazine* reference (11/24/2002) to a "story [that] crescendos to its conclusion."

A gradual *decrease* in the intensity of a crisis would be a *decrescendo*, beginning with a syllable that preferably sounds like "day."

crevasse or crevice? Explorers of the Antarctic soon learn that *crevice* ("KREV-iss") means "a narrow crack in ice or rock" and *crevasse* ("kreh-VAHSS"), the wider of the two words, means "a deep crack in a glacier." You can trip on a crevice, but you can fall into a crevasse.

criteria is or criteria are? Pity the student who asks a professor of English, "What *is* your grading criteria?" instead of "What *are* your grading criteria?" *Criteria* is the plural of the Greek derivative for "a standard of judgment," *criterion*.

Using *criteria* as if it were singular—"criteria is"—has become so common in recent decades that it may eventually achieve acceptability, according to *Merriam-Webster's Collegiate Dictionary*. In an example of that questionable usage, *The Atlanta Constitution* (8/12/1998) published the headline "Criteria for Water Contract Is Disputed." But *The American Heritage Dictionary* emphasizes that the singular *criteria* "is not yet acceptable," and the *Random House Webster's College Dictionary* reports that "*criteria* continues strongly in use as a plural in Standard English."

The anglicized plural, *criterions*, is listed as an alternative to *criteria* in major dictionaries and in Paul W. Lovinger's *Penguin Dictionary of American English Usage and Style*. But *criterions* is not recognized by such usage sources as *Garner's Modern American Usage*, *The New Fowler's Modern English Usage*, and the stylebooks of the Associated Press, *The New York Times*, and *The Wall Street Journal*. Even less welcome in usage circles is *criterias*.

Example of risk-free usage, from *USA Today* (5/19/2000): "The criteria [for certification of beaches by the Clean Beaches Council] address water quality, cleanliness, public safety and environmental management." (See also entry for *media*.)

criticise or criticize? This is one of the words spelled by Americans with a *z* and by the British with an *s*.

criticize* or *critique?   In dictionaries, *criticize* means "to make judgments as to merits or faults" or "to find fault with." Inasmuch as *criticize* is often interpreted in the second sense ("finding fault"), the verb *critique* comes in handy when your intended meaning is "to evaluate." A professor who continually *criticizes* student papers is more likely to demoralize the students than a professor who *critiques* the student papers.

Critique originally was (and still is) a noun for "an essay or article reviewing a literary or artistic work." Its use as a verb was opposed, for no stated reason, by Henry W. Fowler in his influential 1926 *Dictionary of Modern English Usage.* That opposition was echoed by other commentators, including most of the usage panel of the 1975 and 1985 *Harper Dictionary of Contemporary Usage* (who condemned the verb *critique* as "pretentious," "ugly," "stupid," "horrible," and "ghastly").

But another member of the Harper usage panel, author Isaac Asimov, vigorously defended *critique* as a useful, neutral alternative to the negative-sounding *criticize.* So did Roy H. Copperud in *American Usage and Style* (1980), Robert Claiborne in his *Our Marvelous Native Tongue* (1983), and the Merriam-Webster staff in their *Dictionary of Modern English Usage* (1989). Such defenders of the verb *critique* have noted that it has been serving as a neutral alternative to *criticize* since the middle of the 18th century.

***culinary:* two flavors of sound**   Nobody will throw a pie in your face if you use the British pronunciation of this adjective for cookery, "CULL-inary." But you'll show good taste on the American side of the Atlantic if you say "CUE-linary."

cult* or *religion?   Scholars generally use *cult* nonjudgmentally, to mean "a system of religious worship, especially with reference to rituals and beliefs." That is the only sense of the word that you'll find in, for example, *The Columbia Encyclopedia.*

But dictionaries additionally list the more widely used, *derogatory* sense of *cult*, as "a religious group whose beliefs are regarded as outlandishly false." In a typical example, headline writers applied the word *cult* to a Ugandan Christian sect in March 2000 reports that more than nine hundred participants in a prayer meeting, mostly women and children, had been deliberately burned to death to "speed their entry into heaven."

Usage tip: Unless you're addressing scholars, use *cult* only when your intent is derogatory.

cupidity: a story of love and greed The noun *cupidity*—echoing the Roman name for the god of love, Cupid—evolved from a Latin word for "ardent desire" into a 16th-century English word for "excessive longing or lust," then acquired today's sense of "greed; excessive desire for wealth or possessions." (See also "*psyche* or *Psyche?*")

curious is a curious word If you write that somebody is a *curious* person, make sure your context clearly shows whether you mean "driven by curiosity" or "odd, peculiar."

currently may be expendable Check statements such as "She's currently visiting France" to see if you can remove *currently* without sacrificing any meaning. You usually can.

currently or presently? *Currently* means, of course, "at present, now." And that meaning has also been widely and acceptably conveyed by *presently* "more or less continuously since 1485," according to *Merriam-Webster's Dictionary of English Usage.* As *The New York Times Manual of Style and Usage* notes, however, many of today's "precise writers" use *presently* only in its other sense: "in a short while, soon."

Risk-free advice: Inasmuch as *presently* has conflicting meanings, one of which arouses criticism, take the advice of *The Wall Street Journal Guide to Business Style and Usage* and remove *presently* from your vocabulary. The cause of clear communication will be served if you turn instead to *now* or *soon*, depending on the meaning you intend.

curricula or curriculums? Both are standard plurals for *curriculum* ("course of study"), but purists will appreciate your using the Latin *curricula* for this Latin word.

curriculum vita or curriculum vitae? Early in 1996, the University of Nevada, Las Vegas, circulated a notice stating that applications for a position of associate professor of telecommunications "must include an up-to-date *curricu-*

lum vita." The university should have asked applicants to include their curriculum *vitae* ("VEE-tie").

Vitae is correct in this Latin term that literally means "the course of a life" because *vitae* is the required genitive (possessive) form of *vita* ("life") in the phrase "of a life."

The plural of this academic version of the résumé is *curricula vitae*.

"custom more honored in the breach than in the observance" For many people, this cliché refers to a desirable rule of behavior that is more likely to be violated than obeyed. But don't use it in that sense around people who know their Shakespeare.

The phrase originated with a comment Hamlet made about his stepfather's custom of getting drunk. Hamlet's point was that it is more *honorable* to violate such an objectionable custom than to observe it.

cut it out To maximize the readability and power of your writing, remove every word that does not contribute to meaning, clarity, or rhythm. As one of the twentieth century's greatest prose stylists, *1984* author George Orwell, wrote in an essay, "If it is possible to cut a word out, always cut it out." For example, you should remove the italicized portions of such common phrases as *"one should* note that" and "as *is the case* with."

The most famous salute to succinctness, "Brevity is the soul of wit," appeared in *Hamlet,* when the word *wit* meant "intelligent discussion." In another oft-quoted acknowledgment that it's nice to be concise, Roman statesman Pliny the Younger wrote in one of his many letters that survive today as a record of life in ancient times, "I apologize for this long letter; I didn't have time to shorten it."

An instructive example of what happens when you trim wordy writing was published in a public-relations journal in 1977 by William A. Spencer, a university relations officer at Indiana University, Indianapolis. Spencer began with this 38-word sentence: "When a coat of paint that is yellow in color is applied to the four walls of a typical room, the room can be made apparently brighter in appearance and an ambience of cheerfulness can be effectively implemented." Spenser reduced it to an equally informative statement of nine words: "For a brighter, cheerier room, paint the walls yellow." (See also next entry and "readability and reality.")

cut out statements that go without saying   A journalism student of mine wrote a story reporting that a basketball coach was "rooting for his team to win." Needless to say, that statement was needless to say.

A more common form of space-wasting statement was identified by writing instructor Keith Hjortshoj in Cornell University's *Arts and Sciences Newsletter* of Spring 1990: He observed that students "tend to dump everything they can recall onto the page" when they believe that their teacher rewards sheer volume. Hjortshoj quoted another instructor as saying that such students "assume the teacher will meet them halfway and find the right answers somewhere in the debris."

Though data-dumping may pay off in some academic situations, the practice is poor training for those who hope to succeed in the world beyond the classroom. Good writing, readability researcher Rudolf Flesch pointed out, is like an iceberg: "Nine-tenths of the material the writer has assembled stays below the surface and is never used."

cute warning   If you use the word *cute*, you may give some people an acute pain.

In a *Los Angeles Times* op-ed essay (3/24/1993), Jenijoy La Belle, a professor of literature at Caltech, warned of "the current epidemic use of *cute*." She wrote: "How often have you shown a friend something you like—a sleek new outfit, a recently redecorated room or maybe an elegant antique chair—and your friend, expected to utter approval, says, 'Cute!' How has it come about that for a good many of us, *cute* is the only adjective we have for something we sanction aesthetically?" She concluded: "Expunge the word from your vocabulary. . . . The only time the word should drop from your lips is when it is preceded by an 'a' and describes an angle less than 90 degrees."

Actually, when *cute* entered the English language in the 18th century, it was a shortened form of *acute* in the sense of "keenly perceptive or discerning, shrewd." As an abbreviation, it was often preceded by an apostrophe.

In 19th-century America, *cute* took on the meaning of "attractive, pretty, especially in a diminutive, dainty, or delicate way." In pursuit of that meaning, *American Heritage Dictionary* researchers discovered an 1838 reference to "cute gals."

In the 20th century, *cute* acquired a disparaging meaning—"contrived [counterfeit] charm"—as in "just too cute" (Christopher Isherwood), "embarrassingly cute" (Arthur M. Schlesinger Jr.), and "Don't get cute with me" (as uttered by cynical private eyes in Hollywood movies). (See also entries for *cool* and *neat*.)

cutting edge is getting crowded   An enormous number of institutions, programs, and products are now said to be on the *cutting edge*.

To cite a typical example, CBS chairman Leslie Moonves told a news conference (1/17/2005) that he was planning "cutting edge" changes in the format of the *CBS Evening News*.

If you want to preserve the value of this phrase, use it only in the dictionary sense of "the most advanced position." For example, *Barron's*, the Dow Jones business and financial weekly, advised investors (10/23/2000) that Texas Instruments—the company that introduced the silicon transistor in the 1950's— "is on the cutting edge once more." (See also "devalued words.")

Cynics weren't cynical   Today's cynics—those who are contemptuously distrustful of human nature—are quite different from the original Cynics. The Cynics were members of a sect of ancient Greek philosophers who believed that virtue is the only good and that the essence of virtue is self-control to eliminate materialistic desires.

How did the idealistic *Cynic* become today's bitter *cynic*? According to word historians, many Cynics acquired a reputation for pointing out the lack of virtue in others, and thus the word *Cynic* over the centuries became synonymous with "faultfinder." After a few more centuries, the "faultfinding" *Cynicism* became the "contemptuous" *cynicism* that is in our language today.

Incidentally, some scholars believe that the word *Cynic* was adapted from a Greek word for *dog*, because a famous member of their sect—a banker turned beggar named Diogenes of Sinope—lived like a wandering, homeless dog in order to demonstrate his liberation from material possessions. And though it was just a myth that Diogenes wandered around in broad daylight carrying a lantern to look for an honest man, he seems to have been justifiably credited with coining the aphorism "The love of money is the root of all evil."

czar or _tsar_?   Both are acceptable ways to spell "Russian emperor" or "someone in authority" such as a *baseball czar* or a *drug-enforcement czar*. *Czar* is preferred by the stylebooks of the Associated Press, *The New York Times*, and *The Wall Street Journal*. Usage example: A *New York Times* profile (1/27/2001) of the head of the Los Angeles Department of Water and Power, S. David Freeman, recalled that he had served more than a decade earlier as a Texas "public power czar."

Czar, tsar, and *kaiser* ("German emperor") are all adaptations of Julius Caesar's surname, which became a Roman, then European, synonym for *emperor.*

D

dais, lectern, or podium?   The speaker's notes are kept on a *lectern* ("slanted table for holding notes"), which sits on a *podium* ("speaker's or performer's platform") that in turn sits on a larger platform called a *dais* (pronounced "DAY-iss").

dale or vale?   Both are literary synonyms for "valley." *Vale* also is used for "the world as the scene of one's earthly existence," as in the sorrowful phrase "this vale [valley] of tears."

dame or Dame?   Though *dame* is a generally offensive slang term for "woman" in America, the capitalized *Dame* is an official title of a female member of the Order of the British Empire, equivalent to that of a knight, or the official title of the wife of a knight or baronet.

The title is never used with the last name only. Note that Dame Agatha Christie, for example, can be referred to as Dame Agatha but not as Dame Christie.

Damocles ate his words   According to an ancient Greek legend, a nobleman named Damocles was a sycophantic flunky at the court of Dionysius the Elder, a king of Syracuse. King Dionysius, tired of hearing the unctuous Damocles talk endlessly about how wonderful it must feel to have the power of the throne, decided to show Damocles that even a mighty ruler must live in the shadow of fear. So Dionysius invited Damocles to a sumptuous banquet, at which Damocles quickly lost his appetite because he had to sit under a sword suspended by a mere hair. Today the phrases *sword of Damocles* and *Damoclean sword* mean "an imminent danger."

dangling participles   See "participles that dangle."

dash but don't be rash   When used sparingly, the dash adds panache, in that word's sense of "boldness." But when used excessively, the dash adds panache in that word's sense of "flamboyance" ("the state of being too showy").

Dashes—separating a phrase or clause from the rest of sentence—should often be replaced by commas (as in this needlessly dashed sentence).

When you want to dump the dashes but cannot appropriately substitute commas—maybe the interruption is too abrupt, as it is here—the sentence should be rewritten or broken in two. On the other hand, dashes can be useful for emphasis—they really can be—when you want to briefly interrupt your reader's train of thought. A single dash, as noted in Follett's *Modern American Usage*, can be useful for separating the final part of a sentence when your goal is to emphasize or summarize—as with this very phrase.

dastardly: you can't be serious   To avoid risk with *dastardly*, use it only as a playful synonym for *despicable*. For example, tongue-in-cheek columnist Alan Abelson of *Barron's* (2/14/2000) speculated that "virtual vandals" had staged the previous week's business-interrupting "dastardly attacks" on commercial Internet sites in order to help "the notorious Greenspan Gang"—those sharing the approach of Fed Chairman Alan Greenspan—cool off the economy.

The *Encarta World English Dictionary* says *dastardly* is used "humorously or melodramatically." *Merriam-Webster's Dictionary of English Usage* reports that *dastardly* "has been kept in use by its overtones of rhetorical denunciation and the stage villain of melodrama." *The Columbia Guide to Standard American English* observes that *dastardly* is "a word rather hard to take seriously."

Oddly, most other dictionaries and usage guides ignore *dastardly*'s playful connotation. When such sources comment at all about the word, they take sides on the question of whether *dastardly* should mean "despicable" or "despicable cowardice." Inasmuch as nobody disputes the idea that dastardly persons or acts are indeed *despicable* ("deserving to be despised"), you can't go wrong if you use *dastardly* only in that sense.

Historical background: When the noun *dastard* entered English in the 15th century, it meant "dullard," as in "stupid or insensitive person." *Dastard* sometime thereafter acquired the meaning of "coward." By the 16th century, the adjective *dastardly* was being used to describe acts of "despicable cowardice."

For many people in modern times, *dastardly* became just plain "despicable"—a change opposed by Fowler's 1926 and 1965 *Dictionary of Modern English Usage* but accepted by the 1996 *New Fowler's Modern English Usage*.

data is or **data are?**   Use *data* as singular or plural. But be consistent. Don't rattle your reader by saying, for example, "the data shows" in one part of a piece of your writing and "the data show" in another.

   Data—the plural of the singular noun *datum*, a Latin derivative meaning "something given"—is uniformly accepted in formal English in the plural sense of "items of information." For example, note the headline for a *New York Times* article (7/31/1998) about the possible volcanic origin of life: "Data Back Idea That Life Grew Out of Inferno."

   But the additional sense of *data* as a synonym for the singular mass noun *information*—a meaning widely adopted in computer science and related fields—now has the blessing of many usage commentators, including a majority of the *American Heritage Dictionary* usage panel. It is acceptable to say, for example, "Much scientific data supports the value of that new technology."

   Datum survives in English mostly as a technical word for "a fact or proposition used to draw a conclusion or make a decision."

daylight saving or **daylight savings?**   The correct phrase is *daylight saving time*.

dead end or **dead-end?**   *Dead end* is a noun phrase (meaning "something, such as a street, with no exit" or "a situation with no chance of progress"). The hyphenated word, *dead-end*, serves as an adjective (meaning "terminating in a dead end," as in "dead-end street") and an intransitive verb (meaning "to come to a dead end," as in "a street that dead-ends at the park").

deadly or **deathly?**   *Deadly*, of course, means "threatening or causing death," as in "deadly poison." *Deathly* means "deathlike," as in this *New York Times* headline (11/27/2001) for a story about a corpse-strewn city in Afghanistan that had just been liberated from Taliban soldiers: "In Kunduz, a Deathly Peace Takes Hold."

dean or **doyen?**   *Dean*—derived from Greek and Latin words for "a leader of ten monks in a monastery"—is a formal title in education or religion, or an informal title of respect for the senior or otherwise most respected person in a group or category.

Doyen, a French coinage with the feminine form *doyenne*, was originally used to convey both the formal and the informal meanings of *dean*. But *doyen/doyenne* now is used only in the informal sense.

Usage examples: The table of contents of the March 1997 *Vanity Fair* magazine listed an article about the late crusading author Jessica Mitford, calling her "the doyenne of muckraking." *The New Yorker* (12/15/1997) referred to Letitia Baldrige as "the etiquette doyenne."

Pronunciation guide: *Doyen* and *doyenne* are both preferably pronounced "doy-EN." If you want to show off your awareness that the terms are from France, say "dwa-YANH" for the male and "dwa-YEN" for the female.

debut: can you do it?   You can't go wrong if you use *debut* ("day-BYOO") or *début* ("DAY-byoo") as a noun meaning "first public appearance," "beginning of a career," or "the formal introduction of a young woman into society." But you just might find yourself in the middle of a continuing controversy if you use *debut* as an intransitive verb ("The singer *debuts* here tomorrow") or a transitive verb ("The company will *debut* its new computers next month").

The verbified *debut*, which has been traced back to 1830, is listed in leading dictionaries and approved by *The Columbia Guide to Standard American English*. Moreover, *The New York Public Library Writer's Guide to Style and Usage* says the verbified *debut* has gradually won respectability as a result of the fact that it now "appears regularly in such respected newspapers as *The Washington Post* and *The New York Times*." But the verbification of the noun *debut* has been rejected by many word guardians, including Morton S. Freeman (in his *Handbook of Problem Words and Phrases*) and most usage panelists of the *Harper Dictionary of Contemporary Usage* and *The American Heritage Dictionary*. (See also "noun verbification.")

debutant or **debutante?**   A *debutante* is "a female making a debut, especially into society." Dictionaries will tell you that a *debutant* is anyone, male or female, making a debut, but many people will assume that both *debutant* and *debutante* refer to females.

decertification or desertification?   *Decertification* ("withdrawal of certification") is not to be confused with a word that has emerged from the discipline of ecology, *desertification* ("the changing of fertile land into desert"). A *Los Angeles Times* editorial (10/5/1998) noted, "Numerous studies show that *desertification* leads not only to famine but to social fragmentation."

decimate: not quite destroyed   If you want to help preserve a useful word distinction, don't imitate newscasters who say *decimate* when they mean *destroy.* Careful communicators use *decimate* to mean "destroy a large percentage of." For example, a *New York Times* article (1/2/2001) recalled that "hunting decimated trumpeter swans in the 1800's, and pushed them close to extinction."

Decimate, which is related to such *ten*-based words as *decimal* and *decade,* originally referred to the ancient Roman method of disciplining mutinous army units by executing a randomly chosen tenth of their members.

decisions to make   If you decide to include a hyphen to write about a *decision-maker* or *decision-making,* you can cite the authority of *The Oxford English Dictionary.*

But you won't find any support for using a hyphen in *decision theory,* the term for "a statistical decision-making technique based on assigning probabilities to various factors and assigning numerical consequences to the outcome." The same is true for *decision tree,* which is "a diagram in which the selection of each branch requires that some type of logical decision be made."

declare is more than you can say   *Declare,* which is often wrongly used as a simple synonym for *say,* means "state emphatically or positively, or for the record." Don't use *declare* unless you really mean it, as in declaring independence, war, or your love.

décor or decor?   This noun for "decorative style, as of a room"—from the French verb *décorer* ("to decorate")—is preferably decorated with an accent and preferably pronounced "DAY-core."

decry or descry?   *Decry* means "to strongly denounce." *Descry* means "to discern something difficult to catch sight of, to see something by looking carefully."

deduction or *induction*?   See "*a posteriori* or *a priori*?"

deep or *deeply*?   The adverb *deeply* modifies verbs, as in "deeply involved."
Deep can be either a "flat" form of the adverb *deeply* (as in "deep down") or an
adjective (as in "deep pit"). (See also "adverbs that look like adjectives.")

de facto or *de jure*?   The Latin phrase *de facto* (pronounced "dih FAK-toe"
and literally meaning "from fact") is used as an English adverb or adjective to
mean "actually, actual, existing in fact, as opposed to being legally or otherwise
formally established"). *De facto*'s less commonly used Latin-derived opposite,
de jure (pronounced "dih JOOR-ee" and literally meaning "from law"), means
"legally, legal, by legal right."
   Usage example of the two expressions in their usual role as adjectives:
"Though General Strongarm's government has not achieved de jure [legally rec-
ognized] status, nobody doubts that he is his nation's de facto [actual] leader."
De facto is also used in nongovernmental contexts: "Though she is listed as just
another member of the board of directors, she is the corporation's de facto chief
executive officer."

defective or *deficient*?   *Defective*, an adjective containing the noun *defect*,
means "having a defect," as in "a defective computer." *Deficient*, an adjective
containing the letters of the noun *deficit*, means "insufficient," as in "a deficient
education."
   Reminder: *Defective* means a lack of quality, and *deficient* means a lack of
quantity.

define your terms   A 12-year-old Florida girl won $5,000 in the 69th National
Spelling Bee by correctly spelling *vivisepulture*, defeating a 13-year-old Texas girl
who missed *cervicorn*. So reported the *Los Angeles Times* (5/31/1996).
   Does that news item frustrate you because it doesn't define *vivisepulture* and
cervicorn? Well, you might want to remember that frustration so that you won't
inflict similar annoyance on people who receive communication from you.
   The *L.A. Times* story actually came from the Associated Press, but don't
blame the AP. The original, uncut AP story defined the noun *vivisepulture* ("the
act of burying alive"), the adjective *cervicorn* ("branching like antlers"), and
such contestant-defeating words as *sidereal* ("of or pertaining to the stars"), *lac-*

ertillian ("of or pertaining to lizards"), *monostich* (pronounced "MAHN-ah-stick" and meaning "a poem consisting of a single line"), and *hypocorism* (pronounced "hy-POCK-a-rism" and meaning "the practice of calling someone by pet names").

defining with *when* and *where*   *Marriage*, according to oral kindergarten-class definitions published every now and then by columnist Jack Smith, "is when two people like each other [and] you have a baby" (1/24/1991), or is "when you have a wedding" (1/4/1993). *Family* "is when they barbecue for you in the backyard" (10/11/1993). *Jealousy* is "when someone's pretty and you want to be as pretty" (1/4/1993).

"Is when" and similar "is where" definitions are charming when they come from the mouth of a five-year-old. But they are embarrassing when they come from grownups, including college students who compose sentences like one that appeared in a campus newspaper: "A summary probation is when the convicted person is not required to report to a probation officer." Remember that nouns must be equated with nouns: "A summary probation is a *type of probation* in which the convicted person is not required to report to a probation officer."

defuse* or *diffuse*?   *Diffuse* ("scatter widely") is sometimes confused with *defuse* ("remove the fuse; make less dangerous, tense, or hostile").

Here's an example of such confusion from a *Chronicle of Higher Education* electronic-edition news item (8/24/1998): "The association released a new book on racial preferences in employment that the group's executive officer describes in the foreword as an effort 'to diffuse [should be *defuse*] the rhetoric by adding the perspective of empirical study.'"

degrees   See "academic degrees, titles, and departments."

deist* or *theist*?   *Deist* means someone who subscribes to deism, "the belief in a God who created the universe but assumed no control over it." *Theist* means someone who subscribes to theism, "the belief in a personal God as creator and ruler of the world."

***déjà vu*: seeing is believing**   This preferably italicized expression, which in French means "previously seen," emerged from early 20th-century psychology as a term for "the feeling that one has previously seen or experienced something that actually is being encountered for the first time."

Awareness of this psychological phenomenon can be traced at least as far back as the time of the ancient Greek philosopher Plato, who cited instances of the phenomenon as evidence of reincarnation—memories of a previous life.

Today, *déjà vu* is often used in the simple sense of "something previously seen or experienced." For example: Novelist-essayist Salman Rushdie wrote in a *New York Times* op-ed essay of 5/30/2002, "The present Kashmir crisis [bringing India and Pakistan to the brink of nuclear war] feels like a *déjà vu* replay of the last one."

The simple "seen before" sense of *déjà vu* has been given the blessing of leading dictionaries and *The Columbia Guide to Standard American English*. But you'll avoid the possibility of accusations of loose usage if you restrict *déjà vu* to its precise meaning, as the *illusion* of having seen or experienced something before.

delivery or **deliverance**?   Both these words once meant "rescue, liberation," as in being "delivered from temptation." Today, you may pray for *delivery* ("the carrying and turning over") of the check that is supposed to be in the mail, or you may pray for *deliverance* ("rescue, liberation") from junk mail.

delusion or **illusion**? *Delusion* means "a false *belief*," as in "delusions of grandeur."

Illusion means "a false *perception*," as in American journalist-politician Horace Greeley's Civil War–era observation that "the illusion that times that *were* are better than those that *are* has probably pervaded all ages."

deluxe or **de luxe**?   This French term, literally meaning "of luxury" and in practice meaning "particularly luxurious and elegant," is preferably spelled as one word in America.

demonetize, demonic, and **demotic**   *Demonetize* ("deprive of monetary value, as in withdrawing gold from use as money") is a negative derivative of the Latin *moneta* ("money").

Demonic ("fiendish, like a demon") comes from the Latin *daemon* ("evil spirit").

Demotic ("of the people" or "pertaining to the informal, everyday, popular form of a language") is related to *democracy* in the sense that both words were derived from the Greek *demos* ("the common people").

demur or demure?   *Demur* (which rhymes with *recur*) is a verb for "registering disagreement, raising objections, hesitating because of doubts."

Demure (which rhymes with *sure*) is an adjective for "reserved, modest, coy."

denouement or dénouement?   The accent mark for this word is acceptable but not needed. With or without the accent mark, *denouement* (derived from the French *dénouer*, meaning "to untie") is pronounced "day-noo-MAHN," and it means "the outcome of the plot of a novel, play or film, or the end result of a real-life sequence of events." "In the denouement," explains *The Oxford Companion to the English Language*, "mysteries are solved, errors rectified, misunderstandings explained, and rewards and penalties allocated."

Usage example: *The New York Times* reported (7/28/1998) that the investigation of President Clinton by independent counsel Kenneth W. Starr had "moved inexorably toward a denouement."

depart: never leave home without your preposition   Do not depart from the use of *from* with *depart*, as in the airline-schedule abbreviation "Depart Chicago 10:45 a.m." The phrase "Depart Chicago" illogically suggests that you are doing something to Chicago—taking it apart?—rather than just leaving it. (See also "*escape*.")

deplore or lament?   To *deplore* is "to express disapproval about somebody's behavior." To *lament* is "to mourn, often publicly and loudly."

deprecate or depreciate?   Dictionaries record the fact that these words are sometimes used as synonyms of "belittle, mildly disparage." But such usage invites confusion and criticism. To avoid those risks, use *deprecate* in the sense of "to express disapproval of," and use *depreciate* in the sense of "to lessen the value or price of." People who lack self-esteem often make *self-deprecating* comments; sellers are distressed to find that their property has *depreciated* since they bought it.

de rigueur's requirements   The adjective *de rigueur* ("required by fashion, etiquette, or custom") is a French import that should be pronounced "duh ree-

GUR." It is often mispronounced by English-speaking users as if it began with the sound of "day," and it is often misspelled by those who aren't aware that *rigueur* has two *u*'s.

Usage example from *Harper's Bazaar* (10/1998): "I try to imagine myself . . . wearing what it was de rigueur [fashionable] to wear only 15 years ago."

derisive or derisory?   Both these adjectives mean "mocking, jeering, scoffing." But you should save *derisory* for its separate meaning: "ridiculous, worthy of derision [ridicule]." People who make *derisory* remarks might expect *derisive* laughter in return.

desert or dessert?   A "free desert" was featured in a restaurant sign reproduced in a *Los Angeles Times* bloopers column (5/13/2004), along with this sarcastic comment: "You wonder, how do they get it on that little cart?" What the restaurant intended to offer, of course, was a free *dessert*—not a huge *desert* such as the Sahara.

Remind yourself to use two *s*'s—one for "sweet" and one for "sugary"—when you are referring to the final course of a meal. Our name for that end-of-the-meal course, *dessert,* comes from the French *desservir* ("unserve, clear the table").

If you *desert* ("abandon") somebody, you leave that person in a *deserted* condition, as if in a *desert*, an area in which environmental conditions (such as lack of rainfall) prevent the existence of most or all forms of life. Note that a desert is not necessarily a place that is hot. (See also "*just deserts* aren't fattening.")

despite the fact that   A long-winded way of saying *although*.

destiny: can yours be mastered?   Politicians give you false hope when they urge you to master your *destiny*, according to language columnist Edwin Newman. In a Newman column reprinted in his 1988 book, *I Must Say*, he observed: "Nobody, not even presidents of the United States, can determine, decide, or improve his destiny or anyone else's. *Destiny* is, by definition, inevitable. . . . That is what the word means."

You'll find confirmation of Newman's position in Paul W. Lovinger's year-2000 *Penguin Dictionary of American English Usage*, and in the current dictionary definitions of *destiny* by Merriam-Webster ("a predetermined course of events"), American Heritage ("the preordained or inevitable course of events considered as something beyond the power or control of man"), and Oxford ("that which is destined or fated to happen").

If you decide to run for office as a destiny-buster, you may want to cite the somewhat elastic definitions of *destiny* by *Webster's New World College Dictionary* ("the *seemingly* [italics added here and in next quote] inevitable or necessary succession of events") and the Random House dictionaries ("the predetermined, *usually* inevitable or irresistible, course of events").

One of the most enlightening definitions of *destiny* was penned in 1911 by social critic Ambrose Bierce in his *Devil's Dictionary*: "A tyrant's authority for crime and a fool's excuse for failure."

destroy is destructive enough *Destroy* should not be qualified by a word like *completely* or *partially*, because destruction means "complete elimination." For the same reason, don't completely or partially *demolish* or *annihilate*.

devalued words Thanks to generations of exaggerated claims from advertising and show business, almost nobody is awed by the *amazing*, the *fabulous*, or the *fantastic*. Almost nobody is impressed by the *stupendous*, the *tremendous*, or the *colossal*. Almost nobody marvels at the *marvelous*, wonders at the *wonderful*, or thrills to the *thrilling*. Almost nobody dreads the *dreadful*, is appalled by the *appalling*, is horrified by the *horrible*, or is terrified by the *terrible*.

The devaluation of some of our most powerful words would be remarkable ("attracting notice for being extraordinary") if *remarkable* itself had not been reduced to the level of a meaningless filler. (See also entries for *awesome, fabulous, incredible, ubiquitous,* and *unique*.)

device or devise? Be careful to distinguish the noun *device* ("a thing made for a particular purpose") from the verb *devise* ("contrive, plan, invent").

diagnosis: not good for patients Never ask a physician to diagnose a patient. A physician is trained to diagnose a patient's *condition*.

dialect: in the ear of the beholder? No matter how you use the word *dialect*, you may be accused of using it incorrectly.

Dictionaries define *dialect* as a geographical, occupational, or class variety of a language, differing from the standard variety in such aspects as pronunciation, vocabulary, and grammar. That seems clear until you start applying *dialect* to the real world. For example, is Standard American English actually a dialect of what we Americans call British English? If American English is really a language, with its own dialects, at what point do those dialects qualify as languages? Does a dialect become a language, as has been cynically suggested, only when the people who use the dialect form their own army?

Another problem: In some usage, based on dictionary definitions that list *dialect* as *non*standard, *dialect* is just a linguistic classification. In other usage, based on dictionary definitions that list *dialect* as *sub*standard, the word *dialect* is an insult. Note that *The Associated Press Stylebook* contains the following warning: "Quoting dialect, unless used carefully, implies substandard or illiterate usage."

Suggestion: You might want to follow the example set by the authors of *The Story of English*, the companion volume to the PBS television series of that name. They avoided the fuzziness and the derogatory implications of the word *dialect* by replacing that term with the simple, neutral word *variety.*

dialectal, dialectic, or **dialectical?** Both *dialectical* and *dialetic* can mean "regional language variation," but linguists prefer *dialectal.* If you go along with that preference, you can save *dialectic* for its role as a noun meaning "the practice of logical argumentation," and you can save *dialectical* for its role as an adjective meaning "of or pertaining to logical argumentation."

dialogue debates On the question of spelling, American and British dictionaries list *dialogue* as the most common form and *dialog* as the variant form.

On the question of meaning, *dialogue* denotes "a conversation, often including a discussion of conflicting views, between two or more persons." Some usage commentators have insisted that *dialogue* be limited to two, on the grounds that the word begins with a prefix meaning "two," the Greek *di-.* But *dialogue* actually begins with the Greek prefix *dia-,* which has such meanings as "through" and "across."

On the question of using *dialogue* as a verb, the risk-free answer is to refrain. You can find the verb *dialogue* in dictionaries and even in the works of Shakespeare, Coleridge, and Carlyle. But you would be wise to take your cue from the fact that this usage has been rejected as bureaucratic by 98 percent of the usage panel of *The American Heritage Dictionary*.

diaspora or *Diaspora*?   The word *Diaspora*, which was derived from a Greek word for dispersion, originally referred to the forced expulsion and dispersion of the Jews from Israel in the sixth century B.C.

Today, the uncapitalized *diaspora* refers to the communities of Jews still living in nations outside of Israel or to other communities of people living outside their traditional homeland. For example, an article in *The New York Times* (1/10/1998) focused on "the Kurdish diaspora," consisting of the stateless Kurds dispersed through parts of Turkey, Iraq, Iran, and Syria. The word *diaspora* is also used for the widespread dispersion of an entity such as a language or a culture.

dichotomy: long division   *Dichotomy* has long been established as a scientific term for "division into two parts." In nontechnical usage, as leading dictionaries attest, *dichotomy* is used in the sense of "division into two parts that are sharply distinguished, opposed, or contradictory."

Nontechnical usage example from *The Oxford Guide to English Usage*: "An absolute dichotomy between science and reason on the one hand and faith and poetry on the other."

Dickens: a man of his words   From memorable characters in the novels of Charles Dickens (1812–1870), we speak of a *Scrooge* ("miser") and a *Fagin* ("trainer of thieves"). From the names of other Dickens characters, we have the adjectives *Micawberish* ("exhibiting seemingly unjustified optimism"), *Pecksniffian* ("pretending to have high moral principles, hypocritical"), and *Pickwickian* ("of the use of words or ideas in a sense different from the usual one").

Dickensian refers to Dickens' literature or the cruel conditions and treatment of the poor, especially children, portrayed in his novels. (See also next entry.)

dickens is devilish   There is nothing Dickensian about the lowercase *dickens* in such expressions as "a dickens of a scolding" and "What the dickens!" That *dickens* is a euphemism for *devil*, judging from its first known use in Shakespeare's *Merry Wives of Windsor*: "I cannot tell what the dickens his name is."

diction: take your choice   What does it mean if people are praised for their *diction*?

Benét's Reader's Encyclopedia defines *diction* as "word choice, with all that such choice implies in questions of correctness, clarity and style." That source and Follett's *Modern American Usage* acknowledge that *diction* is often popularly equated with "correctness and clarity of word *pronunciation*" but should be restricted to its original meaning of word *choice*.

The Merriam-Webster, Random House, and American Heritage dictionaries, as well as *The New Oxford American Dictionary* and *The Oxford English Dictionary*, list both definitions.

If you use this tricky word, make sure your intended meaning is unmistakable, as in this example: A *Wall Street Journal* essay (4/9/1998) about the 100th anniversary of the birth of singer-actor Paul Robeson recalled "his splendid diction" as the star of Shakespeare's *Othello*. Obviously, *The Wall Street Journal* meant *diction* to be interpreted as word pronunciation, inasmuch as the excellent word *choices* had been made centuries earlier by Shakespeare.

dictionary definition lineup   Definitions are listed in historical order in *The Oxford English Dictionary*, *Webster's New World College Dictionary*, and *Merriam-Webster's Collegiate Dictionary*. As *Webster's New World* notes, "The most common present-day meaning of a word may appear near the end of an entry." The *Random House Webster's College Dictionary* starts with "the most frequently encountered" meaning. *The American Heritage Dictionary* begins with "the central and often the most frequently sought meaning of a word."

Your dictionary, like your computer, should not be used until you've studied its instructions.

dictionaries: use them for more than a spell   People who use dictionaries only as spell-checkers are missing out on other important dictionary services.

Dictionaries show how a word or words in an expression (such as *déjà vu*) should be pronounced, broken into syllables, and placed in a sentence. Dictionaries tell what preposition a word may require and what part or parts of speech the word may "perform." Dictionaries identify a word's "inflected" forms, which means forms of the word that reflect various grammatical functions, such as the plurals and possessives of nouns, past-tense forms of verbs, or the comparative and superlative forms of adjectives (as in the comparative *braver* and the superlative *bravest*). Dictionaries classify verbs as transitive (requiring a direct object, as with *mention*), intransitive (*not* requiring a direct object, as with *recline*), or both. Dictionaries classify words as standard, non-standard, colloquial (informal), slang, archaic (old-fashioned), or vulgar or otherwise offensive. Many dictionaries provide listings about people and places.

And, oh yes, dictionaries list word meanings—as well as words (synonyms) with meanings that are similar to the one you happen to look up.

dictionaries: Webster's name is fair game   If someone tells you to "look it up in Webster's," ask "Which one?" The name *Webster's* can be attached to any dictionary, contrary to a widespread public misconception reinforced by articles such as one by a *Los Angeles Times* staff writer (8/23/1996) that referred to "Merriam-Webster Inc., publisher of Webster's dictionaries." Merriam-Webster publishes only the *Merriam-Webster* dictionaries. That company is not responsible for all the other dictionaries adorned with the name *Webster's*.

Noah Webster—a Connecticut farm boy who fought in the Revolution and became a lawyer, educator, and journalist dedicated to the cause of establishing a distinctly American culture—helped establish the identity of the American language by producing the seventy-thousand-word, two-volume *American Dictionary of the English Language* (1828). Upon Webster's death in 1843, the publishing rights to his dictionary were purchased by George and Charles Merriam, who in 1847 published a revision edited by Noah Webster's son-in-law, Professor Chauncey A. Goodrich of Yale College. That revision became the first Merriam-Webster unabridged dictionary. According to *The New York Times*, the Merriam-Webster company never registered the separate name *Webster*, and therefore the name "quickly entered the public domain, available to anybody who wants to use it."

Today's many varieties of Webster's—in addition to Merriam-Webster's unabridged and collegiate dictionaries—include the *Random House Webster's College Dictionary*, the *Random House Webster's Unabridged Dictionary*, Simon & Schuster's *Webster's New World College Dictionary*, *Webster's II New Riverside University Dictionary*, *The New Lexicon Webster's Dictionary of the English Language*, and *Webster's New Universal Unabridged Dictionary*.

dietician or **dietitian?**   The preferred spelling for a specialist in *dietetics* ("the study of nutrition") is *dietitian*. Memory tip: *Dietitian* provides *t* for two.

different may make no difference   The adjective *different* after a number—as in "three different countries"—is usually redundant.

Different should be removed from "three different countries" because countries obviously differ from one another. Likewise, anyone who talks about visiting Boston "three different times" is being redundant because repeated visits anywhere occur at different times. And it's redundant to talk about "renting three different movies," because people presumably don't rent multiple copies of the same movie.

Use *different* after a number only when you want to emphasize the *difference* ("Three different desserts will be served at the dinner") or the *number* ("Norman Thomas campaigned for the presidency six different times").

different from or different than?   As Paul W. Lovinger wrote in his *Penguin Dictionary of American English Usage and Style,* "You cannot go wrong with *different from.*" In similar fashion, Harry Shaw wrote in his *Errors in English and Ways to Correct Them,* "[Always] use *different from* and be safe, never sorry."

To be "safe, never sorry," use the preposition *than* to follow adjectives that express the comparative degree—as in smaller, larger, shorter, taller, slower, faster *than.* But for the adjective *different,* which expresses a contrast but not the comparative degree, use the preposition *from.* Risk-free usage examples: "That house is *newer than* the other houses in the neighborhood, which explains why the house looks *different from* the others."

Though *different than* is widely used in speech, its use in writing is rejected by language critics as "incorrect" (according to *The American Heritage Book of English Usage*), as "inferior" (according to *Garner's Modern American Usage*), and as "nonstandard" (according to Follett's *Modern American Usage*). The *Associated Press Stylebook* states without comment that "*different* takes the proposition *from,* not *than.*"

Another prescriber of *different from, The New York Times Manual of Style and Usage,* acknowledges that some authorities accept *different than* as necessary before a clause, as in "Newspaper writing is different than it was 25 years ago." But that manual and other usage sources recommend that such sentences be changed so that *different from* can be justified by being placed before a noun: "Newspaper writing is different from what [or the way] it was 25 years ago." (See also "*as* and *than* comparisons need to be complete.")

dilapidated: a word of caution   Merriam-Webster researchers report that this word for "fallen into partial ruin or decay" has "very occasionally" been spelled *delapidated* since the 17th century. But that is considered a misspelling.

dilemma: a problem only if you make it so   A *dilemma* is not just a problem, predicament, or difficult choice, according to usage commentators. In line with the word's traditional use, illustrated by the phrase "on the horns of a dilemma," they say a *dilemma* is a problem involving "a choice between two equally undesirable alternatives" (for example, the choice between a tax increase and a reduction in public-safety services).

Dilemma has had that meaning since the mid-17th century, when the word emerged in everyday English from a Greek-derived term in rhetoric for "an argument that forces an opponent to choose one of two unfavorable alternatives."

Merriam-Webster wordwatchers, in their *Dictionary of English Usage*, contend that today's popular use of *dilemma* as a simple synonym for *problem* is now as acceptable as the traditional "horns of a dilemma" usage. But if you violate the "horns of a dilemma" definition, you will be defying such sources as *The Oxford English Dictionary*, Fowler's *Dictionary of Modern English Usage*, *The New Fowler's Modern English Usage*, Follett's *Modern American Usage*, Bernstein's *Careful Writer*, Ciardi's *Second Browser's Dictionary*, Garner's *Modern American Usage*, Lovinger's *Penguin Dictionary of American English Usage and Style*, 74 percent of the usage panel of *The American Heritage Dictionary*, and the stylebook editors of *The New York Times*, *The Washington Post*, *The Wall Street Journal*, and the Associated Press.

diplomates are not spouses of diplomats   Diploma, a Latin word for "document that serves as a letter of introduction," spawned our English *diploma* ("document introducing someone who has completed a course of study") as well as our word *diplomat* ("someone who traditionally receives a letter introducing that person as an ambassador or other person skilled in tactful negotiation").

A *diplomate* is "a physician or other professional with a diploma showing board certification in a specialty."

disassemble or dissemble?   *Disassemble* means "take apart." *Dissemble* means "feign, act hypocritically, disguise the real nature of, give a false or misleading appearance to."

disassociate or dissociate?　The risk-free answer is *dissociate.*

As *The Oxford English Dictionary* notes, the verb *disassociate* ("to withdraw from association") entered the language in 1603, with its shorter variant, *dissociate,* emerging 20 years later. Today, *dissociate* is more frequently used, according to *Merriam-Webster's Dictionary of English Usage,* the *World Almanac Guide to Good Word Usage,* and *The Columbia Guide to Standard American English.* The longer version, now listed in dictionaries as a variant of the shorter version, is described as "needless" by Follett's *Modern American Usage* and as "widely condemned" by *The New Fowler's Modern English Usage.*

Usage example: *The New York Times* (10/21/2000) reported that former president Jimmy Carter had decided "to dissociate himself from" the national Southern Baptist Convention, the country's largest Protestant denomination, because parts of its "increasingly rigid" doctrines violated the "basic premises of [his] Christian faith."

disc jockeys should never play floppy disks　The spelling question—*disc* or *disk?*—has no answer that will please everybody.

The Associated Press Stylebook prescribes *disc,* except for the *disks* involved with computers. The stylebooks of *The Washington Post* and the *Los Angeles Times,* along with the *Harper Dictionary of Contemporary Usage,* prescribe *disk,* except for the *discs* used in sound recordings. *The New York Times Manual of Style and Usage* tells its writers to use "*disk,* not *disc,*" except for *discotheque.* Dictionaries are neutral, and Copperud's *American Usage and Style* dismissed the distinction between *disc* and *disk* as "a useless one."

Suggestion: To reduce your risk of offending people who may care about this spelling question, use *disc* for sound recordings and *disk* for computer products. Also, try not to write about anything *else* that is thin, flat, and circular.

disclose, divulge, and reveal only what's been hidden　The Postal Service does not *disclose, divulge,* or *reveal* the current price of postage stamps. But it will freely give that information to anyone who asks. *Disclose, divulge,* and *reveal* apply only to the telling of information that has been kept secret.

discomfit or discomfort?　The verbs *discomfit* and *discomfort* are commonly used interchangeably. But careful communicators observe the distinctions cited in dictionaries.

As distinguished from *discomfort* ("to make uncomfortable"), the word *discomfit* has the sense of "confuse, baffle, disconcert, perplex, embarrass." A houseguest is *discomforted* by a lopsided chair and *discomfited* if the chair collapses.

Discomfit is sometimes equated with "foil, thwart, frustrate the plans of," and a few writers still use *discomfit* in its archaic sense of "vanquish, rout, defeat in battle." Unlike *discomfort*, the word *discomfit* changes form as a noun: *discomfiture* ("confusion, embarrassment").

discover, invent, or develop?   Physicist Albert Einstein *discovered* laws of physics that enabled physicist Theodore H. Maiman to *invent* the laser. Maiman's invention, in turn, enabled engineers to *develop* today's many laser devices and applications.

discreet or discrete?   Separate the *e*'s in *discreet* ("showing good judgment, capable of preserving prudent silence") and you get a word with a distinctly separate meaning. *Discrete* means "distinctly separate, detached, distinct." Example: "The energy of light is transmitted not in a continuous stream but in *discrete* particles called photons."

When using the lesser known of this soundalike pair, *discrete*, you obviously need to make sure your meaning is clear from your context. The noun from *discrete* is *discreteness*, and of course the noun from *discreet* is *discretion*.

Warning: If you want to say that some things are not *discrete*, you'd better say exactly that instead of using the authentic but easily misunderstood *indiscrete*.

discrepancy or disparity?   A *discrepancy* ("inconsistency") may be discovered between the defendant's testimony and that person's statement to police. The defense attorney may stress the *disparity* ("marked inequality") between the formidable financial resources of the prosecution and the limited financial resources of the defense.

discriminating or discriminatory?   The meaning of the adjective *discriminatory*—"prejudiced"—is unmistakable.

But the adjective/verb *discriminating* suggests either "prejudice" or "excellent judgment in making distinctions." Anyone who uses *discriminating* must employ excellent judgment to make sure that the intended meaning is clear.

disinterested: a word of caution   Be careful where you use *disinterested*. Word connoisseurs will recognize this adjective as a compliment, meaning "not motivated by self-interest and therefore impartial." But other people will assume *disinterested* means "uninterested, indifferent." If you suspect that your audience will misinterpret *disinterested*, substitute the word *impartial*.

The word *disinterested* actually began as a synonym for *uninterested*, in the 17th century. *Disinterested* didn't acquire its sense of impartiality until the 18th century. Then *uninterested* crept back as an alternative meaning of *disinterested* in the early 20th century. And the revived old use of *disinterested* as a synonym for *uninterested* has become so widespread that you'll find it as an alternate definition in many of today's dictionaries.

disorient or disorientate?   See "*orient or orientate?*"

dissatisfied or unsatisfied?   If you are *dissatisfied* ("displeased, discontented") with something, you definitely do not like it. If you're *unsatisfied* ("unfulfilled, unappeased"), your only problem may be that you did not get enough.

dissension or dissent?   If you turn up the volume on *dissent* ("a difference of opinion"), you get *dissension* ("partisan and contentious quarreling").

distasteful or tasteless?   *Distasteful* means "causing or showing dislike." *Tasteless* means "having or showing a lack of taste." (See also "*tasty* history.")

distinct, distinctive, or distinguished?   *Distinct* can mean "easily or notably distinguishable from others," "easily perceived or unmistakable," or "very likely." Make sure your context clearly communicates your meaning, as in "Her promotion is a distinct [very likely] possibility."

Don't frustrate your reader by writing that something is *distinct from* ("different from") something else unless you proceed to identify the difference. Here's an example of such frustrating communication from an information-technology report: "*Agent*-based access management systems are distinct from *proxy*-based access management systems." That sentence tells readers what they can conclude by themselves—that systems with different names are different. But the writer leaves the reader in the dark about what that difference consists of.

Distinctive means "standing out [because it is easily distinguishable from others]." *Distinguished* means "outstanding [in the sense of *superior*]." Usage example: "An insecure person may drive a *distinctive* car in the hope that others will think he is *distinguished*."

dived or **dove?**   If the past tense of *drive* is *drove*, should the past tense of *dive* be *dove*? Although formal usage favors *dived*, some usage commentators approve both. Others regard *dove* as an error.

Your risk-free choice is *dived* ("She dived into the pool"). And that is your *only* choice for the past participle ("She had dived before").

dock: don't wait on it   Dictionaries list *dock* as "the water-filled space between two piers, used for receiving a ship while in port." In that sense, an arriving ship slips "into a dock." So, if you are going to meet one of the passengers, you'd better not try to wait on the dock.

Some of our dictionaries, reflecting a common American usage, include a definition of *dock* as a synonym for *pier*. But the only way to be risk-free on this matter is to wait on a *pier* until the boat *docks*.

doesn't or **don't?**   The answer to this question illustrates the changing nature of "right" and "wrong" in language usage.

When *don't* emerged in the 17th century, it was used as a contraction for both *do not* and *does not*. Hence, leading writers for hundreds of years used expressions such as "he don't" and "she don't." That usage gradually became "wrong" after the emergence of a new contraction, *doesn't*, in the 19th century.

Don Quixote and his adjective   Four centuries have elapsed since Spanish novelist Miguel de Cervantes penned *Don Quixote de la Mancha*. But time has not dulled the vivid impression left by this comedic story of a country gentleman so crazed by reading the popular romances of chivalry that he convinces himself he is a knight who is destined to ride off to right the wrongs of the world.

In the most famous misadventure of Don Quixote ("key-HOAT-ee"), he encounters a group of windmills that he thinks are "monstrous giants." When he tilts at (uses his lance to attack) one of the windmills, the lance gets stuck in the sail, and he is lifted up and then thrown down in humiliating defeat. That scene inspired a widely used phrase, *tilt at windmills*, which means "to take on impossible or ridiculous challenges."

All such behavior of Don Quixote inspired the adjective *quixotic* ("kwik-SOT-ik") which means "caught up in the pursuit of unreachable goals, driven by impractical idealism." Usage example: The *Los Angeles Times* (6/18/2000) referred to consumer advocate Ralph Nader's "quixotic quest for president on the Green Party ticket." (See also "Kafka and his adjective," "Lucullus and his adjective," "Proteus and his adjective," and "Sisyphus and his adjective.")

donut* or *doughnut? *Donut* is an informal spelling variant of *doughnut*.

dos and don'ts* or *do's and don'ts? *The New York Times Manual of Style and Usage* prescribes *dos and don'ts*, maintaining that one should "use no apostrophes to form the plurals of . . . words being discussed as objects." But some style guides—*Words Into Type*, for instance—support the use of an apostrophe in forming the plural of such words. Note that if, for clarity, you use an apostrophe before the *s* in *do's*, the apostrophe already present in the contraction *don't* makes it unnecessary to add an extra one before the *s* in *don'ts*. (See also "apostrophes that show signs of abuse.")

***dotage* and *dote*: too much and too little** The verb *dote* can mean "to show excessive fondness habitually" (as in parents who dote on a particular child to the exclusion of others) or "to show a decline of mental faculties" (usually as a result of senility). Likewise, the noun *dotage* can mean "the showing of excessive fondness" or "the showing of a decline of mental faculties."

If you want to go with the flow of current usage, let *dote* have the sense of "too much," and let *dotage* have the sense of "too little," as in the decline of mental faculties.

double comparison Doubly emphatic comparisons were acceptable when penned by Shakespeare. In Shakespeare's *Julius Caesar*, for example, Antony refers to the wound given to Caesar by his good friend Brutus as "the *most unkindest* cut of all." But thanks largely to objections raised by 18th-century grammarians, *more* and *most* gradually came to be regarded as redundant when used with adjective forms that already express the comparative (*-er* endings) or superlative (*-est* endings) degree.

In another use of once-standard double comparison, Shakespeare frequently added intensity to *worse*—employing a form, *worser*, that today is considered a mark of an inadequate education.

double entendre or *double entente*?

Double entente—a rarely used import from France that we italicize and pronounce with its French accent, "doo-blahn-TAHNT"—literally means "double understanding" and by extension denotes "a double-meaning word or phrase."

Double entendre, a *former* French way of saying "double understanding," is used today only in English, to convey the idea of "a play on words in which the secondary meaning is risqué."

Given that *double entendre* is considered fake French, you have your choice of pretending it is French by italicizing it and pronouncing it "doo-blahn-TAHN-dra" or dropping the italics and using the more honest pronunciation, "*double* ahn-TAHN-dra."

double negatives that are a no-no

Double negatives such as "I don't have none" were used from Chaucer to Shakespeare and beyond as a form of emphatic negation. But, because two negatives make a positive in the logic of *Latin* grammar, Latin-trained 18th-century English grammarians rejected emphatic double negatives as illogical. Subsequently, English and American usage commentators adopted the view that emphatic double negatives are "nonstandard."

Today, emphatic double negatives are sometimes used for dramatic effect. For example: According to *Parade* magazine (8/2/1997), comedian Rodney Dangerfield "built an enormously successful career" with his double-negative punch line, "I don't get no respect." But as noted in *Merriam-Webster's Dictionary of English Usage*, the emphatic double negative "is [now] widely perceived as a rustic or uneducated form." If you use that form, don't expect respect.

double negatives that are not unacceptable

A phrase such as *not unacceptable* is a grammatically acceptable double negative called a *litotes* ("LIGHT-o-tease"), which is Greek for "understatement for effect." A litotes is defined as a deliberately weak positive expressed by the negative of its opposite.

Examples: According to *The Salt Lake Tribune* (4/I5/2000), "Not unlike what has happened in the United States, fathers in [Cuba] are staking a claim to the [traditionally maternal] role of caregiver." A *Smithsonian* article (August 2000) stated that the raccoon-like ringtail "cat" is "not uncommon in metropolitan areas."

It is not unworthy of notice that litotes, like the "not unworthy" phrase at the beginning of this sentence, is overused in pretentious communication. Use litotes only when understatement for effect is not uncalled for.

If you become addicted to litotes, you'll find a recommended cure in a footnote to George Orwell's *Politics and the English Language* (1946). Orwell suggested that you memorize this sentence: "A not unblack dog was chasing a not unsmall rabbit across a not ungreen field."

double passive   See "passive voice should not be silenced."

double possessive   See "possessives that double up."

dour* rhymes with *cure   But it is not easy to cure someone who is *dour* ("stern, harsh, forbidding, gloomy, silently ill-humored").

***downhill* can go both ways**   Beware of saying "It's all downhill from here." That could mean that a situation is going to be increasingly better (you'll be coasting) or increasingly worse (everything is deteriorating).

***downstage* or *upstage*?**   *Downstage* is the front part of a stage, close to the audience. *Upstage* is the rear part of a stage, away from the audience.

Ever wonder why we use *upstage* as a verb meaning "to steal attention from someone else"? Wouldn't an actor attract more attention by moving to the front? The answer is that by moving to the rear, the actor can force the other performer in a dialogue to face away from the audience.

Draco and his adjective   Draco ("DRAY-ko") was an Athenian legislator who in 62I b.c. was supposedly responsible for developing a code of criminal law that became known for its cruel severity.

Draco's reputation survives today in the adjective *draconian* ("drah-KO-nian"), which means "extremely harsh." For example, *U.S. News & World Report* (3/20/2000) published an article about the anticipated extension of the human life span, quoting some ethicists who "foresee a dangerous future where overpopulation leads to draconian rules about childbearing."

Dr. Dryasdust and his adjective   The adjective *dryasdust* ("pedantically boring") is from Dr. Jonas Dryasdust, a fictitious pedant satirized in the prefaces of some of the novels of Scottish novelist-poet Sir Walter Scott (1771–1832).

drink, drank, drunk, drunken   "He decided not to *drink* today, because yesterday he *drank* until he realized that he *had drunk* too much as a result of being with *drunken revelers*."

The *Random House Webster's Unabridged Dictionary* says, "Perhaps because of the association of *drunk* with intoxication, *drank* is widely used as a past participle in speech by educated persons and must be considered an alternate standard form." Example: "By noon, the children at the party *had drank* [technically, should be *had drunk*] all the soda."

drowned or was drowned?   Use *was drowned* only if the drowning involved foul play.

drug the verb is no drag   *The Salt Lake Tribune* (3/22/2000) quoted the vice president of a Utah firearms company as charging that a major gun manufacturer had been "politically drug [should have been *dragged*] into giving away their own rights" by agreeing to a government safety proposal that included childproof locks.

In Standard English, the verb *drug* means not *drag* but "administer a drug."

dryad or dyad?   In Greek mythology, the word *dryad* (from the Greek word *drys* for "oak") at first meant "oak-tree nymph" and then "tree nymph"—a nature goddess who dwelled within, and protected, trees. A story about the ill-fated love between a dryad named Eurydice and the musician Orpheus has been celebrated in many operas and dramas.

A *dyad* is a pair of individuals maintaining a sociologically significant relationship.

dryer or drier?   *Dryer* is the preferred spelling for "a device that dries." That leaves *drier* for "more dry."

dubious doubts   The adjective *dubious* has five flavors of doubt: just plain "doubtful," "causing doubt," "of doubtful [questionable] quality or character," "of doubtful [unpredictable] outcome," and "inclined to doubt [wavering in opinion]."

You will need to rely on your context to convey your intended meaning. For example, *dubious* clearly meant "of doubtful quality" in a *New York Times* article (2/3/2001) about a report attributing television's inaccurate election-night coverage of the Bush-Gore race to "dubious polls and the competition to be first in calling winners."

due to circumstances you can control   Back in 1965, Lucile V. Payne said in her *Lively Art of Writing* that *due to* should be completely avoided, on the grounds of being a "graceless phrase, even when used correctly." A quarter century later, in 2003, Bryan A. Garner said in *Garner's Modern American Usage* that people who take pride in their writing style "may wish" to take Payne's advice and thus "avoid even correct uses of the phrase."

Graceless or not, *due to* is still widely used today. So you'd better know about the *due to* usage approved by "all grammarians," according to Paul W. Lovinger's year-2000 *Penguin Dictionary of American English Usage and Style*. In that regard, you will be in the Risk-Free Zone for the phrase *due to* if you use it only in the adjectival sense of "caused by," usually following some form of the verb *to be* (*is, are, was,* and so on). Example: The *Los Angeles Times* (8/12/1994) quoted a meteorologist as saying that a near-record heat wave was "due to [caused by] a strong high pressure system."

Now, let's examine "incorrect" use: You may encounter what *The Columbia Guide to Standard American English* calls "a residue of [linguistically] conservative unhappiness" if you join the many people who use *due to* as a compound preposition meaning "because of." Example of disputed usage: A Tennessee roadblock sign—photographed by *The New York Times* (6/18/2003)—said "ROAD CLOSED DUE TO FOG."

The New York Public Library Writer's Guide to Style and Usage says the "because of" use of *due to* is "well on its way to standard status because of widespread, long-established usage." But the guide adds that "careful writers" still use *due to* only for "caused by."

Usage advice: If you decide *due to* is worth the risk of being called graceless, you might at least restrict its use to the sense of "caused by," to avoid the risk of being called careless. So, remember that "most accidents are *due to* [caused by] carelessness."

due to the fact that is usually too much ado   Try replacing *due to the fact that* with *because*, as in "They were late due to the fact that [because] their car had a flat tire."

dumb requires smarts   Don't attempt to use *dumb* in its original sense of "lacking the power or speech," as in "deaf, dumb, and blind." The word is now irreversibly associated with stupidity. People who cannot speak should be called *mute*.

Dumpster should not be trashed   Newspapers frequently make the mistake of lowercasing *Dumpster*, which is the trademark name for a brand of large metal bin designed to be hoisted onto a specially equipped truck for emptying or hauling away. (See also "*yo-yo* and *zipper*: why they're in the same entry.")

Dutch courage   This is an ethnic insult, meaning "courage from drinking liquor." According to the *Encarta World English Dictionary*: "Derogatory expressions containing *Dutch* stem from the rivalry between the Dutch and the English in the 17th and 18th centuries." (See also "ethnic verbs: a form of group libel.")

Dutch designations   The adjective *Dutch*, of course, means "of or relating to the Netherlands [Holland]." But the word's original meaning—"of or relating to Germany, Austria, Switzerland, and the Low Countries [the Netherlands, Belgium, and Luxembourg]"—explains the continued use of *Pennsylvania Dutch* for certain Americans of German descent.

dyeing or dying?   Some people are *dying* to see what happens to their social life if they use *dye* ("coloring matter") for *dyeing* their hair. Note that *dyeing*, the word for "coloring," includes *dye*, the word for "coloring matter."

E

each: singular or plural?   Think of the pronoun *each* as "each one." That will remind you to correctly say "each [one] *is*" rather than "each [one] *are*." That also applies to the phrase *each and every*, as in "Each and every [one] lawmaker ideally serves [not *serve*] only the public."

Some usage commentators condone—others condemn—the use of *each* as if it meant *all* in phrases such as "Each [all] *of them* vote." You should be safe from criticism if you keep thinking of *each* as singular: "Each [one] of them *votes*."

The use of *each* as an *adjective* requires a singular noun ("each *member*"). But when the adjective *each* follows a subject that's plural, the verb agrees with the plural subject: "The *members* each *contribute* to the club's charity." (See also "*everyone* and *everybody*: singular or plural?")

each and every: are they both necessary?   The emphatic phrase *each and every*—as in "Each and every one of us must protect the environment"—has been widely used by writers but widely condemned by usage critics.

Most of the condemnation focuses on the phrase's redundancy, given that the word *each* and the word *every* convey the same message. But—according to *Merriam-Webster's Dictionary of English Usage* and Roy H. Copperud's *American Usage and Style*—the phrase *each and every* has also been denounced by the critics as a cliché, a pomposity, and a bit of bureaucratic bombast. And the last three editions of Strunk and White's *Elements of Style* contemptuously dismissed the phrase as "pitchman's jargon."

Risk-free advice: As lawyer-lexicographer Bryan A. Garner writes in his *Modern American Usage*, "Unless you need a special emphasis, avoid this trite phrase."

each other or one another?   Despite deep-seated disagreement about this question, you can't go wrong if you apply *each other* to two people and *one another* to more than two.

In compliance with that rule, two friends help *each other*, but (to quote author Jared Diamond's op-ed essay in *The New York Times*, 1/1/2005) the various Mayan kings "had to concentrate on fighting one another."

These compound pronouns—expressing a reciprocal action or relationship—have been used interchangeably by distinguished writers for more than four hundred years. And today's widespread continuation of that interchangeable usage is endorsed by *The Columbia Guide to Standard American English, Webster's New World Guide to Current American Usage, The New Fowler's Modern English Usage,* and the editors of the Random House and Merriam-Webster dictionaries. And apparently nobody was linguistically outraged by a *Newsweek* report (1/17/2005) that "Hollywood's reigning golden couple," Brad Pitt and Jennifer Aniston, had issued a joint statement of separation in which they professed continuing "love and admiration for one another." But usage sources including 64 percent of the *American Heritage Dictionary* usage panel and the stylebooks of the Associated Press and *The New York Times* follow an 1823 British grammar-book rule requiring that *each other* refer to two persons and that *one another* refer to more than two.

each other's or **each others'?**   The answer is always *each other's*: "The two children shared each other's [not *each others'*] toys." You can't pluralize the possessive of *each other* because *each other* itself does not exist as a plural. Romeo and Juliet loved each other, not each others.

Likewise, the possessive of *one another* is *one another's*, never *one anothers'*. Good neighbors help one another, not one anothers.

eager or **anxious?**   See "*anxious* or *eager*?"

Earth or **earth?**   *Earth* is properly capitalized when it is viewed as part of the cosmos ("The astronauts photographed *Earth*") but otherwise lowercase ("heaven and *earth*").

earthly or **earthy?**   *Earthly* is used mostly to mean "of the earth as opposed to heavenly or divine," as in "earthly pleasures." But it can also mean "possible, conceivable," as in "no earthly excuse."

The word *earthy* can mean "uninhibited in the sense of natural" or "uninhibited in the sense of being crude or off-color," as in "an earthy sense of humor."

easy **does it**   Aside from being an adjective (as in "easy street"), *easy* is acceptable as an adverb in such idiomatic expressions as *Easy does it, Take it easy*, and *Easy come, easy go.*

Usage example of *easy* as an adverb: *The Wall Street Journal* editorialized (1/15/2004) that "no one can say that business scandal culprits are getting off easy." (See also "adverbs that look like adjectives.")

The *easily* form of the adverb must be used before a past participle, as in "easily pleased" or "easily removed."

Echo: **no sir**   Though an old song celebrates Little Sir Echo, the original *Echo* of Greek mythology was a woman.

The story of Echo, one of several nymphs (goddesses of nature), is an example of how some mythology provided a pre-scientific explanation for natural phenomena—in this case, the reflection of sound waves. According to one version of Echo's story, you hear Echo's voice repeating your words because of an incident in which she agreed to help Greece's supreme god, Zeus, in one of his amorous adventures by engaging in a distracting conversation with Zeus' wife, Hera. When Hera discovered the trick, she punished Echo by making her mute except for the repetition of the sounds of others. Echo's handicap caused her to be cruelly rejected by the man she loved, Narcissus. In despair, Echo hid in a cave and died of grief, leaving only her echoing voice. (See also "*Narcissus, narcissus*, and *narcissism.*")

ecology **or** *environment*?   *Ecology* is "the study of the interrelationships of organisms and their environments." Some dictionaries note that *ecology* is also used in the sense of those interrelationships *themselves*. But that usage invites confusing statements about "the impact on the ecology," making *ecology* sound like nothing more than a synonym for *environment* ("general surroundings").

economic **or** *economical*?   One way to avoid *economic* ("money") problems is to practice an *economical* ("money-saving") lifestyle.

To avoid embarrassment, never say *economical* when you mean *economic*. An ad in the *Los Angeles Times* (4/24/2004) got it wrong: An "acclaimed speaker" invited readers to hear how she overcame her "personal and economical problems" by adopting "a spiritual perspective."

ecstacy or **ecstasy**?   The answer is *ecstasy*.

Ecstasy, which literally means "out of oneself," was inspired by the ancient Greek belief that one's spirit can leap from one's body in an excess of emotion. The word's modern sense is "a state of overwhelming emotion such as rapturous delight, beyond reason and self-control." But that is no excuse for forgetting that it should be spelled with *-asy* rather than with the more common English word ending *-acy*. (See also "spelling traps.")

edification is not necessarily fun   If you say "for your edification" when you mean "for your enjoyment," you're not just pretentious. You're wrong.

The verb *edify*, from a Latin verb meaning "to build, as in build a temple," means "to help build character by providing instruction that is morally or spiritually uplifting."

edifice is not just any building   Usage commentators regard the noun *edifice* as appropriate only for a building that is notably large or imposing, like a mansion, castle, or cathedral. If you use *edifice* when all you mean is "building," you may be accused of having an edifice complex.

editor in chief or **editor-in-chief**?   (See "spelling compound words.")

-ee or **-er**?   People in a category ending in *-ee* commonly are receivers of the action of people in a category ending in *-er*. For example, an *employee* receives a job from an *employer*, and a *mortgagee* receives a mortgage from a *mortgager*.

Follett's *Modern American Usage* warns that these suffixes sometimes get mixed up, as when people who pledge donations to charity are wrongly called *pledgees*. That source maintains that pledgees are actually the charities that receive the pledges from pledgers. (See also "*lessee* or *lessor*?")

effect or **affect**?   See "*affect* or *effect*?"

effete is no longer productive   Here's useful advice about *effete* from the 2003 *Chicago Manual of Style*: "Because of its ambiguity, the word is best avoided."

Effete, derived in the 17th century from the Latin *effetus* ("that which has given birth and is no longer fruitful"), was originally used to describe domestic animals that could no longer produce offspring. But for most of its existence, *effete* has been used in the figurative sense of *sterile*—"exhausted, worn out, unproductive, having lost its vitality"—as in "an effete society."

Beginning in the 1920's, *effete* gradually acquired its currently popular sense of "decadently overrefined, self-indulgent, foppish, degenerate [and more recently] effeminate." *The Oxford English Dictionary* and leading American dictionaries list the "decadent" *effete* along with the literal and figurative "sterile" *effete*.

e.g. or i.e.?   A common error in conversation and casual writing is to use *i.e.* in place of *e.g.*

The abbreviation *e.g.* stands for *exempli gratia*, a Latin phrase meaning "for example." Memory tip: Associate *e.g.* with "eg-zample." The abbreviation *i.e.* stands for *id est*, which is Latin for "that is [to say]," and is used to introduce an identification or paraphrase of, or an explanation for, what has just been said.

Note that *e.g.* and *i.e.*, like the English phrases they substitute for, should be followed by a comma or a colon. Usage examples: "Shortages of qualified applicants seem to be chronic in certain occupations, e.g., nursing and schoolteaching." "The majority ethnic group in Sri Lanka (i.e., the Sinhalese) were involved in a long conflict with the minority Tamils."

egoist or egotist?   If you use *egoist* as a synonym for *egotist* ("self-centered person"), you can find justification in dictionaries; in the title—*The Egoist*—of George Meredith's 1879 novel about a self-centered man; and in comic-strip character Mary Worth's description (12/3/1995) of a self-centered man as "an opinionated egoist."

But you'll win points from purists if you save *egoist* for its other dictionary meaning: "an adherent of egoism, the doctrine that society is best served when individual members of society act in their own self-interest."

egregious is more than outstanding   *Egregious* originally meant "outstanding" but now means "outstandingly bad, notorious, outrageous."

either and neither: singular or plural?   Your risk-free answer is to consider *either* and *neither* singular and choose a singular verb. For example: "*Either* [meaning, one or the other] parent *is* able to give you the information. But *neither* [meaning, not either one] *is* home." (See also "*one of* those plural problems.")

either and neither may be pronounced either way But you are less likely to attract undue attention to yourself if you say the first syllable in each of these words with an *ee* sound.

either . . . or and neither . . . nor: singular or plural? When *either* or *neither* is a correlative conjunction—one used as part of a pair of mutually related conjunctions—as in *either . . . or* and *neither . . . nor*—you will be risk-free if you abide by the rules cited in the remainder of this entry.

Use a singular verb if both subjects in the sentence are singular. Example: "Either the boy's *mother* or his *aunt is* usually able to drive him to soccer practice. But neither the boy's *mother* nor his *aunt is* able to do so this time."

Use a plural verb if both subjects are plural. Example: "Apparently, either the *Canadians* or the *Japanese are* going to be first to develop the new technology. But neither the Canadians nor the Japanese *are* willing to disclose their plans."

If one subject is singular and the other plural, avoid awkwardness by taking the time to restructure your sentence. If you are pressed for time, match the verb with the subject after *or/nor*. Example: "Either the Jacobsens or *Alice is* able to solve the problem. Either Alice or the *Jacobsens are* able to solve the problem." "Neither the Jacobsens nor *Alice is* willing. Neither Alice nor the *Jacobsens are* willing. (See also "conjunctions used in pairs," "*not only . . . but also,*" and "parallel problems.")

eke out a living if you want to Here is an illustration of the need to keep your reference library up to date.

Both the 1926 first edition and the posthumous 1965 second edition of Henry W. Fowler's *Dictionary of Modern English Usage* declared that you "cannot eke out a living"—meaning that it is wrong to use *eke out* in the sense of "obtain or sustain with great difficulty." Fowler ruled that *eke out* can be used only in its original, centuries-old sense of "adding to something," as in "eke out [supplement] your income with odd jobs." But as the revised third edition, *The New Fowler's Modern English Usage*, noted in 1998, "eke out a living" has been used since the early 19th century, and "both constructions are now standard."

Usage example: *The New York Times* (1/25/2002) reported that "thousands of Chechen families eke out an isolated existence in bomb-damaged homes."

"elegant variation"   This sarcastic term was coined by Henry W. Fowler, and used in his *Dictionary of Modern English Usage*, to shame "second-rate writers, those intent rather on expressing themselves prettily than on conveying their meaning clearly." Fowler's point was to warn that readers are easily confused if writers needlessly vary the identification of a subject.

Here is an example of a student writer making one person (italicized below) sound like three: "The *23-year-old girl* sat in class listening to the professor. Meanwhile, the guys in the class had their attention focused on *the beautiful girl* sitting near the front of the class. *Eve Jones* is a Los Angeles native who grew up in the Roland Heights area . . ." (For another Fowlerism, see "slipshod extension.")

elegy or **eulogy?**   An *elegy* ("ELLA-gee") is a poem or song of mourning, especially one that laments the death of someone or something. The adjective *elegiac* ("ella-JEYE-ick") means "expressing sorrow for that which is forever gone," as in a reference in *Smithsonian* magazine (May 1997) to author Peter Matthiessen's "elegiac book," *Wildlife in America*.

A *eulogy* ("YOO-lah-gee") is an expression of praise, especially a speech praising someone who has died. The verbal form is *eulogize* ("to praise highly in speech or writing").

elemental or **elementary?**   *Elementary* means "simple, introductory." *Elemental* means "fundamental, essential, basic" or "resembling a force of nature in power or effect."

elite: one little word with a lot to remember   It's spelled with one l. It's preferably pronounced "ah-LEET" rather than "ay-LEET" or "AY-leet." It's singular when you focus on an elite *group* but plural when you focus on the elite group's *members*.

Also, you need to make clear whether you're using *elite* in the sense of people who are "the best" or "the most powerful."

The least of your worries about this word is the question of whether or not to write it with an accent mark—*élite*. That form is optional in American English and preferable in British English.

elixir or **elixir of life?**   From the medieval practice of alchemy, *elixir* and the full term *elixir of life* both refer to "a substance by means of which it was hoped to change base metals into gold" or "a substance believed to indefinitely prolong life." Today *elixir* is a synonym for any supposed cure-all.

ellipse, Ellipse, or *ellipsis*?

The uppercase *Ellipse* is the egg-shaped lawn behind the White House. The *Ellipse* is so named because the lowercase *ellipse* ("a closed curve in the shape of an egg") comes from a Greek word meaning "to fall short," and an egg-shaped form was thought to fall short of a perfect circle.

The lowercase *ellipse* is also a rarely used, clipped form of *ellipsis*, which refers to "the falling short of completeness" in a quoted statement by the omission of a word or phrase that the context makes unnecessary. An *ellipsis* can also mean the three dots that mark such an omission.

elocution or *locution*?

Both these nouns can be traced to the Latin *elocutio* ("speaking out"). To quote *The Oxford Companion to the English Language*: *Elocution* is "the study and practice of oral delivery, including control of breath, voice, stance, and gesture." *Locution,* a "speaking out" orally or in writing, is "a formal, technical, sometimes pedantic term for a word, phrase, or idiom, especially if regarded as characteristic of a social or regional group, [as in] Irish locutions." (For another pair of words derived from the Latin word for "speaking out," see the next entry.)

eloquence or *grandiloquence*?

A *New York Times* obituary (7/10/1996) about the famous lawyer Melvin Belli recalled that sometimes "his *eloquence* ['speech that is vivid, moving, forceful'] became *grandiloquence* ['speech that is pompous']."

else: a word that's possessed

Notice that *else* possesses the idea of possession in phrases such as "somebody else's" and "everybody else's." Phrases such as "somebody's else" and "everybody's else" are considered by usage commentators to be nonstandard.

But the possessive form for "who else" can be "*whose* else" when a noun does not immediately follow. ("Whose birthday cake is that?" "Jane's. Whose else could it be?")

else: some "additional" advice

Else can be used as a synonym for "additional," as in the observation that "there was nothing else she could do."

But *else* is often used as an addition that's needless in combination with the prepositions *but, except,* and *besides.* For example, *else* should be omitted from the sentence "No one *else* but Roger seemed to enjoy the party."

***Elysian Fields*: no waiting**   In Greek mythology, virtuous people who died were admitted to the beautiful and peaceful Elysian Fields of Elysium. But you needn't wait to go there. *Elysian Fields* is the English translation of the name of the most famous boulevard in Paris, the extremely wide, tree-lined *Champs-Élysées.*

e-mail, email, or E-mail?   All three of those abbreviations of *electronic mail* are correct. But *e-mail* is currently preferred by leading dictionaries and usage manuals, and that form is used exclusively by such influential publications as the *Los Angeles Times, The New York Times,* and *The Wall Street Journal.* The same is true for *e-commerce, e-business, e-books,* and *e-tail* ("electronic retail").

E-mail is a collective noun, as in "How much e-mail did I receive during the weekend?" But just as you would not pluralize the collective noun *mail,* you should not pluralize *e-mail.* Instead of saying that you received 10 *e-mails,* say that you received 10 *e-mail messages.* Note, however, that *e-mails* is a well-established form of the transitive verb *e-mail,* as in "Jacob e-mails love notes to Jeanie every day."

e-mail warning   Like conversation, e-mail is usually edited less carefully than hard copy. The result can be professional embarrassment, as in this excerpt from an October 2002 e-mailing from the American Society of Journalists and Authors: "Once again, ASJA is offering its' annual Lunch-With-An-Editor/Agent Raffle. This year we're offering 11 top flight editors and agents . . ."

As every member of that society should know, there is no apostrophe in the possessive pronoun *its.* And the writer of that ASJA message should have realized that the failure to hyphenate the compound adjective *top-flight* resulted in an unintended reference to top editors and agents who specialize in flight. (See also "*its, it's,* or *its*'?" and "hyphens protect the meaning of these adjectives.")

embarrass: double trouble   *Embarrass,* which can be traced to an Italian verb meaning "put behind bars" (*imbarrare*), entered English in the 17th century with the meaning "hamper the movement of." Its present meaning—"dis-

concert, cause shame to, make uncomfortably self-conscious"—applies to anyone who forgets that it is spelled with a double *r* and a double *s*. (See also
"spelling traps.")

emigrant, immigrant, émigré, or migrant?   *Emigrant* and *immigrant* refer
to persons who move from one nation or region with the intention of permanently settling in another. The person is an *emigrant* relative to the place of
departure and an *immigrant* relative to the place of arrival.

A person *emigrates* with only one *m* from a country but somehow must
acquire a second *m* in order to *immigrate* to or into another country.

An *émigré* is someone who emigrates, especially for political reasons.

Migrant means one who moves from one region to another—for instance,
in search of seasonal work—without intending to settle in the new place permanently.

éminence grise has a misleading color   This term—imported from France,
pronounced "aimee-nahns GREEZ," and sometimes replaced by its English
equivalent, *gray eminence*—means "the power behind the throne, a person who
secretly exercises influence in the shadows by serving as a manipulative adviser."

Ignorance about this term's origin has produced some confusion about its
usage. As noted by Merriam-Webster's *Word Histories*, the use of *éminence grise*
or *gray eminence* as a synonym for *elder statesman* and *grand old man* is based
on the false assumption that the term refers to an eminent (distinguished) person
with gray hair. In typical examples of that error, the *Los Angeles Times*
(7/7/1999) referred to John Kenneth Galbraith as "the 90-year-old *éminence
grise* of economists," and the same newspaper (8/11/2002) called 62-year-old
Caltech physicist Kip Thorne "an *éminence grise* in black-hole research and
gravitational-wave studies."

Incidentally, University of Virginia English Professor E. D. Hirsch Jr. misin-
formed readers of his popular *Dictionary of Cultural Literacy* that the original
Éminence Grise was Cardinal Richelieu (1585–1642), who directed the domestic and foreign policies of France as chief minister of Louis XIII. The fact was
that Richelieu, as a Roman Catholic cardinal, was formally addressed as *His
Eminence* and informally known as *Éminence Rouge* (Red Eminence, from the
color of his robes.) In contrast, the informal title *Éminence Grise* (Gray
Eminence) was acquired by the gray-robed Father Joseph (François Le Clerc du

Tremblay (1577–1638), a Capuchin monk, mystic, and diplomat who was rumored to have exercised evil, behind-the-scenes influence as a "shadowy cardinal" in his role as Cardinal Richelieu's confidant and adviser.

A 1941 book about Father Joseph, written by English novelist-essayist Aldous Huxley and titled *Grey Eminence,* contributed significantly to our language's wide use of *éminence grise* and its English equivalent.

eminent, immanent, or imminent?   *Eminent* ("outstanding") writers distinguish *immanent* ("inherent") from *imminent* ("about to happen").

eminent or pre-eminent?   *Pre-eminent* should be saved for its special meaning of "more eminent [outstanding] than all others." Example from *The New York Times Book Review* (11/19/2000): "Arlene Croce is widely acknowledged as the pre-eminent dance critic of her generation."

Emmies or Emmys?   The plural form for the award presented annually since 1949 by the Academy of Television Arts and Sciences is *Emmys.* According to *Webster's New World Dictionary of Media and Communications,* "The original name was *Immy,* [the slang name for] the image-orthicon tube used in television, but the name changed as a result of a typographical error."

emote is not just emotional   The verb *emote,* which emerged from *emotion* in early 20th-century America, literally means "to express emotion." But it is often used to mean "to express emotion excessively or insincerely, as one might do on the stage." Usage example: "A trial lawyer who emotes is likely to alienate judges and juries."

emotional or emotive?   Writers who take pride in maintaining useful word distinctions use *emotional* to mean "*expressing* emotion" and *emotive* to mean "*arousing* emotion." For such precise writers, people become *emotional* about *emotive* controversies.

empathy or sympathy?   Use *empathy* for the ability to identify with the feelings or thoughts of someone else. Use *sympathy* for the spontaneous reaction of pity.

emulate or *imitate*?   Don't imitate people who use *emulate* as if it were just a synonym for *imitate*. The standard meaning of *emulate*—to quote *The American Heritage Dictionary*—is "to strive to equal or excel, especially through imitation."

enact or *enact into law*?   The verb *enact* means "to make into law." Therefore, the addition of *into law* is redundant.

enclave: use one accent at a time   This French import, meaning "a territory enclosed within foreign territory," is preferably pronounced "EN-clave." People who say "AHN-clave" are mixing French and English accents. A consistently French pronunciation would be "AHN-clahv." (See also "*envelop* or *envelope*?")

energize or *enervate*?   *Enervate*, sometimes wrongly used as if it meant *energize* or *innervate* ("to give energy to"), means "to drain the energy from, to deprive of strength or force."

enlightenment or *Enlightenment*?   An *enlightenment* can be "the act of enlightening" or "the state of being enlightened." The capitalized *Enlightenment*, preceded by the word *the*, refers to the 17th- and 18th-century philosophical movement—in politics, religion, and related areas—that emphasized reason and experience over dogma and tradition.

English vintages   "In the simplest terms," says *The Story of English* by McCrum, Cran, and MacNeil, "the language was brought to Britain by Germanic tribes, the Angles, Saxons, and Jutes, influenced by Latin and Greek when Saint Augustine and his followers converted England to Christianity, subtly enriched by Danes, and finally transformed by the French-speaking Normans."

Old English, the language of the Anglo-Saxons in England, dates from about the middle of the fifth century to the early 12th century.

Middle English emerged about the time of the Norman conquest of England (1066)—incorporating many Latin and French words of the Norman French—and began evolving into *Early Modern English* in the mid-15th century.

enhance nobody   Apply *enhance* ("increase, as in value or reputation") only to qualities and conditions, not to people.

enormity: a wicked word Nobody will fault you if you use *enormity* to mean "great wickedness," as in "the enormity of the 9/11 attack on the World Trade Center." But you will invite criticism if you join the many people who use *enormity* to mean "great size or extent," as in CNN anchor Wolf Blitzer's reference (7/29/2004) to "the enormity of the challenge" faced by John F. Kerry as he prepared to spell out his goals for the nation in his acceptance speech for the Democratic presidential nomination.

Though the *Random House Webster's College Dictionary* says that "*enormity* has been in frequent and continuous use in the sense [of] *immensity* since the 18th century," that source notes that "many people . . . continue to regard *enormity* in the sense of great size as nonstandard."

Support for restricting *enormity* to its "wicked" sense can be found in *The King's English* by Kingsley Amis, Fowler's *Modern English Usage,* Follett's *Modern American Usage,* Strunk and White's *Elements of Style, The Oxford English Dictionary,* and *The New York Times Manual of Style and Usage.*

Atlantic Monthly language columnist Barbara Wallraff issued this appeal in her *Word Court* book (published in 2000): "If we are moral people, we should strive to retain *enormity* as one of few words adequate to decry historic events on the scale of the Serbian slaughter of Albanians in Kosovo in 1999, the mid-1990s genocide in Rwanda, and Hitler's Holocaust."

The American Heritage Dictionary warns that "writers who ignore the distinction, as in 'the enormity of the President's victory' or 'the enormity of her inheritance,' may find that their words have cast unintended aspersions or evoked unexpected laughter." *Webster's New World Guide to Current American Usage* advises that "anyone who applies the word *enormity* to something that is of enormous size or extent is lucky to get off with a charge of loose usage: The offense is ordinarily classified as illiteracy."

enquire or inquire? Both are acceptable spellings of this word for "ask about" or "make an investigation," as can be inferred from the names of *The Philadelphia Inquirer* and *The Cincinnati Enquirer.* But by far the most common form is that prescribed by the Associated Press: *inquire.* Merriam-Webster researchers report that "when *enquire* does appear in American English, it is usually in bookish or formal contexts."

In British English, according to the 1993 *New Shorter Oxford English*

Dictionary, "recent usage tends to distinguish *enquire* = ask, *inquire* = make investigation, [but] the distinction is not made in North America."

en route or **on route?**   This expression, a French phrase meaning "on the way (to)" or "along the way," entered English in the 19th century as both an adverb and an adjective for "on or along the way." Though our preferred pronunciation sounds like "on root," the expression should be spelled "*en* route." It is so well established in English that it does not require italics.

ensure or **insure?**   See "*assure, ensure,* or *insure?*"

enthuse inspires no enthusiasm   The verb *enthuse* ("express enthusiasm")—an early 19th-century American back-formation of the noun *enthusiasm*—is one of the least-respected words in the dictionary. For example, consider the stern warning in *Garner's Modern American Usage* that *enthuse* is "avoided by writers and speakers who care about their language."

The *Random House Webster's College Dictionary* observes that "despite its long history and frequent occurrence, *enthuse* is still strongly disapproved of by many." *The American Heritage Dictionary* reports that "*enthuse* is not well accepted" and has been rejected by 76 percent of its usage panel. *The New York Public Library Writer's Guide to Style and Usage* notes that "*enthuse* is still not an acceptable word to most authorities." *The New Fowler's Modern English Usage* reports that *enthuse* "in general is held at arm's length by serious writers."

Strunk and White's *Elements of Style* condemned *enthuse* as "an annoying verb." The stylebook of *The Washington Post* brands *enthuse* as a colloquialism that should be avoided in standard usage, and the *Longman Guide to English Usage* declares that *enthuse* "should be avoided in serious writing."

Risk-free recommendation from *The Columbia Guide to Standard American English*: "Don't *enthuse*; *show enthusiasm* or *be enthusiastic*."

entomology, etymology, and ***folk* etymology**   *Entomology* is the study of insects.

Etymology, to quote David Crystal's *Cambridge Encyclopedia of the English Language,* is "the study of the origins and history of the form and meanings of words" and phrases.

Folk etymology consists of popular misconceptions, or at least questionable assumptions, about the origins and history of words and phrases. (See also "acronym-initialism imposters" and entries for *cold slaw*, *helpmate*, *OK*, and *rule of thumb*.)

entrée: food or access?

Entrée ("AHN-tray") means "main dish" and also "permission to enter, access." So you would be accurate, though rather silly, if you wrote that somebody "gained *entrée* to a dinner party just to sample the *entrée*."

Entrée (French for "entry") became the English word *entry* in the 13th century. In the 18th century, *entrée* reentered English without any change in spelling, with the meaning "act of entering" and then "permission to enter." Soon, the British also began using *entrée* to designate a small dish served at a formal dinner, after the appetizer, as an "entrance" to the main dish. American restaurants, condensing the formal dinner, eliminated the "entrance" dish but kept the fashionably French word *entrée* to designate the main dish.

envelop or *envelope*?

The French-derived verb *envelop* ("en-VEL-up") means "to enclose, surround."

The noun *envelope* ("EN-velope") means "something that envelops." In addition to being a folded paper that envelops a letter, an envelope can be "a set of limitations for safe performance of an aircraft or other technological system." That second definition explains why people are said to be "pushing the envelope" when they take any risk of testing the limits or bending the rules.

Usage example: The *Los Angeles Times* (1/24/2001) ran a headline, "Rocket Boys Still Pushing the Envelope," about retired space scientists and engineers contributing to medical technology.

envy or *jealousy*?

These words are close, but there is a distinction between them that some usage commentators believe is worth preserving.

Envy is a longing to possess what someone else has. *Jealousy* typically involves suspicion and resentment arising from a fear that a rival will deprive you of something you value.

The adjective *jealous* was thoughtfully defined in social critic Ambrose Bierce's *Devil's Dictionary* as "unduly concerned about the preservation of that which can be lost only if not worth keeping."

***Epicurean* has conflicting meanings**   The capitalized adjective *Epicurean* is defined in *Webster's New World College Dictionary* as "fond of sensuous pleasure, especially that of eating and drinking." But the dictionary's other definition— "of Epicurus or his philosophy"—has quite a different meaning. The ancient Greek philosopher Epicurus founded a school of philosophy, Epicureanism, that held pleasure to be the highest and only good. But he believed that real pleasure is attained through prudence, honor, justice, and intellectual rather than physical satisfaction.

***epidemic* proportions**   An *epidemic* ("widely prevalent") disease may be *endemic* ("restricted to a certain locality"), *pandemic* ("spread over a wide geographic area"), or *epizootic* ("affecting a large number of animals"). All four words are also nouns, as in a *Detroit Free Press* reference (6/23/1998) to "the global pandemic of HIV."

Endemic is often used to describe anything undesirable that's prevalent in a particular field or area, as in a *USA Today* opinion essay (1/11/2005) questioning Iraq's ability to "rise above the culture of corruption endemic to the region."

epigraph, epigram,* or *epitaph?   *Epigraph* means "an inscription, usually on a building or statue," or "a quote prominently displayed in a book." *Epigram* means "a short, witty poem or saying." *Epitaph* ("EP-ah-taf") means "an inscription on a tomb."

epiphany* or *Epiphany?   An *epiphany* is a moment of dramatic revelation, divine or otherwise. As a proper noun, *Epiphany* is the Christian festival of the Twelfth Night (January 6), celebrating what Christians believe to be the revelation to the Magi (three wise men) of Christ's divine nature.

episcopal, Episcopal,* or *Episcopalian?   The lowercase adjective *episcopal* means "of or relating to a bishop."

Capitalize the adjective in references to the Episcopal Church, a member of the international Anglican Communion associated with the Church of England.

Never say Episcopalian *Church,* because *Episcopalian* is strictly a noun identifying Episcopal Church members.

epithet: not born to be bad   Many people assume *epithet* means only "an abusive or contemptuous word or phrase," as in this *Chronicle of Higher Education* headline (6/12/1991): " 'Politically Correct' Has Become an Epithet."

As dictionaries note, however, *epithet* also retains its original, 16th-century meaning of "a descriptive term that may express not only contempt but also praise or no opinion at all." That earlier sense of *epithet* includes descriptions used *with* or *as* a name, such as *Catherine the Great* or the *Great Emancipator*. Some influential usage books, including Fowler's *Dictionary of Modern English Usage* and Bernstein's *Careful Writer*, classified the original, "descriptive term" *epithet* as the only correct one.

In view of this unsettled dispute, Copperud's *American Usage and Style* and Wilson's *Columbia Guide to Standard American English* recommend that you use your context to make your intended meaning absolutely clear. For example, your reader will know you are not referring to descriptive terms of praise if you write that two angry people "hurled" epithets at each other. And the *Financial Times* (6/10/2000) clearly used *epithet* in its complimentary sense when it reported that author Susan Sontag was described by the epithet Most Intelligent Woman in America.

epithet or expletive?   Be careful not to confuse *epithet* with *expletive* ("an exclamatory word or phrase, usually obscene or profane").

Expletive deleted ("the removal of an obscene or profane remark") became a famous phrase in 1974, with publication of the Watergate-scandal transcripts of taped conversations between President Nixon and his aides.

eponymous means never having to say you're anonymous   The adjective *eponymous* means "of, relating to, or being an *eponym*." The noun *eponym* (from the Greek "upon a name") means "a person's name from which a word has been derived," "the person whose name is used in that manner," or "the word derived from a person's name."

Other examples: The magnolia tree was named in honor of French physician-botanist Pierre Magnol ("MAH-nyol"), a 17th-century pioneer of plant classification. And the tight-fitting, torso-covering leotard was named in honor of Jules Léotard, a 19th-century French trapeze artist who popularized that garment. An *ampere* (from French physicist-mathematician André Marie Ampere) is a unit of electric current that one *volt* (a unit of electric potential, named after

Italian physicist Alessandro Volta) can send through one *ohm* (a unit of electrical resistance, named after German physicist Georg Simon Ohm).

One of the best-known eponyms is *boycott*, from Charles C. Boycott (1832–1897), a retired British army officer who went to work as the manager of a British earl's estate in Ireland. In 1880, Boycott refused tenant demands for lower rents, proceeding instead to serve writs of eviction. Though he was behaving like other land agents, Irish nationalists made an example of him by making sure that no Irish tenants would work for him. Forced to harvest his crops with workers from Ulster, guarded by soldiers, Boycott left Ireland that same year. The following year, the rent crisis eased when the British established fair-rent tribunals. Soon after, the term *boycott* was being used to identify nonviolent coercive tactics in general, then "a joining together to prevent dealings with" in particular. (See "*herculean* or *Herculean*?" "Jeremiah and his noun," "Kafka and his adjective," "*Murphy's Law, Parkinson's Law,* and the *Peter Principle*," "Potemkin's unreal estate?" "Procrustes and his adjective," and "*psyche* or *Psyche*?")

equal does not add up   *Equal* ("the same as") is an absolute condition—like *complete* and *perfect*—and therefore not subject to qualification.

Some permissive sources, including *Merriam-Webster's Dictionary of English Usage*, approve of "more equal" on the grounds that it really means "more *nearly* equal." But you do not need to risk giving the appearance of having an illogical mind—by saying "more equal"—when all you need to say is "more *nearly* equal," if that is what you mean.

equally as: use one or the other   The phrase *equally as* contains a redundancy. Use either *equally* or *as,* depending on the structure of your sentence.

Here are examples with the redundant word in brackets: "He types [equally] as fast as his friend." "She plays the piano equally [as] well."

equanimity isn't fair   While crime boss John Gotti was being sentenced to life imprisonment in a federal court in Brooklyn on June 23, 1992, hundreds of his supporters outside chanted, waved American flags, and displayed signs demanding, among other things, "Equanimity Under the Law." Those signs illustrated a common confusion of *equanimity* ("calmness") with *equity* ("justice, fairness").

A subtler problem: the confusion of *inequity* (any "unfairness") with *iniquity* (unfairness so gross that it's "wicked, sinful or depraved").

err is easy to do but hard to say   The verb *err* (a relative of the noun *error*) is probably best known in the phrase "to err is human," from an 18th-century poem by Alexander Pope. The poet illustrated in rhyme the traditional and currently most respectable pronunciation: not the *err* that sounds like *air* but the *err* that rhymes with *prefer*.

Whichever pronunciation you prefer, note that *err* can mean "make a mistake" or "commit a wrong, such as a sin."

escape: does it need *from*?   *Escape* ("break loose, avoid") seems to be breaking loose from the word *from*. Until that escape is complete, you might want to follow the traditional rule: Use *escape from* when you mean "break loose," as in "escape from prison." Use only *escape* when you mean "avoid," as in "escape punishment."

espresso or expresso?   Italians say *caffè espresso* (literally, "coffee that's pressed out") or just *espresso* when they mean the strong coffee made by forcing steam through ground coffee beans. Many English speakers say *expresso* when they mean *espresso*, and you'll find that spelling listed as an acceptable variant in some of our dictionaries. Other sources, including Norman Lewis' *New American Dictionary of Good English*, call *expresso* a "nonword."

-ess: an insufferable suffix?   The French-derived feminine suffix *-ess* is accepted in social-role words such as *princess* and *duchess*. But you are in the Risk Zone of sexism today if you use *-ess* occupational words, as in *stewardess* for *flight attendant*.

Say what you will about the controversial Russian-born poet-philosopher-novelist Ayn Rand (1905–1982), but think twice before you imitate a writer in the *Los Angeles Times Magazine* (8/16/1998) who called her a "poetess." You'll find that word in dictionaries but not in the vocabulary of today's careful communicators.

Actress is still generally considered acceptable, inasmuch as acting roles are almost always gender-specific. Nevertheless, many women in that profession now prefer to be called *actors*.

essence, in essence, of the essence   The *essence* is "that which makes something what it is." *In essence* means "essentially." *Of the essence* means "of the greatest importance."

essential, essentiality, essentially, quintessence, quintessential The adjective *essential* means "absolutely necessary, pertaining to or constituting the *essence* of a thing."

The noun *essentiality* refers to "the essential quality, fact, or thing."

The adverb *essentially* means "fundamentally, basically."

Quintessence (combining *essence* with the Latin word for "fifth") meant to the ancients "the fifth and highest essence after the four elements of earth, air, fire, and water." (The ancients called that highest essence *ether*, and they believed it filled the heavens.) Today, *quintessence* means "the pure, concentrated essence of something" or "the purest manifestation of something."

The adjective *quintessential* means "being the most typical" or "being the purest embodiment of something." A *New York Times* front-page obituary (12/27/2000) for actor Jason Robards referred to him as "the quintessential interpreter of [playwright Eugene] O'Neill's desperate truth-tellers."

etc.* needs no *and An *and* before *etc.* (the abbreviation for the Latin *et cetera*) is redundant, because the expression means "and other things of the same kind."

Avoid *etc.* when the "other things of the same kind" are not easy for your reader to infer. For instance, if you write that the requirements for a certain job are "a college degree, American citizenship, etc.," your job-hunting reader will be frustrated.

Etc. also should be avoided in lists of persons. The Latin *et al.* for "and others"—note the period after *al.*, an abbreviation of *alii*, but not after the complete word *et*—is used for shortening a long list of authors for a book.

ethic, ethics,* or *ethos*? The noun *ethic* refers to "a set of principles or a guiding philosophy," as in "the Protestant ethic" or "a materialist ethic."

Ethics, the most commonly used term of the three, denotes "the rules governing conduct." (See also "*ethics* or *morals*?")

Ethos, pronounced "EE-thos," means "a set of distinguishing beliefs or practices of a person or group." For example, according to a foreign correspondent for the *Los Angeles Times* (1/10/1998), "Smoking is an intimate part of the Balkan ethos—like tea-drinking in England and popcorn-eating at American movies."

ethicist or **moralist?**   Though dictionaries define both *ethicist* and *moralist* as "a specialist in ethics," your only safe choice for that use is *ethicist*. The word *moralist* is risky because it has the additional, pejorative meaning of "a self-righteous person who tries to impose his or her set of beliefs on others." A moralist is apt to *moralize* ("engage in self-righteous lecturing of others").

ethics is or **ethics are?**   Though political *ethics is* a subject that politicians like to discuss, their own political *ethics are* often deplorable.

ethics or **morals?**   These nouns referring to proper conduct have been used interchangeably for generations. But today's tendency is to use *ethics* for conduct that is public and *morals* for conduct that is private. For example, some media critics have questioned the professional *ethics* of radio personality Laura Schlesinger because she solicits call-in questions about the *"moral* dilemmas" of marriage as "Doctor Laura," though her doctoral training was in physiology rather than human relations.

Ethics and *morals* can apply to the same subject, as in a *New York Times* editorial (8/4/2001) stating that research projects on human cloning "raise moral and ethical issues." But the personal-behavior word, *morals,* would be inappropriate in a discussion of a company's questionable business practices, and the professional-context word, *ethics,* would be inappropriate in a reference to a person who is cruel to children or animals.

ethnic and racial classifications   Some social commentators envision a time when there will be no hyphenated Americans—just Americans—and perhaps even a time when people throughout the world will identify with the single category *human beings.* But in today's world, the conscientious communicator must keep informed about the changing standards of acceptability of the various "ethnic" and "racial" classifications.

What was acceptable yesterday does not apply to today. For example, from 1920 to 1940 the U.S. Census applied the pseudoscientific "Hindu race" to Asian Indians. And the 1890 U.S. Census asked residents of African descent to classify themselves as "black," "mulatto," "quadroon," or "octoroon," depending on their percentage of African ancestry. During the 20th century, many Americans of sub-Saharan African ancestry changed their descriptions of themselves from "colored" to "Negro" to "black" and then to "African-American." According to a report in *The New York Times* of August 29, 2004, " 'African-American' has rapidly replaced 'black' in much of the nation's political and cultural discourse." But that article added: "Many [have] argued that the term 'African-American' should refer to the descendants of slaves brought to the United States centuries ago, not to newcomers who have not inherited the legacy of bondage, segregation and legal discrimination. [And] some immigrants and their children prefer to be called African or Nigerian-American or Jamaican-American, depending on their countries of origin."

Children of "racially mixed" marriages may acquire the classification of their mother (as did abolitionist lecturer-writer Frederick Douglass, the "illegitimate" son of a "white" man and a "Negro" slave) or their father (as has civil-rights attorney and law professor Lani Guinier, daughter of "white" Jewish Genii Guinier and the late Ewart Guinier, a "black" civil-rights pioneer, labor leader, and Harvard professor). Also, many people of multiple heritages resent being pressured into accepting *any* label, including "multiracial."

Until the civil-rights revolution, drinking fountains and other public facilities in the American South were designated for "white" and "colored," but the term *colored* would seem to be acceptable today only in the title of the National Association for the Advancement of Colored People (now usually referred to by its initialism, *NAACP*). On the other hand, as reported by *The American Heritage Dictionary*, "the terms 'person of color' and 'people of color' have been revived for use in formal contexts . . . as a rough substitute for *minorities* because these [non-white] groups are not in fact in the minority in many parts of America."

Negro seems to be acceptable today only in historical references and in the title of the United Negro College Fund. And we typically now have such group titles as the Congressional Black Caucus and the National Association of Black Journalists.

When *Negro* was acceptable, during the mid-20th century, *Black* generally was not. Then *Negro* and *Black* switched places. Now, as *The New York Times* reports, *Black* has given way in many quarters to *African-American*. Both of those terms were used to describe the same person in a *Los Angeles Times* obituary (1/4/2005) for "Shirley Chisholm, the first black woman elected to Congress and the first African American to seek a major party nomination for president."

The terms *Asiatic* and *Oriental* are regarded by many *Asian Americans* as offensive, except when *Oriental* is applied to objects. Americans from *Vietnam, Laos,* and *Cambodia* are sometimes collectively referred to as *Indochinese,* but that term is for many an unpleasant reminder of an old imperialist designation, *French Indochina.*

Many of the indigenous Asian people whose ancestors discovered and settled in America thousands of years before the arrival of Columbus wish to be called *Native Americans.* According to *The New York Times Manual of Style and Usage,* however, "the term *Native American(s)* is rejected by some Indians because government programs extend it to others (Eskimos, Aleuts, Native Hawaiians, and Pacific Islanders) along with them." The European-named *Eskimos* of the Arctic coastal regions of North America and Greenland regard themselves as *Inuit* (their word for "people"). (See also *"aboriginal* and *aborigine* can both be proper," *"Brit* or *Briton?" "Hispanic, Latino,* or neither?" *"Moslem, Muslim,* or *Mohammedan?"* and *"race*: a question of reality.")

ethnic-term pronunciation   *Italian* and *Arab* are properly pronounced with "short vowels" at the beginning—*i* as in *it,* and *a* as in *arrow.* The pronunciations "eye-talian" and "ay-rab" suggest a lack of cultural respect.

ethnic verbs: a form of group libel   Inasmuch as the main purpose of dictionaries is to record how language is used—not necessarily how language *should* be used—dictionaries dutifully include words they classify as "offensive." For example, the Random House dictionaries warn about the offensive nature of the term *Indian giver* ("one who gives a gift and then takes it back"), which originated in the early 19th century from what Random House researchers call "a misconception about the customs of Native Americans." At any rate, nothing that dictionaries record along those lines is more offensive than ethnic verbs.

Some of those libelous verbs are so deeply ingrained in our language that they are taken for granted, even by people in public life who are ordinarily sensitive about ethnic issues. For example, the verb *welsh* ("to refuse to fulfill an obligation or pay a debt")—perceived by the Welsh as an ethnic insult, though *The New Fowler's Modern English Usage* says the word's origin is in doubt—was used in 1995 by California's governor and Republican presidential hopeful

Pete Wilson when he accused State Assembly Democrats of "trying to welsh" on a budget agreement. Governor Wilson reacted to criticism of his blunder by sending a letter of "regret" to the Welsh-American Legal Defense, Education and Development Fund.

As a seasoned politician, Wilson clearly had no intention of insulting any group of potential voters, just as most of the people who use the verb *gyp* ("swindle, cheat, defraud") probably have no idea that *gyp* insults the Romany people, who are mistakenly called Gypsies. (See also "*Gypsy, Gipsy,* or neither?")

A defense of ignorance would seem to be considerably less justified for those who use the group-libel expressions *jew* ("cheat by sharp business practice") and *jew down* ("get a price reduced by haggling").

-*ette* is not for women   The suffix *-ette* is appropriate for denoting smallness, as in *kitchenette, novelette, sermonette,* and *towelette.* But as the *Random House Webster's Unabridged Dictionary* notes, "English nouns in which the suffix *-ette* designates a feminine role or identity have been perceived by many people as implying inferiority or insignificance." To demonstrate your sensitivity on this issue, avoid such outdated words as *usherette, bachelorette,* and *suffragette.* (See also "sexism on the job" and "*suffragette* or *suffragist?*")

***even:* don't let it wander**   For clarity, make sure you place the word *even* directly in front of the word it modifies. Note the change in meaning in this two-part example: "*Even Jill* works on holidays." "Jill works *even on holidays.*" (See also "*only* the adverb causes trouble.")

ever so often* or *every so often?   *Ever so often* means "frequently." *Every so often* means "occasionally."

everlasting truths   If you say someone *said* something that is eternally true, put the truth in the present tense: "He insisted that the Earth *is* round."

***every:* singular or plural?**   *Every* is plural in sense but singular in grammar. So *every* takes only singular verbs, as in "Every employee in that department is [not *are*] going to get a raise." Usage tip: Think of *every* as if it were *every single.* (See also "*everyone* and *everybody:* singular or plural?")

everyday or every day? The one-word adjective *everyday* means "common," as in "Traffic jams are an everyday occurrence."

The two-word *every day* ("one day after another") can serve as an adverb, as in "The doctor sees the patient every day," and as an adjective-noun combination, as in "Every day the patient's condition improves."

everyone and everybody: singular or plural? Should *everyone* [meaning *everybody*] do *his* duty? Or *their* duty?

Most usage commentators insist that *everyone/everybody* is always singular. Indeed, everyone would seem to agree that it would be wrong to say "Everyone [or everybody] *are* here."

But many people today violate grammar by saying "*Everyone/everybody* should do *their* duty," to avoid the appearance of sexism or the awkwardness of resorting to the phrase *his or her*. A grammatical solution to those problems is to make the subject plural, as in "All of us should do our duty." (See also "pronouns can be agreeably nonsexist.")

everyone or every one? Both are grammatically singular. But *everyone* (a synonym for *everybody*) refers to an entire group, as in "*Everyone/everybody* dislikes paying taxes." The phrase *every one*, usually followed by *of*, emphasizes the separate individuals in a group, as in "Every *one* of you in this office must work harder."

every other warning When you use the phrase "every other," make sure you clearly indicate whether you mean "all" or "half." Note the ambiguity here: "Billy went to school with the flu, and every other child [all the other children, or half the other children?] in his classroom caught it."

evoke, invoke, or provoke? These verbs are derived from the Latin verb *vocare* ("to call").

Evoke means "to call out, elicit, summon," as in a *New York Times* reference (11/22/2000) to "films that evoke the futility of war."

Invoke means "to call upon and hence appeal to." Example: "The preacher said it was time to invoke a higher power."

Provoke means "to call forward or incite to some act, or incite to a response such as anger." Example: "The lawyer did not want to provoke the judge."

ex- or ***former*?**   Say *ex-*, as in "ex-mayor," for informal usage. Say *former* for formal usage.

exalt or ***exult*?**   *Exalt* means *glorify* ("make glorious or elevate by bestowing honor, praise, or admiration"). In the King James Bible (I Kings 1:5), it is written, "Adonijah the son of Haggith exalted himself, saying I will be king."

Exult means *rejoice* ("feel joy"). A *New York Times* headline (8/26/1998) reported, "Blue-Collar Town Exults in Its Little Leaguers."

example or ***exemplar*?**   An *exemplar* can be "an original or archetype" but is usually "an example or model worthy of imitation." Setting an example of the most widely accepted use of *exemplar*, pioneering biologist Ernst Mayr wrote in his 1997 book, *This Is Biology*: "There is no reason to consider physics as an exemplar [of scientific method] merely because it was the first well-organized science."

examples are exemplary   Professional communicators know that examples are exemplary ("commendable, worthy of imitation") because examples help readers and listeners understand and remember what is being communicated.

Moreover, examples are absolutely necessary when their absence would cause readers and listeners to be frustrated. Here is an instance—from *The New York Times* (7/27/1994)—in which a writer recognized that a statement cried out for examples. The statement: "Throughout [movie star Audrey Hepburn's] career, she used time-honored, sometimes time-worn gestures and expressions to convey emotions." The examples followed immediately in parentheses: "(The widened eyes and the tremulous chin; the hands clasped behind the back when you were lost in thought; the arms outstretched when you were rejoicing.)"

exceedingly or ***excessively*?**   *Exceedingly* means "extremely." *Excessively* means "overly."

excellence or ***excellency*?**   *Excellency* as a synonym for *excellence* ("eminence, superiority, a state of excelling") is an archaic usage for which *The Oxford English Dictionary* lists citations from the 15th through the 18th century. (In 1614, the English poet Richard Carew published a work he called *The Excellencie of the English Tongue*.) Today, *Excellency* (note the capitalization) is "a title of political or religious honor, or a person so entitled."

except you and I or **except you and me?**   *Me* is correct, because the personal pronouns in this phrase are objects of the preposition *except*. (See also "*me* is nothing to be afraid of.")

"exception proves the rule": hold your tongue   You'd be wise to forget that this expression exists. It has a technical meaning among lawyers and a completely different technical meaning among scientists. But if you imitate the many people who use this phrase in ordinary conversation, you'll be speaking nonsense.

The nonsensical interpretation is so deeply established in everyday conversation that you'll find it in John O. E. Clark's *Word Wise: A Dictionary of English Idioms.* "Exception proves the rule: A general principle is proved to be valid if it cannot be applied to a particular instance." In plain English, that means that a rule is actually confirmed if it's contradicted. For example, a boss tells an employee, "You say you always show up for work on time, but I found out that you arrived quite late all last week." The employee attempts to defend his inconsistency by responding, absurdly, "Well, my recent lateness is the exception that proves the rule." That employee should be fired not for lateness but for linguistic lunacy.

"The exception proves the rule" does make sense in legal lingo. That expression in court means that if the law specifies an exception to a rule, that proves the rule exists. For example, a sign forbidding overnight street parking is proof that there is a rule permitting parking there at other hours. To impress judges in such cases, the lawyer will say *Exceptio probat regulam in casibus non exceptis,* which is Latin for "The exception proves the rule in the cases not excepted."

When scientists say that "the exception proves the rule," they use the word *prove* in its lesser-known sense of "subjecting to a technical testing process," as in "proving ground" and "The proof of the pudding is in the eating." Scientists prove (meaning "test") a proposed rule by searching for exceptions. For example, exceptions *disprove* "rules" that all roses are red and that all snakes are dangerous.

exceptionable or **exceptional?**   *Exceptionable,* derived from the rare use of *exception* to mean "objection," is a risky synonym for the perfectly clear word *objectionable.* As Professor J. N. Hook warns in his *Appropriate Word,* your use of *exceptionable* when you mean *objectionable* will cause many people to think you mean *exceptional* (as in "unusually excellent"). Likewise, your use of *unexceptionable* ("not objectionable") will cause many people to think you mean *unexceptional* ("commonplace").

Recommendation: Enter this Risk Zone only if you have an exceptionally attentive audience such as that enjoyed by the distinguished *New York Times* Washington correspondent R. W. Apple Jr., who on January 21, 1997, characterized President Clinton's second inaugural speech as "a cautious, centrist address filled with appeals for national unity and other unexceptionable homilies." Note that Mr. Apple's readers probably took pride in recognizing not only *unexceptionable* but also *homilies* (the plural of a synonym for "a sermon, especially one that is boring and cliché-ridden").

***exceptional* confusion**   When you use *exceptional*, ask yourself if your context clearly shows which of its two standard meanings you intend. Do you mean "unusual" or "unusually *excellent*"? If you are using *exceptional* to describe schoolchildren, do you mean "gifted" or "handicapped"? Some usage commentators object to the potentially confusing use of *exceptional* to mean "handicapped," but that usage has been established for decades.

exclamation pointers   The exclamation point should be used the way responsible motorists use their horn: only as a last resort.

As linguist R. W. Burchfield writes in his *New Fowler's Modern English Usage*: "Excessive use of exclamation marks . . . is a certain indication of an unpracticed writer or of one who wants to add a spurious dash of sensation to something unsensational."

Exclamation points "irritate the eyes," physician-essayist Lewis Thomas wrote in his *Et Cetera, Et Cetera: Notes of a Word-Watcher*. "They are, as well, pretentious, self-indulgent and in the end almost always pointless. If a string of words is designed to be an astonishment . . . the words should be crafted to stand on their own, not forced to jump up and down by an exclamation point." Thomas playfully but pointedly proposed that writers contemplating the use of an exclamation point be compelled, "by law if necessary," to undergo a seven-day waiting period.

If your desire to use an exclamation point ever becomes uncontrollable, write an essay about the *!Kung* people of southwestern Africa. As noted in the *!Kung* entry of *The American Heritage Dictionary*, *!Kung* is spelled with an exclamation point that represents clicking sounds that serve as a series of consonants in the !Kung language.

exhibit or exhibition?   An *exhibit* is a single attraction at an *exhibition*.

exhilarating, exorbitant, exuberant   Careless spellers often drop the *h* from *exhilarating* ("enlivening") and add a needless *h* to *exorbitant* ("exceeding customary limits") and *exuberant* ("full of unrestrained enthusiasm").

exist or subsist?   *Subsist* means "to continue to exist, manage to survive," as in a *Smithsonian* magazine article (April 1997) about Komodo dragons, the largest lizards in the world, that "subsist in the wild" of Indonesia.

expatiate or expostulate?   You may be wasting time if you *expostulate with* someone ("reason earnestly against something that a person intends to do or has done") if that person *expatiates upon* ("discusses at great length or in great detail") every trivial topic that comes up in conversation.

expect: do you suppose?   The use of *expect* in the sense of "suppose"—as in "I expect she was pleased"—has been categorized as "vulgar or carelessly collo- quial speech" by *The Oxford English Dictionary*.

Today's dictionaries on both sides of the Atlantic generally list the "suppose" sense of *expect* as either colloquial or informal. *The Random House Dictionary of the English Language* reports that the "suppose" sense of *expect* "is encoun- tered in the speech of educated people but seldom in their writing."

You can expect to avoid criticism if you use *suppose* when that is your mean- ing and if you save *expect* for "consider likely" or "consider obligatory."

expensive is what things are   The *price* of a product may be high but never *expensive*. Only the *product* can be expensive. (See also entry for *thrifty*.)

explain or explicate?   Both words mean "to make understandable, interpret, account for." But you should use *explicate* only for "engaging in learned and lengthy examination or analysis."

Usage example: *New York Times* book reviewer Michiko Kakutani pointed out (1/16/1998) that South African author Nadine Gordimer wrote "novel after novel [in which] she has explicated the consequences that [apartheid] had on the lives of individual men and women."

explain requires an explanation   Contrary to what some student writers assume, *explain* is not just another synonym for *say*. *Explain* means to clarify something, as in "He explained that he was late because of a traffic jam." In a statement such as "She explained that she had spent the first 20 years of her life in France," *explained* should be replaced by *said* unless her statement answered the question, for example, of why she spoke French well.

explicit: a word of warning   Be careful that your context explicitly conveys your intended meaning. *Explicit* ("fully and clearly expressed, leaving nothing implied") has acquired an additional meaning as a result of the word's frequent use in the phrase *sexually explicit*. Record companies now warn parents about "explicit lyrics," and the *Random House Webster's Unabridged Dictionary* has extended the traditional definition of *explicit* to include "described or shown in realistic detail [as in] explicit sexual scenes."

explode is not always violent   *Explode* entered English in the 16th century from the Latin *explodere* ("to drive off the stage with hisses and boos"). From that Latin meaning developed our original and still-current use of *explode* to mean "reject, disapprove, disprove, discredit." For example: "Scientists long ago exploded the belief that the Earth is flat."

Explode did not mean "burst with destructive force" until the late 19th century.

exploit for good or evil?   The noun *exploit* (with emphasis on the first sylla-ble) clearly means "bold deed," as in "the exploits of computer-game heroes."

But the verb *exploit* (with emphasis on the second syllable) can be confusing, because it has three distinctly different meanings: "use productively," "use unethically," or "publicize." Any of those meanings could be intended in this sentence: "That engineering firm misses no opportunity to exploit its most tal-ented employees." Use the verb only when your context makes your intended meaning unmistakable: "That engineering firm always exploits its achievements in national advertising campaigns." "That engineering firm has been widely praised for exploiting the latest technology." "That engineering firm has been accused of exploiting undocumented workers."

explosion or *implosion*?   Both are sudden and violent. The first is outward, as in the explosion of a bomb. The second is inward, as in the 9/11 implosion (collapse) of the World Trade Center.

Just as *explosion* can be used figuratively, as in "population explosion," so can *implosion*: In a review of the Clinton administration's foreign policy, *The New York Times* (12/28/2000) recalled that in 1995 "Mexico was facing economic implosion, the result of a dive in the value of the peso after years of financial mismanagement and corruption."

exquisite problems   Some usage commentators say *exquisite* should be pronounced with the emphasis on the first syllable. That pronunciation is listed in the preferred position in *The American Heritage Dictionary* and *Webster's New World College Dictionary*. But, if you feel more comfortable emphasizing the second syllable, you can cite the preference for that pronunciation in the Merriam-Webster and Random House dictionaries.

A more serious problem is the daily devaluation of this once-powerful adjective—meaning "the highest possible excellence"—by (for example) shopping-channel hucksters using it to describe just about any merchandise being promoted at a given moment. (See also "devalued words.")

extemporaneous or *impromptu*?   *Extemporaneous* describes a public speech or other performance that may have been conceived in advance but is delivered without a text. *Impromptu* describes a public speech or performance that is spontaneous.

extent or *extant*?   *Extent*, of course, is a noun that refers to size or range. *Extant* is an adjective meaning "still existing," as in a *Wall Street Journal* reference (5/28/2002) to the British-ruled Iberian peninsula of Gibraltar as "Europe's oldest extant colony."

"eyes only for you"?   When people sing "I only have eyes for you," they are defying logic by putting the word *only* in wrong place. But as columnist Jack Smith noted (9/24/1991), the song is correct from the standpoint of idiom. "Can you imagine," Smith rhetorically asked his readers, "singing 'I have eyes for you only'?" (See also "*only* the adverb causes trouble" and "idioms do their own thing.")

F

fabulous: a victim of devaluation   Once upon a time, *fabulous* meant "belonging to fable, mythical, legendary." By the early 17th century, *fabulous* had acquired an additional, powerful meaning as "something so astonishing that it resembled fable, myth, or legend."

Though those meanings of *fabulous* are still listed in dictionaries, they have been all but smothered since the 1960's by the informal *fabulous* and its abbreviated form, *fab,* that serve as generic sounds of approval for everything from the Beatles to bagels. Today, as linguist R. W. Burchfield writes in his *New Fowler's Modern English Usage,* the all-purpose *fabulous* and *fab* "are used with abandon by the young and the moderately educated." (See also "devalued words.")

facile: too easy?   *Facile* is one of those words whose meaning you must make clear in your context. A common dictionary definition of *facile* is "easy, effortless," as in "facile tasks." But this word is often used in the sense of another dictionary definition: "superficial, not profound or sincere," as in "the candidate's facile solution to the problem."

faction now has a confusing twin   The five-century-old word *faction* ("a clique or group within a political or other organization") must now be distinguished from the 1960's-minted *faction* that is a blend of fact and fiction.

The newer *faction,* a form of writing or filmmaking that focuses on real events or people in a fictional narrative, is commonly referred to in film and TV as *docudrama.* The process of combining fact and fiction is called *factionalization.*

factious or fractious?   *Factious* means "divisive, tending to break up into groups." *Fractious* means "quarrelsome."

factitious or fictitious?   *Factitious* describes something "produced artificially and insincerely"—for example, "a factitious display of affection by two movie stars who actually detest each other."

A *factitious* grassroots movement would be one that is actually controlled by a special-interest group. A *fictitious* ("false, imaginary") grassroots movement would be one that doesn't exist.

factoid: a little fact or a lot of falsehood?   The noun *factoid* was introduced by Norman Mailer in his 1973 biography of Marilyn Monroe to denote so-called facts that "have no existence before appearing in a magazine or newspaper, creations [that] are not so much lies as a product to manipulate emotion [among the general public]." But within a decade, *USA Today* and other media began using the term to mean "a little, briefly stated fact."

Though Mailer's definition of *factoid* is the only one listed in *The Oxford English Dictionary* and the *Random House Webster's Unabridged Dictionary*, the *Encarta World English Dictionary* correctly reports that *factoid* has acquired the additional meaning of "a small and often unimportant bit of information." Recent example: *Reader's Digest* (March 2005) published a reader's sarcastic complaint that the Oregon Commercial Motor Vehicle manual "afforded me the opportunity to learn this important driving factoid: 'According to accident reports, the vehicle that trucks and buses most often run into is the one in front of them.'"

Users of *factoid* need to make sure they communicate which of the two meanings they intend: a trivial bit of information, or a falsehood so widely circulated that it is generally accepted as a fact.

facts: can they be trusted?   It would be comforting to know that we live in a world in which we can be sure about *facts*. Unfortunately, we don't. But you can do something about the problem.

The word *fact*, according to the Merriam-Webster and Random House dictionaries, *The American Heritage Dictionary*, and *Webster's New World College Dictionary*, is now widely used not only for something true but also something only *alleged* to be true. For example, a *New York Times* review of a biography of painter Arshile Gorky (7/11/1999) stated that "almost every fact [Gorky] ever shared about himself was a complete fiction."

The "allegation" sense of *fact* is communicated when the word is "loosely used," according to the ultimate authority on the English language, England's *Oxford English Dictionary.* But America's leading dictionaries and usage manuals grant the "allegation" definition their full acceptance. For example, *The American*

Heritage Book of English Usage states that "*fact* has a long history in the sense [of] 'allegation of fact'" and therefore such phrases as *true facts* and *real facts* "are often useful for emphasis." Such emphasis was evident when TV host Hugh Downs wrote in his introduction to the 1993 *Project Censored Yearbook* that people in a democracy need "true facts," and media scholar Ben H. Bagdikian wrote in the 1992 edition of his *Media Monopoly* that people need "accurate facts."

In response to criticism by some usage commentators that a phrase such as *true facts* is redundant, Kenneth G. Wilson defends *true facts* in his *Columbia Guide to Standard American English* by arguing that "many things alleged to be facts turn out not to be factual after all." But that argument—which also appears in *Merriam-Webster's Dictionary of English Usage*—does not really address the issue. Things that are alleged to be *facts* are obviously alleged to be *true*. They are not alleged to be *allegedly* true. Likewise, we should not redefine *truth* as "alleged truth" or *accuracy* as "alleged accuracy" just because many statements that purport to be truthful or accurate turn out to be false.

If you want to defend precision in this matter, restrict your use of the word *fact* to the sense of "something that is true." And instead of questioning *facts*, question *assertions*.

facts count, but *information* doesn't   See "nouns that don't count."

faculty for or *faculty of*?   If a university president is complimented about his faculty *for* management, that means he is receiving praise for his management skills. If the university president is complimented about his faculty *of* management, that means he is receiving praise for the professors at his campus who teach courses on management.

When you use *faculty*, your context should make clear whether you mean "ability, aptitude, power of the mind" or "members of a learned profession."

faint or *feint*?   Be careful not to write *faint* (a noun or verb referring to an abrupt, usually brief loss of consciousness) when you intend to write *feint* (a noun or verb referring to an action or movement intended to distract or otherwise mislead).

"falling between the cracks" is absurd   The expression "fall through the cracks" is frequently misstated as "fall between the cracks." That absurd mistake is so common that you can find it even in a *New York Times Magazine* article (12/19/2004): "She claims her charity application fell between the cracks."

In an example of correct usage, a psychiatrist wrote in a *New York Times* essay (8/26/1999) that violent racists "continue to fall through the cracks of the mental health system."

farther or **further?**   As two forms of the comparative degree of the adjective and adverb *far*, the words *farther* and *further* are commonly used interchangeably. But usagists are unanimous in asking you to use the *far* word, *farther*, for physical distance, as in "moving farther from his office," and to use *further* for nonphysical distance, as in "moving further from his principles."

Note that you must use *further* as an adjective meaning "additional," as in "further delay," and as a verb meaning "advance," as in "further your career." (See "*continual* or *continuous?*" "*convince* or *persuade?*" "*fewer* or *less?*" "*imply* or *infer?*" "*lay* or *lie?*" "*lend* or *loan?*" and "*that* or *which?*")

fated or **fêted?**   This pair can cause confusion in speech because they are both pronounced "FAYT-id." Moreover, the first word has two meanings.

Fated usually means "destined, predetermined by fate." But it can also mean "destined for destruction, doomed." In the latter sense, *The American Heritage Dictionary* cites "the fated city of Troy."

The soundalike *fêted* means "honored with an elaborate ceremony such as an outdoor festival or feast." Here's a usage example from a *New York Review of Books* article (1/15/1998) by travel writer Pico Iyer: "The Dalai Lama thus finds himself in the disheartening position of being fêted around the world even as he is thwarted in the one central mission of his life [Tibet's liberation from China]."

faun or **fawn?**   *Faun*, from Roman mythology, is a noun that refers to any of a group of rural deities represented as men with the horns, ears, and tail of a goat, and sometimes its legs. *Fawn* is a noun meaning "young deer" and a verb meaning "to seek favor or attention by flattery and obsequious behavior."

faux: watch your step   *Faux* (which has the same pronunciation as *foe*) is an adjective imported from France, meaning "false, fake, artificial," as in "faux fur." *Faux pas* (ending in the sound "pah") literally means "false step," and in practice means "an embarrassing social blunder."

favored or *favorite*?   Feel free to use qualifiers like *most* and *least* with the adjective *favored* ("regarded favorably").

But the adjective *favorite* ("preferred above all others") is an absolute. Either something is the favorite or it isn't. Therefore, you cannot logically qualify it, as in phrases like "most favorite" and "least favorite."

faze or *phase*?   *Faze* ("to disturb, disconcert, embarrass") is not an alternate spelling of *phase* ("a stage or aspect").

fearful or *fearsome*?   *Fearsome* means "frightening." But *fearful* can mean either "frightening" or "frightened."

Risk-free recommendation: For "frightening," use *fearsome*. Forget *fearful*. If you mean "frightened," say so.

February: **should you follow *January*?**   Many people apply the pronunciation pattern of *January* to *February*—"FEB-*yoo*-ary"—using the pronunciation that dictionaries list as an alternate choice. But you risk criticism if you don't use the harder-to-pronounce first choice: "FEB-*roo*-ary."

feckless **means a lack of "feck"**   This is one of many words whose meanings are easy to remember once you know their origin.

The story of *feckless* can be traced to 15th-century Scotland, where the people shortened the word *effect* to *feck*. From *feck* came the words *feckful* ("effective") and *feckless* ("ineffective"). *Feckful* stayed in Scotland, but *feckless* was adopted by both British and American English.

Feckless has acquired such extended meanings of "ineffective" as *incompetent, futile, irresponsible, lazy, weak,* and *worthless*. But if you restrict *feckless* to the simple sense of *ineffective*, you will serve the cause of clarity.

feel bad or *feel badly*?   Don't accept *Newsweek*'s statement (6/25/2001) that "everyone feels badly when people lose their jobs." To learn why that statement is unacceptable, see "verbs that link subjects with adjectives."

feel good or *feel well*?   If you feel *good*, that can mean you are in a good *mood* or in good *health*. But you might as well restrict *feel good* to mood, because *feel well* is restricted to health. Usage example: "Gabbi feels *good* when her diabetic mother feels *well*." (See also "*good* or *well?*" and "verbs that link subjects with adjectives.")

feet or **foot?**   Obviously, dimensions are specified in one *foot* or two or more *feet*. But Standard English requires that someone who is six *feet* tall should be referred to as a six-*foot* person. Likewise, an object that is six *feet* long is described as a six-*foot* object.

felicitous **choices**   If you use this easily misunderstood adjective, derived from a Latin noun for happiness (*felicitas*) and related to a noun of ours for happiness (*felicity*), you'll need to make sure your context makes your meaning clear.

Felicitous can mean "strikingly apt or appropriate, admirably and pleasingly suited to the occasion," as in "a felicitous style." So say *The Oxford English Dictionary*, *The Concise Oxford Dictionary*, *The New Oxford American Dictionary*, *Webster's New World College Dictionary*, and the *Random House Webster's Unabridged Dictionary*.

But *felicitous* is defined not only as "apt" and "pleasingly suited" but also as "pleasant, delightful" by the *Longman Dictionary of the English Language* and the college-edition Random House, American Heritage, and Merriam-Webster dictionaries.

Likewise, the noun *felicity* can mean both "appropriate style or apt expression" and "happiness or source of happiness." Usage example of the second meaning: Nature writer David Quammen, reviewing for *The New York Times* (7/6/1997) a book about the evolution of our planet's 2,700 species of snakes, criticized people who take for granted the stupendous wonder of biological diversity as if it were one of "the trivial, marginal felicities [pleasing features] of nature."

If you succeed in using this word in a way that makes your meaning absolutely clear, you deserve *felicitations* ("congratulations").

ferment or **foment?**   Political extremists *foment* ("incite") discontent in order to cause *ferment* ("a state of agitation, unrest"). Usage example of *ferment*: A London *Economist* article (10/10/1998) about political upheavals in Southeast Asia said, "Political ferment still bubbles."

Fermentation is the bubbling chemical change caused by the action of an organic substance such as yeast on complex chemical compounds—for example, the process by which yeast enzymes convert grape sugar into ethyl alcohol.

fervent or fervid?   Both mean "characterized by warm, glowing enthusiasm." But *fervid* may be used to imply that the enthusiasm is overheated. For example: "She was frightened by his fervid display of affection."

fetish is not just any yen   If you're talking to a word connoisseur, don't confess that you have a *fetish* (as in "yen, craving") for candy. *Fetish* literally means "an object worshipped by primitive people because of its supposed magical power." Figuratively, *fetish* means "any object or idea that receives irrational reverence" or the "irrational reverence" itself. In psychology, a *fetish* is an object (such as an article of clothing) that becomes the focus of a sexual fixation.

fewer or less?   Be proud of yourself if you observe the two-century-old distinction between these words.

Fewer refers to a plural quantity, as in an *Economist* article (1/17/2004) about corporate mergers resulting in "fewer banks." *Less* refers to a single amount, as in a *New York Times* article (5/27/2004) about a trucking company that gave its drivers classes on how to use "less diesel fuel."

Reminders: Eating *fewer* calories results in *less* fat. Having *fewer* employed people obviously means *less* employment.

By the way, maintaining a distinction between *fewer* and *less* can contribute to clarity. "Frank's troubles are *less* than mine" means "Frank's total amount of grief is not as large as mine." "Frank's troubles are *fewer* than mine" means "Frank's problems are not *as numerous* as mine."

fey: a strange word   A little knowledge about this little word can be deceiving.

If you have encountered *fey* in literary classics dating back to the Old English epic *Beowulf,* you are familiar with the word's age-old sense of "doomed to die, dying, deadly." But as *The Oxford English Dictionary* reports, the literary sense of *fey* is now regarded as archaic except for what the *OED* calls its surviving "popular use" in Scotland.

Fey eventually came to mean "strange in behavior like somebody about to die." By extension, *fey* in British and American English now means strange in behavior in any of the following ways: unreal, eccentric, visionary, enchanted, spellbound, magical, otherworldly, whimsical, elfin, shy.

Note that each of the words after the colon in the previous sentence will convey your meaning more precisely than *fey.*

fiancé or fiancée?   The single-*e* spelling is the male from and the double-*e* spelling the female form for "a person engaged to be married." The term is derived from an Old French word for "promise," which was derived from a Latin word for "trust."

fight with or fight against?   The statement that someone "fought *with* the French" leaves us guessing about whether that person fought *on the side of* the French or *against* them. Change "fight with" to a phrase that leaves no doubt, such as "fight on the side of" or "fight against" or "oppose."

fillers: listen to your own   All of us are painfully aware of the use by others of conversational fillers such as *like, you know,* and the non-words *er, uh,* and *um.* If you tape one of your own conversations, you might be surprised to learn how frequently you use fillers to cover your pauses in thought.

If you are afflicted with Filler Syndrome, try replacing your fillers with total silence. Your silences won't last long, and they may prompt people to pay more attention to what you say. (See also "*like* as a filler" and "*you know* is too well known.")

firmament isn't really firm   Derived from the Latin *firmamentum* ("a strengthening, support"), *firmament* is a poetic way of referring to the sky as "the arch or vault of heaven."

Perhaps it was the misleading look and sound of *firmament* that caused an editorial writer for the *Pasadena* (Calif.) *Star-News*—on the day after Southern California's major earthquake of January 17, 1994—to refer to the region's frequent and sudden "movements of the firmament." (California's earthquakes aren't *that* bad.) The writer should have written "movements of *terra firma*" (the Latin phrase meaning "solid ground"). (See also "Latinisms.")

first two or two first?   *First two,* as in "the first two runners to cross the finish line," is clear and acceptable.

Two first is avoided by careful writers because it is ambiguous. "The *two first* finishers" might mean the finishers who placed first and second or two finishers who both placed first.

first or firstly?   Usage commentators urge you not to mix *firstly* in enumerations with *second, third,* etc. For the sake of consistency, they recommend *first, second, third,* etc., or *firstly, secondly, thirdly,* etc.

Overall, the usage commentators favor *first, second, third,* etc.

firth, fjord, or ford?   A word we imported from Norway, *fjord* (also spelled *fiord*), denotes "a long, narrow inlet [passage of water] from the sea, bordered by steep cliffs." *Fjord* produced *firth,* a Scottish word that stands for either "a long, narrow inlet from the sea" or "an estuary [a broad mouth of a river into which the tide flows]."

The word *ford* is a noun for a place where a river or other body of water is shallow enough to be crossed on foot. And *ford* is also a verb, meaning "to cross at a ford."

fishing for a plural?   The plural of *fish* is also *fish,* except for references to species of *fishes.* (See also "plurals that are also singular" and "*schools of fish* are not accredited.")

flaccid: the pronunciation isn't flabby   This word meaning "flabby, lacking firmness, soft and limp" is preferably pronounced with a firm "FLACK-sid."

flack or flak?   "Too Much Flak Downs a Flack." That was the heading for a *Time* magazine article (10/7/1991) about *flak* (a slang term for criticism abusive enough to be compared to the *flak* that means *anti-aircraft fire*) causing the firing of a prominent *flack* (a somewhat disparaging American slang term for *press agent*).

Flack and *flak* occasionally show up in print with their spelling switched. To avoid contributing to that confusion, remember that the press-agent *flack* contains a *c,* as in *communications.*

If the spelling of *flak* looks strange to you, there's a reason. *Flak* was the World War Two German acronym for *Flieger* ("aircraft") *Abwehr* ("defense") *Kanone* ("cannon"). After Allied planes were shot down by *flak* (anti-aircraft cannon) fire, the word *flak* began to refer to the anti-aircraft shells and explosions. *Flak* subsequently acquired the extended meaning of "barrage of criticism." And press agents—now called publicists or public relations practitioners—became known as "flak-catchers."

flail or flay?   To *flail* is to whip, typically in a swinging motion. To *flay* is to whip so vigorously that the skin is removed.

flair or flare?   A person who has an aptitude for using fireworks may be said to have a *flair* for *flares*.

Usage example for *flair*: *The Economist* reported (3/4/2000) that "the Indian economy . . . is starting to reap handsome benefits from its flair for the information-technology and knowledge-based industries that may drive the world economy in years to come."

flammable or inflammable?   These words are synonyms for "combustible." Trucks carrying gasoline or explosives are usually marked *flammable* because that newer, 19th-century coinage was adopted in the 1920's as a replacement for *inflammable* by the National Fire Protection Association. The association, and subsequently other organizations involved in fire safety, were motivated by concern that some people might wrongly assume that *inflammable* means *not* flammable. (The prefix *in-* does indeed mean *not* in a host of words, such as *independent, inhospitable, infrequent,* and *indivisible*.)

Strunk and White's *Elements of Style* recommended, "Unless you are operating a truck [with combustible cargo] and hence are concerned with the safety of children and illiterates, use *inflammable*." (See also "*invaluable* information.")

flat adverbs   See "adverbs that look like adjectives."

flaunt or flout?   *Flaunt* ("show off boastfully") and *flout* ("treat with contemptuous disregard") are frequently confused with each other.

For example, the *Los Angeles Times* (12/28/2000) used *flout* when it should have used *flaunt* in reporting that Japanese teenage shoppers "who once hid their Uniqlo [clothing] bags in shame because of their cut-rate image now flouted the newly cool brand." The reverse error was made in President Clinton's "Middle-

Class Bill of Rights" speech in December 1994, when he said that "some people take advantage of the rest of us by flaunting our immigration laws."

Examples of *correct* usage from *The New York Times*: A book reviewer (8/27/2000) condemned "a work that flouts most principles of scientific scholarship." A *Times* foreign correspondent, filing a story (11/21/2000) from the military dictatorship of Myanmar (formerly Burma), wrote that "the generals and their families are getting rich and flaunting it."

flautist or flutist?   A musician who plays the flute is preferably called a *flutist* in American English and a *flautist* in British English.

Our American preference, *flutist,* has been traced back to 1603. The British preference, *flautist,* was adapted by the English from the Italian word *flautista* in 1860.

fleshly or fleshy?   For Chaucer and his contemporaries, both *fleshly* and *fleshy* meant "plump." Today the meaning "plump" is assigned to *fleshy*. The word *fleshly* now denotes "sensual, carnal, lascivious, worldly, of or pertaining to the flesh or body."

flicker with hope or despair?   Like a picture that could be perceived as either a sunrise or a sunset, the image of something *flickering* ("burning unsteadily") could be promising or depressing.

For example, a *Los Angeles Times* headline about the mood of L.A. during the summer of 1992—"Optimism Flickers on the 4th [of July]"—could have meant that optimism was flickering on or off. Readers had to wait until the fourth paragraph to learn that optimism had "fizzled like a damp fuse."

If you use *flickering* imagery, make sure your intended meaning is clear, as in this opening sentence of an article in *The New York Times Magazine* (7/5/1992): "A smile of triumph flickers around the mouth of Dan Quayle."

flier or flyer?   An associate professor of journalism at the University of Texas at Austin wrote a letter (11/11/1991) asking colleagues around the nation to post a notice about faculty openings in his department. In the second line of the letter, he referred to the notice as a *flier*. Four lines later, he spelled it *flyer*. Which was correct?

Flier is preferred in American English, *flyer* in British English. They both spell a small handbill or circular, a person or animal that flies, a trapeze performer, one of the steps in a straight flight of stairs, or a part of a machine having a rapid motion.

flotsam or jetsam? *Flotsam* is "floating debris, goods lost by shipwreck." *Jetsam* is "that which has been *jetti*soned, goods thrown overboard to lighten a vessel during an emergency."

flounder or founder? A fish out of water *flounders* ("thrashes about, struggles awkwardly"), but a ship *founders* ("sinks"). A statement that a "ship founders and sinks" is a redundancy. Memory tip: *Founder* comes from a Latin word for *bottom*, as in *foundation*.

In their figurative senses, *flounder* suggests that failure is still avoidable, but *founder* speaks of failure that has actually happened. Usage example: *The New York Times* reported (11/26/2000) that negotiations for a treaty to curb global warming collapsed "after a tense all-night bargaining session foundered on last-minute disputes between European and American negotiators."

With the verb *founder* having the same form as the noun *founder*, you can expect now and then to see an embarrassing error such as the following from the *Huntsville* (Ala.) *News* (1/10/1996): "Michael Batterberry, a foundering editor of *Food Arts* magazine . . ."

fluorescence and fluorine: catch the *flu* These words, which begin with *flu*, are often misspelled as if they began with *flour*.

Fluorescence involves the emission of light, as in a *fluorescent* lamp, from a substance such as the mineral *fluorite* while that substance is being acted upon by radiant energy, such as ultraviolet or X-rays.

Fluorine, the most reactive of all chemical elements, is used in various industrial compounds.

focus is not just for groups Never begin writing about something until you are able to express your theme or goal in a single, sharply focused sentence that you write as a memo to yourself. Example: "I intend to show that a satisfying summer vacation can be spent in one's hometown."

After you have completed your first draft, delete everything not relevant to your goal, even if you must sacrifice material you consider fascinating. If you discover, however, that everything you have deleted is more interesting than what remains, consider the possibility that you need a new topic. In that case, rewrite your theme-sentence memo and then delete everything not relevant to your *new* theme.

folk etymology   See *entomology, etymology,* and *folk etymology.*

follow **these prepositions**   Heads of state usually are *followed by* body-guards whose job it is to *follow* their instructions in case someone *follows through* on a terrorist threat uncovered by other agents who *follow up* on rumors of such activity.

food of the gods   The ultimate culinary compliment is to refer to a dish of food as *ambrosia* (from a Greek word, *ambrotos,* for "immortality"), because in Greek mythology *ambrosia* was "the food of the gods, conferring immortality." If you want to describe something as "divinely delicious," your fail-safe choice is *ambrosial.*

A divinely delicious drink can be called *nectar,* because in Greek mythology *néktar* was the name for "the life-giving drink of the gods." *Nectar,* of course, also means pure fruit juice or the life-perpetuating, sweet secretion of a plant that attracts insects or birds that pollinate the plant's flower. Note that the adjective that means "of the nature of nectar"—*nectarine*—is identical to the delicious-sounding noun for the fuzzless peach.

fooling your reader is foolish   "It's not easy being a dad, especially when you have 240 kids," a journalism student of mine wrote at the beginning of his feature story. "Yes, you read right, 240!" That feature-story lead was a foolish attempt to deceive the reader, who would soon discover that the story was about a university official who served as an adviser to the university's 240 international students.

Here's a reader-deceiver that managed to slip into *Discover* magazine (3/1993): "William Waycott has a really tiny head. Oh, he started off with an ordinary, regulation-size head, mind you. But with hard work and a lot of perseverance, he managed to shrink it down to a quarter of its original size. If Waycott has his way, we'll all have tiny heads soon." In the next sentence the writer reveals—surprise!—that he has been writing about a plant physiologist who is working on the development of smaller, consumer-convenient heads of lettuce.

Leave deception to magicians and (insert here whatever other professional group you associate with deception). If you really have a good story to tell, begin with a compelling but non-deceiving aspect of that story.

In the case of the "dad with 240 kids," the student writer could have made a legitimate bid for the attention of the reader by beginning with an interesting anecdote that illustrated the adviser's dedication to his job. In the lettuce-head story, the curiosity-driven readers of *Discover* would have been better served if the writer had taken the trouble to show *how* plant physiologists are (to quote the article) "monkeying around with nature's vegetable bin." Or the writer could have begun by focusing on the compelling debate over whether or not we *should* be monkeying around with nature.

footnotes decoded   The abbreviation *c.* or *ca.* (*circa*) means "about," as in "circa 1942." The abbreviation *cf.* (*confer*) means "compare," as in "compare another source." (Note that *cf.* does not mean simply "see," though it is often used that way.)

The abbreviation *et al.* (*et alii*) means "and others," as in "Jones, Smith, et al." in a listing of co-authors. Note the period signifying that *al.* is an abbreviation of *alii*.

The abbreviation *et seq.* (*et sequens*) means "and the following"; and *f.* or *ff.* means, "and the following page or pages."

The abbreviation *ibid.* (*ibidem*) means "in the same place" and refers to the work mentioned in the immediately preceding citation. *Op. cit.* (*opere citato*) means "in the work cited" and refers to a previously mentioned publication of the author. *Passim* means "throughout" and refers to the idea that a subject can be found in various places of a cited publication. The abbreviation *q.v.* (*quod vide*, meaning "which see") recommends that you see a previous citation.

forbear or **forebear**?   *Forbear* is a verb meaning *to refrain* ("show self-restraint"). *Forebear* is a noun meaning *ancestor* ("someone who came be*fore*").

forbid: a **bad** past tense   The past tense of this verb, *forbade*, is preferably pronounced "for-BAD."

forceful or *forcible?*   A person or a speech can be *forceful* ("powerful, effective") but not *forcible* ("accomplished with physical force").

forefront is not where it's *at*   Say "*in* [not *at*] the forefront," just as you would say "*in* [not *at*] the vanguard." Both *forefront* and *vanguard* mean "a movement or trend's leading position."

forego or *forgo?*   To *forgo* means "to do without," as in a *New York Times* article (9/7/2000) about "computer-adept high school students [who] forgo college in favor of entering the red-hot technology field."

   Forgo can also be spelled *forego*. But you will avoid needless confusion if you save *forego* to mean "to go be*fore*, to precede."

foreign: a question of perspective   Dictionaries define *foreign* as "of or pertaining to another country or nation." But in our age of enhanced multicultural awareness, *foreign* is in some cases yielding to *international*. For example, universities refer to students from other countries as *international* students, and the staff of Cable News Network have been instructed by their founder, Ted Turner, that "any person, event, etc., not part of the United States be referred to as *international* rather than *foreign*."

foreword or *forward?*   The noun *foreword* ("a preface or introductory note to a book") is sometimes confused with the adjective, adverb, or verb *forward*.

   Forward, as an adjective, can mean "belonging to the front, eager, bold, progressive, precocious, made in advance." As an adverb, *forward* (also spelled *forwards*) can mean "toward the front, toward the future, in the prescribed direction, into consideration." As a verb, *forward* can mean "to help advance, to send on [as to another address]."

former, latter: two ways to spell *annoying?*   Your use of *the former* (meaning "the first of two cited persons or things") or *the latter* ("the last of two cited persons or things") can be annoying when those phrases force your reader to stop and reread. A simple solution is to replace those phrases with the name of the person or thing you're referring to.

formidable pronunciation *Formidable*—meaning "hard to overcome," "awe-inspiring," or "arousing fear"—is preferably pronounced with the stress on the first syllable. Many Americans have been influenced by a British tendency to say "for-MID-able," but even the British *New Fowler's Modern English Usage* says that pronunciation is "not recommended."

forte: should you hold the *fort*? Be prepared to be "corrected" no matter how you pronounce the *forte* that comes to us from an Old French word meaning "strong" and that in English is a noun meaning "strong point, a skill at which a person excels."

The most common American pronunciation of this word is "FOR-tay." And that is the pronunciation preferred by 74 percent of the usage panel of *The American Heritage Dictionary*. But that dictionary's own editors say that the "strong point" *forte* "should properly be pronounced" like *fort*, inasmuch as the "FOR-tay" pronunciation really applies to the pronunciation of the *forte* that is the Italian-derived adverb, adjective, and noun used in music notation and meaning "loud and *forceful*."

Merriam-Webster's Dictionary of the English Language declares that, inasmuch as the "strong point" *forte* qualifies as an English word and there is "no etymologically respectable pronunciation available" for it, we should feel free to pronounce it "as we see fit." But that source acknowledges that "FOR-tay" has "incurred vociferous disapproval" for being an Italian pronunciation of a French word and that the supposedly proper pronunciation, "fort," distorts the pronunciation actually used by the French—"for"—in talking about *their* "strong point," *le fort*.

Risk-free exit from this mess: Don't hesitate to use *forte* in your writing, as in a *New York Times Magazine* article (1/9/2000), "Finland's Forte," about that nation's achievements in classical music. But in your spoken communication, replace *forte* with *specialty*, *special skill*, *strong point*, or *expertise*.

forthcoming or forthright? *Forthright* means "candid, straightforward."

Forthcoming has an overlapping meaning: "candid, open, cooperative." But *forthcoming* is risky because it can also mean "approaching, soon to be available." The statement "Police Chief Smith's announcement was forthcoming" can mean either that the announcement was candid or that it was coming soon.

If you risk using *forthcoming*, make sure your context unmistakably points to your intended meaning. Example: *Time* magazine (8/15/1994) reported in an article on the Clinton-era Whitewater hearings that members of Congress had accused Deputy Treasury Secretary Roger Altman of being "less than forthcoming [cooperative] about the department's contacts with the White House over an investigation into the failed S&L at the center of Whitewater."

fortitude is a matter of character   Contrary to widespread misusage, *fortitude* does not mean "physical strength." It means "the strength of mind that enables a person to face misfortunate courageously."

fortuitous: a chancy word   If you are married and you accidentally encounter a former lover, think twice before you describe the encounter to your spouse as *fortuitous*.

Though *fortuitous* ("for-TOO-itus") means "accidental, by chance," your spouse may think you mean "fortunate." That is because (to quote *Garner's Modern American Usage*) "the word is commonly misused for *fortunate*, in itself a very unfortunate thing."

Fortuitous (originating in a Latin word for "chance") entered the English language as a term for "happening by chance" in the mid-17th century. But ever since the early 20th century, so many people have mistaken *fortuitous* for "fortunate" that some U.S. dictionaries list "fortunate" in addition to the original definition. And *fortuitous* has acquired widespread acceptance in the combined sense of "by fortunate chance," according to *The Columbia Guide to Standard American English*, Kingsley Amis' *King's English* usage guide, and *The American Heritage Dictionary*.

Nevertheless, the "happening by chance" definition is still the only one prescribed by *The Oxford English Dictionary, The New Fowler's Modern English Usage*, Strunk and White's *Elements of Style*, Follett's *Modern American Usage, The New York Public Library Writer's Guide to Style and Usage*, the *Columbia Journalism Review's* "Language Corner," and the stylebooks of *The New York Times, The Wall Street Journal*, and *The Economist*.

"fortune telling" and "mind reading"   Careful nonfiction writers use attribution ("she said," "he noted," and so on) to avoid giving the false impression that they can predict the future or read minds.

Regarding this "fortune telling": If a politician *says* he will never agree to a tax increase, careful writers do not report that the politician will never agree to a tax increase. Nobody can predict what the politician, or anybody else, will actually do. Careful writers report only what they know, which in this case is that the politician *says* he will never agree to a tax increase.

Likewise, careful writers heed warnings against "mind reading"—warnings such as this one from the 1996 edition of Edward Jay Friedlander and John Lee's *Feature Writing for Newspapers and Magazines*: "Don't Mind-Read. When writing about people and using the occasional paraphrase to season your direct quotes, there's a tendency to drift into word construction such as 'The mayor feels that big business is wrecking the economy.' Don't. It's better to say 'The mayor *says* big business is wrecking the economy.' The same advice holds for describing emotions. Don't say 'The senator was angry.' Tell us 'The senator shook his fist at the audience and demanded silence.' We'll get the idea. Mind reading is for clairvoyants and has no place in [professional writing]."

If that advice sounds overcautious, consider a feature story reprinted in the January 1992 *Harper's Magazine* from the March 6, 1991, issue of the Sebring, Florida, *News-Sun*. The writer of the newspaper feature story, which was about a hometown serviceman's experiences in the Gulf War, told readers that the serviceman "did feel homesick but he knew that a lot of people were counting on the allied troops [and he did not] think so highly of those who protested the war." By omitting attribution—by not saying, for example, that the serviceman *said* he felt homesick—the newspaper writer became an unintentional accomplice to a hoax. Three months after publication of the newspaper article (*Harper's* reported), the serviceman was abruptly discharged for "fabricating his stories of combat in the Middle East [when] he was in fact at an Air Force base in North Dakota during the war."

"Mind reading" is generally okay if you are telling an anecdote ("It was his first job interview, and he was terrified . . ."). But use attribution even with an anecdote when you want your reader to know that you have some doubt about the story's accuracy ("The suspect's mother gave this version of the events leading up to the crime . . .").

forum, Forum, forums, fora   The word *forum* signifies "a place for public discussion or the public discussion itself." The capitalized *Forum* refers to the "place of public assembly in ancient Rome."

Though dictionaries list *fora* as a variant of the plural *forums*, the Latin-faithful *fora* is almost unknown outside of pedantic prose.

***forward* or *forwards*?**   This word is spelled *forward* as an adjective and *forward* or *forwards* as an adverb. In the adverbial use, *forward* is favored in American English, *forwards* in British English. (See also "*afterward* or *afterwards*?*" "*backward* or *backwards*?*" "*foreword* or *forward*?*" and "*toward* or *towards*?*")

***foyer*: it's now English**   Don't apologize if anyone criticizes you for pronouncing *foyer* ("lobby, anteroom, entrance hall") just the way it looks. In English, the pronunciation "FOY-er" is preferred over the French-flavored "FOY-ay."

Foyer is derived from *foier*, an Old French word for "fireplace," because theater audiences used to go to a room with a fireplace to keep warm between acts. But English speakers who really want to show off by pronouncing *foyer* with a French accent should say "FWA-yay."

***fragmentary* or *fragmented*?**   *Fragmentary* means "*consisting* of fragments, incomplete." *Fragmented* means "*broken* into fragments."

fragments   See "sentence fragments are impostors."

***Frankenstein*: a monstrous mistake**   The nameless monster created by Baron Frankenstein in Mary Wollstonecraft Shelley's 1818 Gothic novel is often erroneously called *Frankenstein*. Likewise, the phrase *a Frankenstein* is now widely used to identify any invention that threatens to destroy its creator.

That confusion of the invention with its inventor was so common by the 1920's that Fowler's *Dictionary of Modern English Usage* called it "almost, but surely not quite, sanctioned by custom." The 1996 *New Fowler's Modern English Usage* said, "This use is so widespread and so embedded in the language now that it looks unlikely to be dislodged."

Editor Erik Wensberg, in his 1998 revision of Wilson Follett's *Modern American Usage*, ruled that *a Frankenstein* is as "legitimate" as *a Ford*. But Baron Frankenstein never sold Frankensteins. And Professor J. N. Hook, in his *Appropriate Word*, wisely recommends that you "avoid risk of ridicule by saying '*a Frankenstein monster.*'"

free gift   See "*gift* should be freed of redundancy."

French phrases beginning with *au* Even if your French is flawless, your readers and listeners may say *au revoir* ("good-bye") to you if you habitually make yourself sound pretentious by saying *au contraire* for "on the contrary," *au naturel* for "naked," *au fait* for "well informed," or *au fond* for "fundamentally."

Somewhat less risky is the often-useful phrase *au courant*, pronounced "oh koo-RAHN" and meaning "fully informed on current affairs."

Less risky still is *au pair* ("oh PAIR"), a brief way of saying "a young foreigner who usually does housework and helps care for the children of a household in exchange for room and board, a small salary, and a chance to learn about the host country." The literal French meaning of *au pair*, "as an equal," is fitting because an *au pair* traditionally is treated more like a member of the family than a professional nanny.

You run no risk at all if you refer to common French descriptions of cuisine, such as *au gratin* ("topped with buttered breadcrumbs or grated cheese or both and then browned in an oven"). (See also next entry.)

French toast Here's an alphabetical toast to French terms that are used in Standard English.

Agent provocateur ("AH-jon pro-voc-ah-TUHR"), literally, agent of provocation; actually, a person assigned to incite others to commit criminal acts. *Aide-de-camp* ("ED-de-COM"), confidential adviser to a senior officer, trusted assistant. *Amour* ("a-MOOR"), a love affair, especially one that is illicit. *Amour propre* ("a-moor PROP-rah"), literally, love of self; actually, self-esteem. *Ancien régime* ("AHN-see-en ray-ZHEEM"), the old order, as in France before the revolution of 1789 or any established system that no longer exists. *Avant-garde* ("ah-vant-GARD"), an adjective meaning innovative, or a noun for an innovative group, in both cases especially applying to the arts. *Belles-lettres* ("bell-LET-rah"), literature of a serious, artistic nature. *Blasé* ("blah-ZAY"), nonchalant, world-weary. *Bonhomie* ("bon-om-ME"), good nature, pleasant disposition. *Bon mot* ("bon MOH"), witty remark. *Bon vivant* ("bon vee-VANT"), literally, good living; actually, a refined person who enjoys the good things in life. *Bon voyage* ("bon voy-AHJ"), good journey, meaning "have a good trip." *Cadre* ("KAH-dray"), a group trained to lead a larger group, as in a political movement. *C'est la guerre* ("say lah GAIR"), such is war, such is life (an expression of resignation). *Chez* ("shay"), at the home or place of. *Cinéma vérité* ("see-nay-MAH vay-ree-TAY"), cinema of truth, a style of cinema that emphasizes realism. *Contretemps* ("CON-truh-tom"), literally, against time; actually, an unforeseen event that disrupts the normal situation. *Coup d'état* ("coo day-TAH"), sudden overthrow of the government; *coup de théâtre* ("coo duh tay-AHT-ra"), a sudden, major turn of events in a play or real life; *crème de la crème* ("KREM duh la KREM"), literally, cream of the cream; actually, the very best; *cri de coeur* ("cree duh KUHR"), cry from the heart, heartfelt plea. *Cul-de-sac* ("kuhl-duh-SACK"), literally, bottom of a sack; actually, dead-end street. *De trop* ("duh TROH"), literally, in excess; actually, excessive. *Du jour* ("doo ZHURE"), literally, of the day; actually, prepared for a given day. *Élan* ("ay-LAHN"), distinctive style or flair, dashing quality. *Enfant terrible* ("ahn-FAHN teh-REEB-la"), literally, terrible child; actually, a person whose unconventional behavior creates embarrassment. *En masse* ("on MAHSS"), as a group, all together. *Ennui* ("on-WEE"), boredom. *Entre nous* ("on-truh NOO"), between ourselves, confidentially. *Esprit de corps* ("es-SPREE duh CORE"), literally, spirit of the group; actually, a group's enthusiastic devotion to a cause. *Fait accompli* ("feht ac-kom-PLEE"), accomplished fact, presumably irreversible. *Faux pas* ("foe PAH"), literally, false step; actually, social blunder. *Finesse* ("fin-NESS"), to handle with a deceptive strategy. *Gauche* ("GOsh"), literally, left, perhaps in reference to our usually weaker left hand; actually, awkward, lacking social grace. *Genre* ("JHAN-reh"), a category of artistic achievement, characterized by a distinctive quality such as style or content.

Others include: *Joie de vivre* ("zhwa de VEE-vra"), enthusiasm for life, high spirits. *Laissez faire* ("less-ay FAIR"), literally, allow to do; actually, an economic doctrine advocating government non-interference in commerce. *Lèse majesté* ("LEZ maj-i-stay"), literally, injured sovereignty; actually, high treason, a crime committed against the supreme power of the state. *Louche* ("loosh"), disreputable, of questionable taste or morality. *Macabre* ("muh-KAH-breh"), gruesome, from the Old French phrase *Danse Macabre*, the Dance of Death in which Death leads us all to the same final end. *Manqué* ("mon-KAY"), unfulfilled in the realization of one's ambitions, as in an artist manqué. *Mélange* ("may-LANZH"), miscellaneous mixture. *Mot juste* ("moh ZHUST"), precisely the right word. *Noblesse oblige* ("no-BLESS oh-BLEEZH"), literally, nobility is an obligation; actually, the obligation of people of high social position to behave kindly toward others. *Nouveau riche* ("NOO-vo REESH"), a newly rich person, usually used pejoratively. *Oeuvre* ("UHR-vr"), the complete works of a writer, artist, or composer. *Outré* ("oo-TRAY"), eccentric, bizarre.

And still others: *Rapprochement* ("rah-prosh-MON"), reestablishment of friendly relations, especially between nations. *RSVP*, the abbreviation for *répondez s'il vous plaît* ("ray-PON-day seel voo pleh"), respond please [to this invitation]. *Sang-froid* ("san-FRWA"), literally, cold blood; actually, calmness and composure under strain. *Savoir faire* ("sav-wah FAIR"), literally, to know how to do; actually, sophisticated knowledge of what to do or say in social behavior. *Sobriquet* ("so-brih-KAY"), nickname. *Soigné* ("swa-NYAY"), well groomed. *Tour de force* ("toor deh FORCE"), literally, feat of strength; actually, powerful exhibition of skill. *Voilà* ("vwah-LA"), literally, see there; actually, an interjection used to express satisfaction with something shown or accomplished. *Volte-face* ("volt-FAHS"), about-face, reversal of policy.

(See also entries for *accouterments, adieu, à la, ambiance, billet doux, bon appétit, cache, cause célèbre, chaise longue, charivari, chic, coup de grâce, déjà vu, dénouement, de rigueur, double entendre, elite, éminence grise, en route, entrée, faux, fiancé, forte, frisson, gourmand, haute, idée fixe, je ne sais quoi, mêlée, mésalliance, mise en scène, née, objet d'art, papier-mâché, pâté, pièce de résistance, raison d'être, rendezvous, restaurateur, soiree,* and *vis-à-vis.*)

frequently or **often**? These adverbs are usually interchangeable. But the *Random House Webster's Unabridged Dictionary* cites the following distinctions: "*Often* implies numerous repetitions, sometimes, regularity of recurrence: *We often go there; frequently* suggests especially repetition at comparatively short intervals: *It happens frequently.*" (See also "*often:* is it *t*-time again?")

freshman: a nonsexist alternative In recent years, some American campuses have replaced the term *freshman* with *first-year student*. The British have had an alternative for decades: the slang term *fresher*. But if you use that in the United States, people are likely to respond, "Fresher than what?"

friable or **fryable**? Eggs are *fryable* ("capable of being fried"). Cookies are *friable* ("easily crumbled or broken").

friendly advice The proper preposition to go with *friend* is usually *of*, as in "He's a friend of mine." Use *with* only when *friend* is plural, as in "make friends with."

As noted by *The Columbia Guide to Standard American English*, "[Friend] *to* has a rather old-fashioned air but still occurs: *She is a friend to every stray animal*." But *Merriam-Webster's Dictionary of English Usage* notes that *to* is the most appropriate choice for *friendly*, as in "His boss is always friendly to him."

***frisson*: catch this cold**   If you are not familiar with *frisson* (a French word pronounced in English as "free-SONE"), you can catch and retain the meaning by noting its "cold" history.

The Latin word *frigere* ("to be cold") inspired the Old French word *friçon* for "a trembling" (as in the act of trembling when you're cold), which inspired *frisson* with its meaning of "a shiver of excitement."

Usage example from a *New Yorker* cartoon (10/8/2001): At one end of a couch, a man types on his laptop computer. At the other end, his neglected wife turns toward him and says, "All I ask for is an occasional frisson."

"from Dan to Beersheba" or "David and Bathsheba"?   Both phrases are from the Bible. But the first is about places, the second about people.

As recorded in Judges 20:2, *Dan* was the northernmost limit of the Holy Land, *Beersheba* the southernmost. Hence, for those who know their Bible, *from Dan to Beersheba* means "everywhere, all over the place."

David and Bathsheba is a 1952 Darryl F. Zanuck movie, in which King David (played by Gregory Peck) loves Bathsheba (Susan Hayward), the wife of one of King David's captains.

***fruit* or *vegetable*?**   The scientists who study plant life, botanists, use *vegetable* only as an adjective (meaning "having to do with plants"), as in *vegetable* (plant) *matter* or *vegetable* (plant) *kingdom*. For botanists, such edible vegetable matter as lettuce and spinach are *leaves*, potatoes are *tubers*, and the matured ovaries of seed plants—including apples, pears, bananas, and tomatoes—are fruits. (See also "*tomato*: ripe for argument?")

***fulsome*: too full of risk?**   If you use *fulsome* the way it is frequently understood, to mean "abundant," you'll risk the ire of word guardians. If you use *fulsome* as defined by the word guardians, to mean "insincerely, offensively excessive," your message is likely to be widely misinterpreted. No wonder

British novelist-critic Kingsley Amis declared in his posthumously published 1997 usage guide, *The King's English*, that *fulsome* was "not to be used henceforth by careful writers."

Fulsome was easy to deal with when it entered Middle English in the 13th century as a form of the hyphenated word *full-some* ("abundant, plentiful"). But as noted by Adrian Room's *Dictionary of Changes in Meaning*, the word *fulsome* began to acquire its present "insincerely, offensively excessive" sense in the 14th century, and that sense prevailed by the 16th century. Now, according to the American Heritage dictionaries, the "abundant" *fulsome* is obsolete, and today's only correct sense of *fulsome* "combines the idea of fullness or abundance with that of excess or insincerity."

But as *Webster's New World College Dictionary* and *The New Fowler's Modern English Usage* report, the "insincerely excessive" fulsome is being challenged by a revival of the old "abundant" fulsome. As a reflection of this confusing situation, the *Random House Webster's College Dictionary* defines *fulsome* as "disgustingly excessive" and also as "comprehensive, abundant." Similarly, *Merriam-Webster's Collegiate Dictionary* defines *fulsome* as "disgusting, overdone" and also as "copious, well-rounded."

Risk-free suggestion: Instead of using *fulsome*, especially in "fulsome praise," use *excessive* or *abundant* or whatever other expression clearly conveys your intended meaning. Thus, not only will you avoid being misunderstood, you will also avoid the need to remember that the first syllable of *fulsome* is not completely *full*.

fun is okay to have   Feel free "to have fun [enjoyment]" or "to *be* fun [a *source* of enjoyment]." But as noted in *The American Heritage Dictionary*, your use of *fun* as an adjective (meaning "enjoyable," as in "fun times") can "raise eyebrows among traditionalists." In the words of *The New Fowler's Modern English Usage*, the adjective *fun* "has not yet gained admission to the standard class of adjectives in that, in serious writing, it (so far) lacks a comparative [*funner*] and a superlative [*funnest*]."

The adjectival *fun* and *funner* appear frequently in commercials, as in a September 2000 radio commercial promising that the Los Angeles County Fair that year would be "funner." But to quote *The New York Times Manual of Style and Usage*: "Though the commercials may someday win respectability for *fun* as an adjective (*a fun vacation*), the gushing sound argues for keeping the word a noun."

Usage advice: Your use of *fun* as an adjective in formal communication may cause some people to make fun of you. You also risk ridicule if you use *fun* as a *verb*—as in "He funs [makes or plays jokes] a lot" or "She was just funning [behaving playfully]."

fungous or fungus?   *Fungous* is a spelling variant of the adjective *fungal* ("of or like a fungus"). The noun *fungus* identifies any member of the *Fungi* ("FUN-jeye") kingdom of organisms, including mushrooms, molds, and yeasts.

further clarification   See "*farther* or *further?*"

fury or Fury?   The lowercase *fury* can refer to the intense violence of an inanimate force such as a storm, or the violent or otherwise intense anger of a person. The adjective *furious*—as in "The boss was furious"—suggests an intensely angry reaction.

The capitalized *Fury* can refer to anyone likened to the three Furies of Greek and Roman mythology. They were terrifying winged goddesses with snakes for hair who were said to punish perpetrators of unavenged crimes. In an article titled "Furious Paula," *The Economist* (1/17/1998) compared Paula Corbin Jones, the sexual-harassment accuser of President Clinton, to an "avenging Fury." The redundant *avenging* and a caricature of Jones wearing a hairdo of snakes were helpful to readers who were not familiar with the Furies of classical mythology. (See also "redundancy: a vice and a virtue.")

fused participles   See "participles: the confusion of fusion."

future plans   The *future* in *future plans* is redundant, unless you are comparing plans for the immediate future with plans for the distant future. It is perfectly acceptable to say, for example, "My *plan* is to finish college and get a job; *future plans* include graduate school and marriage."

G

gainsay or naysay?   With *gain* related to the *gain* in "against" and *nay* meaning "no," the verbs *gainsay* and *naysay* both mean "deny, reject, contradict, oppose."

The verb *gainsay*—as in "She could neither *say* [confirm] nor *gainsay* [deny]"—is classified by *The Oxford English Dictionary* as "purely literary" and borderline "archaic."

Though the verb *naysay* is rarely used today, the noun *naysayer* is widely used for "a person who expresses a negative view." For example: A *Time* article (1/22/2001) about *The Surrendered Wife*, "a controversial new book [arguing] that an acquiescent wife is the key to a happy marriage," said that the author, Laura Doyle, "refers naysayers to her pleased disciples [in] *Surrendered Wives* circles [that] have sprouted in cities like Los Angeles and Chicago."

gallant: the adjective and noun   A man described as *gallant* ("GAL-ant")—brave, noble-minded, exceptionally polite and attentive to women—is called a *gallant* ("guh-LAHNT").

Gallicism   The word *Gallicism* ("GAL-ih-sizm")—derived from *Gaul*, the name for the ancient region of western Europe that included today's France—means a French expression used in another language. (For French expressions in English, see "French phrases beginning with *au*" and "French toast.")

Galvani's shocking words   Our language would have fewer words today if Luigi Galvani (1737–1798) had not changed his career goals. Born and raised in Bologna, in what was then Italy's Papal States, Galvani intended to study theology and enter a monastic order. Instead, though he remained faithful to his religion, he devoted his life to science.

As a physician-biologist, Galvani conducted experiments in comparative anatomy that laid the groundwork for our later understanding of the electrical impulses that activate muscles. Galvani's name became the source of some technical terms in electricity, including *galvanometer* ("an instrument that determines the presence, direction, and strength of an electric current in a conductor").

By the mid-19th century, the verb *galvanize* acquired what is now its most common popular meaning: "stimulate forcefully, as if by electricity." The January/February 2005 issue of the Sierra Club magazine, *Sierra*, quoted environmental writer-editor Shoshana Berger: "I'm very encouraged by the galvanization of people in their 20s right now around political and environmental issues." (See also "*eponymous* means never having to say you're anonymous.")

gambit: is it your move?   A *gambit*—from *gambetto*, an Italian word for the act of tripping someone, as in wrestling—is an opening chess move in which a player sacrifices one or more minor pieces to gain a strategic advantage in position. The extended use of *gambit* as *any* type of initial maneuver should involve a sacrifice in return for an expected advantage, in the view of Follett's *Modern American Usage* and Bernstein's *Careful Writer.*

But *The New York Times Manual of Style and Usage* and 63 percent of the usage panel of *The American Heritage Dictionary* approve the use of *gambit* for any initial maneuver to gain an advantage, regardless of whether sacrifice is involved. And today's dictionary definitions of *gambit* now include such extended senses as "an opening stratagem," "any maneuver by which one seeks to gain an advantage," "a calculated move," and "a remark made to open or redirect a conversation."

If you don't want to gamble on the loose use of *gambit*, use the term only for an opening maneuver involving a sacrifice. Whichever sense you do use, note that "*opening* gambit" leaves you open to the possibility that a chess player will charge you with redundancy. (See also "*stratagem*: don't let it trick you.")

gamble or gambol?   Those who compulsively *gamble* rarely have reason to *gambol* ("frolic").

gamut: run it carefully   Make sure you don't confuse running the *gamut* ("the total range of experience or possibility") with running the *gantlet* (cited in the next entry).

Usage example of *gamut* from *The New York Times* (1/31/2002): "The list of the 2,500 participants [in the 31st annual World Economic Forum] ran the gamut from celebrity C.E.O.s like Bill Gates and Steve Forbes on through Russian oligarchs, kings and prime ministers, ministers, senators and even patriarchs."

gantlet or *gauntlet*?   The candidate-punishing ordeal of the U.S. presidential race of the year 2000 was called a *gantlet* in the national weekly edition of *The Washington Post* (1/17/2000) and a *gauntlet* in *Time* (2/21/2000).

Your risk-free choice for "a punishing ordeal" is *gantlet*. Usage example from *Smithsonian* magazine (June 2002): "One young male [ocelot in Texas] managed to cross a 27-mile gantlet of highways, roads and farmland before being hit by a car and killed." Save *gauntlet* for phrases such as *throwing down the gauntlet* ("issuing a challenge") or *taking up the gauntlet* ("accepting a challenge").

You now know everything you need to know about choosing between *gantlet* and *gauntlet*. Proceed with the rest of this entry only if you think you might enjoy or at least endure some extremely complex word history.

Dictionaries list two separate entries for *gauntlet*, because each *gauntlet* is a separate word with its own history. As if that weren't confusing enough, word guardians disagree about whether one *gauntlet* should really be spelled *gantlet*. The original, 14th-century *gauntlet*, derived from an Old French word for "little glove," was a protective metal glove worn with medieval armor. Knights would throw down their gauntlet to issue a challenge to combat. To pick up the gauntlet was to accept the challenge. The other, 17th-century *gauntlet* (now acceptably spelled *gantlet* in American English) was a European military punishment in which an offender was made to pass between two rows of men who struck at him with a stick or knotted rope. That *gauntlet* was originally a Swedish derivative of *gatlopp* (a compound of "lane" and "course") with the English spelling *gantlope*, but Merriam-Webster word sleuths say that English speakers found it easier to substitute the familiar though inappropriate *gauntlet*.

Merriam-Webster's Dictionary of English Usage says that "the [spelling] distinction of *gantlet* for 'punishment' and *gauntlet* for 'glove' seems to have arisen in the U.S. in the 19th century." Today, *Webster's New World College Dictionary* and the *Harper Dictionary of Contemporary Usage* give equal weight to *gantlet* and *gauntlet* for the "punishment" word. Though most leading U.S. dictionaries list *gantlet* as the secondary spelling for the "punishment" word, *gantlet* has been prescribed for the "punishment" word by Bernstein's *Careful Writer*, Garner's *Modern American Usage*, Lovinger's *Penguin Dictionary of American English*

Usage and Style, and the stylebooks of *The New York Times*, *The Washington Post*, *The Wall Street Journal*, the *Los Angeles Times*, and the Associated Press.

gaslight is hazardous to your mental health Syndicated columnist Maureen Dowd observed (3/8/2000) that George W. Bush's strategy in the Campaign 2000 Republican presidential primaries "was to gaslight [his rival], the volatile senator [John McCain]."

Gaslight is listed in dictionaries as a noun, for the old-fashioned gas-burning lamp or the light produced by such a lamp. But Dowd and many others use *gaslight* as a verb, meaning "to attempt to drive someone crazy." As classic-movie buffs know, the *gaslight* verb is derived from the 1944 movie *Gaslight*, in which Ingrid Bergman gave an Oscar-winning performance as a Victorian (gaslight-era) bride whose husband tries to drive her crazy to prevent her from discovering that he had murdered her aunt.

gauge, gage, or guage? This word, which serves as a verb for "measure" and a noun for "measuring instrument," is correctly spelled *gauge*. People who spell it *gage* run the risk of being accused of using a generally discarded old alternative. The version spelled *guage* does not measure up at all.

gay news Is there anyone who hasn't heard the news that today's only risk-free way to use *gay* is as an adjective meaning "homosexual"? Apparently so, to judge from *National Journal* editor Michael Kelly's use of *gay* in the word's original but now eclipsed sense of "merry" in his syndicated column (8/5/1998): "Some months back, when we and the Lewinsky scandal were young and gay . . . "

The "merry" *gay* entered English from Old French in the 14th century. Word historians speculate that the "homosexual" *gay* had its origin in *gay*'s 17th-century association with "wanton" sexual behavior in slang phrases such as *gay woman* ("prostitute"), *gay man* ("womanizer"), and *gay house* ("brothel"). According to the *Random House Webster's Unabridged Dictionary*, "This sexual world included homosexuals too, and *gay* as an adjective meaning 'homosexual' goes back at least to the 1900's." By the middle of the 20th century, notes R. W. Burchfield in *The New Fowler's Modern English Usage*, "homosexual men made it abundantly clear that they used the word *gay* of themselves, and wanted the public at large to use it too."

The 1989 *Merriam-Webster's Dictionary of English Usage* reported that the "merry" *gay* "is still with us." But that source noted even then that the "homosexual" *gay* had created a "potential for unintended humor or serious miscommunication." And as novelist-critic Kingsley Amis wrote in his posthumously published 1997 *King's English*, "anybody who can read" must now know that the "homosexual" *gay* has prevailed. Amis wrote for that book shortly before he died that "in this very spring of 1995 some old curmudgeon is still frothing on about it in the public print and demanding the word 'back' for proper heterosexual use. [But] this is impossible."

gender: just for words?   Henry W. Fowler ruled in his *Dictionary of Modern English Usage* (1926) that *gender* should be restricted to grammatical gender, as in the Latin and Romance-language classification of nouns as masculine, feminine, and neuter. Fowler declared, "To talk of persons or creatures of the masculine or feminine *gender*, meaning of the male or female sex, is either a jocularity (permissible or not according to context) or a blunder." Today, Fowler's ruling is upheld by *The Economist Style Guide*; and the Fowler opinion about *gender* is in fact shared by "most authorities," according to usage-guide author Morton S. Freeman.

But *gender* in the "male/female" sense has been traced all the way back to the 14th century by *The Oxford English Dictionary*. Moreover, the executive editor of the Random House dictionaries, Sol Steinmetz, has written to the letters section of *The New York Times* (1/18/1991) that the "male/female" sense of *gender* is "well established in English and recognized by current dictionaries as standard." In defense of phrases such as *gender gap*, Steinmetz contended that "it is clearer to speak of a 'gender imbalance' than of a 'sex imbalance,' which could be taken for a hormonal disorder." Making that same point, *The New York Public Library Writer's Guide to Style and Usage* observes that the word *sex* "might inadvertently connote 'sexuality' [in a phrase such as] 'gender politics.'"

Recommendation: Using *gender* in the "male/female" sense, referring to people, is worth the risk of being criticized by zealous followers of Fowler, considering the alternative of using such misleading phrases as *sex gap* and *sex politics*. Of course, it is correct to continue to use the word *gender* to refer to grammatical categories also.

genuine pronunciation   You *win* the pronunciation contest for this word if you use the preferred pronunciation "win" rather than "wine" for the last syllable.

geographic or geographical?   Dictionaries list both *geographic* and *geographical* as appropriate ways of spelling the adjective that means "of or pertaining to geography." But *geographical* is preferable for this adjective, as in *Merriam-Webster's Geographical Dictionary*, because *geographic* has its own role as a noun, meaning "a treatise on geography," as in *National Geographic*. (See also *"graphic or graphical?" "historic or historical?"* and *"philosophic or philosophical?"*)

German-Americanisms   See entries for *angst, kitsch, leitmotif, Realpolitik, schadenfreude, wunderkind,* and *zeitgeist.*

gerunds are worth knowing   See "participles play three parts" and "participles: the confusion of fusion."

get or secure?   In the sense of "obtain," careful writers use *secure* only to mean "obtain by *effort*." Observing that distinction, you *secure* a loan but *get* a pizza.

ghetto: an echo of history   Word historians suspect that *ghetto* was derived from the Italian *getto* ("iron foundry") and originally *ghettare* ("to pour, throw, cast in metal"). At any rate, *the Ghetto* was the name of an island district near Venice where cannon were cast in an artillery foundry and also where the city's Jews were forced to live beginning in 1516.

Such segregation of Jews had been practiced in Europe for centuries, but the Italian *ghetto* subsequently became Europe's term for "Jewish district." In modern America, *ghetto* (with the plural preferably spelled *ghettos*) came to mean an urban area in which members of any minority (notably African-Americans) were segregated because of discrimination or poverty.

gibe or jibe?   To *gibe* is "to sneer, taunt, ridicule, heckle, mock." You can think of a sneer as a twisted *grin* to help you remember the *g* in *gibe*.

The Oxford English Dictionary and some American dictionaries list *jibe* as an alternate spelling of *gibe*. But professional communicators tend to keep these words separate. *Jibe*, which literally means to shift a ship's boom from one side of the vessel to another, in colloquial American English means "to harmonize or agree." Usage example: "The facts don't jibe with the candidate's speech."

gift should be freed of redundancy   The redundant *free* in *free gift* is commonly used by advertisers as a form of emphasis, as in a *National Geographic* offer of a "free gift" of a world map upon receipt of payment for a year's subscription. But that's no excuse for the rest of us to forget that a gift by definition is something bestowed without compensation. Whether *any* gift is entirely free—free of strings, free of expectations of reciprocity—is another question. (See "redundancy: a vice and a virtue.")

gifting is not as good as receiving   *The American Heritage Dictionary* (third edition) says that *gift* has "a long history" of use as a verb. "Unfortunately," the dictionary adds, "the verbal use of *gift* in Modern English is irredeemably tainted (as is its derivative *giftable*) by its association with the language of advertising and publicity (as in *Gift her with this copper warming plate*)."

Not all usage commentators would agree in blaming "advertising and publicity," but nobody, apparently, disputes the tainted reputation of *gift* as a verb. *Merriam-Webster's Dictionary of English Usage* warns that the verbified *gift*, though dating back to the 17th century, "has drawn scorn and even expressions of despair from some [current] commentators on language."

Risk-avoidance suggestion: Consider such alternatives as *bestow*, *donate*, *give*, and *give as a gift*. (See also "noun verbification.")

gild the lily, but don't blame Bill   Don't get caught boasting that you know that this idiom is a quote from Shakespeare. What Shakespeare actually wrote, in *King John*, was: "To *gild* refined *gold*, to *paint* the *lily* . . . is wasteful and ridiculous excess." Those words in the play were from Lord Salisbury's response to King John's attempt to add the appearance of legitimacy to his seizure of the English throne by staging the "double pomp" of a second coronation. By the way, don't get caught painting an extra *l* in the middle of *lily*.

girl talk   Stuart Berg Flexner, in *I Hear America Talking*, wrote that the word *girl* "entered the English language in the 13th century with the meaning 'maiden, young woman.'" Flexner added, "Its additional meaning of 'female child' didn't appear until 300 years later."

With the rise of modern feminism about a quarter century ago, according to *Los Angeles Times* staff writer Carla Hill (11/19/1997), "*girl* was banned from the vocabulary of smart-thinking men and women when describing any female over 15 . . . .There were no more office girls . . . no more college girls . . . no more career girls . . . no more girl Fridays, script girls or hatcheck girls." Hill added: "With a significant degree of female equity and parity [now] established in the workplace and other institutions, there has been a gradual social warming among women to the once-ostracized *girl*—a curiously defiant celebration of a word formerly fraught with oppression." The result, she reports, is that many career women now feel free to engage in informal "girl talk," to refer to themselves informally as "girls," and to use a phrase of encouragement adopted from the culture of Black American women, "You go, girl." But, says Hill, *girl* as a synonym for *woman* is still not welcome in formal communication—and it is definitely still not welcome when used by men.

glamor or glamour?   *Glamour* is the preferred spelling in American English and the only spelling considered correct in British English. But you should, and the British may, drop the *u* to form *glamorous* and *glamorize*.

   Glamour, which entered English with the sense of "magic spell," originated as a Scottish spelling alternative of *grammar* when that word meant "learning in general" and when learning was associated with a knowledge of the occult. Today, *glamour* is a "bewitching, enchanting attractiveness," often applied to an attractiveness that is illusory.

glance or glimpse?   As verbs, these words both mean "to look briefly." As nouns, they convey separate meanings: A *glance* ("brief act of *looking*") enables you to catch a *glimpse* ("brief *view*"). *Brief* in "brief glance" and "brief glimpse" is redundant.

glean may not be what you gather   Careful communicators do not use *glean* to mean simply "gather," despite that definition of *glean* in the *Reader's Digest* feature called "It Pays to Enrich Your Word Power" (April 2000).

   In American English, *glean* literally means to engage in the slow, painstaking, bit-by-bit collection of grain or other produce left by reapers. Consequently, our usage commentators and dictionaries agree, *glean* figuratively means "to gather [information, usually] bit by bit, slowly and laboriously."

   Example of careful usage: *Glean* clearly meant "to gather information labo-

riously" in a *New York Times* book review (12/31/2000) in which foreign correspondent A. J. Langguth's in-depth history of the Vietnam War was praised for
"new disclosures gleaned from interviews in Vietnam."

glitterati get more exposure than *literati*   *Glitterati*, a blend of *glitter* and
literati ("intellectual elite"), is American media slang for the glittering stars of fashionable society. *Literati* also inspired a word for the elite of the digital era: *digerati*.

goes, as in "he goes/she goes"   If you are trying to make a good impression
in a formal situation—for instance, in a job interview—avoid the adolescent use
of *goes* as a substitute for *says*, as in "He goes, 'Thank you,' and she goes,
'You're welcome.'"

good or *well*?   No matter how hard you try, you can never do *good* in
English. You can do *well* in English (or anything else), because *well* is an adverb,
and only an adverb can modify a verb (in this case, *do*). A student who does *well*
can be described as a *good* student, because an adjective (*good*) is the appropriate part of speech to describe a noun (*student*).

    You're correct if you say you *are* good at something, or you *feel* good about
something, because *are* and *feel* are among the verbs that link a noun or pronoun (for example, *you*) with an adjective (for example, *good*).

    The one context in which it is correct to say *do good* was neatly illustrated in
a *Time* magazine blurb (9/16/1991): "Doing well by doing good, merchandisers
join forces with environmentalists." In the phrase *doing well*, the adverb *well* is
needed to modify the present participle *doing* (a form of the verb *do*); in the
phrase *doing good*, however, *good* is a noun (meaning "an act or acts that benefit others"), and it serves as the object of *doing*. (See also "*feel bad* or *feel
badly*?" "*feel good* or *feel well*?" and "verbs that link subjects with adjectives.")

Gordian knot: a bold solution   The idea of *cutting the Gordian knot*
("finding a quick, bold solution for a perplexing problem") refers to an ancient
Greek myth about Gordius, a peasant who became king of Phrygia because he
happened to ride into the public square in a wagon when the people were
expecting a king who, according to an oracle, would arrive in just that manner.

    In the temple of the god of the oracle, Gordius fastened the yoke of his
wagon to a beam with a rope so ingeniously tied that no one could undo it.

Soon, it was being said that the knot would be undone only by the future master of Asia. Among those who accepted the challenge was Alexander the Great, who failed to untie the knot but then cut it open with his sword and proceeded to conquer Asia.

gorilla *or* **guerrilla?**   *Gorilla* means "a large anthropoid ape." The word *guerrilla*, derived from a Spanish word for war (*guerra*), means "a soldier in an irregular military unit" or, as an adjective, "the kind of war waged by such shoulders." Note that although the one-*r guerilla* is an accepted variant, most style books prefer *guerrilla*.

got *or* **gotten?**   The past tense of *get* is *got*. For the past participle of *get*, you may choose *got* or *gotten*, depending on which one you think sounds better.

Warning: *The American Heritage Book of English Usage* reports that, though both *got* and *gotten* have been serving as past participles since the Middle Ages, "the notion that *gotten* is illegitimate [a non-word] has been around for over 200 years and refuses to die."

Gothic: a tale of many meanings   *Gothic* originally meant "of or relating to the Goths," a barbaric Teutonic tribe that invaded and pillaged Europe during the third to fifth centuries of the Christian Era. Eventually, *Goth* became a synonym for any barbarian.

During the Renaissance, culture snobs used the word *Gothic* (in the sense of "barbaric, crude, grotesque") to describe the western European medieval architecture epitomized by France's Cathedral of Notre Dame. But that derogatory meaning of *Gothic* has faded with time, and the adjective *Gothic* was extended to a medieval style of painting, sculpture, and music, and even to the general sense of "pertaining to the Middle Ages."

In modern times, *Gothic/gothic* has been applied to fictional tales with grotesque subject matter, such as Mary Shelley's *Frankenstein*, and to youths who favor black clothes, hair dyed black, artificially pale skin, and a subcategory of rock music (*goth*) characterized by gloominess.

gourmand *or* **gourmet?**   All you need to know about *gourmet* is that it means "food connoisseur."

But *gourmand* must be handled with care because of its ambiguity. *Gourmand* shares an *n* with *glutton* ("one who eats to excess"), which is one of its dictionary definitions. But *gourmand* can also mean just a lover of food who is a hearty eater or, according to *The Oxford English Dictionary*, a judge of good food.

graceful or gracious? Both words involve *grace* ("refinement, charm, elegance, or a beauty of form, manner, motion, or action"). But they serve different purposes.

Graceful means showing grace in physical motion, as in "a graceful dance," or to a manner of behavior, as in "a graceful reply."

Gracious means "courteous, kind," as in "a gracious welcome," or "characterized by good taste or luxury," as in "a gracious home."

graduated, graduated from, or was graduated from? Today's most widely accepted usage of the verb *graduate* is in the phrase "graduate *from*," as in "Jennifer graduated [received a degree] from Stanford." Don't forget the *from* in *graduated from*. *New York Times* language columnist William Safire warns that without *from*, "the verb 'to graduate' means to make little marks on a test tube, to calibrate, to move someone to the next gradation or step." Safire adds, "To say 'I graduated college' rather than 'I graduated *from* college' is to be a language slob and a discredit to whatever learning factory mailed you a diploma."

Saying "was graduated from college" makes sense if you are using the old-fashioned meaning of *graduate*: "to be granted a degree or diploma." The old-fashioned definition of *graduate*, prevailing roughly from the 15th to the 19th century, was based on the idea that the school was doing the graduating by conferring the diploma or degree. When the modern sense of *graduate* emerged in the early 19th century, some purists objected, and those objections have been echoing here and there in classrooms and elsewhere down to our own time. So when you hear somebody say "was graduated from," you are hearing an echo from the past.

graffiti: a singular problem Not once in a 57-inch story about graffiti (1/8/1992) did the *Los Angeles Times* report that graffiti is a problem. The *L.A. Times Stylebook* (like the stylebooks of *The New York Times* and *The Washington Post*) insists that graffiti *are* a problem. *Graffiti* (pronounced "gra-FEE-tee") is the plural of the Italian *graffito* (literally "a scratching" and figuratively "a crude marking, drawing, or inscription").

Dictionaries cite some singular use of *graffiti* as a "mass noun" for such markings in general, but the plural *graffiti* is never considered a grammatical eyesore.

The Italian *graffiare* ("to scratch") is an archaeological term for scratching symbols on walls, as in the case of "wall scribblings" found at Pompeii and other Italian cities. *Graffiti* and *graffito* were almost exclusively archaeological terms for such scribblings until the 1960's. *Graffito* today remains as unfamiliar to most Americans as *spaghetto*, the Italian singular for *spaghetti*, and *paparazzo* ("buzzing insect"), the Italian singular for the camera-ready *paparazzi* who buzz around celebrities.

grammar and spelling   *Grammar* ("the system of rules implicit in a language") is frequently misspelled *grammer*.

grammar-check warning   Author Ralph Schoenstein complained in a *New York Times* opinion essay (6/13/1998) that the widely used Microsoft grammar-check program had flunked a simple grammar test that he had devised for it. In a typical part of his test, he typed, "Thinking it was open, the door was really closed." The grammar-check program, unable to recognize such an outrageous dangling participle, irrelevantly replied, "The main clause may contain a verb in the passive voice." (Actually, neither clause of that sentence contained a verb in the passive voice.)

Today, the somewhat improved Microsoft grammar-check program is still ignoring major problems like the dangling participle while overreacting to concerns about such matters as the passive voice. The program does not even give correct advice about when to change the article *a* to *an*. The moral of this story is that thorough grammar-checking—like spell-checking and usage-checking—is still up to you. (See also "*a* or *an?*" "active or passive voice?" "participles that dangle," and "spell-check warning.")

graphic or graphical?   Though these are two forms of the same adjective, dictionaries record distinctions that careful communicators preserve.

Graphic is preferred if you mean "of or relating to visual arts," as in "the graphic arts of drawing, engraving, or lettering," or "providing vivid details," as in "a graphic description of dawn in the forest."

Graphical is preferred if you mean "in the form of a graph" or "of or relating to computer graphics," as in "the graphical user interface involving windows, icons, and menus." (See "*geographic* or *geographical?*" "*historic* or *historical?*" and "*philosophic* or *philosophical?*")

graphic or **graphics?**   The noun *graphic* means a visual representation—such as a graph, map, or picture—used to illustrate something.

Graphics is the plural for such visual representations, and it's a singular word for the process of producing and displaying those images. (See also "*-ics* words.")

gratuities are not gratuitous   People whose income depends partly on *gratuities* ("gift, commonly money [a tip] in return for service") do not view such gifts as *gratuitous*.

Gratuitous means "unearned, unwarranted, unjustified, uncalled for," as in "gratuitous criticism" or "gratuitous insult." Usage example: *The New York Times* editorialized (7/6/1997), "Given the absence of a clear threat to Europe and the possibility of so many unpredictable consequences, NATO expansion seems a gratuitous [uncalled-for] risk."

gray or **grey?**   A *New York Times* story (12/29/1995) about a famous old tree in Mexico described its trunk as *gray* in the story's paragraph 4 and as *grey* in paragraph 14.

Given such confusion about the spelling of this word, what should you do? Stay with *gray*. The *a* in *gray* can help you remember the American preference for that spelling, and the *e* in *grey* can help you remember the preference of the English.

gray eminence   See "*éminence grise* has a misleading color."

grayhound or **greyhound?**   You can associate the *e* in the preferred spelling of *greyhound* with the *e*'s in the Near East, where the breed originated. The *grey* in *greyhound* is not a reference to its color, which in most cases is not gray, but rather a reference to an Old English word, *grieg*, meaning a female dog.

Great Britain   See "*British* or *English?*"

greenroom isn't always green   A greenroom, the backstage waiting area for theatrical and television performers, is not necessarily a room that is green. But that relaxing color apparently became associated with greenrooms early in their history.

Webster's New World Dictionary of Media and Communications says, "The earliest such room probably was in the 17th century in Elizabethan theaters, where they . . . sometimes had green shrubbery in them." That source adds, "In the United Kingdom in the 19th century, *green-room gossip* was theatrical shoptalk."

Gresham and "his" law   *Gresham's law*, credited to a 16th-century English financier named Sir Thomas Gresham but actually formulated long before his time, is a theory that bad money will drive good money out of circulation. The idea is that when two kinds of money of equal denomination but unequal intrinsic value (in terms of precious metals) are in circulation, the one with higher intrinsic value will be withdrawn from circulation by hoarders.

The phrase *Gresham's law* is applied today to a wide variety of situations in which the bad drives out the good. For example, columnist Frank Rich wrote in *The New York Times* (8/17/1996) that America's political conventions have become such a waste of media time that they illustrate historian Daniel J. Boorstin's "new Gresham's law of American public life [in which] counterfeit happenings drive spontaneous happenings out of circulation." (See "*Murphy's Law, Parkinson's Law,* and the *Peter Principle.*")

grill or grille?   These words, both stemming from a Latin term for "wickerwork gate," have related but distinctly different meanings.

Grill is a noun for a cooking surface that resembles a grating, and it is a verb for the cooking that occurs on such a surface.

Grille (with its confusing and therefore undesirable variant spelling *grill*) is the noun for the grating that forms a barrier or screen for a window, gate, or the front of a fireplace or car radiator.

grimace does not always rhyme with "face"   This word—a noun meaning "a contortion of facial features indicating pain, contempt, disgust, or embarrassment" or a verb for making such a face—has been pronounced for most of its centuries of life as "gri-MACE."

That pronunciation is still listed as preferred in *Webster's New World College Dictionary*. But today's more common pronunciation is "GRIM-iss," according to a popular pronunciation guidebook, Charles Harrington Elster's *There Is No Zoo in Zoology*, and most dictionaries, including *The American Heritage Dictionary, Merriam-Webster's Collegiate Dictionary, The Oxford English Dictionary*, and the *Random House Webster's Unabridged Dictionary*.

Risk-free advice: If you don't want to invite grimaces by taking a pronounced stand on this issue, use *grimace* only in writing.

grisly, grizzly, or *grizzled?*

Grizzly (derived from a French word for gray, and therefore meaning "gray" or "graying") is often mistakenly used for *grisly* ("horrifying"). The endangered grizzly bear, whose unfortunate scientific name is *Ursus horribilis* ("horrifying bear"), might inspire less horror if more people knew that *grizzly* was assigned to the grizzly bear because the bear's brown hair usually has gray tips.

Caution: Older men are so frequently described as *grizzled* ("'having hair that is gray or graying") that some writers mistakenly use *grizzled* to mean "aging." In an example of that error, a *New York Times* ad (1/5/2004) for the movie *Monsieur Ibrahim* quoted film critic Kevin Thomas as noting that Omar Sharif played a "grizzled, white-haired grocer."

groundhog or *woodchuck?*

Groundhog Day (February 2)—based on the legend that six more weeks of winter can be expected if a hibernating groundhog in Punxsutawney, Pennsylvania, ventures from his burrow, sees his shadow, and resumes his hibernation—could justifiably be called Woodchuck Day.

Groundhog, woodchuck, and *chuck* are some of the informal names of *Marmota monax*, a two-foot-long rodent with a six-inch tail and thick brownish fur that feeds off green vegetation in open fields and ravines in Canada and the northeastern United States.

ground zero: its meaning was changed in one day

The former site of the World Trade Center was clearly indicated when *The New York Times* (8/30/2004) reported that "Vice President Dick Cheney recalled the president's visit to ground zero three days after the attack."

In the just-cited sense, the term is sometimes capitalized. But it should always be lowercase when used to refer to the site or potential site of other disasters, as when the August 2004 *Smithsonian* reported the possibility that the Pacific islands constituting the tiny nation of Tuvalu might be engulfed by storms, floods, and a rising sea level in a "ground zero for global warming." And the Associated Press reported (1/2/2005) that aid was arriving at Indonesia's ground zero, the "shattered western coast of Sumatra [which] bore the fullest, most deadly force of last week's tsunami disaster."

Before the catastrophic destruction of the World Trade Center on September 11, 2001, the meaning of *ground zero* was established in dictionaries as "the point directly above, below, or at which a nuclear explosion occurs." That original *ground zero* was derived from a point on a military map, marked Zero, designating the New Mexico desert site where a tower was built for the first atomic explosion, in the early morning of July 16, 1945.

guarantee or **guaranty?**   You can't lose if you choose *guarantee*. That is because the word that involves "a promise of product performance" *must* be spelled *guarantee*, and the word that involves "a promise to pay another's debt in the event of a default" *may* be spelled *guarantee* or *guaranty*.

guess who   Careful writers promptly and clearly link names with classifications. For example: "A juror in the Smith case complained about court procedures today. Sally Jones, *the juror*, made her complaints known at a press conference." The role played by Sally Jones might not be immediately clear to the reader unless *the juror* followed or preceded her name.

guillotine **was not his machine**   French Revolutionary physician-lawmaker Joseph-Ignace Guillotin (1738–1814) spent much of the latter part of his life trying to correct the false impression that he had invented the razor-sharp instrument that symbolized the vindictive revolutionary bloodbath called the Reign of Terror.

Ironically, Dr. Guillotin's name became associated with that infamous slaughter of thousands of people because of his interest in eliminating class discrimination and reducing cruelty in capital punishment. He won approval for legislation replacing the noose for common criminals and the broadax for errant nobility with a decapitation machine that seemed to be an efficient and therefore relatively humane alternative. Sadly, the device was favored by revolutionary zealots solely because of its efficiency.

The machine, of an apparently unknown inventor, had been used for the execution of criminals of noble birth in England, Scotland, and various other nations of Europe. In its French debut, in 1792, it was called the *louisette*, because the French version was constructed under the direction of surgeon Antoine Louis. But thanks in part to local songwriters who liked to rhyme *Guillotin* with *machine*, the louisette became *la guillotine*. And some sources today, such as *Discovery Channel Online*, perpetuate the widespread myth that "Dr. Guillotine" was the inventor.

In 1959, in an essay called "Reflections on the Guillotine," Nobel Prize–winning author Albert Camus publicized medical studies showing that guillotine executions were often followed by gruesome signs of continued life in the head and body for a period of "minutes, even hours." Guillotine executions gradually became fewer and fewer, with the last one held in 1977. In 1981 France outlawed the guillotine, becoming one of many European nations that have abolished all forms of capital punishment.

gutteral or guttural?   This word for "the sound articulated in the back of the mouth" is often spelled *gutteral* but should be spelled with two *u*'s: *guttural*.

Gypsy, Gipsy, or neither?   *Gypsy* is preferred in American English, and *Gipsy* used to be preferred in British English. But no matter how you spell this word, it is inaccurate historically.

Gypsy is derived from *Egyptian*, because the English wrongly assumed that these dark-skinned nomadic people who started coming to England in the early 16th century must have originated in Egypt. (In France, the same people were thought to come from Bohemia and thus were called *Bohèmes*, producing the British translation *Bohemian*—a synonym for *Gypsy* that eventually acquired the sense of a lowercase bohemian, "a literary or artistic person living an unconventional life.")

Actually, Gypsies were native to northern India, from which they began migrating to Europe about a thousand years ago. In their society, a Gypsy is a *Rom*. The plural of *Rom* is *Roma*, and the adjective to describe these people and their culture is *Romany*. Usage example from *The New York Times* (5/10/2002): "Some 30 European Romany organizations met in May in Lodz [Poland] . . . to set up a continent-wide organization that could give the Roma, as Gypsies prefer to be called, a strong voice in advancing their causes: housing, jobs, education."

H

had better is better with *had*   The idiomatic verb phrase *had better* (meaning "ought to, must") is often shortened to *better* in informal communication such as "You better wash up." But if you want to avoid criticism, you had better remember to keep the *had*, in full or in a contraction such as *you'd better*.

hail or hale?   *Hail* is used to *summon* a taxi, *salute* a leader, or *greet* a friend.

In archaic usage, you *hale* ("haul") things or you were *haled* ("hauled, carted, compelled to go") into court.

People who take care of themselves are *hale* ("healthy") and *hearty* ("strong, physically vigorous"). Note that the second adjective in that phrase is not *hardy* ("capable of enduring fatigue, hardship, or exposure"). (See also "*hardy* soups and *hearty* flowers?")

halcyon: keep it calm   The adjective *halcyon* is sometimes used in the sense of "prosperous," as in a *Barron's* report (10/16/2000) that "some [Wall] Street seers say the halcyon days of the market are over."

But the preferred sense of *halcyon*—"calm, peaceful, tranquil"—accurately reflects its origin in Greek mythology. When Alkyone, the daughter of Aeolus, the god of the winds, learns that her husband has been killed in a shipwreck, she throws herself into the sea. Alkyone is thus transformed into a kingfisher. According to legend, this bird (called *Alkyone* by the Greeks, then *Halcyon* by the Romans) builds a floating nest on the sea at the beginning of each winter. To protect its eggs during two weeks of incubation, the Halcyon makes sure the sea is calm by charming the wind and the waves.

half-mast or half-staff?   Dictionaries use these terms interchangeably to describe the flying of lowered flags as a sign of mourning. But the stylebooks of the Associated Press, *The Washington Post*, *The New York Times*, and *The Wall Street Journal* prescribe *half-mast* only for flags on ships and at naval stations, *half-staff* elsewhere. Ship flags hang from a structure called a mast.

Halloween or Hallowe'en?   The first is preferred in American English, the second in British English.

halve price: don't buy it   The real bargain, of course, is *half* price. The *half* in that phrase is an adjective relating to "one of two equal portions." *Half* (also a noun) a loaf is better than none. But if you crave both *halves* (the plural of the noun *half*), you'd better be present when somebody decides to *halve* (the verb for "divide in half") it.

hangar or hanger?   Your clothes are likely to get very dirty if you put them on *hangars*. The second *a* in *hangar* should remind you that it's a shed for airplanes.

hanged or hung?   The verb *hang* has two past-tense forms. *Hanged* is the form used to refer to people who have ended up on the gallows: "The sheriff *hanged* the man at dawn." "*Hanged* at dawn, the man was buried by noon." *Hung* is used to refer to inanimate objects: "I *hung* the picture on my bedroom wall." "*Hung* crookedly, the picture looked terrible."

harass: one spelling and two pronunciations   *Harass*, derived from an Old French word meaning "set a dog on," now means "hound, persecute, torment, repeatedly attack or annoy." And if you don't want to be hounded by the spelling police, don't double the *r*.

 The word has traditionally been pronounced in British and American English with the accent on the first syllable. And you run some risk of being criticized by traditionalists if you use the widely adopted new American pronunciation that accents the second syllable.

hardscrabble is no game   *Hardscrabble* originated as a late-18th-century Americanism combining the adjective *hard* ("involving a great deal of effort") with the verb *scrabble* ("scrape or dig frantically, as with the hands").

 As a noun, *hardscrabble* means "barren or almost barren farmland." But it's usually an adjective meaning "yielding a minimum return for one's labor," as in "the hardscrabble life of a sweatshop worker."

 Usage example: An article in *Business Week* (5/1/2000) focused on "a hardscrabble little village in central Mexico where families . . . eke out a living . . . coaxing corn out of the dry clay soil."

***hardy* soups and *hearty* flowers?**   No, thank you. Soups may be described as *hearty* ("nourishing"), and flowers may qualify as *hardy* ("robust, able to survive harsh weather").

Hearty also means "pleasantly warm, outgoing," as in "a hearty handshake."

***harlot,* *helot,* or *hellion*?**   *Harlot* means "prostitute." *Helot* means "slave." *Hellion* means "disorderly, rowdy, mischievous person."

***haute* is a high-class adjective**   This French import, pronounced "oat" and written without italics, means "high-class." *Haute* is commonly seen in the phrases *haute couture* (preferably pronounced "koo-TUR") for "high fashion" and *haute cuisine* (preferably pronounced "kwih-ZEEN") for "gourmet cooking."

Usage example: *A Los Angeles Times* headline (8/24/1997) for a story involving long-range, high-society Christmas-party reservations promised revelations about "Where Haute Holiday Cheer Will Be Spread."

***have your cake* logically**   They say that "you can't have your cake and eat it too," meaning that you can't have it both ways. But they are wrong.

If you have your cake, nothing can stop you from eating it. Logically the saying should be "You can't eat your cake and have it too," which is how this proverb was expressed before it somehow got reversed. In the 16th-century words of John Heywood's *Proverbs*: "Wolde you bothe eate your cake, and haue your cake?"

If you decide to use this expression correctly, don't worry about being the only one who ever does so. Harvard law professor Christopher Edley Jr., in the national weekly edition of *The Washington Post* (7/15/1991), wrote that the first President Bush, on the issue of race relations, wanted "to eat his cake and have it too."

havoc,* as in *cry,* *play,* and *wreak   "Long ago," James Rogers writes in his *Dictionary of Clichés*, "the cry 'Havoc!' was a signal or order to soldiers to seize spoils or to pillage. Gradually the meaning shifted toward destructive devastation in general, not necessarily by soldiers, but even by inanimate things, such as a storm."

Today, to *cry havoc* means "to warn of danger or disaster." To *play havoc with* can mean "to destroy, to ruin, or to create disorder." And to *wreak* (pronounced "reek") *havoc on* means to "inflict widespread destruction." (See also "*wreak havoc* or *wreck havoc?*")

head over heels in nonsense   This expression for "topsy-turvy [upside down, in a state of confusion]"—as in "head over heels in love"—makes no sense. The position "head over heels" is obviously our *normal* position.

The upside-down-in-love expression should be "heels over head," which is how the idea was worded originally, in literature dating back to the 14th century. But beginning in the 18th century, the expression somehow went topsy-turvy itself. Consequently, in our time, *Cosmopolitan* magazine (April 2000) featured an article entitled "How to Know If Your Boy Friend Is Head Over Heels." And a *Parade* magazine article on marriage (3/17/2002) noted that "early in their relationships, couples typically are head over heels in love." (See also "*love*: lost and found.")

headquarter is not formal   *Headquarter* is widely used informally as a transitive and intransitive verb, as in "They headquartered him in Providence" and "He headquarters in Providence."

In *formal* communication, the more appropriate usage would be "They *assigned* him to Providence" and "He *makes his headquarters* in Providence."

headquarters is or headquarters are?   A plural *headquarters* is preferred for location, as in a *New York Times* reference (1/25/2001) to the fact that "Lucent Technologies' headquarters are in Murray Hill, N.J." But a singular *headquarters* is preferred for authority: "Headquarters *has* approved her promotion."

healthful is not healthy   *Healthy* and *healthful,* used interchangeably for more than four hundred years, began acquiring distinctive meanings during the late 19th century. As a result, careful users of the language learned that food that is *healthful* ("health-giving") helps us be *healthy* ("in possession of good health").

Atlantic Monthly language columnist Barbara Wallraff suggests in her book *Word Court,* published in the year 2000, that the word *healthful* ("health-giving") may be dying. She cites evidence, from government and the media, that the word *healthy* is being widely used not only in its own sense of "possessing good health" but also in the *healthful* sense of "health-giving." In other words, healthy people now eat *healthy food* and pursue a *healthy lifestyle.* (An article in the 5/23/2000 issue of *USA Today*, for example, told readers about a woman who lost 80 pounds in 15 months by exercising and eating "healthy foods.") Wallraff adds, however, that she herself likes to preserve the distinction between *healthy* and *healthful* "on the ground that where it is easy to denote a difference in meaning with different word forms—well, why not do it?"

Risk-free usage: The Associated Press reported (12/31/2001) that U.S. Surgeon General David Satcher "noted that in inner cities, fast-food restaurants often crowd out sources of more healthful foods."

heart or **rote?**   You can memorize something by *heart* or by *rote*. But memorizing by *rote* ("a mechanical procedure") is without understanding.

heart-rending: avoid the grief of misspelling   This word for "heartbreaking, arousing deep sympathy, expressing or causing intense grief" may be spelled with or without a hyphen but must not be spelled or pronounced heart-*rendering.*

Example of correct usage: When one hundred North Koreans visited South Korea to see relatives from whom they had been separated by war a half century earlier, *The New York Times* reported (8/16/2000): "In one heart-rending scene after another, mothers embraced children long given up for dead, brothers and sisters struggled to identify adults they knew until now only as children, wives steeled themselves to meet husbands long since wedded to other spouses, and vice versa."

heaven or **Heaven?**   One cannot resist observing that Heaven only knows why the stylebooks of the Associated Press and *U.S. News & World Report* list this word only as the common noun *heaven*. Thank Heaven for more sophisticated listings—such as those in *The New York Times Manual of Style and Usage* and *The American Heritage Dictionary*—that also cite a capitalized *Heaven* as "the abode of God."

Of course, the lowercase *heaven* is appropriate for "a place or condition of great happiness" and in such exclamations of surprise as *good heavens* and *heavens above.*

heinous pronunciation   You'll be committing a *heinous* ("shockingly evil, grossly wicked") offense against Standard American pronunciation if you say this word in any way other than "HAY-niss."

Helen of Troy: facing reality   The phrase from Greek mythology about "the face that launched a thousand ships" is supposed to emphasize Helen of Troy's great beauty, but it really illustrates humanity's capacity for great folly.

A Trojan prince, Paris, went to Greece to abduct Helen—a mortal daughter of Zeus who was married to King Menelaus of Sparta—and took her to be *his* wife in Troy. After the Trojans refused King Menelaus' demand for Helen's return, he persuaded his brother, King Agamemnon of Mycenae, to lead a huge Greek army that set sail for Troy in a thousand ships. The result was the 10-year Trojan War, the rescue of Helen, the death of Paris, and the fiery destruction of Troy.

helpmate **or** *helpmeet*?   The 18th-century coinage *helpmate* ("helpful companion, spouse") evolved from *helpmeet*. The earlier word, *helpmeet*, arose from a popular misunderstanding of a verse from Genesis in the King James Bible: "And the Lord God said, It is not good that man should be alone; I will make him *an help meet* for him."

Many readers of the King James version of the Bible assumed that the verse referred to the about-to-be-created Eve as a "help meet" for Adam, and *helpmeet* thus became a synonym for "wife." But the *meet* in that verse was not a noun. It was *meet* the adjective ("suitable, appropriate"), and the intended meaning of the phrase was that God would create Eve as "a help[er] *suitable* for" Adam.

Today, the more common word is *helpmate*, and its dictionary definition embraces wife or husband.

"he or I is right" or "he or I am right"?   Verbs must agree with their subject in person as well as number. But what do you do when the subject consists of pronouns of different persons joined by *or*, *nor*, or *not only . . . but also*?

According to *Webster's New World Guide to Current American Usage*, most grammarians say you should make the verb agree with whichever pronoun is *closer*. So, you are in step with the grammatical consensus if you say "He or I *am* right" or "I or he *is* right." But your *best* answer would be to avoid such awkwardness by rewriting your sentence.

herculean **or** *Herculean*?   The uppercase adjective *Herculean*, "of or pertaining to Hercules," produced the lowercase adjective *herculean* that can mean either "*possessing* great strength," as a herculean weight-lifter does, or "*requiring* great strength," as a herculean task does.

Usage example: The Associated Press (10/13/2000) circulated a feature story about the Chinese government's "herculean effort" to conduct a census of its population of about 1.26 billion.

If more people knew the Hercules story of Greek mythology, not just the Hollywood version, the word *herculean* might also mean "born unlucky." True, he led an exciting life as Greece's "greatest hero" and "the strongest man on earth," to quote classical scholar Edith Hamilton's book *Mythology*. But as one of the children resulting from Zeus' seductions of mortal women, Hercules bore the guilt of his own birth in the eyes of Zeus' furiously jealous wife, Hera. When Hera tried to kill the infant Hercules in his crib with two deadly snakes, he easily crushed them to death. But in Hercules' adulthood, Hera succeeded in punishing him horribly by taking possession of his mind long enough to make him kill his beloved wife and three sons.

Though Hercules' friends tried to assure him that he was not to blame for the death of his family, he regarded himself as a murderer. After a friend talked Hercules out of committing suicide, he sought atonement by performing 12 seemingly impossible and often dangerous tasks that became known as "the Labors of Hercules."

Even then, Hamilton noted, Hercules "was never tranquil and at ease," and he was fated to acquire more guilt by killing a young servant with a careless thrust of his arm and later deliberately killing a good friend to avenge an insult from the friend's father. Eventually Hercules had himself burned to death on a funeral pyre, and in heaven Hera finally forgave him for being born.

hermitage or ***Hermitage***?   The word *hermitage*, literally "a hermit's home," can refer to any place where one can live in seclusion. The capitalized form can stand for the estate of Andrew Jackson, the world-famous museum in St. Petersburg that used to serve as a palace for the czars, and a rich, full-bodied wine produced in southeastern France and named after a village there called Tain L'Hermitage.

heroics: not always heroic   You are in the Risk Zone if you use *heroics* in its literal sense of "heroic behavior." *Heroics* today is more likely to be perceived as "flamboyant behavior intended to *seem* heroic."

hew or **hue**?   If you are not careful, your fingers will write one of these homophones (words that sound alike) when your brain intends to use the other.

Even a nationally renowned defender of good usage, the late columnist and author Jack Smith, was caught by his readers misstating in his column that the 1991 RAND calendar didn't seem to "hue to any theme." He had meant to write *hew* ("adhere or conform strictly"), as in "hew to the official line." In a correct use of *hew*, *The New York Times Magazine* (3/27/2005) referred to a Pentecostal movement that "continues to hew to tenets that most other denominations consider radical."

Another meaning of *hew*—oddly, the only definition you'll find in *NTC's* [*National Textbook Company's*] *Dictionary of Easily Confused Words*—is "to cut, fell, or give form to something with heavy blows" of an instrument such as an ax.

The word *hue*—derived from the Old English word *hiw* ("form, appearance, color")—means "appearance, aspect," as in "a man of somber hue," and also means, of course, "a color or shade of a color."

A separately evolved *hue*—from an Old French verb, *huer* ("to shout")—survives today only as an echo of the Anglo-Norman phrase *hu e cri* (literally, "shout and cry"). A *hu e cri* was a loud outcry alerting bystanders of their legal obligation to join in the chase of a fleeing criminal. In our modern era, when civic-minded bystanders are more likely to call 911, *hue and cry* means "a public expression of alarm or opposition," as in a *New York Times* report (1/28/1997) that many Australians were "raising a hue and cry" about fast-multiplying stray cats.

hinderance or **hindrance**?   *Hinderance* was the approved spelling in the 18th century, but the only form of the word that is now widely accepted is the two-syllable *hindrance*. This word can mean either "an obstruction" or "the act of obstructing."

Hispanic, Latino, or neither?   Agreement is lacking about the appropriate name for the 38.8 million Americans identified both as *Hispanic* and as *Latino* by the U.S. Census Bureau in 2002. That inconsistency occurs frequently in the media, as in this sentence from *The Wall Street Journal* (4/19/2002): "Spurred by census data showing fast Latino demographic growth, advertising aimed at U.S. Hispanics has outpaced overall advertising growth."

As noted by *U.S. News & World Report* writer Linda Robinson (5/11/1998),

"The label Hispanic obscures the enormous diversity among people who come (or whose forebears came) from two dozen countries and whose ancestry ranges from pure Spanish to mixtures of Spanish blood with Native American, African, German, and Italian, to name a few hybrids."

According to the 1993 *Columbia Guide to Standard American English*, the terms *Hispanic* and *Hispanic-American* "apply specifically to Spanish-speaking people of Latin American origins who now live in the United States, [and those] terms seem to be acceptable to all." But those terms are not acceptable to a group called the Mexican Empowerment Committee. A message from that committee to the news media, published in the June 1994 *Quill* magazine (of the Society of Professional Journalists), declared that *Hispanic* "is unacceptable when referring to the 18-million-plus Mexican and Mexican-American population in the United States. . . . It is insulting to include us . . . when you use this term that denies us our Native Mexican (non-European) roots . . . our true heritage, which is Mestizo: mixed Native Mexican and Spanish. When referring to the general Spanish-speaking population and those of Mexican descent . . . please use . . . Mexican/Latino population; Mexicans and other Latinos of California; Mexican and Latino population of the U.S.; or 'Latino,' if you must, but please, never Hispanic."

Earl Shorris, author of *Latinos: A Biography of the People*, noted in a *New York Times* op-ed essay (10/29/1992) that the term *Latino* is preferred by Mexican-American and other Spanish-speaking groups in California, *Hispanic* is preferred by Cubans in Florida, and *Mexican-American* and *Chicano* are preferred in Texas.

The National Council of La Raza accepts the classification *Hispanic* and has proposed that Hispanics be designated by the Census Bureau as a race rather than just an ethnic group. But *Latinos* author Shorris argued in his essay, "The group cannot be defined racially, because it includes people whose ancestors came from Asia to settle in the Western Hemisphere thousands of years ago, as well as people from Europe, [including] the Iberian Peninsula, and Africa."

A possible solution to the *Hispanic/Latino* controversy was suggested by David Gonzalez in an article about the topic he wrote for *The New York Times* (11/15/1992): "In a recent national survey of Hispanic political attitudes, researchers may have found a key to the issue: Most Hispanics/Latinos prefer to identify themselves as Puerto Rican, Colombian, Dominican or just plain American."

***historic* or *historical*?**   These adjectives have been used interchangeably for a couple of centuries. For today's precise writers, however, a novel that makes history, like *Uncle Tom's Cabin*, is *historic*. A novel *about* history is *historical*. (See also "*geographic* or *geographical*?" "*graphic* or *graphical*?" and "*philosophic* or *philosophical*?")

***histrionics* or *hysterics*?**   The first is a deliberate, dramatic display of emotion. The second is an involuntary emotional outburst. (See also "*hysteria*: the controversy and the confusion.")

***hoards* shouldn't rove**   You can write about "roving *hordes* [large crowds]." But *hoards* are "carefully hidden supplies of something valuable."

***Hobson's choice:* take it or leave it**   *Hobson's choice* dates back about four centuries to Cambridge, England, where innkeeper and stable-keeper Tobias Hobson required that customers choose whichever horse happened to be standing nearest his stable door, or go without. So Hobson's choice meant *no choice at all.*

Today *Hobson's choice* is widely used in the sense of "a *difficult* choice." For example, U.S. Senator Robert C. Byrd of West Virginia argued in a *New York Times* op-ed essay (10/15/1999) that "the Senate was faced with the Hobson's choice of approving a [Comprehensive Test Ban] treaty about which too little was understood or rejecting a treaty of tremendous potential to reduce the proliferation of nuclear weapons."

But that newspaper's stylebook instructs its own staff writers to use *Hobson's choice* only in its original sense of "no choice at all." Likewise, the "no choice at all" meaning is the only definition listed in *Brewer's Dictionary of Phrase and Fable, Bartlett's Familiar Quotations, The Columbia Guide to Standard American English, The Penguin Dictionary of American English Usage and Style, The Oxford English Dictionary, The American Heritage Dictionary,* and the unabridged dictionaries of Merriam-Webster and Random House.

Recommendation: If you use *Hobson's choice*, make sure your choice of meaning is clear.

***hoi polloi:* have they become hoity-toity?**   You may decide the expression *hoi polloi* ("hoy puh-LOY") is more trouble than it's worth.

A Greek term that literally means "the many," *hoi polloi* has been widely used by English-language writers as a term for "the common people, the masses." Example: The *Los Angeles Times* (11/19/2000) used the title "Houdini of the Hoi Polloi" for an article about a magician who performs for people on the street.

But *hoi polloi* in spoken English has ironically acquired a common opposite meaning, "the snobby elite," according to *Merriam-Webster's Dictionary of English Usage*. That source suggests that "the new sense" of *hoi polloi* may have been prompted partly by the expression's sound of "haughtiness and condescension, much like that of *hoity-toity*, a term that has undergone a similar extension of meaning in the 20th century from its former sense, 'frivolous,' to its current sense, 'marked by an air of superiority.'"

Even if you remain faithful to the original sense of *hoi polloi* ("common people"), your use of the expression "the hoi polloi" may cause you to be accused of redundancy by purists who know that *hoi* is Greek for *the*. But if you "correctly" use *hoi polloi* without *the*, you risk being accused of pedantically violating the same type of English idiom that ignores the fact that the syllable *al* meant *the* in the Arabic origins of *algebra* and *alcohol*. (See also "redundant bilingualisms.")

hoist: going up or blowing up?

Hoist generally means "to raise into position," as in a *New York Times* report (4/14/2000) that "the Cuban flag was hoisted high by Cuban exiles today."

But that is not what *hoist* means in the famous phrase from *Hamlet*, "hoist with one's own petard." *Hoist* in that context means "hurt, ruined, destroyed," in this case, by one's own trap. As for *petard*: In days of yore, soldiers were in danger of being blown to bits by their own *petard*, a gunpowder-filled case that was used for blowing a hole in an enemy barricade.

holism: a good word with a tainted reputation

The word *holism* was coined by South African political figure Jan Christiaan Smuts (1870–1950) in a book he wrote in 1926 called *Holism and Evolution*. For Smuts, *holism* was "a synthetic tendency in the universe, and is the principle which makes for the origin and progress of wholes in the universe," culminating in mind and personality.

Holism subsequently became a word for the fertile insight that the whole is greater than the sum of its parts—that all systems, from atoms to humans to the cosmos, are the product not only of their parts but also of the interaction of their parts. From that insight grew such approaches to human problems as systems analysis, ecology, and a holistic approach to medicine that focuses on the interaction of mind and body.

Unfortunately, the adjective *holistic* has been exploited in recent decades by so many irresponsible healers that *holism* and *holistic* are now tainted with a connotation of quackery. If you use *holism* or *holistic*, make sure your reader knows where you are coming from.

homage: honor its first letter The preferred pronunciation of *homage* ("a public expression of reverence, respect, or honor") is "HAHM-idge." You may say "AHM-idge" if you want to risk using the pronunciation that most dictionaries list as the secondary choice. But don't even think about using the pronunciation "HOME-idge."

At any rate, you *pay* homage to a hero, *do* homage to the hero's memory, or *write a/an homage* as a tribute to the hero.

Usage example: An article in *The New York Times* (9/27/2000) told about plans for the formal unveiling of "a city monument at Foley Square in Lower Manhattan that pays homage to African-American slaves."

home in or hone in? The risk-free form of this phrase—which means "to target, to focus attention"—is *home in*. Usage example: According to *The New York Times* (5/8/2001), "A new drug that homes in on cancer cells has achieved striking preliminary results in treating a kind of leukemia and may also be effective against a rare stomach tumor."

Merriam-Webster researchers say the expression *home in (on)* emerged in the mid-20th century from the use of *home* as a verb that at first meant "return home from a distance" (as with homing pigeons) and then "move toward a target" (as in the field of missile technology).

The phrase *hone in (on)* makes no sense, inasmuch as *hone* means "to sharpen, make more effective." But thanks to sloppy pronunciation and spelling, *hone in* became a mass-media variant of *home in*. For example, *People* magazine (9/10/1984) reported that "Springsteen hones in on the plights and victories of the common man."

Despite the frequent use of *hone in*, you are advised to stay with *home in* by *Merriam-Webster's Dictionary of English Usage*, *The Columbia Guide to Standard American English*, *Garner's Modern American Usage*, and the stylebooks of *The New York Times* and *The Wall Street Journal*. Save *hone* for usages like the following from *The New York Times* (11/11/2002): "No country has honed its image with more care than Thailand, [with one result being] nearly $7 billion a year in tourism revenue."

homely doesn't rhyme with *comely* *Homely*, meaning "plain, unattractive," is pronounced the way it looks. But *comely*, meaning "of pleasing appearance," is pronounced "KUM-ly."

In British English, incidentally, *homely* means "simple, informal."

homily hazard Users of *homily* need to make clear whether they mean "a sermon" or "a sermon-like lecture that is boring and characterized by false piety."

It should be needless to note that *homily* must be distinguished from *hominy* ("hulled and dried kernels of corn"). But that advice was indeed needed by *The Indiana Gazette* of Indiana, Pennsylvania (11/21/1999), when it published the headline about "Cardinal O'Connor Delivering Hominy."

homogeneous or homogenous? *Homogeneous* means "composed of parts or people of the same kind," as in "a homogeneous suburb." So does *homogenous*, but you should preserve its special meaning, "similar in structure to something else because of common origin," as in "homogenous biological organs."

homograph, homophone, or homonym? *Homograph* (literally, "same writing") refers to words that are spelled alike but have different pronunciations and meanings. ("Let's not get into a *row* [fight] just because they seated us in the wrong *row*.")

Homophone (from the Greek, literally meaning "same sound") refers to words that have the same sound but different spellings and meanings. ("That was quite a *feat* for someone with sore *feet*.")

Homonym (literally, "same name") refers to words that have different meanings but the same sound (homophones), the same spelling (homographs), or both. ("He couldn't *bear* to share his lunch with a *bear*.")

honcho: heading for trouble? The slang phrase *head honcho* is widely used in the sense of "leader, boss," as in a reference to "the head honcho of the umbrella group of state [securities] regulators" in an article in *Barron's*, the Dow Jones business and financial weekly (2/14/2000).

But if you use *head honcho*, you risk being accused of redundancy. That is because *honcho* itself means the head person ("leader, boss"), according to word connoisseur John Ciardi and the American Heritage, Merriam-Webster, and Random House dictionaries, among others.

Ciardi, in his *Good Words to You*, traced *honcho* to Korean War GI slang, "once the label for the head man of a native village, later for the officer or NCO [noncommissioned officer] ramrodding a work detail or military unit." The GI's, according to Ciardi, had originally borrowed *honcho* from the Japanese *hancho* (*han* meaning "small military unit such as a squad" and *cho* meaning "leader").

hopefully can sentence you to criticism   The adverb *hopefully* is risk-free if you use it to modify a verb or an adjective, and thus to mean "in a hopeful manner." Here is a completely acceptable, verb-modifying example from *The New York Times* (9/6/2000): "In anticipation of China's 2008 Olympic bid, the city [of Beijing] is fervently and hopefully preparing for the event."

But you will invite criticism if you imitate the many people who use *hopefully* as a sentence modifier, in which the meaning is "It is to be hoped that." For example, you would be in the Risk Zone if you used *hopefully* like this: "Hopefully, China will improve its human-rights record by the time it hosts the Olympics." That usage of *hopefully* is rejected by numerous usage commentators on the grounds that it is either illogical or ambiguous.

Some critics call the sentence-modifying *hopefully* illogical because it is a state-of-mind adverb and therefore doesn't conform to the normal pattern of such sentence modifiers as *fortunately* and *strangely*. When *fortunately* and *strangely* are attached to the beginning of a sentence, they clearly mean "It is fortunate that" and "It is strange that." But it would obviously be absurd to say "It is hopeful that." (Because it would likewise be absurd to say "It is regretful that," the word *regretfully* has a separate, sentence-modifying form, *regrettably*, meaning "It is regrettable that." Usage commentators have suggested that a comparable sentence-modifying form for *hopefully* would be *hopably* or *hopedly*, but no such word has been adopted into the language.)

Even if you accept the pattern-bending interpretation of *hopefully*, in the sense of "It is to be hoped that," there are critics who charge that you are non-sensically attributing an emotion, hopefulness, to no one in particular. And other critics argue that readers can never be sure whether the sentence-modifying *hopefully* means "It is to be hoped that" or "in a hopeful manner." For example,

"Hopefully, China will improve" can be interpreted to mean not only "It's to be hoped that China will improve" but also "China is hopeful about improving."

Though the sentence-modifying *hopefully* "seems here to stay," according to the 2003 *Chicago Manual of Style*, that usage is widely opposed by language guardians. According to Strunk and White's *Elements of Style*, the sentence-modifying *hopefully* "is not merely wrong, it is silly." Leo Rosten, expressing the consensus of his fellow usage panelists of the *Harper Dictionary of Contemporary Usage*, said the sentence-modifying *hopefully* "is absurd, no matter who uses it or approves of it." Morton S. Freeman says in *Words to the Wise*, "Among careful writers, the prevailing opinion is to reject this usage." *The Oxford English Dictionary* warns that the sentence-modifying *hopefully* "is avoided by many writers."

The sentence-modifying *hopefully* has also been rejected by the stylebooks of the Associated Press, *The New York Times*, *The Wall Street Journal*, the *Los Angeles Times*, *U.S. News & World Report*, and *The Economist*; by Wilson Follett's *Modern American Usage*, John O. E. Clark's *Word Perfect*, *The New York Public Library Writer's Guide to Style and Usage*, and Paul W. Lovinger's *Penguin Dictionary of American English Usage and Style*; and by 73 percent of the usage panel of *The American Heritage Dictionary*.

horrible, horrid, horrific, or horrifying? All four adjectives can mean "causing horror." But because *horrible* and *horrid* are often used to describe something that is merely objectionable, you are well advised to use *horrific* or *horrifying* to describe a source of literal horror.

For example, a *Los Angeles Times* article (6/19/1998) about South Africa's "inquiry into apartheid-era weapons programs that were aimed at the country's black population" was headlined "Horrific Tales Emerge in Apartheid Hearings."

hover rhymes with lover You can associate that preferable pronunciation with the two meanings of the verb *hover*: Lovers know what it feels like "to float in the air" and "to linger at or near a place" of the loved one.

how is that? You face two risks if you use *how* in place of *that*, as in "The speaker told her audience *how* [meaning *that*] she got her first newspaper job when she was only 16." First, many usage commentators frown on such usage except for informal communication. Second, the *how* that was supposed to mean *that* can be wrongly perceived to mean "by what means." In the example just given, many people would mistakenly think the speaker told the audience the circumstances accounting for her having begun her newspaper career at such an early age.

however or **how ever?**   *However* is an adverb meaning "in whatever manner" and a conjunctive adverb meaning "nevertheless." The adverbial phrase *how ever* is an emphatic way of saying *how*, as in "How ever did *he* get elected?" It is correct to use a space if *ever* could be moved to a different place in the sentence: "How did *he* ever get elected?" (See also "*whatever* or *what ever?*")

however: the start of something new   The conjunctive adverb *however* is the source of a common error when it is used as a synonym for the coordinating conjunction *but*. For example, the following "sentence" with *however* is actually two sentences (or two independent clauses) wrongly joined by a comma: "I pity him, however I don't know how to help." Grammarians refer to this problem as a comma splice or comma fault.

Solution: Use a period to separate the two sentences or a semicolon to separate the two independent clauses before *however* when you use it to mean *but*. Otherwise, replace the *however* with *but*. For example: "I pity him. However, I don't know how to help." "I pity him; however, I don't know how to help." "I pity him, but I don't know how to help."

However doesn't cause a comma-splice problem when it is used in the sense of "in whatever way, no matter how." For example: "He has trouble finding my house, however [no matter how] he approaches it." (See also "sentences that run on into adverbs.")

humanism, Humanism, and humanists   The often-capitalized *Humanism* of the Renaissance refers to the revival of the ancient Roman *studia humanitatis*: studies (of philosophy, poetry, and so on) that supposedly demonstrate human superiority over the other animals.

Today, the word *humanist* means either a scholar in the *humanities* (including philosophy, poetry, music, art, and literature) or a believer in *humanism* (a moral philosophy based on human as distinguished from religious values). And today's humanists are accused by some thinkers of perpetuating the age-old belief in human superiority over all other life forms.

***humor* or *wit*?**   *Humor* and *wit* are both "that which is intended to produce amusement." But *wit*, from Old English *wit an* ("to know"), is an intellectual exhibition of cleverness. A circus clown exhibits humor. A politician exhibits wit.

***hungry* has no national anthem**   The word *hungry* is easily misspelled. For example: *Mrs. Byrne's Dictionary of Unusual, Obscure, and Preposterous Words* defines the adjective *bulimic* as "constantly hungary." Perhaps Mrs. Byrne committed that blunder while hungering for Hungarian goulash.

***hurricane* or *typhoon*?**   Asia's *typhoon* is our *hurricane* ("a violent tropical cyclone with winds moving at more than 70 miles an hour, often accompanied by torrential rains").

husband* as in *husbandry   The meaning of the verb *husband* ("to manage thriftily") and the noun *husbandry* ("careful management of resources, such as in agriculture") echo the origin of the noun *husband*.

Our noun *husband* ("married man") was derived from Old English as a combination of the Old Norse words *hús* ("house") and *bóndi* ("occupier and tiller of the soil"). So *husband* originally meant "male head of a household," a role that required careful and often frugal management.

Today, you need not be male or married in order to "husband [manage thriftily and thereby conserve] your resources."

hyphens change the meaning of these verbs   *Recollect* ("make an effort to remember") is not to be confused with *re-collect* ("to collect again"), *recover* ("get better") is not to be confused with *re-cover* ("cover again"), *recount* ("relate") is not *re-count* ("count again"), *reform* ("improve") is not *re-form* ("form again"), *refunding* ("returning funds") is not *re-funding* ("funding again"), and *resign* ("give up [a position]") is not *re-sign* ("sign again").

hyphens protect the meaning of these adjectives   Compound adjectives— those composed of more than one word—usually need hyphens for clarity. (For the exceptions, see next entry.)

Remove the hyphen in "all-American" and you would create an absurdity in the following blurb from a newspaper ad for a TV docudrama about crime cultist Charles Manson (*New York Times*, 5/16/2004): "How did one man turn all-American teens into cold-blooded killers?"

The hyphenated *more-qualified applicants* means applicants with better qualifications; the unhyphenated version means a larger *number* of qualified applicants. Without their hyphens, a car dealer's *little-used car*—one with desirably low mileage—becomes a small car that might well have hundreds of thousands of miles on the odometer, and *my best-selling book* turns into the best book I've written on the topic of effective sales techniques.

Many compound adjectives need hyphens just to save the reader from having to read and digest each word of the compound adjective separately. For example, the hyphen in the phrase "*ill-equipped* plumber" saves the reader from thinking for a moment that the plumber is ill. And though the phrase "*out-of-the-box* thinking" instantly tells your reader that the thinking is daringly unconventional, the omission of the hyphens would momentarily delay that message while the reader mentally processed the words *out*, *of*, *the*, and *box*, and then figured out that the four words were parts of one adjective that describes the type of thinking.

Likewise, you force the reader to do needless work if you do not hyphenate compound adjectives that can appear either before or after a noun, as in *a short-tempered man* or *a man who is short-tempered*, *a cost-effective change* or *a change that is cost-effective*, *an open-minded judge* or *a judge who is open-minded*.

Sometimes the failure to hyphenate a compound adjective causes no problem for the reader. For example, nobody could mistake the meaning of *The Zero Tolerance Approach to Punctuation*, which was the subtitle of a 2004 bestseller. But the failure to hyphenate the compound adjective "zero-tolerance"—in a book about punctuation—was an embarrassment gleefully noted by at least one reviewer.

hyphens never need to protect these adjectives   You're in violation of English usage if you hyphenate compound adjectives that begin with an *-ly* adverb. That's because the *-ly* end of the adverb—in such phrases as *an extremely dedicated student*, *a carefully written term paper*, and *a highly educated graduate*—does the same job as a hyphen by announcing that the adverb is linked in meaning to the next word.

Also, hyphens are not needed for clarity in compound adjectives consisting of proper names, as in *French Canadian cuisine* and *African American art*. Note too that some compound adjectives, such as *homesick*, need no hyphen because they have become one word. (See also "spelling compound words.")

hyphens in suspension When hyphens join words to form a compound word, as in "*round-the-clock* availability," the hyphens are like links in a chain. But those hyphens may be partially unattached ("suspended") in a set of compound words that share the same end-word. For example, instead of "*one-quart, two-quart,* and *three-quart* cans," you may save space by using suspended hyphens: "*one-, two-,* and *three-quart* cans."

hyphens in titles Though a hyphen is needed in titles that *combine* duties, like *secretary-treasurer*, no hyphens are needed for multiple-word but single-duty titles such as *attorney general, secretary general*, and *surgeon general*. Likewise, you should not hyphenate *editor in chief*, unless you work for a publication (for example, *Time* magazine) whose style prescribes *editor-in-chief*.

***hysteria*: the controversy and the confusion** *Hysteria* ("an uncontrollable outburst of emotion") is derived from a Greek word for *womb* and originated with the belief in ancient Greece that the condition of hysteria was peculiar to women because it was caused by disturbances in the uterus. (Note the related word *hysterectomy*, meaning "surgical removal of the uterus.") Women are likely to be offended—especially when they are aware of the word's history—at hearing a man patronizingly tell a woman, "Now, let's not get hysterical."

Hysteria means something quite different in psychiatry. It is the name for a mental disorder, also known as *conversion hysteria* and *conversion disorder*, in which such physical symptoms as paralysis and blindness may occur solely because of a psychological conflict or need.

The adjective *hysterical* also has conflicting meanings. It can describe an emotional outburst involving uncontrollable weeping. Or it can mean nothing more serious than "causing unrestrained laughter."

I

"*i* before *e*" exceptions   See "spelling tips."

I or *me*?   See "*me* is nothing to be afraid of."

-*ic* or -*ical*?   See "*classic* or *classical*?" "*comic* or *comical*?" "*economic* or *economical*?" "*geographic* or *geographical*?" "*graphic* or *graphical*?" and "*historic* or *historical*?"

icon epidemic   *New York Times* columnist Russell Baker warned (1/24/1997) that the use of the word *icon* (in the sense of "a person or thing that is an object of devotion") had become an "epidemic." Baker wrote, "Wherever you turn, another writer [in newspapers, magazines, and books] is hurling icons." Indicting his own newspaper for "iconning" numerous persons including Virginia Woolf, Frank Sinatra, and Che Guevara, Baker ended his column with a desperate plea: "Will no one save America from iconicization?"

Only days after Baker's plea, his paper "iconned" Thomas Jefferson and Jimmy Stewart. And the paper has continued "iconning" without restraint. For example, in the year 2000, *The New York Times* iconned Bill Clinton, James Dean, Elvis Presley, dancer Katherine Dunham, environmentalist Erin Brockovich, the Red Delicious apple, the Liberty Bell, and Coney Island's Thunderbolt roller coaster.

The word *icon*, derived from the Greek *eikon* ("image"), can also refer to "images of a sacred personage" (as in Eastern Orthodox wood-panel paintings of Christ or of saints or angels). More recently, of course, *icon* acquired the additional meaning of "a symbol of functions and resources on a computer screen."

Iconoclast, originally "one who destroys sacred images," now usually means "one who seeks to overthrow traditional ideas or institutions." UCLA art historian Albert Boime's iconoclastic 1998 book about revered national monuments, including the Statue of Liberty and the Lincoln Memorial, was called *The Unveiling of the National Icons: A Plea for Patriotic Iconoclasm in a Nationalist Era.*

Other *icon*-related words include *iconostasis* ("a church partition on which icons are placed"), *iconophile* ("connoisseur of icons"), *iconolatry* ("the worship of icons"), and two words referring to "the scholarly study of icons," *iconology* and *iconography*.

-*ics* words: some are singular and plural   When an *-ics* word refers to a field of study, the word takes a singular verb: "Acoustics *is* the study of sound." But such a word becomes plural if it is used to refer to characteristics or behavior: "The acoustics in that auditorium *are* terrible."

Here are other examples:

"Ethics *is* the study of the nature of morals." "That politician's ethics *are* disgraceful."

"Politics *is* the study of government." "Office politics *are* sometimes responsible for the resignation or dismissal of valuable employees."

"Mathematics *is* the language with which God has written the universe," said Galileo Galilei, physicist and astronomer (1564–1642). "Students in a physics class discover that the mathematics [mathematical procedures] *are* relatively easy when the problem is fully understood."

***ID* or *I.D.*?**   See "acronym-initialism punctuation."

***idée fixe* is easier to pronounce than to get rid of**   The French-derived *idée fixe*, ("fixed idea, obsession"), and its plural, *idées fixes*, are both pronounced "ee-day FEEKS."

idioms do their own thing   An idiom, as defined by *The American Heritage Dictionary*, is "a speech form or an expression of a given language that is peculiar to itself grammatically *or* cannot be understood from the individual meanings of its elements." In the words of *The Dictionary of Cultural Literacy*, by E. D. Hirsch Jr., Joseph F. Kett, and James Trefil: "Just as each person has a unique, characteristic signature, each language has unique idioms. In fact, the word *idiom* comes from the Greek root *idio*, meaning 'a unique signature.'"

Idiomatic usage has us say *near miss* when we mean *near collision*, and *fat chance* when we mean *slim chance*. It equates *slow down* with *slow up* but requires that our cars *break down* though our relationships *break up*. And we must write *down* an idea but make *up* a story.

Idiomatic usage determines that *good evening* means *hello* but *good night* means *good-bye*. Such usage distinguishes *settle down, settle up*, and *settle on*. Likewise, such usage distinguishes an American phrase for prompt action, *right away*, from the British *straight away*.

Do not waste time seeking logical explanations in a realm in which we bear *in mind* but learn *by heart* and *contract* a disease but *catch* a cold. If anyone questions the logic of your idiom, do not let that person *get your goat* or cause you to be *beside yourself*. Don't *give up* even if you're *fed up*. Just *get down to brass tacks* by *begging to differ*. *Point out* that technical criticism of idiomatic usage is *beside the point* and is therefore *neither here nor there*. (See also " 'It's I' or 'It's me'?" and "*the*: when should it go before a noun?")

idioms get lost in translation   If you're communicating in English to an international audience, remind yourself that idioms you take for granted may be taken in an entirely wrong way by people who did not grow up in an English-speaking environment.

Three oft-cited examples of idiomatic misunderstanding, perhaps all fictional, are a sign in a Hong Kong tailor shop ("Ladies Have Fits Upstairs"), a sign in a Vienna hotel ("In case of fire, do your utmost to alarm the hotel porter"), and a sign in a Moscow hotel lobby ("If this is your first visit to our country, you are welcome to it").

Note that not all abuses of our idioms occur overseas. For example, members of a Los Angeles writers' group were recently informed by e-mail that a literary reading had been canceled, and that the members should "please look out for future readings!" Obviously, the members should have been advised to "*look for* future readings." The phrase *look out for* is appropriate only as a warning, as in "Look out for pickpockets."

***idiosyncracy* or *idiosyncrasy*?**   The prescribed spelling for the word that stands for "characteristic or mannerism peculiar to an individual" ends in *-asy*.

***i.e.* or *e.g.*?**   See "*e.g.* or *i.e.*?"

***if* or *whether*?**   To satisfy word guardians about this question, follow these rules:

Use *if* for what's iffy: "Call me today if you can." Use *whether* for choices:

"Let me know whether you're planning to call me today or tomorrow." Otherwise, feel free to choose *if* or *whether*: "She was trying to decide if (whether) she should accept the job offer." (See also "*whether* or *whether or not?*")

if clauses should not be followed by *then*   Consider this common offer: "If you scratch my back, I'll scratch yours." If you add the word *then*—"If you scratch my back, *then* I'll scratch yours"—you'd be adding a word that contributes nothing to your message. And you might be contributing momentary confusion, because the word *then* in that type of sentence could be interpreted to mean either "as a consequence" or "at that particular time."

The *then* in such sentences is permitted by *The Columbia Guide to Standard American English* when the introductory *if* clause is "very long," as in that source's example: "If we get there in time and the guests have not arrived, then we can ask about tomorrow's schedule." But sometimes you can make the sentence easier to read by reversing it: "We can ask about tomorrow's schedule if we get there in time and the guests have not arrived."

if and when or unless and until you become a lawyer   Lawyers have found those usually needless phrases useful for legal documents, because lawyers understandably would rather risk committing the sin of wordiness than risk committing the more serious offense of omission.

But the rest of us should be aware that thoughtless users of *if and when* and *unless and until* have been scolded for about a century by leading usagists, beginning with usage pioneer Henry W. Fowler. He declared, in a still-quoted condemnation, that a writer who thoughtlessly uses those phrases "lays himself open to . . . suspicions . . . that he likes verbiage for its own sake [or] that he has merely been too lazy to make up his mind between *if* & *when* [or *unless* & *until*]."

If you want to avoid arousing those suspicions, never use *if and when* or *unless and until* without asking yourself if the phrase is really necessary to convey your meaning. For example, the word *if* is sufficient in this statement: "I'll apologize only if he does." But in the following statement the additional word *when* emphasizes important information about time: "We can go on that cruise if and *when* I get my bonus." Likewise, say "I won't apologize unless he does," but say "We can't go on that cruise unless and *until* I get my bonus."

iffy meanings The preposition *if* can sometimes cause confusion when it introduces a clause suggesting uncertainty. Consider this ambiguous sentence: "Make sure he's informed if he's given the promotion." Depending on your intended meaning, the sentence should read "Make sure he's informed whether he's given the promotion" or "If he's given the promotion, make sure he's informed [about something]."

If you say "Tell me if I'm dressed inappropriately," that could mean "Tell me now" or "Tell me if the occasion should ever arise." If you want the advice now, replace *if* with *whether*.

illiterate: a question of ignorance *Illiterate* literally means "unable to read and write." Its extended use, as a synonym for "ignorant," is common but controversial.

When the question of the extended use was put to the usage panel of the *Harper Dictionary of Contemporary Usage*, 49 percent said no for speech and 68 percent said no for writing. That opposition to the "ignorant" *illiterate* was typified by a comment from panelist Barry Bingham Sr., publisher of the *Louisville Courier-Journal* and *Times*: "As in so many other cases, a precise and fully descriptive word is being stretched out of all shape."

illusory or elusory? *Illusory* means "based on an illusion, deceptive."

Elusory, a synonym for *elusive*, can mean "cleverly evasive" or "hard to mentally grasp." For example, the Nobel Prize citation (10/8/1998) for Portuguese novelist José Saramago said he "enables us . . . to apprehend an elusory reality."

images out of focus When you use words to create images, make sure the images make sense. Here, from a student in one of my writing classes, is an image that doesn't quite pass the test: "Just then, worried faces started walking in." Try picturing *that*.

imaginary or imaginative? Carelessness sometimes results in the use of *imaginative* ("showing imagination, having great creative powers") when the needed word is *imaginary* ("existing only in imagination, unreal").

Immaculate Conception or Virgin Birth? The Immaculate Conception is not a reference to the Virgin Birth of Christ. The Immaculate Conception is a

Roman Catholic dogma—proclaimed in 1854 by Pope Pius IX—declaring that the Virgin Mary, unlike the rest of humanity, must herself have been conceived without "the stain" of Adam and Eve's "original sin."

The confusion of those two religious concepts has been widely reinforced by mass media. For example, Rush Limbaugh sarcastically commented on his syndicated radio show (4/2/1997) about a news report of an insurance company's offering a policy to protect women against "immaculate conceptions."

immunity or impunity? *Impunity* means "exemption from punishment." So can *immunity*, as in an ambassador's claim of diplomatic immunity when he or she has violated the laws of the host nation. But *immunity*'s most common meaning is "natural or acquired protection from a disease."

immure or inure? The verb *immure*, derived from the Latin *murus* ("wall"), means "to wall in, to imprison." The verb *inure* (note the single *n*) means "to accustom to hardship, to toughen."

Immure goes with the preposition *in* or *within*; *inure* takes *to*.

impact could have a negative impact on you For risk-free experiences with *impact*, always use it as a noun, never as a verb.

Feel free to use the noun *impact* as a synonym for "forcible contact," as in "the impact of an auto collision." Feel equally free to use the noun *impact* as a synonym for "influence," as in a *New York Times* feature story (2/6/2001) speculating that Vice President Cheney's wife, author and corporate board member Lynne Cheney, "could have a major impact on [White House] policy."

But think twice before you contribute to the widespread use of *impact* as a verb, as in "Many factors impact [have an effect] on consumer confidence." As Bryan A. Garner observes in *Garner's Modern American Usage,* such use is "widely condemned by stylists." For example, *The American Heritage Book of English Usage* reports that 84 percent of the American Heritage usage panel rejected the phrase "to impact on our community," and 95 percent rejected the verb's transitive use, as in "impacting our health." In typical comments, usage panelists branded the verb "bureaucratic," "pretentious," and "vile." In a similarly sweeping rejection of *impact* as a verb, usage panelists of the *Harper Dictionary of Contemporary Usage* denounced the verb with such adjectives as "ugly," "beastly," and "infuriating."

Suggestion: If you experience an overwhelming urge to use *impact* as a verb, switch to the phrase *have* [or *had*] *an impact on.* Example: "Freud's theories impacted [change to *had an impact on*] not only psychology but also philosophy, literature, and advertising."

impassable or **impassible**? If you mistakenly change the ending of *impassable* ("incapable of being passed or traveled") to *-ible*, you have a rarely used word that means "unfeeling, not subject to suffering or pain." Roads are sometimes *impassable* but never *impassible.*

impeach **is just the beginning** Presidents Andrew Johnson and Bill Clinton were *impeached* ("accused of misconduct in public office") by the House of Representatives but acquitted by the Senate. *Impeach* also is used in the general sense of "accuse" or in the sense of "discredit, raise doubts about," as in impeaching someone's motives or testimony.

impeccable or **impeccant**? See "*peccable, peccadillo, peccancy, peccant, peccatophobia.*"

imply or **infer**? The communicator *implies* ("suggests, hints"). The receiver of communication *infers* ("deduces, concludes, draws a conclusion"). To borrow a memorable metaphor from *The Careful Writer*—a classic usage guide by the late Theodore M. Bernstein, who rose on *The New York Times* from copy editor to assistant managing editor—the implier pitches and the inferrer catches.

Infer is frequently used as if it were an elegant way to say *imply.* And that practice is justified by Merriam-Webster and Random House dictionaries on the grounds that it can be found in the work of writers dating back almost to the time when *imply* and *infer* were coined by Sir Thomas More, the English author-statesman (I478–I535).

But Wilson Follett's *Modern American Usage* contends that *infer/imply* usage "has built up a clear [and useful] distinction" that is observed today by educated users of the language. *The Oxford English Dictionary* reports that the use of *infer* to mean *imply* "is widely considered to be incorrect." According to *The HarperCollins Concise Dictionary of English Usage*, the ability to distinguish *imply* from *infer* "functions as a caste mark today." And *Feature Writing for Newspapers and Magazines* by Jay Friedlander and John Lee indicts those who use *imply/infer* interchangeably as "uneducated."

An indication of just how widely the interchangeability of *imply/infer* is rejected may be inferred from the following list of sources that prescribe the separate use of *imply* for "suggest" and *infer* for "deduce": Strunk and White's *Elements of Style,* the Modern Language Association's *Line by Line* editing manual, Morton S. Freeman's *Wordwatcher's Guide to Good Writing & Grammar,* the *Harper Dictionary of Contemporary Usage, Webster's New World Guide to Current American Usage, Garner's Modern American Usage,* Paul W. Lovinger's *Penguin Dictionary of American English Usage and Style,* 92 percent of the usage panel of *The American Heritage Dictionary,* and the stylebooks of the Associated Press, *The New York Times, The Washington Post, The Wall Street Journal,* and the *Los Angeles Times.*

***imposter* or *impostor*?**   Both are legitimate spellings for "a person who deceives under an assumed identity." But the *-or* ending is preferred in both American and British English.

The *act* of deceiving under an assumed identity is called *imposture.*

***impresario*: don't get too impressed**   The word *impresario* ("one who sponsors or produces entertainment, especially the director of an opera company") looks impressive but does not have what *impressive* has—two *s*'s. *Impresario* was adapted from the Italian word *impresa* ("undertaking").

in addition to   See "*together* but alone."

***in behalf of* or *on behalf of*?**   *In behalf of* means "for the benefit of." *On behalf of* means "in place of." Example: "*On* behalf of the scheduled speaker, she appealed for more funds *in* behalf of municipal parks."

***in* interruptions**   With *in* phrases such as *in turn, in effect, in short,* and *in fact,* use commas to separate them from the sentences they interrupt. Usage example from *The Economist* (1/15/2000): "Poverty aggravates health problems . . . and poor health, in turn, aggravates poverty."

***in, into,* or *in to*?**   A silly old joke might help remind you to use these words carefully. A woman says: "My boyfriend is a magician. When he takes me for a ride in his car, he turns into [should be *in to*] a motel."

In is used as a preposition for location and condition: "The boss is *in* his office, and he is *in* a good mood." *In* may also be used as an adverb to show movement: "He went *in* to look for his boss."

The preposition *into* is sometimes needed to make clear that a location has changed. Obviously, saying "Lassie ran *into* the street" is quite different from saying "Lassie ran *in* the street." (Some idiomatic expressions—such as "Go jump in [should be *into*] the lake"—defy the rules.)

Into applies not only to a change in location but also to a change in condition. A frog can turn *into* a prince. But a frog that turns *in* a prince is a stool pigeon. (See also "*on, onto,* or *on to?*")

in lieu of   This is a formal way of saying "instead of." ("My friend was willing to accept an I.O.U. in lieu of money.") It does not mean "because of" or "in light of."

in light of or **in the light of**?   This oft-used expression for "considering, taking into account" refers to the specific light shed by the object of the phrase it introduces. Consequently, Copperud's *American Usage and Style* and other usage sources have prescribed the definite article *the*.

in order to **may be too long**   You can sometimes save space without sacrificing clarity by deleting *in order*. (But see also "*to* can cause confusion.")

in- or **un-** **words**   When the same word can be preceded by either *in-* or *un-*, the *in-* form is likely to be negative and the *un-* form is likely to be neutral. For example, compare the negative *inhuman* with the neutral *unhuman*.

in the event that: **try a little substitute**   Replace those four words with *if*, unless you feel an overwhelming need to use the four-word expression because of its air of formality.

inalienable or **unalienable**?   These are two forms of a word meaning "not to be taken away." Our Declaration of Independence says we are endowed with "certain *unalienable* rights." Usage commentators say the preferred term today is *inalienable*.

inanimate possessives   See "*whose*: for people only?"

incapable **or** *unable*?   *Incapable* suggests a lack of ability that is long-term. ("He's incapable of doing that job.") *Unable* usually suggests a lack of ability caused by temporary circumstances. ("I was unable to reach you last week.")

inchoate: **a question of chaos**   You are in the Safe Zone if you use *inchoate* ("in-KO-it") only in its sense of "not fully developed, immature, in an initial or early stage, imperfect." You'll find that meaning for *inchoate* in *The Oxford English Dictionary* and leading U.S. dictionaries.

Some U.S. dictionaries also include the definition "disorganized, chaotic." According to *Merriam-Webster's Dictionary of English Usage*, "[That] extended use is natural and probably inevitable; what is just begun is also unfinished, incomplete, and often also disorganized or incoherent." But if you use the extended, "chaotic" meaning, be prepared for criticism: A number of usage guides, including J. N. Hook's *Appropriate Word*, regard the second definition as a misusage.

incidentally **or** *incidently*?   As noted by usage commentators Harry Shaw and John L. Dusseau, *incidently* was once in good standing but is now widely regarded as "an illiteracy."

If you choose to defy the standard spelling of *incidentally* (meaning "by way of interjection or digression"), you can defend yourself by pointing out that *incidently* is listed as a rare variant in *Webster's Third New International Dictionary*. But that unabridged volume is too heavy to carry around just to justify the alternate spelling.

including   See "*together* but alone."

incomparable **or** *uncomparable*?   Both mean "not suitable for comparison." But the first implies that this is so because of excellence.

incompetence **or** *incompetency*?   Both words mean "insufficient ability or qualifications." But competent writers reserve *incompetency* for legal contexts, as in "the condition of being mentally unqualified to stand trial or give testimony."

incomplete comparisons   See *"as* and *than* comparisons need to be complete" and "comparisons that aren't."

incredible **confusion**   To avoid *incredible* confusion, make clear whether you are using the adjective *incredible* in its literal sense of "not believable" or its extended sense of "so amazing, astonishing, or strikingly unusual that it's hard to believe."

Incredible was clearly used to mean "not believable" when an *NBC Nightly News* correspondent (7/23/1998) reported that critics of President Clinton regarded as "literally incredible" his initial denial of a sexual relationship with White House intern Monica Lewinsky.

And *incredible* was clearly used in the sense of "amazing" when Walt Disney Pictures' invitation to its $2,000-a-plate "Fantasia/2000 New Year's Eve Gala" promised a showing of *Fantasia 2000* featuring "incredible animation," preceded by a black-tie dinner "topped off with an incredible selection of desserts."

Careless use of *incredible* can leave one's audience wondering which of the two senses is intended, as when Michigan Governor John Engler was quoted by *The New York Times* as calling the 2000 Gore-Bush presidential contest "this incredible election." Careless use of *incredible* can also result in sheer nonsense, as in a June 2004 Book-of-the-Month-Club catalog description of "an amazing true story" as "so incredible, it's hard to believe." (See also *"unbelievable* confusion.")

incredulous **or** *incredible?*   Don't believe it if your neighbors boast to you that they had a vacation that was "absolutely incredulous."

Though *incredulous* meant "incredible"—in the sense of unbelievable—during the time of Shakespeare, its modern meaning is "disbelieving." Appropriate usage: "Filmmaker Oliver Stone spoke about the mainstream media's *incredulous* response to his version of the assassination of President Kennedy."

individuals **need contrast**   Many usage commentators have objected to the use of *individuals* as a simple synonym for *persons* or *people*, as in "three individuals were waiting in the outer office." Critics of that usage contend that it is pretentious and that it undermines the proper role of *individual* as a word contrasting a single person with a larger group: "The rights of society must sometimes yield to the rights of the individual."

***inertia* isn't always inert**   The word *inert* is an adjective meaning "unable to move or act," and *inertia* is a noun that commonly means "resistance to motion, action, or change." But *inertia* in physics means resistance to change in the sense of not only "the tendency of a resting body to remain at rest" but also "the tendency of a moving body to stay in motion."

***infamous* or *notorious*?**   Both these adjectives mean "widely and unfavorably known." But *notorious* is more likely than *infamous* to be used playfully, as in "He's notorious for his taste in ties."

When *notorious* entered the language in the middle of the 16th century, it had a neutral connotation, meaning simply "widely known." Judging from the history of *notorious* recorded in *The Oxford English Dictionary*, the word acquired its pejorative sense as a result of being used in phrases such as "notorious sinner." (See also next entry.)

***infamy* or *notoriety*?**   *Infamy* ("the state of being *infamous* [widely and unfavorably known]") is clearly associated with evil, as when Franklin Delano Roosevelt responded to Japan's bombing of Pearl Harbor by declaring that December 7, 1941, was "a date which will live in infamy." (To learn why he should have replaced *which* with *that*, see "*that* or *which*?")

Notoriety is risky because of its ambiguity. Its primary dictionary definition is "the state of being *notorious* [known widely and usually unfavorably]." But *notoriety* is frequently used informally, especially in the media, as a synonym for "fame."

infinitives   See "splitting infinitives: a needless fear."

***inflection*: more than one change**   Depending on context, an *inflection* is either "a change in pitch or tone of voice," a "change in curvature from convex to concave or vice versa," or "a change in the form of words to reflect different grammatical functions such as the plurals and possessives of nouns, past-tense forms of verbs, or the comparative and superlative forms of adjectives."

***infrastructure*'s three meanings**   *Infrastructure*—combining *structure* with a Latin prefix meaning "below"—is said by word historians to have originated in the early 20th century as a term for "the underlying structure of a nation's military defense system."

Today, infrastructure usually means "the underlying structure of a society's economy, including facilities for transportation, communication, water, and power." A *New York Times* article (1/25/2001) referred to California's sudden shortage of electricity as a "failure of a vital piece of modern infrastructure."

In business and technology, *infrastructure* is the word for what Microsoft's *Encarta World English Dictionary* calls "the system according to which a company, organization or other body is organized at the most basic level."

ingenious or **ingenuous**? An *ingenious* ("clever, resourceful") person may pretend to be *ingenuous* ("lacking in cunning, without artifice") in order to trick you. Such tricky people are described as *disingenuous*.

innocent or **not guilty**? Don't believe media stories about defendants pleading, or being found, *innocent*. The media often use *innocent* rather than the actual plea or verdict of *not guilty* to avoid risking lawsuits over typographical errors or slips of the tongue that omit the important little word *not*. (See also "*not* is not to be taken for granted.")

innovation: **what's new** The word *innovation* means "a new idea, method, or device." Don't get caught saying "new innovation." That's somewhat like saying "Let me tell you what's new-new." If you're referring to the latest in a series of innovations, call it the *latest* innovation, or simply *another* innovation.

inquiry about pronunciation American dictionaries assign the preferential listing to "in-KWIRE-ee" over the British "IN-kwa-ree."

insects and non-insects Spiders aren't insects. Neither are scorpions, ticks, and mites. They are *arachnids*, wingless creatures with eight legs and a body divided into two parts.

Insects (including flies, bees, and butterflies) are usually winged, and they have six legs and a body of three parts.

Insects, arachnids, crustaceans, centipedes, and millipedes are all *arthropods*, invertebrates with segmented bodies and outer skeletons. Arthropods form the world's largest group of animals (more than eight hundred thousand species).

***insidious* or *invidious*?** *Insidious* (from a Latin word for "ambush") means "stealthily treacherous, beguiling but harmful." *Invidious* (from a Latin word for "envious") means "arousing envy or hate, unfairly discriminating."

***insignia is* or *insignia are*?** *Insignia* ("badge or emblem of office, rank, membership, or nationality") entered English in the 17th century as the plural of the Latin *insigne* (pronounced "in-SIG-nee"). But in the 18th century *insignia* began to be used as an English singular, producing the English plural *insignias*.

Today some writers still use *insignia* as a plural for *insigne*, and that practice is acceptable in Standard English and prescribed by Follett's *Modern American Usage*. But the more common practice, approved by most dictionaries and a majority of the usage panel of *The American Heritage Dictionary*, is to use a singular *insignia* and a plural *insignias*.

***intense* or *intensive*?** *Intense* suggests an *inner* strength or concentration, as in "intense pleasure." *Intensive* suggests a strength or concentration from *without*, as in "intensive instruction."

intensive pronouns See "pronouns that are *self*-conscious."

***interment* or *internment*?** The first means "burial"; the second, "confinement."

***intern* or *internist*?** An M.D. must serve as an *intern* ("someone acquiring supervised professional experience") before he or she can practice medicine and perhaps choose to become a specialist such as an *internist* ("a practitioner of internal medicine").

intransitive or transitive? See "verbs: transitive and intransitive."

***intrigue* can be fascinating** *Intrigue* apparently entered English from French in the 16th century, as a noun meaning "intricacy, maze," then "complicated state of affairs," then "plotting or scheming." By the 17th century, *intrigue* was also a *verb*, meaning "to plot or to scheme."

In the early 20th century, *intrigue*'s emerging use in the sense of "arouse curiosity so as to puzzle or fascinate" was opposed by Henry W. Fowler and other usage commentators on the grounds that English already had words like *puzzle* and *fascinate*. But as Sir Ernest Gowers noted in his 1965 revision of Fowler's usage dictionary, *intrigue* had become a useful, one-word *combination* of *puzzle* and *fascinate*. In subsequent years, support for the "fascinating" *intrigue* rose among usage panelists of *The American Heritage Dictionary* from 52 to 78 percent.

intuit: not everybody is into it   *Intuit* ("to know intuitively"), a back-formation from *intuition*, has been around as long as some back-formations that are taken for granted, such as *donate* and *diagnose*. But *intuit* has yet to achieve completely respectable status, judging from the fact that it has been rejected by a majority of the usage panel of *The American Heritage Dictionary*.

invaluable information   If the prefix *in-* means "not" in such words as *incomplete, inseparable, inexperienced, incompetent, inequality,* and *injustice,* why doesn't the adjective *invaluable* mean "not valuable"? Actually, it *does* mean "not valuable"—but *valuable* here means "having a measurable value." An *invaluable* item is so enormously valuable that one cannot measure its value, just as "*incalculable* losses" are too enormous to be calculated.

   Usage example from *The New York Times* (2/18/1997): A review of a TV documentary about Thomas Jefferson cited his "historically invaluable correspondence with John Adams."

iridescent or irridescent?   This adjective, for "displaying a play of lustrous colors like those of the rainbow," has, like *rainbow,* only one *r*.

ironic or ironical?   The preferred form is *ironic*. But the adverbial form is *ironically*.

irony is no coincidence   The brothers Henry W. and Francis George Fowler, in their early 20th-century book, *The King's English*, called the noun *irony* "one of the worst abused in the language." Whether or not that was true in those days, *irony* ("EYE-rah-nee") is widely abused today by those who confuse it with *coincidence*. In a blatant example of that error, an article in the *Los Angeles Times* entertainment section (10/18/1998) began, "The irony of Jonathan Demme directing *Beloved*, the film adaptation of Toni Morrison's acclaimed novel, is that it came about by coincidence."

Notice that *coincidence* plays no role in *The Oxford English Dictionary's* definition of *irony* as "a condition of affairs or events of a character opposite to what was or might naturally be expected." Hence, the adjective *ironic* is appropriate for a fire at a fire station, a burglary at a police station, or actor Christopher Reeve's paralyzing accident in a 1995 equestrian competition after he had just lent his image to a poster promoting riding safety. Usage examples from an editorial in *Psychology Today* (January/February 2001): "But the quest for happiness is probably overrated and is, ironically, the cause of much unhappiness. . . . Religious leaders like the Dalai Lama insist that the only way to achieve real happiness is by making others happy—yet another irony."

Irony also applies to an occurrence so unexpected that it appears to be deliberately perverse. It would be ironic, for example, if consistently tardy dinner guests showed up on time on the one evening when *you* happened to be running late.

In another form of irony, words are used to convey the opposite of their literal meaning, as when a tall person is called Shorty. For a nasty variety of that form of irony, see the next entry.

irony or **sarcasm?**   *Sarcasm* is the word for an ironic expression—one that means the opposite of what it says—that *ridicules.* Derived from a Greek term for "flesh-tearing," *sarcasm* refers to verbal laceration. A sarcastic remark is typically conveyed in speech, with vocal inflection and body language that mocks the literal meaning of the words. Example: "What a great judge of character *you* turned out to be."

irregardless of, irrespective of, or **regardless of?**   Your risk-free choice is *regardless of,* a prepositional phrase meaning "in spite of" (as in "regardless of the cost") or "without regard to" (as in, "regardless of the loan applicant's credit history").

Irrespective used to be an adjective that meant "lacking in respect" or "having no regard for persons or consequences." The word survives today in the prepositional phrase *irrespective of,* but that phrase is a needless, formal substitute for *regardless of.*

Irregardless—which emerged in early 20th-century America, probably as a blend of *irrespective* and *regardless*—has met with what *The American Heritage Dictionary* calls "a blizzard of condemnation." *Irregardless* has been dismissed by grammarians as a nonsensical double negative because it has both a negative prefix, *ir-*, and a negative suffix, *-less*. *Irregardless* has been denounced by usage commentators as nonstandard, substandard, common, vulgar, and semiliterate. Columnist Paul W. Lovinger declares in his *Penguin Dictionary of American English Usage and Style* that *irregardless* "should be shunned." Likewise, lexicographer-lawyer Bryan A. Garner says in his *Modern American Usage* that *irregardless* "should have been stamped out long ago."

issue or problem?   If you succumb to the trendy practice of using *issue* to mean *problem*, you risk sounding pretentious and confusing your listeners. A leaky roof is a problem. A proposed change in your city's building code is an issue. In other words, problems need to be fixed, but issues need to be debated.

is when and is where   See "defining with *when* and *where*."

it and there can hurt or help the start of a sentence   When *it* and *there* are used as "false subjects"—meaningless words at the beginning of a sentence—they may be foes or friends of good writing.

False subjects are often nothing but clutter. For example, notice the improvement when you replace the false subjects *it* and *there* with the actual subjects at the beginning of the following sentences: "*It* is recommended by the car's manufacturer that you change the oil every 3,000 miles." ("The car's manufacturer recommends that you change the oil every 3,000 miles.") "*There* are many motorists who never bother to read their owner's manual." ("Many motorists never bother to read their owner's manual.") An abundance of such false-subject clutter is typical of writing marked by inexperience or laziness.

On the other hand, a false subject is sometimes idiomatically necessary, as in "*It* is raining," "*It* is late," and "*It* is too bad." No matter how hard you try, you won't find a good way to replace the *it* in such expressions.

Moreover, a false subject may be stylistically worthwhile. For example, "*There* is no escape" is a powerful statement precisely because the subject, "no escape," is revealed at the end. If you began the sentence by replacing the false subject *there* with the actual subject, you would have a considerably weakened version, "No escape exists." In a similar example, "*There* are few real heroes" is more powerful than "Few real heroes exist." "*There* are no easy answers" is stronger than "No easy answers exist." And "*There* are new techniques for combating smog" is much less awkward than "New techniques exist with which to combat smog" or "New techniques exist to combat smog with." As Bryan A. Garner advises in his *Modern American Usage*, "If the only real recourse is to use the verb *exist*, then *there is* is perfectly fine."

Another defense of false subjects, cited by Roy H. Copperud in his *American Usage and Style*, involves the dedicated writer's goal of communicating with a sense of rhythm. Consider this sentence from *The New York Times* (7/1/2001): "There has never been a time like this when the world was so small, communication so rapid and the need for a common language so fundamental." The rhythm of that sentence would be shattered if you replaced the false subject *there* with the actual subject: "A time like this has never occurred. . . ."

Sometimes the false subject is useful for rhythmic repetition, as in this introductory paragraph for a feature story in *The New York Times* (7/28/2001): "In a way, all the empty space surrounding Michael Lawson at the baseball stadium only made the day a little finer. *There was no beer being spilled*, no blowhard bellowing into his ear. *There was just the game*, the green field fanning out below him, and row after row of orange, vacant seats." (Italics added.)

italic or **Italic?**   The capitalized *Italic* is an adjective meaning "of or relating to ancient Italy" and a noun meaning "a branch of the Indo-European language family that includes Latin."

The lowercase *italic* is an adjective referring to a form of printing based on a style of right-slanted handwriting favored by Italian scholars of the Renaissance. The italic form of print was introduced as a separate typeface at the beginning of the 16th century by Venetian printer Aldo Manuzio.

Today, italic print is—and you can say "italics *are*"—commonly used with regular (roman-lettering) text to mark words to be emphasized (right *here*), words cited as words (as in "the noun *italics*"), foreign expressions (*nouveau riche*), and distinctive names (including titles of books, plays, movies, periodicals, newspapers, and legal cases).

italicizing foreign expressions   Italicize foreign words and phrases that have not yet blended into the crowd of English vocabulary. How do you decide? Italicize when your dictionary does. For example, the *Random House Webster's Unabridged Dictionary* uses no italics if you choose an hors d'oeuvre but italicizes *hors de combat* ("or duh comb-BAH"), which means "out of combat, out of action, disabled." (See also "dictionaries: use them for more than a spell.")

its, it's, or *its'*?   Many students, assuming that a word can be made possessive only by adding an apostrophe and an *s*, spell the possessive pronoun *its* as if it were *it's* (the contraction for *it is*) or the nonexistent word *its'*. *Its*, like the possessive pronouns *his, hers, theirs,* and *ours*, expresses possessiveness just by being itself.

Usage example of the contraction *it's* and the possessive *its*: A *New York Times Magazine* cover blurb (10/4/1998) for a story about the Caspian Sea oil rush in Azerbaijan declared, "It's old-fashioned capitalism at its most raw."

Caution: No matter how well you know the difference between *its* and *it's*, you are in daily danger of carelessly using one for the other.

"It's I" or "It's me"?   Knock, knock. Who's there? Did you say "It's me"? If so, do not let Grammar Vigilantes make you feel guilty. Though grammar dictates a nominative pronoun like *I* after a linking verb like *is*, this is a case in which grammar must yield to other considerations.

First, there is a valid linguistic reason why millions of people resist saying "It's I." As speakers of English, they are doing what is perfectly normal when they follow a verb with an objective-case pronoun like *me*. ("She saw *me*, I saw *her*, and neither of us saw *them*.")

Second, the informal "It's me" is a fully established English idiom, and an idiom by definition is an expression that is exempt from the rules of logic or grammar. To quote William and Mary Morris in their *Harper Dictionary of Contemporary Usage*: "Here is a case where the preponderance of educated, intelligent people . . . favors the less formal version."

The Columbia Guide to Standard American English notes that "*It's me* and *It's us* are both Standard in all Conversational and most Informal uses, perhaps in part because they occur almost exclusively in speech anyway." *The American Heritage Book of English Usage* says that "constructions like *It is me* have been condemned in the classroom and in writing handbooks for so long that there seems little likelihood that they will ever be entirely acceptable in formal writing." But that same source acknowledges that the "It's me" question is principally relevant only for informal communication, and that "It's I" sounds "pedantic and even ridiculous."

If the nominative-case zealots insist on assailing you for saying "It's me," inform them that it was employed in the writing of Winston Churchill. If that doesn't impress them, ask them if they know any couples who announce their arrival at a friend's home by grammatically but absurdly stating "It's *we*."

If you want to sidestep this problem, respond to the question "Who's there?" by saying "This is [insert your name]." If you pick up the telephone and someone asks for you by name, say "Speaking." (See also "*me* is nothing to be afraid of.")

J

jaguar: **ours is faster**   Don't be confused if you hear the "JAG-yoo-ahr" pronunciation in car commercials. That is the preferred *British* pronunciation for the car and also for the powerful, graceful South American cat after which the car was named. The pronunciation preferred in American English (for both cat and car) has only two syllables: "JAG-wahr."

Janus-faced: **lookin' good or bad?**   Comparing someone to the Roman god Janus can be a compliment or an insult. So you need to make sure your intended meaning for this reference is clear.

Janus was said to have two heads positioned back to back, to simultaneously see the future and the past. Janus began as the god of light, who opened and closed each day. He then became the guardian of beginnings and endings, entrances and exits, gates and doors. And his name was bestowed on the month that became the gateway to each year, January. As a *New York Times* editorial observed (1/1/2001), "New Year's Day is the traditional time for gazing, Janus-like, both forward and backward." Thus, *Janus-like* can describe somebody as "far-sighted."

But beware: *Janus-faced* means "two-faced, hypocritical, deceitful."

Incidentally, the phrase *Janus word* means "*contranym*, a word with contradictory meanings." (See also "contranyms speak with forked tongue.")

jargon **is not really for the birds**   *Jargon* ("JAR-gun"), an Old French word for "chattering of birds," entered English more than five hundred years ago as a term meaning "the inarticulate utterance of birds, or a vocal sound resembling it." The word *jargon* was revived in the 17th century to convey the idea of "confusing, specialized language."

Today, we know that bird language only *seemed* inarticulate, because of the tendency of humans to devalue any language or culture they don't understand. But *jargon* continues to have a derogatory connotation. Though the word is sometimes used as a neutral synonym for "specialized language of a trade or profession," it usually means "a pretentious insider language that is difficult to understand because of its needlessly obscure vocabulary and needlessly complex phrasing,"

Regarding pretentious jargon, an essay in *The New York Times* (12/10/2000) cited a trend in e-commerce technology to turn common words into technical buzzwords, as in the use of *sticky portals* to mean "attention-holding Web sites." To quote the *Times* essay: "This forced march toward new meanings can create costly inefficiencies, says Michael Schrage, co-director of the e-markets initiative at the Media Laboratory of the Massachusetts Institute of Technology. 'When the same word means different things to different people, you're going to spend more time managing meaning than managing the problem,' he warned." (See also "*academese*: an infectious disease.")

jargon of journalese   A random list of infamous journalese "formula phrasing"—published by *Dallas Morning News* writing coach Paula LaRocque in her *Quill* magazine usage column (March 1995)—included *escalating conflict, heated debate, widespread resistance, cautious optimism, heightened criticism, growing indications, cries of protest, bloody coup, defining moment, worst-case scenario, political football, crucial test, litmus test, laundry list, whopping figure, sudden downturn, steep decline, economic crunch, low profile, hard line,* and *bottom line.*

jaundice: more than meets the eye   If you feel bitter about something, you view it with "a jaundiced eye." *Jaundice*, from a Latin word for *yellow*, is a symptom of hepatitis and other diseases, involving a yellowish discoloration of the whites of the eyes, skin, and mucous membranes caused by deposits of bile salts in those tissues. *Bile*, which can mean "bitterness of temper," is the medical term for a bitter and commonly yellowish fluid secreted by the liver as an aid to digestion.

Usage example: The *Los Angeles Times* (1/29/2000) reported that former Senator Eugene J. McCarthy, who blamed dirty politics for his failure to become the Democratic presidential nominee in 1968, watched the 2000 presidential primary race "with a jaundiced eye."

***je ne sais quoi*: expressing the inexpressible**   Do not be surprised if you ask natives of France what *je ne sais quoi* means and you get the response "I don't know what." They really do know what they are talking about. You see, "I don't know what" happens to be the literal English translation of *je ne sais quoi*.

In actual usage, this italicized French import means "a (usually pleasant) quality that is difficult or impossible to describe or express." For example: "The ambassador has a certain *je ne sais quoi* that charms everyone she meets."

Jeremiah and his noun   In one of the books of the Old Testament, called Jeremiah, the Jewish prophet of that name warns in great detail that "God's fury will come forth like fire" in response to social injustice, individual immorality, and the worship of idols. Jeremiah's public condemnations of "those who pollute the land with thy wickedness" inspired our word *jeremiad* ("a righteous prophecy of doom," "a mournful complaint," or a "cautionary scolding").

Here's a usage example of *jeremiad* as "a cautionary scolding": *New York Times* columnist Frank Rich (7/21/2001) cited "a jeremiad on *The Wall Street Journal*'s editorial page this week in which one of its deputy editors chastised the high-brow media, including *The Times*" for surrendering journalistic initiative to the tabloids in the disappearance of Congressman Gary Condit's friend Chandra Levy.

jewellery* or *jewelry?   The first form is British; the second, American.

joyful* or *jubilant?   Both mean "happy." But careful communicators show their respect for the history of the word *jubilant* by using it only in the sense of "shouting for joy, as in the celebration of a victory." *Jubilant* is derived from the Latin *jubilare* ("to shout for joy").

judge* or *jurist?   *Jurist*, often loosely used in American English as a synonym of *judge*, means "a person versed in the law, such as a judge, lawyer, or legal scholar." So a jurist is not necessarily a judge, and a judge is not necessarily a jurist.

Garner's Modern American Usage notes that *jurist* in British English always means "one who has made outstanding contributions to legal thought and legal literature."

judgement or **judgment**?   The spelling of this word touched off a brief argument at an annual senior citizens' spelling bee, covered by the *Los Angeles Times* (8/12/1996). When a contestant spelled out *j-u-d-g-e-m-e-n-t*, a woman in the audience promptly declared that the answer was wrong. The contestant appealed to the event's three-judge panel, who ruled in favor of the contestant after discovering in a dictionary that *j-u-d-g-e-m-e-n-t* is (to quote the *L.A. Times*) "a correct if not the preferred spelling."

Actually, though *judgment* is preferred in American English, *judgement* is preferred in British English.

Warning: Though the spelling preferred by the British, *judgement*, is what *The Columbia Guide to Standard American English* calls "a Standard American variant," that spelling is widely interpreted in the United States as a sign of an inadequate education. (See also entries for *abridgment* and *acknowledgment*.)

judicial or **judicious**?   Both these words are derived from a Latin word for "judgment." But *judicial* means "pertaining to courts of law or to the office of a judge," and *judicious* means "wise, prudent."

Usage example from *The New York Review of Books* (3/9/2000): "It is injudicious [unwise] for a judge to make . . . a public parade of his own politics."

junction or **juncture**?   *Junction* refers to a point in space. *Juncture* refers to a point in time.

A *junction* is "a place where two or more things meet or come together," as in a junction of rail lines or rivers, an intersection of streets, or a connection between two pieces of wood or metal.

A *juncture* is "a point in time made critical, or at least important, by a coming together of events or circumstances." Here's a usage example from syndicated columnist Robert Scheer (2/26/2002): "We have come to an odd juncture in this world's modern history when notions of God are once again routinely employed to justify and counter the most heinous of human actions."

The phrase *at this juncture* is often used as if it were a high-class way of saying nothing more significant than *at this point in time*. But though some dictionaries list that general sense, it is dismissed by word guardians as an example of careless usage.

junta: **more easily seen than said**   U.S. newscasters have a personal reason to dread the replacement of a nation's government by a *junta* ("a group of military officers ruling a country after seizing power"). Our newscasters dread such news because nobody in the English-speaking world is completely sure how to say the word.

You will find the cause of the confusion in language commentator Charles Harrington Elster's guide to what he calls "beastly mispronunciations," *There Is No Zoo in Zoology.* Elster points out that when *junta* entered the English language from Spanish in the early 17th century, its pronunciation was anglicized to "JUHN-tuh," with the first syllable starting out the same way as the word *jump.* In 20th-century America, the preferred pronunciation became the de-anglicized "HUUN-tuh," with that first syllable now starting out the same way as the word *hood.* But that pronunciation is not quite faithful to the original Spanish pronunciation, "HOON-tuh," in which the first syllable rhymes with *moon.*

Elster writes: "The de-anglicized HUUN-tuh, which did not appear in dictionaries before the 1960's, is now preferred by most current authorities. The traditional, anglicized pronunciation JUHN-tuh is most often listed next, and sometimes dictionaries will give the original Spanish HOON-tuh. The hybrid HUHN-tuh, when it appears, is usually listed last."

Risk-free recommendation for newscasters and the rest of us: Until some semblance of democracy is restored in the country of concern, refer to that country's government as a "military dictatorship."

jury-rig **requires no selection of a jury**   As a verb, *jury-rig* literally means "to supply a damaged ship with temporary rigging [sails, masts, etc.]." By extension, *jury-rig* means "to provide a temporary structure, system, or solution" in any urgent situation. *Jury-rigged* is not only the past tense of the verb *jury-rig* but also an adjective meaning "improvised, or constructed for temporary [often emergency] service."

Here's a usage example of the past tense of *jury-rig,* from a *Seattle Times* story marking the tenth anniversary of the disastrous *Exxon Valdez* oil spill of 1989: "A makeshift alliance of oil-spill experts, an innovative Coast Guard commander and dozens of fishermen and boats jury-rigged three walls of oil boom [a floating barrier to contain an oil spill] across the entrance to [a threatened fish hatchery]."

Though the *jury* of the courtroom has been traced to a Latin word for *law*, the origin of the *jury* in *jury-rig* is listed as unknown by the Merriam-Webster dictionaries and *The Oxford English Dictionary* and "a matter of surmise [guesswork]" by *Brewer's Dictionary of Phrase and Fable*. The Random House dictionaries say that "perhaps" the term can be traced to an Old French word, *ajurie*, meaning "aid, help," and the same origin is listed without qualification by *The American Heritage Dictionary*.

just an adverb   Make sure your intended meaning of the adverb *just* is clear from your context.

The adverb *just* can mean *only* (as in "Loans approved in just 24 hours!"), *precisely* ("just right"), *narrowly* ("She just missed getting seriously hurt") or *very recently* ("Your mail just came").

just deserts aren't fattening   When you get your *just deserts*, the pronunciation suggests double-*s desserts*, as in "sugary and sweet." But these *deserts* have only one *s*, because they are the plural of "what one deserves," from the past participle of the Old French verb *deservir* ("to deserve"). (See also "*desert* or *dessert?*")

K

Kafka and his adjective   Need an adjective for a situation that's unbelievably strange, frustratingly complex, or horribly menacing? Consider *Kafkaesque*.

Usage example: *The New York Times* (4/1/1997) reported the "Kafkaesque ordeal" of a Nigerian political dissident who said he fled to America to escape torture at the hands of Nigeria's military dictatorship but that U.S. immigration authorities then kept him in a jail where "guards stomped on him, forced him to kneel naked for hours, pushed his head in a toilet, left him to sleep naked on a bare mattress and subjected him to racist invective."

Kafkaesque reflects the nightmarish content of the best-known writing of the Prague-born, German-language novelist Franz Kafka (1883–1924), who posthumously became one of the most influential writers of the 20th century. In novels such as *The Trial* and *The Castle* and short stories such as "In the Penal Colony" and "The Metamorphosis," says *The Columbia Encyclopedia*, "Kafka presents a world that is at once real and dreamlike and in which individuals burdened with guilt, isolation, and anxiety make a futile search for personal salvation."

key as an adjective unlocks the demon of ambiguity   If you use *key* as an adjective—as in "a key position in the company"—your reader has no way of knowing whether you mean *essential* or merely *important*. Or you could mean *crucial, pivotal, major,* or *fundamental*. To avoid communicating such confusion, replace that *key* with an adjective that says what you mean.

keys you will never mislay   The tourist-attracting Florida Keys—a chain of small coral and limestone islands and reefs—are called *Keys* because the English adaptation of a Spanish word for a low rocky islet or reef, *cayo*, ended up sounding like the *key* that unlocks doors.

kid you not?   *Kid* (originally "young goat") as a synonym for a young human has taken about four hundred years to rise from what *The Oxford English Dictionary* calls "low slang" to its present level of widespread acceptance in the informal spoken and written British and American English.

The word's tone of affection was used by the first President Bush immediately after Operation Desert Storm, when he talked about "bringing our kids home"—meaning "our soldiers"—as soon as possible. But the *Harper Dictionary of Contemporary Usage* has warned that "kid as applied to young children is viewed with distaste by many, including some young people."

kiln: kill the *n*?   Most people pronounce this word for a pottery-baking oven just the way it looks. But ceramists, perpetuating a six-hundred-year-old English practice of dropping a final *n* after *l* in some words, pronounce *kiln* as if it were spelled *kil*.

Incidentally, some ceramists—people who make ceramic objects—call themselves *ceramicists*.

kilt or kilts?   Despite the *-s* attached to *pants* and *trousers*, the traditional pleated skirt of the men of the Scottish Highlands is called a *kilt*. Say "He's wearing a kilt," not "He's wearing kilts."

kin is or **kin are?**   Feel free to use *kin* as a synonym for the plural "kinfolk, relatives," as in "Her kin are all living in this town." But you enter the Risk Zone if you use *kin* as a synonym for the singular "kinsman, relative," as in, "He is *a kin* of mine." The singular *kin* has been traced back to the 13th century, but it is now so rarely used that some word guardians dismiss it as either "archaic" or "an error."

The use of *kin* as an adjective meaning "related"—"He's kin to me"—is acceptable only in informal communication, according to *The Columbia Guide to Standard American English* and *The New Fowler's Modern English Usage.*

kind consistency   Be consistently singular with *this kind* or consistently plural with *these kinds.*

As a "singular classifying noun," *kind* is properly introduced by a singular demonstrative adjective (*this* or *that*) and followed by a singular noun or no noun at all. Examples: "this kind of mistake" and "mistakes of this kind."

Kind should be in the plural only when you are referring to more than one classification: "That sweetener is used in many kinds of food."

kith is not relative   *Kith and kin* was described as a redundant reference to kinfolk by Bill Bryson in *The Mother Tongue: English and How It Got That Way.* But usage commentators point out that *kith* has a separate meaning as a collective term for "friends, acquaintances, neighbors, and countrymen." In support of that view, *kith* researchers point out that *kith* once meant "fellow countrymen." Still earlier, according to *The Oxford English Dictionary,* the word *kith* meant "one's native land."

kitsch: a matter of taste   The noun *kitsch* (from the German, meaning "gaudy trash") identifies "commercially produced art and other products perceived as being of tastelessly poor quality, especially when garish or sentimental." If you are looking for a gift for someone who collects kitsch, buy that person a glow-in-the-dark painting of Elvis Presley on velvet.

In addition to serving as its own adjective, *kitsch* has spawned the adjective *kitschy,* the adverb *kitschily,* and the noun *kitschiness.*

Usage example: In a *New Yorker* cartoon (7/17/2000), a just-arrived flying-saucer passenger, wearing a comic-book-style uniform of tights and a cape, tells a lab-coated scientist of Earth, "Our civilization is thousands of years more advanced than yours, but still sort of kitschy."

knot what he said he was?   A man, picked up for loitering at a seaport, told police that he worked on a ship whose speed averaged six knots an hour. How did the police know he was lying?

People who work on ships do not say *knots an hour*. They just say *knots*. A *knot* is a unit of speed equal to one nautical mile (265 yards more than a statute mile) per hour. In nautical jargon, the ship "makes" a certain number of knots.

The term *knots* originated during the days of sailing vessels, when a log-tied, multiknotted cord was thrown into the water so that the speed could be determined by counting the number of knots pulled out in a given period of time.

kudos is or kudos are?   No matter how praiseworthy your behavior, don't ever expect a kudo. What you can hope for is *kudos* ("praise").

Kudos is as singular as *pathos* ("the quality of eliciting pity"). Just as there is no *patho*, there is no *kudo*, though you may see or hear "a kudo" bestowed on someone in jest or ignorance.

Kydos (Greek for "glory, renown") became *kudos* (a word for "prestige") in British university slang in the 19th century. *Kudos* became a synonym for "praise" early in the 20th century. Today, even if you can't earn kudos, you can buy Kudos (chocolate granola bars).

L

labyrinth or Labyrinth?   The noun *labyrinth*—along with its adjectives, *labyrinthian* and the more common *labyrinthine*—refers to a maze or anything of maze-like complexity, as in a reference in *The New York Times* to "the labyrinthian United Nations bureaucracy" (2/9/1997).

The uppercase *Labyrinth*, in Greek mythology, is the vast maze in which King Minos of Crete hid the monstrous Minotaur, a half man and half bull that had been born to his wife, Queen Pasiphaë, after she had mated with a sacred bull. When King Minos made the Athenians send him young men and women to be forced into the Labyrinth for the Minotaur to eat, the Athenian hero Theseus volunteered to enter the Labyrinth and fight the Minotaur. Theseus managed to slay the Minotaur and was able to find his way out of the Labyrinth by following a trail of thread that he had left on the way in.

The story of the Labyrinth echoes today whenever someone uses the word *clue* ("a fact or thing that guides through complexity"), because *clue* originally meant "a ball of thread" such as that used by Theseus to trace a path through a maze.

"ladies and gentlemen"   The phrase "ladies and gentlemen" is appropriate for addressing audiences, and the terms *ladies* and *gentlemen* appropriately identify individuals in a way that calls attention to their refined, courteous behavior. Otherwise, the appropriate terms are *women* and *men*.

In the words of Rosalie Maggio's *Nonsexist Word Finder*: "Avoid using [*lady*] in place of *woman* unless you intend shadings of meaning that describe someone who is elegant, 'refined,' and conscious of propriety and correct behavior. In most contexts [*lady*] is perceived as (and often is) condescending."

Neither *lady* nor *woman* is appropriate to modify a professional term such as *doctor*. To say someone is a *lady* or *woman* doctor implies that her professional status is somehow different from that of other doctors. (See also "sexism on the job.")

lama or llama?   The South American relative of the camel, the *llama*, has twice as many legs and *l*'s as the high-ranking Tibetan monk, the *lama*.

languid, languish, languor, limp, and limpid   The adjective *limpid* ("clear, transparent, easily understood" or "calm, untroubled") is sometimes confused with *limp* in the sense of "weak or spiritless," as in "a limp handshake." For example, a *Reader's Digest* advertisement (November 1998) absurdly promised readers that a package of Louis Rich Carving Board Chicken Strips would "perk up . . . limpid linguine."

Limpid is also misused as a synonym for *languid* ("lacking energy, showing little or no spirit or animation"). The noun *languor* means "lack of physical or mental energy." The intransitive verb *languish* means "to lose spirit or energy" or "to exist in disheartening conditions."

lark is not just for the birds   In addition to being a noun for "a bird of the family Alaudidae," *lark* is a separately derived noun for "a playful adventure" and a verb for "engaging in playful activity." A book reviewer in *The New York*

Times (10/11/1998) wrote that "literary people have always enjoyed larking about in theological waters."

last or **latest**?   Beware of the ambiguity of *last*. An author's *last* book can be her "final" book or merely her "latest." In sentences in which *last* is unclear, choose a word or phrase whose meaning is unmistakable.

Another ambiguity involving *last* was illustrated in a *Parade* magazine cartoon (1/13/2002) in which a receptionist tells an office visitor, "I scheduled you for 4:45 p.m. because he told me you were the last person he wanted to see."

lath or **lathe**?   A *lath*—which rhymes with *bath*—is a thin, narrow strip of wood, such as that used as a foundation for plaster. A *lathe*—which rhymes with *bathe*—is a machine used for shaping wood, metal, or other hard materials.

Latinisms   The following Latin expressions have become fully established in Standard English, and they are italicized here only because that is the way *Right, Wrong, and Risky* presents every word and phrase under consideration: *ad infinitum* ("to infinity, endlessly"), *ad lib* for *ad libitum* ("freely, unscripted"), *alma mater* (literally "nourishing mother," and meaning "one's old school or college"), *alter ego* ("second self, very close friend"), *amicus curiae* ("friend of the court"), *annus mirabilis* (literally "year of miracles," and meaning "remarkable year"), *carpe diem* (literally "seize the day," and meaning "seize the pleasures and opportunities of the present while you still can"), *casus belli* ("an event causing or at least cited as a justification for a declaration of war"), *caveat emptor* ("let the buyer beware"), *cui bono?* (literally "to whom [is it] a benefit?" and meaning "who stands to gain?"), *e pluribus unum* (literally "out of many, one," and used on American coins, where it means "Out of many states, one nation"), *ergo* ("therefore"), *in absentia* ("while or although not present"), *in flagrante delicto* ("in the very act of committing an offense, red-handed"), *infra dig* ("beneath one's dignity"), *in lieu* ("instead, in place [of]"), *in loco parentis* ("[acting] in the place of a parent"), *magnum opus* ("great work, such as that of a writer or artist"), *mea culpa* (literally "my fault," and meaning "an admission that one is at fault"), *modus operandi* ("method of operation"), *modus vivendi* (literally "manner of living," usually meaning "a temporary agreement between contending parties pending a final settlement"), *ne plus ultra* (literally, "no more beyond," and meaning "ultimate excellence or achievement").

Others include: *per annum* ("by the year, annually"), *per capita* ("for each unit of population, for each person"), *per diem* ("reckoned on a daily basis, paid by the day") *per se* ("by itself, as such, inherently"), *persona non grata* ("unacceptable person, someone who is not welcome"), *pro forma* ("for [the sake of] form, done as a mere formality"), *P.S.* (from *postscriptum,* an addition to a letter), *quid pro quo* ("something given or received for something else"), *rara avis* (literally "rare bird," and meaning "anyone or anything quite rare"), *redux* ("brought back"), *sine qua non* ("without which nothing [of this would be possible], an essential element"), *status quo* ("existing situation"), *sub rosa* ("confidentially, secretly," literally "under the rose," referring to the ancient use of a rose at meetings as a symbol that the participants had taken an oath of secrecy), *sui generis* (literally "of its own kind," and meaning "unique"), *tabula rasa* (literally "blank slate," such as "the mind before it receives the impressions gained from experience"), *terra firma* (literally "firm earth," and meaning "solid ground"), *verbatim* ("word for word"), *vice versa* ("in reverse order from that stated"), and *vox populi* ("voice of the people, public opinion").

(See entries for *ad hoc, ad nauseam, bona fide, corpus delicti, de facto, etc., non sequitur, prima facie,* and *reductio ad absurdum.*)

latitude or longitude?   *Latitude* is the distance north or south of the equator. It is measured in degrees (up to 90) along one of the imaginary globe-circling lines that are parallel to the equator and therefore are called parallels. *Longitude* is the distance in degrees (up to 180) east or west of a meridian (one of the imaginary globe-circling lines that extend from pole to pole) running through Greenwich, England. Chicago, for example, has a latitude of about 41 degrees north and a longitude of about 87 degrees west, which can be written as 41°N, 87°W.

The word *latitude* can also mean "extent" or "freedom from normal limitations," as in this headline in *The New York Times* (8/1/2001): "G.O.P. Delays Effort to Give Bush Latitude on Free Trade."

latter: only for pairs?   *The latter,* like *the former,* applies to pairs. Usage commentators prescribe *the latter* for references to the second of two persons or things mentioned, not to the last-named of three or more.

Latter can also be used to describe something near or nearer to the end, as in "the latter part of the report." In addition, *latter* can mean "belonging to the present or recent times," as in the Mormons' Church of Jesus Christ of Latter-Day Saints.

laudable or **laudatory?**   *Laudatory* ("bestowing praise") is sometimes mistakenly used for *laudable* ("deserving praise"), and occasionally vice versa. Do something *laudable* if you want people to make *laudatory* comments about you.

laurels are no place to rest   The ancient Greeks crowned victors in athletic contests with wreaths made from the leaves of the laurel tree, a Mediterranean evergreen that was said to be held sacred by the god Apollo. Today, we use the plural word *laurels* (a shortened version of the singular *wreath of laurels*) as a synonym for any honor or honors bestowed for achievement. And we are wisely told that we should not "rest on our laurels," meaning that we should not rely on an honor for a past achievement as a substitute for present effort.

A related word, *laureate*, refers to a person (such as a Nobel laureate) who is honored for great achievement. In a tradition dating back to the 17th century, the British government appoints a lifetime poet laureate who writes poetry in celebration of great events. In 1985, the U.S. Congress began appointing an annual poet laureate to serve as a poetry consultant to the Library of Congress.

lay or **lie?**   Usage commentators, cited in this entry's last paragraph, say it's "stupid," "uneducated," and "illiterate" to use *lay* when the intended meaning is *lie*. But people who ought to know better seem totally unaware of the problem. For example, a Southern California crime reporter with a university journalism degree regularly uses the word *lay* in this way: "The gunman told everyone to lay [should be *lie*] down on the floor."

In correct usage, *lay* is a verb that acts directly on an object, and *lie* is a verb that does not. (In the language of grammar, *lay* is transitive and *lie* is intransitive.) Hence, your boss will *lay* you off if you *lie* down on the job.

Lay places or deposits. ("*Lay* [place] your cards on the table." "Chickens *lay* [deposit] eggs.") *Lie* reclines or is situated. ("Our dog likes to *lie* [recline] on our bed." "Canada *lies* [is situated] north of the United States.")

The Oxford English Dictionary suggests that the practice of using *lay* for *lie* was standard as far back as the beginning of the 14th century. But roughly a couple of centuries ago, grammarians began laying down laws that distinguish *lay* from *lie*.

Though some of today's usage commentators regard enforcement of the *lay/lie* laws as a nearly lost cause, you violate those laws at some personal risk: *Merriam-Webster's Dictionary of English Usage* says the ability to properly distinguish *lay* from *lie* has become "a social shibboleth—a marker of class and education." Robert Claiborne wrote in *Our Marvelous Native Tongue* that "not a few people, hearing [*lay* wrongly substituted for *lie*], will deduce that the speaker is poorly educated and/or stupid." (See also "verbs: transitive and intransitive.")

lay and lie: tense situations   *Lie*'s past tense is exactly the same as *lay*'s present tense: *lay*. ("All last week he *lay* in bed, pretending to be sick.")

Lay's past tense is *laid*. ("They *laid* the carpet yesterday.") *Lay*'s present participle is *laying*. ("They're *laying* the carpet now.") *Lay*'s past participle is exactly the same as its past tense: *laid*. ("They had *laid* the original carpets years ago.")

Lie's present participle is *lying*. ("Today, he's just *lying* there.") *Lie*'s past participle is *lain*. (The 8/4/2001 issue of *The Economist* reported that Japan's economy "has lain flat on its back for almost a decade.")

leave alone or let alone?   If you want someone to stop bothering you, should you ask that person to *leave* you alone or *let* you alone? Use either term, unless you're bothered by the slight possibility of encountering someone who is convinced that the only correct answer is *let*.

Both forms have been widely used interchangeably for centuries, and both are acceptable to *The Columbia Guide to Standard American English*, *Webster's New World College Dictionary*, the *Random House Webster's Unabridged Dictionary*, and a majority of the usage panel of *The American Heritage Dictionary*. But a *minority* of that usage panel chose *let alone*, recommending that *leave alone* be saved for the literal meaning of "depart from one who remains in solitude." And the *Harper Dictionary of Contemporary Usage* identified *let alone* as the "preferred" form for "do not bother me" in formal speech and writing.

legalism or legality?   *Legality* means "conformity with the law." *Legalism* means "conformity with the law in a strict, often overly strict, literal manner."

legible or readable?   These adjectives are often used interchangeably. But precise writers use *legible* (as in "legible handwriting") to describe writing that one *can* read, and *readable* (as in "a highly readable textbook") to describe writing that one *wants* to read.

leitmotif, leitmotiv, or motif?   The German import *leitmotif* ("LITE-moh-TEEF")—or *leitmotiv*, if the German spelling is used—and the French import *motif* ("moh-TEEF") both mean "a recurring or principal theme, pattern, or idea."

These words are typically used in literary, artistic, or musical contexts. But they also are widely applied in a general sense, as in a *Chronicle of Higher Education* reference (1/23/1998) to a scholarly study of paranoia as "a leitmotif in political life."

lend or loan?   Don't take the risk of asking someone to *loan* you something.

As noted by *Webster's New World Guide to Current American Usage*, some people are "tormented" when they hear *loan* used as a verb. If you want a risk-free *loan* (the noun), ask someone to *lend* (the verb) you what you need.

Loan as a verb does have its defenders. They include the American Heritage, Merriam-Webster, and Random House dictionaries, whose usage commentators are impressed by the eight-hundred-year history and widespread current usage of *loan* as a verb. John Ciardi, writing in 1980 in his *Browser's Dictionary*, observed that the verb *loan* was "on its way to becoming standard usage." Another defender of *loan* as a verb, Roy H. Copperud, contended in his *American Usage and Style* that "the idea that *loan* is not good form as a verb is a superstition." Kenneth G. Wilson's *Columbia Guide to Standard American English* has listed *loan* the verb as "clearly Standard in American English."

But *loan* the verb is unwelcome among those who use or are heavily influenced by British English. In England, Henry W. Fowler observed in his *Dictionary of Modern English Usage* that "*loan* the verb has been expelled from idiomatic English by *lend*," the *Longman Dictionary of the English Language* advised its readers that *loan* the verb "should be avoided in formal British English," and *The Oxford English Dictionary* dismissed *loan* the verb as "now chiefly U.S."

Such British objections to *loan* the verb, says Wilson's *Columbia Guide*, have caused "several American commentators [to] reject or dislike it." Indeed, *loan* the verb has been rejected in no uncertain terms by Strunk and White's *Elements* of *Style*, Hans P. Guth's *New Concise Handbook*, and the stylebooks of *The New York Times*, *The Washington Post*, and *The Wall Street Journal*.

lengthy or long?   *Merriam-Webster's Dictionary of English Usage* assures us that *lengthy* as a synonym for *long* "has been used by excellent writers for about three centuries." But some usage commentators say you are better off using the shorter word *long* if that is what you mean, because *lengthy*, when used to describe a novel, movie, ceremony, or speech, may unintentionally convey tediousness or *unnecessary* length.

Here's a risk-free suggestion from Theodore M. Bernstein's *Careful Writer*: "The best advice that can be given here about *lengthy* in general is to avoid it and say instead what you really mean—*overlong, tedious, prolix, rather long, very long, longer than necessary*, or even *longish*."

less or fewer?   See "*fewer or less?*"

lessee or lessor?   The *lessor* grants a lease to the *lessee*.

libel or slander?   *Slander* is defamation that is spoken. *Libel* is defamation by any other medium of communication, including recorded speech, print, signs, or effigies.

liberal: which one do you have in mind?   How come the vehemently anti-liberal commentator Rush Limbaugh has never spoken out against the liberal arts? The answer is that, in the realm of words, not all *liberals* are alike.

The only thing all *liberal* words have in common is that they can be traced to the Latin *liber* (meaning "free"), as opposed to *servus* (meaning "servile, slave-like"). Incidentally, a *liber*ated slave in Rome was known as a *libertine* (a word we now use for someone who is overly free in the sense of being morally unrestrained).

Liber, acquiring the suffix *-alis*, produced *liberalis*, which acquired three meanings related to *free*—"free in giving," as in *generous*, "freely available," as in *abundant*, and "worthy of freemen," as in *noble*. In line with the third, elitist meaning, Roman nobles were educated in *artes liberalis* ("liberal arts," mentally challenging, cultural subjects such as logic, rhetoric, and music), whereas the lower classes had to study *artes serviles* ("servile arts," occupational skills involving manual labor). *Liberalis*, with all three of its original Latin meanings, entered English via Old French, in the form of *liberal*, in the 14th century.

In the late 18th century, *liberal* acquired the additional meaning of "free from being strict or literal" (as in "a liberal translation"), and that *liberal* led to a *liberal* that means "free from prejudice, tolerant, open-minded."

By the 19th century, Britain had a Liberal Party that promised to free people from government interference. In the United States, for much of the 20th century the political word *liberal* has suggested "freedom from arbitrary authority and support for reform that would bring about progress." But in recent years self-described conservative commentators like Limbaugh have managed to associate the political term *liberal* (in much of the public mind) with authoritarianism, thus causing some self-described "liberals" to redefine themselves as "moderates."

licence or **license?**   The first is the preferred British spelling; the second, American.

lie or **lay?**   See "*lay* or *lie?*"

life takes three forms   Most compounds formed with *life* are fused, including the nouns *lifeblood, lifeboat, lifeguard, lifeline, lifesaver, lifestyle*, and *lifework*, as well as the noun and adjective *lifetime* and the adjectives *lifelike, lifelong*, and *lifesaving*.

But hyphens are needed for the adjectives *life-giving, life-or-death, life-size*, and *life-threatening*. A hyphen is also needed for the noun *life-form*. However, *life force* is presented as two words, as are the nouns *life belt, life buoy, life cycle, life expectancy, life history, life insurance, life interest, life jacket* (or *vest*), *life net, life preserver, life raft, life science, life sentence*, and *life span*. (See also "spelling compound words.")

lighted or **lit?**   *Lighted* and *lit* are equally acceptable as the past tense and past participle of *light*. Likewise, both are acceptable as adjectives, as in "a *lighted* [or *lit*] candle."

lightening never strikes   Enlightened spellers distinguish *lightening* ("making lighter in weight or color") from the *lightning* caused by a natural electrical discharge in the atmosphere.

light-year is no time at all Many people wrongly assume that *light-year* refers to time. For example: A host on CBS-TV's *Entertainment Tonight* (8/30/1996) observed that "it's been light-years" since the first *Star Trek* series was launched. But a *light-year* is the distance that light travels in one year in a vacuum—nearly six trillion miles.

Note that *light-year* is preferably hyphenated, to make clear that *light* does not describe a year but is rather part of a single concept.

like as a filler A California high school teacher complained—in a *Los Angeles Times* essay (5/5/2002)—that he probably hears "more than 100 super-fluous 'likes' a day." As an example, he quoted a student as asking him, "Do you have, like, a pencil I can borrow?" The teacher also quoted a student's description of her family's trip to Washington, D.C.: "My favorite part was when we went to see, like, the Supreme Court."

A sure-fire way to invite ridicule is to imitate that adolescent habit of using *like* as a conversational filler. Consider the following sarcastic comment from the *Washington Times* (9/29/1997): "California's biggest contribution to the American language is the use of the most versatile word ever—you guessed it, *like. Like*, a word preceding every, like, noun and, like, verb, is almost the only description needed in a world where adjectives are, like, becoming a dying breed."

like as a substitute for mature thought Many of today's teenagers use *like* to introduce their thoughts or to report what they said in an earlier conversa-tion. For example, the *Los Angeles Times* (6/1/2003) quoted a 16-year-old high school girl's reaction to being chosen U.S. delegate in a school version of the United Nations: "My teacher told me, 'You are going to represent the United States,' and I was like, 'Oh, my God. I'm going to be attacked.'"

That usage has become so widespread—notably infecting the speech of enter-tainment celebrities—that it has been the subject of serious examination in jour-nals such as *American Speech*. But its acceptance in Standard American English is unlikely, judging at least from Bryan A. Garner's comment in his *Modern American Usage*: "This [typically teenage] usage . . . in adults . . . shows arrested development."

"like I said" is risky to say See "*as or like?*"

like is a victim of fear   The abuse of *like* is so widespread (see previous entries) that some people are afraid to use it when it's needed. Such people will say, for example, "Nick behaved *as* a fool." That sentence requires the preposition *like,* not the conjunction *as,* to show a comparison between *Nick* and *a fool.*

Likewise, people who say "That candidate, *as* most politicians, avoids the real issues" should use the preposition *like,* not the conjunction *as,* to compare *that candidate* with *most politicians.* (See also "*as* or *like?*")

like or as?   See "*as* or *like?*"

like or such as?   Some usage commentators approve the widespread practice of using *like* and *such as* interchangeably. Others prescribe *like* for showing resemblance and *such as* for introducing examples. For instance: "Brilliant editors *like* Sally exhibit qualities *such as* dedication and diligence."

Risk-free advice: If you maintain that distinction between *like* and *such as,* those who don't care won't notice, and those who do care will have no reason to criticize you. (See also "*such as* this comma issue.")

likely story   You are safe from criticism if you use *likely* in place of the adjective *probable,* as in "She is the likely candidate." You risk criticism if you use *likely* in place of the adverb *probably,* as in "Likely, she will be the candidate." But you can get away with that usage if you add a qualifier like *very, most,* or *quite,* as in "She very likely will be the candidate."

likewise: use it wisely   *Likewise* is not a conjunction and therefore cannot take the place of *and* or *together with.* Incorrect usage: "Their son, likewise their daughter, were late."

Likewise is an adverb, meaning *in like manner* ("do likewise") and *similarly so with me.* Correct usage: Someone says, "Pleased to meet you." You answer, "Likewise."

limit or limitation?   A traffic cop who observes useful word distinctions will never pull you over for violating the speed limitation. The correct word, of course, is *limit,* meaning "furthest extent" or "physical boundary."

Limitation means "restrictive weakness, shortcoming, defect," as in "The governor's intellectual limitations were concealed by ghostwriters." *Limitation* can also mean "a specified period during which an action must be brought," as in "a statute of limitations."

linage or *lineage*?   The two-syllable word *linage* (pronounced "LIE-nij") means the number of lines in a publication (as in "a newspaper's advertising linage"). The three-syllable *lineage* (pronounced "LIN-ee-ij") means "ancestry, lineal descent from an ancestor, the line of descendants of a particular ancestor."

linguistic challenge   Inasmuch as *linguist* and *linguistic* each have more than one meaning, you need to make sure your intended meaning is clear when you use those words.

For more than three centuries, *linguist* has meant "one who is skilled in the use of languages" and also "one who investigates the nature of language itself [a discipline now known as linguistics]."

Linguistic literally means "of or pertaining to *the study of* language," but the word is often used more broadly to mean "of or pertaining to language."

linking verbs   See "verbs that link subjects with adjectives."

lion's share **leaves nothing to be desired**   Be careful how you use this expression among those who are knowledgeable about the origin of literary metaphors.

The *lion's share* is commonly used to mean "the largest portion," as in a *Financial Times* report (5/9/2001) that "a mere 30 [of Egypt's 300 book publishers] receive the lion's share of [that] industry's profits." But the *lion's share* originally meant "all" in one of the stories of *Aesop's Fables*. According to that story, a lion organized a hunt with a goat, a sheep, and a heifer, then declared that all four portions of the captured meal were entirely his: one-quarter for his personal share, one-quarter for his mate and cubs, one-quarter for organizing the hunt, "and as for the fourth portion, let him who will, dispute it with me." The other animals, intimidated by the lion's frown, left him to take his "share."

Usage commentator John Ciardi advised in his *Second Browser's Dictionary* that the erroneous, "largest portion" use of *lion's share* "has been so firmly established that purity [accuracy] would only lead to confusion." A simple way to avoid that confusion, however, would be to ignore the *lion's share* cliché entirely and instead explicitly state that you mean "largest portion" or "all."

liquefy or **liquify**?   Though this verb means "to cause to become liquid," the *liquid*-like spelling *liquify* is listed in dictionaries as merely a "variant form" of the standard spelling, *liquefy*. Based on that standard spelling, the noun for "the process of becoming liquid" is *liquefaction*, and the adjective for "tending to become liquid" is *liquescent*.

lists must stay on one track   Question: What is the error in the following sentence from a paper written by one of my students? "Participation in a debate team helps prepare you for such professions as politics, law, negotiator, and sales representative."

Answer: The first two items in the student's list are professions, but the second two are people. The student should have consistently listed professions or people.

litany or **liturgy**?   *Liturgy* means "any form of public worship."

Litany literally means "a liturgical prayer consisting of a series of invocations and supplications with fixed responses by the congregation." By extension, *litany* means "any widely repeated and usually long recitation or list." Here's a *litany* usage example: Columnist Alan Abelson of *Barron's*, the Dow Jones business and financial weekly (2/21/2000), cited a nationwide "litany of complaints" against a two-hour television presentation entitled *Who Wants to Marry a Multi-Millionaire?* "[It] was demeaning to women, made a mockery of the sanctity of marriage, shamelessly subverted tradition, was blasphemous, obscene, sexist, disgusting, degrading and thoroughly icky."

literally **should be taken seriously**   Don't use *literally* unless you mean it.

Literally should be used only in the sense of "in fact." When it is used loosely, purely for emphasis, the result can be absurd. For example, a journalism student of mine wrote, "I spent the night literally glued to my TV." And a *Los Angeles Times* book reviewer (8/20/2000) quoted a Texas policeman as saying his fellow officers were so pleased by pay raises that they were "literally walking on air."

The nonsensical use of *literally* for sheer emphasis has been condemned by usage commentators at least since the early 20th century. For example, in the 1926 first edition of *A Dictionary of Modern English Usage*, Henry W. Fowler cited atrocious examples of non-literal *literally* that began with the following: "If the [Irish] Home Rule Bill is passed, the 300,000 [pro-British] Unionists of the South & West of Ireland will be literally thrown to the wolves."

Risk-free usage: Say something is literally true only to correct the impression that it is *not* true. For example, when we say somebody "wrote the book" on a subject, we usually don't mean that person actually wrote a book. We mean that person is the leading authority on a subject. But note that *literally* was necessary in an article in *Technology Review* (July/August 1998) stating that electrical engineer Robert W. Lucky "literally wrote the book on data communications, writing a text that was for years the bible of the industry."

livable or **liveable**?   *Liveable* is welcome in British English. But Americans prefer *livable*, removing one *e* (as in *England.*)

live or **reside**?   When skilled writers can say exactly the same thing with either a plain word or a fancy word, they choose the plain one. Don't *relocate* so that you can *reside* at a new *abode*. Instead, *move* so that you can *live* in a new *home*. (See also entry for *abode*.)

livid: a colorful controversy   If you turn *livid with rage*, your face becomes "ashen or pale," not "fiery, bright, crimson, red, or flaming." So say such usage authorities as *The Oxford English Dictionary* and the stylebooks of the Asociated Press and *The Wall Street Journal*.

But as the entry for *livid* in *The Merriam-Webster New Book of Word Histories* notes, "An angry person is at least as likely to be red-faced as pallid." Based on that perception of *livid rage*, "reddish" is currently included in the *livid* spectrum by *Merriam-Webster's Collegiate Dictionary*, the *Random House Webster's College Dictionary*, and *Webster's New World College Dictionary*.

How did *livid*'s color confusion arise? According to Merriam-Webster's *Word Histories*, the word *livid* entered English in the 17th century, from the French version of a Latin adjective for "dull, grayish or leaden blue." *Livid* thus became an English adjective for the "black-and-blue" discoloration associated with bruises. By the end of the 18th century, *livid* acquired the additional meaning of "ashen or pallid" like a corpse. Eventually *livid* became "pale," as in "livid with rage." But because the face of an angry person may also redden, a widely adopted modern sense of *livid* is now "red with rage."

Many dictionaries, reflecting another common usage, include a definition of *livid* that simply denotes *enraged*, thus tacitly inviting you to fill in whatever color the word *enraged* brings to your mind.

Cowardly suggestion: Don't use *livid* until the Crayola company settles the color question once and for all by introducing a crayon in a color called Livid.

loath or **loathe?**   The adjective *loath* means "reluctant, unwilling, disinclined," as in a *New York Times* article (1/2/2001) pointing out that manufacturers of food products "are loath to advertise weight-outs," their deceptive practice of increasing profits by reducing package content.

Add an *e* to *loath* and you get a verb meaning *despise*, as in "I *loathe* hypocrites."

Attach the word *some* to *loath*, to produce *loathsome*, and the result is "repulsively hateful."

locate or **situate?**   *Locate* is a transitive verb that means "find," as in "The student was asked to locate Mexico on the map." *Locate* has also been widely used as an intransitive verb meaning "settle," as in "He wants the family to locate in Mexico." *Merriam-Webster's Dictionary of English Usage* says the intransitive *locate* faced opposition from some usage commentators in the late 19th and early 20th century but is standard today, except possibly in literary writing.

Situate is a little-used transitive verb meaning "to place in a site or situation." More commonly used is the adjective *situated*. That can mean "located," as in "The new factory is situated in Mexico," or it can mean "circumstanced," as in "The managers of the factory are quite comfortably situated."

logical fallacies abound   Review your writing to identify and correct such logical fallacies as the *non sequitur* (a conclusion that does not follow from a premise), the *false analogy* (an irrelevant comparison), the *hasty generalization* (a sweeping conclusion based on insufficient evidence), *the either/or fallacy* (a fallacy that ignores the possibility of alternatives), the *bandwagon fallacy* (the assumption that a viewpoint is valid because it's popular), the *ad hominem argument* (meaning "to the man"; an argument that attacks an opponent rather than the opponent's point of view), and *post hoc, ergo propter hoc* (Latin for "after this, therefore because of this," which applies to the assumption that A caused B simply because A occurred before B).

Review what you write for logical mistakes in general, like the blunder in this headline from the *Los Angeles Times* (12/27/1990): "[Woman's] Musical Talents Overshadow Her Other Limitations." The *other* in the headline absurdly defined the woman's *musical talent* as a "limitation." (See also "*begging the question* is risky business" and "sentences that defy logic.")

loosen or unloosen?   What's the difference between *loosen* and *unloosen?* None. But usage commentators regard *loosen* as better because it is shorter and because *unloosen* seems to contradict itself. (See also "*ravel* or *unravel?*")

lost positives   *Couth* (meaning "refinement"), a jocular back-formation of *uncouth* ("unrefined"), is one of the best known of the "lost positives." Those are words that some people think (or enjoy pretending to think) once existed as prefix-less positives of some of today's common words. Among the many lost positives: *kempt* (from *unkempt*), *sheveled* (*disheveled*), *gruntled* (*disgruntled*), *sipid* (*insipid*), *ept* (*inept*), *ert* (*inert*), and *ane* (*inane*). (See also "back-forming new words.")

love: lost and found   Have you ever wondered why we say of people who dislike each other that "no love is lost between them"? Shouldn't that expression apply to people who care so deeply about each other that none of their love is ever lost? That meaning would be logical, and that indeed was the original meaning, according to *Brewer's Dictionary of Phrase and Fable*.

But somehow the original meaning got lost. Today, the phrase is used only in a negative sense, as in a *New York Times* report (7/20/2004) that "there is no love lost between the [feuding] Israeli and French governments these days." (See also "*head over heels* in nonsense.")

lucked out: how lucky?   *Lucked out* is generally understood to mean "to have had a stroke of good luck." But according to the *Harper Dictionary of Contemporary Usage*, some people still use the World War Two meaning of *lucked out* (quoted here from Wentworth and Flexner's *Dictionary of American Slang*): "to have met with ill fortune or disaster, specifically to be killed."

Lucullus and his adjective   A victorious general of ancient Rome named Lucius Licinius Lucullus ("loo-KUL-us") is remembered today in an adjective that has nothing to do with his military victories. The adjective, *Lucullan* (pronounced "loo-KUL-in"), means "lavish, luxurious," and it celebrates the fact that Lucullus amused himself in his retirement by inviting poets, artists, and philosophers to lavish banquets.

To get the full flavor of the adjective *Lucullan*, read this passage from the ancient Greek biographer Plutarch's *Parallel Lives*: "Lucullus's daily entertainments were ostentatiously extravagant, not only with purple coverlets, and plate adorned with precious stones, and dancings, and interludes, but with the greatest diversity of dishes and the most elaborate cookery, for the vulgar to admire and envy."

***lustful* or *lusty*?**   You will invite criticism if you join the many people who use *lusty* as a synonym for *lustful*, in the sense of "driven by a sexual urge."

Lusty did mean "driven by a sexual urge" some centuries ago. But its primary dictionary meaning now—and that of the related abverb, *lustily*—is "vigorous, robust, active, full of strength and vitality," as in a statement in *The New York Times* (10/5/1998) that "theatergoers lustily cheered."

***luxuriant* or *luxurious*?**   These adjectives originated in a Latin word for "abundance." But while *luxuriant* means "growing abundantly," as in "a luxuriant garden," *luxurious* means "marked by luxury," as in "a luxurious home." Hence, you could compete with the magazine *Better Homes and Gardens* by starting a magazine called *Luxurious Homes and Luxuriant Gardens*.

Merriam-Webster's Dictionary of English Usage and *The New Fowler's Modern English Usage* report that *luxuriant* and *luxurious* have been used interchangeably since the 17th century. And you'll find that loose practice reflected in entries for the two words in Merriam-Webster dictionaries. But "the best policy," advises *The New Fowler's*, "is to endeavor to keep the two words apart." (See also next entry.)

***luxuriate*: one meaning is delightful**   Reflecting the widely practiced interchangeable use of the adjectives *luxuriant* and *luxurious*, dictionaries will tell you that the related verb *luxuriate* can mean "to grow abundantly" or "to take luxurious pleasure, to take great delight." In an example of the "take great delight" meaning, a *New York Times* article (8/15/2000) reported that U.S. Senate candidate Hillary Rodham Clinton "luxuriated in a level of attention [as President Clinton's wife] unimaginable for a candidate conducting her first campaign."

M

Machiavelli and his questionable adjective Florentine statesman and political philosopher Niccolò Machiavelli (1469–1527) is best known as the author of *The Prince*, in which he appears to give advice on how a ruler may gain and maintain power by being amoral and tyrannical.

Scholars differ over whether *The Prince* was to be taken literally as an endorsement of amoral tyranny or as a satire, or perhaps as just a candid description of the ruthless cynicism that abounded in his time in Italian politics. And Machiavelli's more detailed works—his *Discourses* and his *History of Florence*—indicate that he really favored representative government and political morality. But because many readers took *The Prince* literally and did not read his other works, the adjective *Machiavellian* came to mean "marked by expediency, amorality, deceit and cunning, especially in pursuit of political power."

maddening or *madding* **crowd?**   Though crowds can be *maddening* ("*driving* to madness, infuriating"), the oft-used literary allusion is "*madding* ['*acting* madly, frenzied'] crowd."

Far from the madding crowd ("away from turmoil") originated with Thomas Gray's *Elegy Written in a Country Churchyard* in 1750, and it became the title of a Thomas Hardy novel published in 1874.

magazines: **not all need staples**   Did CBS stretch the meaning of *magazine* when it first used that word to describe the TV series *60 Minutes*? Not at all. *Magazine* entered English in the 16th century as an anglicized spelling of *magasin*, a French word for "storehouse." The word was subsequently used to designate a storehouse of ammunition ("ammunition depot"), a chamber to hold cartridges in a gun, and books presented as "storehouses of knowledge."

Magazine as a "storehouse of knowledge" was first applied to a *periodical* in 1731, with the appearance of *The Gentleman's Magazine: or, Monthly Intelligencer*. The word *magazine* in the sense of a periodical subsequently became a common usage, so much so that the word reentered the language of France with its English spelling and new English meaning.

magnet or ***magnate*?**   Writers sometimes write *magnet* ("object with magnetic force") when they mean *magnate* (pronounced "MAG-nate" and meaning "powerful or influential person, especially in business or industry").

magnificent or ***munificent*?**   *Munificent* ("extremely generous") alumni donors were responsible for the construction of the university's *magnificent* ("superb, sublime, splendid, grand") new library building.

majority or ***most*?**   A common error is to use *majority*, which refers to a group constituting more than half of a total, when the appropriate word is *most*. In an example of this error, the *Irvine* (Calif.) *World News* (8/1/2002) reported that "city officials optimistically predicted last week that the majority [should be *most*] of the park could be developed within the next decade."

majority or ***plurality*?**   An election candidate can win by a majority (more than half the votes) or by a plurality (less than half the votes but more votes than were cast for any other candidate).

majority is or ***majority are*?**   Use a singular verb with *majority* when you are using the word to refer to a specific number of votes, as in "A five-vote *majority* is needed in decisions of the U.S. Supreme Court."

When *majority* refers to people or things that are in the majority—that is, people or things that constitute more than half of a total—your choice of *is* or *are* depends on your intended meaning. If you are thinking of the group as a whole, use *is*, as in "The *majority* is America's king." If you are thinking of the individuals making up the group, use *are*, as in "The *majority* of our members *are* opposed to an increase in their dues."

***malaprop*: don't feed the allegories**   The fictional Mrs. Malaprop, whose name was inspired by the French *mal à propos* ("inappropriate"), herself inspired our words *malaprop* and *malapropism* ("the error of substituting a similar-sounding word for the intended one"). In her most memorable word blunder, the pompous Mrs. Malaprop of Richard Brinsley Sheridan's 1775 play, *The Rivals*, referred to someone "as headstrong as an *allegory* on the banks of the Nile." She meant, of course, an *alligator*.

Today, many comedians commit malaprops for laughs. If you don't want people to laugh at your malaprops behind your back, never add a word to your vocabulary until you've looked it up in a dictionary. Even a professional writer will use a word like *allegory* only after checking its precise definition. (See also the entry for *allegory*.)

malign or malignant?   These adjectives have a history of overlapping. But you can't go wrong if you use *malign* for "evil, malicious" and *malignant* for "life-threatening."

manifold or manyfold?   *Manifold* means "characterized by variety," as in "manifold career opportunities." *Manyfold* means "by many times," as in "Housing costs have increased manyfold."

mantel or mantle?   *Mantel* and *mantle* are listed by some dictionaries as spelling variants for "a shelf above a fireplace." But the preferred fireplace-ornamenting form is *mantel*, whose *-el* ending may help you to remember to associate it *only* with the definition that includes the *el*evated "above."

Both *mantel* and *mantle* came from an Old French word for "cloak," and that meaning ("a loose, sleeveless cloak or cape") is preserved today in *mantle*. As noted by *Webster's New World College Dictionary*, the word *mantle* is "sometimes used figuratively, in allusion to royal robes of state, as a symbol of authority or responsibility." For example, in a profile of a newly installed president of Indonesia, Megawati Sukarnoputri, *The New York Times* (7/24/2001) commented that as "the daughter of Indonesia's founding president, Sukarno, [Sukarnoputri] appears to have felt that it was her destiny eventually to inherit his mantle."

By further extension, *mantle* can mean anything that cloaks, covers, suffuses, embraces, enfolds, envelops, surrounds, or encircles. ("A mantle of darkness descended on the remote village.") *Mantle* is also a transitive and intransitive verb, meaning "to cover with, or as with, a mantle, or to be covered in that manner."

In geology, *mantle* is the word for the layer of the earth's interior between the crust and the core.

marathon or **Marathon?**   As a noun, *marathon* refers to the 26-mile footrace. As an adjective, *marathon* applies to situations involving exceptional duration and endurance, as in a reference in the *Financial Times* (6/2/2000) to "a marathon 11-hour cabinet meeting" in Venezuela.

Those forms of *marathon* emerged from the legend of a Greek messenger who is said to have run almost 26 hilly miles from the battlefield of Marathon to Athens one summer day in 490 B.C. to tell of the vastly outnumbered Athenian army's victory over the invading Persians. According to the legend, the weary messenger, Pheidippides, made it to the walls of the Acropolis, cried out "Rejoice, we conquer!" and then dropped dead. Though there is no historical evidence of that incident, Pheidippides' death from exhaustion would be plausible in light of a report by Herodotus, the renowned historian of that time. Herodotus wrote that just prior to the battle at Marathon, a messenger named Pheidippides made a two-day, 150-mile round-trip run between Athens and Sparta in an unsuccessful effort to request Sparta's help in fighting the Persians.

The official marathon distance of 26 miles, 385 yards, is actually a couple of miles longer than the distance between Marathon and Athens. That is because of a decision made during the 1908 Olympics in London for that year's Olympic marathoners to cater to the royal family by starting at Windsor Castle and finishing at the royal box in the London stadium.

marveled or **marvelled?**   Add a second *l* to *marveled, marveling,* and *marvelous* only when you are marveling at the sights while visiting Britain or any other area of the world that uses British English.

marshal or **marshall?**   *Marshal* is the correct spelling of both the noun ("officer of a court, police agency, or military organization") and verb ("to arrange [ideas, things, troops, etc.] in an orderly manner").

Marshall exists only as a proper noun, as in the *Marshall Islands*.

marshmallows aren't totally *mellow*   The marshmallow tastes *mellow* ("soft, sweet, and full-flavored") and is pronounced "marsh-*mellow*." But it is spelled marsh*mallow* because it was once made from the root of the *marsh mallow*, a flowering plant that grows in marshes.

masterful or *masterly?*   *Masterly* means "having the skill of a master," as when the *New York Times* editorialized (6/19/2004) that "the 9/11 commission has done a masterly job of dissecting the Sept. 11 attacks."

Masterful is also widely used in the "skill" sense, but you'll be helping to maintain a useful word distinction if you use *masterful* in its separate function as a synonym for "domineering."

Both words had both meanings until the 18th century. Since then, *masterly* has meant only "skillful," while *masterful* has continued to be widely used in both senses. If *you* use *masterful* in both senses, you can cite the authority of the Merriam-Webster, Random House, and American Heritage dictionaries. But the restriction of *masterful* to the sense of "domineering" has the support of Fowler's *Dictionary of Modern English Usage*, *The New Fowler's Modern English Usage*, Garner's *Modern American Usage*, Copperud's *American Usage and Style*, Follett's *Modern American Usage*, Bernstein's *Careful Writer*, *The New York Times Manual of Style and Usage*, and 67 percent of the usage panel of the *Harper Dictionary of Contemporary Usage*.

material or *matériel?*   *Material* is any kind of substance from which something can be made. *Matériel* (pronounced "muh-teer-ee-EL") is equipment, typically military.

materialism: a lifestyle and a philosophy   *Materialism* can mean not only "a preoccupation with material acquisitions and comforts" but also "the philosophic doctrine that only matter is real and that everything (including thought, feeling, mind, and will) can be explained in terms of physical phenomena."

The philosophy of materialism stands in opposition to the philosophy of idealism, the belief that ideas, thought, and mind are the fundamental forms of reality.

may or *might?*   Did your boss say you *may* get a raise or you *might* get a raise? If your boss uses words with precision, you are more likely to get a raise if the word was *may*. As *New York Times* language columnist William Safire has written (1/28/2001), "*Might* is iffy, hypothetical, perhaps contrary to fact; *may* introduces a real possibility."

maybe or **may be?**   *Maybe* ("perhaps") is an adverb, as in "Maybe Jennifer will apply for the job." *May be* is a two-word verb form requiring a subject, as in "Jennifer may be ready to apply for the job."

mayday is no day   The word *mayday*, an international radiotelephone signal used as a distress call, has nothing to do with the month of May. *Mayday* is from the French *m'aider*, meaning "help me."

me is nothing to be afraid of   Contrary to Hollywood legend, 1930's *Tarzan* star Johnny Weissmuller never said to co-star Maureen O'Sullivan, "Me Tarzan, you Jane."

But the media—including *U.S. & World Report* (7/6/1998) in an item about Ms. O'Sullivan's death at age 87—have widely repeated that line. Perhaps that is because many early film writers did substitute *me* for *I* when they wanted to show that a character spoke like a "savage." And perhaps that is one reason why many people have developed such an aversion to *me* that they have stopped using it even when appropriate.

For example, during the 1992 presidential campaign, Bill Clinton asked voters to "give Al Gore and I a chance." *Me* was needed there as the object of the verb *give*. In a similar mistake, commentator Rush Limbaugh (9/14/1998) reminded his listeners that President Clinton's White House counsel was paid for "by you and I." *Me* was needed there as the object of the preposition *for*.

means is or **means** are?   Her *means* ("financial resources") *are* impressive. The most effective *means* ("strategy") of success *is* hard work. The most effective *means* ("strategies") of success *are* hard work and tenacity.

mecca or **Mecca?**   A pilgrimage to the Saudi Arabian city of *Mecca*, birthplace of Mohammed, is a sacred obligation for devout Muslims. By extension, the lower-case *mecca* is a place that attracts many visitors, commonly with a shared interest, as in "a mecca for nature lovers." (See "*Moslem, Muslim,* or *Mohammedan?*")

mechanics is or **mechanics** are?   Mechanics *is* any mechanical process or the branch of physics dealing with the action of forces on matter. Mechanics *are* people who repair and maintain machinery. (See also "*quantum mechanics can't fix cars.*")

***media, medias, medium, mediums,* and madness** Here's a simple formula for avoiding maddening confusion about these words.

Use *media* as the plural of "a communications, computer, or artistic medium." Use *mediums* as the plural of "a spirit medium, through whom the dead are said to communicate with the living." And forget *medias*, a fake plural that "has raised its ugly head" (to quote *Garner's Modern American Usage*) as a result of the unfortunately widespread use of *media* as a singular word.

Garner says that *media* is now so commonly used as a singular collective noun (like *press*) that such usage "must be accepted as standard." But acceptance of that controversial usage invites linguistic chaos, as in the *Los Angeles Times* coverage (7/2/1998) of the wedding of Barbra Streisand and James Brolin. In that coverage, the word *media* was singular in the story ("the media was kept . . . far away") but plural in the subhead ("media are kept far away").

If you care enough about linguistic clarity to help preserve the plural status of *media*, you can cite the support of Copperud's *American Usage and Style*, Bernstein's *Careful Writer*, Lovinger's *Penguin Dictionary of Usage and Style*, Webster's *New World College Dictionary*, *The New Oxford American Dictionary*, 70 percent of the usage panel of the *Harper Dictionary of Contemporary Usage*, and the stylebooks of the Associated Press, *The Washington Post, U.S. News & World Report, The Economist, The New York Times,* and *The Wall Street Journal*.

Here's some risk-free usage from a *Wall Street Journal* book review (2/6/2002) of author Todd Gitlin's *Media Unlimited*: "The media are so pervasive, so all-encompassing, so unavoidable, Mr. Gitlin claims, that we no longer separate them from ourselves. They become the single medium in which we live." And *The Economist* (12/18/2004) reported, "The media in poor countries are freer and more influential than ever before."

***medieval* or *Medieval*?** In reference to the Middle Ages, write "*medieval* architecture" and "*medieval* attitudes" but "*Medieval* Latin."

By the way, the spelling of this word, with the initial *me* rather than *mid*, is easier to remember if you use the preferred pronunciation beginning with the sound of *me*: "mee-dee-EVIL."

***mediocre* is less than ordinary** One of the dictionary definitions of *mediocre* is "average." But *mediocre* is usually used disparagingly, in the sense of "inferior."

meld: a case of mistaken identity   Be prepared to be *unjustly* accused of abusage if you use *meld* in the perfectly legitimate sense of "combine, blend, merge," as in an article in *The Wall Street Journal* (9/14/1999) about "the melding of entertainment and politics."

Misguided wordwatchers object to the "merge" *meld* because they are not aware that there are two completely different words spelled *meld*. Those wordwatchers have confused the "merge" *meld* (a 1930's Americanism emerging from a probable blend of *melt* and *weld*) with a separate British-American *meld* that appeared in the 1890's with the meaning "to announce or display a card or combination of playing cards in a hand for a score."

In a typical expression of that mistaken identity, the generally reliable Follett's *Modern American Usage* falsely warned in 1966 that the "merge" *meld* was a "misuse." That source added: "The fact is that *meld*, from the German *melden*, means *to announce*. It is a technical term of pinochle [and such card games as gin rummy and canasta]. To make it anything else is a malaprop." (See the entry for "*malaprop*.") If you encounter someone who heeds such misleading advice, refer that person to the entries for the two entirely separate *melds*—each as verb and noun—in *The Oxford English Dictionary* and the U.S. Merriam-Webster, Webster's New World, Random House, and American Heritage dictionaries.

mêlée: don't get confused   Don't let the preferred pronunciation of this French-derived word for "confused hand-to-hand fight, state of tumultuous confusion"—"MAY-lay"—confuse you about its spelling. The French circumflex and acute accent mark are optional.

melliferous or mellifluous?   Both these adjectives are derived from a Latin word for "honey." *Melliferous* means "*forming* or *bearing* honey." *Mellifluous*—with its memory-jogging *fl*—means "*flowing* with honey or other sweetness, smooth," as in "a mellifluous voice."

memento: something to remember   *Memento* ("keepsake, souvenir") begins with *mem-* as in *memory*.

The spelling *momento*, traced back to the 1850's, is seen today in published writing and is listed as an acceptable variant by Merriam-Webster dictionaries. But that form contradicts the word's relation to *memory* and *remember*, and it is rejected as a misspelling by such sources as *Webster's New World College Dictionary* and *Garner's Modern American Usage*.

Of the two forms of the plural, memen*tos* and memen*toes*, the first is preferred by some sources and required by others.

memorabilia is or **memorabilia are?**   Memorabilia *are* memorable things, such as souvenirs. Usage example from a headline in the *Los Angeles Times* (4/12/2000): "Probe Targets Fake Sports and Celebrity Memorabilia."

The singular is *memorabile*, a Latin term listed in our dictionaries but too obscure and therefore too risky to use.

A memorabilia-collecting enthusiast is a *memorabiliast*.

memoranda is or **memoranda are?**   Say "memoranda *are*." The word *memoranda* is the plural of the Latin-derived English word *memorandum*.

The anglicized plural of *memorandum—memorandums*—is prescribed by the stylebooks of the Associated Press, *The New York Times*, and *The Wall Street Journal*.

mendacity or **mendicity?**   *Mendacity*, from the Latin *mendacium* ("a lie"), means "lying."

Mendicity, from the Latin *mendicus* ("needy"), means "begging." The word *mendicant* denotes a beggar or a member of a monastic religious order owning neither personal nor community property.

mental telepathy **requires concentration**   The adjective *mental* in the common expression *mental telepathy* is redundant.

The American Heritage Dictionary says the phrase *mental telepathy* is so well established that any objection to the redundant *mental* "smacks of nit-picking." But it would be just your luck to refer to *mental telepathy* when you are trying to impress an important nitpicker. (See also "redundancy: a vice and a virtue.")

mention **can be dishonorable**   Some student writers incorrectly use *mention* as if it were a simple synonym of *say*, as in " 'I have collected all their rock albums,' he mentioned." When *mention* is used as a verb ("to cite, refer to, specify, speak of"), it can only be transitive, which means it must have a direct object. Examples of correct usage: "He mentioned his plan to travel this summer." "She never mentioned that she had won that prize." (See also "verbs: transitive and intransitive.")

mentor or **Mentor?**   Our word *mentor* ("wise and trusted teacher") came from the *Mentor* in Greek mythology who, as a loyal friend and adviser of Odysseus, was entrusted with the care and education of Odysseus' son, Telemachus.

meritorious or **meretricious?**   *Meritorious*, which derives from a Latin word for "deserving," means "deserving of reward or honor."

Meretricious, which derives from the Latin *meretrix* ("prostitute"), means "whorish, deceitfully attractive, or vulgarly ornamental." Language commentator John Ciardi recalled in his *Good Words to You*: "I once heard a Boston politician in oratorical flight salute a colleague for 'years of meretricious service in city finance.' I suspect he used the word accurately, but more accurately than he knew."

mésalliance or **misalliance?**   *Misalliance*, which is pronounced the way it looks, means "an unsuitable alliance, especially in marriage." *Mésalliance* ("may-ZAHL-ee-ans"), from French, means "a marriage with a person of inferior social position."

metal or **mettle?** A robot shows its *metal* ("metallic substance"), but humans show their *mettle* ("strength of spirit or temperament"). Usage example of *mettle*: A story in *The New York Times* (8/6/1998) about the presidential ambition of Nebraska Senator Kerrey bore the headline "Bob Kerrey Tests His Mettle for 2000."

Metal and *mettle* are examples of *cognates*, words that share a common "parent." In Elizabethan English, *metal*—also spelled *mettle*—had the literal meaning "metallic substance" as well as the figurative meaning "quality of personal temperament." Gradually, *metal* and *mettle* became separate words with today's separate meanings.

metaphors should not mix   Metaphors, typically defined as "figures of speech denoting one thing in place of another to suggest a likeness," have been used by writers and speakers for thousands of years to help their audiences visualize. For example, more than 25 centuries ago, the Greek epic poet Homer wrote of "rosy-fingered dawn." In our own era, a *New Yorker* cinema critic wrote (1/17/2005) that *The Life Aquatic with Steve Zissou* featured Bill Murray as Steve Zissou, "plus a shoal [a large number, as in 'a shoal of fish'] of other stars."

But metaphors do not work if their images are so mixed up that visualization is impossible. Note the impossibility of visualization in the deliberately mixed metaphor Tom Batiuk used in a *Funky Winkerbean* comic strip in which a commencement speaker declared, "As we climb the ladder of success we have to always remember to keep both feet planted firmly on the ground."

metaphor, symbol, or *simile?*   *Metaphor* is now being used not only in the "figure of speech" sense (described in the previous entry) but also in the sense of "symbol," as in this excerpt from an editorial in *The New York Times* (11/13/2002): "Tornadoes have a way of leaving behind the perfect metaphor for the suffering they cause. To see all your possessions scattered across the landscape and to realize that there is no longer any place to put even the possessions that haven't been irreparably damaged, no place for the victims to call home any longer, that is a measure of the emotional force these terrible storms wield."

Though the "symbol" sense of *metaphor* has become so common that it is listed as a definition in dictionaries, it has been emphatically rejected by some word-watchers. For example, cultural historian Jacques Barzun—in "The Press and the Prose," a March 1992 paper he wrote for the Freedom Forum Studies Center— took aim at the journalistic statement "Dresden is a metaphor for mass destruction." Barzun wrote, "Dresden is a symbol, an emblem, a sample, a reminder, a typical case, but metaphor it is not."

Simile, a word related to *similar,* means a figure of speech that serves the same purpose as a metaphor except that the comparison is slightly diluted by *like* or *as.* For instance, instead of metaphorically calling your loved one "an angel," you say she or he is "*like* an angel." Usage example from *National Geographic* (July 2000): A caption for a long-shot photograph of Australia's Ayers Rock said tourists on the rock were "like ants scaling a loaf of bread."

Many similes, like many metaphors, have been so overworked that they deserve a long rest. Some candidates for the simile rest home: *clean as a whistle, dark as night, fit as a fiddle, good as gold, hot as hell, innocent as a newborn babe, light as a feather, meek as a lamb, old as the hills, pretty as a picture,*

quiet as a mouse, right as rain, sober as a judge, thick as thieves, ugly as sin,
and *white as a sheet.*

metempsychosis is not treatable

Metempsychosis, which is related to *psyche* (Greek for "soul"), means "reincarnation, transmigration of the soul, the passing of the soul at or after death from a human or animal to some other human or animal body."

meteoroid, meteor, meteorite, meteorology, meteoric

A *meteoroid* is a piece of interplanetary space rock or metal. If it enters our atmosphere, it is called a *meteor*. If it does not completely burn up as a result of friction with our atmospheric air molecules—if it lands on Earth—it is a *meteorite.*

Meteor is from a Greek word meaning "thing in the air." The study of "things in the air" (atmospheric phenomena) is *meteorology.*

The adjective *meteoric* is widely used in the sense of "similar to a meteor in dazzling swiftness," as in "the meteoric rise" of Upland International stock reported by *Barron's*, the Dow Jones business and financial weekly (2/14/2000).

Midas: a touchy subject

A *Midas touch* means "the uncanny ability to turn any venture into a golden [profitable] one," as in a statement in the *New York Times* obituary for singing cowboy Gene Autry (10/3/1998) that he had "a Midas touch" as an investor in hotels, oil wells, broadcasting stations, and baseball teams.

But you would be wrong to say a successful person is as *clever* as Midas. The original Midas, a character in Greek mythology, was anything but clever.

King Midas of Phrygia (son of the King Gordius who tied the formidable Gordian knot) performed an act of kindness for a friend of the god Dionysus, and the god responded by offering to grant Midas whatever he chose to wish for. Midas unthinkingly wished that everything he touched would turn to gold, and only after his wish was granted did he realize that his touch would turn his loved ones into golden statues and all his food into golden inedibles.

Midas managed to persuade Dionysus to end the golden touch. But Midas' foolishness soon got him in trouble with another god. As the judge in a musical contest between Pan and Apollo, Midas ignorantly awarded the prize to the much less talented Pan. Apollo promptly punished Midas by changing his insensitive ears into those of an ass.

Clearly, among those who are familiar with Greek mythology, calling some-one a Midas is not an unalloyed compliment.

milestone or millstone? A *milestone*, literally "a stone marker on a roadside that shows the distance in miles to or from a given point," usually means "a significant event or turning point."

A *millstone*, literally meaning "one of a pair of cylindrical stones used for grinding grain or other substances in a mill," usually means "a crushing mental or emotional burden," as in "a millstone around one's neck."

militate or mitigate? Here is a common usage blunder: "His looks *mitigated* against him as an actor."

The correct word is *militate*, which means "have a negative effect." You can "*militate* against" but not "*mitigate* against."

Mitigate means "lessen, moderate, alleviate," as in "mitigating the effects of the recession." Usage example from *The Economist* (7/3/1999): "It seems, then, that there are technical fixes in the works that will do much to mitigate the effects of [air travel] turbulence over the coming years."

millennium: you should live so long Some people—surely not you—confuse *millennium* (a period of a thousand years) with *century*. In an example of such confusion shortly before the arrival of the year 2000, a *Pasadena Weekly* article about that Southern California city's Third Annual International Documentary Film Festival recalled that "Thomas Edison [1847–1931] developed the Kinetoscope viewer and Kinetograph camera back in the waning years of the last millennium."

A more common problem is the omission of *millennium*'s second *l* or *n*.

Example of *correct* usage, employing the plural form that some dictionaries prefer to *millennia*: *The New York Times* (7/15/1997) reviewed a book whose theme was that the humanities are in trouble "after being a central part of Western education for more than two millenniums."

Millennium also has the meaning of "a period [in the indefinite future] of general righteousness and happiness." That sense is derived from the thousand-year era that the Bible predicts for the reign of Christ on Earth (Rev. 20:1–7). Belief in that prediction is called *millennialism*, and the believers are *millenarians* (with a single *n* in the middle).

"mind reading"   See " 'fortune telling' and 'mind reading.' "

***minimal* or *minimum*?**   Both *minimal* and *minimum* can be used as adjectives to describe that which is the smallest or very small. But *minimal* should refer to degree, and *minimum* should refer to amount: "The Congressional committee showed *minimal* [an insignificantly small degree of] support for an increase in the *minimum* [legally smallest amount of] wage."

***miniscule* or *minuscule*?**   The correct spelling of this synonym for "very small" is *minuscule* (beginning with *minus*), according to dictionaries and usage manuals. Such sources label *miniscule* a misspelling.

   Usage example from *The New York Times* (2/12/2001): "The human genome is minuscule in size—two copies are packed into the nucleus of each ordinary human cell, itself too small to be seen by the naked eye—but vast in its informational content." Note that the phrase "minuscule in size" would be redundant if it were not contrasted in that sentence with the phrase "vast in its informational content."

***mire* and *quagmire* are not partners in a law firm**   The nouns *mire* and *quagmire* both mean "muddy ground." And because you can sink and get stuck in such stuff, *mire* and *quagmire* have become synonyms for any predicament in which a person can sink and get stuck. But only *mire* can be used as a verb, as in "mired in debt."

***misanthrope, misogamist,* or *misogynist*?**   The first hates people. The second hates marriage. The third hates women.

   The corresponding nouns for referring to the hatred itself—rather than to the person who hates—are *misanthropy, misogamy,* and *misogyny.*

***mischievous*: how to avoid trouble**   Pronounce *mischievous* ("causing trouble, naughty, playfully annoying") with the stress on the first syllable. Do not get caught pronouncing this word the way it was often spelled from the 16th to the 19th century: *mischievious* (rhyming with *devious*).

***mise en scène*: all the world's a stage setting**   *Mise en scène* (an italicized French import pronounced "meez ahn SEN") means the staging of a play, including the setting, props, and arrangement of the actors.

Mise en scène also has the extended meaning of "general surroundings, the physical or social setting in which something occurs."

missile or missle?   If you recall that "a miss is as good as a *mile*," that should remind you that *missile* ends in *-ile*.

misspell: not one to miss   The most embarrassing of all spelling mistakes is to incorrectly spell *misspell* with only one *s*.

Here's an especially embarrassing example: *The Chronicle of Higher Education* (3/13/1998) noted in its Corrections corner that, in a previous issue, the name of an opera and the name of a mathematician had been "mispelled." (See also "spelling traps.")

mnemonic or mnemonics?   *Mnemonics* ("nih-MON-iks") is a singular noun meaning "a technique or system of rules to improve the memory."

Mnemonic can be an adjective ("of or pertaining to mnemonics") or a noun ("memory-assisting device, formula, or code"). For example, "Thirty days hath September, / April, June, and November . . ." is a mnemonic rhyme, or a mnemonic, that helps us remember the number of days in each month.

An expert in mnemonics is a *mnemonist*.

These words come from *Mnemosyne* ("knee-MAS-ah-knee"), the Greek goddess of memory and the mother by Zeus of the nine Muses. (See also "*muse* or *Muse*?")

Moby Dick or Moby-Dick?   The usual version of the title of Herman Melville's classic novel about a ship captain's fatal obsession with a great white whale, *Moby Dick,* is used in the *Random House Webster's Unabridged Dictionary* and also in the title and text of the novel published by the Random House Modern Library. But as *Benét's Reader's Encyclopedia* and other literary reference books will attest, the original, 1851 name of the book and the whale was hyphenated. *Copy Editor* (June–July 2001), a newsletter for the publishing profession, says that "the original source [of literary and other titles] determines correctness."

modifiers: comparative and superlative   See "comparatives and superlatives: what Alice didn't know."

modifiers compounded   See entries on hyphens.

modifiers make mischief when they are misplaced   In grammar, adjectives and adverbs are called *word modifiers*. By extension, to quote the *Random House Webster's Unabridged Dictionary*, a *modifier* is any "word, phrase or sentence element that limits or qualifies the sense of another word, phrase or element in the same construction."

Keep modifiers close to whatever they are supposed to modify. If you don't, you could end up with a statement like this: "For Sale: Piano, by a lady going to Europe with carved legs." Of course, the modifying phrase *with carved legs* belongs with the word *piano*.

In some cases the problem is less obvious. An article in the *Los Angeles Times* (3/17/2005) about the U.S. Senate's vote on drilling for oil in the Arctic National Wildlife Refuge included this sentence: "Displaying large pictures of polar bears and caribou on the Senate floor, opponents argued that the drilling could harm wildlife in an area they call America's equivalent of the Serengeti wildlife refuge in Africa." Though most readers probably did not visualize photographs showing polar bears and caribou frolicking on the Senate floor, it would have been good to reword the sentence to avoid the possibility of that misreading.

Three favorite examples from the collection of *Writer's Digest* grammar columnist Richard Lederer (quoted in his column of January 1994) will help you remember the mischief that misplaced modifiers can cause:

"We saw many bears driving through Yellowstone Park."

"Please look over the brochure that is enclosed with your family."

"At 5:20 yesterday evening, Sean Leary, 24, of Belmont Road, was driving his motorcycle west on the street where he lives at a high speed."

(See also "*only* the adverb causes trouble" and, for the most notorious form of misplaced modifier, "participles that dangle.")

modifiers make mischief when they are two-faced   Watch your writing for what grammarians call "squinting modifiers," which are adverbs or phrases that can be interpreted to modify either what comes before them or what follows. Here's an example from an article on usage in *Harper's Magazine* (April 2001): "People who eat this *often* get sick." Readers of that sentence have no way of knowing if it refers to "people who eat this often" or to people who "often get sick."

Squinting modifiers are inexcusable even when they cause confusion that's only momentary. Consider this headline from *The Oregonian* (7/27/1992): "Man Wearing Scuba Gear Improperly Dies While Diving." The headline writer intended to express the idea of "wearing improperly" but unintentionally communicated the message "improperly dies."

momentarily: **its future is doubtful**   In the future tense, the adverb *momentarily* may cause more confusion than you wish to risk. In a statement such as "She will be there *momentarily*," the word usually means "*in* a moment, shortly." But some word guardians and 59 percent of the usage panel of *The American Heritage Dictionary* insist that *momentarily* means "*for* a moment, a short while." To play it safe, spell out your intended meaning. For instance, instead of saying "Watch—the hummingbird will be at the feeder momentarily," say "Watch—the hummingbird will be at the feeder any moment now" or "Watch—the hummingbird will be at the feeder for only a few seconds."

Momentarily is *not* ambiguous in the present or past tense. In both cases it means only "for a moment, a short while."

momentary or **momentous?**   *Momentary* means "lasting only a moment." *Momentous* means "extremely important."

money talks   Formal style is exemplified by *five dollars*. Informal style, including that of many newspapers, would be *$5*. Publications that ordinarily use figures—such as *$3.5 million*—usually spell out numbers at the beginning of a sentence.

If no cents are involved with the use of the dollar sign, write *$5* rather than *$5.00*. The redundancy of the zeros is useful on checks but needlessly difficult to read in prose.

When a plural number of dollars is used in the sense of a single sum, the amount of money is grammatically singular: "Three and a half million dollars *was* budgeted for road repair."

monologue or **soliloquy?**   TV host Johnny Carson will long be remembered as a master of the comic *monologue* ("discourse by a single speaker"). Hamlet is best remembered for his *soliloquy* ("thinking aloud").

months: named and misnamed   The last four of our twelve months are named as if they were the seventh (*Sept*ember), eighth (*Octo*ber), ninth (*Nove*mber), and tenth (*Dece*mber) months because that is how they were placed in the calendar of the ancient Romans.

The Columbia Encyclopedia (1993) explains: "In its most primitive form, the Roman calendar apparently had 10 months [beginning with *March*, which was named for Mars, the Roman god of war]. To fill out the 365 days, a number of blank days or occasional intercalary [inserted] months were used. Later, January and February were added at the end of the year." *January* (named after the Roman god Janus) and *February* (named after the Februa, a Roman festival of purification), were moved to the start of the year in the 16th century, with the introduction of our present-day Gregorian calendar by Pope Gregory XIII.

The origins of the other names of months: *April* (Aphrodite, the Greek goddess of love, known in Rome as Venus), *May* (the Greek goddess Maia, daughter of Atlas), *June* (the Roman goddess Juno, sister and wife of Jupiter), *July* (Julius Caesar), and *August* (Augustus Caesar).

mood   See "verbs are moody."

moot **point**   *Moot* is another multiple-meaning word that can cause confusion for your reader or listener unless you make sure your context clearly points to your intended meaning.

As *The Columbia Guide to Standard American English* notes, "A *moot question* may be open to discussion, in the process of being discussed, or not worth discussing at all [because the problem has been solved or no longer exists], depending on the sense dictated by context."

For *Dallas Morning News* writing coach Paula LaRocque, *moot* is not worth bothering with. In her usage column for *Quill* magazine (March 1993), she recommended that *moot* be replaced by "debatable, irrelevant, academic, null—whatever is meant."

moral **questions**   See "*ethics* or *morals?*"

more **ambiguity**   Don't make statements in which people have to guess whether you are using *more* to mean "an additional amount" or "in greater degree." For example, if you say you want "more comfortable furniture," that could mean you want *an additional amount* of the type of comfortable furniture that you already have, or it could mean that you want to replace all your furniture with furniture that has *a greater degree* of comfort.

The solution, as with all ambiguity, is to make your intended meaning unmistakable. You could say, for example. "I want more [an additional amount] of the comfortable furniture I recently bought" or "I donated all my furniture to charity because I wanted furniture that's more [in greater degree] comfortable." (See also "ambiguity alert" and "ambiguity can always be cured.")

***more important* or *more importantly*?** The widely used introductory phrase *more importantly*—as in "More importantly, she's reliable"—is denounced as ungrammatical by many usagists because the phrase is an abbreviated way of saying "What is more *important*."

But if you correctly say "More *important*, she's reliable," many people will *think* you're being ungrammatical, because *more importantly* is as well established in professional writing as *more notably*, *more interestingly*, and such sentence-modifying adverbs as *curiously*, *fortunately*, *regrettably*, and *strangely*.

Risk-free solution: Take the advice of reporter-writer David Schoenbrun, one of the usage panelists who commented on this problem for the *Harper Dictionary of Contemporary Usage*: "Write it all out: 'What is more important . . .'"

***more than one* doesn't always add up** Though the phrase *more than one* is plural in meaning, it usually is followed by a singular verb if the phrase precedes a singular noun. It is natural to say, for example, "More than one whale *was* sighted." Grammarians say this has to do with the proximity—the "attraction"—of the singular word *whale* to its verb.

But *more than one* does require a plural verb in sentences in which a singular verb would sound obviously inappropriate: "If there *are* more than one, *they* must share." Note that the *more than one* in that sentence is equated with the plural *they*. (See also "*one of* those plural problems.")

***Moslem, Muslim,* or *Mohammedan*?** Adherents of *Islam* (Arabic for "submission to God") call themselves *Muslims* (Arabic for "one who submits," as in submitting to the will of God).

Our dictionaries list *Muslim* and *Moslem* as equally acceptable. But as *Freeman's Handbook of Problem Words and Phrases* points out, "Most believers in the faith [who number about a fifth of humanity] prefer *Muslim* because it is closer to the Arabic pronunciation."

The term *Mohammedan* once appeared frequently in American and European periodicals, books, and dictionaries. Lest you copy such references, take note: *Mohammedan* is regarded as offensive to adherents of Islam because it falsely suggests that Islam encourages worship of the prophet Mohammed rather than of the one God worshipped by Muslims, Christians, and Jews.

most as a synonym for *almost* *Most* is completely acceptable as an adjective meaning "greatest" and "the majority of," as an adverb meaning "to the greatest degree" and "very," as a noun meaning "the greatest amount," and as a pronoun meaning "the greatest number." But you enter the Risk Zone if you use *most* as a shortened version of the adverb *almost* ("nearly").

The "almost" *most*—as in "Most anyone can start over in America's gambling mecca [Las Vegas]" (*U.S. News & World Report*, 6/28/2004)—has been traced by word historians to 16th-century Scotland. In 1996, Britain's *New Fowler's Modern English Usage* reported that the "almost" *most* "now is effectively limited to some United Kingdom dialects and to American English." On our side of the Atlantic, *The Columbia Guide to Standard American English* and *Merriam-Webster's Dictionary of English Usage* list the "almost" *most* as acceptable only when limited to informal usage.

Many of our word guardians refuse to accept the "almost" *most* even informally. Usage author Morton S. Freeman reports that the majority of grammarians today regard the "almost" *most* as "an example of slovenly speech." Wilson Follett's *Modern American Usage* called it "a patent illiteracy." Among members of *The American Heritage Dictionary's* usage panel, 92 percent voted against its use in writing, and 53 percent voted against its use in speech.

moxie or Moxie? Dictionaries trace the lowercase *moxie* (early 20th-century American slang for "courage, guts") to the uppercase *Moxie* that was once a nationally popular soft drink marketed as a source of "vim and vigor."

The capitalized *Moxie* (whose name word historians have been unable to trace) was introduced in 1884 as Moxie Nerve Food, "a cure-all for nervousness, exhaustion, and insomnia." According to Evan Morris, in his year-2000 collection of columns, *The Word Detective*: "Moxie was enormously popular all over the United States, but in 1906 the passage of the Pure Food and Drug Act put an end to Moxie's medicinal claims, and from then on it was sold as a soft drink. It remained popular . . . but Moxie's star began to wane as the kingdom of Coca-Cola slowly took over the market, and Moxie retreated to its [original and still-current] New England home."

Another capitalized *Moxie* emerged at the end of the 20th century, as a feminist magazine "For the Woman Who Dares."

Mrs.: don't ask what it stands for   Everyone knows *Mr.* is the abbreviation for *mister*. But if you ask people what *Mrs.* means, you're likely to get this uninformative response: "*Mrs.*? It means—uh—*Mrs.*"

As you can learn from dictionaries, *Mrs.* is the abbreviation for *mistress*. But though *mistress* has traditionally meant "the female head of a household," *mistress* today commonly means "a sexual companion other than one's wife." No wonder *Mrs.* has become an abbreviation that stands for nothing other than itself, as in "I'd like you to meet my *Mrs.*"

Mr., Mrs., Ms. plurals   *Messrs.* ("MESS-erz"), *Mmes.* ("may-DAHM"), *Mses.* ("MIZ-iz"). The first two are abbreviations of *Messieurs* and *Mesdames*, the French plural forms for *Mr.* and *Mrs.*

Ms. rarely misses   *Ms.* ("miz") emerged in the mid-20th century and subsequently achieved widespread currency as a title before a woman's surname when her marital status was unknown or regarded as professionally irrelevant or a matter of personal privacy.

Miss and *Mrs.* are still appropriate for women who express a preference for such titles. If a woman adopts her husband's last name, she is *Mrs.* when she is addressed by her husband's full name, as in "Mrs. John Jones." But it is up to her to decide which she wants to be called, "Mrs. Sally Jones" or "Ms. Sally Jones."

muchly ado about nothing?   According to the *Harper Dictionary of Contemporary Usage*, the expression "Thank you muchly" is a misguided attempt at "elegance," because "there is no such word as *muchly*."

Actually, *muchly* (meaning "very much") is a real word, though it is classified as "colloquial" by *Webster's New World College Dictionary* and as "now jocular" by *The Oxford English Dictionary*. The *OED* says *muchly* has a non-jocular history as an adverb meaning "much, exceedingly" that extends at least as far back as the early 17th century. Nevertheless, there is really no need to risk using *muchly* when you have the perfectly acceptable alternative of *very much*. (See also "*thusly* gets almost no respect.")

Murphy's Law, Parkinson's Law, and the *Peter Principle*   *Murphy's Law*, a facetious proposition attributed to U.S. aircraft engineer Edward A. Murphy Jr., states that "if anything can go wrong, it will."

Parkinson's Law, promulgated by British historian C. Northcote Parkinson, states that "work expands so as to fill the time available for its completion."

The *Peter Principle*, introduced by Canadian educator Laurence J. Peter, states that "people in a hierarchy tend to be promoted until they reach their level of incompetence."

muse or Muse?   The *muse* that is a verb ("ponder, become absorbed in thought")—like the verb *amuse*—apparently evolved from an early French word for "open-mouthed stare" and a still-earlier French word for "animal's mouth."

But the *muse* that is a noun ("a source of inspiration, guiding spirit")—along with the nouns *music*, *mosaic*, and *museum*—evolved from the often-capitalized *Muse* ("any of the nine daughters of the Greek god Zeus and the memory goddess Mnemosyne, each of whom guided a different art or science").

Here is a guide to those guides: Muse leader *Calliope* (epic poetry and eloquence), *Clio* (history), *Erato* (love poetry), *Euterpe* (music and lyric poetry), *Melpomene* (tragedy), *Polyhymnia* (sacred poetry), *Terpsichore* (choral song and dance), *Thalia* (comedy), and *Urania* (astronomy).

myriad adds up   The four-century-old noun *myriad*, from a Greek term meaning "ten thousand," means "a very large number." The adjective, which has the same form but surfaced about two centuries later, means "countless." A telescope will show you "a myriad of stars" or "myriad stars" (the noun and the adjective, respectively).

A usage note in *Merriam-Webster's Collegiate Dictionary* (eleventh edition, 2003) acknowledged but dismissed "recent criticism of the use of myriad as a noun." That source attributed the criticism to "the mistaken belief that the word was originally and is still properly only an adjective." The usage note continued: "The noun *myriad* has appeared in the works of such writers as Milton (plural *myriads*) and Thoreau (*a myriad of*), and it continues to occur frequently in reputable English. There is no reason to avoid it."

myself   See "pronouns that are *self*-conscious."

myth: truth or deception?   *Myth* is another word requiring that you make sure your intended meaning is clear from your context.

Derived from the Greek word *mûthos* ("narrative, story"), *myth* stands for what *The Oxford English Dictionary* calls "a purely fictitious narrative usually involving supernatural persons, actions or events, and embodying some popular idea concerning natural or historical phenomena." That concept of myth was the subject of a Joseph Campbell–Bill Moyers TV series and book, *The Power of Myth,* in which mythology scholar Campbell referred to myth as "the penultimate [next-to-last, nearly ultimate] truth—penultimate because the ultimate cannot be put into words."

But the word *myth* can also mean the opposite of truth—"a deceptive vision of reality." For example, U.S. Senator J. William Fulbright warned of what he considered dangerously deceptive visions in a book about America's Cold War foreign policy, *Old Myths and New Realities.* In another realm of reality, anthropologist-author Ashley Montagu (1905–1999) wrote that too many women "are so enslaved to the myths of their own inferiority they are unable to see the truth for the myth."

mythic, mythical, mythologic, or mythological?   Though many dictionaries show these words being used interchangeably, you can demonstrate your appreciation for precise usage by maintaining the distinctions cited in *Webster's New World College Dictionary*:

Use *mythic* for "having the nature of a myth, widely idealized," as in a *New York Times* article (2/8/2001) recalling that aviator Charles Lindbergh's "courageous [1927] solo flight across the Atlantic had made him a hero of mythic proportions."

Use *mythical* for "fictitious, not based on facts," as in the "mythical accomplishments of my political opponent."

Use *mythological* or the less common *mythologic* for "of mythology," as in a phrase such as "a distinguished scholar in mythological studies."

mythy **mouthfuls**   *Mythy*, a little-used adjective meaning "involving or resembling a myth," has the comparative *mythier* and the superlative *mythiest*. *Mythopoetic* and *mythopoeic* are adjectives meaning "of or pertaining to myth-making." *Mythologist*s or *mythographers* collect or write about myths. *Mythicists* are myth interpreters. A *mythos* is a culture's system of basic beliefs and values, as transmitted by myths and the arts. The plural of *mythos* is *mythoi*. A *mythologem* is a basic theme, such as revenge or self-sacrifice, shared by cultures throughout the world. To *mythicize* or *mythify* is to fictionalize fact. A *mythomane* is someone afflicted by *mythomania*, an obsession to tell lies. *Mythoclasts* debunk the myths of *mythmakers*.

N

naïf, naïve, **and** *naïveté*   A naïf ("nah-EEF") is a person who can be described by the adjective *naïve* ("nah-EVE"), which means "unsophisticated, credulous, lacking critical ability and worldly wisdom." The noun for the state of being naïve is *naïveté* ("nah-eve-TAY").

naked **or** *nude*?   When a *nude* artist's model takes a shower, that person is *naked*. *Nude* has a more refined, esthetic connotation than *naked*, which is why you never hear a reference to "nude aggression."

Narcissus, narcissus, **and** *narcissism*   The Greek goddess of retribution, Nemesis, inflicted a severe punishment on the strikingly handsome *Narcissus* for callously breaking the hearts of the nymph Echo and the many others who fell in love with him.

Nemesis made Narcissus suffer much as he had caused others to suffer by having him fall desperately in love with his own reflection in a pool. Unable to reach out for the object of his passion but unable to tear himself away, Narcissus lay beside the pool until he wasted away and was transformed by the gods into the beautiful flower called the *narcissus*.

The term *narcissism* emerged in psychoanalysis in the early 20th century to describe "arrest at or regression to the infantile state in which the self is the object of erotic pleasure."

In nontechnical usage today, *narcissism* means "excessive interest in one's own appearance, importance, or abilities." (See also "*Echo*: no sir.")

naught or _nought_? *Naught* means "nothing," as in "Her lawyer's efforts came to naught." *Nought*, listed in dictionaries as a spelling variant of *naught*, actually has a worth-preserving separate meaning of "zero," as in the British name for our tic-tac-toe, "noughts and crosses."

nauseous: advice that can make you dizzy Many usage commentators do not want to hear you complain that you feel *nauseous*. They contend that *nauseous* means "*causing* nausea," as in a feature story in the *Los Angeles Times* (1/22/1998) that said, "A nauseous blend of construction dust, cigarette smoke, and the odor of decomposing bodies in the morgue two floor below wafts over the jumble of bones that is all that remains of the last czar of Russia."

Guardians of the word *nauseous* say the only proper word for "*feeling* nausea" (from a Greek word for "seasickness") is *nauseated*.

To quote Bernstein's *Careful Writer*, "A person who feels sick is no more *nauseous* than a person who has been poisoned is *poisonous*." That is also the view of Strunk and White's *Elements of Style*, *The Concise Oxford Dictionary*, 76 percent of the usage panel of the *Harper Dictionary of Contemporary Usage*, and the consensus of consultants for Roy H. Copperud's *American Usage and Style*. Copperud commented, "Confusion of [*nauseous* with *nauseated*] is a conspicuous mark of a shaky grasp of language."

In opposition to that view, *Merriam-Webster's Collegiate Dictionary* states: "Those who insist that *nauseous* can properly be used only in the sense of [*causing* nausea] are in error. Current evidence shows [that] *nauseous* is most frequently used to mean physically *affected* with nausea." Supporting that permissive position, the *Random House Webster's Unabridged Dictionary* says that *nauseous* has meant both "*causing* nausea" and "*feeling* nausea" since the early 17th century and that both senses are still in standard use.

The 2003 *Chicago Manual of Style* comments that "the use of *nauseous* to mean *nauseated* may be too common to be called error anymore, but strictly speaking it is poor usage."

Risk-free suggestion: Forget *nauseous*. Instead, say that a nausea-*causing* person is *nauseating* and that a nausea-*suffering* person is *nauseated*.

"nautical" words   *Astronaut, cosmonaut, aquanaut,* and *cybernaut* share endings based on a Greek word for "sailor." The *Argonauts* were heroes of Greek mythology who sailed in a ship called the *Argo* (from a Greek word for "swift") to help a prince named Jason demonstrate his right to be king by engaging in a long and dangerous quest for the magical Golden Fleece of a miraculous flying ram.

***Neanderthal*: a victim of prejudice?**   *Neanderthal* (also spelled *Neandertal*) is widely used to identify someone of subhuman intelligence and social behavior. For example, *Los Angeles Times* columnist Al Martinez (8/11/1998) wrote a tribute to police in which he acknowledged that some police are "uniformed Neanderthals—brutal redneck racists . . . liars and thieves and killers and rapists."

But research now suggests that the brutish reputation of the Neanderthals—who lived in Europe and western Asia from about 300,000 years ago until their population vanished on the Iberian peninsula about 30,000 years ago—may have been shaped by the same type of prejudice that once assigned subhuman status to Native Americans.

Neanderthals—so named because the first of their identified fossils, in 1856, was uncovered in Germany's Neander Valley—had short, muscular bodies, prominent brow ridges, sloping foreheads, and chinless, forward-jutting jaws. Their anatomy, along with early discoveries linking them with rather simple hunting tools, suggested that they were a *Homo sapiens* subspecies or a separate species of humans who were no intellectual match for the modern *Homo sapiens* who arrived in Neanderthal territory about 40,000 years ago and somehow replaced the Neanderthals during the next 10,000 years.

But we now know that the Neanderthal brain was larger than that of the average modern *Homo sapiens*. And recent research, summarized in *Science News* (8/1/1998), associates Neanderthals with relatively sophisticated tools as well as personal ornaments that might well have been symbols of individual social status. *Science News* says, "This emerging view depicts Neanderthals as having a capacity for creative, flexible behavior somewhat like that of modern people."

If you think we are superior to the Neanderthals because we're here and they're not, consider this: We have not yet shown that we can survive as long as they did. (See also "*philistine*: a bum rap?")

near or nearly?   See "adverbs that look like adjectives."

neat no longer counts   Once upon a time, *neat* clearly meant "free from dirt or disorder." But according to *The Glory and the Dream* by William Manchester, the word *neat* became just another slang expression for approval among some American young people at least as far back as 1937: "Girls spoke of boys as smooth, a boy called a girl neat." After many teenagers and adults adopted *neat* as an all-purpose adjective of praise—as in "Your job is really neat," "Neat car you've got!" and "That was a neat movie"—the word has become hopelessly vague.

Anyone still tempted to use *neat* as an all-purpose adjective for approval should rephrase without using any adjective at all. Just tell why you feel the way you do. Say, for example, "That movie really made me laugh!" (See also "adjectives: how many deserve to die?" and "*nice*: a word of distinction.")

necessary evil   You're committing a sin against logic if you use a phrase such as "especially necessary" or "particularly necessary." The adjective *necessary* should not be qualified by adverbs like *especially* or *particularly*, because *necessary*, like *essential*, is an absolute. That means the state of being necessary either exists or it doesn't. There can be no degrees of *necessary*.

If something is necessary, just say so. If not, use an appropriate alternative word, such as *important, useful,* or *helpful*. And with those words, feel free to use qualifiers. For example: "A pleasant personality is especially important [not especially *necessary*] in today's highly competitive job market."

As with all absolute words, you can use a qualifier with *necessary* only when you are acknowledging that the condition does not exist or you are dismissing doubt about its existence. Therefore, you can say something is not, or is, *really* necessary. (See also "absolute advice.")

needless to say is not needed   The phrase *needless to say* is needless nonsense. If there's no need to say something, don't say it.

On the other hand, you are making sense if you say that something "*should* be needless to say." For example: "It should be needless to say that drunk driving is an extremely serious crime."

née needs only the last name   *Née*, which rhymes with *say* and is derived from a French word for "born," is an adjective placed after the name of a married woman to introduce her maiden name.

"Phyllis Baxter, *née* Jones"—meaning "Phyllis Baxter, born Jones"—is correct. But "*née* Phyllis Jones" would be wrong because only a woman's original surname is considered her maiden name.

neither is or neither are?   See "*either* and *neither*: singular or plural?"

neither . . . nor: singular or plural?   See "*either . . . or* and *neither . . . nor*: singular or plural?"

nemesis or Nemesis?   The ancient Greek goddess of retributive justice, *Nemesis*, is the source of our word *nemesis* for "one who imposes retribution" or "something or someone that serves as an obstacle that cannot be overcome."

Usage example of *nemesis* as "one who imposes retribution": A *New York Times* (4/6/1997) headline identified Mississippi Attorney General Michael C. Moore as a "Tobacco Industry Nemesis" for filing "the first lawsuit by a state against the nation's cigarette manufacturers [in 1994 and then waging] a cross-country crusade that has rallied 21 other states to the cause, building the most formidable offensive against the tobacco industry in its history."

nice: a word of distinction   Dictionaries define *nice* as "agreeable, pleasing, pleasant, courteous, considerate." But praise that uses the word *nice* is so vague that it conveys almost no meaning. Notice, for example, the "That's nice" responses of inattentive friends and relatives.

Strunk and White's *Elements of Style* said, "This shaggy, all-purpose word [of praise] should be used sparingly in formal composition." That source acknowledged that *nice* can be useful in another of its dictionary definitions—"precise or exacting, as in 'nice distinction.'" But in that context you are more likely to be understood if you use the word *precise*.

Incidentally, *nice* originally was not at all nice (as in "pleasant"). The Latin *nescius* ("ignorant, not knowing") had its first recorded use in English in 1290, with the meaning of "simple-minded, stupid." In the 14th century, Chaucer used *nice* to mean "wanton, lascivious." From the 15th to the 18th century, *nice* was used in the sense of "coy, reserved, diffident." In the 16th century, *nice* acquired two of its still-current senses: "fussy" and "precise." In the 18th century, *nice* began its modern career as a compliment that damns with vague praise.

nicety isn't necessarily nice   *Nicety* is "a subtle point or detail." The word is often used in the plural, as in "the niceties of diplomatic negotiation."

***nine* usually is complete**   Though *nine* drops its *e* in *ninth*, the word keeps its complete spelling in *ninefold, nineteen, ninety,* and *ninetieth*.

***Nobel* or *Noble* Prize?**   In 1978, the Polish-American critic, journalist, novelist, and writer Isaac Bashevis Singer won the *Nobel* Prize in Literature, one of the awards established by the will of Alfred Bernhard Nobel ("no-BELL"), a Swedish chemist, engineer, and industrialist. But after Singer's death in 1991, the company that made Singer's gravestone identified him as a *Noble* ("virtuous") Laureate. Almost six years elapsed before an engraver was assigned to correct the set-in-stone typo.

Nobel (1833–1896), who said he hoped the destructive power of dynamite and his other explosive inventions would help rid humanity of war, made possible the world's most coveted prizes in peace, literature, physics, chemistry, and the category of "physiology or medicine." (See also next entry.)

Nobel Prizes in Economics have never been awarded   The Nobel Prize in Economics does not exist.

It seems to exist because winners of the "Nobel Prize in Economics" are hailed by much of the media each year. For example, a *Los Angeles Times* article (10/9/2003) reported that "two longtime UC San Diego colleagues won the Nobel Prize in Economics." And an Oscar-winning Hollywood movie (*A Beautiful Mind,* 2001) was made about schizophrenic "Nobel Prize economist" John Forbes Nash Jr. Moreover, the nonexistent award is included in the list of Nobel Prizes in such usually reliable sources as *The Oxford English Dictionary, Webster's New World College Dictionary,* and *The American Heritage Dictionary.* But read on.

The awarding of the actual Nobel Prizes, in the five categories cited in the previous entry, began in 1901. Sixty-eight years later, in an attempt to enhance the public image of economics, members of that discipline succeeded in obtaining the establishment of the awkwardly and confusingly named Bank of Sweden

Prize in Economic Sciences in Memory of Alfred Nobel. As *The New York Times Manual of Style and Usage* advises its writers and editors, the economics prize "is not, strictly speaking, a Nobel Prize." That newspaper and *The Wall Street Journal* carefully refer to the economics award as the Nobel *Memorial* Prize in Economic Science.

New Yorker writer Sylvia Nasar has written (12/20/1999) that "the feeling that the economics Nobel isn't quite as real as the other, older Nobels—and that by implication, economics, the only social science with its own Nobel, isn't really a science at all—has never entirely faded. . . . And, after winning [the previous year's economic prize] medal, Amartya Sen, the liberal Master of Trinity College, Cambridge, said in an interview, 'I've always been skeptical of the prize, but it's difficult to express that until you get it because people think it's sour grapes.'"

Feel free to be even more skeptical of the Ig Nobel Prizes, bestowed annually at a wacky ceremony at which a few real Nobel Laureates sing, dance, and pay mock tribute to "Weird Science" achievements that "cannot and should not be reproduced." Among the Ig Noble winners honored at an October 2004 gala at Harvard University were the developers of a comb-over hairstyle to cover partial baldness and a researcher who discovered that when food is dropped on the floor more women than men will pick it up and eat it.

noisome neighbors?

Noisy neighbors are a nuisance, but *noisome* neighbors are worse. *Noisome* means "foul-smelling, filthy, or otherwise offensive to the point of arousing disgust," as in "the noisome pestilence" cited in the Book of Psalms of the Old Testament.

Noisome, related to *annoy*, is a Middle English compound of *noy* ("annoyance, harm") and *some* ("characterized by").

nom de plume is a fake name for a fake name

Many English-speaking people use *nom de plume* as if it were a French term for "pen name." Indeed, *nom de plume* is so listed in *Larousse's French-English Dictionary*, the *Washington Post Deskbook on Style*, *The Dictionary of Cultural Literacy*, and *The Columbia Guide to Standard American English*. But *nom de plume* was exposed as a "sham" in an early 20th-century book by Henry and Francis Fowler, *The King's English*.

The original French term for an assumed name was *nom de guerre* ("war name"). That term reflects the fact that French knights customarily fought under a pseudonym (as is done today by America's professional wrestlers). Eventually, *nom de guerre* signified any assumed name, including an author's pen name. But in the early 19th century, the British invented a literal "French" term for pen name, *nom de plume*. *The Harper Dictionary of Foreign Terms* sums up the story of *nom de plume* by classifying it as "pseudo-French."

Which term for pen name should you use, *nom de guerre* or *nom de plume?* Why bother with either? Just say *pen name.*

none is or **none are?**   Don't listen to people who tell you they were taught that *none* must always mean "not one" and therefore must always be singular. That error, spread to thousands of teachers by the 1959 edition of Strunk & White's *Elements of Style*, has been corrected in subsequent editions of Strunk & White and has been rejected by other leading usage guides.

The fact is that, at least as far back as the time of the King James Bible, *none* has stood not only for the singular "not one" but also the plural "not any." Moreover, most *none* usage today is plural, as in "None [not any] of humanity's excuses for destroying wildlife *are* valid." The singular usage is usually employed for emphasis: "Of all humanity's excuses for destroying wildlife, none [not a single one] *is* valid."

Recommendation: Use the pronoun *none* as a substitute for the plural phrase "not any," except when you want to use the singular *none* as a substitute for the emphatic phrase "not a single one." If you are otherwise tempted to use the singular *none*, replace it with the clearly understood phrase "not one," as *The New York Public Library Writer's Guide to Style and Usage* suggests.

nonplused confusion *Nonplused* (alternately spelled *nonplussed*) contributes a unique dimension to the concept of "bewildered confusion." If you use this valuable word, try not to join those who are now abusing it. (See usage warning below.)

Derived from Latin words for "no" and "more," *nonplused* means "so confused, so puzzled, so perplexed, so bewildered that one is unable to go, speak, or act further."

The *New York Times* stylebook instructs its writers and editors to use *nonplused* to mean "bewildered to the point of speechlessness." That sense was clearly intended in a *Los Angeles Times* editorial eulogy (1/25/2005) for 30-year

Tonight Show host Johnny Carson. The editorial recalled Carson's famously funny "nonplused stare into the camera."

Usage warning: As an *Oxford English Dictionary* editor, Angus Stevenson, told *The New York Times* (11/12/2002): "[*Nonplused*] has always meant puzzled and confused, but we have evidence that in America some people use it to mean the opposite, as in 'sort of shaken but not stirred,' like 'He was doing his best to appear nonplused.'" Though dictionary editors traditionally describe usage rather than prescribe it, Stevenson told *The Times* that "It's really a mistaken use."

nonrestrictive or restrictive?   Grammarians use those words when they mean "nonessential" and "essential." For important applications of that distinction, see my "commas separating nonessential information" and "*that* or *which*?" entries.

non sequiturs   See "sentences that defy logic."

normal* contains *norm   Though the adjective *normal* is normally used in the sense of "usual, natural," the word is also defined in dictionaries as "serving to establish a standard." That second definition reflects the fact that *normal* is related to *norm* ("authoritative standard, model, pattern") and *normative* ("of or pertaining to a norm or the establishing of a norm").

A third dictionary definition of *normal*, the mathematical sense of "being at right angles, perpendicular," points to the origin of our *norm* words in the Latin *norma* ("carpenter's square, a device that provides a standard for forming right angles"). The Latin *norma* produced the Latin adjective *normalis* as a word that first meant "forming a right angle according to the standard of a carpenter's square," and then came to mean "according to a standard" in general.

Our old term for schools that train teachers, *normal school*, was taken from the French *école normale*, a school that served as a "standard" for other teaching schools. The word *enormous* ("abnormally large") was derived from a Latin adjective for "not normal, abnormal."

***normalcy* or *normality*?**   *The New York Times* reported in a front-page headline of its national edition that war-torn Bosnia was seeking *normality* (6/23/1992). But for the continuation of that story on an inside page, the headline said Bosnia was seeking *normalcy*. Aside from the embarrassing inconsistency, *The Times* had not made a mistake. Both *normality* and *normalcy* are listed as standard by dictionaries and usage manuals.

But your risk-free choice is *normality*, as in a *New York Review of Books* essay (1/17/2002) stating that the people of post-Taliban Afghanistan were "desperate for peace and normality." If you choose *normalcy*, you risk being accused of ignorance by abnormally critical word guardians.

Normalcy became a subject of nationwide controversy in 1920, when Republican presidential candidate Warren G. Harding appealed to war-weary Americans by campaigning for "a return to normalcy." Harding's opponents accused him of ignorantly using a nonword—*normalcy*—when he should have said *normality* (in accordance with the *-ity* nouns formed from such *-al* adjectives as *mortal* and *fatal*). Harding's supporters promptly documented the fact that *normalcy* had been a legitimate, though rarely used, word for "the condition of being normal" since the 19th century. And Harding won the election by the widest popular margin (60.3 percent) recorded to that time. But the myth of Harding's "ignorant" usage persisted. For example, Ernest Klein's *Comprehensive Etymological Dictionary of the English Language* (Elsevier, 1971) accused Harding of "coining" *normalcy* in place of "the correct form . . . *normality*."

nosey or **nosy?**   This adjective, briefly expressing the idea of being "intrusively curious about the affairs of others," is preferably spelled without the complete *nose*. Memory tip: If you stick your nose into other people's business, part of your nose may be bitten off.

no sooner than, then, or **when?**   As a phrase serving as a comparative adverb meaning "as soon as," *no sooner* takes *than*: "No sooner had he arrived *than* [not *then* or *when*] the trouble began."

not is not to be taken for granted   If you are not careful, you can easily forget to include the little word *not* and thus communicate the opposite of what you intend.

Think not? Consider the embarrassment of the British printer who in 1632 produced what came to be known as *The Wicked Bible*, so called because *not* was omitted in the commandment "Thou shalt not commit adultery." Twenty-one years later, in what came to be known as *The Unrighteous Bible*, another British printer left out the *not* in "The unrighteous shall not inherit the kingdom of God."

not only . . . but also   Some usage commentators say the *also* in this conjunctive pair is optional. Others say it's needed only for formal communication. And still others say the *also* is absolutely necessary because it expresses the idea of something that is additional.

Actually, you do tend to lose the meaning of "additional" if you lose *only*. So your risk-free choice is to keep the *only*, as in the following sentence about Nobel novelist Saul Bellow in *The New York Review of Books* (5/31/2001): "Bellow is a supremely entertaining writer not only because he writes beautiful prose but also because he's always topical."

Notice that each conjunction in that mutually related ("correlative") pair introduced a clause beginning with the word *because*. Be sure to follow the conjunctions with matching parts of speech. You would be correct if you wrote "Blake was not only a poet but also a painter" (matching the noun *poet* with the noun *painter*), but you would invite the criticism of grammarians if you wrote "Blake was not only a poet but also he painted" (mismatching the noun *poet* with the pronoun-plus-verb clause *he painted*). (See also "conjunctions used in pairs," "*either . . . or* and *neither . . . nor*: singular or plural?" and "parallel problems.")

notable or noteworthy?   Both of these adjectives mean "worthy of notice." But *notable* also means *noted* ("worthy of notice because of a distinguished reputation"). Remember that *Who's Who in America* contains *noteworthy* information about *notable* people.

nothing is no thing   *Nothing* ("no thing") is singular even if followed by an *except* phrase with a plural noun: "Nothing except a few billboards *spoils* the scenic view."

"noun disease"   The Germans coined the term "noun disease" (*Substantivseuche*) for the objectionable practice of stringing together an overwhelming number of nouns as modifiers.

Professor J. N. Hook gives this example in his *Appropriate Word*: "The teacher lesson-preparation number decrease demand will probably not be granted." When that sentence is cured of noun disease, it reads: "The teachers' demand for a decrease in the number of lesson preparations will probably not be granted."

nouns that can be singular or plural   Does a jury reach *its* verdict or *their* verdict?

The answer to that question depends on what is called notional ("existing in the mind") agreement. *Jury* and some other collective nouns—those that are singular in form but composed of a plural number of individuals—are singular when you wish them to be thought of as a unit and plural when you wish them to be thought of as individuals composing the group. Hence, the jury have *their* disagreements. But later in the week, the jury reaches *its* verdict.

Use the same notional approach for such collective nouns as *couple, pair, family, group, faculty, class, team, crowd, public, audience, chorus,* and *orchestra.*

Some collective nouns—for example, *government, committee,* and *firm*—are viewed as singular in American English and plural in British English. When we want to focus on the plural individuals of such units, we say "*members* of the government [or committee or firm]." (See also "*couple is* or *couple are*?" and "verbs must agree in number with their subject.")

nouns that don't count   People who study English as a second language may need to make a special effort to distinguish *count nouns* from *mass nouns.* A count noun, like *apple,* can be pluralized. A mass noun, like *produce,* cannot. The count noun *fact* can become *facts,* but the mass noun *information* cannot become *informations.*

Furniture stores sell *sofas* but not *furnitures.* No matter how many *airports* you use, you will never lose *luggages.*

Propaganda cannot be pluralized as *propagandas,* and *the poor* cannot be pluralized as *the poors.* But you can say that propaganda *techniques* are used to conceal injustice to poor *people.*

noun verbification   The conversion of nouns into verbs has had a long and respectable history. According to *The New Fowler's Modern English Usage,* such conversion happened in 1578 to *distance,* in 1603 to *silence,* and in 1877 to *telephone.*

But *The New Fowler's* also notes that, in our time, word-guardian resistance to the verbification of nouns "has hardened." That source cites "fierce resistance" to such 20th-century verbified nouns as *author, impact,* and *parent.*

According to Kenneth G. Wilson's *Columbia Guide to Standard American English,* "It is nearly impossible to predict which [verbified nouns] will pass and which will not, but if enough people persist in their objections, such uses can undergo long or even permanent proscription from Standard use." (See also entries for *author, contact, debut, gift, impact,* and *parent.*)

now pending is too much   The *now* is redundant. If something is pending, it is obviously pending now.

nuclear alert   "George W. Bush has a nuclear problem," William Safire wrote in his "On Language" column for *The New York Times* (5/20/2001). "Like Presidents Eisenhower, Carter and Clinton before him, he mispronounces the word *nuclear.* At the Naval War College earlier this month, he tripped over the word a dozen times with great authority, pronouncing it somewhere between Carter's 'nuke-ular' and Clinton's 'nu-ky-ler.' "

Correct pronunciation of *nuclear* ("relating to atomic nuclei," as in "nuclear energy" or "nuclear weapons") is obviously not a requirement for the highest office in the land. But people who take pride in their pronunciation of this word say "NEW-klee-er."

number: singular or plural?   The word *number*—like *total* and *variety*—can be singular or plural, depending on your intended meaning.

"*The* number," "*the* total," and "*the* variety" have a singular meaning, as in "The number of dropouts in that school *was* enormous."

But "*a* number," "*a* total," and "*a* variety" take a plural verb, as in "A number of students *were* listed as dropouts."

number inflation   The phrase *sixty-four-dollar question,* defined by the *Random House Webster's Unabridged Dictionary* as "the critical or basic question or problem," originated with a 1940's radio quiz show in which sixty-four dollars was the largest prize. In the 1950's, television audiences watched a quiz show called *The $64,000 Question.* By the year 2000, four television networks were offering quiz-show contestants a chance to become a millionaire.

Here's a guide to help you cope with number inflation. In the internationally prevailing U.S. system of naming mind-numbing numbers, a thousand thousand is a *million*, a thousand million is a *billion*, a thousand billion is a *trillion*, a thousand trillion is a *quadrillion*, a thousand quadrillion is a *quintillion*, a thousand quintillion is a *sextillion*, a thousand quintillion is a *septillion*, a thousand septillion is an *octillion*, a thousand octillion is a *nonillion*, and a thousand nonillion is a *decillion*.

If you ever need to count beyond a *decillion* (1 followed by 33 zeros), you can go to the *googol* (1 followed by 100 zeros) and then the *googolplex* (1 followed by a googol of zeros). The googol was introduced by U.S. mathematician Edward Kasner (1878–1955), who gave credit for the name to his nine-year-old nephew, Milton Sirotta.

To illustrate a googol's impressive size, Temple University mathematician John Allen Paulos wrote in his book *Beyond Numeracy* that a googol is bigger than the estimated number of particles (protons, electrons, etc.) in the entire universe. Nevertheless, Paulos wrote, you would need a googol multiplied by itself and then multiplied by itself again (a googol cubed) to count the possible sequences of heads and tails if you flipped a penny one thousand times.

number-matching puzzle: are two heads better than one?   Is it grammatically correct to say that "people should make up their own *mind*"? Or, because more than one mind is involved, should you say that "people should make up their own *minds*"?

Before you respond to this oft-debated puzzle, imagine a worried mother calling a doctor about two children of hers who are home with the flu, each of whom has had a fever for two days and has now developed a headache. "They both have a headache" is the correct way to describe the symptom. "They both have *headaches*" would suggest to the doctor that each child has had more than one episode. (The doctor knows, of course, that each child has exactly one head that could be aching.)

Similarly, never hesitate to ask children (plural) to wash their *face*, not their *faces*. (It's hard enough getting some children to wash even that one face of theirs!) And remember that it's unacceptable to accuse passing motorists of thumbing their *noses* at you—unless each of those motorists is a space alien with an extra nose or two.

As *Atlantic Monthly* language columnist Barbara Wallraff advises in *Word*

Court, "Whenever carefully matching number results in ridiculous wording, don't do it." Let's hope people make up their *mind* to follow her advice.

numbers can numb   Suppose you write that a person's chance of winning a contest is 1 in 61,000. Help your reader understand the significance of such odds. In this case, you can inform your reader that 1 in 61,000 means that the chance of winning the contest is less than the chance of being killed by lightning.

Also, take care to avoid the mind-numbing risk of including too many numbers in a sentence, as in the following deliberately exaggerated example: "The 8th grader from 62nd Street scored only 55 percent on the 4-part test as compared with the average of 85 percent scored by the other 325 students at Public School 189."

numerous or numinous?   The mass media do not provide *numerous* ("consisting of a great number, many") examples of the adjective *numinous* ("of or pertaining to a *numen* [divine power or spirit]; filled with a sense of supernatural presence").

But *Time* film reviewer Richard Schickel found a use for the word in the process of panning the science-fiction movie *Contact* (7/21/1997) for being intellectually pretentious and banal. He wrote that the metaphysical climax of the movie turned the "sternly rational" scientist played by Jodie Foster into "numinous jelly."

nymphs or Nymphs?   The *Nymphs* of Greek mythology were goddesses of nature who presided over streams, woods, mountains, and so forth. Lowercase *nymphs* are "sexually desirable young women." *Nymphomania* is "a female psychiatric disorder characterized by excessive sexual desire." (See also *"satyrs."*)

O

O or oh?   Use O (always capitalized, and with no punctuation separating it from the next word) to express religious reverence or poetic earnestness in direct address ("O Lord!" "O Land of Dreams").

Oh, an independent exclamation usually followed by a comma or an exclamation point, expresses such feelings as surprise, pain, and disapproval ("Oh, no!") or serves as a device to attract the attention of a person being spoken to ("Oh, Pat").

objet d'art: an object lesson in spelling   This term for "object of art," borrowed from the French, is often misspelled "*object* d'art," as if the writer had started translating it into English and was then called away on an emergency.

If you need to pronounce it, say "awb-zhai DAHR."

obligated or obliged?   These words are often used interchangeably. But note that you say "Much *obliged*" (not "Much *obligated*") to someone who does you a favor.

You are *obliged by a sense of gratitude* to return the favor. You are *obligated by law* to pay a traffic fine.

obscene is more than some people mean   The adjective *obscene* means more than "causing lustful feelings."

Derived from a Latin word for "repulsive or indecent," *obscene* made its first known appearance in print as a synonym for "disgusting" (sexually and in general) in Shakespeare's *Love's Labor's Lost*. As noted in a Merriam-Webster specialized dictionary, *Coined by Shakespeare*, centuries of usage justify today's extended use of *obscene* to mean "indecent" or "subject to profound disapproval" for any reason. That book cites a famous example of the use of *obscene* to express profound disapproval without any reference to sex: The 19th-century essayist and poet Ralph Waldo Emerson asserted in a lecture that "to live without duties is obscene."

obscure or abstruse?   One way to avoid being *obscure* ("lacking clarity") in your communication is to use plain English to explain subjects that are *abstruse* ("extremely technical and therefore incomprehensible to most people").

observance or observation?   Anthropologists engage in *observation* ("the act of observing") of a tribe's *observance* of ("compliance with") religious rituals.

obsolescent or obsolete?   *Obsolete* means "no longer in use" or "no longer useful." *Obsolescent* means "becoming obsolete."

obvious observations   Careful writers never state what's obvious. When they need to refer to what's obvious, they acknowledge it in passing rather than state it flatly. Wrong way: "*Christmas is approaching*, so merchants are hiring additional salespeople." Right way: "*With Christmas approaching*, merchants are hiring additional salespeople."

Occident **and** *Orient*   The collective term for the countries of the west, the *Occident*, is derived from the Latin *occidens* ("setting" as in "setting sun").

The *Orient*, formerly the countries east of the Mediterranean, now refers to Asia and especially East Asia. The word *Orient*, from the Latin *oriens* ("rising"), reflects the ancient belief that the sun literally rises in the east. As a verb, *orient* literally means to determine your position in relation to the points of the compass.

Figuratively, to *orient* means "to get your bearings." If you lose your bearings, you're *disoriented*. (See also "*orient* or *orientate?*")

occupational mysteries   Leave mysteries to mystery writers. Instead of saying "Lawrence Polan of UCLA," say "Lawrence Polan, the librarian at the UCLA Medical School."

occur **or** *take place*?   Use *occur* for events that are spontaneous: "When did the accident occur?" Use *take place* for events that are scheduled: "When will the hearing about the accident take place?"

octopi **or** *octopuses*?   Are you one of those people who carefully avoid referring to more than one member of the carnivorous mollusks that belong to the genus *Octopus* or related genera? If so, note that *octopi* is acceptable but *octopuses* is preferred. (See also "plurals are not hard to find.")

odds **or** *probability*?   John Allen Paulos, author of *A Mathematician Reads the Newspaper*, says that the media frequently misuse *odds* as a synonym for *probability*.

Paulos explains that the difference between the two can be "crucial," because "the odds of an event can be defined as the probability that it will occur divided by the probability that it will not occur." The probability that a coin will land on heads is *one-half*, but the odds are *one to one*.

Paulos adds: "More serious discrepancies between probabilities and odds occur for events with higher probabilities. . . . What at first glance may seem like semantic nitpicking has significant consequences for public policy and perceptions [about crime and other important issues]."

odyssey or **Odyssey**?   The *Odyssey*, a 2,700-year-old epic poem of Greek mythology attributed to the poet Homer, tells of Trojan War hero Odysseus' perilous adventures during the 10 years it takes him to make his way back from Troy to his wife and home on the Greek island of Ithaca. That classic inspired our word *odyssey* for "a long, difficult journey."

of: to have and have not   Student writers often write *of* when they mean *have*. That is because *have* and its contraction sound like *of* when people in conversation say *could have, should have, would have, could've, should've,* or *would've.*

of is not always welcome   In informal speech, many people add *of* to phrases beginning with *how, that,* or *too* followed by an adjective: "*How* long *of* a movie?" "*That* long *of* a movie?" "*Too* long *of* a movie."

In formal communication, that *of* is generally unwelcome.

Also unwelcome in formal communication is *of* in the popular phrase *off of*—as in "the vase fell off *of* the table."

official or **officious**?   *Official* ("of or pertaining to an office or post of authority") should be carefully distinguished from *officious* ("meddlesome, objectionably aggressive in offering unwanted help").

off-putting: should you put off using it?   The adjective *off-putting* should be avoided, because it is "inexact and clumsy," according to Strunk and White's *Elements of Style.*

But many educated people seem to find the word useful. Examples: *The American Heritage Book of English Usage* states that an expression that is appropriate for a formal letter "may be utterly off-putting in an informal message." And a *New Yorker* magazine obituary for singer Peggy Lee recalled (2/4/2002), "There was something about Peggy Lee that didn't invite a listener all the way in, though that quality, instead of being off-putting, made the intimacy she did allow feel special."

Off-putting may not be one of our most precise words, but it does seem to convey a fairly consistent message. Dictionaries define it as "distracting, annoying, etc." (*Webster's New World*), "tending to disconcert or repel" (*American Heritage*), "repellent, disagreeable" (*Merriam-Webster's*), "provoking uneasiness, dislike, annoyance, or repugnance" (*Random House Webster's*), and "creating an unfavorable impression, causing displeasure" (*OED*).

As for the accusation that *off-putting* is clumsy, only you can say if you find the word off-turning.

often: is it *t*-time again?   *Often* was pronounced with a *t*-sound—"OFF-tun"— until that pronunciation was drowned out by "OFF-un" in the 17th century.

But *often*'s *t*-time has returned. According to *The Random House Dictionary*, so many "educated speakers" now use the *t*-sound that "OFF-tun" has become as "fully standard" as "OFF-un." That source warns, however, that "OFF-tun" is "still sometimes criticized."

oily behavior   The adjective *oily* ("smeared with oil") is often used to describe the slick and smooth behavior of a fawningly flattering bootlicker.

The derogatory *oily*'s synonyms include *smarmy*, which is derived from *smarm*, an old-fashioned oily hair pomade; *oleaginous* ("oh-lee-AJ-uh-nis"), which is derived from a Latin word for olive oil; and *unctuous* ("UNK-chew-us"), which compares the bootlicker's behavior to the application of an *unguent* ("UNG-gwent"), "an ointment or salve for soothing or healing, especially a perfumed oil."

The noun *unction* ("UNK-shun")—which usually means "a religious or other ritualistic anointing with oil"—has the lesser-known meaning of "an insincere, oily display of religious or other earnestness."

OK, O.K., or *okay*?   All three of those forms of this globally adopted American colloquialism are firmly established in published writing, according to *Merriam-Webster's Dictionary of English Usage*. And Roy H. Copperud, in his *American Usage and Style*, saw "no basis for considering [even *okeh*] wrong." But if you are writing for an organization or publication, you should check to see which spelling is acceptable.

Okay is a "don't" in the stylebook of the Associated Press (which prescribes *OK, OK'd, OK'ing, OKs*), the *Los Angeles Times* (which prescribes *OK, OKd,*

OKing, OKs), and *The New York Times* (which prescribes *O.K., O.K.'d, O.K.'s*). In dictionaries, *okay* is generally assigned second or third place in order of preference, or it is isolated in its own entry as a spelling variant. *O.K.* and *OK* alternate for first place in dictionaries and usage books.

The *O.K.* and *OK* spellings are consistent with what many word historians describe as the probable origin of the expression in the abbreviation of *oll korrect*, a jocular phonetic spelling of *all correct. O.K.* was explicitly used as an abbreviation for *all correct* in the first known publication of the expression: an informal social note written by editor C. G. Greene of the *Boston Morning Post* for the edition of March 23, 1839. The following year, *O.K.* became nationally known as the rallying cry of the Democrats' "O.K. Club," which supported the unsuccessful reelection campaign of President Martin "Old Kinderhook" Van Buren, a native of Kinderhook, New York.

old-fashion, old-fashioned, or Old-Fashioned? Though the adjective *old-fashion* appears on many store signs—as in "old-fashion friendly service"—the only correct form is *old-fashioned.*

The uppercase noun *Old-Fashioned* refers to an iced cocktail containing whiskey, bitters, sweetening, water, and pieces of fruit.

Olympian, Olympians, Olympus, Olympics The Greek gods headed by Zeus were called *Olympians,* because they were believed to live atop Mount Olympus, Greece's tallest mountain. The adjective *Olympian* means "relating to the Olympian gods, majestic, superior to all others," as in "Olympian efforts."

A center for the worship of Zeus, Olympia, became the site of the original Olympics—contests of running, long-jumping, boxing, wrestling, chariot racing, and so on, in honor of Zeus. Beginning at least as early as 776 B.C., the ancient Olympic games were held every fourth summer until A.D. 393, when a Christian emperor of the Greece-occupying Roman Empire, Theodosius I, abolished the games as relics of paganism. The modern Olympics began in Athens in 1896.

Greek women, forbidden to participate in or even watch the ancient Olympics, began holding Olympic-style games of their own as early as the sixth century B.C. Women were banned from competition in the modern Olympics until 1912.

omens are not always ominous The noun *omen* refers to something that foreshadows an event that may be good or sinister. But the adjective *ominous* means "serving as an omen of an event of sinister consequences, as in an ominous silence." (See also "*portentous* can be perilous.")

on, onto, or on to?   *On* can be a preposition indicating, say, position: "The squirrel is *on* the roof." It can also be part of a phrasal verb—that is, a two-word verb consisting of the verb itself and an adverbial particle such as *on* or *in* that changes the verb's meaning: "The father *moved on* [meaning *continued*] to the airport gate while his son *held on* [meaning *gripped*] to his hand." When the adverbial particle *on* is followed by the preposition *to*, as in the preceding sentence, the words are separate. Write "moved *on to*" and "held *on to*," not "moved *onto*" and "held *onto*."

Use the single word *onto* as a preposition of motion, meaning "to a position on," as in, "The cat jumped *onto* the bed." *Onto* is also the correct form for the informal preposition meaning "fully aware," as in "I'm onto your tricks."

Ambiguity alert: Don't replace the preposition *onto* with the preposition *on*, though dictionaries list those two words as synonyms. If you say "The cat jumped *on* the bed," that could mean the cat jumped *onto* the bed from some other place or jumped while already at that location, using the bed as a trampoline. (See "*in, into*, or *in to?*")

on or about?   See "*about* or *on?*"

on or upon?   When you have a clear choice between the prepositions *on* and *upon*, choose *on* in order to avoid the needless formality of *upon*. Thus, you can depend *on* (without reaching for *upon*) this advice. Likewise, it would be preferable for you to agree, base, insist, lean, rest, sit, and sleep *on*.

Save *upon* for introducing an event, as in "Once upon a time," "Upon arrival," "Upon receipt," "Upon request," "Winter is almost upon us," and "She suddenly came upon a family of turkeys."

one another   See "*each other* or *one another?*" and "*each other's* or *each others'?*"

one fell swoop is a cruel blow   You risk being accused of ignorance if you use *one fell swoop* in its common meaning of "all at once," as in "The children ate the box of doughnuts in one fell swoop."

Your risk-free alternative is to use *one fell swoop* in its original meaning of "an all-at-once cruel blow." Example from the *Los Angeles Times* (4/25/2002): "With a quarterly loss expected to exceed $50 billion, in one fell swoop the world's largest media company [AOL Time Warner Inc.] will lose more . . . than any company in U.S. corporate history."

The adjective *fell,* a literary word that survives today mostly in dictionaries or concealed in the word *felon,* means "fierce, cruel, savage, dreadful, destructive, deadly." Using that sense of *fell* in 1605, Shakespeare had Macduff compare the killing of his wife and children by Macbeth to a hawk attacking defenseless little birds "at one fell swoop."

one of those plural problems   Don't be misled by the *one* in a clause about *one of* a *plural* number of people or things. The clause as a whole should usually be considered plural. For example, a writer in *The New Yorker* (8/30/2004) observed that "Top Thrill Dragster is one of a new generation of roller coasters that generate their own publicity by setting world records." The plural verb *generate* is correct because its subject is the plural *roller coasters*, not the singular *one*; the sentence places the Top Thrill Dragster in a group of roller coasters that *all* generate their own publicity.

Another example: The "*octopi* or *octopuses?*" entry in this book begins with the question "Are you one of those people who carefully avoid referring to more than one member . . . ?" The suggestion here is that there are many people in this category—people who avoid referring to the plural form of *octopus*—and the sentence asks you whether you are one of them. The verb *avoid* has the plural subject *people*, not the singular subject *one*.

But here is another example, one that seems at first to be an exception to this pattern. It is correct to say "Jerry is the only one of the men I know who *loves* to cook." The reason for the singular verb *loves* becomes clear when the sentence is turned around: "Of the men I know, Jerry is the only one who loves to cook." In this case, Jerry is not being included in a *category*; he is not a member of a group of men who *love* to cook. Rather, he is being singled out; he is the one man I know who *loves* to cook.

Recommendation: Carefully consider what you mean when you say "one of the . . . " If you mean to include someone or something in a category of people or things sharing a characteristic, a plural verb is correct. If you mean to emphasize uniqueness (as signaled by *only one*), a singular verb is correct.

one or more add up   Should you say "one or more *is*" or "one or more *are*"? How about *one or two?* Should that phrase be followed by *is* or *are?*

Both phrases are regarded by usage commentators as plural. So there you are.

one too many   One way to remove clutter from your writing is to look for needless use of the word *one.* For example, the statement "She made my life a happy one" would be shorter and stronger if reduced to "She made my life happy." Notice that the removal of the word *one* resulted in the more appropriate emphasis on the word *happy.*

onerous or **onus?**   The noun *onus* means "burden" or "burden of responsibility," as in a *New York Times* headline (1/3/2001), "I.R.A. Asserts Onus Is Blair's in Peace Effort," for an article about an Irish Republican Army demand that British Prime Minister Tony Blair take responsibility for initiating the next steps toward disarmament in Northern Ireland.

The adjective *onerous* means "burdensome," as in a *Salt Lake Tribune* article (3/14/2000) observing that "it can become onerous to be asked to donate something every other week."

oneself or **one's self?**   *Oneself* is preferred over *one's self.*

Use *oneself* as a reflexive pronoun ("forgive oneself"), for emphasis *after* the pronoun *one* ("one must look out for oneself"), for emphasis *instead* of the pronoun *one* ("Oneself is all you need consider"), and as a way of referring to one's real or normal state ("being oneself again"). (See also "pronouns that are *self-conscious.*")

online, on-line, or **on line?**   The adjective and adverb for being connected to the Internet via a computer can be written *online* or *on-line.*

The hyphenated form, *on-line,* is preferred by the *Random House Webster's College Dictionary* and is the only form listed by *Merriam-Webster's Collegiate Dictionary* and *Webster's New World College Dictionary.* The fused form, *online,* is preferred by Microsoft's *Encarta World English Dictionary* and is the only form listed by *The New York Times Manual of Style and Usage.*

To cite quotes from one edition of *The New York Times* (12/28/2000), you can obtain "online assistance," "go online," and "teach online."

Regarding the two-word phrase *on line, The New York Times* manual says:

"Few besides New Yorkers stand or wait *on line*. In most of the English-speaking world, people stand *in line*."

only the adverb causes trouble   The word *only* causes no usage problem as an adjective meaning *sole*, as in "an only child." But as an adverb often meaning *nothing else*, the word *only* is "perhaps the most misplaced word in English," according to an essay in *The New York Times Magazine* (12/31/2000) by William G. Connolly, a *Times* senior editor and co-author of that newspaper's manual of style and usage.

You must be careful to place the adverbial *only* immediately before the word or phrase you intend to modify. Otherwise, you may communicate a message quite different from what you had in mind.

Consider this sentence: "She said she would donate royalties from her co-authored book about birds *only to the National Wildlife Federation*." Clearly, the meaning of the sentence is that she would donate her royalties only to that organization. But watch the meaning change each time the word *only* changes position:

"She said she would donate *only royalties* from her co-authored book about birds to the National Wildlife Federation." (She would donate nothing but royalties.)

"She said she would donate royalties *only from her co-authored book about birds* to the National Wildlife Federation." (She would donate royalties from no other book.)

"She said she would donate royalties from her *only co-authored book about birds* to the National Wildlife Federation." (She co-authored no other book about birds.)

"She said *only she* would donate royalties from her co-authored book about birds to the National Wildlife Federation." (Her co-author would not donate royalties to the organization.)

"*Only she* said she would donate *royalties* from her co-authored book about birds to the National Wildlife Federation." (Nobody else said it.)

"She *only said* she would donate *royalties* from her co-authored book about birds to the National Wildlife Federation." (She might not actually make the donation.)

(See also "syntax sensitivity.")

***onomatopoeia* has a very sound effect** Communication effectiveness is sometimes enhanced by *onomatopoeia* ("on-ah-maht-ah-PEE-ah"), the use of words (like *crash, mash, smash,* and *sizzle*) whose sound suggests their sense.

***opine* when you have an opinion about an opinion** Dictionaries will tell you that *opine* means "to hold or express an opinion." But that is not enough to guide you in using *opine* intelligently.

A better understanding of *opine* can be found in usage guides. For example, *Merriam-Webster's Dictionary of English Usage* says that *opine,* a 15th-century English coinage that was derived from a Latin word for "believe," is now considered so stilted that many professional writers use it only when they wish to be playful, skeptical, or sarcastic. Echoing that view, Paul W. Lovinger's *Penguin Dictionary of American Usage and Style* says that "*opine* now usually serves journalistic writers seeking to be mildly funny or facetious."

Here's a facetious use of *opine,* from the London *Economist* (2/19/2000): "'Money can't buy friends, but you can get a better class of enemy,' Spike Mulligan, a British comedian, once opined."

***optimal* or *optimum*?** *Optimal* is an adjective meaning "best, most favorable," as in "optimal surfing conditions."

You're allowed to replace *optimal* with *optimum.* But you'll contribute to clarity if you restrict *optimum* to its alternate role as a noun, meaning "best degree, condition, result, or amount," as in "a union negotiator who refuses to settle for anything but the optimum."

For the plural of *optimum,* dictionaries prefer the Latin *optima* over the anglicized *optimums.*

***or* confusion** The conjunction *or* is a clear way to link alternatives in a phrase such as "coffee or tea." But you risk confusion if you use *or* to introduce a synonym for something you just said.

Dictionaries and style manuals support using *or* in this way, as long as you set off the synonymous term with commas. For example, the *Random House Webster's Unabridged Dictionary* gives the phrase "the Hawaiian, or Sandwich, Islands" as an illustration of the use of *or* for a synonym. Likewise, Paul W, Lovinger's *Penguin Dictionary of American English Usage and Style* gives "rock dove, or pigeon" as an example. But people who don't already know that the

Hawaiian Islands used to be called the Sandwich Islands or that *rock dove* is another word for *pigeon* may be baffled if you write, "People came to the Hawaiian, or Sandwich, Islands from many different countries" or "I gave the rest of my lunch to rock doves, or pigeons, at the park."

Recommendation: Don't use a synonym if it's not needed. If it is needed, replace *or* with words that make your meaning unmistakable: "the Hawaiian Islands, *once known as* the Sandwich Islands."

oral or **verbal?**   Writers have been using *verbal* as a synonym for *oral* ("spoken rather than written") for more than four hundred years. Moreover, the synonymous relationship of those two adjectives has been acknowledged by Samuel Johnson's *Dictionary of the English Language* (1755), Noah Webster's *American Dictionary of the English Language* (1828), and the leading dictionaries of our time.

But wordwatchers for the past century or so have been warning that the use of *verbal* to mean *oral* can sometimes be confusing. That is because *verbal* also has the broader meaning of "relating to or associated with words." To quote a usage note in *The American Heritage Dictionary of the English Language*: "Thus the phrase *modern technologies for verbal communication* may refer only to devices such as radio, the telephone, and the loudspeaker, or it may refer to devices such as the telegraph, the teletype, and the fax machine."

Risk-free recommendation: Think of *oral* in terms of *oral hygiene* (your mouth), and you will remember to use *oral* only to refer to words that are spoken, as in an *oral* as opposed to a *written* exam. Think of *verbal* in terms of *verbs* and other words, to help you remember that you can use *verbal* to refer to words, whether spoken or written. And you can use *verbal* to mean "pertaining *only* to words, as opposed to action or reality," as in "support that's just verbal" and "legal distinctions that are purely verbal."

ordinance or **ordnance?**   An *ordinance* is a law, usually local. The word *ordnance* refers to military supplies, including weapons and ammunition.

orient or **orientate?**   Writer-lecturer Phyllis Martin's *Word Watcher's Handbook* declares that the verb *orientate* is "not a word." But *orientate* is a standard word in British English and is quite real in the United States, though its use is regarded by American usage-guide authors Morton S. Freeman and Patricia O'Conner as needlessly long and pretentious.

The verb *orient* (from the French *orienter*, meaning "to place facing the east") was adopted by the English in the 18th century, followed by the longer form in the 19th century. *Orient* and *orientate* developed the extended meanings of "to locate east and thus place oneself in a particular relation to the points of the compass," "to determine one's bearings," and "to adjust to one's circumstances or situation."

Risk-free recommendation: Stay with *orient* in the United States. But feel free to *orient* or *orientate* yourself in England, where linguist R. W. Burchfield has assured readers of his *New Fowler's Modern English Usage* that "one can have no fundamental quarrel with anyone who decides to use the longer of the two words." (See also "verbs pretentiously ending in -*ate*.")

ought and should are not always good   Avoid *ought* and *should* when your audience has no way of knowing whether those words express obligation or expectation.

Consider this: "She ought to [should] be given a raise next week." Depending on the intended meaning, that sentence needs a clarifying substitute for *ought/should*: "She *deserves* to be given a raise next week," or "She will *probably* be given a raise next week."

over and over   Of the 61 ways the *Random House Webster's Unabridged Dictionary* says people use *over*, the most commonly accepted is to use it in place of *above*. And the riskiest is to use it in place of *more than*.

Over has apparently attracted no objection from usage commentators when used in the sense of *above* in such phrases as "the shelf over the fireplace," "the people over him at work," and "a scientific book that's over the head of the average reader."

But as noted by Merriam-Webster researchers, the centuries-old use of *over* in a phrase such as "over [more than] 10,000 spectators" became a victim of unexplained and unjustified criticism by some American usage commentators of the late 19th and early 20th century. And today, according to *Webster's New World Guide to Current American Usage*, the "more than" *over* makes many Americans "uneasy" because their schoolteachers taught them that *over* "should be limited to showing location, as in 'The moon came over the mountain.'"

Indeed, the "more than" *over* has been rejected by the majority of the people consulted for the *Harper Dictionary of Contemporary Usage.*

Some of our nation's usage commentators have also denounced *over* in the sense of *about* ("cry over spilt milk"), in the sense of *on* ("struck over the head"), and in the sense of *across* ("walk over the bridge"). The late *New York Times* language critic Theodore M. Bernstein warned in his *Careful Writer* that *over* makes no sense if it is used to express a comparative *reduction*, as in "Highway deaths are *down* 11 percent in the state *over* the same period a year ago." In that sentence, Bernstein said, *over* should have been replaced by *compared with.*

over- compounds   No space or hyphen is needed in the approximately four hundred compounds prefixed by *over,* from *overabundant* to *overzealous.*

But don't forget the hyphen when *over* is used as a separate word in a compound modifier, as in "over-the-counter pain relievers."

overexaggerated is too stressful   The prefix *over* in this compound is redundant. *Exaggerated* says it all.

oversight: careless or careful?   Here's another word whose meaning you'll have to make clear in your context. If you're referring to a government regulatory agency's *oversight,* for example, the word could mean "an act of careless omission" or "an act of careful supervision."

owing to the fact that   Replace this space-wasting phrase with *because,* unless somebody is paying you by the word.

oxymorons can be sharp or foolish   The word *oxymoron* (combining Greek words for *sharp* and *foolish*) refers to a figure of speech consisting of contradictory elements. Examples: "cruel kindness," "thunderous silence," and what 19th-century English poet John Keats called the poet's "diligent indolence," a state of suspended activity that invites creative thought.

Many of us use oxymorons, such as "Make haste slowly," in everyday speech. But be aware that you risk ridicule if you compose an oxymoron unintentionally, as in a *Boston Globe* headline reprinted for the snickering enjoyment of *New Republic* readers (11/19/1990): "Law Students Start Drive for Mandatory Volunteerism."

P

pachyderm: a pack of meanings   *Pachyderm* is not a synonym for *elephant,* contrary to the impression given by many newspaper stories about this powerful vegetarian. *Pachyderm* is from a Greek word for "thick-skinned," and it refers equally to the elephant, rhinoceros, hippopotamus, tapir, and pig.

padding is not pretty   Padding—stating the obvious, engaging in needless repetition, or citing information that has nothing to do with your topic—is a common strategy for student writers when they discover that they do not have enough relevant material to write about. In professional writing, padding is a serious offense because it wastes space and time.

pair is or pair are?   Say "pair *is*" when that word refers to one entity, and say "pair *are*" when the word refers to two entities. For example, you're thinking of one item when you shop for a pair of shoes. Hence, you're correct if you say "That pair of shoes is [not *are*] just what I was looking for." But you're thinking of two entities when you discuss a pair of jaywalkers.

Grammarians accept both *pair* and *pairs* after a number greater than one ("two pair" or "two pairs"). But if you want to *sound* right as well as *be* right, say *pairs.* That's the most commonly used form for more than one pair, according to *The American Heritage Dictionary* and the *Random House Webster's Unabridged Dictionary.* The "more than one" *pairs* is so common that it's listed as the only correct choice by the *Microsoft Encarta College Dictionary.*

palate, palette, pallet, or pallette?   These nouns—all pronounced "PAL-it"—convey a wide variety of meanings.

The *-ate* in *palate* should help you remember that *palate* means "the roof of the mouth" or "the sense of taste."

The *-ette* in *palette,* like the *–ette* in *kitchenette,* should help you remember the "small" in its definition: "a small board on which an artist mixes pigments for paintings."

Pallet, a spelling variant of *palette*, is also the spelling of three other words. One *pallet* means "a wooden potter's tool with a flat blade," "a tool for stamping letters on the binding of a book," or "a portable platform on which materials are stacked for storage or transportation." Another *pallet* is "a small sleeping pad that is placed directly on the floor." A third *pallet* is "one form of vertical stripe in a coat of arms."

Pallette, which you'll probably never use unless you play Scrabble, means "the part of a suit of armor that protects the armpit."

palindrome is not a sports arena   But it is a form of recreation, and it has been for centuries.

According to *The New York Public Library Desk Reference*, people have been creating *palindromes*—words, phrases, and sentences that read the same forward and backward—since at least as early as the third century B.C. That was the time of the Greek poet, Sotades, who was credited with being the first person to pen a palindrome (from the Greek word *palindromos*, meaning "running back again, recurring").

The back-and-forth palindrome concept today applies not just to sequences of letters, as in *pip*, *pup*, *peep*, and *pop*, but also to sequences of numbers (such as those of the palindromic years 1991 and 2002), to reversed sequences of the basic constituents (nucleotides) in complementary strands of DNA, and to reversed sequences of music in which, for example, a prelude is played more or less backward in a postlude.

But palindromes are mostly about play, with palindrome pals trading palindromes the way stamp collectors trade stamps. For example, if you tell a palindrome collector that you have a "mirror rim," you might be given a "rio memoir."

Palindrome collectors imagine that the first romantic pickup line was "Madam, I'm Adam" and that Napoleon might have said "Able was I ere I saw Elba." They imagine greedy lawyers in ancient Greece urging clients to "Sue Zeus." And they cynically cite a palindromic Latin boast by a dream-team lawyer in ancient Rome, "Si nummi immunis" ("Pay my fee and you go scot-free").

Memorable palindromic sentences may suggest poignant scenes, as when we're told that "poor Dan is in a droop." We're not told why, but perhaps it is because Dan's favorite supermarket has a sign announcing "No lemons, no melon," or because his favorite Chinese restaurant has a sign that says

"Wonton? Not now," or because he is having so much trouble staying on his diet that his doctor told him he's "dessert stressed."

In palindrome legend, a physician is told by a strong-willed patient: "Doc, note, I dissent. A fast never prevents a fatness. I diet on cod." Though no record exists of the physician's response, we can guess that the physician jokingly tells the patient to "sit on a potato pan, Otis." Whereupon the doctor's medical assistant, having overheard the conversation, comments on the situation with a palindromic sentence in which the reversal is based on words rather than letters: "So patient a doctor to doctor a patient so."

Palindrome addicts get their fixes from books with palindromic titles such as Craig Hansen's *Ana, Nab a Banana*, in which a "taco cat" pursues "sleek eels." In Jon Agee's *So Many Dynamos* and *Go Hang a Salami! I'm a Lasagna Hog,* you'll find: "No, Sir! Away! A papaya war is on," "Flo, gin is a sin! I golf!" and "Mr. Owl ate my metal worm." Michael Donner's palindrome encyclopedia, *I Love Me, Vol. I,* responds to the famous palindrome "A man, a plan, a canal—Panama!" with "No, it's a banana bastion."

Another form of wordplay reversal, *chiasmus* ("key-AZ-mus"), involves the reversal of the order of words in two parallel phrases. For example, a recent book about chiasmus is fittingly entitled *Never Let a Fool Kiss You or a Kiss Fool You.* (See also "*anagrams* and *antigrams.*")

palpable: a touching word   *Palpable* literally means "capable of being touched or felt." But it is widely used in its figurative sense of "so vividly perceived as to be *almost* felt."

Usage example from a "Writers on Writing" series in *The New York Times* (1/1/2001): Novelist Rosellen Brown recalled that her goal in her first novel was to present "in a palpable way the feel of a particular set of lives in a particular time and place."

pantheon, Pantheon, or Panthéon?   The word *pantheon* ("all those most highly regarded in a particular field") comes from the uppercase *Pantheon* (literally meaning "of all gods" and actually referring to "the temple in Rome dedicated to all the gods").

Usage example: *The New Yorker* (1/10/2005), reflecting on the scandal-driven withdrawal of former New York Police Commissioner Bernard B. Kerik as President George W. Bush's choice for Secretary of Homeland Security, observed that Kerik "enters the pantheon of celebrated New Yorkers who have been dramatically undone by their own high-handedness or low dealings."

The form with the French accent, *Panthéon* ("pan-tay-ONH"), stands for a national monument in Paris containing the remains of honored men of France—and one of its honored women, Marie Sklodowska Curie, the Warsaw-born chemist who became a Nobel laureate for her research on radioactivity and her discovery of radium and polonium.

papier-mâché: don't paper over this spelling   Note that *papier-mâché* ("paper mah-SHAY")—a French-derived term for material of glued paper pulp that can be molded when wet into various shapes—uses the English pronunciation but not the English spelling for the first word in the hyphenated compound.

paradigm is a shifty word   In the syndicated cartoon *Non Sequitur* (10/7/1999) by Wiley Miller, a beggar in a business suit sits on the sidewalk alongside a sign in which he explains, "Couldn't interface with a new paradigm, whatever the hell THAT means."

Paradigm ("PARA-dime") is an academic and corporate buzzword that has been stretched in so many different ways—to convey the ideas expressed by the words *pattern, paragon, model, system, example*, and *prevailing view*, among others—that it now tends to be more buzz than word.

A 15th-century English derivative of the Greek word for "pattern" (*paradeigma*), the word *paradigm* has long been used as a term in grammar for a list serving as a pattern of the way words can change to reflect a change in number, tense, or the like. (For example: *is/are* and *walk/walked*.)

Paradigm became a buzzword as a result of a 1962 book by physicist and historian of science Thomas Kuhn, *The Structure of Scientific Revolutions*, which sold more than one million copies and was translated into more than a dozen languages. Kuhn defined the concept of a scientific revolution as a *paradigm shift*, by which he meant a shift in a set of basic assumptions. But in the 1973 edition of *Structure*, Kuhn admitted that in his first edition he had used *paradigm* in 22 different ways. No wonder that, as a *New York Times* review (5/28/2000) of a book about Kuhn's book recalled, "most philosophers and historians soon came to the conclusion that Kuhn's signature concept of the paradigm was frustratingly vague."

Nevertheless, as noted by science writer James Gleick in *The New York Times* (12/29/1996), "practitioners of just about every branch of science now claim paradigm shifts almost yearly." And in 1998, the widespread use of the term was mocked in a cartoon in *The Chronicle of Higher Education*, showing a greeting-card display for "birthday," "anniversary," and "major paradigm shift."

But some writers still take "paradigm shifts" seriously and continue to use the word *paradigm* when they mean "model" or "pattern." For example, a *Wall Street Journal* writer (1/16/2004) observed that the efforts of presidential primary candidate Howard Dean to enlist the support of millions of new voters "could change [presumably meaning *shift*] the paradigm for presidential campaigns." The writer of a *New York Times Magazine* subhead (1/30/2005) characterized American military aid to Indonesian tsunami victims as a new "foreign policy paradigm." And *New York Times* columnist David Brooks (2/26/2005) expressed the hope for democratizing "paradigm shifts" in Eastern Europe and the Middle East.

Risk-free suggestion: Forget *paradigm*. Let those who use it shift for themselves.

***paradox* needs your protection**   *Paradox* is a valuable word when used in its precise sense as "a statement or situation that seems self-contradictory until it is explained." Unfortunately, it is often used as a needless synonym for an actual contradiction. And dictionaries now reinforce that abusage by recording both meanings.

Usage advice: Only the "*seems* self-contradictory" definition is used by precise writers, including those who abide by *The New York Times Manual of Style and Usage*. Such careful communicators would consider it redundant to say "*apparent* paradox," a phrase used twice by a professor of anthropology in an article in *The Chronicle of Higher Education* (5/12/2000). Commonly used phrases such as "apparent paradox" and "seeming paradox" are nonsensical in the sense that they mean "a seemingly seeming contradiction."

Here's an example of risk-free usage: Scottish psychiatrist R. D. Laing (1927–1989) "made his name [as an author] with the paradox that madness was the sane response to an insane world," according to Jacques Barzun's history of Western culture, *From Dawn to Decadence*.

paragraphing: a question of moderation   As William H. Roberts notes in his *Writer's Companion*, "The two most common errors in paragraph division are not paragraphing enough and paragraphing too much."

When should you begin a new paragraph? You should do it when you are starting a new thought, when you are switching from direct to indirect quotation or vice versa, or when you discover that your paragraph is longer than you want it to be from a visual standpoint. That visual problem is a special challenge, of course, for publications with narrow columns.

Note that you can make a paragraph out of one sentence—even a sentence as short as one word—when it's appropriate and when you don't do it often.

parallel problems   The failure to maintain parallelism (a consistent, coordinated pattern) is the cause of many awkward sentences.

One type of faulty parallelism results from an awkward pairing of a noun with an adjective: "The girl was *an accomplished athlete* and *smart*." A smoothly parallel sentence would pair a noun with another noun ("The girl was *an accomplished athlete* and *an excellent student*") or an adjective with another adjective ("The girl was *athletic* and *smart*").

Another type of faulty parallelism results from a mismatch of a noun with a verb: "He likes *bird watching* and *to go hiking*." An appropriately parallel sentence would be "He likes *bird watching* and *hiking*." (See also "conjunctions used in pairs," "*either . . . or* and *neither . . . nor*: singular or plural?" and "*not only . . . but also*.")

parentheses   See "brackets and parentheses."

Parkinson's Law   See "*Murphy's Law, Parkinson's Law*, and the *Peter Principle*."

parlay or *parley*?   The verb and noun *parlay* ("PAR-lay") refers to a bet using a previous wager and its winnings. By extension, *parlay* refers to the exploitation of any asset to great advantage, as in "The candidate parlayed family connections into a political career."

The verb and noun *parley* ("PAR-lee") refers to a discussion about a specific matter, especially to settle a dispute with an enemy.

parlous or *perilous*?   Use *perilous* ("dangerous") for something specific, as in "a perilous occupation." Use *parlous* (an old contraction of *perilous*) for something general, such as a "parlous era in the Middle East."

***parochial* is neutral and negative**   The neutral meaning of *parochial* is "relating to a parish, originally an English county subdivision small enough to be served by a single church." In that sense, a "parochial school" is the school of the local parish church.

Because a parish is a relatively small area, *parochial* acquired an additional, negative meaning of "very limited in scope or outlook." Usage example: In a posthumous tribute to art historian Francis Haskell (1928–2000), *The New York Review of Books* (2/24/2000) credited him with making art history "richer and less parochial."

***partial* requires your full attention**   "A *partial* investigation" can mean one that is *incomplete* or one that is *biased*. If your context doesn't clearly show your intended meaning, use another word.

A glaring example of the word *partial*'s ambiguity occurred in a headline in *The State News* of Lansing, Mich. (1/28/1992): "Partial Jury Chosen for Tyson Trial."

participles play three parts   Participles—verb-based words with the endings *-ing*, *-ed*, *-d*, *-t*, *-en*, or *-n.* as in *baking* and *baked*—can serve as more than verbs. They are indeed participial verbs in phrases such as "have been baking" and "having baked." But they are participial adjectives in the phrases "baking soda" and "baked beans."

In the terminology of some grammarians, the *-ing* form can also be a participial noun, known alternatively as a verbal noun or most commonly as a gerund. In "Baking is often preferable to frying," both *baking* and *frying* are participial nouns, verbal nouns, or gerunds.

participles that dangle   Verb forms commonly ending in *-ing* or *-ed*—as in the present participle *talking* and the past participle *talked*—become grammar-violating dangling participles when they are so carelessly connected to a sentence that they seem to refer to the wrong subject.

Here's an example of a dangling participial phrase often cited by writing instructors: "*Having looked shabby* for years, Arthur remodeled the house." As a result of that dangler, poor Arthur (rather than the house) is wrongly described as looking shabby. To undangle a participle, make sure the participial phrase is directly followed by its subject: "Having looked shabby for years, *the house* was remodeled by Arthur."

Often, dangling participles occur when the writer follows the participle or participial phrase with something *possessed by* the subject of the participle. Copy editors often cite this sentence as an example: "Walking down the street, his pencil fell out of his pocket." The problem, of course, is that he, not his pencil, was walking down the street. You can fix the sentence either by placing *he* after the participial phrase ("Walking down the street, *he* lost the pencil that had been in his pocket") or by adding the subject *he* to the first part of the sentence ("*As he walked* down the street, his pencil fell out of his pocket").

Other dangling participles refer to the wrong subject in a sentence in which the correct subject is not even directly mentioned. Here's a typical example from the *Irvine* (Calif.) *World News* (2/1/2004): "Heading deeper into the canyon, the sycamores and oak trees begin to close in." That sentence irrationally has the *trees* "heading deeper into the canyon." To cure such a sentence of its dangling participle, you need to cite the subject and make sure it adjoins the participial phrase: "Heading deeper into the canyon, *one* discovers that the sycamores and oak trees begin to close in." Alternatively, you can rewrite the participial phrase to include a subject: "*As we head* deeper into the canyon, the sycamores and oak trees begin to close in."

Participles also may dangle later in the sentence. "We must design new automobile engines using every available resource" absurdly suggests that we develop new car engines that will menace the entire planet by using every available resource. To fix the problem, connect the participle with its subject: "Using every available resource, *we* must design new automobile engines." (See also "*based on* confusion.")

participles: the confusion of fusion   Suppose a woman is upset because her husband habitually leaves dirty dishes in the sink. Should she say to her erring spouse, "I hate you"? Of course not. And neither should she say, "*I hate you* leaving dirty dishes in the sink." For one thing, her husband might storm out of the house after her first three words. For another, it's ungrammatical. To state clearly and grammatically that she hates her husband's *behavior*, not her husband, she should say, "I hate *your* leaving dirty dishes in the sink."

In that example, *leaving* is a gerund—the *-ing* present participle of the verb *leave*, used as a noun. When a noun or a pronoun precedes the gerund, the possessive form of that noun or pronoun (*Tom's, the dog's, my, your*) should be used.

Note, for example, the possessive case before the gerund *being* in *Newsweek* columnist's Jonathan Alter's observation (2/24/2003) that "oddsmakers reassure us that the chances of any one person's being victimized by terrorism are small."

This rule applies even to inanimate objects, as in the possessive-case *book's* in an article that biographer Marion Meade wrote for *Brill's Content* magazine (March 2000): "As biographers know, there is mighty little likelihood these days of a book's being optioned [by television and film companies]."

The *failure* to use the possessive case for a noun or pronoun before a gerund is called a *fused participle*. That awkward term for this grammatical offense was "invented" by early 20th-century usagist Henry W. Fowler "for the purpose of labeling & so making recognizable & avoidable a usage considered by the inventor to be rapidly corrupting modern English style." Today's usagists tend to be more tolerant of the fused participle, but they acknowledge that it is worth your attention.

In *defense* of the fused participle, *The American Heritage Book of English Usage* notes that it "has been used by respected writers for 300 years and is perfectly idiomatic. Moreover, there is often no way to 'fix' the construction by inserting the possessive." That source points out, for example, that you cannot say, "We have had very few instances of *luggage's* being lost." Likewise, you cannot say, "What she objects to is *men's* making more money." But such problems are easily solved if you simply rewrite the sentence: "We have had very few instances in which luggage was lost." "What she objects to is the fact that men make more money."

Here's risk-free advice: Avoid fused participles by switching to the possessive case or by rewriting your sentence. Fuse your participle only if you want to emphasize the identity of the noun or pronoun: "Was it *you* making all that noise?"

particular people   Whenever you use the word *particular* in referring to a person, make sure your context clearly indicates whether you mean "specific" or "choosy."

If you are not particularly careful with *particular*, you could end up with some hopelessly ambiguous sentences, such as the following one in a feature story submitted to me by one of my journalism students: "She told the receptionist at the campus housing office that she wanted to share an apartment with a particular student."

parting shot or **Parthian shot?**   Both of these phrases mean "a hostile remark or gesture made upon leaving."

Parthian shot, recalling the ancient country of Parthia that corresponds to today's northeastern Iran, is identified by Fowler's *Dictionary of Modern English Usage* (1965 edition) as the "parent phrase." The phrase recalls what Fowler described as "the tactics of the Parthian mounted archers, who would discharge a volley into the enemy while moving smartly out of range of retaliation."

passed or **past?**   *Passed* is the past tense and past participle of the verb *pass*. The word *past* won't work as a verb but is appropriate as a noun, adjective, adverb, or preposition.

Usage examples: Junior *passed* his exam. A car *passed* ours. Time *passed*. Those statements refer to the *past* (noun), which is why they are in the *past* (adjective) tense. If you have bills that are *past* (adverb) due, mail the payments in the drive-by mailbox when you go *past* (preposition) the post office.

passive voice should not be silenced   Did some well-meaning teacher make you swear never to use the passive voice? If so, you swore off a style of communication that can be as helpful as it is harmful.

The passive voice—the verb form showing a subject receiving rather than engaging in action—is a notorious way of beating around the bush. Note that the *active*-voice airport sign "Watch Your Luggage" delivers its message with fewer words and more impact than would the *passive*-voice sign "Your Luggage Should Be Watched" or the *double-passive*-voice sign "It *Is Required* That Your Luggage Be Watched." The passive voice also encourages evasiveness, as when an advertiser says a product "*is recognized* as the best" (by whom?); a technical writer says a process "has been successfully tested" (by whom?); a writer in a scholarly journal says a theory "has been discredited" (by whom?); or a blundering bureaucrat declares that "mistakes *were made*" rather than "I made a mistake."

But the passive voice is preferable when you want to emphasize the *receiver* of action, as in "Elvis Presley has been found hiding in a Las Vegas retirement home." The passive voice is also preferable when you don't know the agent of action ("More FBI files have been stolen"); when you want to place the agent of action at the end of your statement for the purpose of emphasis ("A local businessman has been kidnapped by his former wife"); when you want to emphasize the action itself ("An overdue library book was returned yesterday in a package dropped by parachute"); or when you choose passive voice for variety amid a series of sentences using the active voice.

Here are examples of appropriate active/passive voice from the front page of *The New York Times* (8/15/2001): In the *active* voice, an *agent of action*, the tobacco industry, was justifiably emphasized in the headline "Tobacco Industry Still Advertises in Magazines Read by the Young." In the *passive* voice, a *receiver of action*, costly emphysema surgery, was justifiably emphasized in the headline "Costly Emphysema Surgery Is Challenged by Researchers."

pâté or *pate*? You need the circumflex over the *a* and the acute accent over the *e* to distinguish *pâté* (a French word, pronounced "pah-TAY," for "meat paste") from *pate* (our Middle English word, rhyming with *date*, for "the top of the head").

pathetic fallacy isn't pitiful The word *pathetic* is commonly used in its dictionary sense of "contemptibly inadequate," as in "a pathetic salary." But a less common dictionary sense of *pathetic*, "pertaining to the arousal of feeling," applies to *pathetic fallacy*. That term was coined as a synonym for *anthropomorphizing* ("falsely ascribing human feelings to natural phenomena") by British art critic John Ruskin in the third volume of his *Modern Painters* (1856). Ruskin invented the term *pathetic fallacy* as a criticism of poets who attributed human emotions to nature, as in "cruel storms," and thereby contributed to "falseness in all our impressions of external things."

patrician or *plebeian*? In ancient Rome, *patricians* were members of the nobility, as opposed to the common-folk *plebeians*. Today, *patrician* means "aristocrat," "upper-class person" or "a person of refined manners and tastes." And *plebeian* means "a member of the lower classes" or "someone who is unrefined, coarse, vulgar." The short form, *plebe*, refers to a lowly first-year student at the U.S. Military Academy or the U.S. Naval Academy.

patronize carefully When you use *patronize*, make sure you clearly show whether you mean "be a customer of" or "treat with condescension."

peaceable or *peaceful*? A *peaceable* ("preferring peace") person may live in an area that's not at all *peaceful* ("characterized by peace"). Those are today's usual meanings of *peaceful* and *peaceable*, though the words have been used interchangeably since the 14th century.

peak-a-boo-boo   *Peak* ("high point") is sometimes carelessly written in place of *peek* (the noun and verb for "glance") and *pique* (a noun meaning "fit of resentment" or a verb meaning "excite, arouse, provoke").

peccable, peccadillo, peccancy, peccant, peccatophobia   These "pecka"-sounding words are derived from the Latin verb *peccare* ("to sin"). They mean, in the order of their appearance, "liable to sin," "minor sin," "sinfulness," "sinful," and "an abnormal fear of sinning."

Impeccable ("not liable to sin") is commonly used as an emphatic synonym for "faultless." *Impeccant* means "free from sin, blameless."

pedal or peddle?   You *pedal* a bike. And in a car, you press your foot against the gas *pedal*. Salespeople *peddle* their wares.

pedantry fools nobody   Pedantic writing is characterized by words that are needlessly long and obscure, often employed in a futile attempt to conceal a lack of original or useful ideas.

Pioneer usage commentator Henry W. Fowler wrote that "the display of superior knowledge is as great a vulgarity as a display of superior wealth." But Fowler acknowledged that the term *pedantry* "is relative: "My pedantry is your scholarship, his reasonable accuracy, her irreducible minimum of education, & someone else's ignorance."

pejorative: a disparaging word   *Pejorative* means "having negative connotations, tending to disparage or belittle." Careful communicators take pains to learn not only which words are *inherently* pejorative but also which words may be pejorative for certain times, places, and audiences. (See also entries for *dame*, *exploit*, *scheme*, and *wonk*.)

Usage example from *The New York Times* (12/24/2001): "Such [unsolicited] e-mail, known by its pejorative appellation, *spam*, has been annoying Internet users for years."

Warning: Resist the temptation to misspell this word as if it began with *per*.

penultimate: less impressive than it looks   Some people, including advertising writers for the Ralph Lauren Purple Label collection, are not satisfied with describing something as the *ultimate* ("last, maximum, highest, farthest, final"). Seeking to go *beyond* ultimate, they reach for *penultimate*—as in Ralph Lauren's "penultimate collection from this master of distinctive style"—not realizing that *penultimate*, which actually means "next to last," represents a step down.

Example of correct usage: *The New York Times* (5/14/2000) noted that beatification, the Roman Catholic Church's proclamation that a deceased person is one of the blessed, "is the penultimate step before sainthood."

people or persons?   Once upon a time, many usage commentators were partial to *persons* for the plural of *person*. Today, you are more likely to encounter *people*, except in legal documents and in references to a small, exact number.

Feel free to trust your ear on this decision. For example, "we the people" obviously sounds better than "we the persons." Likewise, you are not likely to hear people singing about "persons who need persons."

per your instructions   Here are your risk-free instructions for the Latin preposition *per*.

As a *general* rule, avoid phrases that combine the Latin *per* with English words. For example, change *per day* to *a day*. Change *per your instructions* (or *request*) to *according to your instructions* (or *request*). And change *as per* to *in accordance with*.

As Roy H. Copperud noted in his *American Usage and Style*, "The consensus is heavily against *per* where *a* or some other native [English] expression will do." Bryan A. Garner, in his *Modern American Usage*, quotes usage commentators as saying that *per your request* is "business jargon at its worst" and that *as per* is "horrible commercialese." Garner adds that the *as* in *as per* is redundant, inasmuch as that *per* means *in accordance with* all by itself.

Exceptions to the rule: The combining of *per* with an English word is acceptable idiom in *per hour*, *per mile*, *miles per hour*, *per gallon*, and *per person*. As the *Harper Dictionary of Contemporary Usage* states, "In all other instances, *per* should be avoided, with [such words as] *a*, *by*, or *in accordance with* (depending on the context) used instead."

Feel free to use *per* in the following all-Latin phrases that are fully established in English: *per annum* ("by the year, annually"), *per capita* ("for each unit of population, each person"), *per diem* ("reckoned on a daily basis, paid by the day"), and *per se* ("by itself, as such, inherently"). (See also "Latinisms.")

percent or **per cent?**   Both are correct. But *percent* is the more common form, and it is prescribed by the stylebooks of the Associated Press, *The New York Times, The Washington Post, The Wall Street Journal,* and the *Los Angeles Times.*

Per centum (Latin for "by the hundred") became part of the English language in the 16th century. Later, it was abbreviated *per cent.,* with a final period. Then the period wore off. Finally, for many users of the language, the two parts merged.

percent is or **percent are?**   Say *is* if the noun following *percent* is singular: "Ten percent of the proposed tax *increase is* likely to be eliminated." Say *are* if the noun following *percent* is plural: "Ten percent of this year's tax *dollars are* likely to be consumed by inflation."

percent or **percentage points?**   The difference between *percent* and *percentage points* can be enormous. Remember that if, for instance, the poverty rate goes from 10 to 20 percent, that is not an increase of only 10 *percent.* Though the figure rose 10 *percentage points,* the poverty rate doubled—which is an increase of 100 percent. For every person living in poverty the last time a count was made, there is now an additional person.

perfect: **can it get any better?**   The adjective *perfect* ("PER-fect"), like *unique,* is an absolute. Either something is *perfect* ("ideal, flawless, beyond improvement") or it is not. Therefore, you are illogical if you qualify *perfect* with words like *more* or *most.*

When this usage question is discussed, someone is likely to argue that our nation's founders declared in the Preamble to the U.S. Constitution that their purpose was "to form a more perfect union." The answer to that challenge is that our nation's founders were not themselves perfect. If they had been, they would have edited that phrase to read "a more *nearly* perfect union."

If you feel an overwhelming urge to emphasize a state of perfection, try the word *pluperfect*, which literally means "more than perfect" but is actually just a way to express perfection with added emphasis. Usage example: In an article about a shortage of lifeguards, *The New York Times* (6/18/2000) recalled a time when "much of teenage America would have agreed [that] lifeguarding was the pluperfect summer [job]."

In grammar, the *pluperfect tense* (also called the *past perfect tense*) expresses action completed before a specified or implied past time. Example: "Mike saw that his friends *had arrived* before he did."

perfect: the verb   Definitions of the verb *perfect* ("per-FECT") range from "improve" to "bring to a state of supreme excellence."

Be aware that you can't *perfect* something unless it is *perfectible* (often misspelled "perfect*able*," perhaps because that word means "cap*able* of becoming perfect").

perfect strangers really are   Many punning jokes have been made about the expressions *perfect stranger* and *perfect fool*. Actually, those expressions conform to one of the perfectly correct definitions of *perfect*: "absolute."

Perfect can also mean "lacking nothing," "without defect," "excellent in all ways," "thoroughly skilled," or "completely appropriate."

period or semicolon?   See "colon or semicolon?"

periodic ambiguity   *Periodic* is usually understood to mean "at regular or predictable intervals." (This is also the sense of the related noun *periodical*, a publication issued at regular intervals.) You therefore risk ambiguity if you use *periodic* in its other dictionary meaning: "occasional."

periods that do double duty   If a sentence ends with an abbreviation requiring a period, you don't need a second period to complete the sentence. ("The quack pretended to be an M.D.")

perquisite or prerequisite?   *Perquisite*, informally known as a *perk*, is "an extra gain," such as the free use of a company car. A *prerequisite* is "a requirement that must be satisfied in advance."

persona is still a mask   The old Latin meaning of *persona* ("a mask, especially as worn by actors") was extended by Jungian psychology to mean "the public image people present to perform their role in society."

Today *persona* is commonly applied to the public image of celebrities, as in *New York Times* columnist Frank Rich's comment (1/29/1997) that Bill Cosby and his murdered son, Ennis, became "indistinguishable from their public personae as merchandised under the brand name Huxtable in hundreds of hours of TV sitcoms and such adjunct products as the best-selling book *Fatherhood*."

As a separate term in literary criticism, first applied in 1909 by the poet Ezra Pound, *persona* means "the speaker in a literary poem or the narrator in a fictional narrative."

personal friend: too personal?   *Personal* is redundant in that expression, unless you are distinguishing between categories such as *personal* friends and *business* friends. (See also "redundancy: a vice and a virtue.")

personnel is or personnel are?   *Personnel* is singular in the sense of a "collective body," plural in the sense of "employees."

perspective or prospective?   Many of my student writers mistakenly used the noun *perspective* when they meant the adjective *prospective*.

Perspective literally means "the art of picturing a scene in depth on a flat surface" and figuratively means "the ability to see the actual way that things relate to each other." *Prospective* means "potential, likely, expected, future." *Prospective* students might visit a college campus to gain *perspective* on what it is like to be a student there.

perspicacity or perspicuity?   The first means "acuteness of perception or understanding." The second means "that which is clearly expressed or lucid." The corresponding adjectives are *perspicacious* and *perspicuous*.

peruse or read?   Use *peruse* only when you mean "read carefully, thoroughly." If you employ *peruse* as merely a synonym for "read," according to *The Oxford English Dictionary* and *The American Heritage Dictionary*, you'll be guilty of loose use.

perverse or **perverted**?   Take care with this pair. A *perverse* person is "stubborn." A *perverted* person is "corrupt, deviating from what is right or normal."

Peter Principle   See *"Murphy's Law, Parkinson's Law,* and the *Peter Principle."*

Ph.D. should be abbreviated intelligently   You have just seen the way to abbreviate "doctor of philosophy."

phenomena is or **phenomena are**?   Say *are,* because *phenomena* is the plural of *phenomenon* ("a marvel, a rare or significant fact or event").

The plural form *phenomenons* is listed in some dictionaries as an alternate plural, but that variant is unnecessary, unappealing, and, to many usage commentators, unacceptable.

The slang word *phenom* is considered appropriate only in sports journalism.

philistine: a bum rap?   If you call someone a *philistine* in its commonly accepted dictionary sense of "crude, materialistic, uncultured," you could be accused of being the one who is uncultured.

You can try to defend your pejorative use of *philistine* by pointing out that the word is included in Hugh Rawson's *Wicked Words* and that the Bible tells us that the Israelites regarded the Philistine Goliath and all his countrymen from neighboring Philistia as uncultured brutes. But a 30-year study by archaeologists Trude and Moshe Dothan of Hebrew University in Jerusalem (detailed in their 1992 book, *People of the Sea*) shows that the ancient Philistines developed one of the most advanced civilizations of their time. According to the Dothans and other archaeologists, the Philistines achieved excellence in art and architecture and were clever enough to engage in copper smelting more than a thousand years before the Romans did.

True, the Bible assures us that the Philistine Goliath's brawn was no match for the brain of David. But in another Bible story the Philistine Delilah used her brain quite successfully to neutralize the brawn of Samson.

philosophic or **philosophical**?   *Philosophical* is listed in dictionaries as the preferred member of this pair of adjectives meaning "of or related to philosophy" or "rational, calm, and accepting life's defeats in the [supposed] manner of a philosopher." (See also "*geographic* or *geographical*?" "*graphic* or *graphical*?" "*historic* or *historical*?")

philter tip   What sounds like *filter* but isn't? The answer is *philter*, "a love potion." *Philter* is also a verb, meaning "to enchant with or as if with a philter."

phoney or _phony_?   The *phony* spelling of this 1900-vintage Americanism for "fake, counterfeit, false" is currently genuine throughout the United States. The British take theirs with a spot of *e*.

   Phony has several fake etymologies (versions of the word's history), according to Craig M. Carver's *History of English in Its Own Words*. Research (now discredited) traced *phony* to *funny* and even to the practical jokes played by early users of the *phone*. Carver writes: "*Phony* probably originated in the earlier English slang term *fawney* (a gilt brass ring), from the Irish *fainne* (ring). In the 1890's, a *fawney* man was a seller of bogus jewelry."

pidgin is not a bird   The word *pidgin*—meaning a simplified, "auxiliary" language (such as *pidgin English*) that is formed to bridge the communication gap between people who have no common language—is widely believed to have originated (somehow) in a Chinese mispronunciation of the English word *business*.

pièce de résistance: can you resist?   This French import (pronounced "pyes dah ray-zee-STAHNS") literally means "piece of resistance," with *resistance* in this context conveying the meaning of "staying power, lastingness" and hence "outstanding."

   In the words of *Webster's Third New International Dictionary*, a *pièce de résistance* is "the outstanding item of a group," "the prize piece or main exhibit," "the showpiece of a collection." The term is also widely used to identify "the principal dish of a meal."

ping-pong or _Ping-Pong_?   This term for table tennis must be capitalized, because it's a trademark. The lowercase *ping-pong* is an informal verb meaning "move rapidly back and forth." (See also "*yo-yo* and *zipper*: why they're in the same entry.")

piety and pious are perilous   These words can communicate the opposite of what you mean if you don't use them in a context that makes your intended meaning absolutely clear. *Piety* can mean "a religious or other devotion" or "a *pretense* of such devotion." Likewise, the adjective *pious* can mean "exhibiting religious or other devotion" or "*pretending* to exhibit such devotion."

Usage example: *Piety* clearly means "religious devotion" in Thomas Cahill's reference in his *Desire of the Everlasting Hills: The World Before and After Jesus* (Doubleday, 2000) to "a gang of priest-pretenders whose piety was not so much suspect as nonexistent."

piteous, pitiable, or pitiful?   All three of these words mean "arousing pity." But *pitiful* and *pitiable* are also used to mean "arousing pity mingled with contempt," as in "a pitifully inadequate library" or "a pitiable lack of character."

According to the *Random House Webster's Unabridged Dictionary*, *piteous* "refers only to that which exhibits suffering and misery," but *The American Heritage Dictionary* defines it instead as "exciting pity, pathetic."

Recommendation: When you want to add a touch of contempt, use *pitiful* or *pitiable* rather than *piteous*.

plagiarism as piracy   *Plagiarism* ("stealing another's work or idea and claiming it as one's own") derives from the Latin *plagarius* ("sea raider, plunderer").

An offense regarding the word itself is to forget that *plagiarism* has an *i* in the middle.

playwright or playwrite?   You can *write* plays. You can teach play*writing*. But you cannot be a *playwrite*. The correct spelling for a person who writes plays is *playwright*, with the same ending as *shipwright, wheelwright,* and other names for people who make things.

Usage example: *The New York Times* (8/25/1999) published an obituary of "Norman Wexler, a playwright and screenwriter."

pleaded or pled?   The risk-free past tense of *plead* is *pleaded*.

Pled is listed as colloquial (informal) in some of our dictionaries and as unacceptable in the stylebooks of the Associated Press, *The New York Times*, and *The Wall Street Journal*.

plenitude or plentitude?　　The original, risk-free form of this word for "abundance" is *plenitude*. Though *plenitude's* spelling variant, *plentitude*, has been around almost five centuries, it is widely regarded as a spelling error influenced by the word *plenty*.

plenteous or plentiful?　　Both mean "abundant." But word connoisseurs say you should save *plenteous* for a poetic context.

plethora is too much　　*Plethora* ("PLETH-ara") means "excessive abundance," because the word originally meant a "pathological condition involving excessive blood or other bodily fluid."

　　Warning: Many people now use *plethora* loosely, to mean just plain "abundance." So, to be correct and also clear, use *plethora* only when you make its excessive quality obvious, as in this report from *The Economist* (5/27/2000): "With an unchanged electoral system ensuring the continued existence of a plethora of pointless parties, Italy is unlikely to find political stability." (See also next entry.)

plethora: singular and plural　　*Plethora* ("excessive abundance") is a singular noun with a rarely used plural, *plethoras*. But as *Merriam-Webster's Dictionary of English Usage* notes, "Writers who view *plethora* as a lump use a singular verb; those who view it as a collection of discrete items use a plural verb."

plural versus possessive: the *s* factor　　Inasmuch as the letter *s* is typically used for both the plural and the possessive—as in the plural *boys* and the singular possessive *boy's*—you'd better check to make sure you write what you mean. Cautionary example: A recent letter soliciting enrollment at a Southern California court-reporting school embarrassingly referred to "the *schools* reputation for excellence." (Italics added.)

plurals are not hard to find　　A brochure advertising an English-usage seminar for businessmen tells a story about a zookeeper writing a letter to an animal supplier. The zookeeper wrote, "Please send me two mongooses." That didn't sound right, so he changed it to "Please send me two mongeese." That sounded worse, so then he wrote, "Please send me a mongoose. And while you're at it, please send me another mongoose."

　　To solve problems with plurals, you don't have to invest time and money in an English-usage seminar. Any dictionary will tell you that the zookeeper was right the first time. (See also "dictionaries: use them for more than a spell.")

plural-sounding *-ics* words   See "*-ics* words: some are singular and plural."

plurals that are also singular   Some nouns have identical singular and plural forms, including *chassis, corps, deer, falls, fowl, gallows, moose, sheep, species, straits, sweepstakes, swine,* and *vermin.* The same is true of *Burmese, Chinese, Japanese, Portuguese,* and *Vietnamese.* (See also "*series is* or *series are?*")

***plus* should not subtract from your writing**   *Plus* is completely acceptable as a preposition meaning "increased by," as in "Two plus two is four." But the informal, advertising-style use of *plus* as a conjunction meaning "also"—"Plus you get a free clock-radio"—is not welcome in formal writing. (See also "*together* but alone.")

***poetaster*: not like a wine taster**   *Poetaster,* which means "a poet who is inferior," is pronounced "POET-aster." The suffix *-aster* denotes the inferiority.

Here are some lesser-known *-aster* put-downs: *medicaster, philosophaster, criticaster* and (for the petty, pedantic grammarian) *grammaticaster.*

***point in time*: still untimely**   "Point in time" is a wordy, bureaucratic, pedantic, annoying way of saying *now* ("this point in time"), *then* ("that point in time"), and *sometime* ("some point in time").

Also, beware of wasting time by changing "a long time" and "during that time" to "a long *period of* time" and "during that *period of* time" or "during that time *frame.*"

politic* or *politick?   *Politic* is an adjective meaning "diplomatic, tactful, prudent, expedient." Usage example from *U.S. News & World Report* (2/24/1997): "Despite the politic words of Gen. [Barry] McCaffrey [President Clinton's drug czar], U.S. officials . . . are increasingly operating on the assumption that Mexican cooperation means little as long as [Mexico's drug] cartel leaders run free and official corruption lets them."

Politick is a verb meaning "to engage in politicking (the practice of politics)."

politics is or *politics are?*   See "-*ics* words: some are singular and plural."

pore or *pour?*   The verb *pore* ("to read or study carefully, to gaze intently at") is sometimes mistakenly written *pour* ("to make flow"). An example of that error was cited in the September–October 1998 newsletter of the Society for the Preservation of English Language and Literature: "A staff writer for *The San Diego Union-Tribune* recently wrote: 'Becker and co-authors Jack Canfield, Mark Victor Hansen and Carol Kline poured [should be *pored*] over 5,000 stories. . . .'"

port or *starboard?*   Hint for landlubbers: From the perspective of a ship's captain, *port* means "left," and both words are shorter than *starboard* and its synonym, "right."

portentous **can be perilous**   If you use the adjective *portentous*, make sure you do so in a context that enables your audience to know which of the word's meanings you intend to convey.

The noun *portent* means "something that foreshadows an event of sinister consequences." Hence, the adjective *portentous* can mean "ominous," as in a *New York Times* opinion essay (1/5/2001) in which a 1960's White House press aide recalled the 13 terrifying days of the Cuban missile crisis: "I first realized something portentous was going on when, on a presidential trip to Chicago, we abruptly returned to Washington."

Portentous is also used by some writers as a synonym for "pretentious, pompous, self-important," as in a *New York Times* report (10/6/1998) that many members of the House Judiciary Committee "said portentously that their debates and votes [regarding the decision to hold impeachment hearings for President Clinton] would be remembered for generations."

To add to the potential confusion about *portentous*, it can also mean "amazing, awe-inspiring, or marvelous."

possessive punctuation prescriptions   See "apostrophes for possessives."

possessives that don't really possess   Follow standard possessive punctuation when inanimate subjects are involved, even though they are incapable of literally possessing (as in "owning") anything: "the building's roof," "a day's pay," "two weeks' vacation," "your money's worth." (See also "*whose*: for people only?")

possessives that double up Suppose you want to say "He's a friend of my dad." That's fine. But many people would say "He's a friend of my *dad's*," a form of usage that is called a double possessive (also known as double genitive) because it includes both the possessive *of* and the possessive *'s*.

Is the double possessive also acceptable? Yes, say the language guardians who regard that form as an expression that has earned idiomatic respectability through long use. Here's an example from *Fortune* magazine (6/28/2004): "I borrowed some books from a friend of my dad's." Defenders of the double possessive additionally argue that a phrase such as "a friend of my dad's" is correct because you would need to say "a friend of *his*" rather than "a friend of *he*," though both *of* and *his* denote possessiveness.

Other language guardians accept the double possessive for pronouns (as in "a friend of *hers*, *his*, or *theirs*") but not for nouns (as in "a friend of my *dad's*"). These critics note that saying "a friend of my dad's," with the blatant possessiveness of the apostrophe, raises the question "A friend of your dad's *what*?" In the light of that criticism, the *friend* in "a friend of my dad's" may not be a friend of the dad at all but rather a friend of the dad's wife, lawyer, or dentist.

Risk-free recommendation: For clarity and acceptability, at least in formal writing, say "a friend of my dad [or *my father*, in formal contexts]." But beware: A phrase such as "a painting of Picasso" could be as ambiguous as any double possessive. That phrase could mean a painting that he painted, a painting someone made of him, or a painting in Picasso's own collection. To avoid ambiguity in such cases, make sure your meaning is clear from your context, or spell out what you mean. For example: "She owns two Picasso paintings."

potato **puzzle** *Potato* became one of America's least misspelled words during Campaign 1992, after Vice President Dan Quayle had embarrassed himself in front of dozens of reporters by instructing a 12-year-old boy in a classroom spelling bee to add an *-e* to the boy's correct spelling of *potato*.

The Associated Press reported the following week that the *-oe* ending for *potato* had been used by George Washington, but the AP added that Washington himself had been an eccentric speller whose *potatoe* defied the spelling traced back to 1587 by *The Oxford English Dictionary*.

Historians can only guess at what might have happened if Quayle had been invited back to that classroom and asked to guide the students in making the *p*-word plural. Would Quayle, overreacting to his gaffe, have served up *potatos*? If so, he would have been wrong again. The plural of *potato*, like the plural of *mosquito*, needs *-es*. (See also "spelling traps.")

Potemkin's unreal estate?   A major figure in Russian history is remembered in our language today for something he might not have done.

He was army officer Grigori Aleksandrovich Potemkin, who helped Catherine the Great seize power and became one of a series of men who served the empress as both lover and political adviser. In 1783, Potemkin masterminded Catherine's conquest and annexation of the Crimea. Four years later, as governor-general of the Crimea and other newly acquired Black Sea provinces, he organized Catherine's triumphant tour of that region. According to a rumor circulated at the time, he ordered the construction of elaborate fake villages made of cardboard, like those you might see today on a movie set, along her carefully planned route. He was thus said to have tricked Catherine and accompanying foreign leaders and diplomats into thinking that Russian rule in the region had produced prosperity.

The rumor about such a ruse, apparently started by one of the diplomats on the tour, was "at best, an extreme exaggeration" (to quote *The Columbia Encyclopedia*) and only "an apocryphal tale" (*Encyclopaedia Britannica*). But the phrase *Potemkin village* became a term, still used today, for any "deceptively imposing façade." For example: *The New York Times* reported (2/26/2002) that "Enron Energy Services, another money-losing unit [of the Enron Corporation], spent hundreds of thousands of dollars to build a Potemkin village trading floor to impress equity analysts invited to a conference, though the unit had no trading function."

***potpourri*: a medley of meanings**   A *potpourri* ("poh-puh-REE") is "a sweet-smelling mixture of dried flower petals and spices, preserved in a vase." It also can mean a musical medley, a literary anthology, or a miscellaneous collection of any kind.

***practicable* or *practical*?**   Doubling the size of American cars would be *practicable* ("*possible* to put into practice, feasible") but not *practical* ("*worth* putting into practice, useful").

Of these two words, only *practical*—which has many meanings—can describe a person. A practical person is one who is "level-headed, efficient, and unspeculative."

pragmatism: philosophy and attitude   The American-born philosophy of *pragmatism*—introduced in 1878 in *Popular Science Monthly* by philosopher-logician Charles Sanders Peirce (1839–1914) and subsequently championed by philosopher-psychologist William James (1842–1910) and philosopher-educator John Dewey (1859–1952)—spawned many philosophies called pragmatism, some contradicting others.

But *The Columbia Encyclopedia* and other reference sources today note that *pragmatism*—a word derived from the Greek root *pragma*, meaning "practical matter"—identifies a philosophical approach that consistently rejects all hypotheses that fail the test, or are too speculative to be put to the test, of experiment or practical experience.

In everyday language, *pragmatism* means "a practical attitude," as in a headline about Republican members of Congress collaborating with Democratic President Bill Clinton and thus "Choosing Pragmatism Over Partisanship" (*Washington Post* national weekly edition, 8/12/1996).

precipitate or precipitous?   As adjectives, these words have been used interchangeably for centuries, and they are listed as synonyms in some dictionaries. But careful communicators today use *precipitate* (and its related adverb, *precipitately*) only to describe an action that is abrupt, rash, hasty, or headlong, as in "a precipitate rush to judgment." *Precipitous* (and its adverb, *precipitously*) is used to describe something that's extremely steep either physically or figuratively, as in "the campfire's precipitous edge" or "a precipitous drop in price."

Precipitate as a *verb* means "to cause to happen, especially suddenly or prematurely," as in "to precipitate a confrontation between the union and management." Another meaning of the verb *precipitate* is "to fling or hurl down," a sense reflected in the noun *precipitation* ("falling products of condensation [rain, snow, hail] in the atmosphere").

Memory tip: *Precipitate* shares an *a* with *abrupt*, and *precipitous* shares an *s* with *steep*.

predicate: the noun and the verb The noun *predicate* ("PRED-ih-kit") refers to the part of a sentence, including a verb, that talks about the subject. For example, the predicate in the following sentence consists of everything that comes after *cat*: "Gabbi's cat loves to be taken for a walk."

The verb *predicate* ("PRED-ih-kate"), derived from a Latin verb for "proclaim," became an English synonym for "assert." With the emergence of American English in the 18th century, the verb *predicate* acquired the additional meaning, "to base [*on* or *upon*]," as in "to predicate one's philosophy on the sacredness of all life." Language purists denounced the "to base" *predicate* as an error until the 1970's, and such denunciations may still be found in outdated reference libraries. But you can tell anybody who criticizes you for using the "to base" *predicate* that it is now fully accepted by our usage commentators as the dominant definition in the United States and is as acceptable as the "to assert" definition among usage commentators in Britain.

Usage example of the "to base" *predicate*: University of Illinois media scholar Robert W. McChesney wrote in his 1999 book, *Rich Media, Poor Democracy:* "Professional journalism was predicated on the notion that its content should not be shaped by the dictates of owners and advertisers, or by the biases of editors and reporters, but rather by core public service values."

prelude: an introduction to its pronunciation Though many speakers pronounce this word "PRAY-lood," dictionaries consistently list that pronunciation as secondary to "PREL-yood."

And though *prelude* is commonly used as a noun ("an introduction to a performance, action, event; an introductory musical composition"), it is also a verb ("to serve as a prelude, to play a prelude"). Usage example: *Benét's Reader's Encyclopedia* tells us that a Henry James novel about an actress, *The Tragic Muse*, "preludes James's excursion into playwriting in the 1890s."

premier or premiere? *Premier* (literally, "first") is a French-derived noun meaning, "first minister, prime minister" and an adjective meaning "first in status, supreme."

A related noun with an added *-e*, *premiere* (sometimes *première*), is "a first public presentation."

premises is* or *premises are?   The answer is always *are*.

The word *premises* obviously takes a plural verb when it's the plural of *premise*, "a proposition upon which an argument is based or a conclusion is drawn." For example: "Valid *premises are* no guarantee of valid conclusions."

Not so obviously, *premises* in the sense of "property" takes a plural verb whether the meaning is plural or singular. For example: "These *premises* [a single building, or a tract of land with one or more buildings] *are* off-limits to the public."

Both *premises*, derived from a Latin expression for "things mentioned before," emerged in the Middle Ages as a reference to things mentioned at the beginning of a legal document. That meaning was extended to ideas (premises) mentioned at the beginning of a logical argument, and then to a single idea (a premise) upon which an argument is based. The original, legal-expression *premises* was also extended to land and buildings mentioned at the beginning of a legal document. But the "property" *premises* never developed a singular form.

prepositions make a difference   As Follett's *Modern American Usage* warned, "Nothing gives away the . . . insensitive writer like the misused preposition."

The prepositions include *about, above, across, after, against, along, amid, among, around, at, before, behind, below, beneath, beside, between, beyond, by, concerning, despite, down, during, for, from, in, including, inside, into, like, near, of, off, on, onto, over, past, round, since, through, throughout, till, to, toward, under, until, unto, up, upon, with, within,* and *without*.

What do they have in common? According to *The Cambridge Encyclopedia of the English Language*, "A preposition is [a member of a class of words that] expresses a relationship of meaning between two parts of a sentence, most often showing how they are related in space or time: *We sat* on *the beach. They left* at *three*."

Your problem is choosing which prepositions go with which words for which purpose. Unfortunately, you can't solve prepositional problems by memorizing general prepositional rules. General prepositional rules don't exist. Prepositional choices for each word evolved separately, idiomatically, through custom rather than logic, so when you're in doubt, you'll need to check individual words in the dictionary to learn about their prepositional relationships.

If you grew up speaking and reading American English, you effortlessly absorbed many of our language's prepositional usages. You know, for example, that your home is *on* a certain street, not (as in British English) *in* that street.

And with other native speakers of English you know when to bear *up*, *down*, and *with*, and when to take *after*, *down*, *for*, *in*, *off*, *on*, *over*, *to*, and *up*.

But whether or not American English is your native language, you need lifelong reading and reliance on a dictionary if you want to consistently pick proper prepositions. (See also "*confused* by prepositions?" and "*follow* these prepositions.")

prepositions you end sentences with   Are you afraid to end sentences with a preposition because somebody told you not *to*? Well, fear no more.

Fowler's *Dictionary of Modern English Usage* dismissed such fear as nothing but "a cherished superstition." Burchfield's *New Fowler's Modern English Usage* says such fear is based on "entrenched myth." *Garner's Modern American Usage* says, "Good writers don't hesitate to end their sentences with prepositions if doing so results in phrasing that seems natural." In the words of *Webster's New World Guide to Current American Usage*: "Most grammar books have stopped insisting that a sentence not end with a preposition. This so-called rule, which has tyrannized schoolchildren for centuries, was nonsense to begin with, having been invented by English writers who considered it elegant to impose Latin sentence structure on their language."

The Latin-inspired prohibition against the terminal preposition in English was promoted (and perhaps introduced) by English poet-playwright-essayist John Dryden in a 1672 piece of criticism that he called *Defence of the Epilogue*. The silly rule was subsequently circulated by a number of grammarians, as well as by lexicographer Noah Webster in his 1784 grammar. "So," say Merriam-Webster researchers, "the 19th century began with three widely used, standard school texts formidably opposing the preposition at the end of the sentence. The topic entered the general consciousness through schoolteachers, and, as we have seen, it persists there still."

Terminal prepophobia (a term just invented for this sentence) can result in extremely awkward phrasing in English, as was illustrated in a legendary incident involving Winston Churchill. Sir Winston is said to have become so annoyed when an overzealous secretary rearranged a terminal preposition in one of his memos that he scribbled on the memo, "This is the type of arrant pedantry up with which I will not put."

Of course, you should rewrite sentences (and clauses) whose terminal prepositions *cause* awkwardness, as if we were to "pledge allegiance to the republic, which we stand *for.*" But modern usage commentators urge you to use terminal prepositions whenever they help your phrasing go with the flow.

Usage commentators also note that the terminal preposition may sometimes be essential, to let your reader clearly understand where you're coming *from.* Such advice is not worth arguing *about.* Nor is it to be sneezed *at.* As a matter of fact, that is advice you can count *on.*

So feel free, when it's appropriate, to laugh your head *off.* And don't listen to anyone who tells you to laugh off your head. Anyone who tells you to do that will have a lot to answer *for.*

prescribe or proscribe?   Hit one wrong key in typing *prescribe* ("issue guidance, give medical directions") and you get *proscribe* ("forbid").

Proscribe is fundamentally risky. No matter how carefully you use it, people may think they are hearing or reading *prescribe.*

presently a problem   *Presently* can mean "at present," "now," or "soon." For clarity, substitute whichever of those expressions conveys your intended meaning.

pretence or pretense?   *Pretense* is the usual spelling in American English. *Pretence* is the usual spelling in British English.

preternatural or supernatural?   *Preternatural,* which for centuries served as a synonym for *supernatural,* now serves a separate purpose as a powerful word of praise, meaning "surpassing the normal, extraordinary."

Usage example: Novelist John Updike wrote in *The New York Review of Books* (10/19/2000): "Born in 1872, [author Max Beerbohm] early developed a preternatural poise and grace as a writer and a caricaturist."

preventative or preventive?   For a clue to the answer to this question, notice the name of the *American Journal of Preventive Medicine.*

Both *preventive* and *preventative* have been used for more than three hundred years, and *The Columbia Guide to Standard American English* says that "each is standard as both adjective and noun." But *preventative* was panned as "not a correct word" in William and Mary Morris' *Harper Dictionary of*

Contemporary Usage and was dismissed as "a needless lengthening of an established word" in Fowler's *Dictionary of Modern English Usage*. Though R. W. Burchfield says in *The New Fowler's Modern English Usage* that both forms are acceptable, he cites evidence that the shorter form is used much more frequently, and he prescribes that form "for most contexts."

prima facie: **facing this pronunciation**   If you want to show off your knowledge of this Latin phrase (meaning "at first sight, on the face of it, at face value"), don't spoil the effect by mispronouncing it. Don't say "*PRIM*-uh FAY-*see*." Say "*PRY*-muh FAY-*shee*" (the preferred pronunciation), "PRY-muh FAY-shee-*ee*," or "PRY-muh FAY-*shuh*."

Prima facie may be used not only as an adjective (as in "a prima facie violation") but also as an adverb (as in "She had, prima facie, a strong argument"). In law, *prima facie evidence*—constituting a *prima facie case*—is that which establishes a fact or raises a presumption of a fact unless contested.

principal **or** *principle*?   *Principal* and *main* both contain the letter *a*, and *principal* is a noun that means "the main person" or an adjective that describes something as "the main thing."

Principle, always a noun, ends with the same two letters as one of its synonyms, *rule*. Other synonyms for *principle* are "doctrine" and "fundamental truth."

prior **offense**   You are committing an offense against English if you use the phrase *prior to* as a substitute for the preposition *before*, according to the "Language Corner" of the *Columbia Journalism Review* (November/December 1996).

That source says: "What in heaven's name is wrong with *before*? We don't have to follow the lead of . . . the academics, doctors, lawyers, and bureaucrats of all stripes, public and private, for whom *prior to* is mandatory because *before* is plain English and they can't have *that*."

A more tolerant view of this usage is expressed by *The Columbia Guide to Standard American English*, which says *prior to* is a standard substitute for *before*, though "sometimes it may be thought pretentious or stuffy."

Risk-free hint: Why be a bore when you can stay with *before*?

pristine* began *old* and became *new Pristine—derived from *pristinus*, a
Latin word for "ancient"—entered the English language in the 16th century as
an adjective meaning "belonging to the earliest state or period, primitive."
Pristine seems to have acquired its additional, extended meanings—evolving
from "primitive" to "uncorrupted and unpolluted" to "free from dirt or decay"
to "new and pure"—in early 20th-century America.

Some word guardians in England have stubbornly rejected the extended
meanings. For example, England's *Economist Style Guide* states emphatically
that "*pristine* means *original condition*, not *pure* or *clean*." But the extended
meanings are listed after the original meaning in *The New Shorter Oxford
English Dictionary*; the extended meanings are "becoming increasingly difficult
to find fault with," in the view of *The New Fowler's Modern English Usage*; and
we are assured by *Merriam-Webster's Dictionary of English Usage* that the
extended meanings are "in current standard use on both sides of the Atlantic."

Example of risk-free usage of *pristine* in the sense of "original condition":
The New York Times (6/9/1997) observed that "Kamchatka, in Russia's Far
East, is one of the last pristine places on the planet."

***problematic* is a problem** The adjective *problematic*—the short, preferred
form of *problematical*—can be confusing because it can mean "problem-filled"
but often means "doubtful." If somebody tells you that repairing your computer
will be problematic, it could mean that the repair will be difficult, but it could
also mean that the repair may not be possible.

Risk-free solution: If you mean "problem-filled," say so. Use *problematic*
only to mean "doubtful," and use it only in a context that makes your meaning
unmistakable. For example, an editorial in the Dow Jones financial weekly,
Barron's (2/2/2003), endorsed President George W. Bush's State of the Union
message on Iraq but then expressed doubt about the practicality of Bush's proposals for America's ailing economy: "Much more problematic was his prescription for reinvigorating the economy, not least because it leans heavily toward
time-release rather than immediate effect."

***proceed* with caution** Do not *proceed* to the shopping mall. Just *go*. To *pro-
ceed* when you decide to *go* is pretentious. Moreover, according to some usage
commentators, it is inaccurate. For many precise communicators, *proceed*
means "continue after a pause," as in "The train proceeded after having its

engine repaired" or "The trial proceeded after order was restored in the court-room." *Proceed* also means "to come forth from a source," "to begin and carry on an action, process, or movement," and "to move along a course."

Proceed is often misspelled *procede* (duplicating the ending of *precede*). *Procedure* is sometimes misspelled *proceedure*.

Procrustes and his adjective Procrustes was a bandit in Greek mythology who would seize travelers, tie them to his iron bedstead, and make them fit the space by either stretching or amputating their limbs. This sadistic criminal, whose name was derived from a Greek word meaning "one who stretches," was eventually slain in his own bed by the Athenian hero Theseus.

The adjective *Procrustean*, acceptable in upper or lower case, means "impos-ing strict uniformity by arbitrary methods." School systems here and abroad are sometimes accused of subjecting children to a Procrustean curriculum, meaning one that disregards individual differences and talents. Any system that arbitrar-ily imposes uniformity can be called a Procrustean bed.

***prodigal son* was no conservative** *The New York Times* and the *Los Angeles Times* should have consulted a dictionary and a Bible before each news-paper published a story (11/3/1999) describing U.S. Senator Bob Smith as "prodigal" in the headline and a "prodigal son" in the text.

The stories about Smith, a New Hampshire Republican chosen the previ-ous day to head the Senate's powerful Environment and Public Works Committee, labeled him "prodigal" and a "prodigal son" because he had just rejoined the Republican Party after a brief campaign for president as an Independent. Those stories thus perpetuated the widespread misconception that *prodigal* means "wandering" and *prodigal* son means "someone who wanders away and then returns."

Actually, *prodigal* means "recklessly extravagant," a description that the devoutly conservative Senator Smith would undoubtedly regard as appropriate for his political adversaries rather than for himself. In a parable of Jesus about the value of repentance, as told in the King James Bible (Luke 15:11), the prodi-gal son was a young man who indeed wandered off, after obtaining his share of the family property from his father. But the prodigal son was called prodigal ("wasteful") because he squandered his share of the family wealth by patroniz-ing "harlots" and by otherwise engaging in "riotous living." The prodigal son eventually returned home and confessed his sins, an act of repentance that won him forgiveness from his father.

Here's an example of correct usage: Cultural historian Jacques Barzun wrote in his history of Western culture, *From Dawn to Decadence*, that "one cannot pour all human and material resources into a fiery cauldron [such as World War I] and expect to resume normal life at the end of the prodigal enterprise."

***professors*: not all can be trusted**   A professor is an educator who has been awarded the highest rank in a university pecking order that includes associate professors, assistant professors, lecturers, and teaching assistants.

But the noun *professor* also means "one who professes," and the verb *profess* means not only "teach as a professor" and "claim skill in or knowledge of" but also "take a vow, as in a religious order," "declare, as in declaring a belief or feeling," and "declare *insincerely*."

Risk-free recommendation: Inasmuch as the verb *profess* signals insincerity in much of today's usage, use it only for that purpose and make your meaning clear in your context. For example: "Though he is one of the world's most ruthless dictators, he takes every opportunity to profess his love of democracy."

***prone, prostrate, recumbent,* or *supine*?**   All these adjectives mean "lying down." But they denote different positions. *Prone* means "lying face down." *Supine* means "lying face up." (Remember the *up* in *supine*.) *Prostrate* means "lying flat, usually prone, often out of adoration, submission, grief, or exhaustion." *Recumbent* means "lying down in any position of comfort for rest or sleep." Be careful not to spell *prostrate* as if you were referring to the gland, *prostate*, surrounding the neck of the bladder in male mammals.

pronouns are personal in three ways   During President George W. Bush's early months in office, he was widely ridiculed for saying, "You teach a child to read and he or her will pass a literacy test" (*New York Times*, 3/17/2001). What he wished he had said, of course, was "he or *she*."

Presidents and everyone else should be reminded that English personal pronouns come in three case forms: *nominative, objective,* and *possessive.*

In the *nominative* case are *I, you, he, she, we, they,* and *who.* ("He loved Juliet.")

In the *objective* case, the personal pronouns are *me, you, him, her, us, them,* and *whom*. ("Juliet loved him.") *You* is the only personal pronoun that is both objective ("Colleagues respect you") and nominative ("You respect colleagues").

In the *possessive* case, the personal pronouns are *my, his, her, our,* and *their*. Note that *her* is the only possessive pronoun ("her book") that is also an objective pronoun ("They booked her for a talk show").

pronouns are preferably followers   When you make a pronoun follow the noun it replaces, you're helping the reader know who or what the pronoun stands for. For example, say "*Stan* had an old car, which *he* decided to donate to charity" rather than "Since *his* [whose?] car was old, Stan donated it to charity."

The word *Stan* in the first two examples above is called an *antecedent*, which means "something that came before" or, in grammar, "the subject that comes before the pronoun that replaces it." Here are two more sentences containing antecedents and pronoun replacements: "*The vice president* [the antecedent] arrived so late that *he* [the pronoun replacing *the vice president*] missed the meeting." "*John* [the antecedent] caught *his* [the pronoun replacing *John's*] train."

If you betray the meaning of *antecedent*—if you make it *follow* the pronoun—you risk reader frustration, especially if there is another noun that might be the antecedent or if there are many words separating the pronoun from the noun it replaces. Here's an unfortunate two-sentence example from a *New York Times Book Review* essay by Pulitzer Prize–winning historian Michael Kammen (7/6/1997): "We still have a lot to learn from [19th-century French historian Alexis de] Tocqueville, but above all, perhaps, that we must not appropriate or misuse him for partisan purposes. When his [Toqueville's? Guess again!] fellow Republicans chose him to be Speaker of the House after the party's 1994 Congressional sweep, Newt Gingrich prescribed Tocqueville as essential reading for his colleagues to understand their agenda."

In short sentences, however, there is nothing wrong with antecedent reversal, as in the following heading from *Newsweek* (4/8/1996): "A public debate over its mission divides the Fed." Note that putting the antecedent and the pronoun in the preferred order in that sentence—"A public debate over the Fed's mission divides it"—would have left the reader unsure of which noun the word *it* was replacing, the debate or the Fed or the mission. If the reader will not have any difficulty connecting the antecedent with the pronoun, reversing the order is sometimes the best solution.

pronouns are prone to getting lost   In the rush of writing and speaking, a pronoun may become separated from its antecedent (the noun to which the pronoun refers). The result of such a misplaced pronoun can be as embarrassing as the following paragraph from an article contributed by cookbook author Clifford A. Wright to the Food section of the *Los Angeles Times* (1/23/2002): "I first tried kohlrabi leaves in a spaghetti *alla carbonara* my kids had been asking me to fix. I decided to toss them in too, really just to get rid of them. But the resulting dish was so good it became part of my repertoire."

Let that seeming tale of culinary crime remind you that each pronoun should refer to the most recently named noun that is consistent with the nature of the pronoun. For example, *them* should be used only when the most recently named persons or things are its intended antecedent. If a pronoun cannot be placed properly, its antecedent should be used instead. That means the food writer should have said, "I decided to toss the kohlrabi leaves in too, really just to get rid of them."

For practice, consider this sentence: "Ken tried to tell Ben what he needs." Does that mean Ken tried to talk about *Ben's* needs or his own? Depending on the intended meaning, the sentence should be changed to "Ken tried to tell Ben what Ben needs" or "Ken tried to express his needs to Ben."

pronouns can be agreeably nonsexist   Many people today are so afraid to appear sexist that they violate a basic grammatical rule about noun-pronoun agreement rather than use *he* or *his* as generic pronouns.

For example, a *New Yorker* ad (11/20/2000) made the following romantic promise for the purchaser of Microsoft Reader: "Never be lost for words when you need the perfect quote to sweep your partner off their feet." Notice that the writer of that sentence ungrammatically matched the singular noun *partner* with the plural pronoun *their*. The result was that the partner ended up with the feet of some other people.

In such sentences, you don't need to sacrifice noun-pronoun agreement to avoid a gender-specific pronoun. You can change the sentence so that the pronoun is unnecessary. You can write, for example, "Never be lost for words when you need the perfect quote for a romantic occasion."

Another solution in some cases is to switch to a plural noun to agree with the plural pronoun. For instance, "Every teacher should try to treat all their students fairly" can easily become "Teachers should try to treat all their students fairly."

If you decide you must keep your subject singular, note that even the extremely awkward *his or her* or *his/her* is less objectionable than noun-pronoun disagreement. So is the traditional, generic *his*, as in a *Newsweek* observation (7/30/2001) that "nobody wants radioactive cargo chugging by his town."

pronouns: indefinitely singular or plural?   Only singular verbs go with the indefinite pronouns *another, each, either, nobody,* and *no one*. ("No one *is* here.")

Only plural verbs go with the indefinite pronouns *both, many,* and *several*. For example: "Both *are* here."

Singular *or* plural verbs go with the indefinite pronouns *all, any, most, none,* and *some*. Those indefinite pronouns are singular when they refer to *quantity* ("mass" nouns) but plural when they refer to a *number* ("count" nouns). For example: "*All* good clothing *is* expensive, but *all* his suits *are* unusually expensive because they are made to order."

pronouns that are *self*-conscious   Pronouns ending in *-self* are appropriate as "intensive" or "reflexive" pronouns. An *intensive pronoun* is one that emphasizes the identity of the subject. ("The magician himself was amazed by what happened next.") A *reflexive pronoun* is one that is acted upon by its own subject. ("The gymnast hurt herself.")

But watch yourself. You risk severe criticism if you use these pronouns in places where personal pronouns without *-self* would do the job. As Bryan A. Garner explains in his *Modern American Usage*, pronouns ending in *-self* should "reflect an antecedent." Here are two examples of risky usage, with risk-free changes in brackets: "My wife and myself [*I*] arrived early." "It was a pleasant evening for my wife and myself [*me*]."

The just-cited risky uses of pronouns ending in *-self* have been common for more than four centuries in the informal speech and writing of leading political and literary figures, according to *Merriam-Webster's Dictionary of English Usage*. But that source acknowledges that various language commentators for at least a century have branded such usage unacceptable for formal English on the grounds of being "nonstandard, colloquial, unstylish, self-indulgent, self-conscious, old-fashioned, timorous, and snobbish." So let that be a lesson to a student in a university English-composition class who wrote me that a guest lecture I had given to her class "was informative and beneficial to both myself [should be *me*] and my classmates."

pronunciation requires sound advice Desi Arnaz was paid big bucks to make people laugh at his mispronunciations of English in the classic sitcom *I Love Lucy*. One entire episode, for example, was based on the humorous consequences of his character's confusion of the word *radio* with *rodeo*. But if your mispronunciations cause people to laugh behind your back, it's no joke.

Check pronunciations in a dictionary. When you find more than one acceptable pronunciation for a word, pick the preferred one (listed first). (See also entries for *anecdote, asterisk, February*, and *shibboleth*.)

proofreading: everybody needs it As former *Editor & Publisher* columnist Ray Erwin once jokingly advised writers of news, "Proofread your writing to see if you any words out." That advice was obviously ignored when *The New York Times* published the following sentence in its national edition of June 19, 1997: "He did not enter a plea because does not yet have a lawyer."

Of course, you also need to make sure you did not include too many words, as *The New York Times* (1/31/1998) did in the following sentence: "Senator John Ashcroft, Republican of Missouri, called for the President to resign if the accusation [about White House intern Monica Lewinsky] *are is* true." And you need to check to see if you unconsciously substituted one word for another, as did the Southern California *USA Track & Field Guide* for November–December 1993: "First place men and women finishers will be awarded Commemorative *Plagues*." (Italics added.)

While you are at it, proofread aloud. When you hear as well as view what you have written, you may discover errors that sight alone did not catch. Bear in mind, too, that your concentration may be more focused when you read aloud, because your thoughts are less likely to wander.

prophecy* or *prophesy? Beware of a typographical error that can turn the noun *prophecy* ("prediction") into the verb *prophesy* (which rhymes with *eye* and means "predict").

Usage example of the verb *prophesy*: An essay in *The New York Review of Books* (3/18/1999) reminded readers that "the electronic age did not drive the printed word into extinction, as [Marshall] McLuhan prophesied in 1962."

protégé* or *protégée? *Protégé*—pronounced "PRO-tah-zhay" and derived from the past participle of a French word meaning "to protect"—means "one whose welfare, training, or career is protected by someone with influence." The extra *e* in *protégée*, as with *fiancée*, designates the feminine form.

Usage example from *The New York Times* obituary of Beat Generation poet Allen Ginsberg (4/6/1997): "Returning home to Paterson [New Jersey], Mr. Ginsberg became a protégé of William Carlos Williams, the physician and poet, who lived nearby."

Proteus and his adjective   In the world of Greek mythology, people could learn about their future and get brilliant answers to their problems by going to a cave-dwelling prophet named Proteus. But those who sought his services had to surprise, seize, and bind him. Otherwise, he would elude anyone who approached him by changing into a lion, dragon, a tree, or anything else of his choice. And in a non-human form he was no prophet.

The myth of Proteus inspired the adjective *protean*, which means "readily assuming different forms." Usage example: *The New York Times* (9/27/2000) described Hillary Rodham Clinton's role as first lady in these words: "a spectacularly protean performance, veering from secretive boss of a failed health care plan to self-effacing advocate for children, from suspect in an Arkansas land deal to victim in America's biggest political sex scandal."

proved or **proven?**   Which of these two forms of the past participle of *prove* should you use? For example, should you say the prosecution has *proved* or *proven* its case?

The criticism-proof answer is the original form, *proved*, not the variant *proven*. The word *proven* is criticism-proof only as an adjective, as in a *Financial Times* reference (6/10/2000) to the fact that Saudi Arabia and the other Gulf oil states "own almost half the world's proven oil reserves."

provenance is not in Rhode Island   The noun *provenance*, from a French verb meaning "to originate," literally means "place of origin," and is commonly used at art and antique auctions to mean "proof of authenticity and prior ownership."

The word *providence* ("the benevolent guidance of God") became the upper-case *Providence* (Rhode Island's capital and largest city), named by English clergyman Roger Williams when he founded the city in 1636 as a haven for religious dissenters.

proverbial usage   The word *proverb*, of course, means "a short, popular expression of wisdom," such as "A stitch in time saves nine." (See also next entry.)

Proverbial means not only "of or pertaining to the characteristics of a proverb" but also "having been made the subject of a proverb or of any popular reference." Usage example of the extended meaning of *proverbial*: A *New York Times* feature story (8/6/1998) told of a married couple who left their hotel room looking as if it had been "hit by the proverbial hurricane."

proverbs and other sayings   The word *saying* ("a pithy expression of wisdom") has a variety of synonyms with slightly varying meanings: *maxim* ("a concise statement of a truth or a rule of conduct"), *motto* ("a maxim accepted as a guiding principle"), *aphorism* ("a short, often witty saying expressing an important truth"), *apothegm* ("a short, witty saying"), *saw* ("a familiar saying that may have been distorted through long use"), and *proverb* ("a saying expressing a folksy truth").

A *Smithsonian* article (September 1992) profiling "the world's top proverb expert," University of Vermont folklorist Wolfgang Mieder, quoted him as warning that proverbs are "not necessarily true." By way of illustration, Mieder was quoted as asking: "If 'Absence makes the heart grow fonder,' why do we say 'Out of sight, out of mind'? And if 'He who hesitates is lost,' how come you have to 'Look before you leap'?"

Mieder, whose 50 books on proverbs include the Oxford University Press *Dictionary of American Proverbs*, has discovered that some proverbs can be classified according to "universal types." For example, the general idea that "one of something is worth vast numbers of something else" is found in "One picture is worth a thousand words" (reportedly introduced for the first time in 1921 in a *Printer's Ink* article by advertising man Fred R. Barnard). Other proverbs with that pattern are "One good head is better than a hundred strong hands" (English), "A friend is better than a thousand silver pieces" (Greek), "A moment is worth a thousand gold pieces" (Korean), "A single penny fairly got is worth a thousand that are not" (German), and "Silence is worth a thousand pieces of silver" (Burmese).

proximity is close enough   Inasmuch as *proximity* means *closeness,* the *close* in *close proximity* is redundant. (See also "redundancy: a vice and a virtue.")

***pseudo*: don't be swayed**   Some years ago, a Hollywood B-movie producer became notorious for repeatedly denouncing film critics as "SWAY-dough" intellectuals.

Pseudo (as in *pseudonym, pseudoscience,* and *pseudo-event*)—a Greek-derived combining form used in scores of English words to denote "fake, false, counterfeit"—should be pronounced "SOO-dough."

***psyche* or *Psyche*?**   The word *psyche* rhymes with *Nike* (the athletic shoes named after the Greek goddess of victory). It means "human soul, spirit, mind." And *psyche*—along with *psychiatry* and *psychology* and the many other words beginning with *psycho*—can be traced to a princess named Psyche in the mythology of ancient Rome.

The princess Psyche attracted the worshipful glances of so many men that she aroused the jealousy of even the goddess of love, Venus. So Venus spitefully told her son, the love god Cupid, to make Psyche fall in love with someone who would make her miserable. But when Cupid beheld Psyche, he himself fell in love with her. She agreed to marry him even though he did not allow her to know who he was, and he came to her only at night and made her promise never to look at him in the light. When Psyche broke her promise by bringing a lamp to bed, Cupid deserted her for being untrustworthy.

Psyche was so eager to win Cupid back that she begged for help from the gods, but they did not want to offend Venus. Desperate, Psyche appealed to Venus, who pretended to offer help on condition that Psyche undertake a series of cruel tasks. After Psyche had performed several such tasks, Cupid on his own decided he could not live without her. He rejoined her and made sure Venus would show some respect for her by arranging with the god Jupiter (known in Greece as Zeus) to turn Psyche into a goddess. Psyche thus became the immortal personification of the human soul; and the marriage of Psyche and Cupid became an everlasting union of Soul and Love.

***psychic income* doesn't motivate mediums**   The word *psychic* is an adjective meaning "mental as opposed to physical," as in *psychic income* ("subjective rather than financial job benefits").

Psychic is also an adjective meaning "sensitive to supernatural forces," and a noun referring to someone who is supposedly endowed with that sensitivity.

Pulitzer and his prizes   The Pulitzer Prizes for American journalism, letters (books, drama, poetry, and so on) and musical composition are paid for from the income of a fund left by newspaper publisher Joseph Pulitzer ("PUH-litzer") to the trustees of Columbia University. The prizes have been awarded annually since 1917, six years after Pulitzer's death.

Born in Hungary in 1847, Pulitzer emigrated to the United States in 1864. He served in the Union army during the Civil War, was elected to the Missouri legislature and the U.S. House of Representatives, and achieved fame as the publisher of the St. Louis *Post-Dispatch* and the New York *World*. In addition to endowing the Pulitzer Prizes, Pulitzer left funds to found Columbia University's Graduate School of Journalism.

punctilious or **punctual?**   A *punctilious* (note the single *l*) person is attentive to the fine points of proper behavior, usually including the idea of being *punctual* ("prompt").

punctuation is a toolbox   When your only tool is a hammer, according to a wise saying, every problem looks like a nail. In the same manner, some people write as if all, or nearly all, punctuation problems can be solved with only a dash, or only a comma, or only a colon, or only a semicolon. Such people need to be reminded that punctuation marks are tools with specialized functions, and that those tools are no more interchangeable than is a hammer with a saw.

Just as carpentry tools evolved to extend the power of our hands, punctuation evolved to extend the power of our writing. Punctuation was added to writing because writing lacked the interpretive assistance of the volume, tone, pitch, stress, pauses, facial expressions, gestures, and body language of spoken communication.

Hence, punctuation tells readers when to pause (,), when to stop briefly so they can prepare for a closely related statement (;), and when to come to what the British call a full stop (.). Punctuation helps readers instantly identify quotes ("), questions (?), promises of further information (:), statements that are parenthetical ( ), interruptions of a sentence (—), and statements that are exclamatory (!). And the punctuation called capitalization helps readers distinguish a common noun, such as a *white house*, from a proper noun, the *White House*.

(See also "brackets and parentheses," "capital punishment," "colon or semicolon?" the many entries on commas, "dash but don't be rash," "exclamation pointers," the entries on hyphens, "questions that should not be marked," and the entries on quotation marks and on quotations.)

punctuation that puzzles   "What do you do when two different punctuation marks are called for at the same location in a sentence?," a student asked in a note to the instructor. The *wrong* answer is to include both, as in the just-cited example of a question mark followed by a redundant comma.

The instructor's instruction—"Retain only the question mark because that serves the stronger purpose"—was consistent with the consensus of usage commentators. Note that this last sentence illustrated the answer to *another* punctuation puzzle: Omit the period at the end of a sentence included within another sentence. On the other hand, do include a question mark when appropriate in the middle of a sentence: "When does this plane take off? was the question on everyone's mind."

punctuation at the close of a quote   See "quotation marks and terminal punctuation."

puns: the payoff may be grins or groans   All puns are risky. A pun that amuses some may annoy others.

For example, judge for yourself a caption for an Associated Press photograph in *The New York Times* (9/6/2000), "Russian President Is Overthrown," showing judo black-belt holder Vladimir Putin floored in a playful match with a 10-year-old schoolgirl in a visit by the Russian leader to Tokyo.

Above all, beware of puns that may creep into your writing when you're not watching. Here is an example, reprinted in the March 1994 *American Journalism Review* from *Life Insurance Selling* magazine: "Even in the dead of winter, however, we must all put on our trench coats and expose ourselves to as many people as possible."

pupil or *student*?   *Pupils* become *students* when they enter high school. They remain *students*, even beyond the university, if they pursue lifelong learning. But *students* can become *pupils* again by taking personal lessons from a master practitioner of the arts.

***purposefully* or *purposely*?**   *Purposefully* is usually a compliment, meaning "determinedly, with determination." Example: "She strode purposefully across the playground to confront the bully."

Purposely is often a criticism, meaning "on purpose, intentionally." Example: "He purposely neglected to tell his supervisor that the factory was going to be visited by government inspectors."

pushing the envelope   See "*envelop* or *envelope?*"

***Pyrrhic victory*: no cause for celebration**   A *Pyrrhic victory* is one that has been achieved at too heavy a price, like the victory in which Pyrrhus, King of Epirus, lost his best officers and many of his other men in a battle with the Romans at Asculum in 279 B.C. Pyrrhus was quoted by the Greek biographer Plutarch as saying, "Another such victory over the Romans, and we are undone."

Here's a modern example of *Pyrrhic victory* usage, from an *Economist* news item on the Internet (6/5/2002): "[German] Chancellor Schröder has won his court battle over his claim that he does not dye his gray-free auburn locks. But it could turn out to be a Pyrrhic victory. Many feel the chancellor has made himself a laughing-stock by taking such a matter to court."

Q

***quandary* or *quandry*?**   *Quandary* (preferably pronounced "QWAN-dah-ree" and meaning "dilemma, a state of uncertainty about what to do") is sometimes misspelled *quandry* because many people pronounce it that way.

Usage example: In war-torn Kosovo, the Serbian province inhabited mostly by Albanians, the head of American peacekeeping troops there told *The New York Times* (2/3/2001): "We are kind of in a quandary. We very much believe in human rights. [But] we also have a mandate to disrupt the insurgency [of armed Albanians] as much as we can."

***quantum*: a little giant**   *Quantum*, from the Latin *quantus* ("how much"), is a technical noun in physics for the smallest unit of radiant energy. But as a nontechnical adjective meaning "sudden and significant," *quantum* suggests large-ness, as in "a quantum increase in productivity."

Quantum jump technically refers to the abrupt transition of an atomic or molecular system from one energy level to another. Figuratively, *quantum jump* and *quantum leap* mean any "sudden, significant change."

The plural of *quantum* is *quanta*.

quantum mechanics can't fix cars   *Quantum mechanics* is the mathemati-cal formulation of *quantum theory*, which was developed by 20th-century scien-tists to explain the behavior of matter on the ultra-small scale of molecules, atoms, and elementary particles such as electrons and quarks.

quarrelsome or querulous?   A person who is *quarrelsome* ("tending to start arguments") may also be *querulous* ("complaining, fault-finding").

quarry: the prey and the place   Two words with completely different ori-gins share the spelling and pronunciation *quarry* ("KWAR-ee"). One *quarry* means "that which is hunted or otherwise pursued; animal or human prey." The other *quarry* means "an open excavation or pit from which stone or another useful material is obtained."

quasi: more than a prefix   The Latin *quasi* ("as if, as it were") serves English as a prefix, adjective, and adverb meaning "almost, somewhat, more or less."

The *quasi* prefix helped produce *quasi-stellar* ("resembling a star") object, better known by its acronym, *quasar*. *Quasi* can be pejorative ("tending to dis-parage or belittle") in the sense of "not genuine," as in a reference in the journal *Current History* (October 1998) to "quasi democracies of Indonesia [and] the Philippines." Note that *quasi-stellar*, a compound adjective, is hyphenated, but no hyphen is needed in the compound noun *quasi democracy*.

Quasi has several "respectable" pronunciations, according to *Merriam-Webster's Dictionary of English Usage*. That source recommends that you rhyme *quasi* with "Ray's eye" if you want to use the most common pronuncia-tion, and with "Ozzie" if you want to sound like Caesar.

questionable request   You don't need a question mark to terminate "a request courteously disguised as a question," says *The Chicago Manual of Style*. An example from that source: "Would you kindly respond by March 1."

***questionnaire*: a question of spelling**   To fill out the word *questionnaire* correctly, don't forget to double the *n*.

questions that should not be marked   Use a question mark when a question is actually being asked—"Are you paying attention?"—but not when a question is simply being referred to. "I asked if you were paying attention" is not a question; it's a statement that includes a reference to a question.

   Here's an example of a question with an *inappropriate* question mark, published in a dispatch from Naples, Italy, in *The New York Times* (11/5/1993): "Underlying the election of Nov. 21, though, the question is not so much who will govern the city but whether it can be governed at all?" (See also "questionable request.")

***quick* or *quickly*?**   When grammarians summon help, do they say "Come *quick*" or "Come *quickly*"? Both are correct, though *quickly* is preferred in formal usage. *Quick*, like *slow*, can function either as an adjective or as a "flat" form of an *-ly* adverb. (See also "adverbs that look like adjectives.")

***quiescent* or *quiet*?**   Though *quiescent* is from a Latin word meaning "to be quiet," *quiescent* means not just "quiet" but "inactive, motionless, tranquil, in repose." *Quiescent* is usually pronounced "kwi-ES-ent" but it may be pronounced with the beginning sound "kwee."

quintessential   See the entry for "*essential*."

quotation cuts   When you quote from a publication or public statement, indicate deletions of one or more words by inserting three dots. Some writers and editors use four dots—a sentence period plus the usual three dots—when the end of a sentence has been deleted or when the omission consists of a sentence or more. But if a quoted sentence is *intentionally* being left incomplete—for instance, to show that a speaker's voice has trailed off in the middle of a sentence ("I don't really think she . . .")—it is correct to use three dots instead of four.

In published interviews, professional writers do not use the three-dot ellipsis unless they need to show that a quote has been edited from a published source. Otherwise, newspaper and magazine interviews would resemble Morse code.

quotation-mark irony: make sure it's deliberate   Be alert to the possibility of using quotation marks that unintentionally indicate irony.

For example: If you write in office e-mail that "our boss is quite a 'leader,'" you're suggesting with the quotation marks around *leader* that the boss is no leader at all. Whether that is your intended message or not, you may need to find yourself a new boss.

quotation marks and terminal punctuation   When do punctuation marks—question marks, exclamation points, colons, semicolons, periods, and commas—go inside closing quotation marks, and when do they go outside?

British English follows the logical practice of placing a punctuation mark inside if it appeared in the original material, outside if it did not. American English adheres to the British practice except in the case of commas and periods. Under our peculiar American "law," commas and periods go inside the closing quote even if (as in this sentence) the quoted material consists of only one word.

How did this irrational usage of ours get started? According to William and Mary Morris' *Harper Dictionary of Contemporary Usage*, early American typesetters decided that "the quotation mark helps fill the small spot of white that would be left if the comma or period came outside the quote."

quotation marks that aren't needed   No need for quotation marks in this example: "He said he would 'resign' from his government post." The *resign* needed no quotes because we didn't learn anything by being informed that *resign* was the actual word he used.

When you're paraphrasing what somebody has said, do not use quotation marks for a word or phrase that the speaker happened to use unless the word or phrase is particularly dramatic or otherwise unusual. Quotation marks *would* be needed for the final phrase in this sentence: "He said he would resign from his post because it was 'painfully boring.'"

quotations: direct and indirect   Some fragmented quotes—involving a mixture of indirect and direct quotation—can produce an illogical statement.

Example: "He said he 'feels happy.'" The person being quoted is unlikely to have said, "I *feels* happy." The problem here is easily solved by removing the quotation marks from "feels happy." Alternatively, if it is important to show that you are using his exact words, retain the quotation marks and place an extra word or two inside: "He said, 'I feel happy.'"

Some fragmented quotes, though logical, contain an awkward switch in pronouns: "*He* said that it 'doesn't bother *me*.'" A simple solution is to make the entire quote indirect ("*He* said that it doesn't bother *him*") or, sometimes, to use a direct quote instead ("He said, 'It doesn't bother me'"). Note that when you make a quote indirect and move a quoted verb out of quotation marks, you may need to change the verb's tense. "He said that he 'will go to the meeting because the issue interests me'" would become "He said that he *would* go to the meeting because the issue *interested* him." (See also "tense must make sense.")

quotations within quotations   Use single quotes for a quote within a quote. ("I told my opponent, 'You'll never get me to change my position,' but he didn't believe me.")

Don't be confused by the quotation marks in publications written in British English. Such publications usually use single quotes for general purposes and double quotes for a quote within a quote.

quoting more than one paragraph   If a direct quotation continues for more than one paragraph, begin each new paragraph with quotation marks. But do not *end* any paragraph with quotation marks until you have reached the end of the last paragraph of the continuous quotation.

quoting sources   In a direct quotation longer than one sentence, do not keep your reader in suspense about the identity of the person being quoted. Identify your source within, or at the beginning or end of, the first quoted sentence.

Do not repeat the attribution during the remainder of an uninterrupted direct quotation. *Do* repeat the attribution each time you begin a separate quotation segment, even if your source has not changed. (Of course, you can use an appropriate pronoun rather than the person's name if the antecedent for the pronoun is clear.)

When you use attribution to introduce a single quoted sentence, the proper punctuation before the quotation marks is a comma. (For example: "Joe said,

'You can count on me.'") When your attribution introduces a quotation longer than a sentence, use a colon.

If you start a long quotation with a sentence fragment, close the quote at the end of the fragment. Then reopen the quote with a new sentence, preferably in a new paragraph, containing attribution such as "she continued."

When you switch sources, identify the new source immediately, at the beginning of a new paragraph of quoted material.

quoting without context   The riskiest place for a direct quote is in your first sentence.

Heed this warning from an article in the June 1992 *Quill* magazine of the Society of Professional Journalists, penned by Paula LaRocque, assistant managing editor and writing coach of *The Dallas Morning News*: "The worst place to present [quotes] is at the beginning. . . . They have no context. The readers don't know who's speaking, why, or why it matters. Without context, even the best quotations are wasted."

R

race: **a question of reality**   Dictionaries say that the word *race* is used in the sense of "subspecies," meaning "a genetically distinct population." "But," notes an in-depth article in the Science section of *The New York Times* (8/22/2000), "the more closely that researchers examine the human genome—the complement of genetic material encased in the heart of almost every cell of the body—the more most of them are convinced that the standard labels used to distinguish people by 'race' have little or no biological meaning." In the words of one of the scientists interviewed for that article, "Race is a social concept, not a scientific one."

Many of the world's most prominent scientists—including the late paleontologist-author Stephen Jay Gould (1941–2002)—have declared that *race* should be removed from the vocabulary of science because the term implies the existence of a distinct category that simply doesn't exist.

In *Saying What You Mean*, Robert Claiborne contends that the application of race to humans is "almost invariably inaccurate or confusing" and is often used as a rationalization for "discrimination, brutality, and murder." No human racial classification, says Claiborne, "tells you anything useful about the peoples concerned, except that they resemble one another in some ways (they also invariably differ from one another in other ways)."

But despite the mounting evidence that *race* is scientifically meaningless, the general public and people in public life probably will continue to use the word for some time to come. "Everyone believes that races exist and we all function as if they did," *The New York Times* was told (1/10/1998) by Yolanda Moses, a former president of the American Anthropological Association. Indeed, the year-2000 census forms asked all Americans to identify themselves by choosing one or more of the five "racial" categories: Asian, white, American Indian/Alaska Native, Black/African-American/Negro, and Native Hawaiian/Pacific Islander. In addition, the Census Bureau provided a blank space for anyone to write in "Some other race."

Recommendation: If you use the word *race*, you cannot go wrong if you do so in the sense of a social rather than scientific classification. (See also "ethnic and racial classifications.")

rack or **wrack?**   This pair can confuse even a professional wordsmith. For example, the assistant editor of *The Wall Street Journal*'s editorial page, Melanie Kirkpatrick, referred (12/23/1997) to a "heart wracked [should have been *racked*] by doubt."

A heart or a whole person can be *racked* ("tortured, tormented"), as if being stretched on a medieval *rack*. In the same sense, a person can be nerve-*racked* but is not likely to be nerve-*wracked*. The word *wrack* is an old spelling variant of *wreck* and today means "wreck, destroy," as in the cliché *wrack and ruin*.

When you seriously challenge your mental capacity, *rack* ("stretch") your brain, but don't *wrack* ("destroy") it. A sports score is *racked up* (not *wracked up*), because *racked up* comes from poolroom scorekeeping by means of counters on an overhead frame or *rack*.

raise or **rear?**   According to an old saying, "The British raise plants and animals, and they rear children, but Americans raise all three."

That's true. *Raise* has become completely acceptable in referring to the upbringing of children in Standard American English.

raise or **rise** (nouns)?   If you go to work in England, don't expect a raise. There, the word is *rise*.

Except for that difference, *rise* is an appropriate synonym for "increase" in both British and American English. Examples: England's *Economist* (2/7/1998) reported that President Clinton "announced a rise of 4% in government spending." A *New York Times* headline (2/18/2000) said: "[Federal Reserve Chairman] Greenspan Warns of Another Rise in Interest Rates."

raise or **rise** (verbs)?   You can't go wrong if you use *raise* as a transitive verb (one requiring a direct object) and *rise* as an intransitive verb (one not requiring a direct object).

As noted in the *Random House Webster's Unabridged Dictionary*, "To *raise* something is to cause it to *rise*." For example: "If you raise the curtain, the audience will see it rise."

raison d'être is beyond reason   This French import is not just a synonym for "reason." *Raison d'être* ("RAY-zone DET-ra") means "a reason or justification for *existence*." The *Random House Webster's Unabridged Dictionary* cites this example: "Art is the *raison d'être* of the artist."

ranging from: don't forget the range   Use the expression *ranging from* only when a *range* ("limits between which variation is possible") really exists. "From dollars to yen" is not a *range*, but "from one cent to a dollar" is.

rapt or **wrapped**?   Department stores expect their gift-*wrappers* to pay *rapt* ("deeply absorbed") attention to their job.

Usage example of *rapt*: The *New York Times* (1/19/2001) reported that the U.S. Senate Judiciary Committee, considering the nomination of John Ashcroft for attorney general, "listened raptly" when a Missouri judge, Ronnie White, testified that he had lost his chance to be a federal judge because Ashcroft as a U.S. senator had misrepresented him as being soft on crime.

rarely ever or **rarely if ever**?   In the phrase "rarely ever," the word *ever* is redundant because it adds nothing to the "seldom" meaning of *rarely*. But "rarely if ever" is useful because *if* adds the idea of "if at all."

ravage or **ravish**?   *Ravage* poses no usage problem, as long as you remember that it means "to plunder" or "to cause great damage." A town can be *ravaged* by an invading army or by a storm.

But the verb *ravish* and its adjective and noun must be used with caution. In rare usage listed by dictionaries, *ravish* conveys the "plundering" sense of *ravage*. More commonly, though, *ravish* means "to abduct" or "to rape."

Ravish also means "to overwhelm with an emotion such as joy," so that musicians who play the drums breathtakingly well can *ravish* audiences without fear of what a punster might call legal repercussions.

The adjective *ravishing* means "entrancing, inspiring joy or delight," as in "a ravishing smile."

Be especially careful how you use the noun *ravishment*. It can mean either "rapture" or "rape."

ravel or **unravel**?   Those words have the same meaning. But don't show off by saying *ravel*. Use the version—*unravel*—that is clearly understood. (See also "*loosen* or *unloosen*?")

readability and reality   The best-known research on the question of how writers can maximize their readability was conducted about half a century ago by educator-editor-author Rudolph Flesch. His "Flesch score" for measuring readability—used by many word-processing programs today—awards high marks for short words, short sentences, short paragraphs, active verbs, and personal pronouns.

But note: For the sake of variety and therefore greater impact, don't hesitate to use some long words, some long sentences, some long paragraphs, some passive verbs, and some impersonal pronouns.

real or **really**?   As an adjective and nothing but an adjective, *real* can modify only nouns. *Real* is misused in a sentence such as "Harry was real sorry." Depending on your intended meaning, say either that Harry was "*really* [truly] sorry" or that he was "*very* [extremely] sorry."

really **should be used rarely**   Preserve the impact of the adverb *really* ("truly") by using it only as a contrast to what is false.

Don't describe a message as "really important" unless you're comparing it with messages that only *seem* important. Don't say that a product "really performs better than the others" unless you're responding to a suspicion that it doesn't. Don't say that you "really don't mind working overtime" unless people assume that you do. In those examples, all you usually need to say is that the message is important, the product performs better, or you don't mind.

Feel free, however, to use *really* as an interjection ("a grammatically isolated word expressing an emotion"), meaning "indeed." For example: "Really, I won't put up with his insults anymore." (See also "*very* is usually unnecessary.")

***Realpolitik* is all too real**   This italicized and usually capitalized word, adopted from German and pronounced "ray-AHL-poh-lih-TEEK," means "practical politics, especially a political policy based on power rather than ideals."

***Realtor*: a capital job**   The American occupational title *Realtor* doesn't apply to every real-estate agent; it designates a member of the National Association of Realtors. Because *Realtor* is a registered trademark, it must be capitalized.

The preferred pronunciation of *Realtor* has two syllables: "REEL-ter." If you pronounce it with three, be sure to say "REE-uhl-ter" rather than the incorrect (though often heard) "REEL-ah-ter."

***rebound* or *redound*?**   The verb *rebound*—which contains most of the word *bounce*—means "bounce back." For example, a *New York Times* headline reported (6/12/2000): "Oil Industry Rebounds in Canada As It Becomes Top U.S. Supplier." *Rebound* is also a noun, for "the act of rebounding." Example: A *New York Times* editorial (9/2/1998) titled "Rebound on Wall Street" commented on the fact that "the stock market bounced back yesterday."

The verb *redound* means "to have a result that contributes to a person's honor or disgrace." ("Her good deeds *redounded* to her credit.")

***rebut* or *refute*?**   NBC news anchor Tom Brokaw (9/11/1998) reported that President Clinton's lawyers had issued a statement *refuting* charges that Clinton had committed impeachable offenses. Later in his broadcast, Brokaw substituted the word *rebutting*, giving the misleading impression that the verb *refute* was just a synonym for *rebut*.

To *rebut* is to offer an opposing argument ("to deny the truth or accuracy of"), as when a trial lawyer offers a *rebuttal* ("counterargument") in court. Only rarely is a lawyer able to *refute* ("prove false, disprove") an opposing argument. To help you remember that *rebut* denies whereas *refute* disproves, note that *rebut* contains an argumentative *but*, and *refute* contains an *f* as in *false*.

Usage example of *rebut*: According to a contributor to *The New York Times Book Review* (2/27/2000), *New Republic* senior editor John B. Judis hoped in his book, *The Paradox of American Democracy* "to rebut [offer an opposing argument to] a common school of sociology . . . that holds that a small 'power elite' acts to stymie fundamental reform in the United States."

Usage example of *refute*: So many people in recent decades have used *refute* when they mean *rebut* that dictionaries now define *refute* as meaning not only "disprove" but also "deny." But usage commentators approve of *refute* only to mean "disprove," as in a *Modern Maturity* article (March–April 2000) observing that "the notion that most . . . creative people dry up at 50 is quickly refuted [disproved] by a glance at the recent past." The article pointed out—to cite here only a few examples—that Pablo Picasso painted his *Rape of the Sabines* at 81, Dame Agatha Christie oversaw production of the movie version of her *Murder on the Orient Express* at 84, and Frank Lloyd Wright designed New York's Guggenheim Museum at 91.

recall, recollect, or **remember?**   Though these memory-retrieval verbs are often used interchangeably, you'll earn the admiration of word connoisseurs if you use *recall* and the somewhat old-fashioned *recollect* only when the act of remembering requires concentrated effort. When little or no memory-retrieval effort is required, use *remember*.

Risk-free usage: "'Remember that you are under oath,' the prosecutor instructed the defendant's friend, 'and tell the jury what you can recall about the behavior of the defendant on the morning after the crime.'"

Of the three verbs examined in this entry, *remember* is your only choice for recognizing someone or something ("Remember me?"), emphasizing an assertion ("Remember that honesty is the best policy"), serving as a reminder of something that needs to be done ("Remember to brush your teeth"), bearing someone in mind ("I shall remember him in my will"), and extending greetings ("Remember me to your parents").

recur or **reoccur?**   The verb *recur*, the adjective *recurrent*, and the noun *recurrence* generally refer to something that happens *repeatedly*, like the flu season.

Reoccur, *reoccurrent*, and *reoccurrence* generally refer to something happening for *the second time*, like lightning striking twice in the same place.

reductio ad absurdum: an absurd contradiction?   The phrase *reductio ad absurdum* (Latin for "reduction to an absurdity") refers to a technique in logic in which a hypothesis is proved by demonstrating that its negation involves an absurdity.

But *reductio ad absurdum* is usually interpreted to mean the *dis*proof of a hypothesis by demonstrating the absurdity of its consequences. Indeed, that is the only interpretation listed in most dictionaries, with the notable exception of the listing of both interpretations by *Webster's New World Dictionary*.

Risk-free recommendation: If you use the less popular definition cited at the beginning of this entry, you'd better let your audience know that you know you are contradicting the common interpretation.

redundancy: a synonym for *tautology*?   Dictionaries say a redundancy is a tautology, and a tautology is a redundancy. But careful communicators disagree. They use *redundancy* to mean a "closely placed repetition of the same sense in a different *word* or *phrase*" (see examples in next entry), and *tautology* to mean "a closely placed repetition of the same sense in a different *idea* or *statement*" or "a statement that contributes no new information."

In the field of logic, a tautology is—in the definition of *The American Heritage Dictionary*—"an empty or vacuous statement composed of simpler statements in a fashion that makes [the statement] logically true whether the simpler statements are factually true or false." That dictionary gives "Either it will rain tomorrow or it will not rain tomorrow" as an example.

redundancy: a vice and a virtue   The word *redundancy*, derived from a Latin word for "overflow," is commonly defined as "repetition that is unnecessary." But it can also mean "repetition for the sake of clarity or emphasis" or "repetition of parts or all of a message to circumvent transmission errors."

The need for clarity may be served in spoken communication when you use the redundant *12* in "12 noon" and "12 midnight" and the redundant *a.m.* and *p.m.* in "8 a.m. tomorrow morning" and "8 p.m. tonight."

Emphasis is often cited as a justification for redundancy in advertising.

Consider, for example, "*garden* vegetables" and "*oven-baked* rolls." Likewise, redundancy is often used for emphasis in everyday conversation, as when an irate customer swears never to "return to that store *again*." Repetition to circumvent transmission errors occurs routinely in the writing of checks, as in the redundant last two zeros in a check entry for *$500.00*. Redundancy is also widely accepted in certain idiomatic expressions, such as *null and void, rant and rave*, and *wrack and ruin*.

But a pointless redundancy wastes space and time. Moreover, it is likely to cause readers to engage in a frustrating search for an extra meaning that isn't there. For example, consider a *New York Times* story quoting "respected national security experts" (7/4/2004). That phrase left the reader wondering if some national security experts are not respected. If so, wouldn't they no longer qualify as experts? Moreover, how can anybody become an expert in anything without achieving respect?

Now, consider the potential for puzzlement in such pointless pleonasms (redundancies) as: *actual* fact, adequate *enough*, *advance* planning, *and* etc., alongside *of*, *armed* gunman, *at a* later *time*, *brief* glimpse, *completely* eliminated, connect *together*, continue *on*, *craven* coward, enclosed *herewith*, equally *as*, estimated at *about*, fall *down*, fewer *in number*, *general* trend, *helpful* assistance, *huge* throng, *important* essentials, joined *together*, large *in size*, *mutual* affinity, *new* innovation, *new* recruit, *one* half, *overly* simplistic, pizza *pie*, *pleasantly* cordial, *past* history, *possible* choices, *puzzling* mystery, rain *activity*, raze *to the ground*, red *in color*, reflect *back*, *sad* misfortune, *serious* crisis, *sudden* impulse, sufficient *enough*, *sworn* affidavit, *tiresome* cliché, *totally* destroyed, *toxic* poison, *unexpected* surprises, usually *but not always*. (See also "*body*, as in victim," "*gift* should be freed of redundancy," "redundant bilingualisms," and "*until*: watch what you're up to.")

redundant acronyms and initialisms   The initialism for automated teller machine, *ATM*, is often referred to as ATM *machine*. And in a misuse of the acronym for a personal identification number, *PIN*, a letter from South African Airways (5/11/2004) advised customers that they could obtain information from the airline's Contact Center only by using their personally assigned "PIN number."

Such redundancies are so common that you can even find one in the carefully edited *American Heritage Dictionary*. In the year-2000 edition, a usage note near the top of page 1949 refers to the computer-world initialism for Hypertext Markup Language, *HTML*, as HTML *markup language*.

redundant bilingualisms   Though the United States is a nation of immigrants, most of the nation's native speakers of English are unilingual. Therefore, many Americans redundantly say "Sahara *Desert*," unaware that *sahara* means *desert* in Arabic; "*Mount* Fujiyama," unaware that *yama* is Japanese for *mountain*; "Rio Grande *River*," unaware that *rio* is Spanish for river; and "Sierra Madre *Mountains*," unaware that *sierra* (from a Spanish word for *saw*) is a Spanish-derived English word for a range of mountains characterized by a serrated (saw-toothed) outline.

Early in 2005, the owner of Southern California's Anaheim Angels baseball team was ridiculed by cartoonists, commentators, and late-night television comedians when he decided to rename his team the Los Angeles Angels of Anaheim. The new name, designed to be more marketable, thus redundantly identified the team as "the the Angels *Angels*," inasmuch as the city name *Los Angeles* is Spanish for *the angels*. The city of L.A. originated in 1791 as a settlement known as *El Pueblo de Nuestra Señora la Reina de los Angeles de Porciúncula* or *The Town of Our Lady the Queen of Angels of the Little Portion*. Its official name became *El Pueblo de la Reina de Los Angeles*.

Usage advice: Some apparent bilingual redundancy is unavoidable, as in the English *the* followed by the Spanish *the* in references to the many organizations and institutions associated with a place name like *Los Angeles*. You'd be absurdly obsessive to delete the word *the* in referring, for example, to "*the* Los Angeles County Museum of Art," "*the* Los Angeles Philharmonic Orchestra," or "*the* Los Angeles Police Department." In all such cases, the reference clearly is to a place called Los Angeles, not to any actual angels. (See "*hoi polloi*.")

regard or ***regards*?**   For a formal substitute for "concerning" or "about," note that customary usage requires "*as* regards" but "*in* regard to" and "*with* regard to."

Turning to other meanings of *regard* and *regards*, remember that you *regard* ("consider, look upon") someone as a friend, and that you have *regard* ("respect, affection") for that person. But you send that person your *regards* ("respectful, affectionate good wishes").

reign or rein? These sound-alike words are easily confused, especially because they both can be used in connection with government.

The noun *reign* means "the exercise of sovereign power, as by a monarch," "the period during which a monarch rules," or simply "dominance." The verb *reign* means "to exercise sovereign power" or "to be predominant." Memory tip: *Reign* is the last part of the word *sovereign*.

The noun *rein* literally means "the leather strap that restrains a horse." By extension, *rein* means not only "a means of restraint or guidance" but also "a means by which government and other power is exercised." Hence, a monarch's *reign* may end when an invader seizes the *reins* of government.

The verb *rein* means "restrain," as in the following sentence from *The Wall Street Journal* (3/28/2002): "Time and again during the past few years, problems in Japan's banking system or financial markets have threatened to spin out of control, only to be reined in at the last moment by the government."

Usage examples from *The New York Times*: "Gen. Augusto Pinochet . . . reigned over Chile as a dictator for 17 years" (10/18/1998). "[Saudi Arabia's Crown Prince Abdullah] gathered up the reins of power during the protracted illness of his half-brother, King Fahd" (12/4/2000).

reiterate: how's that again? If you use *reiterate* in the usual way, as a synonym for "say or do again," almost everyone will understand you. But some word guardians will accuse you of redundancy. That is because the rarely used *iterate* (from the Latin *iterum*, "again") itself means "say or do again." *Reiterate* therefore has the literal sense of "say or do again once again," which would be appropriate only if someone is repeating more than once. Indeed, some precise writers use *reiterate* only in the sense of "say repeatedly."

That would seem to leave you with *iterate* when you just want to say "say again." But *iterate* is so little known, outside of technical and scholarly writing, that your use of it would mystify most people.

Risk-free solution: Instead of saying *reiterate* or *iterate*, say "repeat," "restate," "say again," or "say repeatedly," depending on your intended meaning. Whatever you do, never say "reiterate again," because that would mean "say or do *again-again-again.*"

rejoin: a verb with two lives   In addition to being a verb meaning "reunite" or "be reunited," *rejoin* is a separate verb meaning "to issue a rejoinder [a statement of response, often to a reply]."

Usage example: A *Los Angeles Times* article (5/9/2000) about Elian Gonzalez, the six-year-old Cuban boy caught in a custody fight between his Miami relatives and his Cuban father, reported that after a government-assigned pediatrician approved of "rescuing" Elian from the Miami relatives, a psychologist they hired "rejoined by stating that . . . removing him from the care of his relatives . . . would likely produce 'irreversible emotional damage.'"

rejoinder, retort, or riposte?   *Rejoinder* means "an answer, often to a reply." *Retort* means "a rejoinder that's hostile." *Riposte* ("rih-POST")—a term in fencing for a quick thrust after evading an opponent's lunge—can mean "a quick verbal thrust in response to a retort."

In the following joke, the punch line is a *rejoinder*: A psychiatrist, asked by a patient for a diagnosis, says to the patient, "I think you're in a state of denial." The patient replies, "No, I'm not!" To change that punch line from a rejoinder to a *retort*, have the patient reply, "No, I'm not, you fool!" To which the psychiatrist's *riposte* could be, "If I'm a fool and you're paying me for therapy, what does that make you?"

reluctant or reticent?   Contrary to widespread misusage, *reticent* has a narrower meaning than *reluctant*. *Reticent*—originating in the Latin *reticere* ("to keep silent")—means "reluctant to speak."

Defenders of the "reluctant to speak" meaning of *reticent* may be fighting a lost cause, judging from the observation of *The Columbia Guide to Standard American English* that *reticent* "is now developing a new meaning of 'hesitant or reluctant.'" For example, an article in *Fortune* magazine (8/9/2004) recalled that Arnold Schwarzenegger's wife, Maria Shriver, had originally been "reticent" about encouraging him to run for governor.

Likewise, *The New Fowler's Modern English Usage* reported that "evidence is accumulating that [*reticent* is currently] being used to mean 'reluctant to act,' and dragging the noun [*reticence*] along in the same direction." *The New Fowler's* added that the ultimate acceptance of *reticent* to express simple reluctance "has an air of inevitability about it." But that source warned that such usage "is nonstandard at present." And *Atlantic Monthly* usage columnist

Barbara Wallraff wrote in *Word Court* (Harcourt, 2000), "I am reluctant to accept the shift in meaning—and not reticent about saying so."

Risk-free recommendation: Use *reticent* only to mean "reluctant to speak," and make sure your context makes your intended meaning clear. Here's an example of clear use, in a *New York Times* headline (5/24/2004) about U.S. Speaker of the House J. Dennis Hastert: "Hastert, the Reticent Speaker, Suddenly Has Plenty to Say."

remediable or remedial?   The adjective *remediable* means "*capable* of being remedied." The adjective *remedial* means "*intended* as a remedy."

renaissance or Renaissance?   As a lowercase noun, *renaissance* means "revival, renewal, rebirth, resurgence, reawakening." ("San Franciscans are reveling in a cultural and economic renaissance," the *Los Angeles Times* reported on August 16, 1996.)

As an uppercase noun, *Renaissance* refers to "the great revival of art, literature and learning in Europe from the 14th to the 17th century."

A *renaissance man* or *renaissance woman* is "one who has acquired profound knowledge or efficiency in several fields." The quintessential *renaissance man*, Leonardo da Vinci (1452–1519), was a Renaissance painter, poet, sculptor, musician, philosopher, naturalist, architect, engineer, and inventor. In his spare time, he conducted research in physics, astronomy, geology, and biology.

rendezvous more than once?   *Rendezvous*, pronounced "RON-day-voo," is spelled the same way but pronounced "RON-day-vooz" in the plural.

Rendezvous can mean a prearranged meeting (for spacecraft or lovers) or a prearranged meeting *place* (military or social). Originating as a French word for "present yourselves," *rendezvous* is believed to have entered English in the late 16th century as a word for a place where troops are to assemble.

renown or renowned?   Be careful not to write the short word *renown* (a *noun* for "fame, eminence") when you mean *renowned* (an *adjective* for "famous, celebrated"). In an embarrassing example of that mistake, Cal State University Dominguez Hills ran an online promo (1/18/2005) about a continuing-education television series hosted by "Gene Parrish, the renown public radio/television personality."

Also, when you reach for the full word *renowned*, be careful of sloppy spelling, as in the following sign I saw a few years ago in the window of the Gas Lamp Quarter Antique Store in San Diego: "Wyatt Earp, the most famous lawman of the Old West, was renouned as a crack shot." Another misspelling, *reknowned*, has appeared in some prominent newspapers, including the *Cleveland Plain Dealer* (1/17/2005) and the *St. Petersburg Times* (1/18/2005). *Reknowned* can be frequently found among orthographically challenged advertisers on the Internet, where you'll have no trouble finding, for example, "reknowned" speakers, artists, and spirit mediums.

rent the air?   *Rent* is more than the noun and verb involving payments for the use of someone's property. *Rent* is also a noun and the past tense and past participle involving the act of *rending* ("violently ripping"). That *rent* has the additional meaning of "piercingly disturb with sound," as in a *Los Angeles Times* news story (3/1/1997) reporting that "gunfire rent the air."

repair is two verbs and two nouns   The verb *repair* that is a synonym for *fix* is derived from a Latin word meaning "put in order." As a noun, that *repair* means "the process or an instance of repairing" or "general condition after repairing."

Related words: *reparable* ("possible to repair") and *reparation* ("the process of repairing or of making amends by means of compensation").

The other verb *repair* started as a Latin word for *repatriate* ("return to one's country") and then came to us from Old French and Middle English words for *return*. In modern English, *repair* means "to go or go customarily." Usage example: Ugandan President Yoweri Museveni "often repairs to his cattle ranch," according to an article about that African leader in *Time* (9/1/1997). As a noun, that *repair* means "the *act* of going or going customarily" or "a place one goes to or goes to customarily."

repel or repulse?   Freeman's *Words to the Wise* and other usage books prescribe *repulse* for "*drive away*, spurn, snub," and *repel* for "*cause repulsion* in." That prescription is filled in this sentence: "She repulsed him [drove him away] because he repelled [caused repulsion in] her."

The American Heritage Dictionary reported in its third edition (1992) that "in recent years . . . there has been an increasing tendency to use *repulse* in the sense 'cause repulsion in.' . . . Still, writers who want to stay on the safe side may prefer to use only *repel* when the intended sense is 'cause repulsion in.'"

repertoire or repertory?   As *The New Fowler's Modern English Usage* notes, *repertoire* ("REP-er-twar") and *repertory* (rhyming with "story") are "essentially the same word, being the French and English equivalents of Latin *repertorium* ('an inventory, a catalogue')." Indeed, one meaning of *repertory* is *repertoire* ("the songs, plays, operas, and other pieces that a player or company is prepared to perform" or "any range of skills of an individual or group").

But *repertory* is preferably used in its special sense of "a theater or theatrical group that presents works from a particular repertoire." *Repertory* is often used as an abbreviated way of saying *repertory company*.

replete isn't *complete*   *Replete*—frequently misused as a synonym for *complete* or *equipped with*—means "abundantly supplied." Usage example: "The Book of Job is replete with legal metaphors," William Safire wrote in *Lend Me Your Ears: Great Speeches in History*.

replica: more precious than you think?   In today's typical use of *replica*, *The New York Times* (2/3/2001) referred to "a replica of a first century A.D. street market" in a story about the opening of a Bible theme park in Orlando, Florida.

Such use of *replica*, as a "model," is widely accepted. But do not use *replica* with that meaning in fine art. Among professional artists, as noted by *The Oxford English Dictionary*, a replica is "a copy of a work of art, properly one made by the original artist."

replicate should be left to experts   *Replicate* is appropriately used in the technical sense of "copy exactly, as in repeating the exact results of an experiment." You risk being regarded as pretentious if you use *replicate* as a substitute for such plain words as *copy*, *duplicate*, or *repeat*.

reprieve has its limits   *The New York Times* (6/1/2000)—in one of its rare usage mistakes—reported that Texas Governor George W. Bush was about "to grant a temporary reprieve for a man scheduled to be executed." That distinguished newspaper's writers and editors should have been alert to the redundancy of "temporary reprieve": *Reprieve* means a temporary halt. (See also "redundancy: a vice and a virtue.")

reprise rhymes with *breeze* Say "ree-PREEZ." So let's have no *reprise* ("repetition, recurrence, resumption") of the pronunciation that rhymes with *surprise*. The same goes for *reprise* as a verb meaning "repeat, resume."

requirement or requisite? *Requirements* are demands that must be met. *Requisites* are objects that must be included.

respective and respectively should be used thoughtfully The adverb *respectively* ("separately, in the order just named") is sometimes useful and sometimes useless.

The word was useful when *The Wall Street Journal* reported (3/18/2002) that Enron International's chief executive, Rebecca Mark, and its president, Joe Sutton, "received bonuses of $54 million and $42 million, respectively, for work on an Indian power plant project." In that statement, the word *respectively* communicated the message that the first-named person received $54 million and the second-named person received $42 million. Without *respectively*, the sentence would have indicated that each person received, or at least had a share of, both bonuses.

The word *respectively* was useless when *The Journal Gazette* of Fort Wayne, Indiana, advised its readers (7/15/2001) that "because of the [Fort Wayne police] department's reporting policies, an attempted robbery or burglary is classified as an actual robbery or burglary, respectively." In fact, that redundant *respectively* was worse than useless, because it encouraged readers to engage in the futile effort of reviewing a statement that was already complete.

The adjective *respective* can also be useful or useless. *Respective* is useful in this sentence: "Each day, Betty drives her two children to their respective schools." Without the word *respective*, the sentence might be interpreted to mean that Betty drives both children to the same schools (perhaps an elementary school and a music school) each day. But *respective* is useless in this statement: "At three o'clock each day, all the children in that school return to their respective homes."

restaurateur or restauranteur? The English language adopted *restaurateur* ("restaurant owner or manager")—literally meaning "one who restores [you and your energies]"—from French about two centuries ago. Today, though the anglicized *restauranteur* is common in English speech, the original French word (without the *n*) is preferred in English writing.

restive or **restless?**   The careless use of *restive* as a synonym for *restless* has been documented for many years by usage guides. Back in 1975, historian-usagist Jacques Barzun confided to readers of his *Simple and Direct: A Rhetoric for Writers* that he had "given up" on hoping that people would maintain the distinction between these two adjectives. But not everybody has given up on this cause.

The American Heritage Book of English Usage and the British *New Fowler's Modern English Usage* urge their readers to carefully separate *restless* in the sense of "characterized by inability to rest or relax" from *restive* in the sense of "balky, unruly, difficult to control."

Examples of the precise use of *restive*: A *Newsweek* (2/28/2000) story about Iran focused on "a skilled political operator [who] maneuvers between restive youth and a rigid old guard." *The New York Times* (11/19/2000) published a story about "a far western outpost" in China where "a Muslim majority lives restively under Chinese rule."

restoration or **Restoration?**   The word *restoration* ("renewal, reestablishment") becomes *Restoration* when reference is made to the reestablishment of the English monarchy that began in 1660 after the collapse of the republican government that had been led by Oliver Cromwell. Nearly a couple of centuries later, the French had their own Restoration, with the return of the Bourbon monarchy after the defeat and exile of Napoleon.

resume spelling your *résumé?*   Without the acute accents, the noun *résumé* ("a summary of qualifications") can be mistaken for the verb *resume* ("to begin again").

resurrectionist used to have a profane meaning   Though *resurrectionist* can mean "a believer in resurrection" or "a person who resurrects something literally or figuratively," the word is also a synonym for the 18th- and 19th-century-English "resurrection man" who used to exhume and steal dead bodies in order to sell them to medical schools for dissection.

revel or **revile**?   If you *revel* (pronounced "REV-il" and meaning "to engage in noisy and lively festivities") late at night, your neighbors may *revile* (pronounced "re-VILE" and meaning "to speak abusively about") you.

Revel can also mean "to take great pleasure or delight [in]," as in "She reveled in her new freedom."

reverent and **Reverend**: **adjectives of respect**   The lowercase adjective *reverent* means "showing respect." The uppercase adjective *Reverend* means "deserving respect."

Just as public officials are referred to as *the Honorable* (or *the Hon.*) So-and-So, clergymen are referred to as *the Reverend* (or *the Rev.*) So-and-So.

The Reverend Dr. Martin Luther King Jr. means *the revered* Dr. Martin Luther King Jr. And *the very revered* is the descriptive address for *the Very Reverend* Harry S. Pritchett Jr., dean of New York City's Episcopal Cathedral of St. John the Divine. As noted by Professor Hans P. Guth in his *New Concise Handbook*, the standard American English usage is "the Rev. George Price," or "the Rev. Mr. Price," not "the Rev. Price," "the Reverend," or "Rev. Price."

Reverend is used in *some* churches as if it were a *noun* that expresses a title like *Professor* or *Doctor*, and a member of their clergy may be referred to by name as "Reverend Jones" or by occupation as "a reverend." But dictionaries list *reverend* as an adjective, except for *informal* use as a noun.

Moreover, the adjectival phrase *the Reverend* (or *the Rev.*) preceding the name is prescribed by *The Penguin Dictionary of American Usage and Style*, by *The New Fowler's Modern English Usage* and by the stylebooks of the Associated Press, *The New York Times*, *The Washington Post*, *The Wall Street Journal*, and the *Los Angeles Times*.

Risk-free recommendation: Introduce or refer to a member of the clergy as "*the* Reverend Mr./Ms. So-and-So" unless a church spokesperson instructs you otherwise.

reversal or **reversion**?   *Reversal*, the noun form of the verb *reverse*, means "the act of putting in an opposite direction." *Reversion*, the noun form of the verb *revert*, means "a return to a former condition, return to a former owner."

In the frequently used phrase *revert back*, the word *back* is redundant.

***revolting*: use this word carefully**   If you write that the students at a certain university are *revolting*, make sure your context makes clear whether you mean to say they are "rebelling" or "repulsive."

***revolve* or *rotate*?**   Earth *rotates* ("spins, turns") on its axis and *revolves* ("orbits, circles") around the Sun.

***rhapsodically* extravagant**   This adverb literally means "in the manner of a rhapsody, an ancient Greek epic poem or a musical composition suggestive of improvisation." The adverb's more common, extended meaning is "in a manner that is extravagantly enthusiastic."

Usage example: A *New York Times* editorial (2/8/2001), expressing concern about the anti-environmentalist reputation of President George W. Bush's Secretary of the Interior, Gale Norton, observed that "when Ms. Norton talks rhapsodically about protecting 'national [wilderness] treasures,' she is usually talking about the national parks, which under law cannot be [opened up for oil and gas exploration] anyway."

***rhetoric*: a Jekyll-and-Hyde word**   This is another case in which you'll have to rely on your context to clarify your intended meaning.

Rhetoric is "the art of speaking or writing effectively and persuasively" (or the study of that art). As dictionaries confirm, however, *rhetoric* is now understood to also mean "empty talk, language that is insincere."

***right* or *rightly, wrong* or *wrongly*?**   See "adverbs that look like adjectives."

***ritzy* is in the eye of the beholder**   If you use this slang word, make sure your intended meaning is clear.

Ritzy is from the palatial Ritz Hotels opened by Cesar Ritz in Paris (1898) and London (1905). For people who crave the last word in luxury, *ritzy* means "elegant, posh, smart, fashionable, exclusive." For people who are offended by those who *put on the ritz* ("ostentatiously display wealth"), *ritzy* means "showy, flashy, pretentious, snobbish, snooty."

***riven* as in *driven* apart**   *Riven*, which rhymes with *driven* and means "torn apart," is the past participle of *rive*, which rhymes with *drive* and means "to tear apart." A person who *rives*, which rhymes with *drives*, is a *river* that rhymes with *driver*.

Usage example from *The New York Times* (10/28/2000): "From the moment of [our nation's] founding, it was riven with conflict: agrarian vs. rural, patrician vs. plebeian, Old World loyalists vs. New World iconoclasts, Indian vs. settler, German vs. French, slave vs. freeman." (See also *"patrician or plebeian?"*)

rivet: the noun and verb   Some people find it riveting ("engrossing") to watch construction workers engaged in the bolt-installing act of riveting. The verb *rivet*—from an Old French verb meaning "to attach"—literally means "to securely fasten or hold with a *rivet* [metal bolt]." Figuratively, the verb means "to securely hold attention."

Insider's tip: If you can arrange to review movies for your local newspaper or TV station, make sure you say each film is "Riveting!" Pretty soon, movie companies may begin inviting you on all-expenses-paid junkets to meet the stars.

rob or steal?   Nobody can be charged with *robbing* jewelry or other property. The object of robbery must be a person or an establishment, such as a jewelry store. Thieves do not *rob* jewelry; they *steal* it.

Romance as an adjective   The phrase *Romance languages*—referring to French, Spanish, Italian, Portuguese, Romanian, and some lesser-known languages—is a reminder that those languages evolved from Latin, the language of the ancient *Romans*.

Romans counted on this   In Roman numerals, the numbers 1 through 10 are written I, II, III, IV, V, VI, VII, VIII, IX, and X. The large numbers are L = 50, C = 100, D = 500, and M = 1,000.

romantic or Romantic?   The lowercase adjective *romantic* can mean "expressing love" or "unrealistic." As author-columnist Richard Hitchins notes in *The New York Review of Books* (5/31/2001), "a romantic 'interlude' is rather a good thing, but a romantic 'scheme' is rather not."

For example, *romantic ideas* can be affectionate or impractical.

The usually capitalized *Romantic* means "of or pertaining to [usually capitalized] Romanticism, a literary and artistic movement in Europe during the late 18th and early 19th century." Characteristics of the Romantic style included a mystical reverence for nature along with an emphasis on emotion and imagination over intellect and rules.

rout or route?   *Rout*, which rhymes with *bout*, is a noun meaning "overwhelming defeat, disorderly retreat," and it's a verb meaning "to defeat overwhelmingly."

Route, as a noun for "highway or other course for traveling," rhymes with *boot* or *bout*, in that order of frequency. *Route*, as a verb meaning "send by a specified route," is usually pronounced like *rout*.

rule of thumb: don't be an accomplice   Carpenters once employed a "ruler of thumb," using the length of the thumb's first joint to make approximate measurements of an inch. Whether or not those carpenters actually used that phrase, their "thumb-ruler" practice probably explains why people for at least three centuries have been using the phrase *rule of thumb* for any procedure or way of thinking that usually does the job without scientific precision. (For example, here's a rule of thumb that some people use when encountering a person for the first time: "Be suspicious if that person won't look you in the eye.")

The expression itself remains useful, and there's no reason you should not use it. But you should be aware that *rule of thumb* in recent decades has become widely linked to a separate meaning that has no basis in reality. That's because somebody, somewhere, began spreading the false notion that the phrase *rule of thumb* actually originated in some ancient sexist practice—supposedly later adopted in English and American law—allowing a man to beat his wife if the beating instrument was no thicker than a thumb.

Nobody has ever been able to identify such a rule, ancient or otherwise. But its existence has seemed plausible because wife-beating has long been tolerated in many parts of the world. Given that tragic, continuing behavior, the mythical, wife-beating origin of the phrase *rule of thumb* has gained acceptance by sheer repetition. For example, it has been cited as if it were established fact by a few judges, by several journalists, a textbook on women's studies (*Women: A Feminist Perspective*, Mayfield Publishing, 1989), and even by the group of scholars and lawyers who prepared a report on wife abuse for the United States

Commission on Civil Rights, *Under the Rule of Thumb: Battered Women and the Administration of Justice* (1982).

The false story about the sexist origin of *rule of thumb* has been exposed repeatedly, as in David Wilton's book *Word Myths* (Oxford, 2004) and, a decade earlier, in Henry Ansgar Kelly's "Rule of Thumb and the Folk Law of the Husband's Stick" (*Journal of Legal Education*, 9/1/1994). But the myth seems destined to survive the debunking.

Suggestion: Forgive those who innocently perpetuate the myth. But don't become their accomplice in promoting this item of linguistic ignorance.

run-on sentences   See "sentences that run on."

ruthless: **what happened to *ruth*?**   Dictionaries define *ruthless* as "having no ruth [compassion], pitiless." *Ruth* as a synonym for *compassion* is extinct today, though you'll find its fossil in a famous line of poetry by Milton: "Look homeward, Angel, now, and melt with ruth."

S

saccharin or *saccharine*?   The noun for the sugar substitute *saccharin* requires an *e* to become the adjective for "overly sweet or sentimental."

sacreligious or *sacrilegious*?   This word is often misspelled and mispronounced as if it contained the word *religious*. The correct spelling is *sacrilegious*, because it is the adjective formed from *sacrilege*, pronounced "SACK-rah-lij" and meaning "disrespectful treatment of a sacred person, place, thing, or idea." The correct pronunciation of *sacrilegious* is "sack-rah-LEE-jus."

sacrosanct: **is nothing sacred?**   Be careful with *sacrosanct*. It literally means "regarded as sacred, beyond criticism." But when not used in a specifically religious context, *sacrosanct* often is used ironically, with the result that it means "supposedly beyond criticism."

Sahara says it all   See "redundant bilingualisms."

said can be said again   Don't look desperately for synonyms for *said* when you are repeatedly quoting somebody. As Robert Claiborne wrote in *Saying What You Mean*, "Straining after substitutes [for *said*] is the mark of an amateurish writer."

If you use an alternative to *said*, make sure it is appropriate. Don't *emphasize* without emphasis, *explain* without explanation, or *declare* without a formal *declaration*. Don't *affirm* unless something is being declared true, *state* unless something is set forth in detailed formality, *assert* unless something is being expressed strongly, or *reveal* unless something that was hidden is being uncovered. (See also "*disclose, divulge,* and *reveal* only what's been hidden.")

said or *says*?   The past-tense verb *said* is used in newspaper news stories, but the present-tense *says* is used for the sake of vividness in newspaper headlines and in many news stories in broadcasting.

In newspaper feature stories and all other non-news pieces in print and broadcasting, *says* conveys the idea that the time of a quote is irrelevant, as in "A dermatologist, Dr. Hugo Moore, *says* suntanning is America's most foolish fashion." But *said* would be appropriate if the writer reports that the dermatologist made that statement at the time of his installation as president of a professional society.

Saint or *St.*?   Spell it out with people. Abbreviate it with places.

salad days: **not for dieters**   In Shakespeare's *Antony and Cleopatra*, the queen of Egypt refers to her former love for Caesar as something that happened during "my salad days, when I was green in judgment." In modern English, this figure of speech still means "green, in the sense of young and inexperienced."

sanction: **for approval and disapproval**   As a verb, *sanction* means "to authorize, approve."

As a noun, *sanction* means "authorization, approval." But it can also mean "a form of punishment, such as trade restrictions, imposed by a nation or nations to show disapproval of another nation's actions."

This is yet another word that requires that a writer make sure the meaning is clear from the context.

***sanguinary* or *sanguine*?**   The adjective *sanguinary* means "bloody, accompanied by bloodshed," as in a *New Yorker* film critic's description (7/27/1998) of the Steven Spielberg movie *Saving Private Ryan* as "surely one of the most sanguinary pictures ever made by a big Hollywood studio."

The adjective *sanguine*—derived, like *sanguinary*, from the Latin word for blood, *sanguis*—means "optimistic." Usage example: "I am even less sanguine than [19th-century English naturalist Alfred Russel] Wallace about possibilities for predicting the future," wrote paleontologist-author Stephen Jay Gould in the September 1998 *Natural History* magazine.

That "optimistic" meaning of *sanguine* reflects the medieval belief that one's temperament depends on the relative amounts in each person's body of four fluids, called "humors." People with a ruddy face and hopeful disposition were called *sanguine* because their predominant bodily fluid was assumed to be blood. People who were slow and stolid were called *phlegmatic* because their predominant fluid was assumed to be phlegm. If melancholy ("black bile") predominated, the person was *melancholic* ("gloomy"). If choler ("yellow bile") predominated, the person was *choleric* ("irritable, hotheaded").

***sans*: do without it?**   According to Professor J. N. Hook's *Appropriate Word*, only "show-offs" use the French word *sans* in English. Stick with the plain English word *without*.

But *sans* is correct in a term used by graphic designers and typesetters, *sans serif* (sometimes spelled *san-serif*). It refers to a type font without serifs, the little lines (often horizontal) that extend at an angle from the main strokes that make up the letters in many type fonts.

sarcasm   See "*irony* or *sarcasm*?"

***satyrs* or *Satyrs*?**   The *Satyrs* ("SAY-ters") were ancient Greek deities of the woods and fields, who had the bodies of men but the horns and feet of goats, and who spent their time drinking and chasing nymphs (goddesses of nature).

Lowercase *satyrs* are lecherers, some of them victims of *satyriasis* ("a psychiatric disorder characterized by excessive preoccupation with sexual gratification or conquest, and attributable to feelings of inadequate masculinity").

Satyriasis ("say-ter-RI-eh-sis") is also called *Don Juanism*, from the legendary Spanish nobleman famous for his seductions. But a *Don Juan* is simply "a womanizer." (See also "*nymphs* or *Nymphs*?")

say, how about that Tom Swift?   In imitation of the style of the old Tom Swift adventure books, Americans during the 1950's traded such *Tom Swifties* as " 'I don't have a drinking problem,' Tom gulped."

Unless you are trying to revive the Swifties game, don't refer to something that was *said* by using a verb that refers to something that was *done*. Examples of such illogical usage: " 'I agree,' she *nodded*." " 'Have a doughnut,' he *smiled*." " 'I hate doughnuts,' he *grimaced*." A person can nod to indicate her agreement, but when actual words are uttered, they cannot be "nodded." Likewise, smiling and grimacing communicate emotions but do not convey actual words. A person might smile or grimace while speaking, but he cannot "smile" or "grimace" the utterance itself.

Simple editing takes care of the problem. Change "she nodded" to "she said, nodding" or "she said with a nod." Change "he smiled" to "he said, smiling" or "he said with a smile"—or make it a separate sentence, disconnected from the words uttered: " 'Have a doughnut.' He smiled at her. 'I made them myself,' he added."

If you do play the Swifties game, try playing a variation that's grammatical: " 'This knife won't cut,' Tom said bluntly."

scan: a three-faced word   If your boss asks you to *scan* a report, you'd better find out exactly what he means. He may want you to enter it into a computer or to study it. If he wants you to study it, he may want you to do so carefully or superficially.

Scan as a noun means any examination involving motion, such as "a scan of the horizon." For a couple of hundred years, *scan* as a verb has meant *scrutinize*, as in moving one's eyes "to examine carefully." Many careful communicators still use *scan* the verb that way. But a contradictory meaning that emerged in the 1920's—"to examine hurriedly, superficially" as in "scanning the headlines"— now tends to dominate *scan* usage.

If you use the verb *scan* in the sense of "study," make sure that your context makes your meaning clear. For example: "Take a minute to scan this report" or "I want you to spend the whole week, if necessary, scanning this report."

scarce or **scant**?   Both these words are sometimes used in the sense of "insufficient, inadequate." But *scarce* has its own sense of "rarely encountered," and *scant* has its own sense of "barely sufficient."

sceptics or **skeptics**?   You'll find sceptics in England, skeptics in the United States.

schadenfreude: a compact German import   The imported noun *schadenfreude* ("SHAHD-n-froi-deh") entered English in the late 19th century to identify an idea not conveyed by any single word previously introduced in our language. A combination of *harm* (the German noun *Schaden*) and *joy* (the German noun *Freude*), *schadenfreude* means "pleasure derived from another's misfortune."

Such pleasure is typically mixed with a feeling of guilt, according to a recent book about *schadenfreude*, John Portmann's *When Bad Things Happen to Other People*.

Usage example: In a *New Yorker* cartoon (8/4/2003), the cover of a magazine called *Schadenfreude Monthly* promises "scads of gruesome pictures" about an "obnoxious heiress's cosmetic surgery [that] goes horribly wrong!"

scheme: not the American plan   Do not be misled by references to the British use of the word *scheme* to mean "plan," as in "the British health scheme." On our side of the Atlantic, *scheme* commonly connotes a plan that is dishonest.

schism: a split over pronunciation   You will find something of a *schism* ("a separation into factions over issues of belief or practice") involving this word's pronunciation.

The preferred pronunciation begins like *sizzle*—"sizzem"—according to the Merriam-Webster and Random House dictionaries, *The American Heritage Dictionary*, *Webster's New World College Dictionary*, and *The Oxford English Dictionary*. Moreover, "sizzem" is the only pronunciation prescribed by *The New Oxford American Dictionary*.

But *The Oxford English Dictionary* says, "The pronunciation 'skiz'm,' though widely regarded as incorrect, is now frequently used for this word and its derivatives in the U.K. [United Kingdom] and North America."

Risk-free recommendation: If you pronounce this word "correctly"—as "sizzem"—many people will not understand you. Of those who do, many may think you are ignorant or pretentious. The simple solution to this dilemma is to use *schism* only in your writing, and then only when you are reasonably certain that your readers will know what it means.

schmooze is a valuable verb You'll find the Yiddish word *schmooze* (rhymes with snooze) in American and British dictionaries because it conveys a unique sense of chatting. As defined by *The American Heritage Dictionary of the English Language*, *schmooze* (also spelled *shmooze*) means "to converse casually, especially in order to gain an advantage or make a social connection."

This verb can be transitive (acting directly on an object), as when a politician schmoozes a wealthy campaign contributor, or intransitive (without a direct object), as when a politician schmoozes *with* a wealthy campaign contributor. The word can also be used as a noun, if you want to "have a schmooze." (See "*chutzpah*: dare to use it correctly.")

Usage example: A front-page *Los Angeles Times* story (1/7/2005) about the naming of a new head of Viacom Inc.'s Paramount Pictures contained this headline and sub-headline: "A Carefully Crafted Rise to Paramount's Top: Schmoozing, skill and calculation took Brad Grey from gofer to studio chief, many say." The article suggested that Grey's rise was partly attributable to his having schmoozed, among others, "legendary talent manager Bernie Brillstein [and] power hitters such as the late Brandon Tartikoff, then president of NBC Entertainment." (See "*chutzpah*: dare to use it correctly.")

schools of fish are not accredited The *school* in "school of fish" derives from the Old English *scolu* and a Modern English sense of *shoal*, both of which denote either "multitude" or "multitude of fish swimming together." *Shoal* also spells the completely separate word that means "an area of shallow water."

Our word for the human *school* comes from a Greek word for "leisure" (*schole*), because the ancient Greeks associated leisure with the opportunity to pursue knowledge.

scissors is or **scissors are?** Say *scissors are*, or *a pair of scissors is*. Do the same with *clippers, pincers, pliers, shears,* and *tweezers.*

Scot, Scots, Scottish, Scotch, scotch A *Scot* lives in Scotland with other *Scots*, preserving *Scottish* culture and raising *Scottish* terriers. The adjective for broth and tape is *Scotch*. The verb *scotch* means "stamp out, put an end to."

scrimp and save: a redundancy? No. Extremely poor people *scrimp* ("economize") just to survive, often without being able to *save* ("put aside") anything.

sculp, sculpt, or **sculpture?** The back-formations *sculp* and *sculpt* (both meaning "to sculpture") have gained wide acceptance in recent decades. But they were dismissed by dictionaries as "jocular" early in the 20th century, and you may encounter some lingering resistance to them.

Simple solution: As Theodore M. Bernstein reminded readers of his *Careful Writer*, the word *sculpture* is not just a noun but also "a perfectly good verb."

sea changes that occur on land The first known use of *sea change* (currently meaning "major change or transformation") was by Shakespeare in *The Tempest*: *Full fathom five thy father lies, / Of his bones are coral made: / Those are pearls that were his eyes: / Nothing of him that doth fade, / But doth suffer a sea-change / Into something rich and strange.*

Usage example from the *San Francisco Sunday Examiner & Chronicle* (4/23/2000): "Now that technology enables us to work anywhere, . . . home offices [are] going through a sea change."

seasonable or **seasonal?** The first of this often-confused pair means "appropriate for a season, timely," and the second means "of or relating to a season, occurring in a particular season."

Seasonable winter clothes are those that are appropriately warm for that time of year. Economists refer to *seasonal* variations in employment.

see: more than meets the eye In addition to meaning "perceive with the eye," the verb *see* can be used in many other ways: "I see [perceive mentally] a brilliant future for that student." "I don't see [imagine] that happening." "I see [regard] them as dedicated parents." "I'll see [find out] who's at the door." "I try to see [recognize] only the good in people." "I think she would like to see [keep company with] him often." "I hope the doctor will see [admit, as for consultation] me soon." "I'll see [escort] you home." "I'll see [make sure] that the place is cleaned up." "I see [understand] what you're getting at."

As a noun, *see* means "seat or center of authority, office of a bishop." The Holy See—the "see [center of authority] of the bishop of Rome [the pope]"—is a synonym for the Vatican. Usage example from *The New York Times* (5/13/2001): "The Holy See has moved at its own pace for centuries."

self-confessed: guilty of redundancy   The *self* in *self-confessed* is not needed.

semicolonitis   Writers and editors who suffer from what I call semicolonitis have a compulsion to sprinkle sentences with semicolons as if those punctuation marks were paprika being sprinkled on a salad. Semicolons are supposed to add sense, not seasoning. For their proper use, see "colon or semicolon?"

sensibility or sensitivity?   Both these words denote "the capacity to respond *to* or be affected *by* something." But they have different shades of meaning.

Sensibility, to quote the *Random House Webster's Unabridged Dictionary*, "is, particularly, [the] capacity to respond to aesthetic and emotional stimuli, [as in] 'the sensibility of the artist.'" A *New York Times* obituary for film director Akira Kurosawa (9/7/1998) said he had "a painter's eye for composition, a dancer's sense of movement, and a humanist's quiet sensibility."

Sensitivity, depending on the context in which it is used, can mean "sympathetically responsive to the feelings of others" or "overly responsive to what others *do* and therefore easily annoyed."

sensual or sensuous?   *Sensuous* is often used as if it's a synonym of *sensual* ("pertaining to the gratification of physical appetites, especially sexual"). But *sensuous* has a separate history that is respected by word connoisseurs.

Sensuous was coined by the 17th-century English poet John Milton when he decided that the English language needed a nonsexual adjective meaning "appealing to the senses, especially those involved in the appreciation of poetry, art, and music."

sentence adverbs   See "commas for sentence adverbs."

sentence fragments are impostors A sentence fragment masquerades as a sentence, with a capital letter at the beginning and a period at the end. But you can distinguish a sentence fragment from a complete sentence by the fact that the fragment does not convey a complete thought. The fragment is either an isolated phrase—such as "Just before midnight"—or an isolated dependent clause—such as "Because he returned just before midnight." Note that the just-cited phrase and dependent clause would make sense only if they were a response to someone's question.

In another example of a sentence fragment, a university student of mine with severe writing deficiencies submitted a homework essay that began with the fragment that I've italicized: "*The professor who has been teaching 30 years.* He finally retired." To avoid that error, the student could have written, "The professor, who has been teaching 30 years, finally retired."

The Oxford Companion to the English Language acknowledges that the word *sentence* is "notoriously difficult to define." So, until linguists solve that centuries-old problem, we must rely on the centuries-old traditional definition of a sentence as "a grammatical unit that expresses a complete thought." As *The Oxford Companion* concedes, the "complete thought" definition of a sentence raises the additional question of how the term "complete thought" should be defined. Putting that new question aside for the moment, let's consider some sentences to see if they fit with our commonsense notions of "complete thoughts."

If you walk up to a stranger in the street and say "A bag of popcorn," the stranger will think you are strange. In that situation, "A bag of popcorn" does not express a complete thought and is therefore nothing but a sentence fragment. But "A bag of popcorn" does express a complete thought if it's your response when your companion at a movie theater asks if you would like something at the candy counter. In that situation, "A bag of popcorn" is actually an abbreviation of the sentence "I would like a bag of popcorn."

Even the single word "Never" can be a complete sentence, if it is a response to a question. Are there more examples that can be cited of apparent sentence fragments that are really complete sentences? *Yes. Absolutely. Definitely. Of course. No doubt about it.*

sentences should not be choppy Good writing involves a pleasing mix of short, simple sentences with relatively complex sentences that link major and subordinate information. *Choppy writing* consists of a series of short sentences that tend to confuse the reader by giving equal emphasis to major and subordinate information.

Here is an example—from Diana Hacker's *Rules for Writers*—of how three choppy sentences can be combined into one sentence in which the subordinate ideas are included in an introductory phrase:

Choppy: "The huts vary in height. They measure from 10 to 15 feet in diameter. They contain no modern conveniences."

Improved: "Varying in height and measuring from 10 to 15 feet in diameter, the huts contain no modern conveniences." (Notice that the appropriate emphasis—in this case, at the end of the sentence—was given to the information "no modern conveniences.")

sentences that defy logic   A sentence composed of unrelated facts can produce a *non sequitur* ("nahn SEK-wi-tuhr," Latin for "it does not follow"), an illogical conclusion such as an inference that does not follow from a premise or from something previously stated.

Here's an example of a non sequitur: "Born in Detroit, he loved to play the piano." That sentence implicitly defies logic because the content of the second part of the sentence has no relationship with the content of the first part.

In these variations of that sentence, logic has been restored: "Born in Detroit, he spent most of his life making cars." "Born into a family of musicians, he loved to play the piano."

sentences that run on   Contrary to what you may have been taught by educators whose own education about grammar was incomplete, a "run-on sentence" is not a sentence that runs on too long. It is a sentence that runs into another. In other words, a run-on sentence is an inappropriate joining of independent clauses—clauses that can stand alone as sentences—as in "Mary had a little lamb its fleece was white as snow."

The other form of a run-on sentence is the "comma splice," alias "comma fault," which is an inappropriate joining (splicing) of independent clauses with a comma: "Mary had a little lamb, its fleece was white as snow."

All run-on sentences can be cured in three ways: Turn the second independent clause into a separate sentence. Join the independent clauses with a semicolon. Join the independent clauses with a comma that's followed by a coordinating conjunction: "Mary had a little lamb, *and* its fleece was white as snow." (The other coordinating conjunctions are *but, for, nor, or, so,* and *yet*.)

You can cure some run-on sentences if you can turn the first clause into a dependent clause by introducing it with a subordinating conjunction. In the following example, the addition of the bracketed subordinating conjunction cures a comma splice: "[Though] my wife loves to read historical novels, I don't care for them at all." Other subordinating conjunctions (those that introduce a dependent clause and show that clause's relationship with the clause that follows) include *although, after, as, because, before, if, once, since, unless, until,* and *while*.

Comma splices are acceptable only when the two independent clauses are short, alike in form, and extremely easy to read. The following example is from *New York Times* columnist Paul Krugman (6/15/2004): "I report, you decide."

sentences that run on into adverbs Many unacceptable comma splices occur because the writer assumes that two independent clauses have been joined by a comma and a coordinating conjunction (see list in above entry) when in fact the writer has used a conjunctive *adverb*. Failure to recognize a conjunctive adverb is the cause of the comma splice in this example: "He studied hard for the course, nevertheless he failed."

Here's how to repair sentences of this kind: Replace the conjunctive adverb (for example, *nevertheless*) with a conjunction (*but* or *and*). Or, if you keep the conjunctive adverb, precede it by a semicolon and follow it with a comma: "He studied hard for the course; nevertheless, he failed."

Other conjunctive adverbs are *accordingly, afterwards, also, anyhow, besides, consequently, earlier, furthermore, hence, however, indeed, instead, later, likewise, meanwhile, moreover, nonetheless, otherwise, similarly, still, then, therefore,* and *thus*.

sentences with delayed meaning Should professors of other ethnic groups be given the opportunity to teach African-American studies? That's an interesting subject for debate. But there is no debate about the fact that the question begins with a phrase—"professors of *other ethnic groups*"—that makes no sense to the reader until the end of the sentence. Such problems are easily corrected. For example: "Should the opportunity to teach African-American studies be given to professors of other ethnic groups?"

***sententious* or *sentient*?**   *Sentient* ("conscious, capable of sensation") must be distinguished from *sentientious*, which *itself* has meanings that must be carefully distinguished: "terse, pithy, epigrammatic" or "given to excessive moralizing."

***separate* or *seperate*?**   Students who want to get an A in spelling are careful to spell this word with an *a* in the middle. (See also "spelling traps.")

sequence of tenses   See "tense must make sense."

serial comma   See "commas are advisable before the last item in a series."

***series is* or *series are*?**   The answer is both. The word *series* can mean "*one set* of related things occurring in succession" or "*more than one set* of related things occurring in succession."

Usage examples: "*A series* of storms *is* expected." "*Two series* of storms *are* expected." (See also "plurals that are also singular.")

***serve* or *service*?**   Serve people. Service things.

***sesquipedalian* spells show-off**   This adjective, from Latin for "a foot and a half," is used to describe show-off words that seem that long. One of the most famous sesquipedalian words is the 28-letter *antidisestablishmentarianism* ("opposition to those who oppose an established order"). But that word is humbled by a 45-letter monster that can be found in *Webster's Third New International Dictionary: neumonoultramicroscopicsilicovolcanoconiosis* ("a lung disease caused by breathing volcanic or other fine dust"). (See also "short words are long on impact.")

***set* or *sit*?**   *Set*, a transitive verb, requires an object. *Sit*, an intransitive verb, requires only a subject. After you *set* ("place the usual things on") the table, you may *sit* ("take a sitting position").

Exceptions: The sun intransitively *sets*. Hens intransitively *set* (or *sit*) on their eggs. (See also "verbs: transitive or intransitive?")

seven sevens   The number *seven*, considered in many cultures to have mystical influence, has figured prominently in the history of language and thought.

Babylonians, Egyptians, and other ancient peoples believed in seven sacred planets. The ancient Greek historian Herodotus wrote about an Arabian oath in which blood was smeared on seven stones. Ancient Jewish farmers observed every seventh year as a year of rest for the land, known as a Sabbatical year.

Here's some background about seven other sevens.

Seventh heaven ("a state of great joy and satisfaction") is in Christian theology the highest of heaven's seven levels of beatitude ("supreme blessedness or happiness").

The *seven sacraments* of Roman Catholics are baptism, confirmation, the Eucharist, penance, holy orders, matrimony, and anointing the sick.

The *seven deadly sins*—those punishable by an eternity in hell—are pride, greed, lust, envy, gluttony, anger, and sloth. They were identified by Christian writers as early as the sixth century and discussed definitively in the *Summa Theologica* by the 13th-century theologian Thomas Aquinas.

The *seven wonders of the world*, an ancient list of human-built spectacles, was compiled from reports by Hellenic travelers. The list consisted of the pyramids of Egypt; the Hanging Gardens of Babylon; Phidias' 40-foot, gold-plated statue of Zeus at Olympia; the huge, art-filled Temple of Artemis at Ephesus; the monumental tomb (Mausoleum) of King Mausolus at Halicarnassus; the Colossus of Rhodes, a 100-foot bronze statue of Helios, the sun god; and the 440-foot lighthouse on the island of Pharos, off Alexandria.

The *seven hills of Rome,* on or about which the ancient city of Rome was built, are the Palatine, the Capitoline, the Esquiline, the Aventine, the Caelian, the Quitrinal, and the Viminal.

The *Seven Gods of Luck*—a favorite subject of Japanese folksong, painting, and theater—are deities associated with good fortune and happiness. The Seven are often depicted in their "treasure ship" together with magical implements that include an inexhaustible purse and keys to a divine treasure house.

The *seven seas* in ancient Rome were a group of lagoons near what is now Venice. Today, the seven seas are "all the planet's seas," or, specifically, the North and South Atlantic, the North and South Pacific, and the Arctic, Antarctic, and Indian Oceans.

sewage, sewer, or *sewerage?*   A *sewer* system of underground pipes conveys waste matter called *sewage* to treatment plants that are part of a *sewage*-treatment or *sewerage* system.

sexism on the job   Moving toward gender neutrality, the U.S. Department of Labor's *Dictionary of Occupational Titles* changed *public relations man* to *public relations practitioner*, *shoe repairman* to *shoe repairer*, and *yardmaster* to *yard manager*. In similar changes made by the Bureau of the Census, *airline stewardess* became *flight attendant* and *fireman* became *firefighter*.

The *Random House Webster's College Dictionary* notes that "*actress, heiress* and *hostess* remain in active use, though many women prefer the terms *actor, heir* and *host*."

sexism and personal pronouns   See "pronouns can be agreeably nonsexist."

sexism, *man*, and *mankind*   You are in the Risk Zone today if you use *man* or *mankind* when you mean *humanity* or *humankind*, as in "Man's fate hangs in the balance." *The American Heritage Dictionary* reports that 81 percent of its usage panel still accepts the generic use of *man*, but only 58 percent of the panelists who are women accept that usage.

Sensitive writers today are replacing *man-made* with *synthetic, man in the street* with *average person, forefather* with *ancestor*, and *founding fathers* with *founders*.

***shall* or *will*?**   The *old* rule for the auxiliary verbs *shall* and *will*, emerging in the 19th century and taught to schoolchildren through much of the 20th century, was to use *shall* for the first person ("*I* shall") and *will* for the second and third person ("*You* and *they* will"). But leading usage commentators from the 1940's onward have been dismissing that rule as grammatically groundless and so contrary to what people actually write and say that the rule has become irrelevant. The phrase "I shall"—in routine messages such as "I shall see you tonight"—is now regarded as old-fashioned and pretentious.

Use *will*—"I will," "you will," "they will"—except in the following circumstances: expressions of determination ("I shall return," "We shall overcome"); requests for permission or agreement ("Shall I call you a cab?" "Shall we dance?"); and statements of obligation ("Jurors shall not discuss the case with friends or relatives").

***shambles*: no ordinary mess**   For centuries, *shambles* meant "slaughterhouse." Today, a *shambles*—plural in form, singular in meaning—is "a scene of great destruction" or just "a scene of great disorder."

shameful or shameless? A *shameless* ("lacking a sense of shame") person is not inhibited about engaging in behavior that is *shameful* ("causing shame; disgraceful").

shear or sheer? To *shear* is "to cut or trim with shears or a similar instrument." By extension, *to shear* means "to deprive of something as if by cutting." ("The dictator was *shorn* of his power.")

Sheer is an adjective meaning "thin, fine, transparent," as in "sheer stockings," or "without qualification or exception, in a complete manner," as in "sheer stupidity."

"*Sheer* [complete] madness" was obviously implied in the punning title "Shear Madness" for an article in *U.S. News & World Report* (8/11/1997) about controversial coal-mining operations that were removing (shearing) the tops of mountains in West Virginia.

sherbert or sherbet? For this frozen mixture of fruit, milk, and egg-white, place your *bet* on *sherbet*. You may hear and see a lot of *sherbert*, but some word guardians consider it a mispronunciation and a misspelling.

The term entered English in the early 17th century, from an Ottoman Turkish word for "cold fruit drink." Starting with as many as 14 English spellings, it evolved two that reflected its principal pronunciations, *sherbet* and *sherbert*. By the 18th century, *sherbet* became dominant. Though *sherbert* made a comeback in the 20th century and is now accepted as a second choice by some dictionaries, *The Columbia Guide to Standard American English* warns that you may encounter "purists" who accept only *sherbet*.

Incidentally, word historians have traced the fruit-flavored ice called *sorbet* to French, which obtained it from Italian, which obtained it from the same Turkish word that gave us *sherbet*.

shibboleth: a life-and-death pronunciation People who don't pay enough attention to their pronunciation should be reminded of the story behind *shibboleth* ("slogan, catchword, usage distinguishing members of a group").

The Old Testament Book of Judges says *shibboleth* (Hebrew for either "stream" or "ear of grain") was used by ancient Israel's Gileadite army as a battlefield password, because the Gileadites knew that their enemies, the Ephraimites, had difficulty pronouncing the sound *sh*. In retreat, members of the enemy army attempted to sneak across the Jordan River on foot at a shallow site occupied by the Gileadites. As each soldier attempted the crossing, he was asked by the Gileadites to say the password *shibboleth*. The Old Testament tells us that "forty and two thousand" were slain because they responded with the mispronunciation "SIB-olith."

shined or *shone?*   The general practice in American English is to use *shined* transitively (with a direct object) and *shone* intransitively (without a direct object). For example: "While Jonathan *shined* his shoes in preparation for proposing to Rosie, he noticed that the moon *shone* brightly."

short words are long on impact   One of world's most respected periodicals, the London *Economist*, has the following entry in its style guide: "Short Words: Use them. They are often Anglo-Saxon rather than Latin in origin. They are easy to spell and easy to understand. Thus prefer *about* to *approximately*, *after* to *following*, *let* to *permit*, *but* to *however*, *use* to *utilize*, *make* to *manufacture*, *plant* to *facility*, *take part* to *participate*, *set up* to *establish*, *enough* to *sufficient*, *show* to *demonstrate*, and so on."

Richard Lederer writes in his *Miracle of Language*: "If a long word says just what you want, do not fear to use it. But know that our tongue is rich in crisp, brisk, swift, short words. Short words are bright, like sparks that glow in the night." (Did you notice that the crisp, brisk quote you have just read consists entirely of words of one syllable?)

should have or *should of?*   See "*of*: to have and have not."

should **is not always good**   See "*ought* and *should* are not always good."

showed or *shown?*   A student took a needless risk by writing this sentence in a college newspaper: "My experience with the recycling program has showed me a lot of [things] that I wouldn't have learned in class." The student should have written "has shown."

Nobody disputes the use of *showed* as *show*'s past tense. But though *showed* has also been acceptable for centuries as a past participle, as in "has showed," the more common and more widely recommended choice is "has *shown*."

showstopper: **cause for applause?** Hold your applause until you determine if this informal word is being used in its theatrical or its technological sense.

Showstopper is defined in *Webster's New World Dictionary of Media and Communications* as "a performance, such as a song, that is so enthusiastically received by an audience that the show pauses to allow for [prolonged] applause." And, as noted by the Random House and American Heritage dictionaries, the meaning of *showstopper* has been extended to any "spectacularly arresting person or thing."

But in engineering and computer science, *showstopper* has emerged as a term for something that literally "stops the show" by presenting an insurmountable obstacle. In those contexts, *showstopper* means "a problem that makes success impossible." For example, *The Chronicle of Higher Education* (4/4/1997) quoted NASA planetary scientist Everett K. Gibson Jr. as saying, "We feel . . . there are no showstoppers to the ideas that we presented last August [about the possible discovery of fossilized life on Mars]."

shrank **or** *shrunk*? People who *shrink* ("draw back, as in retreat or avoidance") from criticism are well advised to use *shrank* for the past tense and *shrunk* for the past participle. Here are *shrank* and *shrunk* in action: "The dry-cleaning fellow *shrank* another one of my sweaters. So I told him that he *has shrunk* my clothes for the last time."

O. J. Simpson prosecutor Christopher Darden was wrong when he said, "The [murder] gloves appear to have *shrank*." Darden should have said *shrunk*. Likewise, the Walt Disney people chose the wrong form of *shrink* when they titled their 1989 movie, *Honey, I Shrunk the Kids*. They should have used *shrank*.

To help you remember how to use *shrank* and *shrunk*, try chanting the following mantra: *shrink-shrank-shrunk, sink-sank-sunk, drink-drank-drunk*.

shuttle **contains four words** The phrase "shuttles back and forth" is redundant. *Shuttle* means "to move back and forth."

sic **says "not a typo"** This always-italicized Latin word (for "thus, so, in this manner") is used within brackets in quoted matter to inform readers that something is accurately quoted though it is false or otherwise eyebrow-raising. For example: "He boasted that he had once been good friends with President Donald [*sic*] Reagan."

simplistic **is more than** *simple*   *Simplistic* is not a synonym for *simple*. The word *simplistic* means "overly simplified." Therefore, the oft-used phrase "too simplistic" redundantly means "overly overly simplified."

Simplistic is derived from the little-used noun *simplism*, which dictionaries define as "an act of oversimplification that ignores important details."

Correct usage: *Time* magazine observed (2/28/2000) that "it's simplistic to say that when TV *shows* bad behavior, it *induces* bad behavior among the audience."

since **ambiguity**   The word *since* conveys useful messages about time in its role as a preposition (meaning "continuously from") or as an adverb (meaning "from then until now").

But in its role as a conjunction, *since* can be unclear, its message about time sometimes becoming confused with an alternative message about cause. Consider the conjunctive *since* at the beginning of the following sentence: "Since Irwin married Marilyn, he's taken up tennis." That could mean merely that he's taken up tennis *during the period after* he married Marilyn. Or it could mean he's taken up tennis *because* his wife is a devoted tennis player. (See also "ambiguity alert," "ambiguity can always be cured," and "*as* ambiguity.")

single out **carefully**   If you are thinking about singling out a couple of your co-workers, think again. You can single out only one person, group, or thing at a time.

singular: **its fate was not unique**   *Singular*, like *unique*, used to unmistakably mean "one of a kind." But as the Fowler brothers observed early in the 20th century in their *King's English*, "slovenly use" caused *singular* to be reduced in the public mind so that it meant "remarkable."

Today's dictionaries define *singular* as "one of a kind" as well as "remarkable." If you use this muddy word, you will need to clarify your intended meaning with your context.

Sisyphus and his adjective   In Greek mythology, Sisyphus was a cruel king of Corinth who showed disrespect for the god Zeus and consequently was condemned to the eternal frustration of repeatedly pushing a heavy rock to the top of a steep hill, only to have the rock keep rolling back down.

Use the adjective *Sisyphean* (pronounced "sis-a-FEE-un" and meaning "endlessly laborious or futile") to describe a task so maddeningly frustrating that it can be compared to the punishment inflicted on Sisyphus.

Sometimes a Sisyphean task is identified by a direct reference to Sisyphus himself. For example, *U.S. News & World Report* (11/25/1996) published a political essay observing that "campaign finance reform is Sisyphus's work; the stone always rolls back downhill."

sleight or slight?   The slight addition of the letter *e* changes *slight* to a word meaning "cunning, dexterity," as in "*sleight* of hand." The pronunciation remains the same.

slew serves as a verb and a noun   In addition to being the past tense of *slay*, the word *slew* is a noun for "large amount or number" (from the Irish Gaelic *sluagh*, which means "multitude").

Usage example from *The Philadelphia Inquirer* (9/6/1998): "The phrase *age-defying* already is appended to a slew of personal-care products."

"slipshod extension"   Why do many precise, valuable words lose their precision and much of their value? According to Henry W. Fowler's *Dictionary of Modern English Usage*, such linguistic erosion is caused by the "slipshod extension" of a word's precise meaning.

"Slipshod extension is especially likely to occur," said Fowler, "when some accident gives currency among the uneducated to words of learned origin." Fowler added that a person who engages in slipshod extension is "injuring the language, however unconsciously, both by helping to break down a serviceable distinction, and by giving currency to a mere token word in place of one that is alive. He is in fact participating in what has been called the crime of verbicide." (See also "devalued words" as well as entries for *aggravate, alibi, anticipate, decimate, dilemma, simplistic, singular,* and *transpire.*)

slow or slowly?   See "adverbs that look like adjectives."

small or little?   Though these adjectives are synonyms, *little* has the connotation of "pleasingly or charmingly small." That's probably why you have never heard any stories about Small Bo Peep.

smell or ***reek*?**   When accused by a woman of "smelling," the great lexicographer Samuel Johnson (1709–1784) is said to have corrected her usage: "Nay, madam. *You* smell [perceive an odor]. I *reek* [give off an unpleasant odor]."

sneaked or ***snuck*?**   Your risk-free choice is *sneaked*, though *snuck* appears to be gaining some long-withheld respect.

When *snuck* emerged as an American variant of *sneaked* in the late 19th century, professional writers regarded it as a sign of ignorance. And today, *snuck* is dismissed as a nonstandard form to be used "only in quotations" (*Wall Street Journal* stylebook), to be "restricted to a frivolous context" (*Penguin Dictionary of American English Usage and Style*), and not to be used at all "by people who use proper English" ("Dear Abby" column of 4/9/2002).

But *The American Heritage Dictionary* reports that, despite the disapproval of *snuck* by 67 percent of its usage panel, "*snuck* appears in the work of many respected columnists and authors." The *Random House Webster's Unabridged Dictionary* reports that *snuck* is now "widely used by professional writers and educated speakers." *Merriam-Webster's Collegiate Dictionary* says that so many writers and speakers are using *snuck* that it "has risen to approximate equality with *sneaked*." *Merriam-Webster's Dictionary of English Usage* maintains that *snuck* even "stands a good chance to become the dominant form."

Risk-free recommendation: For now, use *snuck* only with a playful wink, as in this *Los Angeles Times* headline (7/28/1997) about the movie *My Best Friend's Wedding*: "The Film Musical That Snuck Up on Gen-X."

so **what?**   The conversational use of *so* as an intensifier meaning "very, extremely," as in "He was *so* handsome," has "a certain air of silliness" when it is used in writing. So said Henry W. Fowler in his 1926 *Dictionary of Modern English Usage*, and that is the consensus of usage commentators today.

Apart from the offense of "silliness," the intensive *so* has been found guilty of conveying an incomplete thought because it is an unfinished comparison. To complete the comparison, you need to say something like "He was so handsome that people thought he might be a movie star."

To stay on the good side of usage commentators, follow *so* with *that* in your writing when the conjunction *so* introduces a clause of *purpose*: "She frequently worked overtime *so that* she could save for an overseas vacation." But according to 83 percent of the usage panel of *The American Heritage Dictionary*, you don't need *that* to follow *so* when *so* introduces a clause of *result*: "She wanted to visit Europe next summer, *so* she began saving for the trip by working overtime."

so-called, unquote   If you want to express skepticism—for example, in reference to a person's reputation as a genius—write *the so-called genius* or *the "genius."* Inasmuch as you can express your skepticism with either *so-called* or quotation marks, writing *the so-called "genius"* would be redundant.

soiree should not be rushed   Try to spot the error in the following e-mailed invitation: "Join the Angeles Chapter as we celebrate the Sierra Club Outings Centennial with a soiree at Rancho Santa Ana Botanic Garden. Toast 100 years of outdoor fun, Saturday, November 17, 2001, 1:30 p.m."

The error in that invitation is in the scheduled time: 1:30 p.m. The word *soiree* ("swah-RAY") is derived from the French word *soir* ("evening"), as in the French expression *bonsoir* ("good evening"). Hence, *soiree* means "a social gathering, usually held for some purpose other than just socializing, that takes place *in the evening.*"

solecism: an ancient offense   As colonists have tended to do all through history, the ancient Greeks who colonized Soloi in Cilicia (in what is now southern Turkey) began to speak a variation of their native language. Back in Greece, that nonstandard manner of speaking Greek was sneeringly referred to as *soloikos,* and *soloikos* produced *soloikismos,* a Greek word for "speaking incorrectly." As handed down to us from the Latin *soloecismus,* our word *solecism* denotes "a nonstandard or ungrammatical usage."

sometime or _some time_?   "When she visits our city *sometime* [a time that's indefinite] next summer, she hopes we'll be able to spend *some time* [an interval or period] with her."

To test which form is appropriate, try inserting *quite* before *some.* If *quite* makes sense, you need *some time.* ("I haven't been to Chicago in quite some time.")

sop for Cerberus   A *sop* is a piece of bread or other food that is sopped ("soaked") in a liquid such as milk or gravy. Metaphorically, a *sop* is any offering given to appease, placate, or pacify.

A *sop for Cerberus* is literally a morsel of food used by characters in Greek mythology to temporarily pacify Cerberus ("SUR-beris"), the three-headed, dragon-tailed dog guarding the gate of Hades. By extension, a *sop for Cerberus* is any gesture of appeasement, such as a political leader's award of a government position to a rival.

In general usage, a *Cerberus* is "a formidable guard."

sources: when should they be identified?   There's no need to cite a source for information that's obvious, such as the fact that a presidential election is approaching. But responsible writers cite a source for information that's so questionable or debatable that it would cause readers to respond, "Says who?" A report that a major presidential candidate intends to withdraw would need a cited source.

Note, too, that you do not need to cite a source for information that's readily available, such as the published estimates of the current population of China. But you would need a source if you said those estimates are erroneous.

Fight the temptation to act like a know-it-all. Do not pass along sourceless information that you couldn't possibly have acquired on your own, such as the quality of food in a restaurant you've never patronized.

sources: when should they be trusted?   "A serious error [in the teaching of critical thinking] is failing to evaluate the credibility or reliability of sources," says a report on critical-thinking instruction recently published by George Washington University.

Help your reader evaluate your source's "credibility or reliability" the same way a trial lawyer establishes the credentials of a witness. If your source is supposed to be an authority in a particular field, summarize the source's accomplishments in that field.

Anybody can boast of prestigious-sounding awards, buy an academic degree from a diploma mill, operate a practice as a "therapist," or carry a business card that says "author, lecturer, and consultant." What institution granted the award or degree? What training does the "therapist" have? What has the author published? Who was the publisher? Where were the lectures presented? Who, if anyone, actually hired your source to be a consultant?

Sparta and its adjectives   Sparta, a militaristic city-state of ancient Greece, inspired the adjective *spartan* ("of or relating to Sparta and its people; frugal, austere, characterized by self-discipline and self-denial"). Usage example: *The New York Times* (1/25/2001) reported that the ailing communications-equipment giant Lucent Technologies had adopted "a spartan strategy" involving the elimination of more than ten thousand jobs.

The people of Sparta were also known for the extreme brevity of their speech. And because Sparta was the capital of a region called Laconia, Sparta inspired the adjective *laconic* ("terse, marked by the use of few words, concise even to the point of seeming rude").

specially or **especially**? *Specially* means "for a special purpose." ("She was specially trained for that assignment.") *Especially* means "markedly, to an exceptional degree." ("He said he felt especially honored because the prize was awarded by his colleagues.")

specie or **species**? *Specie*, sometimes mistaken for the singular of *species*, means "money in coin." *Species* is both singular and plural for the entity described in the next entry.

species are classy The basic unit of living things is the *species*, a collection of all individuals that share the same gene pool and are capable of interbreeding and producing fertile offspring. (A horse and a donkey can interbreed, though they are different species, but the resulting mule is sterile.)

An international system of taxonomy ("the science of classification"), based on the work of Swedish botanist-explorer Carolus Linnaeus (1707–1778), requires that organisms have a name (usually in Latin or Greek) consisting of a lowercase *species* preceded by a group of closely related species designated by an uppercase *genus*. Both parts of the name are italicized.

As *Homo sapiens* (Latin for "wise man"), we are the only surviving species of the genus *Homo*, which once included the likes of *Homo erectus* and *Homo habilis*. By contrast, bats survive today in some 200 genera comprising about 1,000 species, and orchids can be found in about 450 genera comprising more than 10,000 species. (*Genera* is the plural form of the word *genus*.)

Related genera are classified as members of a *family*. Related families are members of an *order*. Related orders are members of a *class*. Related classes are members of a *phylum* in the animal kingdom (*Animalia*) and *division* in the plant kingdom (*Plantae*). Family, order, class, and phylum or division designations are not ordinarily italicized.

Some scientists recognize separate kingdoms for organisms that are not clearly plant or animal, such as *fungi*, *protists* (protozoans, slime molds, and other one-celled organisms with a visible nucleus), *monerans* (bacteria, blue-green algae, and other organisms lacking a distinct nucleus), and *archaea* (organisms that resemble bacteria but are chemically and genetically more primitive).

As noted in *Smithsonian* magazine (December 1996), scientists who identify previously unknown species sometimes take playful advantage of the privilege of assigning a name to "their" species. For example, an entomologist who specializes in identifying new species of ground beetles of the genus *Agra* chose to name one of them *Agra vation*.

specious or **spurious?**   *Spurious* means "fake, counterfeit, not genuine." *Specious* means "not genuine but *appearing* to be genuine."

The adverb for *specious* is *speciously*, and the quality or state of being specious is *speciousness* or *speciosity*.

spell-check warning   No spell-check program could have detected the wrong word in a *New York Times* report (1/1/2002) that bank accounts in Argentina had been "party frozen," or the wrong word in a *Los Angeles Times* movie review (2/22/2002) that referred to "a daughter who sleeps around to support her heroine habit," or the wrong word in a 2003 California Employment Development Department flier advising students to conclude a job interview by thanking the employer for "there time."

spelling bee sting   Next time you're confronted by a pretentious speller, you may want to ask that person to spell *desiccate* ("to thoroughly remove water from, as in a process for preserving food"). Rare is the person who knows that *desiccate* has one *s* and two *c*'s. (See also "spelling traps.")

spelling compound words   Don't look for a rule about spelling compound nouns and adjectives—that is, nouns and adjectives formed from a combination of two or more words. You can't even rely on professional editors about this matter, as witness the fact that *The Wall Street Journal* (3/8/2002) identified someone as a magazine's "editor-in-chief," though the *Journal*'s own style guide prescribes the unhyphenated *editor in chief*.

For guidance on spelling compound words, you must turn to dictionaries. There, depending partly on which dictionary you choose, you'll find that *home run* is what is called an open compound but *homesick* is closed and *homegrown* is acceptably closed or hyphenated. In dictionaries you'll discover, for example, that a *coffee shop* is open but a *coffeehouse* is closed, that *life cycle* is open but *lifestyle* is closed, and that you must hyphenate *self-esteem* and all other *self-* starting nouns. (See also "*life* takes three forms.")

spelling tips Do not excuse your spelling mistakes by telling yourself that you are a bad speller. Remember that few of us ever spelled well enough to compete in the annual National Spelling Bee.

Instead of looking for excuses, cultivate two habits that spell good spelling even for the worst speller. When in doubt, consult a dictionary. To learn when to *be* in doubt, read voraciously ("in the manner of someone with an insatiable appetite").

When your dictionary lists more than one spelling, read the dictionary's front matter to learn how to interpret the order of the alternatives and the meaning of the words *or*, *also*, and *variant*. Often the first-listed spelling is the preferred one (especially if two spellings are presented out of alphabetical order), but the word *or* may signal that the spellings are considered equally correct. The words *also* and *variant* are typically used for spellings that are not the preferred forms. It is risky to choose these variants. Some dictionaries include them only because they are in use, not because they are correct.

As you may have been told in school, use *i* before *e* except after *c* or when sounded like *a* as in *neighbor* and *weigh*. But note the exceptions italicized in the following sentence: "*Neither* of the *society*'s *scientists seized* the chance to engage in that *weird* species of *leisure*."

spelling traps Some of the most commonly misspelled words are: *absence, absorption, acceptance, accessible, accustom, achievement, acquiesce, address, adolescence, affidavit, anonymous, Antarctic, argument, assess, auxiliary, basically, beginning, beneficial, bookkeeping, boundaries, bulletin, buoyant, bureaucracy, caffeine, camaraderie, cancellation, category, changeable, colossal, commitment, committed, compatible, competent, conceivable, condemn, conde-*

scend, conscience, conscientious, correlate, counselor, courageous, debtor, definitely, development, disastrous, discipline, dissipate, drunkenness, dumbbell, effervescent, eighth, enforceable, exaggerate, extemporaneous, exhilarate, fascinate, February, fictitious, forehead, forfeit, fortunately, genealogy, good-bye, government, and *handkerchief.*

Others are *hemorrhage, heroes, hierarchy, hoping, hundredth, hygiene, hypocrisy, indispensable, inferred, innocuous, innuendo, inoculate, inveigle, irresistible, laboratory, liaison, likable, likelihood, livelihood, loneliness, lovable, marriageable, miscellaneous, murmur, nickel, ninety, ninth, noticeable, occasion, occurred, oneself, parallel, pastime, permissible, picnicking, precede, questionnaire, queue, rarefy, resistance, resuscitate, salable, separate, serviceable, sheriff, siege, silhouette, simultaneity, sizable, skiing, stopping, stupefy, superintendent, susceptible, synonym, temperament, truly, tying, unmanageable, usable, usage, vacuum, villain, weird, writing, written, xylophone, yacht, yield,* and *zealous.*

(See entries for *abridgment, accidentally, accommodate, acknowledge, admissible, ageism, aging, anoint, bandanna, cauldron, coleslaw, commemorate, consensus, ecstasy, embarrass, fluorescence, glamour, greyhound, harass, hindrance, impresario, incidentally, iridescent, judgment, memento, minuscule, mischievous, misspell, sacrilegious, sherbet, supersede,* and *vacillate.*)

spirals go both ways   When you say something such as the cost of living is *spiraling,* you need to say whether you mean *up* or *down.* Remember that spiral staircases go both ways.

Usage examples: *The Wall Street Journal* (9/4/1998) reported that movie production and marketing costs "have spiraled *so high* that even some movies grossing $100 million at the U.S. box office—the classic benchmark for blockbuster status—wouldn't turn a profit." And in a 1998 book called *The Professor and the Madman,* author Simon Winchester described the "*downward* spiral" of a scholar's mental illness.

splitting infinitives: a needless fear   Many people are needlessly afraid of splitting an infinitive—inserting an adverb or other word between *to* and a verb—as in *to gradually recover* or *to boldly go.*

As *The American Heritage Book of English Usage* points out, "People have been splitting infinitives since the 14th century, and some of the most noteworthy splitters include John Donne, Samuel Pepys, Daniel Defoe, Benjamin Franklin,

Samuel Johnson, William Wordsworth, Abraham Lincoln, George Eliot, Henry James, and Willa Cather."

But split infinitives were forbidden by Latin-trained English grammarians of the 19th century, apparently because Latin infinitives (like Greek infinitives) were all single words and therefore could not possibly be split. The absolute rule against splitting English infinitives was repealed by leading usage commentators decades ago, though the *Cliffs Writing Proficiency Examinations Preparation Guide* sternly warns wannabe schoolteachers: "No split infinitives."

Fowler's *Dictionary of Modern English Usage*, Follett's *Modern American Usage* and other usage guides say you should split an infinitive when the split contributes to clarity or rhythm. Strunk and White's *Elements of Style* concedes that "some infinitives seem to improve on being split" and cites the split infinitive in the following sentence: "I cannot bring myself *to really like* the fellow." That source also approves a split infinitive when there is a need to emphasize an inserted adverb, as in "to *diligently* inquire." *The Chicago Manual of Style*, which listed the split infinitive as a "debatable error" in its thirteenth edition (1982), told readers of its fourteenth edition (1993) that "in many cases clarity and naturalness of expression are best served by a judicious splitting of infinitives" and called the practice "sometimes . . . perfectly appropriate" in its fifteenth edition (2003).

Sometimes a split infinitive is the only alternative to awkwardness and inaccuracy. That was true, for example, when *The New York Times* (7/16/1994) split an infinitive to tell its readers that "Microsoft Corporation . . . agreed *to immediately abandon* a number of important licensing practices." The phrase *to abandon immediately* would have been awkward, and the only other choices, *immediately agreed to abandon* or *agreed immediately to abandon*, would have inaccurately applied immediacy to the agreement rather than the abandonment.

But never split an infinitive if the result is awkward. For example, *to dangerously live* should be unsplit so that it reads *to live dangerously*. Likewise, it is better to unsplit clumsy, multiple splits such as *to painlessly, prudently, and profitably consolidate your debts* by putting the adverbs at the end.

splitting verbal phrases: another needless fear Don't be afraid to split a verbal phrase with an adverb, as in "had *scarcely* parted," "should *probably* go," and "will *never* be." The insertion of adverbs in verbal phrases prevents the awkwardness and ambiguity that would result if you were to separate an adverb from the verb it modifies.

As *Dallas Morning News* writing coach Paula LaRocque pointed out in her column for *Quill*, the magazine of the Society of Professional Journalists (May 1993): "The split verbal phrase is not an error. Good writers and speakers split them all the time."

The good writers of *The New York Times* follow this advice in their newspaper's stylebook: "An adverb used with a compound verb [that is, a verbal phrase] should normally be placed between parts of the verb (the way *normally* is, a few words back in this sentence, and the way *usually* is, in the next example): *He will usually take the opposing side.*"

The stylebook of the Associated Press offers this example of a split verbal phrase that is necessary to avoid ambiguity: "Those who lie are *often* found out." A writer or editor who is afraid to split a verbal phrase might foolishly allow this ambiguity: "Those who lie *often* are found out." Readers of that sentence would have no way of knowing if it is a warning for all liars or only those "who lie often."

If you look back at the paragraph above, you'll see that the same type of ambiguity problem would have arisen if I had replaced "splitting a verbal phrase *might foolishly* allow" with "*splitting a verbal phrase foolishly* might allow." In the latter version, the reader would think I was expressing concern only about verbal phrases that are split foolishly. (See also "modifiers make mischief when they are two-faced.")

Spoonerisms London-born William Archibald Spooner (1844–1930)—an Anglican priest who for many years lectured in history, philosophy, and divinity at Oxford University, is commemorated in today's dictionaries for his *spooner-isms* ("the transposition of sounds in two or more words, usually the initial sounds, to form an amusing combination"). Two examples are "hush my brat" for "brush my hat" and "scoop of boy trouts" for "troop of boy scouts."

Some dictionaries identify Spooner's spoonerisms as just slips of the tongue, blunders similar to what linguists call *metathesis* ("the transposition, within a word, of letters, syllables, and sounds," as in *aks* for *ask*). But many of the blunders attributed to Spooner seem intentional or even fictional, in the light of their consistently creative comedy. Consider these oft-quoted examples: Spooner reprimands a student who "hissed my mystery lecture," and then adds, "You have tasted two worms." Officiating at a wedding, he tells the bridegroom, "It is kisstomary to cuss the bride." And to someone at the wedding who is seated in the wrong place, he says, "I believe you're occupewing my pie. May I sew you to another sheet?" When he visits a friend's country cottage for the first time, he comments appreciatively, "You have a nosy little crook here."

Whether those particular spoonerisms were spontaneous or spurious, the phenomenon itself is undeniably real. Note, for example, a correction published in the *Des Moines Register* (9/17/1994) after that newspaper ran a notice about the upcoming First Federated Church's Back to School Bash. The correction explained that the event featured a "car bash." What the newspaper had reported was that the church had invited the school-bound children to a "cash bar."

squalor is filthy enough   The radio adviser known as Dr. Laura (6/22/2001) urged a listener to notify child-protective services about a child living "in filth and squalor." The *filth* in that phrase was redundant. As noted in the Merriam-Webster, Random House, and American Heritage dictionaries, among others, the word *squalor* means "wretched filth caused by neglect."

squinting modifiers   See "modifiers make mischief when they are two-faced."

stadiums or stadia?   Both are acceptable, but the usual English plural of *stadium* is *stadiums*.

stalactite or *stalagmite*?   *Stalactite* is spelled with a *c*, as in the cave *ceiling* from which it hangs. The corresponding cave formation that goes from the ground up, *stalagmite*, has a *g*, as in *ground*. Both are deposits of calcium carbonate formed by the dripping of water.

stamp or *stomp*?   *Stomp* means "to tread on violently." So does *stamp*, but you should save *stamp* for such separate uses as "stamp one's foot in anger" and "stamp out [eliminate] ignorance."

stanch or *staunch*?   Some usage commentators approve the use of these words interchangeably. But you can avoid the risk of criticism by using *staunch* strictly as an *adjective* ("steadfast, resolute"). That usage leaves you free to use *stanch* strictly as a *verb* ("stop the flow, often of a liquid such as blood").

Usage example of *stanch* from *The Wall Street Journal* (4/23/2002):

"Struggling to stanch losses in an extremely difficult operating environment, Lucent Technologies said yesterday that it planned to cut 6,000 more jobs."

***stat* or *stet*?** Doctors in hospital dramas who punctuate their emergency orders with *stat* are using an abbreviation for *statim* (Latin for "immediately").

Stet (Latin for "let it stand") is what editors write when they decide against a change they've entered on a manuscript.

***state of the art* is the most** This noun and its hyphenated adjective, *state-of-the-art*, are "tainted by association with salesmen's jargon," according to *Garner's Modern American Usage*.

If you choose to risk such guilt by association, remember when you use this term that it cannot be qualified with an adjective like *most* because it means "the most advanced level of technological development." Note the redundant *most* in the following sentence from a press release (3/3/2000) circulated in the U.S. for a Chinese airline: "China Southern Airlines features the Boeing 777, the most state-of-the-art aircraft in the world."

***stated* or *said*?** See "*said* can be said again."

***stationary* or *stationery*?** The adjective is *stationary* ("fixed in position, not moving"). The noun is *stationery* ("writing material"). Spelling tip: Note that *stationery* shares its *er* with *paper* and *letter*.

***status* should be stated** The "proper" pronunciation is "STAY-tus," not "STAT-us," according to language commentator Charles Harrington Elster's pronunciation guide, *There is no Zoo in Zoology*. And "STAY-tus" is awarded the preferred listing by the Merriam-Webster, Random House, and American Heritage dictionaries. If you strongly prefer "STAT-us," you can cite support from *Webster's New World College Dictionary*.

Stentor was a loudmouth In the Greek mythology recorded in Homer's *Iliad*, a Trojan War herald named Stentor had a voice as loud as that of 50 men combined. Hence, the adjective *stentorian* means "having a voice that is extremely loud and powerful."

stereotype   See entries for *cliché.*

stank or *stunk*?   Both are acceptable for the past tense of *stink*, but *stank* is more common than *stunk*, especially when the verb is followed by *of*. So you can't go wrong if you restrict *stunk* to its mandatory role as the past participle, as in "has stunk."

stoic or *Stoic*?   The noun *stoic* ("STOH-ick") means "one who submits without complaint to hardship or suffering," like adherents of the Stoic philosophy founded about 300 B.C. by the Greek philosopher Zeno of Citium.

The adjective *stoic* and its variant, *stoical*, usually mean "uncomplaining about hardship or suffering" but can also mean "impassive, not feeling or showing emotion." In an example of the most common meaning of *stoic*, *Newsweek* reported (2/17/1997) that Washington Metro subway riders "endured the morning rush hour in stoic silence."

Zeno taught his followers that the key to happiness was virtue (moral excellence) and that virtue could be attained by repressing feelings of both grief and joy and by calmly accepting all occurrences as unavoidable results of divine will or the natural order. Stoics and the philosophy of Stoicism were so called because Zeno lectured to his followers from a place in Athens called the *Stoah Poecile* (Greek for "Painted Porch").

stomach this   See "*abdomen, belly, stomach,* or *tummy?*"

straight or *strait*?   A nail is much easier to *straighten* ("unbend") than to *straiten* ("squeeze and make narrow").

Straight comes to us from the Middle English *strecchen* ("to stretch"). *Strait* came to English in the 16th century from the early French adjective *estreit*, which came from the Latin *strictus*, past participle of *stringere* ("to bind tight"). A violent person may be "bound tight" in a *straitjacket*. Someone who is narrow-minded about manners and morals is *strait-laced*.

The *straight* in "straight and narrow" is a misspelling of a warning in the King James Bible to avoid the temptingly wide gate of destruction—"because *strait* [narrow] is the gate, and narrow is the way which leadeth unto life."

strait or **straits**?   Both are acceptable forms of a singular noun meaning "a narrow passage of water connecting two large bodies of water." Example: *The Straits* was the former name of *the Strait of Gibraltar* connecting the Atlantic Ocean with the Mediterranean Sea.

Straits can also mean "a condition of distress or need," as in a *Financial Times* reference (1/8/2002) to "the dire straits in which the [airline] industry finds itself."

stratagem: **don't let it trick you**   *Stratagem* often is misspelled *strategem* and mistakenly used as a synonym for *strategy*, as in a *Los Angeles Times* article (9/5/2000) about the pioneering "marketing strategem [should be *strategy*]" of Internet companies providing home delivery of groceries and other products in as little as half an hour.

Stratagem, from a Greek word for *general*, is a synonym for *trick*, and it specifically means "a military maneuver designed to deceive an enemy" or "any clever scheme involving deception." The word ends in *-agem* rather than *-egem* because it entered English from French in the 15th century, more than three centuries before *strategy* entered English from Latin.

In an example of the correct use of *stratagem*, an article in *The New Yorker* (4/23/2001) told about a divorce lawyer's "delighting in . . . stratagems [that expose] weakness in his adversaries."

strategy, **tactic**, or **tactics**?   *Strategy* in the military sense means "the science and art of military command as applied to the overall planning and conduct of large-scale combat operations." *Strategy* in the civilian sense means "any long-range plan of action designed to accomplish a specific goal."

A *tactic* is any maneuver for achieving a goal. *Tactics* is the plural of *tactic* or a singular word referring to the technique of achieving the goal designated by a strategy.

stricture: **watch your context**   Depending on your context, *stricture* can mean either "adverse criticism" or "something that restrains, limits, or restricts."

strided or **strode**?   The past tense of *stride* is *strode*, not *strided*.

style: **both versions are important**   In writing, *style* means two different things: a manner of *expression* (polished, formal, informal, bureaucratic, conversational, and so on) or a system of *rules* involving such mechanical matters as capitalization and abbreviation.

subconscious or *unconscious*?   Both forms of this noun and adjective refer to "mental processes of which the individual is not aware." *Subconscious* sounds right to many people because it conveys the idea of mental activity occurring beneath (*sub-*) the level of consciousness. But *unconscious* is the established term among behavioral scientists.

Usage example: Harvard biologist Edward O. Wilson wrote in his 1998 book, *Consilience*, that "Freud's conception of the unconscious, by focusing attention on hidden irrational processes of the brain, was a fundamental contribution to culture."

Psychiatrist Sigmund Freud, who earned an M.D. from the University of Vienna in 1881, issued his first major statement about his "theory of the unconscious" in 1912. Previously, German physicist/physiologist Hermann von Helmholtz had introduced the idea of "unconscious inferences" and German philosopher Eduard von Hartmann had published a three-volume *Philosophy of the Unconscious*.

The Oxford English Dictionary notes that *the unconscious* is "applied to mental processes of which a person is not aware but which have a powerful effect on his attitudes and behavior, specifically in Freud's psychoanalytic theory."

subject-verb agreement   See "verbs must agree with their subject."

subjunctive   See "verbs are moody."

such as **this comma issue**   Use commas to separate "such as" phrases that are not essential to the message of the sentence: "Typical vending-machine snacks, *such as candy bars and potato chips*, are justifiably referred to as junk food." "She has visited Europe's major cities, *such as London, Paris, and Rome*." Notice that in both of these sentences the removal of the "such as" phrase would not destroy the message.

Don't use commas when "such as" phrases are essential to the message: "Courses in subjects *such as math and physics* are necessary as preparation for many careers in science." Notice that the removal of *that* "such as" phrase would destroy the message. (See also "commas separating nonessential information" and "*like* or *such as*?")

***such* unfinished thoughts**   "This is *such* a hot day!" is acceptable in informal conversation. In writing, you need to complete the thought: "This is such a hot day that I think I'll cancel my shopping plans." Otherwise, change the statement: "This is an unusually hot day!"

***suffragette* or *suffragist*?**   For a historical reference to "a woman who militantly advocated the right of women to vote," many feminists prefer *suffragist*. The argument against *suffragette* is that the suffix *-ette* is belittling, as in *usherette* ("little usher"). Indeed, according to the *Harper Dictionary of Contemporary Usage,* "the *-ette* ending was given to the word *suffragist* in [19th-century] England to deride those women demanding the right to vote."

***supersede*: don't cede it**   This word—meaning "to replace, typically because what is replaced is obsolete"—has been wrongly spelled *supercede* for centuries. But the only acceptable spelling remains *supersede*.

***suppose to* or *supposed to*?**   You are *supposed to* remember that you should never use *suppose to.*

***surprise, astonish,* or *astound*?**   In an oft-told apocryphal tale, the wife of English lexicographer Samuel Johnson catches him kissing the upstairs maid. Johnson's wife exclaims, "I am surprised!" Dr. Johnson responds, "No, madam; *I* am surprised. *You* are astonished."

Astonish, derived from the Latin *attono* ("to strike by thunder"), refers to an intensity of surprise that leaves one "thunderstruck, stunned." If Dr. Johnson and the maid had been surprised in a situation that was even more shocking, Johnson's wife might have been *astounded* ("overwhelmed with amazement").

***surreal*: beyond reality**   The adjective *surreal* ("bizarre, dreamlike") emerged from the noun *surrealism,* the name of an early 20th-century movement in literature, art, and philosophy.

Surrealism, introduced in 1924 by the Freudian French writer André Breton in his *Manifeste du surréalisme,* sought a reality under the surface by exploring irrational combinations of images and symbols as revealed in dreams and spontaneous "automatic" writing and painting.

Usage example of *surreal* in the sense of "bizarre" from a political commentary in *The New York Times* (12/21/2000): "Given the surreal closeness of Election 2000, and the impeachment of the sitting president less than two years ago, the White House transition from Bill Clinton to George W. Bush has so far been a stroll."

suspect: **an offense against sense**   In police jargon, the word *suspect* is used not only to refer to a person who is suspected of having committed a crime but also, nonsensically, to refer to the person who *actually* committed the crime. As Bill Walsh says in *Lapsing Into a Comma*: "The word is often misused . . . in crimes where there are no suspects. If the only witness to a homicide saw the killer drive away in a blue sedan, the witness saw just that: the killer. Who, exactly, would the 'suspect' be?"

Examples of the illogical usage abound in small newspapers, as when the crime reporter for the *Irvine* (Calif.) *World News* (7/31/2003) wrote that a gas station had been held up by a "suspect . . . wearing a blue ski cap." Sometimes that usage even infects major metropolitan newspapers, as in a *Los Angeles Times* picture caption (5/20/2001) showing a news photographer being held hostage at gunpoint "by one of the robbery suspects barricaded in a gas station in a Buenos Aires suburb after [the news photographer] got too close."

In an example of correct usage, *The New York Times* (7/21/2001) published a story that began: "Prompted by new insights into the psychology of eyewitnesses to crimes, New Jersey is changing the way it uses witnesses to identify suspects."

suspicion: **keep it in its place**   *Suspicion* has been widely used as a verb in fictional dialogue employing nonstandard language, as when Tom Sawyer says, "Anybody would suspicion us that saw us." *The Oxford English Dictionary* records some use of *suspicion* as a verb as far back as the early 17th century. But in today's standard British and American English, *suspicion* is strictly confined to nounhood.

suspicious: **a word that's suspect**   Caution: Your description of someone as *suspicious* can be interpreted as meaning that the person "suspects" or that the person "is suspected." Make sure your intended meaning of *suspicious* is made clear by your context: "His strange behavior made the police suspicious." (See also "contranyms speak with forked tongue.")

***swam* or *swum*?** Almost everyone knows to say "she *swims*" and "she *swam*." The insufficiently known past participle is *swum*, as in "she has swum for a long time."

***swatch, swath,* or *swathe*?** A *swatch* is "a sample of cloth or other material."

A *swath* is literally "a row of cut grain or grass." Figuratively, *swath* means any "long, broad strip," as in a Reuters news dispatch (10/10/2000) about "a wide swath of southern Chile [that] was on alert Monday as dangerous levels of ultraviolet radiation hit peaks because of the depletion of the protective ozone layer over the Antarctic."

To *cut a swath* means to "attract notice."

Swathe is a verb meaning "to bind or wrap" or a noun for whatever material is used in that act.

***syllabuses* or *syllabi*?** Either the Latin *syllabi* or the anglicized *syllabuses* can be used for the plural of *syllabus* ("outline of a course"). *Syllabi* has been given the preferred listing in the Merriam-Webster and Longman dictionaries. But *syllabuses* is the choice of Fowler's *Dictionary of Modern English Usage*, *The Oxford English Dictionary*, *Webster's New World College Dictionary*, the American Heritage and Random House dictionaries, and the stylebooks of *The New York Times* and the Associated Press. In usage and in scholarly acceptance, *syllabuses* appears to be leading.

By the way: To *syllabize* is not to create a syllabus but rather to divide words into syllables.

***syndrome* as its own syndrome?** A Sunday-supplement editor at a Los Angeles newspaper was in the habit of using *syndrome* for nearly every conceivable condition or situation: "The Skateboard Syndrome," "The Summer Vacation Syndrome," "The Rent-or-Buy Syndrome," "The Holiday Syndrome," and so forth. The editor was cured of this loose usage when one of his staff writers anonymously submitted a tongue-in-cheek article entitled "The *Syndrome* Syndrome."

Syndrome ("a pattern of symptoms that characterize a physical disease or mental disorder") can be used in the figurative sense of "a pattern of behavior characterizing an undesirable social condition." An example of the figurative sense: The Pentagon's long silence about widespread exposure of U.S. Gulf War troops to Iraqi chemical-weapons toxins was deplored in a *Los Angeles Times* editorial (8/29/1996) entitled "Secrecy Syndrome."

synonym doesn't always spell *substitute* Many people acquire the false notion in school that *synonym* can be fully defined as "a word with the same meaning as another word." The full definition of *synonym* is "a word with a meaning that is the same as *or similar to* the meaning of another word." Often, that means you can't choose a synonym randomly any more than a golfer can randomly choose a club from his bag.

The noun *cougar* can substitute for *mountain lion*, because they are exact synonyms. But the verb *desire* is not interchangeable with the synonyms listed for it in *Webster's Dictionary of Synonyms*: *wish*, *want*, *crave*, and *covet*. That source explains: "*Desire*, in its most effective use, emphasizes strength and ardor of feeling. *Wish*, especially in poetic language, often connotes longing for the unattainable. *Want* is frequently used in place of *wish* . . . when the latter is felt to be slightly more formal than the object or the context requires. *Crave* carries a stronger implication of physical or mental appetite or need than the preceding terms. *Covet* implies inordinate and eager or passionate longing, often for something [that] belongs to another."

syntax sensitivity *Syntax*, as *The Columbia Guide to Standard American English* defines it, is "the term for that aspect of grammar that describes word order, the relationships among words, and the structure of phrases, clauses and sentences." And as noted by linguist David Crystal in his *Cambridge Encyclopedia of the English Language*, "Word order is at the heart of syntax, [and consequently] the meaning of the sentence alters fundamentally once the order varies."

The sentence "Paul often telephones Pearl" obviously means something quite different from "Pearl often telephones Paul." But sometimes the significance of word order requires a deeper level of attention. For example, the phrase "Clara's *new first* car" communicates the idea that she has acquired her first car, and it happens to be new. But "Clara's *first new* car" means that this is *not* her first car but rather the first that is new.

A change in word order can also produce a change in emphasis. For example, a routine request to "turn off the TV" can become a possibly angry command to "turn the TV *off*."

T

table talk   If you want to postpone discussion of a topic at a formal meeting in Britain, do not ask that it be *tabled*. In that part of the English-speaking world, *to table* means "to put on the table for discussion, bring something forward for action."

tantalize means "torment terribly"   The verb *tantalize*—"to torment with the sight of something desired but out of reach"—can be used with the greatest precision if you keep in mind the shocking story of its origin.

The story, as recounted by classical scholar Edith Hamilton in her book *Mythology*, involves a king named Tantalus who was honored by the gods "beyond all the mortal children of Zeus." He was the only mortal allowed to dine with the gods, and they even accepted his invitation to dinner at his palace.

To quote Hamilton: "In return for their favor, he acted so atrociously [when the gods visited Tantalus' palace for dinner] that no poet ever tried to explain his conduct. He had his only son Pelops killed, boiled in a great cauldron, and served to the gods. Apparently [Tantalus] was driven by a passion of hatred against them which made him willing to sacrifice his son in order to [prove they were not all-knowing and] bring upon them the horror of being cannibals."

At the gruesome dinner party, the gods discovered the awful truth as soon as the son's flesh was served to them. Outraged, they condemned Tantalus to eternal thirst and hunger in Hades, where he stood in a pool whose water drained away whenever he bent down to drink and where overhanging limbs of fruit trees were blown aside by the wind whenever he tried to reach the fruit.

P.S. The gods restored the life of Pelops (Tantalus' son), and he lived happily ever after.

tartar or _Tartar?_   The lowercase *tartar* that means "someone who is ill-tempered, ferocious, or violent" is derived from the uppercase *Tartar* that means "a member of the central Asian tribes who invaded western Asia and eastern Europe in the Middle Ages." An obituary for violinist Yehudi Menuhin in *The Economist* (3/20/1999) said his Russian-born mother "was of Tartar stock, and, as some might say, a tartar."

Another *tartar*, with a separate word history, is the hard, yellowish deposit that forms on teeth from a mixture of saliva and food particles.

tasty history Back in the 18th and 19th centuries, you could buy clothing that was tasty. That's because *tasty*, which originally meant "pleasing to one's taste buds," acquired during those centuries the additional meaning of "pleasing to one's sense of good taste." By the beginning of the 20th century, that second meaning was being conveyed adequately, as it is now, by the word *tasteful*.

Echoes of *tasty* ambiguity can still be heard today in the word *tasteless*, which can mean either "lacking flavor" or "unpleasing to one's sense of good taste."

technical terminology translation When you must use technical terminology, have mercy on your readers. Translate.

The computer term *megabyte of memory* is meaningless to many people, until it is equated with the capacity to store the entire text of the Bible. Likewise, a reference to a noise level of *150 decibels* may become meaningful only when it is likened to the noise of a riveting gun.

teenager or *teen-ager*? *The New Yorker* and newspapers that follow Associated Press style use *teen-ager*. But you can't go wrong with *teenager*, which is the sensible, easy-on-the-eyes choice of dictionaries and *The New York Times*.

temblor or *tremblor*? The preferred word for an earthquake is not *tremblor* but *temblor* (from a Spanish word for "trembling").

temerity or *timidity*? *Temerity* refers to behavior that is "foolishly bold." *Timidity* refers to behavior that is "timid," which can mean "shy" and/or "fearful."

An employee afflicted by temerity asks for an undeserved raise during a period of layoffs. An employee afflicted by timidity is afraid to ask for a highly deserved raise from a prosperous company.

tense must make sense   Don't engage in time travel within a sentence—changing your verbs from one tense to another—unless you do so to make a point. In other words, never switch tenses by accident or even deliberately just for the sake of variety.

Ordinarily, keep your verbs in the same time zone. For example: In the present tense, you write, "She *says* she *is reading* the report." In the past tense, you write, "She *said* she *was reading* the report."

Looking toward the future from the present, you write, "She *says* she *will read* it." Looking toward the future from the past, you write, "She *said* she *would read* it."

Consider the tenses in the following statements about an unhappy man: If you write, "He *says* he *is* unhappy," that means he's unhappy right now. If you write, "He *said* he *was* unhappy," that means he was unhappy when he said it. But if he was unhappy at some point *before* he said it, you should write, "He *said* he *had been* unhappy."

Combine past and present tenses with reference to a past observation or discovery involving something that remains true today: "He *discovered* that the universe *consists* [not *consisted*] of many galaxies."

***tepid* or *torpid*?**   *Tepid* means "lukewarm, halfhearted." *Torpid*—the adjective that goes with the noun *torpor*—means "sluggish, lethargic."

terminal prepositions   See "prepositions you end sentences with."

***than* or *then*?**   *Than* is a conjunction in clauses of comparison: "Jane performed better *than* Paul." *Then* is an adverb of time: "They *then* adjourned."

***than* comparisons need to be complete**   See "*as* and *than* comparisons need to be complete."

***that*: needed and not**   The word *that* can be a space-waster or a confusion-preventer. *That* is a space-waster when its removal has no effect on meaning or readability: "He said (that) he reads poetry." "She told him (that) she writes poetry." "He loved the poems (that) she gave him."

But *that* is sometimes needed to preserve your meaning. Try reading the following sentence without *that*: "Please tell Jeff (that) Kent can't attend the meeting." Note how your apparent meaning would change if you removed the word *that* from "I know that you . . . ," "I recommend that you . . . ," and "She said to tell you that people . . . "

You also need *that* when a time element intervenes between the verb and the clause: "He said *yesterday* that the factory would shut down." The removal of *that* would result in the misleading implication that the factory was going to be shut down yesterday.

Note also that the word *that* is needed for clarity when it introduces a clause that parallels a previous clause: "He announced *that* his retirement was definite and *that* he would name his successor." The second *that* clearly extends the announcement to include the decision to name his successor.

that or **which**?   Here's the rule: *That* defines; *which* merely informs.

That introduces essential information, because it defines what you're referring to. For example, according to *National Geographic* (12/2003), Japan's samurai warriors "lived by a code *that valued death over defeat.*"

Which introduces nonessential information, regardless of how interesting that information may be. Therefore, *which* would have been appropriate if the just-cited *National Geographic* article had said the samurai warriors "lived by a rigid code of death before dishonor, which is common among warriors in many cultures."

The Columbia Guide to Standard American English says the *that/which* rule is one "almost no one follows perfectly in other than Edited English and few can follow even there." Indeed, many professional writers routinely use *which* for *that*. But your mastery of the *that/which* rule will win you the respect of "the best American editors," according to *Garner's Modern American Usage*. And, what is more important, your communication will be clearer.

Regarding the issue of clarity, consider this example from a travel-tip article in the *Los Angeles Times* (5/12/2002): "Hospital cafeterias, which are open to the public, charge half the price of the average hotel restaurant." If that sentence were changed to refer to "hospital cafeterias that are open to the public," the message would be that travelers could save money on meals only at certain hospital cafeterias.

Even when clarity is not an obvious problem, you should get in the habit of using the relative pronoun *that* to introduce a clause defining the immediately preceding subject, as in "the computer *that Larry just bought.*" In that example, "the computer" is singled out from all other computers in the world by the defining clause, "that Larry just bought." In the terminology of grammar, the *that* clause is "essential" to the subject. Grammarians also say the *that* clause is "restrictive," because it restricts the subject to its unique identification.

And remember to use a comma followed by the relative pronoun *which* to introduce a clause with nondefining information, as in "Larry's new computer, *which he bought on sale at an electronics exhibition,* has greatly increased his productivity." The phrase "Larry's new computer" precisely identifies the subject, so the comma and *which* are needed to tell us that the upcoming clause informs but does not define. Note that you can remove *which* clauses and still have a sentence that makes complete sense.

If your adherence to the *that/which* rule ever makes you feel lonely, recite to yourself the following list of sources that have supported it: Fowler's *Dictionary of Modern English Usage, The New Fowler's Modern English Usage,* Strunk and White's *Elements of Style,* Bernstein's *Careful Writer,* Copperud's *American Usage and Style, The New Oxford American Dictionary,* Freeman's *Words to the Wise, The American Heritage Dictionary,* the Modern Language Association's *Line by Line,* Clark's *Word Perfect, The Concise Oxford Dictionary, The New York Public Library Writer's Guide to Style and Usage,* Follett's *Modern American Usage,* Lovinger's *Penguin Dictionary of American English Usage and Style,* and the stylebooks of *The New York Times, The Wall Street Journal,* The Associated Press, and *The Economist.* (See "*which*-hunting.")

that or **who?**   Syndicated columnist James J. Kilpatrick (7/12/1998) issued "an order forbidding the use of *that* as a relative pronoun for clearly human entities." For references to humans, he "ordered" the use of *who* and nothing but *who.* For example, he changed "a teacher *that*" to "a teacher *who.*"

Kilpatrick's edict is worth obeying for anyone who wants a *who/that* rule that is simple and free of risk. Use the relative pronoun *that* only for things.

"As for animals," notes *The New York Times Manual of Style and Usage,* "use *who* if the animal's sex is known or if it has been personalized with a name." And be aware that an increasing number of people now believe the personhood of *who* should be applied to all animals.

the way to start a sentence?   Did someone make you afraid to start a sentence with *the*? If so, you can overcome that foolish fear by paying attention to the widespread use of the initial *the* in professional writing. For example, a randomly selected copy of the national edition of *The New York Times* (1/20/2005) had 11 initial-*the* sentences on the front page.

Of course, you should resist the temptation to use *the* as the first word of sentence after sentence or paragraph after paragraph.

the: when does it sound like *thee*?   The definite article should sound like *thee* before a word that begins with a vowel sound, as in "the AMA" and "the NAACP." When *the* comes before a consonant sound, as in "the BBC" and "the USA," say "thuh," except when you want to stress *the* as if it had a few extra *e*'s, as in "*the* Bill Gates." (See also "*a* pronunciation.")

the: when should it be included in a newspaper's name?   You'll find bad advice about this question in a book that careful writers, editors, and publishers have consulted for decades: *The Chicago Manual of Style*. This otherwise sensible manual says, "When newspapers and periodicals are mentioned in text, an initial *the*, even if part of the official title, is lowercased (unless it begins a sentence) and not italicized."

That manual, like all stylebooks, offers extensive, valuable advice about style consistency. But style consistency can never justify inaccuracy.

In New York City, there's a magazine that calls itself *New York*. And that's what you should call it—*New York* magazine. But there are other periodicals that call themselves *The New Yorker*, *The New York Review of Books*, and *The New York Times*. They, too, should be called what they call themselves. (Of course, it's OK to refer to "a *New York Times* reporter," because "a *The New York Times* reporter" would be intolerably awkward.)

the: when should it go before a noun?   If you're a native speaker of American English, you'll almost always find the answer to that question by trusting your ear. In other words, the answer is found in idiom, which is language usage based purely on custom.

For example, nobody needs to tell an adult native speaker of our language that you should make *the bed* before you go *to bed*. Our children know they should be careful when they walk *to school*, so they can avoid the need to go *to the hospital.* And studious children may *go to the library* before they *go home.*

Likewise, you know it's correct to say *the United States* and *the Dominican Republic,* but it's wrong to say *the Canada* or *the Haiti.* And you don't write "Vatican says"—omitting *the*—unless you're writing a telegram or a newspaper headline.

If you are not a native speaker of American English, you may need to find guidance on specific answers to this usage question by asking someone who is. (See "idioms do their own thing.")

theater or **theatre?**   *Theater* is the preferred spelling in American English, and note that the word *American* contains an *-er* reminder for you. *Theatre* is British. The same distinction applies to *amphitheater/re, caliber/re, center/re, luster/re, meager/re* and *meter/re.*

Newspaper stylebooks such as those of *The Washington Post* and the *Los Angeles Times* prescribe the American *theater,* except for proper names that include the British *theatre.* Hence, "Ford's *Theatre* was the *theater* where Lincoln was shot."

The Associated Press Stylebook prescribes *theater* even for theaters that call themselves *theatres.* That AP rule, while upholding the principle of consistency, violates the higher principle of accuracy. The AP has no more justification for changing the spelling of a theatrical site than it would have for changing *Barbra* Streisand's first name back to her original *Barbara.* Curiously, the AP stylebook adopts the opposite policy when it prescribes the prevailing American spelling *flier* over *flyer* while permitting exceptions for trains or buses with proper names that use the spelling *flyer.*

Why does *The New Yorker* magazine spell its Broadway section *Theatre* but refrain from such British spellings as *cheque, kerb, programme, pyjamas,* and *tyre* in the magazine's pages? That's because America's theatrical world was under considerable British influence when the Broadway stage was founded, and American theater owners today seem to think that the British *theatre* adds a touch of class. You may notice the same pretentious spelling at your neighborhood multiplex.

their, there, or **they're?**   Don't expect a computer spell-checker to help you distinguish *their* ("belonging to them") from *there* ("in that place") and *they're* ("they are").

theirs or there's?   These words are often used interchangeably by amateur writers. *There's* is the contraction for "there is." *Theirs* is a plural possessive pronoun.

then or than?   See "*than* or *then*?"

theory is not always "just a theory"   The word *theory* has two distinct meanings, both listed by dictionaries as standard. In everyday language, *theory* means "speculation, conjecture." But a *scientific theory*, as defined by the *Hammond Barnhart Dictionary of Science*, is "an explanation or model based on observation, experimentation, and reasoning, *especially* one that has been *tested and confirmed* [italics added] as a general principle helping to explain and predict natural phenomena." That is why you will never hear a scientist refer to Einstein's theory of relativity as "*just* a theory."

there is a good way and a bad way to start a sentence   See "*it* and *there* can hurt or help the start of a sentence."

therefor or therefore?   The common adverb meaning "consequently" is spelled with a final *e*. The word *therefor*, with the accent on *-for*, is a rarely used adverb meaning "for that, for it, in return for that." ("She told us her decision and the reason *therefor*.")

thesaurus: don't be intimidated   Are you afraid to ask a bookstore clerk for a *thesaurus* because you aren't sure how to pronounce the word? Fear no more. Associate the pronunciation of *thesaurus* with the pronunciation of *brontosaurus* and *tyrannosaurus*, and you will remember that *thesaurus* is accented on the *saur*.

Thesaurus, which is Latin for "something stored up, storehouse, treasury," entered English in the 19th century as an archaeological term for a "temple-like treasury." Then *thesaurus* became a metaphor: "a treasury of words or information about a particular subject." In 1852, *thesaurus* became "a treasury of words organized by their meanings" as a result of the publication of English physician-scholar Peter Mark Roget's *Thesaurus of English Words and Phrases Classified and Arranged So As to Facilitate the Expression of Ideas and Assist in Literary Composition.*

Getting back to your visit to the bookstore: You'll find many books now called *Roget's Thesaurus*. From the most recently published editions, choose the one you find easiest to use.

third world or *Third World*?

This term is uppercase in some quarters (for example, the *Los Angeles Times*) and lowercase in others (*The New York Times*).

The term, coined by Charles de Gaulle to designate the generally underdeveloped parts of the world that were not part of the West or the Soviet bloc, has retained a post–Cold War meaning of "underdeveloped [sometimes euphemistically called *developing*] nations."

Usage example from *The New York Times* (2/25/2002): "The global export of electronic waste, including consumer devices, computer monitors and circuit boards, is creating environmental and health problems in the third world."

this or *that*, *these* or *those*?

A choice between *this* or *that*—or, in the plural, between *these* and *those*—is usually made on the basis of proximity in space and time.

To begin with the realm of space, *that* object and *those* objects are usually not as close as *this* object and *these* objects. The exception occurs in a comparison of two equidistant objects that are referred to as "*this* one" and "*that* one" in order to distinguish one from the other.

Turning to the realm of time, *that* and *those* subjects usually have been cited already, and *this* and *these* subjects usually are about to be cited. The exception here is that *this* and *these* refer to previously cited subjects that are continuing to be examined: "This [previously cited] tax proposal must be carefully studied now in the light of recent economic developments."

A famous example of the correct choice of *these* rather than *those* appears in our Declaration of Independence: "We hold *these* [about-to-be-cited] truths to be self-evident, that all Men are created equal, that they are endowed by their Creator with certain unalienable Rights, that among *these* [previously cited rights that are still being examined] are Life, Liberty, and the Pursuit of Happiness."

thrifty: what money can't buy

Apply *thrifty* to people, not products. "Thrifty people shop for low-priced products." (See also "*cheap* prices are impossible to find.")

throe or throes?   *Throe* ("a severe spasm of pain") is much less common than *throes* ("an agonizing struggle").

Usage example of *throes* from *The New York Review of Books* (11/18/1999): "Now, governments are trying to respond in various other ways, both inside and outside the UN, to the plight of people in the throes of disaster."

thusly gets almost no respect   You need supreme self-confidence to use this much-maligned variant of the adverb *thus* (meaning "in this or that manner, to this extent, because of this").

Thusly, which word sleuths suspect was coined in the mid-19th century as a humorous American variant of *thus*, has been taken seriously by almost nobody in America's usage establishment. Descriptions of *thusly* have ranged from "superfluous" (Theodore M. Bernstein's *Careful Writer*) to "an abomination" (William and Mary Morris' *Harper Dictionary of Contemporary Usage*).

The American Heritage Dictionary reports that *thusly* has "gained some currency in educated usage, but it is still often regarded as incorrect." *The Columbia Guide to Standard American English* warns that "to some people [*thusly*] is still jocular at best." *The New Oxford American Dictionary* declares that "*thusly* as a substitute for *thus* is always incorrect." *Webster's New World College Dictionary* lists *thusly* as "colloquial." The Random House dictionaries award *thusly* a listing as a legitimate word, but they add a usage note warning that some speakers and writers, and usage guides generally, regard *thusly* as "a pointless synonym for *thus*."

Thusly's apparently sole defender is Merriam-Webster. That publisher's unabridged and collegiate dictionaries treat *thusly* as standard. Merriam-Webster's usage dictionary acknowledges that *thusly* is inappropriate as a substitute for *thus* in usage such as "Thus we see" and "We thus see" but maintains that *thusly* is now a common and desirable alternative to *thus* after a verb and before a colon, as in "running thusly: [in this way]" and "described thusly: [as follows]."

Suggestion: Stay with *thus* where appropriate. Where *thusly* seems preferable (as in the last two examples), you have the choice of bravery (using *thusly*) or expediency (substituting "in this way" or "as follows").

tidal wave or tsunami?   "Thank you for your concern about my safety in the wake of last Sunday's devastating tidal wave," 87-year-old mathematician-physicist-author Arthur C. Clarke wrote to his world of admirers on his website (12/29/2004) from his home in Sri Lanka, one of the nations ravaged by 2004's catastrophic tsunami.

The British-born writer understandably used the Western term *tidal wave* as a synonym for *tsunami*. But the Western term is inaccurate, because the earthquake-generated disaster that struck Clarke's Sri Lankan home and devastated shores from Thailand to Somalia had nothing to do with tides.

Tsunami (pronounced "tsoo-NAH-me" and literally meaning "harbor wave") is an English transliteration of a Japanese term for a series of gargantuan sea waves caused by an earthquake or volcanic eruption on the ocean floor. *Tsunami* has now replaced the misleading *tidal wave* among geologists around the world, including those at the Pacific Tsunami Warning Center near Pearl Harbor. But the confusion showed up even in a *Newsweek* cover story called "After the Tsunami" (1/10/2005), in its reference to "a tidal wave [that] killed more than 150 people in Hawaii in 1946."

tight or **tightly?**   Like *slow*, the word *tight* can be an adverb with or without adding an *-ly*. *The American Heritage Book of English Usage* prescribes the adverb *tight* "following verbs that denote a process of closure or constriction, such as *squeeze*, *shut*, *close*, *tie*, and *hold*." But that source notes that you need *tightly* when you place the adverb in front of such verbs. Thus, a house is "shut tight" but "tightly shut." (See also "adverbs that look like adjectives.")

'til, till, or **until?**   See "*until, till, or 'til?*"

"tilt at windmills"   See "Don Quixote and his adjective."

times: more or less?   Do not emulate the advertising hype that says a food product has "three times less fat" (or sugar, or some other undesirable ingredient). *Times* refers to multiplying, not dividing. To advertise the product grammatically, you could say that it has "*one-third* the fat" of competing products, or that the competing products have "three times *as much*" fat.

titan or ***Titan?***   The word *titan* refers to "a person or entity of enormous size, strength, power, or influence."

In an example of *titan* referring to a person, *The New York Times* editorialized (6/16/2000) that "the shape of Vladimir Putin's presidency could well be determined by the unfolding clash between the Russian leader and the small group of business titans who control much of their nation's wealth."

In an example of *titan* referring to an entity, the *Los Angeles Times* (7/22/2001) reported that "MTV has grown into a marketing titan and set off a dramatic shift of power in the record industry."

The original *Titans* were a family of gigantic gods in Greek mythology, led by Cronus (known to the Romans as Saturn), who ruled until they were defeated by the Olympian gods, led by Zeus (known to Romans as Jupiter).

The nouns *titan* and *Titan* have matching adjectives, *titanic* and *Titanic*. The 20th-century noun *Titanic*, when italicized, refers, of course, to the enormous British luxury liner that sank after colliding with an iceberg in the North Atlantic on its maiden voyage in April 1912, and later to the blockbuster movie with that name.

to* or *too? In proofreading, check each *to* and *too* to make sure you have chosen the appropriate word.

The confusion of *to* with *too* is so easy to make that you will find it on the first page of the 1978 edition of Professor Roy H. Copperud's *Handbook for Journalists* at USC's School of Journalism: "Students cannot start work on the [student newspaper] staff *to* [sic] soon."

***to* can cause confusion** Consider this ambiguous headline for an Associated Press story (7/25/1992) about the first President Bush: "Bush Cancels Trip to Confer on Iraqi Defiance." Does the headline mean that a trip the president planned for the purpose of conferring on Iraqi defiance has now been canceled ("Bush Cancels Trip-to-Confer-on-Iraqi-Defiance"), or does it mean that the president has canceled a trip to an unspecified destination so that he can confer on Iraqi defiance instead ("Bush Cancels Trip, to Confer on Iraqi Defiance")? As we learn only when we read the text, President Bush in fact canceled a vacation trip so that he could attend a conference on Iraqi defiance instead.

To avoid such ambiguity, sacrifice brevity for clarity. "My daughter skipped the class to make ceramic pots," for example, can be changed to "My daughter skipped the class *at which ceramic pots were being made*" or "My daughter skipped the class *so that she could* make ceramic pots *instead*."

"to all intents and purposes"   This idiom, traced to Henry the Eighth's phrasing of a law back in 1546 ("to all intents, constructions, and purposes") has been used by outstanding writers for centuries. But some critics regard the idiom as a long-winded way of saying *in effect.*

If you use the phrase, sometimes written *"for* all intents and purposes," take care not to make the common mistake of writing "to [or *for*] all *intensive* purposes."

"to the manner born" or "to the manor born"?   The phrase comes from Shakespeare. Hamlet, describing himself as "to the *manner* born," means that there is an expectation of certain behavior from him and that he can easily meet the expectation, as if he were born to it. But the phrase is often mistakenly rendered as "to the *manor* [mansion] born" and is used to label someone as an aristocrat or a member of a privileged class. For example, a *New York Times* article (12/22/1997) about the *Social Register* said that book "acts as the last word on who is merely rich and who is to the manor born."

A television comedy may be responsible for some of the confusion. Entitled *To the Manor Born*, the British show—which originally aired in 1971–1981—was popular in the United States as well. Despite the confusion, the correct phrase was used in a headline for a *Los Angeles Times* feature story about Republican presidential candidate George W. Bush (7/30/2000): "To the Manner Born, Bush Finds His Own Way."

toe or *tow* the line?   Many people who hear this expression—meaning "to make a strenuous effort to do one's duty or obey the rules"—assume it's based on the image of somebody who makes a strenuous effort to *tow* (pull) a line. But the expression is *toe the line,* or *toe the mark,* based on the image of a competitive runner who touches a line or mark with the toe in readiness for the start of a race.

Example of correct usage: *The Wall Street Journal* (11/19/2003) began an editorial about government censorship in Singapore by raising the question "How does an authoritarian government get its journalists to toe the line without having to micromanage them?"

together but alone   When a noun goes "together" with one or more other nouns, it remains grammatically alone and therefore takes a singular verb.

For example, you are correct in saying, "*England*, together with other nations, *has* supported the United Nations." The same rule applies to nouns accompanied by other nouns introduced by *as well as, in addition to, including, with,* and *plus*.

tomato: ripe for argument? "Probably no pronunciation in our American language is more argued about than that of the simple vegetable, the *tomato*," observes the *Harper Dictionary of Contemporary Usage*.

Actually, the tomato is a *fruit* that's *used* as a vegetable. And you should be able to avoid arguments about its pronunciation in most of the United States if you say "tuh-MAY-toh." But be aware that the British "tuh-MAH-toh" comes naturally to many people in New England and the South.

tortuous or torturous? Both these adjectives are derived from a Latin word for "twist." But though *tortuous* means "twisted or winding," *torturous* means "causing torture." Remember that, of these two words, *torturous* contains more of the word *torture*.

Tortuous and *torturous* are so easily mistaken for each other that you must be careful not to use either in an ambiguous context. For example, your reader would wonder if you meant "twisted" or "causing torture" if you wrote, "He had to drive all night on *torturous* roads."

Usage examples: A *New York Times* article (11/13/2000) recalled "four years of tortuous [twisted] negotiations [for] a treaty aimed at curtailing global warming." *New York Times* columnist Bob Herbert devoted a column (1/15/2001) to an H.I.V.-infected drug addict who "has recently made a torturously [painfully] difficult effort to turn her life around."

toward or towards? *Toward* is the favored form for this preposition in American English, *towards* in British English. (See also "*afterward* or *afterwards?*" "*backward* or *backwards?*" and "*forward* or *forwards?*")

trademark: keep it together Though *trademark* is one word, note *trade practice, trade wind,* and *trade name*.

trade names See "*yo-yo* and *zipper*: why they're in the same entry."

transcendent or **transcendental?**   Both of these words mean "surpassing, superior, supreme, going beyond ordinary limits," but *transcendental* is more likely to be found in contexts having to do with philosophy or religion.

transitions   A vital element of readable writing is the use of appropriate transitional words and phrases that connect ideas within and between sentences. For example, the conjunction *but* signals your reader that you are about to introduce a contrasting idea. (See also "*but* ins and outs.")

As Kessler and McDonald note in *When Words Collide: Media Writer's Guide to Grammar and Style*, our language contains transitions that link thoughts (*again, also, and, besides, likewise, moreover*), transitions that compare similar ideas (*as well as, in the same way, resembling, similarly*), transitions that contrast ideas (*although, conversely, nevertheless, otherwise, still, yet*), transitions that show sequence and time (*afterward, during, earlier, later, next, simultaneously, while*), transitions that show cause and effect (a*ccordingly, consequently, due to, therefore, thus*), transitions that provide emphasis (*certainly, indeed, surely, undoubtedly*), and transitions that summarize (*thus, in brief, in conclusion, in sum*).

translate or **transliterate?**   Transliteration requires more work than ordinary translation. *Transliterate* means "write something in the characters of another alphabet," as with English translations of Arabic, Hebrew, Greek, and Chinese.

translucent or **transparent?**   *Translucent* material, such as frosted glass, diffuses light so that objects beyond cannot be seen clearly. *Transparent* material, such as the glass in most windows, permits the passage of light without interference.

transpire: a non-happening?   The risk-free way to deal with the verb *transpire* is to avoid it.

Transpire is often needlessly used by the media as a snooty substitute for the perfectly good word *happen*, as in this sentence from *Time* magazine (9/15/2003): "That kind of diligence may be a clue to what transpired on his final day." If you use *transpire* that way, you risk being accused of pretentiousness. You also risk offending word guardians, including those who abide by *The*

New York Times Manual of Style and Usage. That manual says *transpire*'s only correct meaning is "leak out, become known." But if you use *transpire* in that sense, almost nobody will understand you.

Transpire, which combines Latin terms for *across* and *breathe,* arrived in England from France in the 16th century as a scientific word for "the escaping of vapor through the pores of a membrane." That technical sense of *transpire* is still used by botanists. For them, *transpire* denotes the way trees return much of their absorbed water to the atmosphere as a result of the "leaking out" and subsequent evaporation of water from their leaves.

During the 17th century, *transpire* acquired the additional, figurative sense of "leak out, become known." Subsequently, when writers began referring to "what has transpired [become known]," many readers mistakenly assumed that it meant "what has *happened.*" The "happening" *transpire* apparently began to take hold in the late 18th century, and it was acknowledged by Noah Webster in his dictionary of 1828. But according to Merriam-Webster researchers, "Around 1870 the ['happening'] sense began to be attacked as a misuse on the grounds of etymology." And American Heritage researchers say that "language critics have condemned [the 'happening' *transpire*] for more than 100 years as both pretentious and unetymological."

Here are samples of that condemnation: *Transpire* for *happen* was listed as "a notorious misuse" by Henry W. Fowler's *Dictionary of Modern English Usage,* a "do-not-use" by Sir Ernest Gowers' *Complete Plain Words,* and "a needless and even harmful change" by Theodore M. Bernstein's *Careful Writer.* The use of *transpire* for *happen* is listed as "misused" by *The New Oxford English Dictionary,* a "famous misuse" by Kingsley Amis in his *King's English,* ill advised for "careful writers" by *The Oxford American Dictionary,* "loose and pompous" by *The Penguin Dictionary of American Usage and Style,* "disputed" by the *Longman Guide to English Usage* and the Random House dictionaries, and "unacceptable" by Wilson Follett's *Modern American Usage* and John O. E. Clark's *Word Perfect.* And you are advised to "leave *transpire* to botanists" by R. W. Burchfield's *New Fowler's Modern English Usage,* Robert Claiborne's *Saying What You Mean,* and Bryan A. Garner's *Modern American Usage.*

transverse or **traverse?**　*Transverse* is an adjective, meaning "across, crosswise." *Traverse* is a verb, meaning "to cross, travel across."

triumphal or ***triumphant*?**   In August 1994, Paris staged a *triumphal* ("celebrating a triumph") parade to mark the 50th anniversary of the liberation of that city by *triumphant* ("victorious") Allied troops.

***trivial* pursuits**   *Trivia* is acceptable to many usage authorities as either a plural or a singular noun, meaning either "insignificant matters" or "an insignificant matter." But if you use *trivia* as a singular noun, you may hear from Latinists. They insist that *trivia* can only be plural, because it is the Latin plural of *trivium*.

The original Latin meaning of *trivium* was "the meeting place of three roads," where Romans, like people in modern cities who loiter on street corners, would stop and talk about insignificant matters. The noun *trivium* produced the Latin adjective *trivialis,* meaning "like what you would encounter at a crossroads, everyday, ordinary."

The capitalized *Trivia* was the Roman goddess of crossroads.

***troop* is not always a group**   *Troop* means "group" when you're referring to a small number, as in "a troop of boy scouts." But "150,000 troops" does not mean that many groups. It means that many individuals. That's not logical, but it's standard English usage.

troop or ***troupe*?**   A *troop* typically consists of soldiers or animals. A *troupe* is a group of entertainers. A dedicated performer is a "real *trouper.*"

***trousers*: you can't buy one**   Though *trousers* has no singular, you can buy *one pair* of trousers.

trove or ***treasure-trove*?**   The hyphenated compound noun *treasure-trove* entered English in the 14th century and still retains its literal Old French meaning of "treasure [that has been] found," along with today's wider meaning of "any discovery of great value." *Trove,* the *treasure-trove* abbreviation that emerged in the late 19th century, is a completely acceptable variant.

Usage examples of *treasure-trove* and *trove*: A *Smithsonian* magazine article (May 2001) described an exhibition on the American presidency for which experts had to "scour a treasure-trove of historic pictures." A *New York Times* article (4/3/2000) said that "Los Angeles has a trove of art even a New Yorker can love."

truculent has become less menacing   Do not be confused by dictionaries that define *truculent* as "savage, cruel" and also as merely "belligerent, defiant." *Truculent*, derived in the 16th century from a Latin word for *savage*, originally denoted *savage cruelty* but is now used mostly to describe behavior, including speech and writing, that is harsh but hardly horrifying.

true believer   You are in the Risk Zone if you use this term as if it were a compliment, as did the writer of a university newsletter profile describing the director of the campus Educational Opportunity Program as "a true believer in the program."

The term *true believer* originated as the title of a 1953 book about radical political fanaticism by American longshoreman-philosopher Eric Hoffer (1902–1983). Thanks to that book, *true believer* became synonymous with *fanatic* in general.

The literal use of *true believer* as a "thoroughly convinced supporter" is listed in some dictionaries. The Random House and Merriam-Webster dictionaries define *true believer* literally in addition to listing the "fanatic" sense. But the prevalence of the "fanatic" use of the term is suggested by the fact that "fanatic" is the only meaning listed for *true believer* in *The American Heritage Dictionary* and *Webster's New World College Dictionary*.

Risk-free suggestion: Use *true believer* only to mean "fanatic," and only when your context makes your intended meaning clear. Example: Less than three months after the 9/11 attack on the United States, *The New York Times* (11/25/2001) quoted "a senior C.I.A. spymaster" as saying that "now the bad guys are religious fanatics, true believers, almost incomprehensible to us."

truisms are too true   The word *truism* refers to something so obviously true that it goes without saying.

A truism can be a platitude, such as a politician's self-evident declaration that "the future lies ahead." Or it can be something nobody needs to be told about a specific situation. For example, two days after a terrorist bombing had killed scores and injured thousands in Nairobi, Kenya, a correspondent for the *Los Angeles Times* wrote (8/9/1998) that "few Kenyans were able to put [the] terrorist attack behind them."

***try and* or *try to*?**   The risk-free answer is *try to*, as in "Try to call me."

The centuries-old phrase *try and* is common in oral communication, as when a woman in a *New Yorker* cartoon (3/11/2002) turns to her husband and says, "Couldn't you at least try and read my mind?" But *try and* illogically suggests that trying and doing are separate efforts. That's why *try and* is rejected by many grammarians and by 65 percent of the usage panel of *The American Heritage Dictionary*.

Some leading usage books—including *Garner's Modern American Usage*—say that *try and* is an acceptable "casualism" in American English and a fully established "standard idiom" in British English. But that doesn't justify the use of the illogical *try and* when we have a logical alternative, *try to*.

***tryout* or *try out*?**   If you want to *try out* for the team, you'd better not be late for the *tryout*.

***turbid* or *turgid*?**   *Turbid* shares a *b* with its synonym *obscure*. (Other synonyms: "dense, muddy, clouded.")

Turgid, which shares a *g* with *gross*, means "swollen, bloated, pompous." A river can be *turbid* ("muddy") and *turgid* ("swollen"). Figuratively speaking, a political speech can be both *turbid* ("unclear") and *turgid* ("overblown, grandiloquent").

***TV* or *T.V.*?**   One of the most common punctuation mistakes is the use of *T.V.* in place of the logical form, *TV*, for an initialism representing a single word (*television*). The error is especially common in store signs, in advertising, and in syndicated comic strips (as in Bruce Tinsley's *Mallard Fillmore*, which referred to "T.V. Executives" in the strip published on January 4, 2005). (See also "acronym-initialism punctuation.")

two-faced words   See "contranyms speak with forked tongue."

U

ubiquitous is almost never literal   The adjective *ubiquitous* literally means "present everywhere at the same time," as in the Ubiquitarian belief of some Christians that Jesus Christ is simultaneously present in all places. But *ubiquitous* is commonly and acceptably used today to describe things that are "seemingly everywhere," "virtually everywhere," or just "noticeably widespread."

Here are usage examples of today's three nonliteral meanings of *ubiquitous*: A *USA Today* (5/19/2000) article entitled "Ubiquitous Orchids" (5/19/2000) observed that orchids, "once the fawned-over flora of the rich and eccentric, now seem to be everywhere." A *New Yorker* article about the Clinton administration (11/16/2000) said that "televisions are ubiquitous [virtually everywhere] in the White House, usually tuned to the all-news cable networks." The *Financial Times* (6/10/2000) referred to "a ubiquitous [noticeably widespread] chain of dry cleaners in Brussels."

A synonym for *ubiquitous—omnipresent—*is likewise commonly used in a non-literal sense. For example, a *New York Times* dispatch from the Danish island of Greenland (11/30/2000) pointed out that the nationalist flag of Greenland "is omnipresent [noticeably widespread]" there.

ugly words   *The Columbia Guide to Standard American English* assures us that Standard English status has been awarded to the verb *uglify* ("to make ugly") and even to the adverb *uglily* ("in an ugly manner"). But if you use those awkward words, especially the adverb, the response could get ugly.

ultimata or ultimatums?   For this word, the plural form of *ultimatum* (meaning "final, uncompromising demand"), the preferred form is the anglicized *ultimatums*.

unaware or unawares?   *Unaware* is an *adjective* meaning "not aware, ignorant." *Unaware* has also served for centuries as an *adverb*, meaning "unexpectedly, by surprise." But that adverbial role is now played mostly by *unawares*, as in a *Wall Street Journal* report (4/15/2002) that "the Sept. 11 attacks caught the [Central Intelligence Agency] unawares."

unbelievable confusion   Like *incredible*, the adjective *unbelievable* is used in its literal sense of "not believable" and also in the extended sense of "so amazing, astonishing, or strikingly unusual that it's hard to believe." To avoid confusion, make sure your intended meaning is unmistakable. (See also "*incredible* confusion.")

underway or under way?   This term for "in progress, already commenced" is preferably written as two words. But the one-word version is increasingly used and increasingly accepted by dictionaries as a variant. Given the historic tendency for two-word expressions to become a single word, you may sooner or later see *underway* adopted by dictionaries as the preferred form.

underwhelm: a word or just a joke?   *Underwhelm* ("to fail to impress") emerged as the facetious opposite of *overwhelm* sometime in the 1940's. The coinage is credited by some sources to playwright-columnist George S. Kaufman, by other sources to sportswriter Red Smith. *Underwhelm* has made it into dictionaries, but with classifications such as "jocular" and "informal."

unequivocably or unequivocally?   The standard spelling for this adverb, meaning "in a clear, unambiguous manner," is *unequivocally*. Memory tip: *Unequivocally* consists of the adjective *unequivocal* ("clear, unambiguous") with an added *-ly.*

unique: a risky synonym for *unusual*   Nothing will sink your reputation among word guardians faster than your saying that something is "very unique." If you care about what such people think about you, remember that either something is unique or it isn't.

When the English acquired *unique* from the French in the early 17th century, the word was used in the sense of "one of a kind." That precise meaning—consistent with the origin of *unique* in the Latin *unicus* ("single, sole, alone of its kind")—is still faithfully used by careful communicators.

Here's an example of the careful use of *unique*, from *The Wall Street Journal* (5/29/2002): "McDonald's is unique in the fast-food industry in that it owns much of its real estate or has it tied up in long-term leases, giving the company more control over what it can do on the land [to extend its business to non-food items]." And here's an example of the careful use of *uniquely* from a recommendation for a new plier wrench in *Popular Mechanics* (February 2005): "The German manufacturer has created something uniquely useful with its self-locking, cam-actuated, [and one-hand-adjustable] tool that can seize upon a nut firmly and yet release it with ease over and over again."

   Unique became the subject of controversy in the 19th century, when many people began using *unique* in the weakened sense of "unusual." By 1926, Fowler's *Dictionary of Modern English Usage* was blaming "the illiterate" for using *uniqu*e as if it meant merely "remarkable." The 1996 *New Fowler's Modern English Usage* reported that published examples of the weakened sense of the word were as easy to find as examples of the original sense.

   Indeed, nearly everything remarkable has become *very unique*—or *more, most, rather, somewhat, thoroughly,* or *extremely unique.* A 1996 Calvin Klein Barbie was advertised as "the most unique Barbie ever." A 1998 Frank Sinatra Singing Portrait Doll was advertised by the Franklin Mint as "the most unique collectible of its kind." A brochure for *Encyclopaedia Britannica*'s 1998 CD-ROM described its international data cross-referencing as its "most unique feature." An official of the Los Angeles County Economic Development Corporation called the Pasadena-based Art Center College of Design "very unique" in an interview with the *Los Angeles Times* (7/29/2000). Radio commentator Rush Limbaugh (6/14/2001) discussed "a very unique way to raise money for charity." And Michael Barone declared in *U.S. News & World Report* (6/28/2004), "Every nation is unique, but America is the most unique."

   The *Longman Guide to English Usage* notes that the "unusual" *unique* "has aroused a great deal of adverse criticism, and should be avoided in formal writing." *The Economist Style Guide* says "it is nonsense to describe something or someone as *almost/rather/the most unique.*" *The Columbia Guide to Standard American English* advises that comparative forms of the uncomparable *unique* are "best avoided in other than humorous use." The *Columbia Journalism Review*'s Language Corner (March/April 1997) denounced dictionaries that include the "unusual" unique for engaging in "a cave-in."

   Though the current American Heritage, Random House, and Merriam-Webster dictionaries include the "unusual" *unique*, those dictionaries also include usage-note warnings about the opposition to that usage. For example, *The American Heritage Dictionary* cites the opposition of 80 percent of its usage panel.

Risk-free recommendation: Qualify *unique* only when you are affirming or denying its uniqueness, as in "truly unique" and "hardly unique." (See also "*singular*: its fate was not unique.")

unless and until   See "*if and when* or *unless and until* you become a lawyer."

unprecedented: an invitation to embarrassment   *The New York Times Manual of Style and Usage* wisely warns its editors and writers that *unprecedented* is "a dangerous word that should be avoided." A writer who says something is unprecedented is just daring someone to cite a precedent. A much safer alternative is *unusual*.

until, till, or 'til?   *Till* is a perfectly acceptable, though slightly less formal, version of the preposition and conjunction *until*. Usage example: An op-ed essay in the *Los Angeles Times* (8/4/1997) was titled "Sweatshops Won't End Till Workers Have Power."

The word *till* has two *l*'s and no apostrophe, because it is not an abbreviation of *until*. *Till* is actually the older word, emerging at least three centuries before *until* appeared around the year 1200.

Though *'til* is commonly used in informal writing, as in the phrase "up 'til now" in a *Sally Forth* comic strip (8/22/1998), it is widely regarded by usage commentators as a misspelling of *till*. According to *Merriam-Webster's Dictionary of English Usage*, *'til* is, unarguably, a variant spelling of *till* used by writers who do not know that *till* is a complete, unabbreviated word in its own right." *The Columbia Guide to Standard American English* says simply, "Use *till* instead."

Till, of course, is also a noun for "money drawer" and a verb for "cultivate," as in "till the soil."

until: watch what you're up to   First, be aware that *up* is redundant in the common expression "up until." The word *up* is included in the meaning of the preposition *until* ("He waited until ['up to the time of'] midnight") and the conjunction *until* ("He waited until ['up to the time that or when'] she arrived"). *Up until* is viewed as a harmless conversational idiom by *Merriam-Webster's*

Dictionary of English Usage, but you harm your mind, your reputation, and your language every time you communicate a nonsense message such as "*up up to the time of.*"

Second, be aware that the preposition and conjunction *until* can also mean "before," as in "One of the major novelists in English literature, Polish-born Joseph Conrad, knew no English until [before, prior to the time that] he was 21." If you forget that the word *until* can mean "before," you might say something like "Arthur was scrupulously honest until he died"—which could be interpreted as meaning that Arthur became dishonest after his death! Say "Arthur was scrupulously honest all his life" instead.

unwanted or unwonted?   Typo gremlins can make you write an unintentional *unwanted* when you mean to write *unwonted*, which is a formal word for "uncommon, not customary, unaccustomed." (See also "*won't* or *wont*?")

up: the addicting "upper"   The preposition *up* is frequently used in conversation for emphasis, as in *wash up, clean up, hurry up,* and *fix up.* But some people will not look up to you if you use *up* in such phrases as *head up, slow up, free up,* and, of course, *listen up.*

up until   See "*until*: watch what you're up to."

urban or urbane?   Not everybody in an *urban* ("of or relating to a city") environment is *urbane* ("sophisticated, smooth in manner").

usage or use?   If you say *usage* ("customary practice") when you mean *use* ("the act of using"), you'll invite criticism for being not only wrong but also pretentious. Everybody should know by now that "many jobs require the *use* [not *usage*] of a computer."

use or utilize?   Some usage commentators consider *utilize* an unnecessary synonym for *use.* But the words can have distinct roles: "Jones could not figure out how to *use* the new equipment" suggests that Jones was unable to *operate* the equipment. "Jones could not figure out how to *utilize* the equipment" suggests that he did not see how to put the equipment *to good use.*

use to or used to?   *Used to*, in the sense of "in the habit, accustomed," is the correct form. Many people incorrectly write *use to* because they are used to hearing *used to* pronounced as if it were *use to*. Correct example: "He *used to* be punctual."

Exception: In today's American usage, the *d* in *used* is dropped after *did*: "Did he *use* to be punctual?"

V

vacant or vacuous?   If you catch someone looking *vacant* ("empty of thought, expressionless"), don't assume that person is *vacuous* ("stupid").

vacillate has no s   But note that this word for "fluctuate, waver, hesitate" has two *l*'s. (See also "spelling traps.")

vamp: the noun and verb   The noun *vamp* refers to "a seductive woman who exploits men." The verb *vamp* can be transitive ("watch her vamp him") or intransitive ("watch her vamp"). An entirely different *vamp* is a verb meaning "improvise, compose, or recite without preparation." Usage example: A media critic wrote in *The New York Times* (8/8/1998) that "cable news programs have been criticized on the [Monica] Lewinsky matter . . . for vamping without substance."

vandals or Vandals?   People who maliciously deface or destroy property, *vandals*, are named after the *Vandals*, an ancient Germanic tribe that ravaged Gaul and Spain and sacked Rome in the fifth century.

various redundancy accusations   Avoid redundancy accusations involving the adjective *various* by using its risk-free sense of "dissimilar," never its common but debatable sense of "many."

You can safely use the phrase "many and various" because that clearly means "many and dissimilar." But word guardians, including those at *The New Oxford American Dictionary*, maintain that the phrase "various different" is a redundancy because it means "dissimilar dissimilar."

And the phrase "various and sundry" is considered redundant on the grounds that both *various* and *sundry* mean "dissimilar." The phrase "various and sundry" actually "has two strikes against it," in the view of Morton S. Freeman's *Handbook of Problem Words and Phrases.* "It is redundant and a cliché."

vase: too precious?   This breakable collectible should be pronounced "vays" (rhyming with *face*) or "vayz" (rhyming with *faze*). The American use of the British pronunciation, "vahz," is considered by some Americans to be an affectation.

vehemently or violently?   The founder of a political action committee widely regarded as ultraconservative, Utah-based Howard Ruff, was quoted in *The Salt Lake Tribune* (3/23/2000) as saying he was "violently opposed" to Hillary Rodham Clinton's candidacy for the U.S. Senate.

Such use of *violently* in the sense of *vehemently* ("with intensity of emotion or conviction") has become so common that it is listed in dictionaries. But careful communicators restrict violently to threats or acts of violence. For example: "The American colonists reacted violently to British rule."

venal or venial?   *Venal* ("corrupt, mercenary") people may commit sins that are not *venial* ("forgivable"). Usage author Theodore M. Bernstein suggested that you remember *venal* by associating it with *penal*.

venerable need not mean old   If you want to be called *venerable* ("worthy of reverence"), you don't have to wait until you are too old to enjoy it. The full meaning of the adjective *venerable* is "commanding respect by virtue of great age, dignity, character, *or* position." Any one of those "virtues" will qualify you.

veracious or voracious?   A completely *veracious* ("truthful") houseguest does not hesitate to admit being *voracious* ("ravenously hungry").

verbal   See "*oral* or *verbal?*"

verbiage or verbosity?   *Verbiage* is commonly listed in dictionaries as a synonym for *verbosity* ("the quality of being verbose, the practice of using an excess of words"). But as *Merriam-Webster's Dictionary of English Usage* notes,

"*Verbiage* stresses more the superfluous words themselves than the quality that produces them."

To preserve the distinction between these words, indict wordy writers for *verbosity* (the offense) by citing their *verbiage* (the *results* of the offense).

verbified nouns   See "noun verbification."

verbs are moody   English verbs usually change form—for example, from "I *was*" to "they *were*"—according to a pattern called the *indicative mood* (also spelled *mode*, as in "manner"). The indicative mood is also called the normal mood, because it is the pattern speakers of English use automatically, without conscious thought. To use a computer analogy, the indicative mood is the default setting.

But grammarians say that changes in verb form should occur according to a different pattern, called the *subjunctive* mood (or mode), when you are referring to something contrary to fact, such as a supposition or wish. For example, the normal, indicative-mood word *was* becomes the subjunctive word *were* in contrary-to-fact phrases such as "if I were you" or "wishing I were there."

Here are other contrary-to-fact statements for which the subjunctive mood is prescribed: A poor man in the musical *Fiddler on the Roof* sang, "If I were [not *was*] a rich man . . ." Romance novelist Barbara Cartland (1901–2000), according to *The New York Times Magazine* (1/7/2001), "managed to live through the ugliest century of world history as though she were [not *was*] an eternal 11-year-old girl."

There are other contexts in which subjunctive mood is called for. Subjunctive is used for proposals, commands, and statements of necessity: "I suggested that she *go* [not the indicative-mood *goes*]." "She insisted that her friend *be invited* [not the indicative-mood *is invited*]." "It's important that he *be told*." In general, though, subjunctive is used less often than it once was. Most writers would change the last example to a sentence not requiring subjunctive—for example, "It's important to tell him," "It's important for him to be told," or "We have to tell him."

To stay on the right side of the warden at the Correctional Facility, be sure not to use subjunctive when you don't have to. Pay special attention to *if* statements, many of which are simply conditional, not contrary to fact, and thus should not be in the subjunctive mood. A candidate for the presidency, for example, should not preface a promise with the phrase "If I were elected president . . ." The correct version is "If I *am* elected president . . ." After all, if the possibility is so far-fetched that it has to be described as "contrary to fact," the candidate should not bother to run.

verbs must agree in number with their subject This grammatical task may not always be as easy as you think.

You probably have no trouble remembering, for example, that a horse *is* but horses *are*. But people who ought to know better sometimes mistakenly use a singular verb with two singular subjects. In an embarrassing example, the California Employment Development Department issued a 2003 flier advising young people who fill out job applications to "make sure spelling & grammar is correct."

But a singular verb *is* appropriate when two subjects are so closely linked that they can be thought of as one. For instance: "Strawberries and cream was served for dessert."

Note, too, that a plural number of something can be a single quantity. For example: "Fifty dollars [a single price] *is* not too much to pay for such a beautiful gift."

And a singular subject remains singular even if other subjects are linked to it by *with, as well as, in addition to, except, together with,* and *no less than.* For example: "His accent, as well as his clothes, *makes* him stand out from the rest."

Finally, you should guard against the common error of assuming that the subject of a verb is always the closest noun. In an example of that error, Don R. Pember's *Mass Media Law* states that "many elements of the American press is [should be *are*] sorely testing the patience of many of this nation's citizens." The author wrongly matched the singular verb *is* with the closest noun, the singular word *press.* He should have chosen the plural *are* to go with the verb's actual subject, *many elements.*

verbs pretentiously ending in -ate Such verbs are each followed here by preferred alternatives: *Administrate* (administer), *asseverate* (assert), *cohabitate* (cohabit), *coronate* (crown), *defenestrate* (throw from a window), *delimitate* (delimit), *denudate* (denude), *devaluate* (devalue), *eventuate* (happen), *expectorate* (spit), *interpretate* (interpret), *overvaluate* (overvalue), *quotate* (quote), *ruminate* (ponder), *spectate* (observe).

verbs that are irregular   When playwrights and novelists want to show that a character lacks competence in English, they have the character say things like "I *feeled* [instead of *felt*] so tired at the party that I *goed* [instead of *went*] home." In real life, such mistakes result from an inability to recognize the difference between verbs that are *regular* (requiring only an added *-ed* for the past tense, such as *require/required*) and verbs that are *irregular* (requiring individual changes for the past tense, such as *fight/fought*). If you are not sure about a particular verb's past-tense form, look up that verb's entry in a dictionary.

verbs that come first   Be careful to match your noun and verb in number when the verb comes first, as in an inverted (reverse-order) sentence such as this: "Voting against the proposal *was* [should be *were*] Harriet Smith and Melvin Jones."

verbs that go without saying   See "*as* and *than* comparisons that only *seem* incomplete."

verbs that link subjects with adjectives   "Do I feel *badly* about selling cigarettes? No, I do not," the C.E.O. of Philip Morris, Geoffrey C. Bible, was quoted as telling a writer for *The New York Times Magazine* (6/21/1998). *Should* Mr. Bible have felt badly? Not at all. Even if he *had* experienced remorse about the way he made his living, he should have felt *bad*. Saying he felt *badly* about selling cigarettes would be as ungrammatical as saying his company's profits made him feel *gladly*.

As adverbs, *gladly* and *badly* are appropriate for modifying what grammarians call an *action verb*, as in the case of an employee who "*performs* gladly but badly." But *feel* in a statement such as "I feel bad" refers not to action but to a state of being. And verbs that refer to a state of being are called *linking verbs*, because their role is to help communicate a state of being by linking a subject with an adjective. Hence, English grammar permits you to feel *bad* or *glad*, *sad* or *happy*; but you are not allowed to feel *badly*, *gladly*, *happily*, or *sadly*.

Inasmuch as a linking verb is one that expresses a state of *being*, you would be right to guess that the most frequently used linking verb is *to be*. Examples: In the expression "be careful," the verb *to be* links the understood pronoun *you* with the adjective *careful*. The same applies to "be gentle," "be quick," and the slang expression "be cool." Not even the most unconventional speaker of English would urge you to "be coolly."

Other linking verbs express a state of be-ing in such verb-adjective phrases as "*seems* calm," "*sounds* eager," and "*tastes* sweet." Some linking verbs express a state of being in the form of a result, as in such verb-adjective phrases as "*becomes* brave," "*gets* clean," and "*grows* fond."

Here's one more thing to remember about linking verbs. Some verbs—including *feel* and *look*—are linking verbs in one context but action verbs in another. For example, you can feel (linking an adjective) *strong* as Hercules or you can feel (modified by an adverb) *strongly about* your need to increase your strength. Likewise, you can look *strange* if you wear winter clothes in the summer, or you can look *strangely at* somebody else who does. Note, too, that a person can look *good* (an adjective) but can see and hear *well* (an adverb). So you should always ask yourself if a descriptive word following a verb should be or an adjective because it modifies the subject or an adverb because it modifies the verb.

verbs: transitive and intransitive   You may commit embarrassing language errors if you do not master the difference between *transitive* and *intransitive* verbs.

A *transitive* verb is one that requires not just a subject but also what grammarians call a direct object, the person or thing on the receiving end of the verb's action. The verb *throw*, for example, is transitive, because in addition to telling us who or what is doing the throwing (the subject), a sentence using *throw* has to tell us who or what is being thrown (the direct object). Similarly, the verb *recognize* is transitive, because a sentence using *recognize* doesn't make sense unless we know who or what has been recognized. You cannot say simply "I recognized." You have to say something like "I recognized *my neighbor* under the blond wig," "I recognized *the picture* as one I had seen before," "I recognized *her shortcomings*," or "I recognized *that she doesn't like me*." (The direct object can be a clause, as in the last of these three examples.)

An *intransitive* verb, in contrast, needs only a subject. Consider the intransitive verb *languish* ("to become weak or downcast, to exist in disheartening conditions") in the following assertion in a *New York Times* opinion essay (8/13/2000): "Not content to languish at state funerals, Mr. Gore has been the most productive and industrious vice president in modern times." Notice that, as an intransitive verb, *languish* cannot take a direct object, so you're not likely to hear of somebody languishing somebody else.

Here are usage examples from a *Vanity Fair* magazine interview (April 1998) conducted in the London apartment of 87-year-old Luise Rainer, the first star ever to win the best-actress Oscar two years in a row, in 1936 and 1937. The interviewer, Marie Brenner, recalls the first moment of her encounter with the famed actress: "She pulls [transitive verb] me [the direct object] to her with both hands." In Rainer's study, "her two Oscars gleam [intransitive verb] from a high shelf."

People who are not alert to the difference between transitive and intransitive verbs tend to choose *transitive* verbs when they should choose *intransitive* verbs. Such people will say such things as "The cat was *laying* [should be *lying*] on the floor." As a transitive verb form, *laying* requires a direct object, as in "laying *tiles* on the floor."

Some verbs can be used either transitively or intransitively. For example, you can transitively *play chess* or intransitively *play*. An envelope transitively *holds a letter*, but a knot intransitively *holds*. You can transitively state that somebody *said* or *declared* something, or you can intransitively begin or end a quoted sentence with "she said" or "she declared." But you should not begin or end a sentence with "she *mentioned*" or "she *expressed*"—as all too many college students do—because *mentioned* and *expressed* are strictly transitive and therefore always require a direct object. Correct usage would be "She mentioned *his name*," "She mentioned *that she knows me*," and "She expressed *gratitude*."

When in doubt about the *transitive/intransitive* question, consult your dictionary to determine if a verb is accompanied by a symbol such as *v.t.* ("verb transitive"), *v.i.* ("verb intransitive"), or both. (See also "*lay* or *lie*?" "*mention* can be dishonorable," and "*set* or *sit*?")

vertex or **vortex?**   *Vertex* means "highest point," as in the summit of a mountain. *Vertex* is used in anatomy for the highest point of a skull, in astronomy for the highest point reached in the apparent motion of a celestial body, and in mathematics for the point on a triangle or pyramid opposite to and farthest from its base.

Vortex means "whirlpool, whirlwind, whirling mass of fire" or any whirlpool-like situation that draws into its powerful current everything that surrounds it, as in "the vortex of war." The plural of *vortex* is *vortexes* or *vortices* ("VOR-tuh-seize"). The adjective for *vortex* is *vortical*.

very is **usually unnecessary**   *Very* is "possibly the most frequently abused adverb in the English language," says Morton S. Freeman in his *Words to the*

Wise. Freeman adds that "omitting *very* often improves, even strengthens, style, for *very* adds nothing but verbiage while foreclosing the use of more accurate terms." He concedes, however, that *very* is useful when the adverb *likely* is used in the sense of *probably*, as in *very likely*.

vet as a verb   In addition to being an informal synonym for *veterinarian*, the word *vet* is a *verb* meaning "to administer veterinary care" or "to subject to a thorough examination."

Example of the general use: An article in *Newsweek* (12/9/1991) noted that "authors get to vet [examine for accuracy] the manuscripts" of the audio versions of their books.

via is the way   *Via* is widely used today in two senses, one completely acceptable and the other somewhat controversial.

The unchallenged sense, "by way of"—as in "He traveled to Boston via Chicago"—was the meaning *via* had when it was adopted from Latin as an English preposition in the late 18th century.

The additional sense of *via*, "by means of"—as in "The package will be sent via an overnight service"—has been adopted by many professional writers and embraced by leading dictionaries since its appearance early in the 20th century. But this newer sense was ruled incorrect by Bernstein's *Careful Writer* (1965) and by a consensus of usage commentators surveyed for Copperud's *American Usage and Style* (1980).

Merriam-Webster's Dictionary of English Usage reported in 1989 that users of the newer sense "still run the risk of ruffling a few feathers." And the newer sense was listed as an error in a 1996 usage guide, Patricia O'Conner's *Woe Is I*.

viable: worker or survivor?   *Viable* is commonly used to mean "workable, effective," as in "a viable alternative." But word guardians believe that *viable* should be restricted to its literal sense of "capable of living, capable of surviving," as in "a viable fetus."

vicious circle or vicious cycle?   *Vicious circle* is the preferred term for a situation in which an effort to solve a problem makes the situation worse.

Vicious circle is assigned the primary listing in *Webster's New World Dictionary* and the *Random House Webster's College Dictionary*, and it is the *only* term listed for this phenomenon in the *Random House Unabridged Dictionary*, the Merriam-Webster unabridged and collegiate dictionaries, *The Oxford English Dictionary*, and *The New Oxford American Dictionary*.

Explaining the preference for *vicious circle*, the *Harper Dictionary of Contemporary Usage* notes that a circle literally brings you back to where you started; a cycle does not.

victuals: a puzzling pronunciation

This quaint word for "food provisions" is pronounced like its nonstandard spelling variant, *vittles*. The word, from Latin by way of French *vitaille*, originally had English spellings that suggested its present pronunciation. But 16th-century grammarians prescribed the present spelling so that the word would more closely resemble its Latin ancestor, *victualia* ("provisions").

violincello or *violoncello*?

Don't look for a *violin* in the full word for *cello*. The correctly spelled *violoncello* comes from the Italian *violone* ("*big* viola"), not the Italian *violino* ("*little* viola").

vis-à-vis: let's face it

One of the English language's popular French imports, *vis-à-vis* ("vee-zah-VEE") literally means "face to face." As an English preposition with a continental flavor, it means "face to face with, confronted with" and more commonly "in relation to, in comparison with." *Vis-à-vis* is sometimes used in the sense of "with regard to, concerning," but some word-watchers have classified that usage as an error. As a noun, *vis-à-vis* means "counterpart, partner."

vocabulary-expansion strategy

Violinist Jascha Heifetz's daughter, pianist-composer Josefa Heifetz Byrne, made a hobby of collecting odd words. Her collection, published in 1974 under the title *Mrs. Byrne's Dictionary of Unusual, Obscure and Preposterous Words,* ranged from *ablutomania* ("a compulsion for washing oneself") to *zzxjoanw* ("a Maori drum").

Mrs. Byrne's Dictionary is fascinating. But if you expand your vocabulary by randomly memorizing words in her dictionary or (let's say) the 600,000-word *Oxford English Dictionary*, you are likely to acquire words that too few people recognize. Instead, adopt words you discover in general-interest newspapers, magazines, and books.

W

***wait on* can be a turnoff** The use of *wait on* in the sense of *wait for* ("await") is common in some parts of the United States, especially the South. So it was no surprise when President George W. Bush, a former governor of Texas, said in his first State of the Union address, "I will not wait on events while dangers gather." But for more than a century, usage commentators have dismissed that regional sense of *wait on* with such put-downs as "dialect," "slang," and "substandard."

Risk-free advice: Wherever you live, use *wait for* in the sense of *awaiting* someone or something. Use *wait on* in the sense of *serving* someone, in the manner of a store clerk waiting on a customer.

***walking on eggs* or *walking on eggshells*?** For five centuries people have been using the phrase *walking on eggs* to express the idea of "proceeding with extreme caution," as if tiptoeing on eggs to avoid cracking them.

Don't join the modern, mindless switch to *walking on eggshells*. Walking on the already-cracked shells requires no caution.

***wangle* or *wrangle*?** *Wangle* is an informal verb meaning "to engage in, or obtain by, cleverness or trickery," as in a reference in *The New York Times* (12/16/2000) to a physician in poverty-stricken Russia who had to "wangle baby formula" for a patient's infant.

Wrangle is a verb and a noun for "arguing angrily," as in this *New York Times* headline (7/23/2001): "Nations Wrangle in an All-Night Marathon on Climate Treaty."

Wrangle is also a separate verb meaning "to herd and tend livestock, especially horses, on the range." That verb came from the noun *horse-wrangler*, a ranch hand who takes care of saddle horses. *Wrangler* can be an abbreviation for *horse-wrangler* or a separate noun meaning "someone who wrangles, in the sense of arguing angrily."

ware or **wear?**   If you cannot wear it, as in *sportswear* and *swimwear*, then *ware* it, as in *hardware, software, kitchenware,* and *warehouse.*

was or **were?**   *Was* becomes *were* not only to express a plural ("she *was,* they *were*") but also to express speculation, doubt, or a condition contrary to fact. For example: "I wish I *were* able to help you. I could help you if I *were* rich. If I *were* you, I'd borrow the money." (See also "verbs are moody.")

ways to go?   *Ways* as an informal variant of *way* (a noun for "distance")—as in "a long *ways* off"—has been used by such renowned writers as Henry Fielding, Lord Byron, and Stephen Crane. But inasmuch as this usage offends many word guardians, *way* is the safer way to go when you mean *distance.*

When you use *way* as an *adverb*—an informal intensifier of "far" (as in "way off base")—you're employing a well-established usage that has been traced back to the 13th century. But if you hear echoes of early 20th-century usage-critic opposition to *that* use of *way,* be prepared to replace it in your formal communication with *far, by a long distance,* or *by a great amount.*

wean from or **wean on?**   *To wean* literally means "to gradually withdraw a child *from* mother's milk." Figuratively, *to wean* means "to gradually withdraw from *any* dependence." In an example of that expanded usage, *The New York Times* (9/29/1995) reported that "[health-conscious] Argentines are weaning themselves from a steady diet of red meat."

Beginning perhaps in the 1930's, some writers began using *weaned on* as if that phrase meant "raised on," as in "a generation of children weaned on comic-book violence." The new meaning was denounced by language commentator Theodore M. Bernstein in 1965, in his *Careful Writer.* But by 1989 *Merriam-Webster's Dictionary of English Usage* reported that the usage had become so common that "its appearance in dictionaries is just a matter of time."

Subsequently, *New York Times* language columnist William Safire regretfully reported (7/7/1991) that NBC news anchor Tom Brokaw had talked to the nation about "children *weaned on* [raised on] television." Safire mournfully added that the new meaning of *wean* had indeed entered a dictionary: the third college edition of *Webster's New World.* In 1992 the new meaning was included in the entry for *wean* in *The American Heritage Dictionary,* though that meaning was listed with the warning label "Usage Problem."

Suggestion: As Bernstein wrote about this question back in 1965, "the safest course" is to be faithful to the original meaning of *wean* and to make sure people understand you by using *from* with it. For example, note the clarity in this headline from the *Los Angeles Times* (1/12/1992): "Europe Is Weaning Itself From U.S. Economy."

For the "raise, rear, bring up" meaning, Bernstein advised, the safe and simple solution is to say *raise, rear,* or *bring up.*

weaved or wove?   For the literal weaving of material, the past tense is *wove.* For weaving a path or weaving from side to side, say *weaved.*

Webster's is anybody's dictionary   See "dictionaries: Webster's name is fair game."

weeped or wept?   You'll see *weeped* here and there, but the undisputed past tense and past participle of *weep* is *wept.*

well or good?   See "*good* or *well?*"

well-known or well known?   See "hyphens protect the meaning of these adjectives."

whatever or what ever?   Whatever you do with *whatever,* your wisest choice is to keep it as one word unless you choose to use *ever* as an intensive adverb—an optional form of emphasis—in a sentence such as "What *ever* made you choose that movie?" The same rule applies to *however, whenever, wherever,* and *whoever.*

whatever or whatsoever?   *Whatsoever* is an emphatic version of the already emphatic adjective *whatever* that means "of any kind at all." Example: "His political connections gave him no advantage *whatever (whatsoever).*"

when and where   See "defining with *when* and *where.*"

whence knows where it's from   The word *from* is redundant in the phrase *from whence*, inasmuch as *whence* entered our language with the sense of "from where, from which."

The American Heritage Dictionary acknowledges that *from whence* "has been used steadily by reputable writers since the 14th century." But that source adds that, inasmuch as *whence* is usually used nowadays only to impart an archaic tone, any use of the word should be without the added *from* in order to be faithful to the old meaning.

where not to use *where*   The adverb of location, *where*, should not substitute for the relative pronoun *that* or the relative-pronoun phrase *in which*.

For example, *where* should be replaced by *that* in a sentence such as "I see in the newspapers *where* there's another political scandal." That loose use of *where* is dismissed as nonstandard by some commentators and as "an illiteracy" by usage commentator Morton S. Freeman.

Where should be replaced by *in which* in a sentence such as "That is a situation *where* a pilot must make a split-second decision." The word *where* does not belong there, because a situation is not a location.

whereabouts *is* or *whereabouts* are?   If you correctly say "whereabouts is"—because the noun *whereabouts* is a singular word meaning "the place where somebody or something can be found"—most people will think you're wrong. Most people say "whereabouts are" because they wrongly assume the *-s* ending is plural, though this *-s* ending is borrowed from the adverbial suffix *-s* in such adverbs as *whereabouts* ("where"), *hereabouts* ("here"), and *thereabouts* ("there").

Risk-free solution: Instead of saying someone's whereabouts *is* unknown or *are* unknown, say that nobody knows that person's whereabouts. Or just say nobody knows where that person is.

whereas *you don't want to seem pompous*   Avoid the pretentious conjunction *whereas*—meaning "it being the case that" or "considering that"—unless somebody forces you to use it in a legal document or in an extremely formal announcement. *Whereas* is considered so rigidly formal that the plural noun form, *whereases*, stands for bureaucratic jargon in general. ("The mayor had so many whereases in his proclamation that I thought he'd never get to the point.")

wherein should be out   *Wherein* serves no purpose other than to make the user appear "excessively formal" (to quote usage commentators cited by *Merriam-Webster's Dictionary of English Usage*) or "slightly pretentious" (to quote Kenneth G. Wilson's *Columbia Guide to Standard American English*).

Risk-free recommendation: Replace *wherein* with the plain, honest words set off by brackets in the following examples: "Wherein [in what way] did we fail?" "That's the community wherein [where] she had her first taste of politics." "Those were the years wherein [when] he first learned to accept responsibility." "That was the conversation wherein [in which] they realized they were soul mates."

wherever or where ever?   See "*whatever* or *what ever?*"

whether or whether or not?   Your choice between *whether* and *whether or not* is sometimes as obvious as your choice of which shoe (left or right?) goes on which foot.

For example, only *whether* will fit (that is, make sense) for introducing alternatives: "She had a hard time deciding whether to choose the chocolate cake or the fruit tart." And only the phrase *whether or not* will make sense when you mean "regardless of whether": "He decided to take his family on the trip whether or not he got a raise."

Either *whether* or *whether or not* will make sense if you mean *if*: "The mayor did not know whether (or not) she would be able to attend the meeting." But in such sentences many usagists regard *or not* as a space-waster, unless it serves the purpose of emphasis.

which or that?   See "*that* or *which?*"

which *which* is which?   The pronoun *which* can be an ambiguity trap.

Which can refer either to an explicit antecedent ("I love my extra-roomy car, which I just bought") or to the general idea of a preceding clause ("I have a large family, which is why I bought such a roomy car"). Constructions of the second type are "frowned upon by the ultrafinicky," says usage author Theodore M. Bernstein in *The Careful Writer*, but most usage commentators allow the construction if the meaning is clear. But note the following ambiguous use of *which*, cited by Bernstein: "Laboratory animals don't catch the disease, which hampers research." Is research hampered by the disease or by the fact that the laboratory animals don't catch it?

Avoid any uses of *which* that will force the reader to stop and consider the construction carefully. Notice the momentary confusion caused by the phrase *which is* in this sentence from *Newsweek* (3/28/1994): "In December, [U.S. Supreme Court Justice Harry Blackmun] was interviewed on ABC's 'Nightline,' which is highly unusual for a justice." The *which* at first seems to refer to the television program itself and then must be reinterpreted as a reference to the idea of being interviewed on the program.

which-hunting   A preliminary draft of the 1984 Republican platform opposed "any attempts to increase taxes *which* would harm the recovery." Did that mean the party would oppose *all* tax increases or just those that the Republicans considered harmful?

The *which* in the Republican platform statement (rather than *that*) suggested that the party's opposition to taxes was absolute. But the lack of a comma before the *which* suggested otherwise. To make sure the party went on record against *all* tax increases, an anti-tax faction of the party succeeded in inserting a comma before the *which*.

When you proofread what you write, go *which*-hunting. If you find a *which* that defines something, as in "the school which he attends," change *which* to *that*. When you use *which* correctly, for introducing *nondefining* information— "his school, which was recently damaged by an earthquake, will soon be torn down"—do not forget to set off the nondefining information between opening and closing commas. (See also *"that* or *which?"*)

while ambiguity   You can avoid ambiguity with the conjunction *while* by using it only when you are able to clearly convey the meaning "during the time that." For example: "He caught up on his reading while he was recovering from his illness."

In a sentence in which *while* can mean "during the time that" or "in spite of the fact that," replace *while* with one or the other of those meanings, depending on your intended message. Here's a sentence in which that replacement is necessary to eliminate ambiguity: "While [during the time that?] [in spite of the fact that?] he was conducting business in Japan, he spoke nothing but English." If your intended meaning is "in spite of the fact that," you can substitute such shorter expressions as "even though," "although," or "though."

Also, for the sake of instant clarity, replace *while* with *and* or *but* if either of those conjunctions conveys your intended meaning. Examples: "California's capital is Sacramento, while [replace with *and*] New York's is Albany." "Some people have two or more homes, while [replace with *but*] others have none." (See "ambiguity alert" and "ambiguity can be cured.")

who or **whom?**   That remains a valid question, though *whom* was seen to be "fast vanishing from Standard American" back in 1936, in the fourth edition of journalist-critic H. L. Mencken's landmark study of the evolution of American English, entitled *The American Language.*

The still-accepted grammatical rule is that the nominative pronoun *who* is used as the subject of a verb ("*Who* is at the door?") and the objective pronoun *whom* is used as the object of a verb ("The neighbor *whom* we invited").

If you want to test your choice of *who* or *whom*, imagine that you replace the *who* or *whom* relative pronoun with a personal pronoun such as *she* or *her*. You'll see that *who* is correct if you can substitute *she/he* or *they*, and *whom* is correct if you can substitute *her/him* or *them*. For example, "*Who* is at the door?" is correct because *who* can be replaced by *she/he*. And "The neighbor *whom* we invited" is correct because *her/him* is appropriate in the clause "we invited *her/him*."

Notice the correct use of *who* and *whom* in this sentence from *The New York Times* (6/19/2000): "The federal district judge who had been overseeing the case suddenly withdrew and assigned it to a judge whom the defense regards as more independent-minded." *Who* is correct as the subject of the verb *had been overseeing*, and *whom* is correct as the object of the verb *regards*.

Whom is also used as the object of a preposition. Therefore, it is customary to address certain formal correspondence "To whom it may concern," *whom* in that phrase being the object of the preposition *to*. Also, remember that *whom* was the object of the preposition *for* in the title of one of the most famous American novels of the 20th century, Ernest Hemingway's *For Whom the Bell Tolls.*

whom: don't let it wrongly replace *who*   *The New York Public Library Writer's Guide to Style and Usage* recalls "the well-mannered butler in countless British movies who answered the phone or the door and asked, 'Whom shall I say is calling?' Although he sounded very proper, he was wrong." *Who* was needed in the butler's sentence as the subject of the verb *is calling*. The correct usage becomes obvious if you restructure the sentence: "May I say who is [not *whom is*] calling?"

The same error was committed by foreign-policy scholar Gar Alperovitz in a 1998 essay marking the 53rd anniversary of the atomic bombing of Hiroshima and Nagasaki. Alperovitz wrote that President Truman was "strongly influenced by his secretary of state, James F. Byrnes, whom many historians believe wanted to demonstrate the bomb to make Russia more 'manageable' (as he told one scientist)." The ungrammatical use of *whom* for *who* becomes obvious when you take out the aside ("many historians believe") and look at what remains: "whom . . . wanted to demonstrate." As the subject of the verb *wanted*, the nominative *who* is correct.

who's or *whose*?   If you carelessly use one of these words for the other, you will have a lot of company. But *The Columbia Guide to Standard American English* warns that this mistake is often considered evidence of a lack of education.

When you proofread, make sure that your *who's* is a contraction for *who is* or *who has*, and that your *whose* means "of whom" or "of which." (For the acceptability of the "of which" *whom*, see next entry.)

whose: for people only?   Are you committing a grammatical offense if you apply *whose* to an inanimate object, as in "a house *whose* roof needs repair"? Not according to many of today's usage commentators and such all-time literary role models as Shakespeare, Milton, Pope, and Wordsworth.

But be prepared for the possibility that your use of the inanimate *whose* will cause you to be indicted anyway. Opposition to the inanimate *whose* can be traced to a number of 18th-century grammarians who reasoned as follows: *Which* applies to things. *Who* applies to people. *Whose* is the genitive (possessive) case of *who* and therefore cannot apply to things.

Those grammarians influenced so many generations of schoolteachers and students that *Merriam-Webster's Dictionary of English Usage* reports that a survey of college and university teaching assistants showed that 67 percent would mark the inanimate *whose* wrong in a student paper.

But the Merriam-Webster's editors maintain that the inanimate *whose* has been as acceptable as the animate *whose* "since sometime in the 14th century." That, they say, is because English has no genitive case for *which* and therefore no word other than *whose* to express the meaning "of which." In other words, according to this argument, *whose* means not only "of whom" but also "of which." As the Merriam-Webster editors and other defenders of the inanimate *whose* note, the avoidance of the inanimate *whose* results in extremely awkward phrases such as "a house, the roof of which needs repair."

Other sources of solid support for the inanimate *whose* include *The Columbia Guide to Standard American English*, the Language Corner of the *Columbia Journalism Review*, *Garner's Modern American Usage*, *The Random House Webster's Unabridged Dictionary*, a "large majority" of the usage panel of *The American Heritage Dictionary*, and *The Oxford English Dictionary*.

In *The New Fowler's Modern English Usage*, linguist R. W. Burchfield approvingly quotes the following defense of the inanimate *whose* by Henry W. Fowler: "Let us, in the name of common sense, prohibit the prohibition of *whose* inanimate; good writing is surely difficult enough without the forbidding of things that have historical grammar, and present intelligibility, and obvious convenience, on their side."

wiggle or **wriggle**? To *wiggle* is "to move or cause to move with short, quick, irregular motions from side to side." The informal expression *get a wiggle on* means "hurry up." To *wriggle* is "to twist and turn" or "to move by twisting and turning, as does a snake." *Wriggle* can also mean "dodge or equivocate," as in "to wriggle out of a difficulty."

will or **shall**? See "*shall* or *will*?"

will or **would**? Use *will* when you are contemplating the future from the present, *would* when you're contemplating the future from the past. "Betty *says* she *will* call her mother." "Betty *said* she *would* call her mother."

The *Los Angeles Times* generally ignores the distinction and uses *will* in both situations, but the distinction seems to be observed by most professional writers elsewhere, including those who write for *The New York Times*. A *New York Times* editorial (9/27/2000) noted that presidential candidate Al Gore "*says* he *will* make it a point to name justices who respect women's reproductive freedom," and an article in that paper's business section (10/25/2000) reported that "the Xerox Corporation . . . *said* yesterday that it *would* sell pieces of most of its operations." (Italics added.)

A distinction between *will* and *would* is also made on the basis of whether a future development is definite or conditional: "A bill [a law being considered by a lawmaking body such as Congress] *would* cut taxes [on condition that it is passed]." "The newly enacted law *will* cut taxes."

willy-nilly: unwilling ambiguity

If you write "He did the job willy-nilly," does that mean that he did the job "against his will" or that he did it "in a disorganized manner"? The sentence could be read either way, so you'd better make sure you use save *willy-nilly* for contexts in which your intended meaning is absolutely clear.

The "against one's will" meaning has been conveyed by *willy-nilly* ever since the term originated in the early 17th century as a variant of *will I, nill I* ("be I willing, be I unwilling"). In a recent example of that usage, poet William Logan wrote in *The New York Times Book Review* (2/11/2001) that "Shakespeare had some un-Christian notions, but his views of people were, willy-nilly conditioned by Christianity."

But the "disorganized" sense is now so common that it is listed in dictionaries as a standard second definition. Here's an example of *willy-nilly* usage in which the "disorganized" meaning is unmistakable: The *Financial Times* (5/12/2000) quoted John Fisher author of *How to Run a Successful Conference*, as saying "You cannot just put people to speak willy-nilly. You have to consider what to do after lunch, when people are likely to have eaten more than usual and tend to drift off."

wimp has come a long way

According to *The Oxford Dictionary of New Words*, *wimp* was 1920's slang for "young woman" among undergraduates at Cambridge University. Among mid-1960's undergraduates in the United States, *wimp* surfaced with the meaning "effeminate man." By the late 1970's, *wimp* was a U.S. teenage term for someone who is "old-fashioned, especially in dress and appearance." Today, a *wimp* is generally regarded as a "feeble, ineffectual, cowardly person."

Though *The Oxford Dictionary of New Words* and *The Oxford English Dictionary* suggest that *wimp* may be short for *whimper*, Merriam-Webster's *New Book of Word Histories* and John Ayto's *Dictionary of Word Origins* insist that the origin of *wimp* is still a mystery.

No doubt exists, however, that *wimp* has firmly established itself in the language. *Wimp* has already produced the adjective *wimpy*, the verb *to wimp*, the noun compound *wimphood,* and the acronym *Wimps* ("weakly interacting massive particles" suspected of being the invisible matter exercising a gravitational pull on visible stars and galaxies).

winning or winsome?   Do not be misled by some dictionary entries that equate the adjective *winsome* with *winning.* If you continue your dictionary checking, you will discover that *winsome* people have a winning style because they are "attractive in a sweet, engaging way" or endowed with "childlike charm and innocence."

Usage examples: The 18th-century Scottish poet Robert Burns wrote, "She is a winsome wee thing . . . This sweet wee wife o' mine." More recently, *The Virginian-Pilot* (8/7/1998) published an article about a nine-year-old boy with "a winsome, shy smile" who overcame cancer and became an outstanding surfer.

-*wise* endings aren't always wise   Be content with fully established words that end in *-wise,* such as *likewise, otherwise,* and *clockwise.* If you invent your own adverbs that end in *-wise,* you risk becoming known as a wise guy.

wish I was or wish I were?   You need the subjunctive-mood *were* here, because a person wishes only for things that are contrary to fact. (See also "verbs are moody" and "*was* or *were?*")

with can turn *against* you   Beware of writing a sentence in which *with* can sabotage your meaning by conveying the idea of *against.* Instead of writing an ambiguous statement such as "He fought with the Conservative Party in Parliament," clarify your intended meaning by exchanging *with* for either *alongside* or *against.*

The ambiguity of *with* can easily sneak up on you if you are not careful. For example, the writer of IBM's 1991 annual report wanted to emphasize that the company had gained a competitive edge by making better products. But the headline in the report, "Competing With Better Products," could just as easily have been interpreted to mean that IBM was suffering from the problem of having to compete against the better products of its rivals. The message would have been unmistakable if the headline had been "Competing by Making Better Products." (See also "*together* but alone.")

wonderous or *wondrous?*   The correct spelling is *wondrous.*

wonk is not new   Kenneth G. Wilson's *Columbia Guide to Standard American English* (1993) described *wonk* as "a very recent slang coinage"—in the sense of a "scornful" way to refer to "those in the know or in power." Wilson speculated that the "know-it-all" *wonk* might have originated as a backward spelling of *know.* Maybe so. But other *wonks* have been around for at least a century.

The Oxford English Dictionary has a 1900 citation for *wonk* as "a term commonly applied by foreigners to the ordinary Chinese dog," a 1929 citation as "a young naval cadet who [is useless because he] has not yet learned the elements of his job," a number of mid-20th-century Australian citations as "an effeminate male" and also as an Aboriginal pejorative for "white person," and a U.S. citation of 1962 identifying *wonk* as "a disparaging term for a studious or hard-working person." Echoing that last meaning, *Random House Webster's College Dictionary* lists *wonk* as "a person who studies a subject or issue in an excessively assiduous and thorough manner."

According to *Safire's New Political Dictionary*, the term *policy wonk* (which language columnist William Safire defines as "a grimly serious scholar of the tedious side of public affairs") was first used in print when *The New Republic's* Sidney Blumenthal referred to 1984 presidential candidate Walter Mondale's "thralldom to the policy wonks and wise men of the Washington establishment."

won't or wont?   Usage example: "She *won't* [contraction for '*will not*'] eat a heavy meal, because such meals are not her *wont* [a noun rhyming with *gaunt* and meaning 'custom, habit, practice']." *Wont* is also an adjective ("accustomed, inclined") and a verb ("to accustom").

wordiness   See "cut it out" and "cut out statements that go without saying."

word-processing warning   Professor Hans P. Guth warned in his *New Concise Handbook*: "Do not be fooled by the finished appearance of word-processed text. The speed and ease of typing on an electronic keyboard often multiply transposed letters (*wrtier*), run together words (*taggedon*), random misspellings, and miscellaneous glitches." Guth's recommendation: Proofread on the screen, then in typescript.

would have or *would of*?   See "*of*: to have and have not."

wreak havoc or wreck havoc?   A radio talk-show host in Los Angeles recently invited her listeners to call in with responses to the question "Does gossip wreck havoc with your life?" In terms of word usage, the only appropriate answer to that question is no. The correct phrase is "*wreak* havoc," with *wreak* pronounced like "reek" and meaning "to cause, to inflict," and *havoc* meaning "great damage."

Usage example: *The Economist* (12/15/2001) noted that "even short-term disruptions can wreak havoc on the world economy."

writer's block prescription   First, remind yourself that you cannot improve a blank sheet of paper or a blank computer file. In the beginning, it is better to write *anything* than nothing at all.

Try concentrating on what you want to say rather than on how you want to say it. As a veteran author tells an aspiring writer in the movie *Finding Forrester*, write the first draft from the heart, then edit from the head. In other words, put down one idea after another until you are drained of ideas. And do not stop to make a single correction. Then polish. And keep polishing until your gem sparkles.

If that doesn't work, it's time to engage in drastic action. Begin writing about your topic in a deliberately nonsensical way. For example, if you're writing about budget tours of England, begin by saying that the cheapest way to fly there is to hide in a plane's luggage compartment. Again, do not stop to make changes of any kind. Sooner or later, no matter how determined you are to write nonsense, some of what you write will be worth polishing. And polishing. And polishing.

writers should beware of *MEGO*   This acronym, which has earned an entry in the *Random House Webster's College Dictionary*, stands for "my eyes glaze over." When an editor or writing instructor scribbles *MEGO* on a manuscript, that means the writer is boring the reader with information that is inherently uninteresting or is presented in an uninteresting manner.

A writer must focus on what the reader will find useful, entertaining, or inspiring. Moreover, the writer must introduce the relevance of an article or story promptly and clearly. The clear and prompt display of relevance may even outweigh conventional readability factors such as the use of simple words and short sentences, according to a 1991 study of newspaper readability conducted by journalism professor Katherine C. McAdams of the University of Maryland.

writers should keep their promises Two basic challenges that confront every nonfiction writer on every writing project: Does the piece begin with an interesting promise? (For example: "Here's how you can lose weight while eating as much as you want.") And is the promise kept? (Or do you disappoint your reader, as with the "lose weight" promise, by merely recommending self-control?)

Writing projects are doomed from the start if the promise is of no interest to the reader. ("How to decide when it's time to sharpen a pencil.") But the most compelling promise imaginable—for instance, "How to become a millionaire by age 25"—is worse than worthless if the promise is not kept.

writers should not turn purple If you write purple prose—defined by the *Random House Webster's Unabridged Dictionary* as "writing that calls attention to itself because of its obvious use of certain effects"—don't expect an appreciative audience unless you send such prose to the English department of San Jose (California) State University. Each year since 1981, the department has sponsored the Bulwer-Lytton Fiction Contest, in which thousands of entrants from around the world attempt "to compose the opening sentence to the worst of all possible novels."

Here, from software developer Dave Zobel, is the winning entry for 2004: "She resolved to end the love affair with Ramon tonight . . . summarily, like Martha Stewart ripping the sand vein out of a shrimp's tail . . . though the term 'love affair' now struck her as a ridiculous euphemism . . . not unlike 'sand vein,' which is after all an intestine, not a vein . . . and that tarry substance inside certainly isn't sand . . . and that brought her back to Ramon."

The contest is a mock tribute to the pretentious style of English novelist Edward George Bulwer-Lytton (1803–1873). Bulwer-Lytton's opening phrase for his 1830 novel *Paul Clifford*—"It was a dark and stormy night"—became a comic-strip cliché in the never-completed literary work of Charles Schulz's *Peanuts* comic-strip dog, Snoopy. This is the complete sentence as Bulwer-Lytton himself penned it: "It was a dark and stormy night, the rain falling in torrents—except at occasional intervals, when it was checked by a violent gust of wind which swept up the streets and then (for it is in London that our scene lies) rattling along the housetops, and fiercely agitating the scanty flames of the lamps that struggled against the darkness."

writing for the ear   If you take the time to read your writing aloud, you may discover ways to make your sentences sound better. Many, perhaps all, readers read with an "inner ear." They find it pleasing when the sound of writing matches the sense. Take your cue from poets, who let the intended mood determine the sound and rhythm of their writing.

writing for the eye   Imagery makes messages memorable. Consequently, showing can be as important as telling.

For example, in a *Smithsonian* article (June 1999) about Costa Rica's squirrel monkeys, the writer told his readers that those monkeys are remarkably inquisitive. Then, to show that inquisitiveness, he wrote: "Scampering dexterously across small branches, a band of [squirrel monkey] juveniles saw us and came closer. [One] skipped across a thin branch just a few feet away, plopped down in front of us and looked us straight in the eye. As surely as we were studying him, he seemed to be studying us."

Strunk and White's *Elements of Style* wisely urges writers to "prefer the specific to the general, the definite to the vague, the concrete to the abstract." Instead of, "A period of unfavorable weather set in," *The Elements of Style* suggests "It rained every day for a week." Notice that the first sentence did not let you picture what was happening, but the second sentence did.

wunderkind is not necessarily a kid   The German-derived *wunderkind* ("VUN-der-kin'd") literally means "wonder child" but is used in the sense of "a person who achieves success earlier than would be expected in a particular field." Usage example: *The New York Times* (9/5/2001) noted that Carleton S. Fiorina "was viewed as a wunderkind when she was named to head Hewlett-Packard two years ago at the age of 44."

X

Xmas presence Here's another term that's risky though right. Some people think use of this common written abbreviation for *Christmas* is religiously objectionable. But as *The Oxford English Dictionary* notes, the letter *X* has been used as an abbreviation for *Christ* from the "early times" of Christianity onward because *X* represents *chi*, the first letter of Christ's name when spelled in Greek. *OED* word historians have traced the English use of *X* to represent *Christ* as far back as the beginning of the 12th century.

X-ray or X ray?   As a noun, this word is spelled with a capital X and an optional hyphen. But the hyphen is standard when the word is used as a verb or an adjective and is prescribed in all cases by the stylebooks of the Associated Press, *The New York Times,* and the *Los Angeles Times.*

Y

yahoo, Yahoo, and Yahoo!   The lowercase *yahoo* (preferably pronounced "YAY-hoo") means "someone who is crude, insensitive and stupid." The word originated as a capitalized term in Jonathan Swift's 1726 satire, *Gulliver's Travels.* In his fourth and final voyage, ship's physician Lemuel Gulliver visits a country named Houyhnhnmland (pronounced "WHIN-im-land"), where a race of stupid and brutish humans called *Yahoos* has been tamed by a race of intelligent, virtuous, highly civilized horses.

In 1994, Stanford engineering students David Filo and Jerry Yang started a guide to the World Wide Web that they called *Yahoo!* (pronounced "YAH-hoo" and standing for "Yet Another Hierarchical Officious Oracle").

ye olde controversy   If *Ye Olde Gifte Shoppe* sounds more charming to you than *The Old Gift Shop*, you are pronouncing *ye* in a way that has offended some usage commentators.

In the view of Fowler's *Dictionary of Modern English Usage* and some American usage guides, the archaic article *ye* is properly pronounced not "yee" but precisely like the word it stands for: *the.* Their explanation: Early English printers introduced the *ye* spelling of *the* because they used our letter *y* for the bugle-shaped Old English letter (called a *thorn*) that stood for the sound *th.* Among dictionary entries for the *ye* that means *the,* Merriam-Webster lists the pronunciations "yee" and "the" in that order, Random House lists "the," followed by "yee" as a "spelling pronunciation," *Webster's New World College Dictionary* lists "the" with the advice that "yee" is "erroneous or facetious," and *The American Heritage Dictionary* lists only the pronunciation "the."

The archaic *ye* that means *the* is not related to the archaic *ye* that means *you,* which is pronounced "yee" without objection. The "you" *ye,* surviving today in religious and literary contexts, was from the Old English *ge,* with the *g* pronounced like our *y.*

yoga or yogi?   A *yogi* is a person who practices *yoga* ("Hindu postures, breathing exercises, and mental disciplines whose purpose is to achieve spiritual insight and tranquility").

yo-yo and *zipper*: why they're in the same entry   The answer is that both the zipper and the yo-yo used to be capitalized as brand names registered as trademarks.

Yo-yo, the Philippine name for a toy of undetermined origin, was protected as a U.S. trademark early in the 20th century. The word soon became an informal synonym for a person who is stupid or whose opinion changes easily. *Zipper* (from a 19th-century word, *zip,* for the sound made by a fast-moving object) was registered in 1925 as the trademark for B. F. Goodrich overshoes that had a new, sliding fastener that zipped up and down. The word *zipper* became a common noun after other manufacturers adopted the new fastener for other products, and B. F. Goodrich was allowed to legally protect only the name of the company's *Zipper Boots.*

Other brand names that became common nouns include *aspirin, cellophane, celluloid, escalator, linoleum, milk of magnesia, mimeograph, pace-*

maker, pogo stick, thermos, and *trampoline.* Some products today seem equally generic, but they remain legally protected brand names and thus continue to require capitalization: *Aqua-Lung, Band-Aid, Dixie Cup, Dumpster, Frigidaire, Frisbee, Jeep, Mace, Mailgram, Naugahyde, Ping-Pong, Plexiglas, Popsicle, Pyrex, Styrofoam, Tabasco, Technicolor, Teflon, TelePrompTer, Touch-Tone, Vaseline, Velcro,* and *Xerox.*

you know is too well known   The use of *you know* as conversational filler, by many teenagers and all too many adults, has been described by language critic Harry G. Nickles as "perhaps the worst plague that ever infected English."

An exaggeration? Maybe. But, y'know, that extreme comment indicates, y'know, how annoying it can be, y'know, when spoken communication is, y'know, continually interrupted with *y'know.* Y'know?

Want to know how to break that habit? In your future conversations, force yourself to remain silent for as long as it takes for you to think of your next word. Take my word for the fact that the pauses will be less annoying than the fillers. Gradually, most of your pauses will become so brief that they will go unnoticed. And the pauses that are noticeable will enhance your oral communication by adding a touch of suspense.

you you can be fixed   Do not let anyone tell *you you* can't fix the eyesore in this sentence. You can separate the two *you*'s with the word *that.*

Young Turk may be neither   This term—from an early 20th-century revolutionary party in Turkey—now means anyone, regardless of age or nationality, challenging a political or other establishment. Here's an example from a *New York Times* headline (7/21/1998) about Japanese politician Seiroku Kajiyama: "A 72-Year-Old Young Turk in Japan's Premier Race."

your or you're?   Don't forget that you must use your brain, not your word-processing spell-checker, to make sure that you've used *your* to mean "belonging to you" and *you're* to mean "you are." (See also "spell-check warning.")

Z

***zeitgeist* has spirit**   This sometimes-capitalized German noun has become a full-fledged word in English because it serves a uniquely useful purpose. The word *zeitgeist*—combining the German *Zeit* for "time" and *Geist* for "spirit"— means "the spirit of the time; the general trend of thought or feeling characteristic of a particular era." Usage example from *The New York Times* (7/29/1999): "Bob Dylan and Paul Simon . . . are among the best and most expansive songwriters of their time, each with one hand firmly clasping the political and intellectual zeitgeist."

***zenith* or *nadir*?**   The *zenith* is the high point in the sky, from the standpoint of an observer, or the highest point or highest state of anything. The *nadir* is the low point in the observer's sky, or the lowest point or lowest state of anything.

***zephyr* or *Zephyr*?**   The lowercase *zephyr* ("ZEF-er") means "west wind, soft gentle breeze" and comes from the uppercase *Zephyr*, the name of the Greek and Roman god of the west wind, regarded as the most pleasant of the winds.

***zeroes* or *zeros*?**   Both spellings are listed in dictionaries, but the preferred listing is assigned to *zeros*.

***zoology*'s "beastly mispronunciation"**   *There Is No Zoo in Zoology*, a book by language commentator Charles Harrington Elster about what he called "beastly mispronunciations," has been around since 1988. But many people still mispronounce the first syllable of zoology as if it were "zoo." If you look carefully at the word, you'll see that *zoology*—like *biology, sociology, theology,* and many other words referring to branches of knowledge—ends in *-ology* and therefore must begin with the sound "zoh." The second *o* belongs to the second syllable.

zoom: don't let it down   The verb *zoom* is always acceptable for dramatic motion that is *upward*, as in a report for the first quarter of the year 2000 that "net profits zoomed 27% . . . for the 900 companies on *Business Week's* Corporate Scoreboard." Likewise, nobody objects to references to a camera lens that zooms *outward*. But you will encounter resistance from some word guardians if you try to zoom *down*. For dramatic motion downward, use *dive, swoop, plunge,* or *plummet.*

Sources

The American Heritage Book of English Usage. Boston: Houghton Mifflin, 1996.

The American Heritage College Dictionary. 4th ed. Boston: Houghton Mifflin, 2002.

The American Heritage Dictionary of the English Language. 4th ed. Exec. ed. Anne H. Soukhanov. Boston: Houghton Mifflin, 2000. (3d ed., 1992.)

The American Heritage Dictionary of Idioms. Ed. Christine Ammer. Boston: Houghton Mifflin, 1997.

Amis, Kingsley. *The King's English: A Guide to Modern Usage.* First U.S. edition, New York: St. Martin's Press, 1998. (First published in Great Britain by HarperCollins, 1997.)

Angell, David, and Brent Heslop. *The Elements of E-mail Style.* Reading, Mass.: Addison-Wesley, 1994.

The Associated Press Stylebook. Ed. Norm Goldstein. Cambridge, Mass.: Perseus, 2000.

Ayto, John. *Dictionary of Word Origins.* New York: Arcade, 1990.

Bacon, Dennis. *Guide to Home Language Repair.* Urbana, Ill.: National Council of Teachers of English, 1994.

The Barnhart Concise Dictionary of Etymology: The Origins of American English Words. Ed. Robert K. Barnhart. New York: HarperCollins, 1995.

Bartlett's Familiar Quotations. 16th edition. Ed. by Justin Kaplan. Boston: Little, Brown, 1992.

Barzun, Jacques. *Simple and Direct: A Rhetoric for Writers.* New York: Harper & Row, 1975.

Benét's Reader's Encyclopedia. 4th edition. Ed. Bruce Murphy. New York: HarperCollins, 1996.

Bernstein, Theodore M. *Miss Thistlebottom's Hobgoblins*. New York: Noonday Press, 1971; republished with an introduction by Mark Singer, 1991.

———. *The Careful Writer: A Modern Guide to English Usage*. New York: Atheneum, 1972.

———. *Dos, Don'ts and Maybes of English Usage*. New York: Times Books, 1977.

Berry, Thomas Elliott. *The Most Common Mistakes in English Usage*. New York: McGraw-Hill, 1961.

Bierce, Ambrose. *The Devil's Dictionary*. New York: Dell, 1991. (Originally published in 1911.)

Bowler, Peter. *The Superior Person's Book of Words*. New York: Dell, 1990.

Brewer's Dictionary of Phrase and Fable. 16th ed. New York: HarperCollins, 1999.

Brooks, Brian S., and James L. Pinson. *Working With Words: A Concise Guide for Media Editors and Writers*. New York: St. Martin's Press, 1989.

Brooks, Terri. *Words' Worth: A Handbook on Writing and Selling Nonfiction*. New York: St. Martin's Press, 1989.

Bryson, Bill. *The Mother Tongue: English and How It Got That Way*. New York: William Morrow, 1990.

———. *Made in America: An Informal History of the English Language in the United States*. New York: William Morrow, 1994.

———. *Bryson's Dictionary of Troublesome Words*. New York: Broadway Books, 2002.

Buckley, William F., Jr. *Buckley: The Right Word*. New York: Random House, 1996.

Byrne, Josefa Heifetz. *Mrs. Byrne's Dictionary of Unusual, Obscure, and Preposterous Words*. Secaucus, N.J.: Citadel Press, 1974.

Carver, Craig M. *A History of English in Its Own Words*. New York: HarperCollins, 1991.

The Chicago Manual of Style. 15th ed. Chicago: University of Chicago Press, 2003.

Ciardi, John. *A Browser's Dictionary and Native's Guide to the Unknown American Language*. New York: Harper & Row, 1980.

———. *A Second Browser's Dictionary and Native's Guide to the Unknown American Language*. New York: Harper & Row, 1983.

———. *Good Words to You*. New York: Harper & Row, 1987.

Claiborne, Robert. *Our Marvelous Native Tongue: The Life and Times of the English Language*. New York: Times Books, 1983.

———. *Saying What You Mean: A Commonsense Guide to American Usage*. New York: W. W. Norton, 1986.

———. *Loose Cannons and Red Herrings: A Book of Lost Metaphors*. New York: Ballantine Books, 1988.

Clark, John O. E. *Word Perfect: A Dictionary of Current English Usage*. New York: Henry Holt, 1987.

———. *Word Wise: A Dictionary of English Idioms*. New York: Henry Holt, 1988.

The Concise Oxford Dictionary of Current English. 8th ed. Ed. R. E. Allen. Oxford: Clarendon, 1990.

Cook, Claire Kehrwald. *The Modern Language Association of America's Line by Line: How to Edit Your Own Writing*. Boston: Houghton Mifflin, 1985.

Copperud, Roy H. *A Dictionary of Usage and Style*. New York: Hawthorn Books, 1964.

———. *Handbook for Journalists*. Los Angeles: University of Southern California School of Journalism, 1972, 1978.

———. *American Usage and Style: The Consensus*. New York: Van Nostrand, 1980.

Crystal, David. *The Cambridge Encyclopedia of the English Language*. Cambridge, Eng.: Cambridge University Press, 1995.

The Dictionary of Cultural Literacy. See Hirsch, E. D., Jr., Joseph F. Kett, and James Trefil.

Dillard, J. L. *A History of American English*. London: Longman, 1992.

Dusseau, John L. *Bugaboos, Chimeras and Achilles' Heels: 10,001 Difficult Words and How to Use Them*. Englewood Cliffs, N.J.: Prentice Hall, 1993.

The Economist Style Guide. London: The Economist Books. 1991.

Eggenschwiter, Jean. *Writing: Grammar, Usage and Style*. Lincoln, Neb.: Cliffs Notes, 1997.

Ehrlich, Eugene. *The Highly Selective Dictionary for the Extraordinarily Literate*. New York: HarperCollins, 1997.

Einstein, Charles. *How to Communicate: The Manning Selvage and Lee Guide to Clear Writing and Speech*. New York: McGraw-Hill, 1985.

Elster, Charles Harrington. *There Is No Zoo in Zoology and Other Beastly Mispronunciations*. New York: Macmillan, 1988.

———. *Is There a Cow in Moscow? More Beastly Mispronunciations and Sound Advice*. New York: Macmillan, 1990.

Encarta World English Dictionary. New York: St. Martin's Press, 1999.

Evans, Bergen, and Cornelia Evans. *A Dictionary of Contemporary American Usage*. New York: Random House, 1957.

Fiske, Robert Hartwell. *Guide to Concise Writing*. New York: Webster's New World, 1990.

Flesch, Rudolf. *The Art of Readable Writing*. New York: Harper & Row, 1949.

———. *How to Be Brief: An Index to Simple Writing*. New York: Harper & Row, 1962.

Flexner, Stuart Berg. *I Hear America Talking*. New York: Van Nostrand Reinhold, 1976.

Flexner, Stuart Berg, and Anne H. Soukhanov. *Speaking Freely: A Guided Tour of American English From Plymouth Rock to Silicon Valley*. New York: Oxford University Press, 1997.

Follett, Wilson. *Modern American Usage*. New York: Grosset & Dunlap, 1970.

———. *Modern American Usage*. Revised by Erik Wensberg. New York: Hill and Wang, 1998.

Fowler, Henry W. *A Dictionary of Modern English Usage*. Oxford: Clarendon Press, 1926.

———. *A Dictionary of Modern English Usage*. 2d ed. Revised by Sir Ernest Gowers. Oxford: Clarendon Press, 1965.

———. *The New Fowler's Modern English Usage*. 3d ed. Revised by R. W. Burchfield. New York: Oxford University Press, 2000. (Published in Great Britain in 1998.)

Fowler, Henry W., and Francis George Fowler. *The King's English*. 3d ed. Oxford: Clarendon Press, 1930.

Freeman, Morton S. *Words to the Wise*. New York: Meridian, 1983.

———. *A Handbook of Problem Words and Phrases*. Philadelphia: ISI Press, 1987.

———. *The Wordwatcher's Guide to Good Writing and Grammar*. Cincinnati: Writer's Digest Books, 1990.

———. *The One-Minute Grammarian*. New York: Signet, 1992.

Friedlander, Edward Jay, and John Lee. *Feature Writing for Newspapers and Magazines*. New York: HarperCollins, 1996.

Funk & Wagnalls Standard Dictionary. New York: Harper Paperbacks, 1991.

Garner, Bryan A. *Garner's Modern American Usage*. New York: Oxford University Press, 2003.

Garrison, Webb. *Why You Say It*. Nashville, Tenn.: Rutledge Hill Press, 1992.

Gordon, Karen Elizabeth. *The Deluxe Transitive Vampire: The Ultimate Handbook of Grammar for the Innocent, the Eager, and the Doomed*. New York: Pantheon Books, 1993.

———. *Torn Wings and Faux Pas: A Flashbook of Style, a Beastly Guide Through the Writer's Labyrinth*. New York: Pantheon Books, 1997.

Gowers, Sir Ernest. *The Complete Plain Words*. Revised by Sidney Greenbaum and Janet Whitcut. Boston: David R. Godine, 1988.

Graves, Robert, and Alan Hodge. *The Use and Abuse of the English Language*. New York: Paragon House, 1943, 1970.

Green, Jonathan. *Cassell's Dictionary of Slang*. London: Cassell, 1998.

Gookin, Dan, Wally Wang, and Chris Van Buren. *Illustrated Computer Dictionary for Dummies*. San Mateo, Calif.: IDG Books Worldwide, 1993.

Hacker, Diana. *Rules for Writers*. New York: St. Martin's Press, 1985.

———. *A Writer's Reference*. New York: St. Martin's Press, 1989.

Hairston, Maxine, and John J. Ruszkiewicz. *The Scott, Foresman Handbook for Writers*. Glenview, Ill.: Scott, Foresman, 1988.

Hammond Barnhart Dictionary of Science. Maplewood, N.J.: Hammond, 1986.

The HarperCollins Concise Dictionary of English Usage. New York: HarperCollins, 1991.

Harper Dictionary of Contemporary Usage. See Morris, William, and Mary Morris.

The Harper Dictionary of Foreign Terms. 3d ed. New York: Harper & Row, 1987.

Harrison, James S. *Confusion Reigns: A Quick and Easy Guide to the Most Easily Mixed-Up Words*. New York: St. Martin's Press, 1987.

Hayakawa, S. I. *Use the Right Word: A Modern Guide to Synonyms*. Pleasantville, N.Y.: Reader's Digest, 1968.

Heacock, Paul. *Which Word When?* New York: Dell, 1989.

Heffernan, James A. W., and John E. Lincoln. *Writing: A College Handbook*. 2d ed. New York: W. W. Norton, 1986.

Hill-Miller, Katherine. *The Most Common Errors in English Usage and How to Avoid Them*. New York: Arco, 1983.

Hirsch, E. D., Jr., Joseph F. Kett, and James Trefil. *The Dictionary of Cultural*

Literacy: What Every American Needs to Know. 2d ed. Boston: Houghton Mifflin, 1993.

Historical Dictionary of American Slang. Vol. 1, ed. J. E. Lighter. New York: Random House, 1994.

Hook, J. N. *The Appropriate Word.* Reading, Mass.: Addison-Wesley, 1990.

Hudson, Kenneth. *The Dictionary of Diseased English: A Dictionary of Linguistic Fog and Fraud.* New York: Harper & Row, 1977.

Illustrated Oxford Dictionary. New York: Oxford University Press, 2003.

Johnson, Edward P. *The Handbook of Good English.* New York: Facts on File, 1982.

Kessler, Lauren, and Duncan McDonald. *When Words Collide: A Media Writer's Guide to Grammar and Style.* 3d ed. Belmont, Calif.: Wadsworth, 1992.

Kirkland, James W., and Collett B. Dilworth, Jr. *Concise English Handbook.* Lexington, Mass.: D. C. Heath, 1985.

Kolb, Harold H., Jr. *A Writer's Guide.* New York: Harcourt Brace Jovanovich, 1980.

Lakoff, Robin Tolmach. *Talking Power: The Politics of Language.* New York: Basic Books, 1990.

Lederer, Richard. *Crazy English.* New York: Pocket Books, 1990.

———. *The Miracle of Language.* New York: Pocket Books, 1991.

Le Mot Juste: A Dictionary of Classical and Foreign Words and Phrases. New York: Vintage Books, 1980, 1991.

Lewis, Norman. *Word Power Made Easy.* New York: Pocket Books, 1978.

———. *30 Days to Better English.* New York: New American Library, 1985.

———. *The New American Dictionary of Good English.* New York: New American Library, 1987.

Line by Line. See Cook, Claire Kehrwald.

The Little, Brown Handbook. 3d ed. Boston: Little, Brown and Co., 1986.

Longman Dictionary of the English Language. London: Longman, 1984.

Longman Guide to English Usage. London: Longman, 1988.

Los Angeles Times Stylebook. Ed. Frederick S. Holley. New York: New American Library, 1981.

Lovinger, Paul W. *The Penguin Dictionary of American English Usage and Style.* New York: Penguin Putnam, 2000.

Lunsford, Andrea, and Robert Connors. *The St. Martin's Handbook.* New York: St. Martin's Press, 1989.

MacNeil, Robert. *Wordstruck*. New York: Viking Penguin, 1989.

Maleska, Eugene T. *A Pleasure in Words*. New York: Simon & Schuster, 1981.

Martin, Phyllis. *Word Watcher's Handbook: A Deletionary of the Most Abused and Misused Words*. New York: St. Martin's Press, 1982.

McArthur, Tom, ed. *The Oxford Companion to the English Language*. Oxford: Oxford University Press, 1992.

———. *The Oxford Guide to World English*. Oxford: Oxford University Press, 1992.

McCrum, Robert, William Cran, and Robert MacNeil. *The Story of English*. New York: Penguin Books, 1986.

Mencken, H. L. *The American Language*. 4th ed. New York: Alfred A. Knopf, 1936. (22d printing, 1980).

Merriam-Webster's Collegiate Dictionary. 11th ed. Springfield, Mass.: Merriam-Webster, 2003.

The Merriam-Webster Concise Handbook for Writers. Springfield, Mass.: Merriam-Webster, 1991.

Merriam-Webster's Dictionary of Allusions. Springfield, Mass.: Merriam-Webster, 1999.

Merriam-Webster's Dictionary of English Usage. Springfield, Mass.: Merriam-Webster, 1994. (Previously published in 1989 as *Webster's Dictionary of English Usage*.)

The Merriam-Webster New Book of Word Histories. Springfield, Mass.: Merriam-Webster, 1991.

Mitchell, Richard. *The Leaning Tower of Babel*. New York: Simon & Schuster, 1984.

MLA Style Manual. 2d ed. New York: Modern Language Association, 1998.

Morris, Evan. *The Word Detective*. Chapel Hill, N.C.: Algonquin Books of Chapel Hill, 2000.

Morris, William, and Mary Morris. *Morris Dictionary of Word and Phrase Origins*. New York: Harper & Row, 1971.

———. *Harper Dictionary of Contemporary Usage*. New York: Harper & Row, 1975.

———. *Harper Dictionary of Contemporary Usage*. 2d ed. New York: Harper & Row, 1985.

New Dictionary of American Slang. New York: Harper & Row, 1987.

New Lexicon Webster's Dictionary of the English Language. Managing Ed.

Doris E. Lechner. New York: Lexicon Publications, 1989.

Newman, Edwin. *Strictly Speaking*. New York: Bobbs-Merrill, 1974.

———. *I Must Say*. New York: Warner Books, 1988.

The New Oxford American Dictionary. Ed. Elizabeth J. Jewell and Frank Abate. New York: Oxford University Press. 2001.

The New York Public Library Desk Reference. New York: Webster's New World. 1998.

The New York Public Library Writer's Guide to Style and Usage. New York: HarperCollins, 1994.

The New York Times Everyday Reader's Dictionary of Misunderstood, Misused, and Mispronounced Words. Ed. Laurence Urdang. New York: New American Library, 1985.

The New York Times Guide to Reference Materials. Rev. ed. by Mona McCormick. New York: New American Library, 1986.

The New York Times Manual of Style and Usage. New York: Times Books, 1976, rev. 1999.

Nickles, Harry G. *The Dictionary of Do's and Don'ts: A Guide for Writers and Speakers*. New York: McGraw-Hill, 1974.

Nurnberg, Maxwell. *Questions You Always Wanted to Ask About English*. New York: Pocket Books, 1972.

O'Conner, Patricia. *Woe Is I: The Grammarphobe's Guide to Better English in Plain English*. New York: G. P. Putnam's Sons, 1996.

———. *Words Fail Me: What Everyone Who Writes Should Know About Writing*. New York: Harcourt, Inc., 1999.

The Oxford Dictionary of New Words. Compiled by Sara Tulloch. Oxford: Oxford University Press, 1991.

The Oxford English Dictionary. Ed. James A. H. Murray et al. 12 vols. Oxford: Clarendon Press, 1928.

The Oxford English Dictionary, Supplement. Ed. Robert W. Burchfield. 4 vols. Oxford: Clarendon Press, 1972–1986.

The Oxford English Dictionary. 2d ed. Prepared by J. A. Simpson and E. S. C. Weiner. 20 vols. Oxford: Clarendon Press, 1989.

The Oxford English Dictionary, Compact Edition. (Reproduced micrographically in one volume.) Oxford: Clarendon Press, 1991.

The Oxford Guide to English Usage. Oxford: Oxford University Press, 1994.

Partridge, Eric. *Usage and Abusage*. Hammondsworth, Middlesex, Eng.: Penguin Books, 1947, rev. 1973.

Paxson, William C. *The New American Dictionary of Confusing Words*. New York: Signet, 1990.

Perrin, Robert. *The Beacon Handbook*. 2d ed. Boston: Houghton Mifflin, 1990.

Phythian, B. A. *A Concise Dictionary of Confusables*. New York: John Wiley & Sons, 1990.

The Princeton Review Word Smart. New York: Villard Books, 1990.

Random House Webster's College Dictionary. New York: Random House, 2001–2002.

Random House Webster's Unabridged Dictionary. 2001. New York: Random House.

Rawson, Hugh. *Wicked Words: A Treasury of Curses, Insults, Put-Downs, and Other Formerly Unprintable Terms from Anglo-Saxon Times to the Present*. New York: Crown, 1989.

———. *Devious Derivations: Popular Misconceptions—and More Than 1,000 True Origins of Common Words and Phrases*. New York: Crown, 1994.

Reader's Digest Family Word Finder: A New Thesaurus of Synonyms and Antonyms in Dictionary Form. Ed. Stuart B. Flexner. Pleasantville, N.Y.: Reader's Digest Association, 1975.

Reader's Digest Success With Words: A Guide to the American Language. Ed. Peter Davies. Pleasantville, N.Y.: Reader's Digest Association, 1983.

Rees, Nigel. *The Phrase That Launched 1,000 Ships*. New York: Dell, 1991.

Rizzo, Betty. *Priorities: A Handbook for Basic Writing*. New York: Harper & Row, 1985.

Roberts, William H. *The Writer's Companion*. Boston: Little, Brown, 1985.

Robinson, Adam. *Word Smart*. New York: Villard Books, 1990.

Rogers, James. *The Dictionary of Clichés*. New York: Ballantine Books, 1985.

Roget's International Thesaurus. 4th ed. Revised by Robert L. Chapman. New York: Thomas Y. Crowell, 1977.

Room, Adrian. *Dictionary of Changes in Meaning*. New York: Routledge & Kegan Paul, 1986.

Safire, William. *On Language*. New York: Times Books, 1980.

———. *What's the Good Word?* New York: Times Books, 1982.

———. *I Stand Corrected*. New York: Times Books, 1984.

———. *Take My Word for It*. New York: Times Books, 1986.

———. *You Could Look It Up*. New York: Henry Holt, 1988.

———. *Language Maven Strikes Again*. New York: Henry Holt, 1990.

———. *Fumblerules: A Lighthearted Guide to Grammar and Good Usage*. New York: Doubleday, 1990. (Reissued as *How Not to Write: The Essential Misrules of Grammar*. New York: W. W. Norton, 2005.)

———. *Coming to Terms*. New York: Doubleday, 1991.

———. *Quoth the Maven: More on Language From William Safire*. New York: Random House, 1993.

———. *Safire's New Political Dictionary*. New York: Random House, 1993.

———. *Watching My Language*. New York: Random House, 1997.

———. *Adventures in the Word Trade*. New York: Random House, 1998.

———. *No Uncertain Terms*. New York: Simon & Schuster, 2003.

———. *Lend Me Your Ears: Great Speeches in History*. 3rd ed. New York: W. W. Norton, 2004.

———. *The Right Word in the Right Place at the Right Time*. New York: Simon & Schuster, 2004.

Schur, Norman W. *1000 Most Challenging Words*. New York: Facts on File Publications, 1987.

Shaw, Harry. *Dictionary of Problem Words and Phrases*. New York: Washington Square Press, 1975.

———. *Errors in English and Ways to Correct Them*. New York: Harper & Row, 1986.

Shorter Oxford English Dictionary. Oxford: Clarendon Press, 2002.

Simon, John. *Paradigms Lost: Reflections on Literacy and Its Decline*. New York: Clarkson N. Potter, 1980.

Sorel, Nancy Caldwell. *Word People*. New York: American Heritage Press, 1970.

Strunk, William, Jr., and E. B. White. *The Elements of Style*. 4th ed. Boston: Allyn and Bacon, 2000. (1st ed., New York: Macmillan, 1959.)

Thomas, Lewis. *Et Cetera, Et Cetera: Notes of a Word-Watcher*. Boston: Little, Brown, 1990.

United Press International Stylebook. Chicago: National Textbook Co., 1992.

Urdang, Laurence. *The Dictionary of Confusable Words*. New York: Ballantine Books, 1988, 1989.

Wallraff, Barbara. *Word Court*. New York: Harcourt, 2000.

The Wall Street Journal Guide to Business Style and Usage. Ed. Paul R. Martin. New York: Simon & Schuster, 2002.

Walsh, Bill. *Lapsing Into a Comma: A Curmudgeon's Guide to the Many Things That Can Go Wrong in Print—and How to Avoid Them.* Lincolnwood, Ill.: Contemporary Books, 2000.

———. *The Elephants of Style: A Trunkload of Tips on the Big Issues and Gray Areas of Contemporary American English.* New York: McGraw-Hill, 2004.

Washington Post Deskbook on Style. Ed. Thomas W. Lippman. New York: McGraw-Hill, 1989.

Webster's New World College Dictionary. (The official dictionary of the Associated Press.) 4th ed., Foster City, Calif.: IDG Books Worldwide, 2001.

Webster's New World Dictionary of Media and Communications. Ed. Richard Weiner. New York: Macmillan General Reference / Simon & Schuster, 1996.

Webster's New World Guide to Current American Usage. New York: Webster's New World, 1988.

Webster's Standard American Style Manual. Springfield, Mass.: Merriam-Webster, 1985.

Webster's Third New International Dictionary of the English Language. Unabridged. Ed. Philip B. Gove. Springfield, Mass.: G. & C. Merriam, 1961.

Webster's Third New International Dictionary: 12,000 Words: A Supplement. Springfield, Mass.: G. & C. Merriam, 1986.

Webster's II New Riverside University Dictionary. Ed. Anne H. Soukhanov. Boston: Houghton Mifflin, 1988.

Webster's Word Histories. Springfield, Mass.: Merriam-Webster, 1989.

Wentworth, Harold, and Stuart Berg Flexner. *Dictionary of American Slang.* New York: Thomas Y. Crowell, 1960.

Wilber, Rick. *The Writer's Handbook for Editing and Revision.* Lincolnwood, Ill.: NTC (National Textbook Company) Publishing Group, 1997.

Williams, Deborah K. *NTC's Dictionary of Tricky Words.* Lincolnwood, Ill.: NTC (National Textbook Company) Publishing Group, 1996.

Wilson, Kenneth G. *The Columbia Guide to Standard American English.* New York: Columbia University Press, 1993.

Wilton, David. *Word Myths: Debunking Linguistic Urban Legends.* New York: Oxford University Press, 2004.

Winchester, Simon. *The Professor and the Madman: A Tale of Murder, Insanity, and the Making of the Oxford English Dictionary.* New York: HarperCollins, 1998.

————. *The Meaning of Everything: The Story of the Oxford English Dictionary.* New York: Oxford University Press, 2003.

Wired Style: Principles of English Usage in the Digital Age. Ed., Constance Hale. San Francisco: HardWired, 1996.

Word Mysteries and Histories. By the editors of the American Heritage Dictionaries. Boston: Houghton Mifflin Co., 1986.

World Almanac Guide to Good Word Usage. Ed., Martin H. Manser. New York: World Almanac, 1989.

Zinsser, William. *On Writing Well.* 6th ed. New York: HarperCollins, 2001.

————. *Writing With a Word Processor.* New York: Harper & Row, 1983.

About the Author

During much of his multimedia writing career, Mark Davidson taught writing and other communications courses at UCLA, the University of Southern California, West Los Angeles College, and three campuses of the California State University system, where he earned tenure and a full professorship. He retired from teaching in 1999 to concentrate on book projects. He died shortly after completing work on this book, in March 2005.

Davidson, who became a Sackett Scholar as a student at the Columbia University Graduate School of Journalism, worked for many years as a reporter, feature writer, and columnist for metropolitan newspapers and a wire service, as a by-liner for national magazines, and as a producer-host for *Reporter at Large*, his own prime-time Los Angeles TV talk show. He won an Emmy for a series of historical satires he wrote for the internationally syndicated *Dinah Shore Show*. He was an associate editor and writer for *The UCLA Monthly*, a national correspondent for *Science Digest*, a medical research writer for the City of Hope National Medical Center, and the science writer for the University of Southern California News Service.

Davidson's book on systems-science approaches to problem-solving, *Uncommon Sense: The Life and Thought of Ludwig von Bertalanffy, Father of General Systems Theory*, with a foreword by R. Buckminster Fuller, was published by Tarcher/Houghton Mifflin in 1983. It was translated into

Japanese in 2000 and into German in 2005. In the aftermath of 9/11/2001, Davidson was invited to draw on his systems-science worldview to address international scientific conferences at Vienna's University of Technology (2001) and the Republic of Slovenia's University of Maribor (2002).

In 2003, Davidson was awarded a Best Paper designation for his "Art of Disinformation" contribution to the text of an international conference on science and technology in Pori, Finland. At the time of his death, he was working on a book stemming from that essay, about linguistic techniques of mass mind manipulation.